Brief Contents

FOCUS
on WRITING
PARAGRAPHS AND ESSAYS

Fifth Edition

Laurie G. Kirszner
University of the Sciences, Emeritus

Stephen R. Mandell
Drexel University

bedford/st.martin's
Macmillan Learning

Boston | New York

For Bedford/St. Martin's

Vice President, Editorial, Macmillan Learning Humanities: Leasa Burton
Senior Program Manager: Karita France dos Santos
Marketing Manager: Lauren Arrant
Director of Content Development, Humanities: Jane Knetzger
Senior Developmental Editor: Cynthia Ward
Assistant Editor: Paola Garcia-Muniz
Senior Content Project Manager: Edward Dionne
Senior Workflow Project Manager: Jennifer Wetzel
Production Supervisor: Brianna Lester
Project Management: Lumina Datamatics, Inc.
Composition: Lumina Datamatics, Inc.
Text Permissions Editor: Kalina Ingham
Photo Permissions Editor: Angela Boehler
Photo Researcher: Krystyna Borgen, Lumina Datamatics, Inc.
Director of Design, Content Management: Diana Blume
Text Design: Claire Seng-Niemoeller and Lumina Datamatics, Inc.
Cover Design: William Boardman
Cover Image: PJPhoto69/E+/Getty Images
Printing and Binding: LSC Communications

Manufactured in the United States of America.

1   2   3   4   5   6   24   23   22   21   20   19

For information, write: Bedford/St. Martin's, 75 Arlington Street, Boston, MA 02116

ISBN   978-1-319-20739-7   (Student Edition)
ISBN   978-1-319-22993-1   (Loose-leaf Student Edition)

Acknowledgments

Text acknowledgments and copyrights appear at the back of the book on pages 665–666, which constitute an extension of the copyright page. Art acknowledgments and copyrights appear on the same page as the art selections they cover.

Preface

Our goal when we wrote the first edition of *Focus on Writing: Paragraphs and Essays* was to create an appealing text that motivates students to improve their writing and gives them the tools to do so. We developed the popular **TEST** tool specifically for this purpose. The letters that spell **TEST** stand for **T**opic sentence (or **T**hesis statement), **E**vidence, **S**ummary statement, and **T**ransitions; this acronym helps students understand how paragraphs and essays are constructed and teaches them how to begin to revise their own writing by checking for unity, support, and coherence.

In addition to retaining this important and successful feature, the fifth edition of *Focus on Writing* continues to reflect one of our central beliefs: that in college, writing comes first. Accordingly, the text's activities not only get students writing immediately but also encourage them to return to their own writing to apply the new skills they are learning and—with the help of **TEST**—to create a finished draft. We also believe that students learn grammar and editing skills best in the context of their own writing. For this reason, *Focus on* Writing includes Grammar in Context boxes that introduce fundamental concepts where they are most relevant to the student's own writing.

In this fifth edition, we continue to use appealing images and a contemporary design to engage today's visual learners. The text's explanations and instructions have been streamlined throughout to make them as useful as possible. We now offer more coverage of critical reading, and we have included many new readings and updated many exercise topics to reflect the interests and concerns of contemporary students. In addition, we've expanded our coverage of writing with sources to prepare students for their college coursework.

It is our hope that this new edition of *Focus on Writing* will continue to motivate and empower students to become confident writers and capable editors of their own writing.

Organization

Focus on Writing has a flexible organization that permits instructors to teach various topics in the order that works best for them and their students. The book is divided into five units, which are color-coded to help students and instructors more easily navigate the book:

- **Unit 1, Reading to Write,** introduces students to critical reading skills such as note taking and highlighting and also shows them how to approach the various types of reading they will encounter in college.

- **Unit 2, Focus on Writing Paragraphs** (Chapters 2–12), provides a comprehensive discussion of the writing process, illustrating this process as it applies to different kinds of paragraphs.

- **Unit 3, Focus on Writing Essays** (Chapters 13–17), explains and illustrates the writing process as it applies to essays. These chapters include model essays as well as study questions and writing prompts. Chapter 17, Writing with Sources, introduces the research process from finding and evaluating sources through crediting sources in both MLA and APA documentation styles.

- **Unit 4, Revising and Editing Your Writing** (Chapters 18–36), is a thorough review of sentence skills, grammar, punctuation, and mechanics, including numerous practice exercises.

- **Unit 5, Reading Essays** (Chapter 37), is a collection of model essays accompanied by critical reading/thinking questions and writing prompts designed to encourage students to read and understand the texts they encounter.

Features

Central *to Focus on Writing* is our philosophy that students learn to write best by working with their own writing. This philosophy is supported by a number of innovative features designed to make students' writing practice meaningful, productive, and enjoyable.

TEST helps students write and revise. This easy-to-remember acronym is designed to help students keep track of the criteria they can use to check their paragraphs and essays for unity, support, and coherence. By applying **TEST** to their writing, students can quickly see where their drafts need more work.

Focus on Writing activities, which open Chapters 1–14, engage and motivate students. These activities immediately involve students in writing by asking them to respond to a visual and a related prompt. An end-of-chapter prompt sends students back to their writing to apply the new skills they have learned and to work toward a final draft.

Students get the writing help they need—in a clear, step-by-step format. Eleven chapters on paragraph writing and five on essay writing cover the writing process, patterns of development, and writing with sources. Each chapter includes a student-focused case study and an abundance of clear examples and engaging exercises.

Instruction and activities emphasize critical reading and thinking skills. With a full chapter on active reading and a set of critical reading/thinking questions for each professional reading, *Focus on Writing* helps students build essential critical thinking and reading skills.

Grammar coverage is thorough yet accessible. Nineteen grammar chapters clearly and concisely convey the rules of English grammar.

New to This Edition

More material on the reading process and its relationship to writing. Chapter 1, Focus on Active Reading, has been thoroughly revised to reflect an emphasis on integrated reading and writing. The active reading process is now illustrated by a student response to Colin Powell's essay "What Makes American Citizenship Possible."

A new chapter, Writing with Sources (Chapter 17), guides students through the process of writing a research paper, from choosing a topic to evaluating, integrating, and documenting sources. Special attention is given to how to avoid plagiarism, which is an especially challenging issue for today's students. This chapter includes the most recent MLA and APA documentation styles.

New readings with updated topics and perspectives for today's students. Among the new readings are essays by Junot Diaz, Trevor Noah, Sherry Turkle, Hanif Willis-Abdurraqib, Jacqueline Woodson, and others on contemporary topics such as driverless cars, gun safety, racial profiling, ocean pollution, and the pros and cons of social media. This edition also includes more examples of argument, exposing students to a pattern that is central to much of academic writing.

Revised and enhanced exercises. New exercises help students practice the writing and grammar strategies they will use in their own essays.

Strategies for college success such as time-management strategies (Chapter 1) and email etiquette (Chapter 2) are integrated within the reading and writing instruction.

Bedford/St. Martin's puts you first

From day one, our goal has been simple: to provide inspiring resources that are grounded in best practices for teaching reading and writing. For more than thirty-five years, Bedford/St. Martin's has partnered with the field, listening to teachers, scholars, and students about the support writers need. We are committed to helping every writing instructor make the most of our resources.

How can we help *you*?

- Our editors can align our resources to your outcomes through correlation and transition guides for your syllabus. Just ask us.
- Our sales representatives specialize in helping you find the right materials to support your course goals.
- Our *Bits* blog on the Bedford/St. Martin's English Community (**community.macmillan.com**) publishes fresh teaching ideas weekly. You'll also find easily downloadable professional resources and links to author webinars on our community site.

Contact your Bedford/St. Martin's sales representative or visit **macmillanlearning.com** to learn more.

Print and Digital Options for *Focus on Writing*

Choose the format that works best for your course, and ask about our packaging options that offer savings for students.

Print

- *Paperback.* To order the paperback format for the fifth edition, use ISBN 978-1-319-20739-7.
- *Loose-leaf edition.* This format does not have a traditional binding; its pages are loose and hole punched to provide flexibility and a lower price to students (ISBN: 978-1-319-22993-1). It can be packaged with our digital space for additional savings.

Digital

- *Innovative digital learning space.* Bedford/St. Martin's suite of digital tools makes it easy to get everyone on the same page by putting student writers at the center. For details, visit **macmillanlearning.com /college/us/englishdigital**.
- *Popular e-book formats.* For details about our e-book partners, visit **macmillanlearning.com/ebooks**.

- *Inclusive Access.* Enable every student to receive their course materials through your LMS on the first day of class. Macmillan Learning's Inclusive Access program is the easiest, most affordable way to ensure all students have access to quality educational resources. Find out more at **macmillanlearning.com/inclusiveaccess**.

Your Course, Your Way

No two writing programs or classrooms are exactly alike. Our Curriculum Solutions team works with you to design custom options that provide the resources your students need. (Options below require enrollment minimums.)

- *ForeWords for English.* Customize any print resource to fit the focus of your course or program by choosing from a range of prepared topics, such as Sentence Guides for Academic Writers.
- *Macmillan Author Program (MAP).* Add excerpts or package acclaimed works from Macmillan's trade imprints to connect students with prominent authors and public conversations. A list of popular examples or academic themes is available upon request.
- *Bedford Select.* Build your own print handbook or anthology from a database of more than eight hundred selections, and add your own materials to create your ideal text. Package with any Bedford/St. Martin's text for additional savings. Visit **macmillanlearning.com/bedfordselect**.

Instructor Resources

You have a lot to do in your course. We want to make it easy for you to find the support you need—and to get it quickly.

- The **Instructor's Annotated Edition** of *Focus on Writing* contains answers to practice and editing exercises as well as teaching tips within the book's margins, some of which are specific to ESL students. ISBN: 978-1-319-27972-1.
- The **Instructor's Manual** for *Focus on Writing* is available as a PDF that can be downloaded from **macmillanlearning.com**. It includes sample syllabi, chapter overviews, and teaching tips specific to developmental writing.

Acknowledgments

In our work on *Focus on Writing*, we have benefited from the help of a great many people.

We are grateful to those instructors who lent their expertise to the support material for instructors. For this fifth edition, Gina Santoro of Community College of Rhode Island brought a fresh editorial eye to the Instructor's Manual as we streamlined the organization and updated the advice. The contributions previously made by Linda Crawford of McLennan Community College and Timothy Jones of Oklahoma City Community College continue to enhance the Instructor's Annotated Edition.

Instructors throughout the country have contributed suggestions and encouragement at various stages of the book's development. For their collegial support on this and previous editions, we thank Sandra Albers, Leeward Community College; Jaclyn Allen, Bismarck State College; Elizabeth Andrews, South Florida State College; Crystal Bacon, Wenatchee Valley College; Diego Baez, Harry S. Truman College; Phillip Bannowsky, University of Delaware; Monique Blake, Broward College; Reed Breneman, Wake Technical Community College; Robyn Browder, Tidewater Community College; Susan Buchler, Montgomery County Community College; Angelica P. Cerda, South Texas College; Joanna Christopher, John A. Logan College; Sandra K. Chumchal, Blinn College; Shari Clevenger, Northeastern State University; Julia Conway, Bristol Community College; Jack Conway, Bristol Community College; Mary Copeland, San Bernardino Valley College; Emily Cosper, Delgado Community College; Patty Crockett, Bishop State Community College; Laura de la Vina, South Texas College; Karin Deol, Imperial Valley College; Rita Fernandez-Sterling, Miami Dade College, Kendall Campus; Jennifer Ferguson, Cazenovia College; Katherine Firkins, California State University, Northridge; David Freeman, Valencia College; Joyce Gatta, Middlesex Community College; Kendra Haggard, Northeastern State University; Karin Hauschild, Northern Kentucky University; Andrew M. Howard, University of the District of Columbia Community College; Nikkina Hughes, Tarrant County College; Curt Hutchison, Leeward Community College; Spring Hyde, Lincoln College; Patrice Johnson, Eastfield College; Therese Jones, Lewis University; Tracie Justus, Georgia Perimeter College; Ken Kouba, Prairie State College; Kevin Lamkins, Capital Community College; Katherine Lang, Community College of Allegheny County; Aaron Lelito, Erie Community College; Jonathan Lowndes, Broward College; Joshua Mattern, Waubonsee Community College; Angelina Misaghi, California State University, Northridge; Ela Newman, University of Texas at Brownsville; Thomas Nicholas, Prairie State College; John Nordlof, Eastern University; Donna Obrzut, Henry Ford Community College; Donna Pallanti, Albertus Magnus College; Charles Porter, Wor-Wic Community College; Patricia Pullenza, Mesa

Community College; Margaret Quinn, Montgomery County Community College; Minati Roychoudhuri, Capital Community College; Lisa M. Russell, Georgia Northwestern Technical College; Kimberly G. Russell, West Kentucky Community and Technical College; Robin Smith, Towson University; Selena Stewart-Alexander, Eastfield College; Qiana Towns, Davenport University; Brenda Tuberville, Rogers State University; Elizabeth Wallace, Georgia Perimeter College; Eliza Warren, Christian Brothers University; Ann L. Wells, Coconino Community College; and Stephanie Zerkel-Humbert, Maple Woods Community College.

At Bedford/St. Martin's, we continue to be grateful to founder and former president Charles Christensen, former president Joan Feinberg, and former editor in chief Nancy Perry, who believed in this project and gave us support and encouragement from the outset. We thank Vice President for the Humanities Edwin Hill, Executive Program Director Leasa Burton, and Senior Program Manager for Developmental English Karita dos Santos for overseeing this edition. We are also grateful to Edward Dionne, Senior Content Project Manager at Macmillan Learning and to Misbah Ansari, Senior Project Manager at Lumina, for guiding the book ably through production. Thanks also go to Lauren Arrant, Marketing Manager, as well as to Assistant Editor Paola Garcia-Muniz, a valued member of our team. Finally, we thank Cynthia Ward, Senior Development Editor, for her conscientious attention to detail and her creative contributions to the project.

It almost goes without saying that *Focus on Writing* could not exist without our students, whose words appear on almost every page of the book in sample sentences, paragraphs, and essays. We thank all of them, past and present, who gave us permission to use their work.

Finally, we are grateful for the survival and growth of the writing partnership we entered into when we were graduate students. We had no idea then of the wonderful places our collaborative efforts would take us. Now, we know.

Laurie G. Kirszner

Stephen R. Mandell

A Note to Students

Most people agree that the best way to learn to write is by writing. In a sense, then, you are already something of an expert when it comes to writing; after all, you have been writing for years—not just for your classes but also in your everyday life. For example, you update your social media profiles, post and respond to comments, and send messages; you probably text or tweet every day. In these situations, you write fluently and with confidence because you know your audience and you know what you want to say.

As you probably already know, however, college writing is different from this informal writing; "textspeak," abbreviations, and shorthand are not acceptable in academic writing assignments. Still, you can build on what you already know about writing to make your experience work for you in this new setting. As you go through this book, you will learn skills and strategies that will help you learn to write in a variety of contexts with clarity and confidence.

As teachers—and as former students—we know how demanding college can be and how hard it is to juggle academic assignments with work and family responsibilities. We also know that you don't want to waste your time. That's why in *Focus on Writing* we make information easy to find and use and include a variety of features to help you become a better writer.

Boxes

Preview boxes. Each chapter in Units 1–3 starts with a list of key concepts that will be discussed in the chapter. Looking at these boxes before you begin the chapter will give you an overview of what's to come.

Writing prompt boxes. Most chapters in Units 1–3 start with a Focus on Writing activity, accompanied by a visual, that asks you to begin writing about a topic. Later in the chapter, a TEST-Revise-Edit-Proofread prompt guides you to fine-tune your writing.

FYI boxes. Throughout the book, purple-outlined boxes with the letters *FYI* (For Your Information) highlight useful information, explain key concepts, and offer tips for using technology.

Grammar in Context boxes. Throughout the writing chapters, boxes identify key grammar issues. These boxes will help you understand how particular grammatical concepts are relevant to your writing. They also include cross-references to the chapters in Unit 4, Revising and Editing Your Writing, where these concepts are discussed in greater depth.

Word Power boxes. Marginal Word Power boxes define unfamiliar words that appear in the text's explanations and reading selections.

Checklists

Self-Assessment Checklists. Chapters 2 and 13 include Self-Assessment Checklists that enable you to measure your understanding of basic paragraph and essay structure.

Review Checklists. All grammar chapters and some of the writing chapters end with a summary of the most important information in the chapter. You can use these checklists to review material for quizzes or to remind yourself of key points.

TEST Checklists. All paragraph development chapters and both essay development chapters end with checklists that help you check your writing for the **TEST** elements.

Contents

*Asterisks indicate new reading selections.

unit 3 Focus on Essays 179

15   Patterns of Essay Development: Exemplification, Narration, Process, Cause and Effect, and Comparison and Contrast   235

*Asterisks indicate new reading selections.

16 Patterns of Essay Development: Description, Classification, Definition, and Argument 283

*Asterisks indicate new reading selections.

17 Writing with Sources 326

Unit 4 Revising and Editing Your Writing 359

unit 5   Reading Essays   619

37 Readings for Writers   620

*Asterisks indicate new reading selections.

Thematic Table of Contents

*Asterisks indicate new reading selections.

xxix

Language

Media and Society

Race and Culture

Science and Technology

*Asterisks indicate new reading selections.

Parents and Children

About the Authors

During their long collaboration, Laurie Kirszner and Stephen Mandell have written a number of best-selling college texts for Bedford/St. Martin's, including *Patterns for College Writing*, *Foundations First*, *Writing First*, *Focus on Writing*, *Practical Argument*, and most recently, *Focus on Reading and Writing*. **Laurie Kirszner** is an emeritus Professor of English at the University of the Sciences, where she has taught composition, literature, creative writing, and scientific writing and served as coordinator of the first-year writing program. **Stephen Mandell** is a Professor of English at Drexel University, where he founded and directed the basic writing program and has taught composition, literature, speech, and technical and business writing.

Kirszner/Mandell, *Focus on Writing*, 5e, © 2020 Bedford/St. Martin's

1 Reading to Write

1 Focus on Active Reading

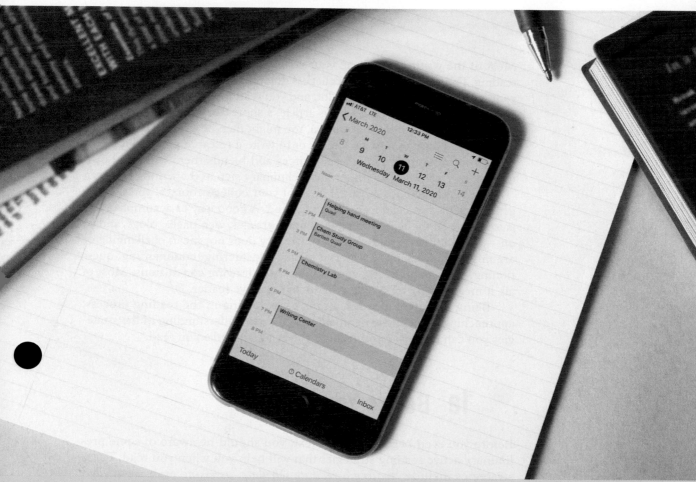

Photo Researchers/Science Source

focus on active reading

Think about what you already know about how to manage your time.
Later in this chapter, you will read and write about a passage on this topic.

In this chapter, you will learn to

- use active reading strategies before you read (1a).
- use active reading strategies as you read (1b).
- use active reading strategies after you read (1c).
- write a response paragraph (1d).

Most of the writing you do in your college courses will be in response to reading. The reading you do in college is different from the reading you do on your own. In college, you read a lot, and you read for a reason. For example, you might be asked to read a news article, a short story, a textbook chapter, or an article in a professional journal. You might then be expected to write an informal response to a writer's ideas or to write a research paper that incorporates information from several sources and blends them with your own ideas. Thus, reading is an important preliminary step in the writing process.

Because reading is essential in all of your college courses, you need to get as much as you can from what you read. A good way to accomplish this is to approach the texts you read—books, articles, web pages, blogs, and so on—with a critical eye. **Reading critically** does not mean challenging or arguing with every idea; rather, it means considering, commenting, questioning, assessing, making connections, and drawing conclusions. Most of all, it means being an active rather than a passive reader.

Being an **active reader** means participating in the reading process: approaching a reading assignment with a clear understanding of the strategies you can use *before* you read, *as* you read, and *after* you read.

 ## 1a Before You Read

Before you even begin reading a text, you should be aware of some preliminary active reading strategies that will help you when you read. These strategies include *creating a reading schedule*, *assessing prior knowledge*, *understanding your purpose*, and *previewing*.

Creating a Reading Schedule

As a college student, you have a lot to do, so planning your reading and study time is very important. One useful time-management strategy is creating a **reading schedule** that maps out how many pages you will read and when you will read them.

For example, if you are assigned to read thirty-six pages in your biology textbook, and the time you have available is between 3 p.m. Monday and 11 a.m. Wednesday, you could map out a reading schedule like the following one.

---

36 pages/3 days = 12 pages per day

Monday: Read pages 1–12 (7:30–8:45 p.m.)

Tuesday: Read pages 13–24 (3:15–4:30 p.m.)

Wednesday: Read pages 25–36 (7:30–8:45 a.m.)

TOTAL PAGES = 36

When creating your reading schedule, be sure to specify exact times for your reading. If you have blocked out specific times, you will be less likely to procrastinate. Also, be realistic about the number of pages you will read each time, and give yourself more time than you think you will need.

PRACTICE

1-1   For practice, create a reading schedule like the one illustrated above for an assignment in one of your classes.

FYI

Preparing to Read

Active reading requires your full attention. Following these guidelines will help you focus as you read:

- **Find a quiet place to study**. If you will be constantly interrupted in your home or dorm room, find an alternative spot, such as the college library, your local public library, a coffee shop, or a bookstore.

- **Read in the same place and at the same time each day**. Block out regular times for reading, and then list your assignments for each week. Once you develop a routine of reading in the same place and at the same time, you'll find it easier to focus, and concentrated reading will become a useful habit.

- **Read when you are alert**. Choose a time of day when you're not hungry or tired.

(Continued)

- **Avoid distractions**. Turn off the television. Silence your cell phone; ignore texts; and resist visiting Facebook, YouTube, Snapchat, Instagram, or Twitter. Every time you look at your cell phone, you'll lose your concentration.

- **Break readings into manageable chunks**. Don't try to finish a long reading in one sitting. Instead, try breaking a chapter into sections and stopping at the end of each section to make sure you have understood what you have just read. Be sure to reread any passages you find confusing.

- **Build in breaks**. Stop at the end of a chapter, a long section, or an article to stretch your legs, get coffee, or take a short walk.

- **Build in rewards for completing assignments**. Once you've completed your reading for the day, reward yourself. For example, text with a friend or order pizza.

Assessing Prior Knowledge

WORD POWER

assessing measuring; determining the value, extent, or significance

prior preceding in time or order

Before you begin a reading assignment, you might want to **assess your prior knowledge**—that is, ask yourself what you already know about a subject and what you still need (or want) to know about it. Assessing your prior knowledge will help you to decide how much time you will need to read and which specific reading strategies to use. For example, if you already know a good deal about animal and plant cells, reading a chapter in your biology textbook about them may not be very difficult for you. However, if you have no idea how animal and plant cells are different, you will probably have to spend more time reading the chapter in your biology textbook.

Questions for Assessing Prior Knowledge

To assess your prior knowledge, start by asking the following questions:

- Can you predict what the reading material will be about?
- What do you already know about the subject?
- How is the text similar to (or different from) other texts you have read?
- Is there anything in your background that helps you relate to or understand the material?
- How interested are you in this subject?
- What do you hope to learn from your reading?

Understanding Your Purpose

Before you begin to read, you should make sure you have a clear understanding of your **purpose** for reading. For example, are you reading to study for a test or quiz? For a research project? To locate information? To complete an assignment? Understanding your purpose, like assessing your prior knowledge, can help you to decide how much time you will need and what reading strategies you will use. For example, if you are reading to prepare for an informal discussion with your study group, you will not need to read as carefully as you might if you were studying for an exam.

Questions for Understanding Your Purpose

To understand your purpose for reading, ask the following questions:

- Why are you reading?

- Will you be expected to discuss what you are reading? If so, will you discuss it in class? In a conference with your instructor?

- Will you have to write about what you are reading? If so, will you be expected to write a brief informal response (for example, a journal entry) or a longer, more formal one (for example, an essay)?

- Will you be tested on the material?

Previewing

Once you have set up a reading schedule, assessed your prior knowledge, and established your purpose for reading, you are ready to **preview**, focusing on *skimming* and *scanning* the text.

Skimming

When you **skim** a text, you read it quickly, to get a sense of the writer's main idea and key supporting points. This strategy is particularly useful when you need to read many pages in a short amount of time. (Skimming can also help you determine if a text will be useful to you.)

As you skim, you look at the text's **visual signals**: the title, the author's name, the first paragraph (which often contains a thesis statement or overview), and the last paragraph (which often contains a summary of the writer's points). You might also look at each paragraph's first sentence, which often states the paragraph's main idea. As you skim, you should also look at other visual signals for clues to content and emphasis—for example, headings, boxed text, and images. (Later on, as you read, you will look at **verbal signals**—the words and phrases the writer uses to indicate which points are emphasized and how ideas are arranged.)

Guidelines for Skimming

When skimming a text, look for these visual signals:

- The title
- The author's name
- The opening paragraph, searching for the sentence that best expresses the main idea
- The closing paragraph, searching for a summary of the writer's ideas
- The first sentence of each of the other paragraphs
- Headings and subheadings
- *Italicized* and **boldfaced** words
- Numbered lists
- Bulleted lists (like this one)
- Graphs, charts, tables, diagrams, photographs, and other visuals
- Any information that is in color

Scanning

Scanning is a purposeful, focused way of looking at a text to locate specific information—often to enable you to answer specific questions about the material. For example, if you need to prepare for a quiz or answer questions on a worksheet, you would scan the text, looking only for specific words and phrases that will give you the information you need.

Guidelines for Scanning

When scanning a text, look for the following elements:

- Bulleted or numbered lists that might enumerate the writer's key points
- **Boldfaced** or *italicized* words
- Organizational words such as *first*, *second*, *third*, *next*, and *finally*
- Proper nouns (capitalized)
- Numbers
- Words set in quotation marks
- Specific words or ideas related to information you are looking for

---

WORD POWER

enumerate to name one by one

When you have finished previewing a text, you should have a general sense of what the writer wants to communicate.

PRACTICE

1-2   Below is a discussion of time management from a first-year college textbook. In preparation for class discussion and other activities that will be assigned throughout this chapter, **skim** the textbook passage. As you skim, try to identify the writer's main idea and key supporting points and perhaps jot them down for future reference.

TIME-MANAGEMENT STRATEGIES

Learning to manage your time is very important for success in college. Here are some strategies you can adopt to make this task easier:

1. *Use an organizer.* New electronic tools are constantly being developed to help you stay organized. For example, Schoolbinder, a free online organizer, can help you manage your time and create a study schedule. If you have trouble blocking out distractions when you are studying, a site like StudyRails can be helpful. For a small monthly fee, this site will help you plan a study schedule and alert you to when it's time to focus on schoolwork. It can also be programmed to block your go-to recreational sites during hours when you should be studying.

   You can use the calendar function on your smartphone or tablet to keep track of deadlines and appointments. At the beginning of the semester, enter key pieces of information from each course syllabus—for example, the date of every quiz and exam and the due date of every paper. (Set the alert function of your calendar two or three days in advance so you have enough time to prepare.)

   As the semester progresses, continue to add assignments and deadlines. In addition, enter information such as days when a class will be canceled or will meet in the computer lab or in the library, reminders to bring a particular book or piece of equipment to class, and appointments with instructors or other college personnel. (If you'd like, you can also note reminders and schedule appointments that are not related to school—for example, changes in your work hours, a dental appointment, or lunch with a friend.) Some students also like to keep a separate month-by-month "to-do" list. Deleting completed items can give you a feeling of accomplishment—and make the road ahead look shorter.

2. *Use a calendar.* Buy a large wall calendar, and post it where you will see it every morning—on your desk, on the refrigerator, or wherever you keep your phone, your keys, and your ID. At the beginning of the semester, fill in important dates such as school holidays, work commitments, exam dates, and due dates for papers and projects. When you

return from classes each day, update the calendar with any new information you have entered into your organizer.

3. ***Plan ahead.*** If you think you will need help from a writing center tutor to revise a paper that is due in two weeks, don't wait until day thirteen to make an appointment; all the tutoring slots may be filled by then. To be safe, make an appointment about a week in advance.

4. ***Learn to enjoy downtime.*** When you have a free minute, take time for yourself—and don't feel guilty about it.

PRACTICE

1-3 Look once again at "Time-Management Strategies." This time, **scan** the passage to look for the following details, noting where you found each piece of information:

- Examples of electronic tools that can help you stay organized
- Suggestions for the best places to put a calendar
- How far in advance you should make an appointment with a writing center tutor

 # 1b As You Read

Once you have finished previewing a text, it is time to begin reading. Two active reading strategies—*marking* up a text and *annotating* a text—can aid your comprehension as you read. In addition, at some point in this stage of the reading process, you will find it helpful to **TEST** the text you are reading.

TESTing a Text

The letters that spell **TEST** form an acronym for the four basic elements of an essay: **T**hesis (main idea), **E**vidence, **S**ummary, and **T**ransitions. **TEST** is a reading strategy that you can use to help you identify these elements in the professional essays and other texts you will encounter in your college courses. As you will discover in Chapters 2 and 13, **TEST** is also a writing strategy that you can use to help you take inventory of the elements in the paragraphs and essays you compose. Using **TEST** to survey a text will help you to get a general idea of what you are reading; it can also help you to see the logic of the writer's discussion and the relationship between the key ideas and the evidence that supports them.

T <u>Thesis</u>—Look for the thesis or **main idea**, which is sometimes stated directly, often (but not always) in the opening paragraphs and often, but not always, in a single sentence. Try to decide why the writer placed the main idea where it is. If the main idea is **implied** (suggested), think about why it is not explicitly stated. If no thesis is included, try to write a sentence that states the main idea in your own words.

E **Evidence**—Look for the evidence that supports the writer's main idea. This evidence can be in the form of facts, examples, statistics, anecdotes based on the writer's observations or experiences, or the opinions of experts. Think about why the writer chose these types of evidence rather than others. Consider whether different evidence or additional support is needed and whether any evidence is irrelevant or unnecessary. Also, ask yourself what information the writer might have omitted, and why. Finally, think about what you can **infer** from the evidence presented.

S <u>Summary</u>—Look for a statement that lists or summarizes the writer's key points or the essay's main idea. (Often, this summary appears in the closing paragraphs.) If no summary is included, write a sentence that could serve as a summary statement.

T <u>Transitions</u>—Look for transitional words and expressions that connect ideas within and between paragraphs. How do these transitions help you to understand the writer's ideas and follow his or her train of thought? Look for **transitional paragraphs**, paragraphs whose purpose is not to supply evidence but rather to move readers from one section of the essay to the next.

When you read essays by professional writers, you should always look for the four **TEST** elements. In some cases, however, you may not be able to easily identify these elements. For example, professional writers may imply a thesis instead of stating it directly or suggest, rather than explicitly summarizing, their main points. In a long or complex professional essay, particularly one whose main idea is controversial, the main idea may appear at the end instead of near the beginning. In addition, the conclusion may not include a summary statement; it may simply suggest the main idea and not summarize it at all.

Despite these variations, looking for the four **TEST** elements as you read is important because it will help you to identify the main idea and the evidence that supports it. This in turn will aid your comprehension and enable you to respond in writing to the writer's ideas.

In the following essay, "What American Citizenship Makes Possible," by Colin Powell, the **TEST** elements have been identified for you.

What American Citizenship Makes Possible

Colin Powell

Taking the Oath of Allegiance to the U.S., June 20, in Washington, DC.

T	Thesis
E	Evidence
S	Summary
T	Transitions

T Thesis

1 Many years ago, after I had become a four-star general and then chairman of the Joint Chiefs of Staff, *The Times* of London wrote an article observing that if my parents had sailed to England rather than New York, "the most they could have dreamed of for their son in the military was to become a sergeant in one of the lesser British regiments."

2 Only in America could the son of two poor Jamaican immigrants become the first African-American, the youngest person and the first ROTC graduate from a public university to hold those positions, among many other firsts. My parents arrived—one at the Port of Philadelphia, the other at Ellis Island—in search of economic opportunity, but their goal was to become American citizens, because they knew what that made possible.

3 Immigration is a vital part of our national being because people come here not only to build a better life for themselves and their children, but to become Americans. With access to education and a clear path to citizenship, they routinely become some of the best, most-patriotic Americans you'll ever know. That's why I am a strong supporter of immigration-law reform: America stands to benefit from it as much as, if not more than, the immigrants themselves.

4   Contrary to some common misconceptions, neighborhoods with greater concentrations of immigrants have lower rates of crime and violence than comparable nonimmigrant neighborhoods, according to a 2015 report from the National Academies of Sciences, Engineering, and Medicine. Foreign-born men age 18–39 are jailed at one-quarter the rate of native-born American men of the same age.

T Transitions

5   Today's immigrants are learning English at the same rate or faster than earlier waves of newcomers, and first-generation arrivals are less likely to die from cardiovascular disease or cancer than native-born people. They experience fewer chronic health conditions, have lower infant-mortality and obesity rates, and have a longer life expectancy.

E Evidence

6   My parents met and married here and worked in the garment industry, bringing home $50 to $60 a week. They had two children: my sister Marilyn, who became a teacher, and me. I didn't do as well as the family hoped; I caused a bit of a crisis when I decided to stay in the Army. "Couldn't he get a job? Why is he still in the Army?"

7   We were a tightknit family with cousins and aunts and uncles all over the place. But that family network didn't guarantee success. What did? The New York City public education system.

8   I'm a public-education kid, from kindergarten through to Morris High School in the South Bronx and, finally, City College of New York. New York University made me an offer, but tuition there was $750 a year. Such a huge sum in 1954! I would never impose that on my parents, so it was CCNY, where back then tuition was free. I got a B.S. in geology and a commission as an Army second lieutenant, and that was that. And it all cost my parents nothing. Zero.

E Evidence

9   After CCNY, I was lucky to be among the first group of officers commissioned just after the Army was desegregated. I competed against West Pointers, against grads from Harvard and VMI and the Citadel and other top schools. And to my surprise, I discovered I had gotten a pretty good education in the New York City public schools. Not only in geology and the military, but also in wider culture. I had learned a little about music, about Chaucer's *Canterbury Tales* and theater and things like that. I got a complete education, all through public schools, and it shapes me to this day.

10   This amazing gift goes back to 1847 when the Free Academy of the City of New York was created with a simple mandate: "Give every child the opportunity for an education." And who would pay for it? The citizens and taxpayers of New York City and State. They did it and kept at it when the Academy became CCNY in 1866, because they knew that poor immigrants were their children. They were the future.

T Transitions

11   They still are. Today some 41 million immigrants and 37.1 million U.S.-born children of immigrants live in the U.S. Taken together, the first and second generations are one-quarter of the population. While some countries, like Japan and Russia, worry that population decline threatens their economies, America's economic future vibrates with promise from immigrants' energy, creativity, and ambition.

Evidence **E**

12 Every one of these people deserves the same educational opportunities I had. It wasn't, and isn't, charity to immigrants or to the poor. Those early New Yorkers were investing in their own future by making education and citizenship accessible to "every child." They knew it—and what a future it became!

13 We still have that model. But today too many politicians seem to think that shortchanging education will somehow help society. It does not. It hurts society. We need people who know that government has no more important function than securing the terrain, which means opening the pathways to the future for everyone, educating them to be consumers, workers, leaders, and citizens.

S Summary

14 We are all immigrants, wave after wave over several hundred years. And every wave makes us richer: in cultures, in language and food, in music and dance, and in intellectual capacity. We should treasure this immigrant tradition, and we should reform our laws to guarantee it.

15 In this political season, let us remember the most important task of our government: making Americans. Immigrants—future Americans—make America better every single day.

★ ★ ★

In this essay, retired general and former Secretary of State Colin Powell presents a powerful argument about the value of immigrants. Noting that he himself is the son of immigrants, he goes on to convince readers that his position is valid.

Instead of stating his thesis explicitly in a single sentence at the end of the first paragraph, a technique that serves beginning writers well, he presents his main idea in paragraph 3, after first introducing himself and establishing his status as a son of immigrants. Paragraph 3 then explains his main idea: that immigrants "become American" and thus become patriotic citizens—and that this in turn benefits the nation.

Powell's essay includes helpful transitions between paragraphs, such as "They were the future. They still are" (paras. 10–11), as well as a transitional paragraph (para. 7). He also includes a summary (para. 14) that stresses the importance of immigrants, and he closes with a strong appeal to his audience (para. 15).

Marking Up a Text

When you **mark up** a text, you use underlining and symbols to identify key ideas. This active reading strategy will help you to understand the writer's ideas and make connections among them when you reread. Be selective as you proceed. You will eventually be rereading every underlined word, phrase, and sentence—so set off only the most important information.

Marking Up a Text

- <u>Underline</u> key ideas—for example, topic sentences.
- Box or circle words or phrases you want to remember.
- Place a check mark (✓) or star (*) next to an important idea.
- Place double check marks (✓✓) or double stars (**) next to an especially significant idea.
- Draw lines or arrows to connect related ideas. ⟶
- Put a question mark (?) beside a word or idea that you need to look up.
- [Bracket] text you want to set off.
- Number the writer's key supporting points or examples.

FYI

Knowing What to Mark Up

You want to identify what is important—but how do you *know* what is important?

- *Look for visual signals.* As a general rule, you should look for the same **visual signals** you looked for when you did your previewing. Many of the ideas you will want to set off will probably be found in material that is visually set off from the rest of the text—opening and closing paragraphs, lists, and so on.
- *Look for verbal signals.* At this stage, you should also look for **verbal signals**—words and phrases that often introduce key points. (These are listed in the box on page 15.)

Together, these visual and verbal signals will give you clues to the writer's meaning and emphasis.

Verbal Signals

As you read, look for the following verbal signals:

- Repeated words and phrases
- Phrases that signal emphasis ("The *primary* reason"; "The *most important* idea")
- Words that signal addition (*also, in addition, furthermore*)
- Words that signal time sequence (*first, after, then, next, finally*)
- Words that identify causes and effects (*because, as a result, for this reason*)

(Continued)

- Words that introduce examples (*for example*, *for instance*)
- Words that signal comparison (*likewise*, *similarly*)
- Words that signal contrast (*unlike*, *although*, *in contrast*)
- Words that signal contradiction (*however*, *on the contrary*)
- Words that signal a narrowing of the writer's focus (*in fact*, *specifically*, *in other words*)
- Words that signal summaries or conclusions (*to sum up*, *in conclusion*)

Here is how one student used underlining and symbols to mark up an excerpt from the newspaper article "What American Citizenship Makes Possible" by Colin Powell.

We were a tightknit family with cousins and aunts and uncles all over the place. But that family network didn't guarantee success. What did? The New York City public education system.

I'm a public-education kid, from kindergarten through to Morris High School in the South Bronx and, finally, City College of New York. New York University made me an offer, but tuition there was $750 a year. Such a huge sum in 1954! I would never impose that on my parents, so it was CCNY, where back then tuition was free. I got a B.S. in geology and a commission as an Army second lieutenant, and that was that. And it all cost my parents nothing. Zero.

After CCNY, I was lucky to be among the first group of officers commissioned just after the Army was desegregated. I competed against West Pointers, against grads from Harvard and VMI and the Citadel and other top schools. And to my surprise, I discovered I had gotten a pretty good education in the New York City public schools. Not only in geology and the military, but also in wider culture. I had learned a little about music, about Chaucer's "Canterbury Tales" and theater and things like that. I got a complete education, all through public schools, and it shapes me to this day.

This amazing gift goes back to 1847 when the Free Academy of the City of New York was created with a simple mandate: "Give every child the opportunity for an education." And who would pay for it? The citizens and taxpayers of New York City and State. They did it and kept at it when the Academy became CCNY in 1866, because they knew that poor immigrants ✱ were their children. They were the future.

The student who marked up the passage above was preparing to write an essay about whether public colleges should be free. Because the passage included no visual signals apart from the paragraph divisions, she looked carefully for verbal signals.

The student began by underlining the writer's main idea in the passage's first paragraph: that New York City public schools made him a success. She then circled the key terms *success*, *lucky*, *amazing gift*, and *opportunity*, which she thought conveyed a sense of the writer's impression of his public school education, and she drew lines to connect these related terms.

The student underlined sentences that supported the main idea, drawing an arrow to connect two related points ("I'm a public-education kid" and "I got a complete education, all through public schools, and it shapes me to this day.") She also bracketed an unfamiliar reference to desegregating the army and put a question mark beside it to remind herself to look it up.

Finally, she underlined and starred some of the passage's closing lines, which she thought summarized the main idea: that poor immigrants, like Powell himself, have benefited from their free education and owe their success to the New York City schools.

PRACTICE

1-4   Review the marked-up passage on pages 19 and 20. How would your own underlining and symbols on this passage be similar to or different from the sample student's? How does the purpose for your reading affect what you might set off?

PRACTICE

1-5   Reread "Time-Management Strategies" (pp. 9–10). As you reread, underline and star the main idea, box and circle key words, checkmark important points, draw lines and arrows to connect related ideas, and so on. Be sure to circle each unfamiliar word and put a question mark above it so that you will remember to look it up later on.

FYI

Using Context Clues

Before you turn to a dictionary to determine the meaning of an unfamiliar word, see if you can figure out the meaning from context clues in the text.

Annotating a Text

Once you have marked up a passage, your next step is to *annotate* it. **Annotating** a passage means reading critically and making notes—of questions, reactions, reminders, and ideas for writing or discussion—in the margins or between the lines. (If you run out of room on the page, you can use sticky notes.) Keeping an informal record of ideas as they occur to you will prepare you for class discussion and for writing. This is the first step in engaging with the text on a deeper level, one in which you analyze and evaluate it.

Questions for Annotating

As you read, keeping the following questions in mind will help you make useful annotations:

- What is the writer saying? What do you think the writer is suggesting or implying? What makes you think so?
- What is the writer's purpose (his or her reason for writing)?
- What kind of audience is the writer addressing?
- Is the writer responding to another writer's ideas?
- What is the writer's main idea? Is it stated or implied? Can you restate the main idea in your own words?
- How does the writer support his or her points? Does the writer use facts? Statistics? Expert opinion? Personal experiences or observations?
- Does the writer include enough supporting details and examples?
- How does the writer signal a shift from one point to the next?
- Does the writer summarize the main idea or key points? If so, where?
- What is the writer's main idea?
- Does the writer seem well informed? Reasonable? Fair?
- Do you understand the writer's vocabulary?
- Do you understand the writer's ideas?
- Do you agree with the points the writer is making?
- How are the ideas presented in this reading selection like (or unlike) those presented in other texts you have read?

FYI

Making Useful Annotations

As you annotate, remember that you should not write too much or too little; good annotations fit in the margins or on a small sticky note. You should *not* write your annotations on a separate sheet of paper. If you do, you will be tempted to write too much, and you can easily lose track of where a particular note belongs or what point it comments on. (Moreover, if you lose the sheet of paper, you will also lose all your notes and thoughts.)

Think of annotations as a study aid that you can consult when you return to the text a few days later. Brief, useful annotations will help you follow the writer's ideas and remember what is most important in the text.

The following passage, which reproduces the student's marked-up text (pp. 16–17), also includes her annotations.

We were a tightknit family with cousins and aunts and uncles all over the place. But that family network didn't guarantee success. What did? The New York City public education system.

I'm a public-education kid, from kindergarten through to Morris High School in the South Bronx and, finally, City College of New York. New York University made me an offer, but tuition there was $750 a year. Such a huge sum in 1954! I would never impose that on my parents, so it was CCNY, where back then tuition was free. I got a B.S. in geology and a commission as an Army second lieutenant, and that was that. And it all cost my parents nothing. Zero.

Is CCNY still free?

After CCNY, I was lucky to be among the first group of officers commissioned just after the Army was desegregated. I competed against West Pointers, against grads from Harvard and VMI and the Citadel and other top schools. And to my surprise, I discovered I had gotten a pretty good education in the New York City public schools. Not only in geology and the military, but also in wider culture. I had learned a little about music, about Chaucer's "Canterbury Tales" and theater and things like that. I got a complete education, all through public schools, and it shapes me to this day.

?

U.S. Army segregated until 1948 (through WWII)

Why is he surprised to find his education was good?

This [amazing gift] goes back to 1847 when the Free Academy of the City of New York was created with a simple mandate: "Give every child the [opportunity] for an education." And who would pay for it? <u>The citizens and taxpayers of New York City and State.</u> They did it and kept at it when the Academy became CCNY in 1866, because <u>they knew that poor immigrants</u> * <u>were their children. They were the future.</u>

In her marginal annotations, the student wrote a brief explanation of the reference to army segregation and asked two questions. She thought that answers to these questions would give her information that would help her develop ideas for her paper on whether public colleges should be free.

PRACTICE

1-6   Reread "Time-Management Strategies" (p. 9). This time, refer to the Questions for Annotating (p. 18), and use them to guide you as you write down your own thoughts and questions in the margins of the passage. As you read, you might note where you agree or disagree with the writer, and briefly explain why or briefly summarize any points you think are particularly important. Be sure to look up any unfamiliar words you have circled and to write brief definitions. Think of these annotations as your preparation for discussing the passage in class—and, eventually, for writing about it.

PRACTICE

1-7   Exchange books with another student, and read his or her highlighting and annotations on "Time-Management Strategies." How are your written responses similar to the other student's? How are they different? Do your classmate's responses help you to see anything new about the passage? Looking again at your own annotations, consider how you might use them to write a response to the suggestions in "Time-Management Strategies."

1c   After You Read

After you finish reading, three additional active reading strategies—outlining, summarizing, and paraphrasing—will enable you to better retain and use the information you have acquired. Once you have a command of the material, you will be prepared to express your reactions by writing a *response paragraph.*

Outlining

Outlining is an active reading strategy that you can use to help you understand a text. Unlike a **formal outline**, which follows strict conventions, an **informal outline** is just a list of a passage's key ideas and supporting points in the order in which they are presented. After you have made an informal outline of a passage, you should be able to see which ideas are more important than others, as well as how the ideas are related.

FYI

Constructing an Informal Outline

To construct an informal outline, follow these guidelines:

1. Write or type the passage's main idea at the top of a sheet of paper. (This will remind you of the writer's focus and help keep your outline on track.)

2. At the left margin, record the most important idea of the first body paragraph or the first part of the passage.

3. Indent the next line a few spaces, and list the examples or details that support this idea.

4. As ideas become more specific, indent further. (Ideas that have the same degree of importance are indented the same distance from the left margin.)

Repeat the process with each body paragraph or part of the passage.

The student who marked up and annotated the excerpt from Colin Powell's "What American Citizenship Makes Possible" made the following informal outline to help her understand the writer's ideas.

Main idea: According to Colin Powell, he—like many other children from poor immigrant families—owes his success to the free public education he received.

        New York City public school experience
            Attended free public elementary and high school
            Attended CCNY
                Free tuition
                B.S. degree
                Army commission

        Army experience
            Became officer
            Realized his education had been good
                Geology and military
                "Wider culture"

PRACTICE

1-8   Make an informal outline of "Time-Management Strategies" (p. 9). Refer to your underlining, symbols, and annotations as you construct your outline. When you have finished, check to make certain your outline accurately represents the writer's emphasis and the relationships among his or her ideas.

Summarizing and Paraphrasing

Once you have **TEST**ed, marked up, annotated, and outlined a passage, you may want to *summarize* or *paraphrase* it to help you understand it better.

Summarizing

A **summary** is a brief restatement, *in your own words*, of a passage's main idea. A summary does not include supporting examples and details, and it does not include your own ideas or opinions. For this reason, a summary is always much shorter than the original passage—usually no longer than a few sentences.

> ### Guidelines for Writing a Summary
>
> To write a summary, follow these guidelines:
>
> 1. Reread your source, and review your outline.
> 2. Consulting your outline, restate the passage's main idea *in your own words,* using synonyms wherever possible and using your own syntax. If you decide to use a distinctive word or phrase from the original passage, put it in quotation marks.
> 3. To avoid accidentally using the exact same language as the original, do not look at the passage when you are writing your summary.
> 4. Be sure to identify the author and title of the source.
> 5. Reread your source to make sure you have accurately summarized the main idea and key supporting details and that you have not included any unrelated or unnecessary material. Also, check to make sure you have not accidentally used the source's exact wording or sentence structure. (If you have, you will have committed **plagiarism**. See 17c Using Sources Responsibly.)

The student who marked up, annotated, and outlined the excerpt from "What American Citizenship Makes Possible" wrote the following summary. Note that her summary includes the author's name and the title of the source.

In "What American Citizenship Makes Possible," Colin Powell attributes his success in life to the free public education he received from kindergarten through college and stresses the value of free college education, particularly for children of immigrants (like himself).

PRACTICE

1-9   Write a summary of "Time-Management Strategies" (p. 9). Use your informal outline to guide you, and keep your summary brief—no more than two or three sentences long.

Paraphrasing

When you **paraphrase**, you put a writer's words into your own, substituting different vocabulary and sentence structure for the writer's. The act of paraphrasing helps you to understand a text better because it requires you to think about exactly what the writer means to say and how he or she says it.

As is the case with summaries, paraphrases do not include your own ideas or your opinions of the writer's statements. Unlike a summary, however, a paraphrase can be the same length as (or longer than) the original.

Guidelines for Writing a Paraphrase

To write a paraphrase, follow these guidelines:

1. Read the passage carefully.

2. Draft your paraphrase, following the order and emphasis of the original. Be sure to include the passage's main idea as well as the key supporting examples and details. Use your own syntax, use synonyms wherever possible, and put any distinctive words you borrow in quotation marks.

3. Reread your paraphrase, comparing it to the original source to make sure it reflects its meaning and emphasis and does not include any of the source's distinctive wording or sentence structure.

4. Be sure to include an in-text citation that references your Works Cited List.

The student who summarized the Colin Powell excerpt paraphrased a few sentences to help her understand his ideas.

ORIGINAL EXCERPT

I discovered I had gotten a pretty good education in the New York City public schools. Not only in geology and the military, but also in wider culture. I had learned a little about music, about Chaucer's *Canterbury Tales* and theater and things like that. I got a complete education, all through public schools, and it shapes me to this day.

PARAPHRASE

Powell learned that his New York City public school education was better than he had thought, giving him a foundation in "wider culture" as well as in subjects such as geology and in military topics. He discovered he had also learned something about subjects such as music, literature, and theater. The public school education he received "shapes [him] to this day" (p. 13).

The student writer knew that she had to avoid using the original excerpt's distinctive words or sentence constructions. When she came across distinctive phrases that were hard to put into different words, she kept the original words but put them in quotation marks to indicate that they were used in her source. (When she had to change the source's *me* to *him* to make it fit into her sentence, she set *him* in brackets to indicate her change.) She was also careful to retain the meaning and emphasis of Powell's ideas. (For more information on writing summaries and paraphrases, see 17b Using Paraphrase, Summary, and Quotation.)

 # 1d   Writing a Response

After you have marked up and annotated a reading selection, you are ready to write a **response**, in which you record your reactions to the writer's ideas.

Because a response is informal, no special guidelines or rules govern its format or structure, and informal style and personal opinions are acceptable.

The student who marked up, annotated, outlined, summarized, and paraphrased material from "What American Citizenship Makes Possible," wrote the following response.

In "What American Citizenship Makes Possible," General Colin Powell, former U.S. Secretary of State, discusses the ways in which immigrants enrich the United States. Summarizing his own experience as the son of poor Jamaican immigrants, Powell stresses the value of the free public education he received not just in elementary and high school but also through college, and he identifies this education as the key factor that led to his professional success. This seems like an exaggeration. He probably had many other important personal experiences and professional interactions that could have led to his success. Besides, a private college—even one he had to borrow money to attend—might have provided an even better education. By stressing how fortunate he was and how greatly he benefited, Powell seems to suggest that the "amazing gift" he received from New York City should be widely available today to students like him. If it were, he believes, it would provide a valuable opportunity for immigrants who cannot afford private college tuition. However, immigrant children could fund their education at private colleges with the help of loans, work-study, and tuition scholarships. Thus, Powell's point—that the children of poor immigrants should have access to free public college education—is questionable. These children may be "the future" of our country, as he says, but that does not mean that their college education should be subsidized.

The process of writing this response was very helpful to the student. The questions she asked suggested some interesting ideas that she could explore in class discussion or in a more fully developed piece of writing.

PRACTICE

1-10 Now that you have practiced the complete active reading process with the textbook excerpt on page 9, "Time-Management Strategies," write a response that explains your thoughts about the time-management strategies presented in the excerpt. In your response, you can discuss why these strategies would (or would not) be useful to you, or you can write about strategies you already use to manage your time.

CHAPTER REVIEW

REVIEW ACTIVITY

Graphic Organizer: *Active Reading Strategies*

Drawing on the information you learned in Chapter 1, use the graphic organizer that follows to map the various strategies that can be applied before, during, and after reading. Also include a brief explanation of how you plan to use each reading strategy this semester.

Before Reading Strategies	During Reading Strategies	After Reading Strategies
Strategy 1: _Creating a reading schedule_	Strategy 1: _____	Strategy 1: _____
I will apply strategy 1 by _Reading at least 15 pages of each textbook on Mon. – Thurs. between 7:00–9:00 p.m._	I will apply strategy 1 by _____	I will apply strategy 1 by _____
Strategy 2: _____		Strategy 2: _____
I will apply strategy 2 by _____	Strategy 2: _____	I will apply strategy 2 by _____
Strategy 3: _____	I will apply strategy 2 by _____	Strategy 3: _____
I will apply strategy 3 by _____		I will apply strategy 3 by _____
Strategy 4: _____		
I will apply strategy 4 by _____		

COLLABORATIVE ACTIVITY

Complete the crossword puzzle by entering the word or words that answer each clue. The answers are drawn from the key terms in Chapter 1 (which are set in boldface), and page numbers are provided to guide you back to the proper place in the chapter.

Hint: Five of the answers consist of two-word terms.

Example (2 Across):

The words and phrases the writer uses to indicate which points are emphasized and how ideas are arranged: VERBAL SIGNALS

ACROSS

2. The words and phrases the writer uses to indicate which points are emphasized and how ideas are arranged (see p. 7)

8. A plan that maps out how many pages you will read and when you will read them (two words) (see p. 4)

9. A reading strategy that helps you identify an essay's four key elements (see p. 10)

10. Clues to content and emphasis, such as headings, boxed text, and images (see p. 7)

13. Taking a purposeful, focused look at a text to locate specific information (see p. 8)

14. Tools to help you manage your time (see p. 9)

15. Putting a passage into your own words (see p. 23)

DOWN

1. Using underlining and symbols to identify key ideas (see p. 14)

3. A process involving strategies that include creating a reading schedule, assessing prior knowledge, understanding your purpose, and previewing (two words) (see p. 4)

4. A technique to help you understand the structure of a reading assignment as well as the ideas it communicates (see p. 21)

5. What you already know about a subject and what you still need (or want) to know about it (two words) (see p. 6)

6. Your reason for reading, such as for pleasure, for information, or to complete an assignment (see p. 7)

7. Writing a brief restatement, in your own words, of a passage's main idea (see p. 22)

11. Reading critically and making notes—of questions, reactions, reminders, and ideas for writing or discussion—in the margins or between the lines (see p. 18)

12. Reading a text quickly and trying to get a sense of the writer's main idea and key supporting points (see p. 7)

review checklist

✔ Being an active reader involves using strategies before, during, and after you read to help you retain and use the information in the text.

✔ Before you read, you should assess your prior knowledge, set a purpose for your reading, and preview the text. (See 1a.)

✔ As you read, **TEST** the text to help you identify its key elements. Also, mark up and annotate the text to help you identify the writer's key ideas. (See 1b.)

✔ After you read, outlining, summarizing, and paraphrasing can help you remember what you have read. (See 1c.)

✔ Once you have marked up and annotated a text, you can write a response paragraph to record your reactions to the writer's ideas. (See 1d.)

unit
2 Focus on Writing Paragraphs

unit
2
Focus on Writing Paragraphs

2 Writing a Paragraph

Huntstock/Brand X Pictures/Getty Images (left), Hero Images/Getty Images (right)

focus on writing

Today's college students may find themselves in either a traditional classroom or a career-oriented setting. What is the most important purpose of college for you—to get a general education or to learn skills to prepare you for a career? Think about this question as you read the pages that follow.

2a Understanding Paragraph Structure

Because paragraphs are central to almost every kind of writing, learning how to write one is an important step in becoming a competent writer. (Although a paragraph can be a complete piece of writing in itself—as it is in a short classroom exercise or an exam answer—most of the time, a paragraph is part of a longer piece of writing.)

A **paragraph** is a group of sentences that is unified by a single main idea. The **topic sentence** states the main idea, and the rest of the sentences in the paragraph provide **evidence** (examples and details) to support the main idea. The sentences in a paragraph are linked by **transitions**, words and phrases (such as *also* and *for example*) that show how ideas are related. At the end of the paragraph, a **summary statement** reinforces the main idea.

Paragraph Structure

Topic sentence —

Evidence —

Summary statement —

> In every paragraph you write, you need to include a main idea, supporting evidence, transitions, and a summary statement. First, state the main idea of the paragraph in a topic sentence. This idea will unify your paragraph. Then, add sentences to provide support for your topic sentence. In these sentences, you present and develop the evidence that will help readers understand your main idea. Next, check to make sure you have linked these sentences with transitions. Finally, write a summary statement, a sentence that reinforces your paragraph's main idea. If you follow this general structure, you are on your way to writing an effective paragraph.

Transitions (boxed)

The first letters of these four elements—**T**opic sentence, **E**vidence, **S**ummary statement, and **T**ransitions—spell **TEST**. Whenever you write a paragraph, you should **TEST** it to make sure it is complete.

FYI

The first sentence of a paragraph is **indented**, starting about half an inch from the left-hand margin. Every sentence begins with a capital letter and, in most cases, ends with a period. (Sometimes a sentence ends with a question mark or an exclamation point.)

PRACTICE

2-1 Bring two paragraphs to class—one from a newspaper or magazine article and one from a textbook. Compare your paragraphs with those brought in by other students. What features do all your paragraphs share? How do the paragraphs differ from one another?

The Writing Process

Writing is a **process**, a series of steps that begins in your college classes when you get an assignment:

- You start by thinking about what you want to say and finding ideas to write about. Then, you identify the main idea you want to get across.
- Once you have material to write about, you arrange the points that support your main idea in an order that makes sense to you.
- When you have decided how to arrange your ideas, you write a draft.
- When you finish your draft, you **TEST** it to make sure it includes all the elements of an effective paragraph.
- Finally, you revise, edit, and proofread.

The steps in the writing process are explained and illustrated in the pages that follow.

Plan

Organize

Draft

TEST

Revise, edit, and proofread

2b Focusing on Your Assignment, Purpose, and Audience

In college, a writing task usually begins with an assignment that gives you a topic to write about. Instead of jumping in headfirst and starting to write, take time to consider some questions about your **assignment** (*what* you are expected to write about), your **purpose** (*why* you are writing), and your **audience** (*for whom* you are writing). Answering these questions at this point will save you time in the long run.

Questions about Assignment, Purpose, and Audience

Assignment

- What is your assignment? Is it included on your course syllabus or posted on the class web page?
- Do you have a word or page limit?
- When is your assignment due?
- Will you be expected to do all of your work outside of class, or will you be doing some work in class?
- Will you be expected to work on your own or with others?
- Will you be allowed to revise before you hand in your assignment?
- Will you be allowed to revise after your assignment is graded?
- Does your instructor require a particular **format**?

Purpose

- Are you expected to express your personal reactions—for example, to tell how you feel about a piece of music or a news event?
- Are you expected to present information—for example, to answer an exam question, describe a scientific process, or summarize a story or essay you have read?
- Are you expected to argue for or against a position on a controversial issue?

Audience

- Who will read your paper—just your instructor or other students as well?
- How much will your readers know about your topic?
- Will your readers expect you to use **formal** or **informal** language?

WORD POWER

format specified arrangement of elements in a document—for example, where to type your name, the date, and the course number

---

WORD POWER

formal language language that is grammatically precise and uses words familiar to an educated audience

informal language language that is used in conversation and personal email; may include contractions and slang

PRACTICE

2-2 The text message and email shown below are addressed to two different kinds of audiences: the text message on the left addresses a friend; the email on the right addresses an instructor. Read these two communications and be prepared to explain how and why they are different in format, style, and word choice.

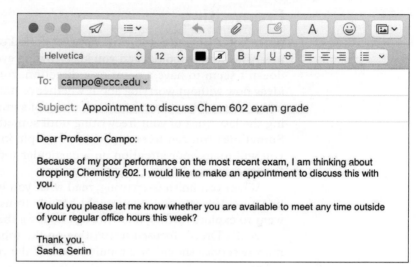

 ## 2c Finding Ideas to Write About

Once you know what, why, and for whom you are writing, you can begin the process of finding material to write about. This process is different for every writer.

In this chapter, you will be following the writing process of Stella Drew, a student in an introductory writing course, who was given the following assignment:

> Should community service—unpaid work in the community—be a required part of the college curriculum? Write a paragraph in which you answer this question.

Before she drafted her paragraph, Stella used a variety of strategies to find ideas to write about. The pages that follow illustrate the four strategies her instructor asked the class to try:

- Freewriting
- Brainstorming
- Clustering
- Journal writing

> **WORD POWER**
>
> **curriculum** all the courses required by a school

FYI

Keep in mind that you do not have to use all four of the strategies listed above every time you write a paragraph. Try out the various strategies, and see which ones work best for you.

Freewriting

When you **freewrite**, you write for a set period of time—perhaps five minutes—without stopping, and you keep writing even if what you are writing doesn't seem to have a point or a direction. Your goal is to relax and let ideas flow without worrying about whether or not they are related—or even make sense. (If you have trouble thinking of something to say, keep repeating the last word of your freewriting until something else comes to mind.) Sometimes you can freewrite without a topic in mind, but at other times you will focus your attention on a particular topic. This strategy is called **focused freewriting**.

When you finish freewriting, read what you have written. Then, underline any ideas you think you might be able to use. If you find an idea you want to explore further, freewrite again, using that idea as a starting point.

Stella Drew's focused freewriting on the topic of whether or not community service should be a required part of the college curriculum appears below.

Community service. Community service. Sounds like what you do instead of going to jail. Service to the community—service in the community. Community center. College community—community college. Community service—I guess it's a good idea to do it—but when? In my spare time—spare time—that's pretty funny. So after school and work and all the reading and studying I also have to do <u>service</u>? Right. And what could I do anyway? Work with kids. Or homeless people. Old people? Sick people? Or not people—maybe animals. Or work for a political candidate. Does that count? But when would I do it? Maybe other people have time, but I don't. OK idea, could work—but not for me.

PRACTICE

2-3 Reread Stella's freewriting on the topic of community service for college students (p. 38). If you were advising her, which of her ideas would you suggest she explore further? Underline these ideas in her freewriting, and be prepared to discuss your suggestions with the class or in a small group.

---

freewrite

Write (or type) for at least five minutes on the following topic: What is the most important purpose of college for you—to get a general education or to learn skills to prepare you for a career?

When you are finished, reread your freewriting, and underline any ideas you think you might be able to use in your paragraph.

Huntstock/Brand X Pictures/Getty Images

FYI

To experience genuine freewriting, try darkening your computer screen while you type. This strategy will prevent you from stopping to reread and analyze what you have already written.

Brainstorming

When you **brainstorm**, you quickly record all the ideas about your topic that you can think of. Unlike freewriting, brainstorming is sometimes written in list form and sometimes scattered all over the page. You don't have to use complete sentences; single words or phrases are fine. You can underline, star, or box important points. You can also ask questions, draw arrows to connect ideas, and even draw pictures or diagrams.

Stella's brainstorming notes on community service appear below.

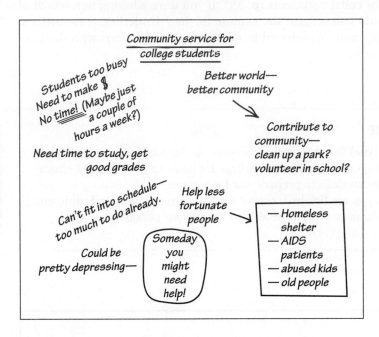

Community service for college students

Students too busy
Need to make $
No time! (Maybe just a couple of hours a week?)

Need time to study, get good grades

Can't fit into schedule—too much to do already.

Could be pretty depressing—

Someday you might need help!

Better world—better community

Contribute to community—clean up a park? volunteer in school?

Help less fortunate people

— *Homeless shelter*
— *AIDS patients*
— *abused kids*
— *old people*

PRACTICE

2-4   Reread Stella's brainstorming notes on community service (above). How is her brainstorming similar to her freewriting on the same subject (p. 38)? How is it different? If you were advising Stella, which ideas would you suggest she write more about? Which ideas should she cross out? Be prepared to discuss your suggestions with the class or in a small group.

Hero Images/Getty Images

brainstorm

On a sheet of paper or on your computer, brainstorm about your assignment: What is the most important purpose of college for you—to get a general education or to learn skills to prepare you for a career? (Begin by writing your topic, "The purpose of college," at the top of the page.)

When you have finished, look over what you have written. Did you come up with any new ideas as you brainstormed that you did not discover while freewriting?

FYI

Usually you brainstorm on your own, but at times you may find it helpful to do **collaborative brainstorming**, working with other students to find ideas. Sometimes your instructor may ask you and another student to brainstorm together. At other times, the class might brainstorm as a group while your instructor records the ideas you think of. However you brainstorm, your goal is the same: to come up with as much material about your topic as you can.

PRACTICE

2-5 Working as a class or in a group of three or four students, practice collaborative brainstorming by following these steps:

- First, decide as a group on a topic for brainstorming. (Your instructor may assign a topic.)
- Next, choose one person to record ideas. (If your group is large enough, you might choose two people to write down ideas, and have them compare notes at the end of the brainstorming session.)
- Then, discuss the topic informally, with each person contributing at least one idea.
- Finally, review the ideas that have been recorded. As a group, try to identify interesting connections among ideas, and suggest ideas that might be explored further.

Clustering

Clustering, sometimes called *mapping*, is another strategy that can help you find ideas to write about. When you cluster, you begin by writing your topic in the center of a sheet of paper. Then, you branch out, writing related ideas on the page in groups, or clusters, around the topic. As you add new ideas, you circle them and draw lines to connect the ideas to one another and to the topic at the center. (These lines will look like a spiderweb or like spokes of a wheel or branches of a tree.) As you move from the center to the corners of the page, your ideas will get more and more specific.

Sometimes one branch of your cluster diagram will give you all the material you need. At other times, you may decide to write about the ideas from several branches, or to choose one or two ideas from each branch. If you find you need additional material after you finish your first cluster diagram, you can cluster again on a new sheet of paper, this time beginning with a topic from one of the branches.

Stella's cluster diagram on the topic of community service for college students appears below.

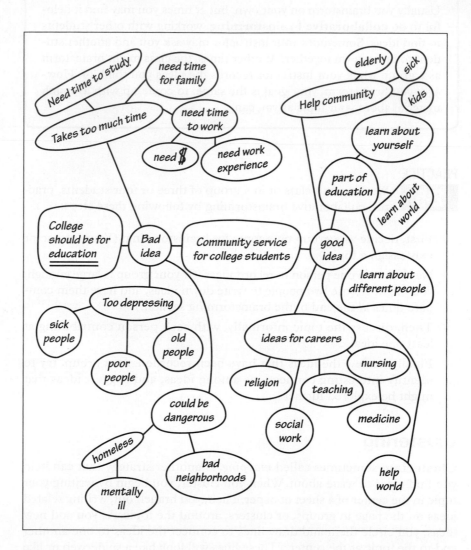

PRACTICE

2-6   Look closely at Stella's cluster diagram on the topic of community service for college students. How is it similar to her brainstorming on the same subject (p. 40)? How is it different? If you were advising Stella, which branches of the cluster diagram would you suggest she develop further? Why? Would you add any branches? Be prepared to discuss your suggestions with the class or in a small group.

make a cluster diagram

Write your topic ("The purpose of college") in the center of a blank sheet of unlined paper. Circle the topic, and then branch out with specific ideas and examples, continuing to the corners of the page if you can.

When you have finished, look over what you have written. Use a highlighter to identify the branches and ideas that you could develop further. Then, add as many new details and branches as you can.

Huntstock/Brand X Pictures/
Getty Images

Keeping a Journal

A **journal** is a notebook or a computer file in which you keep an informal record of your thoughts and ideas. In a journal, you can reflect, question, summarize, or even complain. Your journal is also a place where you record ideas about your assignments and note possible ideas to write about. Here you can try to resolve a problem, restart a stalled project, argue with yourself about your topic, or comment on a draft. You can also try out different versions of sentences, list details or examples, or keep a record of interesting things you read, see, or hear.

Journal writing works best when you write regularly, ideally at the same time each day, so that it becomes a habit. Once you have started making regular entries in your journal, take the time every week or so to go back and reread what you have written. You may find material you want to explore in further journal entries—or even an idea for an essay.

FYI

Journals

Here are some subjects you can write about in your journal:

- *Your schoolwork*: You can explore ideas for writing assignments, reflect on what you have learned, and ask questions about concepts you are having trouble understanding.

- *Your job*: You can record job-related successes and frustrations, examine conflicts with coworkers, or review how you handled problems on the job. Reading over these entries can help you understand your strengths and weaknesses and become a more effective employee.

(Continued)

- *Your reactions to current events*:   Expressing your opinions in your journal can be a good way to explore your reactions to social or political issues. Your journal entries may encourage you to write to your local or school newspaper or to public officials—and even to become involved in community projects or political activities.

- *Your impressions of what you see*:   Many writers carry their journals with them everywhere so they can record any interesting or unusual things they observe. You can later incorporate these observations into essays or other pieces of writing.

- *Your personal life*:   Although you may not want to record the intimate details of your life if your instructor will read your journal, writing about relationships with family and friends, personal problems, hopes and dreams, and so on can help you develop a better understanding of yourself and others.

Here is Stella's journal entry on the topic of community service for college students.

> I'm not really sure what I think about community service. I guess I think it sounds like a good idea, but I still don't see why we should have to do it. I can't fit anything else into my life. I guess it would be possible if it was just an hour or two a week. And maybe we could get credit and a grade for it, like a course. Or maybe it should just be for people who have the time and want to do it. But if it's not required, will anyone do it?

Hero Images/Getty Images

write a journal entry

For your first journal entry, record your thoughts about the topic you have been working on in this chapter: your main purpose for attending college.

2d Identifying Your Main Idea and Writing a Topic Sentence

When you think you have enough material to write about, it is time to identify your **main idea**—the idea you will develop in your paragraph.

To find a main idea for your paragraph, begin by looking over what you have already written. As you read through your freewriting, brainstorming, clustering, or journal entries, look for the central idea that your material seems to support. The sentence that states this main idea and gives your writing its focus will be your paragraph's **topic sentence**.

The topic sentence is usually the first sentence of your paragraph, and it is important because it tells both you and your readers what the focus of your paragraph will be. An effective topic sentence has three characteristics.

1. *A topic sentence is a complete sentence.* There is a difference between a *topic* and a *topic sentence*. The **topic** is what the paragraph is about. A **topic sentence**, however, is a complete sentence that includes a subject and a verb and expresses a complete thought. This sentence includes both a topic and the writer's idea about the topic.

   > **TOPIC**   Community service for college students
   >
   > **TOPIC SENTENCE**   Community service should be required for all college students.

2. *A topic sentence is more than just an announcement of what you plan to write about.* A topic sentence makes a point about the topic the paragraph discusses.

   > **ANNOUNCEMENT**   In this paragraph, I will explain my ideas about community service.
   >
   > **TOPIC SENTENCE**   My ideas about the importance of community service changed after I started to volunteer at a soup kitchen for homeless families.

3. *A topic sentence presents an idea that can be discussed in a single paragraph.* If your topic sentence is too broad, you will not be able to discuss it adequately in just one paragraph. If your topic sentence is too narrow, you will not be able to say much about it.

   > **TOPIC SENTENCE TOO BROAD**   Students all over the country participate in community service, making important contributions to their communities.

TOPIC SENTENCE TOO NARROW	Our school has a community service requirement for graduation.
EFFECTIVE TOPIC SENTENCE	Our school's community service requirement has had a number of positive results.

When Stella Drew reviewed her notes, she saw that they included two different kinds of ideas: ideas about the value of doing community service and ideas about the problems it presents. The material on the value of community service seemed more convincing, so she decided that her paragraph should support a community service requirement. She stated her main idea in a topic sentence.

> Community service is so important that college students should be required to do it.

When Stella thought about how to express her topic sentence, she knew it had to be a complete sentence, not just a topic, and that it would have to make a point, not just announce what she planned to write about. When she reread the topic sentence she had written, she felt confident that it did these things. Her topic sentence was neither too broad nor too narrow, and it made a statement she could support in a paragraph.

PRACTICE

2-7   Read the following items. Put a check mark next to each one that has all three characteristics of an effective topic sentence. Be prepared to explain why some items are effective topic sentences while others are not.

Examples

Speaking two languages, an advantage in today's workplace

_____

Our school should not abandon the foreign language requirement.

_____✓_____

1. The new farmers' market is a valuable addition to our community because it makes it easier for people in the neighborhood to buy fresh produce. _____

2. Eating a balanced diet with plenty of proteins and carbohydrates

_____

3. In this paragraph, I will look at the disadvantages of a large high school. _____

4. The best size for high schools: not too large, not too small.

   _____

5. Participation in sports is important for children because it teaches them how to compete. _____

6. The history of sports goes back to before the earliest civilizations.

   _____

7. Spending a quiet evening at home can have some unexpected advantages. _____

8. Television, the most popular leisure activity in the United States

   _____

PRACTICE

2-8   Decide whether each of the following statements could be an effective topic sentence for a paragraph. If a sentence is too broad, write *too broad* in the blank following the sentence. If the sentence is too narrow, write *too narrow* in the blank. If the sentence is an effective topic sentence, write *OK* in the blank.

Example: Unfortunately, many countries in today's world are involved in conflicts. ____*too broad*____

1. Deciding what to do in life is a difficult task for many young people. _____

2. A college career counselor can help students decide what kind of work they would like to do. _____

3. The college career counseling office has three full-time employees and two part-time employees. _____

4. Safe driving reduces the number of accidents and saves lives.

   _____

5. Different countries, and even different states, have different rules of the road. _____

6. Texting while driving greatly increases the chance of an accident. _____

7. Some students are much happier with their college experience than other students. _____

8. Joining a study group is a good way for students who commute to get to know other students. _____

9. Flu shots are especially important for people in certain high-risk groups. _____

10. Flu shots occasionally result in soreness in the area where the shot was given. _____

Huntstock/Brand X Pictures/
Getty Images

identify your main idea, and write a topic sentence

Look over the work you have done so far, and try to identify the main idea your material seems to support. Are you enrolled in college primarily to get a general education or to prepare for a career? Write a topic sentence that expresses your main idea on the lines below.

Topic sentence: _____

_____

 ## 2e Choosing Supporting Points

After you have stated your paragraph's main idea in a topic sentence, you will need to provide specific **evidence** (examples and details) to **support** your main idea.

When you choose points to support your topic sentence, make sure they are *relevant*, *distinct*, and *specific*.

1. **Relevant** points are directly related to your main idea.

TOPIC SENTENCE   College is important because it teaches students skills they need for their future careers.

SUPPORTING POINTS

- Students learn to write in college, and knowing how to write well is important for any job.
- Students learn to think critically in college, and knowing how to think critically is necessary for almost any career.
- ~~Choosing a career path is difficult.~~

The third supporting point above is not relevant because it does not support the topic sentence. (It does not provide an example of how skills learned in college will help students in their future careers.)

2. **Distinct** points are different from other points you plan to use.

TOPIC SENTENCE   College is important because it teaches students skills they need for their future careers.

SUPPORTING POINTS

- Students learn to write in college, and knowing how to write well is important for any job.
- Students learn to think critically in college, and knowing how to think critically is necessary for almost any career.
- ~~College writing courses will prepare students to write on the job.~~

The third point above is not distinct because it says the same thing as the first point.

3. **Specific** points communicate exactly what you want to say; they are not general or vague.

to write in college, and knowing how to write well is important
- Students learn ~~things in college that will help them~~ in any job.

The original point above is not specific because it does not tell what "things" students learn. The revision clarifies the point the writer uses to support the topic sentence.

As she continued to work on her paragraph, Stella listed several points from her notes that she thought she could write about. After she read through her list of points, she crossed out those that did not support her topic sentence or that overlapped with other points. She decided that the remaining two points on her list would give her enough material to write about in her paragraph.

TOPIC SENTENCE   Community service is so important that college students should be required to do it.

- ~~Community service helps people.~~
- ~~Some community service activities could be boring.~~
- ~~Community service can help the world.~~
- Community service helps the community.
- ~~College students are busy.~~
- ~~Community service takes a lot of time.~~
- ~~Community service might not relate to students' majors.~~
- ~~Community service can be upsetting or depressing.~~
- Community service can be part of a student's education.

PRACTICE

2-9   In each of the following two outlines, a topic sentence and a tentative list of supporting points have been provided. Read each list of points carefully, and consider whether the points support the topic sentence. Cross out any points that are not relevant, distinct, and specific.

1. *Topic Sentence:* Even though some fans may object, professional sports teams should abandon their Indian logos and nicknames.

- Indian logos and nicknames are offensive to many people.
- Indian logos and nicknames misrepresent Indians and perpetuate troubling stereotypes.
- Some Indian tribes have given teams official permission to use tribal names or symbols.
- Many high school and college teams have already abandoned their Indian names and logos.

WORD POWER
perpetuate to cause to last for a long time

- Some sports teams change their names when they move to a different city.

- Tradition is not a strong enough reason to keep racist names and logos.

- Change is difficult, but fans will get used to new names and logos.

- Many people dislike teams' Indian nicknames and logos.

- Changing a name or a logo is not a big deal.

- Team names and logos that are disrespectful of other races and cultures are unacceptable.

2. *Topic Sentence:* The government should ban unpaid student internships because they are unfair.

- Internships can be hard to find.

- Employers benefit financially from interns' free labor.

- Many unpaid interns do boring, menial work and gain few valuable job skills.

- Some students are just looking to boost their résumés and do not mind working for free.

- The government has a responsibility to protect workers from being exploited.

- Without government involvement, few employers will offer to pay their interns.

- Employers are taking advantage of their interns' unpaid work.

- A lot of unpaid interns do not benefit much from their internship experiences.

- Students from low-income families cannot afford to work without pay as wealthier students can.

- Nobody wants to work for free.

- Interns do not have enough power to negotiate with employers for paid positions.

Hero Images/Getty Images

choose supporting points

Review your freewriting, brainstorming, clustering, and journal writing to identify the points that can best support your topic sentence. Write your topic sentence on the lines below; then, list your supporting points.

Topic sentence: _____

_____

Supporting points:

- _____

- _____

- _____

Check carefully to make sure each point on your list supports your topic sentence. Cross out any points that are not relevant, distinct, and specific.

2f Developing Supporting Points

Now that you have identified points that support your main idea, you need to **develop** them, explaining them more fully and making clear how they relate to your topic sentence. One way to develop your points is to provide specific examples. To come up with examples, ask yourself *how? why?* or *what?* for each point.

After Stella chose the two points she was going to use to support her main idea, she went back and added examples to develop each point.

SUPPORTING POINT	EXAMPLES
Community service helps the community. (How?)	—*Volunteers can help feed the homeless.* —*They can tutor in schools.* —*They can work with the elderly.*
Community service can be part of a student's education. (How?)	—*Students can discover what they want to do for a career.* —*Students can learn about their community and the world.* —*Students can learn about themselves and others.*

develop your supporting points

Review your list of supporting points, and then think of examples you can use to develop each point. (If you like, you can make a chart like the one on p. 52 to help you arrange your supporting points and examples.)

Huntstock/Brand X Pictures/Getty Images

2g Making an Outline

After you have decided which points to use to support your topic sentence and chosen examples to develop each point, your next step is to make an informal **outline**. You do this by arranging your supporting points in the order in which you plan to discuss them in your paragraph.

When Stella thought she had gathered all the examples she needed to develop the two points she planned to discuss in her paragraph, she made the following informal outline.

Outline

Topic sentence: Community service is so important that college students should be required to do it.

• Community service helps the community.
  — Volunteers can help feed the homeless.
  — Volunteers can help the elderly.
  — Volunteers can tutor students.

• Community service can be part of a student's education.
  — Students can learn about themselves.
  — Students can learn about others.
  — Students can learn about community.
  — Students can learn about the world.
  — Students can discover what they want to do for a career.

Hero Images/Getty Images

make an outline

Look over your supporting points, and decide which ones you want to include in your paragraph. Then, make an informal outline that arranges your supporting points in the order in which you plan to write about them.

2h Drafting Your Paragraph

Once you have written a topic sentence for your paragraph, selected the points you will discuss, and arranged them in the order in which you plan to write about them, you are ready to write a first draft.

In a **first draft**, your goal is to get your ideas down on paper. Begin your paragraph with a topic sentence that states the paragraph's main idea. Then, following your informal outline, write or type without worrying about correct wording, spelling, or punctuation. If a new idea occurs to you, include it in your draft. Don't worry about whether it fits with the other ideas. Your goal is not to produce a perfect paragraph but simply to create a working draft. Later on, when you revise, you will have a chance to rethink ideas and rework sentences.

Because you will be making changes to this first draft, you should leave wide margins, skip lines, and leave extra blank lines in places where you might need to add material.

When you have finished your first draft, don't make any changes right away. Take a break (overnight if possible), and think about something—anything—else. Then, return to your draft, and read it with a fresh eye.

Here is the first draft of Stella's paragraph on the topic of community service for college students. (Note that she included a brief working title to help her focus on her topic.)

Community Service

Community service is so important that college students should be required

to do it. When college students do community service, they spend their time

doing good for someone or for the community. Working in a homeless shelter,

doing chores for senior citizens, and tutoring children are all examples of community service. Community service activities like these are good for the

community, and they can be more fulfilling for students than playing sports or

participating in school activities. Community service can be an important part of

a college education. Students can learn a lot about themselves and others and

can discover what they want to do with their lives. Community service can also

make the world a better place.

PRACTICE

Reread the first draft of Stella's paragraph. Working in a group of three or four students, list the changes that you think Stella should make. For example, what should she add? What should she cross out? Have one member of your group record all your suggestions, and be prepared to exchange ideas with the rest of the class.

draft your paragraph

Write a first draft of your paragraph about what you hope to get out of your college education. Be sure to state your main idea in the topic sentence and support the topic sentence with specific evidence. Finally, add a working title.

Huntstock/Brand X Pictures/
Getty Images

2i TESTing Your Paragraph

When you have finished your draft, the first thing you should do is "test" what you have written to make sure it includes all the elements of an effective paragraph. You do this by asking the following four **TEST** questions:

T **Topic sentence**—Does your paragraph have a topic sentence that states its main idea?

E **Evidence**—Does your paragraph include specific points that support your topic sentence? Are these points developed with evidence (examples and details)?

S **Summary statement**—Does your paragraph end with a statement that reinforces its main idea?

T **Transitions**—Does your paragraph include transitional words and phrases that show readers how your ideas are related?

If your paragraph includes these four **TEST** elements, you are off to a very good start. If it does not, you will need to add whatever is missing.

When Stella reread her draft, she **TEST**ed it to take a quick inventory of her paragraph.

- She decided that her **topic sentence** clearly stated her main idea.
- She thought she needed more **evidence** to support her topic sentence.
- She noticed that her paragraph had no **summary statement**.
- She realized she needed to add **transitions** to connect her ideas.

Hero Images/Getty Images

TEST your paragraph

TEST the first draft of your paragraph to make sure it includes all four elements of an effective paragraph: **T**opic sentence, **E**vidence, **S**ummary statement, and **T**ransitions. If any elements are missing, add them now.

2j　Revising Your Paragraph

Once you have **TEST**ed your paragraph to make sure it is complete, you are ready to revise it.

Revision is the process of reseeing, rethinking, reevaluating, and rewriting your work. Revision involves much more than substituting one word for another or correcting a comma here and there. In fact, it can mean moving sentences, adding words and phrases, and even changing the direction or emphasis of your ideas.

Using a Self-Assessment Checklist

To get the most out of the revision process, you should carefully reread your draft, using the following Self-Assessment Checklist to guide your revision.

self-assessment checklist

Revising Your Paragraph

✔ Is your topic sentence clearly worded?

✔ Do you have enough evidence to support your topic sentence, or do you need to look back at your notes or try another strategy to find additional supporting material?

✔ Do you need to explain anything more fully or more clearly?

✔ Do you need to add or delete examples or details?

✔ Does every sentence say what you mean?

✔ Can you combine any sentences to make your writing smoother?

✔ Should you move any sentences?

✔ Are all your words necessary, or can you cut some?

✔ Should you change any words to make them more specific?

✔ Does your paragraph end with a summary statement that clearly reinforces its main idea?

Using Peer Review

Sometimes you revise on your own, but at other times—with your instructor's permission—you may be able to get feedback (in the form of oral or written comments) from your classmates. The process of giving and receiving constructive feedback is called **peer review**. Peer review is most productive if you know how to make helpful comments and how to use the comments you get from your peers.

WORD POWER
peer someone with equal standing; an equal

Guidelines for Peer Review

Giving Feedback

- **Be positive.** Remember that your purpose is to help other students improve their writing.

- **Be tactful.** Be sure to emphasize the good points about the writing. Mention one or two things the writer has done particularly well before you offer your suggestions for improvement.

- **Be specific.** Offer concrete suggestions about how the writer could do better. A general comment like "You need more support" is not

(Continued)

as helpful as a more specific comment like "You need support for the point you make in the fourth sentence."

- **Be involved.** If you are giving feedback orally instead of in writing, make sure you interact with the writer. Ask questions, listen to responses, and explain your comments.

- **Look at the big picture.** Don't focus on issues such as spelling and punctuation, which the writer will correct at the editing and proofreading stage. At this point, the clarity of the topic sentence, the effectiveness of the support, and the organization of ideas are much more important.

- **Be thorough.** When possible, write down and explain your comments, either on a form your instructor provides or in the margins of the draft you are reviewing. (If you are reviewing another student's writing electronically, you can add your feedback using "Comments." (In Microsoft Word, the Comments function is in the Track Changes tool. In Google Docs, it pops up on the right when you highlight within the document.)

Using Feedback

- **Be open-minded.** Receive your peers' comments with an open mind. They might notice something important that you missed, and they might help you see something from a different angle.

- **Be selective.** It is up to you to carefully evaluate the suggestions from your peers and decide whether or not their advice will strengthen your draft. Remember, not every suggestion is worth following, but every one is worth considering.

One effective strategy to use when you are reviewing the work of your classmates is to **TEST** their writing. Just as you **TEST** your own drafts, you can use **TEST** to guide your peer review and to help you stay focused on the big picture. Here are the questions you should ask yourself as you review other students' work and make comments.

T **Topic sentence**—Does this paragraph have a topic sentence that states its main idea? If the answer is no, remind your classmate to add a topic sentence that clearly states the main idea of the paragraph.

E **Evidence**—Does this paragraph include specific points that support the topic sentence? Are these points developed with evidence (examples and details)? If the answer to these questions is no, alert the writer to this issue and suggest the kinds of examples and details that he or she might add to better support the topic sentence.

S **Summary statement**—Does this paragraph end with a statement that reinforces its main idea? If the answer is no, remind your classmate to add a summary statement that clearly reinforces the main idea of the paragraph.

T **Transitions**—Does this paragraph include transitional words and phrases that show readers how ideas are related? If the answer is no, point out specific areas where the relationship between ideas is unclear.

Classmates in Stella's peer-review group used **TEST** to make suggestions for revision, working on an electronic draft of Stella's paragraph as part of a homework assignment. Their comments on her first draft, inserted using the Comment function in Word, follow:

Community Service

Community service is so important that college students should be required to do it. When college students do community service, they spend their time doing good for someone or for the community. Working in a homeless shelter, doing chores for senior citizens, and tutoring children are all examples of community service. Community service activities like these are good for the community, and they can be more fulfilling for students than playing sports or participating in school activities. Community service can be an important part of a college education. Students can learn a lot about themselves and others and can discover what they want to do with their lives. Community service can also make the world a better place.

Comment [RK1]: Can title be more specific? What will paragraph be about?

Comment [AJ1]: Good topic sentence!

Comment [RK2]: Good examples

Comment [RK3]: Add examples here?

Comment [AJ2]: TEST element missing—you need a summary statement.

Guided by her **TEST** responses and the Self-Assessment Checklist, as well as by comments from her peer-review group, Stella revised her paragraph, writing her changes in by hand on her typed draft.

Why   Should Be Required
Community Service

Community service is so important that college students should be

required to do it. When college students do community service, they spend

helping a person or organization in their communities. For example, they can work

their time ~~doing good for someone or for the community. Working~~ in a homeless

s do

shelter, ~~doing~~ chores for senior citizens, ~~and tutoring~~ *or tutor or mentor at-risk*

children. ~~are all exam-~~

~~ples of community service.~~ Community service activities like these are good for

are also good for the students who give their time. This work

the community, and they can be more fulfilling ~~for students~~ than playing

also

sports or participating in school activities. Community service can be an im-

portant part of a college education. Students can learn a lot about themselves

, about their communities, about different kinds of people, and about their world. They

~~and others and~~ can discover what they want to do with their lives. ~~Community~~

even

~~service can also make the world a better place.~~ *For example, working in a*

school can lead a student to a career as a teacher. For all these reasons, community

service should be a required part of the college curriculum.

As she made her revisions, Stella did not worry about being neat. She crossed out words, added material, and changed sentences and words. When she felt her revision was complete, she was ready to move on to edit and proofread her paragraph.

2k Editing and Proofreading Your Paragraph

When you **edit**, you check for correct grammar, punctuation, mechanics, and spelling. Then, you go on to **proofread** carefully for typographical errors that your spell checker may not identify, checking to make sure that you have indented the first sentence of your paragraph and that every sentence begins with a capital letter and ends with a period. Finally, you check your essay's **format** to make sure it satisfies your instructor's requirements.

Remember, editing and proofreading are vital steps in the writing process. Many readers will not take your ideas seriously if your paragraph contains grammatical or mechanical errors. You can use the following checklist to guide your editing.

self-assessment checklist

Editing and Proofreading Your Paragraph

✔ Are all your sentences complete and grammatically correct?

✔ Do all your subjects and verbs agree?

✔ Have you used the correct verb tenses?

✔ Are commas used where they are required?

✔ Have you used apostrophes correctly?

✔ Have you used other punctuation marks correctly?

✔ Have you used capital letters where they are required?

✔ Are all words spelled correctly?

✔ For help with grammar, punctuation, mechanics, and spelling, see **Unit 4** of this text.

Before Stella edited her paragraph, she typed in the changes she had made by hand on her first draft and printed out a revised draft. Then, she checked grammar, punctuation, mechanics, and spelling and proofread for typos. The final version of her paragraph appears below.

Why Community Service Should Be Required

Community service is so important that college students should be required to do it. When college students do community service, they spend their time helping a person or organization in their communities. For example, they can work in homeless shelters, do chores for senior citizens, or tutor or mentor at-risk children. Community service activities like these are good for the community, and they are also good for the students who give their time. This work can be more fulfilling than playing sports or participating in school activities. Community service can <u>also</u> be an important part of a college education. Students can learn a lot about themselves, about their communities, about different kinds of people, and about their world. They can even discover what they want to do with their lives. For example, working in a school can lead a student to a career as a teacher. For all these reasons, community service should be a required part of the college curriculum.

TEST
T Topic Sentence
E Evidence
S Summary Statement
T Transitions

E

PRACTICE

2-11 Reread the final draft of Stella's paragraph about the value of community service for college students (above), and compare it with her first draft (pp. 54–55).

Huntstock/Brand X
Pictures/Getty Images

revise, edit, and proofread your paragraph

Use the Self-Assessment Checklist on page 61 (and, if your instructor allows it, feedback from peer review) to help you revise your draft. Then, edit your paragraph, checking grammar, punctuation, mechanics, and spelling—and proofread carefully for typos. When you are satisfied with your paragraph, print it out.

COLLABORATIVE REVIEW ACTIVITY

Working in a small group with other students, study the differences between Stella's first and final drafts. Use the following questions to guide your analysis.

1. Do you agree with Stella's decision not to revise her paragraph's topic sentence?

2. What new supporting material did Stella add to her paragraph? Can you think of any new material she could have added?

3. What did Stella cross out? Why do you think she deleted this material? Do you think she should make additional deletions?

4. Why do you think Stella added "For example" and "also" to her final draft? In her revision Stella added a sentence at the end of the paragraph. Do you think this sentence is necessary? Why or why not?

review checklist

Writing a Paragraph

✔ Be sure you understand paragraph structure. (See 2a.)

✔ Before you start to write, consider your assignment, purpose, and audience. (See 2b.)

✔ Use freewriting, brainstorming, clustering, and journal writing to help you find ideas. (See 2c.)

✔ Identify your main idea, and write a topic sentence. (See 2d.)

✔ Choose points to support your main idea. (See 2e.)

✔ Develop your supporting points with evidence. (See 2f.)

✔ Make an informal outline by arranging your points in the order in which you plan to discuss them. (See 2g.)

✔ Write a first draft of your paragraph. (See 2h.)

✔ TEST your paragraph. (See 2i.)

✔ Revise your paragraph. (See 2j.)

✔ Edit and proofread your paragraph. (See 2k.)

3 TESTing Your Paragraphs

focus on writing

This picture shows students reading and writing on three different digital devices. Which kind of device do you use most often? What do you like about it? What, if anything, do you dislike? Write a paragraph in which you discuss the advantages and disadvantages of reading and composing on one of these devices.

As you learned in Chapter 2, you should **TEST** every paragraph after you finish drafting. **TEST**ing will tell you whether or not your paragraph includes all the elements of an effective paragraph.

T opic sentence
E vidence
S ummary statement
T ransitions

If you **TEST** the following paragraph, you will see that it contains all four elements of an effective paragraph.

Although most people do not know it, the modern roller coaster got its start in Coney Island in Brooklyn, New York. First, in 1888, the Flip Flap Railway, which featured a circular loop, was built. The coaster was the first to go upside down, but it frequently injured riders' necks. Next, in 1901, the Loop-the-Loop, which was safer than the Flip Flap Railway, was built. Then, from 1884 through the 1930s, over thirty roller coasters were constructed in Coney Island. Finally, in 1927, the most famous roller coaster in history, the Cyclone, was built at a cost of over $100,000. Although it began operating over eighty years ago, it is still the standard by which all roller coasters are measured. It has steep drops, a lot of speed, and only lap belts to hold riders in their seats. Still in operation, the Cyclone is the most successful ride in Coney Island history. It is the last survivor of the wooden roller coasters that once drew crowds to Coney Island. With their many innovations, Coney Island's roller coasters paved the way for the high-tech roller coasters in amusement parks today.

> **TEST**
>
> **T** Topic Sentence
> **E** Evidence
> **S** Summary Statement
> **T** Transitions

E

> **WORD POWER**
> **innovation** something newly invented; a new way of doing something

3a TESTing for a Topic Sentence

The first thing you do when you **TEST** a paragraph is look for a **topic sentence (T)**. An effective paragraph focuses on a single main idea, and it includes a topic sentence that states this main idea.

A paragraph is **unified** when all its sentences support the main idea stated in the topic sentence. When you revise, you can make your paragraphs unified by crossing out sentences that do not support your topic sentence and, if necessary, adding sentences that do.

The following paragraph is not unified because it contains sentences that do not support the paragraph's topic sentence. (These sentences have been crossed out.)

The weak local economy has led many people to move away from the rural Ohio community where I was raised. Over the years, farmland has become more and more expensive. Years ago, a family could buy each of its children twenty-five acres on which they could start farming. Today, the average farmer cannot make enough money to buy this amount of land, and those who choose not to farm have few alternatives. ~~After I graduate, I intend to return to my town and get a job there. Even though many factories have moved out of the area, I think I will be able to get a job. My uncle owns a hardware store, and he told me that after I graduate, he will teach me the business. I think I can contribute something to both the business and the community.~~ Young people just cannot get good jobs anymore. Factories have moved out of the area and taken with them the jobs that many young people used to get after high school. As a result, many eighteen-year-olds have no choice but to move away to find employment.

The following revised paragraph is unified. It discusses only the idea that is stated in the topic sentence.

The weak local economy has led many people to move away from the rural Ohio community where I was raised. Over the years, farmland has become more and more expensive. Years ago, a family could buy each of its children twenty-five acres on which they could start farming. Today, the average farmer cannot make enough money to buy this amount of land, and those who choose not to farm have few alternatives. Young people just cannot get good jobs anymore. Factories have moved out of the area and taken with them the jobs that many young people used to get after high school. As a result, many eighteen-year-olds have no choice but to move away to find employment.

TEST

T	Topic Sentence
E	Evidence
S	Summary Statement
T	Transitions

PRACTICE

3-1   The following paragraph is not unified because some sentences do not support the topic sentence. First, underline the topic sentence. Then, cross out any sentences that do not support the topic sentence.

Although many people still get down on one knee to propose, others have found more creative ways to pop the question. Using Jumbotrons, computer games, or even zero-gravity chambers, some people are making the moment truly memorable. Last year, one English graffiti artist asked his girlfriend to marry him by spray-painting his proposal on the side of a building. In 2018, a man used the Sunday crossword puzzle to propose to his girlfriend. As she completed the puzzle, she saw that the answers to several of the clues spelled out her name and a question. Weddings are also becoming more unusual. Some couples are choosing to get married while skydiving or riding bicycles. One couple recently got married in a shark tank. Several brave people have also proposed on television. By buying ad space and recording a brief video clip, they appear on the screen during a favorite show. People are clearly using their imaginations to ask this age-old question in unexpected ways.

PRACTICE

3-2   The following paragraph has no topic sentence. Read it carefully, and then choose the most appropriate topic sentence from the list that follows the paragraph.

While continuing to make its famous interlocking plastic bricks, Lego has created a number of popular video games, such as *Lego Racer* and *Lego Star Wars*. The company also shares ownership of four Legoland amusement parks and owns dozens of retail stores in Europe and North America. In 2014, the company produced a successful feature film called *The Lego Movie*. The company also continues to make products using licensed characters from other movies, such as *Harry Potter* and *Lord of the Rings*, and has its own television series on the Cartoon Network. The Lego Group also offers special programs to accompany its products. For example, the Lego Group has developed an educational branch, Lego Education, which sponsors competitions for students and provides lesson plans and professional development for educators. With such wide-ranging programs and merchandise, the company will likely continue to thrive.

Put a check mark next to the topic sentence that best expresses the main idea of the paragraph above.

1. The Lego Group has been very successful in the video game

   market. _____

2. Because of a decline in sales, the Lego Group is now pursuing the

   education market. _____

3. Today, the Lego Group is much more than just a manufacturer of children's construction toys. _____

4. The founder of the Lego Group, a Danish man named Ole Kirk Christiansen, had a passion for making children's toys. _____

5. By diversifying its products and services, the Lego Group has spread itself too thin. _____

PRACTICE

3-3 The following paragraphs do not have topic sentences. Think of a topic sentence that expresses each paragraph's main idea, and write it on the lines above the paragraphs.

Example: Possible answer: Rock and roll originated in African American music but was reinterpreted by white performers.

Early 1950s African American musicians included performers such as Johnny Ace, Big Joe Turner, and Ruth Brown. Groups like the Drifters and the Clovers were also popular. By the mid-1950s, white performers such as Bill Haley and the Comets, Jerry Lee Lewis, and Elvis Presley were imitating African American music. Their songs had a beat and lyrics that appealed to a white audience. Eventually, this combination of black and white musical styles became known as rock and roll.

1. _____

_____

First, you have to find a suitable job opening. Once you decide to apply, you have to compose your résumé and cover letter to send them to the potential employer. Then, when you are invited in for an interview, you need to decide what you are going to wear and prepare a list of questions to ask your potential employer. Next, review your résumé, and practice answering questions that the interviewer might ask you. At the interview, speak slowly and clearly, make eye contact, and answer all questions directly and honestly. After the interview, send a note to the person who interviewed you, thanking him or her and reinforcing your interest in the job. Finally, if everything goes well, you will get an email or a phone call offering you the job.

2. _____

_____

There are no written records left by the Native Americans themselves. Most of the early European settlers in North America were more interested in staying alive than in writing about the Native Americans. In addition, as the westward expansion took place, the Europeans encountered the Native Americans in stages, not all at once. Also, the Native Americans spoke at least fifty-eight different languages, which made it difficult for the Europeans to speak with them. Most important, by the time scholars decided to study Native American culture, many of the tribes no longer existed. Disease and war had wiped them out.

3b TESTing for Evidence

The next thing you do when you **TEST** a paragraph is to make sure you have enough **evidence (E)** to support the main idea stated in your topic sentence.

Evidence consists of the facts, details, and examples that support your statements. To make a convincing point, you need to support it with evidence. For example, it is one thing to say that gun violence has torn some neighborhoods apart, but it is much more effective to follow this general statement with examples of specific incidents of gun violence in a specific community. The same is true when you describe something you have observed. You could, for example, say that a certain area of campus is peaceful. This statement means little to readers, however, unless you follow it with the details—the tall trees, the grass, the silence—that explain what you mean.

A paragraph is **well developed** when it includes enough evidence to explain and support its main idea. In other words, a well-developed paragraph leaves readers feeling that it is thorough and complete. The following paragraph is not well developed because it does not include enough evidence to support its main idea.

> Although pit bulls have a bad reputation, they actually make good pets. Part of their problem is that they can look frightening. Actually, though, pit bulls are no worse than other breeds of dogs. Even so, the bad publicity they get has given them a bad reputation. Pit bulls really do not deserve their bad reputation, though. Contrary to popular opinion, pit bulls can (and do) make friendly, affectionate, and loyal pets.

The following revised paragraph now includes enough evidence to support the main idea stated in the topic sentence.

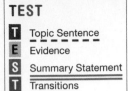

TEST

T	Topic Sentence
E	Evidence
S	Summary Statement
T	Transitions

Although pit bulls have a bad reputation, they actually make good pets. Part of their problem is that they can look frightening. Their wide, powerful jaws, short muscular legs, and large teeth are ideally suited for fighting, and they were bred for this purpose. In addition, some pit bulls—especially males—can be very aggressive toward both people and other dogs. Actually, though, pit bulls are no worse than other breeds of dogs. As several recent newspaper articles have pointed out, the number of reported bites by pit bulls is no greater than the number of bites by other breeds. In fact, some breeds, such as cocker spaniels, bite more frequently than pit bulls. Even so, the bad publicity they get has given them a bad reputation. The problem is that whenever a pit bull attacks someone, the incident is reported on the evening news. Contrary to popular opinion, pit bulls can (and do) make friendly, affectionate, and loyal pets.

E Evidence added

Note: Length alone is no guarantee that a paragraph contains enough evidence to be well developed. A long paragraph that consists of one generalization after another will still not include enough support for the topic sentence.

PRACTICE

3-4 Underline the specific supporting evidence in each of the following paragraphs.

1. Hearing people have some mistaken ideas about the deaf community. First, some hearing adults think that all deaf people consider themselves disabled and would trade anything not to be "handicapped." Hearing people do not realize that many deaf people do not consider themselves handicapped and are proud to be part of the deaf community, which has its own language, customs, and culture. Second, many hearing people think that all deaf people read lips, so there is no need to learn sign language to communicate with them. However, lip reading—or speech reading, as deaf people call the practice—is difficult. Not all hearing people say the same words in the same way, and facial expressions can also change the meaning of the words. If hearing people make more of an attempt to understand the deaf culture, communication between them will improve.

2. One of the largest celebrations of the passage of young girls into womanhood occurs in Latin American and Hispanic cultures. This event is called La Quinceañera, or the fifteenth year. It acknowledges that a young woman is now of marriageable age. The day usually begins with a Mass of Thanksgiving. The young woman wears a full-length white or pastel-colored dress and is attended by fourteen friends and relatives who serve as maids of honor and escorts. Her parents and godparents surround her at the foot of the altar.

When the Mass ends, other young relatives give small gifts to those who attended, while the young woman places a bouquet of flowers on the altar of the Virgin Mary. Following the Mass is an elaborate party, with dancing, cake, and toasts. Finally, to end the evening, the young woman dances a waltz with her favorite escort. For young Hispanic women, the Quinceañera is an important milestone.

PRACTICE

3-5 Provide two or three specific pieces of evidence (examples or details) to support each of the following topic sentences.

1. When it comes to feeding a family, there are several cost-effective alternatives to fast food.

   ■ _____

   ■ _____

   ■ _____

2. A romantic relationship with a coworker can create serious problems.

   ■ _____

   ■ _____

   ■ _____

3. Choosing the right career is harder than I thought it would be.

   ■ _____

   ■ _____

   ■ _____

PRACTICE

3-6 The paragraph that follows does not include enough supporting evidence. Suggest some examples and details that might help the writer develop the topic sentence more fully.

Young adults who move back in with their parents after college face many challenges. Feeling dependent on one's parents after living away from home can be frustrating. Living at home can restrict a person's freedom. Also, some parents can be overbearing and treat the young graduate as if he or she is a child. Of course, the success of the living situation depends on how well the college graduate and his or her parents communicate. Despite these drawbacks, living at home for a while after college can make sense.

 ## 3c TESTing for a Summary Statement

The third thing you do when you **TEST** a paragraph is to make sure it ends with a **summary statement (S)**—a sentence that reinforces your paragraph's main idea. By reminding readers what your paragraph is about, a summary statement helps to further **unify** your paragraph.

The following paragraph has no summary statement.

> Artificial intelligence (AI) is a big concern for many people. Experts such as Elon Musk, Stephen Hawking, and Bill Gates have all expressed doubts about the development of this technology. For example, in a world where self-driving cars are in the majority, will their benefits outweigh the liabilities? Should autonomous vehicles be able to make life and death decisions in the event of a potential accident? Will these decisions comply with human morality, or will goals be misaligned with ours? Also, what about autonomous weapons in a war situation? Will they be able to show mercy to civilians or surrendering enemy fighters, or will they be unable to make such distinctions? The same questions can be asked about AI systems and their ability to interpret data from surveillance cameras, emails, or cell phones.

The summary statement in the following revised paragraph reinforces the paragraph's main idea and brings the paragraph to a close.

> Artificial intelligence (AI) is a big concern for many people. Experts such as Elon Musk, Stephen Hawking, and Bill Gates have all expressed doubts about the development of this technology. For example, in a world where self-driving cars are in the majority, will their benefits outweigh the liabilities? Should autonomous vehicles be able to make life and death decisions in the event of a potential accident? Will these decisions comply with human morality, or will goals be misaligned with ours? Also, what about autonomous weapons in a war situation? Will they be able to show mercy to civilians or surrendering enemy fighters, or will they be unable to make such distinctions? The same questions can be asked about AI systems and their ability to interpret data from surveillance cameras, emails, or cell phones. If we continue to develop advanced AI systems, then we must address the fearsome possibility that one day these systems could begin to act on their own and override their programming.

WORD POWER

autonomous having the ability to act independently

TEST

T Topic Sentence
E Evidence
S Summary Statement
T Transitions

PRACTICE

3-7 Read the following paragraph, which does not include a summary statement. Then, on the lines below the paragraph, write a summary statement that adds unity to the paragraph by reinforcing the main idea stated in the topic sentence. Be careful not to use the same wording as in the topic sentence.

> Founded more than fifty years ago, NASCAR has become one of the most successful spectator sports in the world. In December 1947, Bill France formed the National Association for Stock Car Auto Racing (NASCAR). The first NASCAR race was held at Daytona Beach's auto racecourse in 1948. From this modest start, France turned NASCAR into a highly successful business. Attendance grew 8.2 percent during 1997, and 2,102,000 fans attended the thirty-one NASCAR events in 1998. This was the first time that NASCAR attendance topped the two million mark. By 2012, more than three million people attended NASCAR events annually. Then, in 2013, NASCAR negotiated a ten-year deal with NBC and Fox for a reported $8.2 billion. As a result, these networks now televise NASCAR's most popular events. Today, NASCAR sanctions over 1,200 races at one hundred tracks across the United States.

_____

_____

_____

3d TESTing for Transitions

The final thing you do when you **TEST** a paragraph is make sure the paragraph includes **transitions (T)** that connect ideas in a clear, logical order.

Transitional words and phrases create **coherence** by indicating how ideas are connected in a paragraph—for example, in _time order_, _spatial order_, or _logical order_. By signaling the order of ideas in a paragraph, these words and phrases make it easier for readers to follow your discussion.

- You use **time** signals to show readers the order in which events occurred.

  > In 1883, my great-grandfather came to this country from Russia.

- You use **spatial** signals to show readers how people, places, and things stand in relation to one another. For example, you can move from top to bottom, from near to far, from right to left, and so on.

  > Next to my bed is a bookcase that also serves as a room divider.

■ You use **logical** signals to show readers how ideas are connected. For example, you can move from the least important idea to the most important idea or from the least familiar idea to the most familiar idea.

Certain strategies can help you do well in college. First, you should learn to manage your time effectively.

Because transitional words and phrases create coherence, a paragraph without them can be difficult to understand. You can avoid this problem by checking to make sure you have included all the words and phrases that you need to link the ideas in your paragraph.

Frequently Used Transitional Words and Phrases

SOME WORDS AND PHRASES THAT SIGNAL TIME ORDER

after	finally	phrases that
afterward	later	include dates
at first	next	(for example,
before	now	"In June";
during	soon	"In 1904")
earlier	then	
eventually	today	

SOME WORDS AND PHRASES THAT SIGNAL SPATIAL ORDER

above	in front	on the left
behind	inside	on the right
below	in the center	on top
beside	near	over
in back	next to	under
in between	on the bottom	

SOME WORDS AND PHRASES THAT SIGNAL LOGICAL ORDER

also	in addition
although	in fact
as a result	last
consequently	moreover
even though	next
first . . . second	not only . . . but also
. . . third	one . . . another
for example	similarly
for instance	the least important
furthermore	the most important
however	therefore

The paragraph below has no transitional words and phrases to link ideas.

> During his lifetime, Jim Thorpe faced many obstacles. Thorpe was born in 1888, the son of an Irish father and a Native American mother. He was sent to the Carlisle Indian School in Pennsylvania. "Pop" Warner, the legendary coach at Carlisle, discovered Thorpe. Thorpe left Carlisle to play baseball for two seasons in the newly formed East Carolina minor league. He returned to Carlisle, played football, and was named to the All-American team. Thorpe went to the Olympic Games in Stockholm, where he won two gold medals. Thorpe's career took a dramatic turn for the worse when a sportswriter who had seen him play baseball in North Carolina exposed him as a professional. The Amateur Athletic Union stripped him of his records and medals. Thorpe died in 1953. The International Olympic Committee returned Thorpe's Olympic medals to his family in 1982. Ironically, only in death was Thorpe able to overcome the difficulties that had frustrated him while he was alive.

The following revised paragraph is coherent because it includes transitional words and phrases that connect its ideas.

> During his lifetime, Jim Thorpe faced many obstacles. Thorpe was born in 1888, the son of an Irish father and a Native American mother. <u>In 1904,</u> he was sent to the Carlisle Indian School in Pennsylvania. <u>The next year,</u> "Pop" Warner, the legendary coach at Carlisle, discovered Thorpe. Thorpe left Carlisle <u>in 1909</u> to play baseball for two seasons in the newly formed East Carolina minor league. <u>In 1912,</u> he returned to Carlisle, played football, and was named to the All-American team. Thorpe <u>then</u> went to the Olympic Games in Stockholm, where he won two gold medals. <u>The next year,</u> however, Thorpe's career took a dramatic turn for the worse when a sportswriter who had seen him play baseball in North Carolina exposed him as a professional. <u>As a result,</u> the Amateur Athletic Union stripped him of his records and medals. Thorpe died in 1953. <u>After years of appeals,</u> the International Olympic Committee returned Thorpe's Olympic medals to his family in 1982. Ironically, only in death was Thorpe able to overcome the difficulties that had frustrated him while he was alive.

TEST	
T	Topic Sentence
E	Evidence
S	Summary Statement
T	Transitions

PRACTICE

3-8 Read the following paragraph carefully. Then, select transitional words and phrases from the accompanying alphabetized list, and write them in the appropriate blanks. When you have finished, reread your paragraph to make sure that it is coherent.

TRANSITIONS

by 1960	in 1989
first	in 1993
in the 1970s	today
in 1957	soon afterward

The history of modern-day GPS can be traced back to a small Russian satellite called Sputnik. _____, Russia launched the first artificial satellite into space. _____, American scientists realized that they could use radio signals to track Sputnik's location along its orbit. That observation sparked an idea, and _____, the Navy had developed a satellite navigation system for tracking submarines. This system was the ___ to use continuous signals from satellites in space. _____, the Department of Defense began testing satellites for a proposed Global Positioning System, or GPS. The first GPS satellite was launched into orbit _____ and the twenty-four-satellite system was declared fully operational _____. ____, GPS satellites circle the Earth twice a day, sending signals from an altitude of more than 12,000 miles to help people navigate the world.

TEST · Revise · Edit · Proofread

Review the paragraph you drafted in response to the Focus on Writing prompt on page 64. Next, **TEST** your paragraph to make sure it includes a topic sentence, evidence, a summary statement, and transitions, and revise your draft accordingly. Then, edit and proofread your paragraph.

EDITING PRACTICE

TEST the following paragraph to make sure it is **unified**, **well developed**, and **coherent**. Begin by underlining the topic sentence. Then, cross out any sentences that do not support the topic sentence. If necessary, add evidence (details and examples) to support the topic sentence. Next, decide whether you need to make any changes to the paragraph's summary statement. (If the paragraph includes no summary statement, write one.) Finally, add transitional words and phrases where they are needed.

In 1979, a series of mechanical and human errors in Unit 2 of the nuclear generating plant at Three Mile Island, near Harrisburg, Pennsylvania, caused an accident that changed the nuclear power industry. A combination of stuck valves, human error, and poor decisions caused a partial meltdown of the reactor core. Large amounts of radioactive gases were released into the atmosphere. The governor of Pennsylvania evacuated pregnant women from the area. Other residents then panicked and left their homes. The nuclear regulatory agency claimed that the situation was not really dangerous and that the released gases were not a health threat. Activists and local residents disagreed with this. The reactor itself remained unusable for more than ten years. Large demonstrations followed the accident, including a rally of more than 200,000 people in New York City. Some people came just because the day was nice. By the mid-1980s, as a result of the accident at Three Mile Island, new construction of nuclear power plants in the United States had stopped.

COLLABORATIVE ACTIVITY

In a newspaper or magazine, find an illustration or photograph that includes a lot of details. Then, write a paragraph describing what you see. (Include enough details so that readers will be able to "see" it almost as clearly as you can.) Decide on a specific spatial order—from top to bottom or from left to right, for example—that makes sense to you, and follow this order as you organize the details in your paragraph. Finally, trade paragraphs with another student, and offer suggestions that could improve his or her paragraph.

review checklist

TESTing Your Paragraphs

✔ A topic sentence states a paragraph's main idea. (See 3a.)

✔ A paragraph should include enough evidence—examples and details—to support its main idea. (See 3b.)

✔ A paragraph should end with a summary statement that reinforces its main idea and helps to unify the paragraph. (See 3c.)

✔ A paragraph should include transitional words and phrases that indicate how ideas are connected. (See 3d.)

4 Exemplification Paragraphs

Student Services

FIRST FLOOR
Dean of Students
Disability Services
Student Affairs

SECOND FLOOR
Writing Center
Career Development
Advising

THIRD FLOOR
Counseling and Wellness Center
Center for International Students
Student Life

focus on writing

Most colleges have a student services center, where students can get information and advice on making the most of the programs and support the school provides. Brainstorm to develop a list of the programs and services your school offers (or should offer) to help students adjust to college. (If you prefer, you may choose a topic from the list on the following page instead.) You will return to your topic and review your brainstorming later in the chapter when you write your exemplification paragraph.

additional topics for exemplification

Qualities of effective teachers

Qualities that make a great athlete

Challenges older students face

Challenges of your job

Things you can't do without

Three positive things about your neighborhood, school, or workplace

In Chapters 2 and 3, you learned how to write effective paragraphs. In Chapters 4 through 12, you will learn different ways of organizing your ideas within paragraphs. Understanding these patterns of paragraph development can help you organize ideas and become a more effective, more confident writer.

 ## 4a Understanding Exemplification

What do we mean when we tell a friend that an instructor is *good* or that a football team is *bad*? What do we mean when we say that a movie is *boring* or that a particular law is *unjust*? To clarify general statements like these, we use **exemplification**—that is, we give **examples** to illustrate a general idea. In daily conversation and in school, you use specific examples to help explain your ideas.

GENERAL STATEMENT	SPECIFIC EXAMPLES
Today is going to be a hard day.	Today is going to be a hard day because I have a math test in the morning, a lab quiz in the afternoon, and work in the evening.

GENERAL STATEMENT	SPECIFIC EXAMPLES
My car is giving me problems.	My car is burning oil and won't start on cold mornings. In addition, it needs a new set of tires.

An **exemplification paragraph** uses specific examples to explain or clarify a general idea. Personal experiences, class discussions, observations, conversations, and readings can all be good sources of examples. (For information on writing exemplification essays, see 15a.)

When you TEST an exemplification paragraph, make sure it follows these guidelines:

T An exemplification paragraph should begin with a **topic sentence** that states the paragraph's main idea.

E An exemplification paragraph should present **evidence**—in the form of examples—that supports and clarifies the general statement made in the topic sentence. Examples should be arranged in **logical order**—for example, from least to most important or from general to specific. The number of examples you need depends on your topic sentence. A broad statement will probably require more examples than a relatively narrow one.

S An exemplification paragraph should end with a **summary statement** that reinforces the paragraph's main idea.

T An exemplification paragraph should include **transitions** that introduce the examples and connect them to one another and to the topic sentence.

Some Transitional Words and Phrases for Exemplification

When you write an exemplification paragraph, be sure to include appropriate transitional words and phrases. These transitions help readers follow your discussion by indicating how your examples are related and how each example supports the topic sentence.

also	furthermore	the most important
finally	in addition	example
first . . . second . . .	moreover	the next example
(and so on)	one example . . .	then
for example	another example	
for instance	specifically	

Paragraph Map: Exemplification

Topic Sentence

Example #1

Example #2

Example #3

Summary Statement

Model Paragraph: Exemplification

The following paragraph uses several examples to support the idea that some countries change their names for political reasons.

TEST

T	Topic Sentence
E	Evidence
S	Summary Statement
T	Transitions

Examples presented in logical order

E

New Government, New Name

When countries change their names, it is often for political reasons. Sometimes a new government decides to change the country's name to separate itself from an earlier government. For example, Burma became Myanmar when a military government took over in 1989. Cambodia has had several name changes as well. After a coup in 1970, it was called the Khmer Republic. Then, in 1975, under communist rule, it became Kampuchea. Gaining independence from another nation is another reason for a country to change its name. For instance, in 1957, after gaining independence from Great Britain, the Gold Coast became Ghana. Another name change occurred when Zimbabwe gave up its former British name, Rhodesia, several years after winning independence. Finally, after the collapse of the Soviet Union in 1992, the country of Yugoslavia broke up into the independent states of Serbia, Croatia, Bosnia, and Herzegovina as well as the Province of Kosovo and Metohija, which declared its independence from Serbia in 2008. These name changes can be confusing, but they reveal the changing political climate of the countries in which they occur.

—Kim Seng (student)

grammar in context

Exemplification

When you write an exemplification paragraph, always use a comma after the introductory transitional word or phrase that introduces an example.

For example, Burma became Myanmar in 1989.

For instance, the Gold Coast changed its name to Ghana in 1957.

Finally, after the collapse of the Soviet Union in 1992, the country of Yugoslavia broke up into the independent states of Serbia, Croatia, Bosnia, and Herzegovina.

For information on using commas with introductory transitional words and phrases, see 34b.

Analyzing an Exemplification Paragraph

Read the exemplification paragraph below; then, follow the instructions in Practice 4-1.

Jobs of the Future

College students should take courses that prepare them for the careers that will be in demand over the next ten years. For example, the health-care field will have tremendous growth. Hundreds of thousands of medical workers—such as home-care aides, dental hygienists, and registered nurses—will be needed. Also, there will be an ongoing demand for workers who can operate and repair the specialized machines used in hospitals, labs, and other medical settings. In addition, a wide range of "green" jobs will become available as many industries work to strengthen their environmental policies. For example, construction workers, architects, and landscapers will be needed to create eco-friendly living and working spaces. Finally, education will be an attractive area for job seekers in the coming years. Many new teachers, especially those who are experienced with e-learning, will be needed to replace the teachers who retire during the next ten years. Students who know what jobs will be available can prepare themselves for the future.

—Bill Broderick (student)

PRACTICE

4-1   1. Underline the topic sentence of the paragraph above.

2. List the specific examples the writer uses to support his topic sentence. The first example has been listed for you.

health-care jobs

_____

_____

3. Circle the transitional words and phrases that the writer uses to connect ideas in the paragraph.

4. Underline the paragraph's summary statement.

PRACTICE

4-2   Following are four possible topic sentences for exemplification paragraphs. Copy the topic sentences on a separate sheet of paper. Then, list three or four examples you could use to support each topic sentence. For example, if you were writing a paragraph about how difficult the first week of your new job was, you could mention waking up early, getting to know your coworkers, and learning new routines.

1. There are many things you can do to protect your online privacy.

2. Internships give students valuable opportunities to develop job skills.

3. Many recent movies feature strong female characters.

4. Some reality television shows insult the intelligence of their viewers.

4b Case Study: A Student Writes an Exemplification Paragraph

Here is how one student, Sarah Herman, wrote an exemplification paragraph.

When Sarah was asked to write a paragraph on a challenging job, she had little difficulty deciding what to focus on. She had just finished a summer job waiting tables in a beach community on the New Jersey shore—by far the most challenging job she had ever had. Once Sarah decided to focus her paragraph on this difficult work experience, she drafted the following topic sentence.

Waiting tables on the Jersey shore was the most challenging job I ever had.

identify your main idea, and write a topic sentence

Look back at the brainstorming you did in response to the Focus on Writing prompt on page 79, and choose several programs or services to write about. Then, draft a topic sentence that communicates the main idea your paragraph will discuss.

_____

_____

After Sarah drafted her topic sentence, she listed several examples to support it.

Restaurant too big

Boss disrespectful

No experience

Kitchen chaotic

Customers rude

Tips bad

list examples

List some examples that can support your topic sentence and help you develop your exemplification paragraph about programs or services that your school offers (or should offer) to help students adjust to college life.

_____

_____

_____

_____

_____

_____

Next, Sarah eliminated the examples on her list that she thought did not directly support her topic sentence. Then, she made an **informal outline**, arranging the remaining examples in the order in which she thought she could discuss them most effectively—in this case, from the least important to the most important example.

TOPIC SENTENCE   Waiting on tables was the most challenging job I ever had.
1. No experience
2. Customers rude
3. Tips bad
4. Boss disrespectful

make an outline

Create an informal outline for your paragraph by arranging your list of examples in a logical order—for instance, from the least important to the most important example. Make sure you include only those examples that directly support your topic sentence.

Using her informal outline as a guide, Sarah wrote the following draft of her paragraph.

Waiting tables on the Jersey shore was the most challenging job I ever had. I had little experience as a food server. The first day of work was so bad that I almost quit. The customers were rude. All they wanted was to get their food as fast as possible so they could get back to the beach or the boardwalk. They were often impolite and demanding. The tips were bad. It was hard to be pleasant when you knew that the people you were waiting on were probably going to leave you a bad tip. Finally, the owner of the restaurant did not show us any respect. He often yelled at us, saying that if we didn't work harder, he would fire us. He never did, but his constant threats didn't do much to help our morale.

draft your paragraph

Using your informal outline as a guide, draft your exemplification paragraph.

When she finished her draft, Sarah scheduled a conference with her instructor, who suggested that her paragraph would be stronger if she made some of her examples more specific. For example, what experience did she have that made her want to quit? Exactly how were customers rude? Her instructor also reminded her that she needed to **TEST** her paragraph. As she **TEST**ed her paragraph, Sarah assessed her draft.

- She checked her **topic sentence** and decided that it was effective.
- When she evaluated her **evidence**, she realized she needed to add more examples and details and delete irrelevant materials.
- She noticed that she did not have a **summary statement**, so she planned to add one at the end of her paragraph.
- She decided she needed to add more **transitions** to make it easier for readers to follow her discussion.

After **TEST**ing her paragraph, Sarah revised her draft. The draft below, which has been edited and proofread, includes all the elements that Sarah looked for when she **TEST**ed her paragraph.

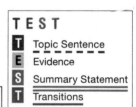

T E S T
T Topic Sentence
E Evidence
S Summary Statement
T Transitions

My Most Challenging Job

Waiting tables on the Jersey shore was the most challenging job I ever had. First, I had never worked in a restaurant before, so I made a lot of mistakes. Once, I forgot to bring salads to a table I waited on. A person at the table complained so loudly that the owner had to calm him down. I was so frustrated and upset that I almost quit. Second, the customers at the restaurant were often rude. All they wanted was to get their food as fast as possible so they could get back to the beach or the boardwalk. They were on vacation, and they wanted to be treated well. As a result, they were frequently very demanding. No one ever said, "excuse me," "please," or "thank you," no matter what I did for them. Third, the tips were usually bad. It was hard to be pleasant when you knew that the people you were waiting on were probably going to leave you a bad tip. Finally, the owner of the restaurant never showed his workers any respect. He would yell at us, saying that if we didn't work harder, he would fire us. He never did, but his constant threats didn't do much to help our morale. Even though I survived the summer, I promised myself that I would never wait tables again.

E

TEST · Revise · Edit · Proofread

Look back at the draft of your exemplification paragraph. Using the **TEST** checklist below, evaluate your paragraph to make sure it includes a topic sentence, evidence, a summary statement, and transitions. Then, revise your draft accordingly. Finally, edit and proofread your paragraph.

TESTing an exemplification paragraph

Topic Sentence Unifies Your Paragraph

☐ Do you have a clearly worded **topic sentence** that states your paragraph's main idea?

☐ Does your topic sentence state an idea that can be supported by examples?

Evidence Supports Your Paragraph's Topic Sentence

☐ Does all your **evidence**—the examples you present—support your paragraph's main idea?

☐ Do you need to add more examples?

Summary Statement Reinforces Your Paragraph's Unity

☐ Does your paragraph end with a **summary statement** that reinforces your main idea?

Transitions Add Coherence to Your Paragraph

☐ Do you use **transitions** to introduce each example your paragraph discusses?

☐ Do you need to add transitions to make your paragraph clearer and to help readers follow your ideas?

5 Narrative Paragraphs

NASA

focus on writing

On July 21, 1969, astronauts from the *Apollo 11* spaceflight took their first steps onto the surface of the Moon. Brainstorm to decide on a significant local, national, or international event that you remember. (If you prefer, you may choose a topic from the list on the following page instead.) You will return to your topic and review your brainstorming notes later in the chapter when you write your narrative paragraph.

additional topics for narration

A difficult choice

An embarrassing situation

A dangerous experience

An experience that had an impact on you

An instance of injustice

 5a Understanding Narration

Narration is writing that tells a story. For example, a narrative paragraph could tell how an experience you had as a child changed you, how the life of Martin Luther King Jr. is inspiring, or how the Battle of Gettysburg was the turning point in the Civil War. (For information on writing narrative essays, see 15b.)

When you **TEST** a **narrative paragraph**, make sure it follows these guidelines:

T A narrative paragraph should begin with a **topic sentence** that states its main idea, letting readers know why you are telling a particular story.

E A narrative paragraph should present **evidence**—events and details—in **time order**, usually in the order in which the events actually occurred. Effective narrative paragraphs include only those events that tell the story and avoid irrelevant information that could distract or confuse readers.

S A narrative paragraph should end with a **summary statement** that reinforces the paragraph's main idea.

T A narrative paragraph should include **transitions** that connect events to one another and to the topic sentence.

Some Transitional Words and Phrases for Narration

As you arrange your ideas in a narrative paragraph, be sure to use clear transitional words and phrases. These signals help readers follow your narrative by indicating the order of the events you discuss.

after	first . . . second . . . third	specific dates
as	immediately	(for example, "In 2006")
as soon as	later	suddenly
before	later on	then
by the time	meanwhile	two hours (days, months,
earlier	next	years) later
eventually	now	until
finally	soon	when

Paragraph Map: Narration

> **Topic Sentence**
>
> *Event #1*
>
> *Event #2*
>
> *Event #3*
>
> **Summary Statement**

Model Paragraph: Narration

The student writer of the following paragraph presents a series of events to describe the creation of a viral video.

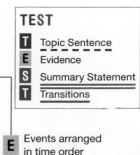

T	Topic Sentence
E	Evidence
S	Summary Statement
T	Transitions

E Events arranged in time order

Fifteen Minutes of Fame

Creating a viral video isn't easy. Before I created my first viral video, I spent hours watching some of the most famous online videos like "Charlie Bit My Finger" and "The Evolution of Dance." I even watched "The Dancing Baby," which debuted in the late 1990s and is considered one of the very first viral videos. Once I had done my research, I started drafting ideas for my own video. As soon as I finalized my concept for filming a flash mob lip syncing and dancing at the local shopping mall. I invited all of my friends and family to participate. We practiced for a few days and then put the plan into action. Two hours after filming, I uploaded the video to YouTube. Then I waited. Eventually, the number of views started to rise. Before I knew it, the video had over thirty thousand views and the local newspaper was calling to see if they could interview me. Although my video only went viral locally, the hard work was worth it when I got my fifteen minutes of fame on the local news.

—Christine Clark (student)

grammar in context

Narration

When you write a narrative paragraph, you tell a story. As you become involved in your story, you might begin to string events together without proper punctuation. If you do, you will create a **run-on**.

INCORRECT (RUN-ON)	Two hours after filming, I uploaded the video to YouTube then I waited.
CORRECT	Two hours after filming, I uploaded the video to YouTube. Then I waited.

For information on how to identify and correct run-ons, see Chapter 24.

Analyzing a Narrative Paragraph

Read this narrative paragraph; then, follow the instructions in Practice 5-1.

A lighthearted adventure turned into an international rescue effort when the Wild Boars youth soccer team became trapped in a cave in Thailand. After practice on June 18, 2018, the boys and their coach went to Tham Luang cave to do some exploring. While the group was in the cave, heavy rains began to fall, flooding the cave and trapping the group inside. Over the next week, Thai Navy divers searched the cave, but they were hampered by strong currents, poor visibility, and tight passageways. Meanwhile, an international rescue mission was taking shape with the arrival of thousands of volunteers, including cave and rescue experts, military personnel, and divers, from the United States, Britain, Australia, and other countries. On July 2, British divers discovered the boys and their coach huddled on a narrow ledge more than two miles from the entrance. However, the joy of finding them turned immediately to the challenge of getting them out. The international rescue team considered several options before deciding on a plan. Divers would use special stretchers to transport each person safely out of the cave. By the end of the day on July 8, the first four boys had been rescued. The next day, divers retrieved four more boys. On July 10, eighteen days after entering the cave, the last four boys and their coach were rescued. The dramatic rescue of the Wild Boars was a success, thanks to the teamwork of people from all over the world.

—Francis Orlando (student)

PRACTICE

5-1

1. Underline the topic sentence of the paragraph on page 92.

2. List the major events discussed in the paragraph. The first event has been listed for you.

The boys and their coach went to explore a cave.

_____

_____

_____

_____

_____

_____

3. Circle the transitional words and phrases that the writer uses to link events in time.

4. Underline the paragraph's summary statement.

PRACTICE

5-2

Following are four possible topic sentences for narrative paragraphs. List three or four events that could support each topic sentence. For example, if you were recalling a barbecue that turned into a disaster, you could tell about burning the hamburgers, spilling the soda, and forgetting to buy paper plates.

1. One experience made me realize that I was no longer as young as I thought.

2. The first time I _____, I got more than I bargained for.

3. I didn't think I had the courage to _____, but when I did, I felt proud of myself.

4. I remember my reactions to one particular event very clearly.

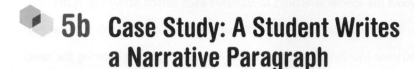

5b Case Study: A Student Writes a Narrative Paragraph

Here is how one student, Todd Kinzer, wrote a narrative paragraph. When Todd's instructor asked the class to write a paragraph about an experience that had a great impact on them, Todd began by listing some experiences that he could write about.

> Accident at camp—Realized I wasn't as strong as I thought I was
>
> Breaking up with Lindsay—That was painful
>
> Shooting the winning basket in my last high school game—Sweet
>
> The last Thanksgiving at my grandparents' house—Happy and sad

As Todd looked over the experiences on his list, he realized that he could write about all of them. He decided, however, to focus on the last Thanksgiving he spent at his grandparents' house. This occasion was especially meaningful to him because his grandfather had died shortly after the holiday.

Todd began by freewriting on his topic. He typed whatever came into his mind about the dinner, without worrying about spelling, punctuation, or grammar. Here is Todd's freewriting paragraph.

> Thanksgiving. Who knew? I remember the smells when I woke up. I can see Granddad at the stove. We were all happy. He told us stories about when he was a kid. I'd heard some of them before, but so what? I loved to hear them. We ate so much I could hardly move. They say turkey has something in it that puts you to sleep. We watched football all afternoon and evening. I still can't believe Granddad is dead. I guess I have the topic for my paragraph.

NASA

freewrite

Look back at the brainstorming you did in response to the Focus on Writing prompt on page 89. Choose one experience from your notes, and then freewrite about that experience. Be sure to write nonstop, without worrying about spelling, punctuation, or grammar.

After he finished freewriting, Todd arranged the main events he planned to write about in an informal outline that reflected the order in which they occurred.

Grandfather cooking

Grandfather told stories

Sat down for Thanksgiving dinner

Watched football on TV

make an outline

Create an informal outline for your paragraph by arranging the events you remember from your childhood experience in the order in which they occurred. (Keep in mind that you will add details to develop these events when you draft your paragraph.)

NASA

Using his informal outline as a guide, Todd drafted the following paragraph.

> Last Thanksgiving, my grandparents were up early. My grandfather stuffed the turkey, and my grandmother started cooking the other dishes. When I got up, I could smell the turkey in the oven. The table was already set for dinner, so we ate breakfast in the kitchen. My grandfather told us about the Thanksgivings he remembered from when he was a boy. When we sat down for dinner, a fire was burning in the fireplace. My grandmother said grace. My grandfather carved the turkey, and we all passed around dishes of food. For dessert, we had pecan pie and ice cream. After dinner, we watched football on TV. When I went to bed, I felt happy. This was my grandfather's last Thanksgiving.

draft your paragraph

Using your informal outline as a guide, draft your narrative paragraph.

NASA

Todd knew his draft needed a lot of work. Before he wrote the next draft, he tried to recall what other things had happened that Thanksgiving. He also tried to decide which idea was the most important and what additional supporting information could make his paragraph stronger. Todd emailed his draft to his instructor, and his instructor returned the draft along with her comments. After considering his instructor's suggestions and **TEST**ing his paragraph, Todd decided to make the following changes.

- He decided that he needed to add a **topic sentence** that stated his paragraph's main idea.
- He decided that he needed to add more details and examples and to delete irrelevant sentences so that all his **evidence** would support his main idea.
- He decided to write a stronger **summary statement**.
- He decided that he needed to add **transitions** to indicate the time order of the events in his paragraph.

After **TEST**ing his paragraph, Todd revised and edited, checking grammar, punctuation, mechanics, and spelling. Then, he proofread carefully for typos. The final draft below includes all the elements Todd looked for when he **TEST**ed his paragraph.

Thanksgiving Memories

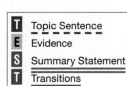

T	Topic Sentence
E	Evidence
S	Summary Statement
T	Transitions

E

   This past Thanksgiving was both happy and sad because it was the last one I would spend with my grandfather. The holiday began early. At five o'clock in the morning, my grandfather woke up and began to stuff the turkey. About an hour later, my grandmother began cooking corn pie and pineapple casserole. At eight o'clock, when I got up, I could smell the turkey cooking. While we ate breakfast, my grandfather told us about Thanksgivings he remembered when he was a boy. Later, my grandfather made a fire in the fireplace, and we sat down for dinner. After my grandmother said grace, my grandfather carved and served the turkey. The rest of us passed around dishes of sweet potatoes, mashed potatoes, green beans, asparagus, cucumber salad, relish, cranberry sauce, apple butter, cabbage salad, stuffing, and, of course, corn pie and pineapple casserole. For dessert, my grandmother served pecan pie with generous scoops of ice cream. After dinner, we turned on the TV and the whole family watched football all evening. That night, I remember thinking that life couldn't get much better. Four months later, my grandfather died in his sleep. For my family and me, Thanksgiving would never be the same.

TEST · Revise · Edit · Proofread

Look back at the draft of your narrative paragraph. Using the **TEST** checklist below, evaluate your paragraph to make sure it includes a topic sentence, evidence, a summary statement, and transitions. Then, revise your draft accordingly. Finally, edit and proofread your paragraph.

NASA

TESTing a narrative paragraph

T opic Sentence Unifies Your Paragraph

☐ Do you have a clearly worded **topic sentence** that states your paragraph's main idea?

☐ Does your topic sentence give readers an idea of why you are telling the story?

E vidence Supports Your Paragraph's Topic Sentence

☐ Do you include enough information about the events you discuss?

☐ Does all your **evidence**—events and details—support your paragraph's main idea?

☐ Do you need to include more events or details in your narrative?

S ummary Statement Reinforces Your Paragraph's Unity

☐ Does your paragraph end with a **summary statement** that reinforces your main idea?

T ransitions Add Coherence to Your Paragraph

☐ Do your **transitions** indicate the time order of events in your paragraph?

☐ Do you need to add transitions to make your paragraph clearer and to help readers follow your ideas?

6 Process Paragraphs

Bloomberg/Getty Images

focus on writing

The picture shows a screen from the popular game *Candy Crush*, an app that so far has been installed over 500 million times. Brainstorm to develop a list of games you know well and could explain to others. (If you prefer, you may choose a topic from the list on the following page instead.) You will return to your topic and review your brainstorming later in the chapter when you write your process paragraph.

additional topics for process

How to apply for financial aid

How to shop online for bargains

A process you perform every day

How to find an apartment

How to prepare for a storm or another natural disaster

 # 6a Understanding Process

When you describe a **process**, you tell readers how something works or how to do something. For example, you could explain how the optical scanner at the checkout counter of a food store works, how to hem a pair of pants, or how to start a blog. A **process paragraph** tells readers how to complete a process by listing steps in time order. (For information on writing process essays, see 15c.)

When you **TEST** a process paragraph, make sure it follows these guidelines:

T A process paragraph should begin with a **topic sentence** that identifies the process you are explaining and the point you want to make about it (for example, "Parallel parking is easy once you know the secret" or "By following a few simple steps, you can design a résumé that will get noticed").

E A process paragraph should discuss all the steps in the process, one at a time. These steps should be presented in strict **time order**—the order in which they occur. A process paragraph should present enough **evidence**—examples and details—to explain the steps and make the process clear to readers.

S A process paragraph should end with a **summary statement** that reinforces the paragraph's main idea.

T A process paragraph should include **transitions** that connect the steps in the process to one another and to the topic sentence.

Some Transitional Words and Phrases for Process

Transitions are very important in process paragraphs. They enable readers to clearly identify each step—for example, *first*, *second*, *third*, and so on. In addition, they establish a sequence that lets readers move easily through the process you are describing.

after that,	first	subsequently
after this	immediately	the first (second,
as	later	third) step
as soon as	meanwhile	the next step
at the same time	next	the last step
at this point	now	then
during	once	when
finally	soon	while

Paragraph Map: Process

Topic Sentence
Step #1
Step #2
Step #3
Summary Statement

There are two types of process paragraphs: *process explanations* and *instructions*.

Model Paragraph: Process Explanations

In a **process explanation**, your purpose is to help readers understand how something operates or how something happens—for example, how a hurricane forms or how fracking works. With a process explanation, you do not expect readers to perform the process.

In the following process explanation paragraph from a psychology exam, the writer explains the four stages children go through when they acquire language.

Children go through four distinct stages when they learn language. The first stage begins as soon as infants are born. By crying, they let people know when they need something or if they are in pain. The second stage begins when children are about a year old and are able to communicate with single words. For example, a child will use the word *food* to mean anything from "I'm hungry" to "feed the dog." The third stage begins at about twenty months. During this stage, children begin to use two-word sentences, such as "dada car" (for "This is dada's car"). Finally, at about thirty months, children begin to learn the rules that govern language. They learn how to form simple sentences, plurals, and the past tense of verbs. No matter what language they speak, all children follow the same process when they learn language.

—Jennifer Gulla (student)

TEST

T Topic Sentence
E Evidence
S Summary Statement
T Transitions

E Steps presented in time order

Model Paragraph: Instructions

When you write **instructions**, your purpose is to give readers the information they need to perform a task or activity—for example, to fill out an application, to operate a piece of machinery, or to help someone who is choking. Because you expect readers to follow your instructions, you address them directly, using **commands** to tell them what to do (*check the gauge* . . . *pull the valve*).

In the following paragraph, the writer gives a humorous set of instructions on how to get food out of a defective vending machine.

Man vs. Machine

There is a foolproof method of outsmarting a vending machine that refuses to give up its food. First, approach the vending machine coolly. Make sure that you don't seem frightened or angry. The machine will sense these emotions and steal your money. Second, be polite. Say hello, compliment the machine on its selection of goodies, and smile. Be careful. If the machine thinks you are trying to take advantage of it, it will steal your money. Third, if the machine steals your money, remain calm. Ask nicely to get the food you paid for. Finally, it is time to get serious. Hit the side of the vending machine with your fist. If this doesn't work, lower your shoulder and throw yourself at the machine. (A good kick or two might also help.) When the machine has had enough, it will drop your snack, and you can grab it. If you follow these few simple steps, you should have no trouble walking away from vending machines with the food you paid for.

—Adam Cooper (student)

TEST

T Topic Sentence
E Evidence
S Summary Statement
T Transitions

E Step-by-step instructions presented in time order

grammar in context

Process

When you write a process paragraph, you may find yourself making **illogical shifts** in tense, person, and voice. If you shift from one tense, person, or voice to another without good reason, you may confuse readers.

CONFUSING (ILLOGICAL SHIFT)　First, the vending machine <u>should be approached</u> coolly. <u>Make sure</u> that you don't seem frightened or angry. (illogical shift from passive to active voice)

CLEAR　First, <u>approach</u> the vending machine coolly. <u>Make sure</u> that you don't seem frightened or angry. (consistent use of active voice)

For information on how to avoid illogical shifts in tense, person, and voice, see Chapter 27.

Analyzing a Process Paragraph

Read this process paragraph; then, follow the instructions in Practice 6-1.

An Order of Fries

I never realized how much work goes into making French fries until I had a summer job at a potato processing plant in Hermiston, Oregon. The process begins with freshly dug potatoes being shoveled from trucks onto conveyor belts leading into the plant. During this stage, workers pick out any rocks that may have been dug up with the potatoes because these could damage the automated peelers. After the potatoes have gone through the peelers, they travel on a conveyor belt through the "trim line." Here, workers cut out any bad spots, being careful not to waste potatoes by trimming too much. Next, the potatoes are sliced by automated cutters and then deep-fried for about a minute. After this, they continue along a conveyor belt to the "wet line." Here, workers again look for bad spots, and they throw away any rotten pieces. At this point, the potatoes go to a second set of fryers for three minutes before being moved to subzero freezers for ten minutes. Then, it's on to the "frozen line" for a final inspection. The inspected fries are weighed by machines and then sealed into five-pound plastic packages, which are weighed again by workers who also check that the packages are properly sealed. Finally, the bags are packed into boxes and made ready for shipment to various restaurants across the western United States. This process goes on twenty-four hours a day, seven days a week, to bring consumers the French fries they enjoy so much.

—Cheri Rodriguez (student)

PRACTICE
 6-1

1. Underline the topic sentence of the paragraph on pages 102–103.

2. Is this a process explanation or instructions?

_____

How do you know? _____

3. List the steps in the process. The first step has been listed for you.
The potatoes are unloaded, and the rocks are sorted out.

_____

_____

_____

_____

_____

_____

4. Circle the transitional words and phrases that the writer uses to move readers from one step to the next.

5. Underline the paragraph's summary statement.

PRACTICE
6-2

Following are four possible topic sentences for process paragraphs. List three or four steps that explain the process each topic sentence identifies. For example, if you were explaining the process of getting a job, you could list preparing a résumé, looking at ads in newspapers or online, writing a job application letter, and going on an interview. Make sure each step follows logically from the one that precedes it.

1. Getting the lowest prices when you shop is not a simple process.

2. Getting the most out of a student-teacher conference requires some preparation.

3. Crate-training a puppy can be a tricky process.

4. Choosing an outfit for a job interview can be challenging.

 ## 6b Case Study: A Student Writes a Process Paragraph

Here is how one student, Manasvi Bari, wrote a process paragraph. When Manasvi was assigned to write a paragraph in which she explained a process she performed every day, she decided to write about how to get a seat on a crowded subway car. To make sure she had enough to write about, she made the following list of possible steps she could include.

Don't pay attention to heat
Get into the train
Get the first seat
Look as if you need help
Get to a pole
Don't travel during rush hour
Choose your time
Be alert
Squeeze in

After looking over her list, Manasvi crossed out steps that she didn't think were essential to the process she wanted to describe.

~~Don't pay attention to heat~~
Get into the train
Get the first seat

Look as if you need help

~~Get to a pole~~

~~Don't travel during rush hour~~

~~Choose your time~~

Be alert

Squeeze in

list the steps in the process

Choose one game from the brainstorming you did in response to the Focus on Writing prompt on page 98, and then list the steps you need to discuss in order to explain how to play the game. (Assume that your readers know nothing about the game you are describing.)

Bloomberg/Getty Images

_____

_____

_____

_____

_____

_____

Now, cross out any steps that you don't think readers will need in order to understand how to play the game.

Once she had decided on her list of steps, Manasvi made an informal outline, arranging the steps in the order in which they should be performed.

Get into the train

Be alert

Get the first seat

Squeeze in

Look as if you need help

Bloomberg/Getty Images

make an outline

Create an informal outline for your paragraph by arranging the steps for playing your game in the order in which they should be performed.

At this point, Manasvi thought that she was ready to begin writing her paragraph. Here is her draft.

> When the train arrives, get into the car as fast as possible. Be alert. If you see an empty seat, grab it and sit down immediately. If there is no seat, ask people to move down, or squeeze into a space that seems too small. If none of this works, you'll have to use some imagination. Look helpless. Drop your books, and look as if the day can't get any worse. Sometimes a person will get up and give you a seat. If this strategy doesn't work, stand near someone who looks as if he or she is going to get up. When the person gets up, jump into the seat as fast as you can. Don't let the people who are getting on the train get the seat before you do.

Bloomberg/Getty Images

draft your paragraph

Using your informal outline as a guide, draft your process paragraph.

Manasvi showed the draft of her paragraph to a writing center tutor. Together, they **TEST**ed her paragraph and made the following decisions.

- They decided that she needed to add a **topic sentence** that identified the process and stated the point she wanted to make about it.
- They decided that her **evidence**—the examples and details that described the steps in her process—was clear and complete.
- They decided that she needed to add a **summary statement** that reinforced the point of the process.
- They decided that she needed to add **transitions** that helped readers follow the steps in the process.

After **TEST**ing her paragraph, Manasvi revised her paragraph. The final edited and proofread draft includes all the elements that Manasvi looked for when she **TEST**ed her paragraph.

Surviving Rush Hour

Anyone who takes the subway to school in the morning knows how hard it is to find a seat, but by following a few simple steps, you should be able to get a seat almost every day. First, when the train arrives, get into the car as fast as possible. Be alert. As soon as you see an empty seat, grab it and sit down immediately. Meanwhile, if there is no seat, ask people to move down, or try to squeeze into a space that seems too small. If none of this works, the next step is to use some imagination. Look helpless. Drop your books, and look as if the day can't get any worse. Sometimes a person will get up and give you a seat. Don't be shy. Take it, and remember to say thank you. Finally, if this strategy doesn't work, stand near someone who looks as if he or she is going to get up. When the person gets up, jump into the seat as fast as you can. By following these steps, you should be able to get a seat on the subway and arrive at school rested and relaxed.

TEST

T	Topic Sentence
E	Evidence
S	Summary Statement
T	Transitions

E

TEST · Revise · Edit · Proofread

Look back at the draft of your process paragraph. Using the **TEST** checklist on page 108, evaluate your paragraph to make sure it includes a topic sentence, evidence, a summary statement, and transitions. Then, revise your draft accordingly. Finally, edit and proofread your paragraph.

Bloomberg/Getty Images

TESTing a process paragraph

T opic Sentence Unifies Your Paragraph

☐ Do you have a clearly worded **topic sentence** that states your paragraph's main idea?

☐ Does your topic sentence identify the process you will discuss?

☐ Does your topic sentence indicate whether you will be explaining a process or giving instructions?

E vidence Supports Your Paragraph's Topic Sentence

☐ Have you included all the steps in the process?

☐ Have you included enough **evidence**—examples and details—to explain the steps and make the process clear to readers?

☐ If your paragraph is a set of instructions, have you included all the information readers need to perform the process?

S ummary Statement Reinforces Your Paragraph's Unity

☐ Does your paragraph end with a **summary statement** that reinforces your main idea?

T ransitions Add Coherence to Your Paragraph

☐ Do your **transitions** move readers from one step in the process to the next?

☐ Do you need to add transitions to make your paragraph clearer and to help readers follow your ideas?

7 Cause-and-Effect Paragraphs

Ikon Images/Alamy

focus on writing

Look at the picture above that shows various electronic devices. Then, freewrite to decide on a particular electronic device that had a significant effect on you or your family. (If you prefer, you may choose a topic from the list on the following page instead.) You will return to your topic and review your freewriting later in the chapter when you write your cause-and-effect paragraph.

additional topics for cause and effect

The effects of bullying

The reasons you decided to attend college

A decision that changed your life

How a particular event affected you

Why students drop out of high school

7a   Understanding Cause and Effect

Why is the cost of college so high in the United States? How does smoking affect a person's health? What would happen if the city increased its minimum wage? How dangerous is the flu? All these questions have one thing in common: They try to determine the causes or effects of an action, event, or situation.

A **cause** is something or someone that makes something happen. An **effect** is something brought about by a particular cause.

CAUSE	EFFECT
Increased airport security ⟶	Long lines at airports
Weight gain ⟶	Health problems
Seat belt laws passed ⟶	Traffic deaths reduced

A **cause-and-effect paragraph** examines or analyzes reasons and results. It helps readers understand why something happened or is happening or shows how one thing affects another. (For information on writing cause-and-effect essays, see 15d.)

When you **TEST** a cause-and-effect paragraph, make sure it follows these guidelines:

T   A cause-and-effect paragraph should begin with a <u>**topic sentence**</u> that tells readers whether the paragraph is focusing on causes or on effects—for example, "There are several reasons why the cost of health care is so high" (causes) or "Going to the writing center has given me confidence as well as skill as a writer" (effects).

E A cause-and-effect paragraph should present **evidence**—examples and details—to support the topic sentence and explain each cause and effect. Causes or effects should be arranged in **logical order**—for example, from least to most important.

S A cause-and-effect paragraph should end with a **summary statement** that reinforces the paragraph's main idea.

T A cause-and-effect paragraph should include **transitions** that connect causes or effects to one another and to the topic sentence.

Some Transitional Words and Phrases for Cause and Effect

Transitions in cause-and-effect paragraphs introduce individual causes or effects. They may also show the connections between a cause and its effects or between an effect and its causes. In addition, they may indicate which cause or effect is more important than another.

accordingly	moreover	the first (second, third)
another cause	since	reason
another effect	so	the most important cause
as a result	the first (second,	the most important effect
because	third, final) cause	therefore
consequently	the first (second,	
for	third, final) effect	
for this reason		

Paragraph Map: Cause and Effect

Topic Sentence

Cause (or effect) #1

Cause (or effect) #2

Cause (or effect) #3

Summary Statement

Model Paragraph: Causes

The following paragraph focuses on **causes**.

TEST

T Topic Sentence
E Evidence
S Summary Statement
T Transitions

Why Young People Don't Vote

There are several reasons why young adults don't vote in national elec-
tions. The first is that they don't think their vote is important. Nothing could
be further from the truth, however. When young people vote, they help set
the social agenda. By voting, they are able to weigh in on the things that
they care about. By not voting, they give the impression that they don't care
about issues such as abortion, gun control, and the environment. Another
reason young people don't vote is that they don't realize that policies put in
place now will affect them in the future. For example, will Social Security be
available to them when they retire? Will student debt make it impossible for
them to save or to buy a house? Only by exercising their right to vote will
young people make their voices heard about these and other vital issues.
Finally, many young people don't understand that it is their civic duty to
vote. The right to vote—especially for women and minorities—was achieved
only after a number of hard-fought battles had been won. People in many
other countries are not able to vote and, for this reason, do not get to select
their leaders. This situation should make it clear that for our form of government to work, everyone—including young people—must participate in the
democratic process. For these reasons, young people should realize that their
votes count and that they should vote in every election.

Causes arranged in logical order **E**

—Moniquetta Hall (student)

Model Paragraph: Effects

The following paragraph focuses on **effects**.

TEST

T Topic Sentence
E Evidence
S Summary Statement
T Transitions

The Negative Effects of Climate Change

Climate change caused by global warming would have several negative
effects. One effect would be an increase in the number of intense storms.
Large hurricanes and other types of storms would damage property and
kill many people. Another effect would be a rise in sea level. As the earth
warms, the polar ice would melt and raise the level of the earth's oceans.

Effects arranged in logical order **E**

Coastal cities and low-lying areas would probably be flooded. Still <u>another</u>
effect would be the spread of certain kinds of diseases. Many diseases, now
found only in warm areas, would spread to areas that were once cool but
then became warm. Malaria and yellow fever, for example, could become as
common in the United States as they are in Africa and Southeast Asia. <u>Finally,</u>
climate change associated with global warming would affect agriculture.
Farming areas, such as the Midwest, where American farmers grow corn and
wheat, would become dry. <u>As a result</u>, there would be food shortages, and
many people could go hungry. <u>No one knows for certain what will happen, but</u>
<u>if global warming continues, our lives would certainly be affected.</u>

E Effects arranged in
logical order

—Jackie Hue (student)

grammar in context

Cause and Effect

When you write a cause-and-effect paragraph, you should be careful
not to confuse the words *affect* and *effect*. *Affect* is a verb meaning "to
influence." *Effect* is a noun meaning "result."

One ~~affect~~ would be an increase in the number of storms. (*effect* is
a noun)
effect

No one knows for certain what will happen, but if global warming
continues, our lives will certainly be ~~effected~~. (*affect* is a verb)
affected

For more information on effect *and* affect, *see 23g.*

Analyzing a Cause-and-Effect Paragraph

Read this cause-and-effect paragraph; then, follow the instructions in
Practice 7-1.

Disaster Tourism

People taking disaster tours can have good reasons for doing so. First,
disaster tourism enables people to see a disaster area in real time, without
any media manipulation. For people such as educators and historians, this
is important. They want to visit a disaster site so that they can understand

what happened and connect the disaster to historical events. This is the case with tours of the killing fields in Cambodia and of the Auschwitz-Birkenau concentration camps in Poland. Second, some disaster tourists come to help, not just to visit. For example, after the devastating 2015 earthquake in Nepal that killed almost nine thousand people, tourists cleared rubble, prepared food for locals, and gave comfort to the injured. Finally, some disaster tourists want to help publicize the scope of the damage. They hope that, by doing so, they will be able to focus attention on the area and bring in more aid. After Hurricane Katrina, for example, some New Orleans residents credited disaster tourism with helping to attract volunteers and bringing in badly needed dollars to the area. Contrary to their critics, disaster tourists can help, not hinder, efforts to rebuild devastated areas.

PRACTICE

 7-1

1. Underline the topic sentence of the preceding paragraph.

2. List the causes the writer describes. The first cause has been listed for you.

Disasters are reported on by the media. Since disaster coverage can be

biased, many people want to see disaster areas for themselves.

_____

_____

3. Circle the transitional words and phrases that the writer uses to identify causes.

4. Underline the paragraph's summary statement.

PRACTICE

7-2   Following are four possible topic sentences for cause-and-effect paragraphs. For each topic sentence, list the effects that could result from the cause identified in the topic sentence. For example, if you were writing a paragraph about the effects of excessive drinking on campus, you could list low grades, health problems, and vandalism.

1. Having a baby can change your life.

2. Being bilingual has many advantages.

3. Social media have affected me in several ways.

4. Impulse buying can have negative effects on a person's finances.

PRACTICE

7-3   List three causes that could support each of the following topic sentences.

1. The causes of teenage obesity are easy to identify.

2. Chronic unemployment can have many causes.

3. The high cost of college tuition is not easy to explain.

4. There are several reasons why professional athletes' salaries are so high.

7b Case Study: A Student Writes a Cause-and-Effect Paragraph

Here is how one student, Sean Jin, wrote a cause-and-effect paragraph. When Sean was asked to write a cause-and-effect essay for his composition class, he had no trouble thinking of a topic because of a debate that was going on in his hometown about building a Walmart Superstore there. He decided to write a paragraph that discussed the effects that such a store would have on the local economy.

Sean's instructor told the class the main problem to watch for in planning a cause-and-effect essay is making sure that a **causal relationship** exists—that one event actually causes another. In other words, just because one event follows another closely in time, students should not assume that the second event was caused by the first.

With this advice in mind, Sean brainstormed to develop a list of possible effects a Walmart would have on his small town. Here is Sean's list of effects.

Provide new jobs
Offer low-cost items
Pay low wages
Push out small businesses

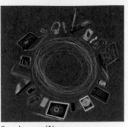

Ikon Images/Alamy

list effects

Choose one event from the freewriting you did in response to the Focus on Writing prompt on page 109. Then, brainstorm to develop a list of the effects that the event has had on you.

_____

_____

_____

_____

_____

_____

After reviewing his list of effects, Sean drafted a topic sentence that introduced his topic and communicated the point he wanted to make about it. Here is Sean's topic sentence.

Walmart can have good and bad effects on a small town.

Ikon Images/Alamy

write a topic sentence

Review your list of effects, and then draft a topic sentence for your cause-and-effect paragraph.

_____

_____

Next, Sean made an informal outline that arranged the effects on his list in a logical order. This outline helped him check to make sure he had included enough examples to explain each effect and to support his topic sentence. Here is Sean's outline.

Good effects

Provides new jobs

    —Store needs many employees

    —Many people out of work in rural town and need jobs

Offers low-cost items
   —Families on a budget can buy things they usually can't afford
   —Walmart prices lower than most other stores' prices

Bad effects

Pays low wages
   —Walmart pays less than other stores

Pushes out small businesses
   —Forces many small businesses to close
   —Local businesses can't match low prices or wide selection

---

make an outline

Create an informal outline for your paragraph by arranging your list of effects in a logical order—for example, from least to most important.

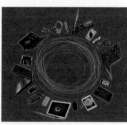

Ikon Images/Alamy

After completing his outline, Sean wrote the following draft of his paragraph.

> Walmart can have good and bad effects on a small town. It provides jobs. A large store needs a lot of employees. So, many people from the area will be able to find work. Walmart's prices are low. Families that don't have much money may be able to buy things they can't afford to buy at other stores. Not all of Walmart's effects are positive. Walmart pays employees less than other stores. Walmart provides jobs, but those jobs don't pay very much. When Walmart comes into an area, many small businesses are forced to close. They just can't match Walmart's prices or stock as much merchandise as Walmart can.

---

draft your paragraph

Using your informal outline as a guide, draft your cause-and-effect paragraph.

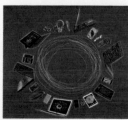

Ikon Images/Alamy

When he finished his draft, Sean went to the writing center and met with a tutor. After going over his draft with the tutor and **TEST**ing his paragraph, Sean made the following decisions.

- He decided that he needed to sharpen his **topic sentence** to tie his discussion of Walmart to the small town in which he lived.
- He decided to provide more **evidence** to support his topic sentence—for example, what exactly does Walmart pay its salespeople?
- He realized that he needed to add a **summary statement** to reinforce his main idea.
- He decided to add **transitions** to identify positive and negative effects.

Now Sean was ready to revise and edit his paragraph. The final edited and proofread draft includes all the elements Sean looked for when he **TEST**ed his paragraph.

Walmart Comes to Town

TEST

T Topic Sentence
E Evidence
S Summary Statement
T Transitions

E

When Walmart comes to a small town like mine, it can have both good and bad effects. The first and most positive effect is that it provides jobs. A large Walmart Superstore needs a lot of employees, so many people will be able to find work. In my rural town, over 15 percent of the people are out of work. Walmart could give these people a chance to improve their lives. Another positive effect that Walmart can have is to keep prices low so families on tight budgets will be able to buy things they cannot afford to buy at other stores. My own observations show that many items at a local Walmart are cheaper than those at other stores. Not all of Walmart's effects are positive, however. One negative effect Walmart can have is that it can actually lower wages in an area. My aunt, a longtime employee, says that Walmart pays beginning workers $11 an hour. This is less than they would get in stores that pay union wages. Another negative effect Walmart can have is to drive other, smaller businesses out. When Walmart comes into an area, many small businesses are forced to close. They just cannot match Walmart's prices or selection of merchandise. It is clear that although Walmart can have a number of positive effects, it can also have some negative ones.

TEST · Revise · Edit · Proofread

Look back at the draft of your cause-and-effect paragraph. Using the **TEST** checklist below, evaluate your paragraph to make sure it includes a topic sentence, evidence, a summary statement, and transitions. Then, revise your draft accordingly. Finally, edit and proofread your paragraph.

Ikon Images/Alamy

TESTing a cause-and-effect paragraph

T opic Sentence Unifies Your Paragraph

☐ Do you have a clearly worded **topic sentence** that states your paragraph's main idea?

☐ Does your topic sentence identify the cause or effect on which your paragraph will focus?

E vidence Supports Your Paragraph's Topic Sentence

☐ Do you need to add any important causes or effects?

☐ Do you need to explain your causes or effects more fully?

☐ Does all your **evidence**—examples and details—support your paragraph's main idea?

S ummary Statement Reinforces Your Paragraph's Unity

☐ Does your paragraph end with a **summary statement** that reinforces your main idea?

T ransitions Add Coherence to Your Paragraph

☐ Do your **transitions** show how your ideas are related?

☐ Do your transitions clearly introduce each cause or effect?

☐ Do you need to add transitions to make your paragraph clearer and to help readers follow your ideas?

8 Comparison-and-Contrast Paragraphs

	OLD WORDS	NEW MEANINGS
GREEN	yellow + blue	good for the planet
FRIEND	a person you know	a random person
ORGANIC	living matter	made naturally in a factory

© Maria Scrivan

focus on writing

This chart shows old words that have acquired new meanings. Brainstorm to develop a list of three or four words that you think have acquired new meanings. (You can also do an Internet search with the terms "old words, new meanings.") Then, make your own chart that lists the old and new meanings of the words you have listed. (If you prefer, you may choose a topic from the list on the following page.) You will return to your topic and review your brainstorming later in the chapter when you write your comparison-and-contrast paragraph.

additional topics for comparison and contrast

Two popular sports figures

Men's and women's attitudes toward relationships, shopping,
 or conversation

Two cars you would consider buying

Two websites

Two people, places, or objects

 8a **Understanding Comparison and Contrast**

When you buy something— for example, a set of headphones, a smartphone, a computer, or a car—you often comparison-shop, looking at
various models to determine how they are alike and how they are different.
In other words, you *compare and contrast*. When you **compare**, you consider how things are similar. When you **contrast**, you consider how they
are different. A **comparison-and-contrast paragraph** can examine
just similarities, just differences, or both similarities and differences. (For
information on writing comparison-and-contrast essays, see 15e.)

Before two things can be compared, however, they need to have a
basis for comparison: The items need to have enough in common so
that a comparison is logical. For example, you could not compare people
and apples (they have nothing in common). You could, however, compare
people and chimpanzees—both are mammals, both live in complex social
groups, and both are capable of communication.

When you **TEST** a comparison-and-contrast paragraph, make sure it
follows these guidelines:

T A comparison-and-contrast paragraph should begin with a **topic
sentence** that tells readers whether the paragraph is going to discuss
similarities, differences, or both. The topic sentence should also make
clear the main point of the comparison—why you are comparing or
contrasting the two subjects (for example, "The writers Toni Morrison
and Maya Angelou have similar ideas about race and society" or "My
parents and I have different ideas about success").

121

E A comparison-and-contrast paragraph should include enough **evidence**—examples and details—to make the similarities and differences clear to readers. A comparison-and-contrast paragraph should discuss the same or similar points for both subjects, one by one. Points should be arranged in **logical order**—for example, from least to most important.

S A comparison-and-contrast paragraph should end with a **summary statement** that reinforces the paragraph's main idea.

T A comparison-and-contrast paragraph should include **transitions** that indicate the two subjects being compared and connect the points you make about each subject.

Some Transitional Words and Phrases for Comparison and Contrast

Transitions make your paragraph more coherent by showing readers whether you are focusing on similarities (for example, *likewise* or *similarly*) or differences (for example, *although* or *in contrast*). Transitions also tell readers when you are changing from one point (or one subject) to another.

although	one difference . . . another difference
but	one similarity . . . another similarity
even though	on the contrary
however	on the one hand . . . on the other hand
in comparison	similarly
in contrast	though
like	unlike
likewise	whereas
nevertheless	

There are two kinds of comparison-and-contrast paragraphs: *subject-by-subject comparisons* and *point-by-point comparisons*.

Subject-by-Subject Comparisons

In a **subject-by-subject comparison**, you divide your comparison into two parts and discuss one subject at a time. In the first part of the paragraph, you discuss all your points about one subject. Then, in the second part, you discuss the same (or similar) points about the other subject. (In each part of the paragraph, you discuss the points in the same order.)

A subject-by-subject comparison is best for paragraphs in which you discuss just a few points. In this situation, readers will have little difficulty remembering the points you discuss for the first subject when you move on to discuss the second subject.

Paragraph Map: Subject-by-Subject Comparison

> **Topic Sentence**
>
> *Subject A*
>   Point #1
>
>   Point #2
>
>   Point #3
>
> *Subject B*
>   Point #1
>
>   Point #2
>
>   Point #3
>
> **Summary Statement**

Model Paragraph: Subject-by-Subject Comparison

The writer of the following paragraph uses a subject-by-subject comparison to compare sociologists and anthropologists.

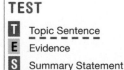

TEST

T Topic Sentence
E Evidence
S Summary Statement
T Transitions

Sociologists vs. Anthropologists: What's the Difference?

Both sociologists and anthropologists study human behavior, but there are key differences between these two types of scientists. In their studies of human behavior, sociologists look at the structure of groups and how people interact within these groups. They focus on social relationships, examining how human behavior is influenced by social groups in a given place and time. Sociologists primarily study patterns of relationships in industrialized societies, with research by sociologists helping to shape public policy on social issues such as desegregation, divorce, and gender equality. Unlike sociologists who concentrate on societies and social interactions, anthropologists focus on cultures and cross-cultural differences. Anthropologists explore all aspects of human life from past to present, gathering information from people all over the world and from all periods of history. In addition, anthropologists look at

Subject A:
Sociologists

Subject B:
Anthropologists

E human behavior by examining everything about a particular culture, from its tools and art to its language and social structure. <u>Although</u> anthropologists initially concentrated on non-Western cultures, their studies have now included industrialized societies. The work anthropologists do includes searching for fossils to study human origins as well as helping law enforcement agencies solve crimes. <u>Even though sociologists and anthropologists share a common interest in studying human behavior, their focus is actually quite different.</u>

—Jeanne Jones (student)

Point-by-Point Comparisons

When you write a **point-by-point comparison**, you discuss a point about one subject and then discuss the same point for the second subject. You use this alternating pattern throughout the paragraph.

A point-by-point comparison is a better strategy for long paragraphs in which you discuss many points. It is also a better choice if the points you are discussing are technical or complicated. Because you compare the two subjects one point at a time, readers will be able to see one point of comparison before moving on to the next point.

Paragraph Map: Point-by-Point Comparison

Topic Sentence

Point #1
    Subject A

    Subject B

Point #2
    Subject A

    Subject B

Point #3
    Subject A

    Subject B

Summary Statement

Model Paragraph: Point-by-Point Comparison

In the following paragraph, the writer uses a point-by-point comparison to compare two characters in a short story.

T	Topic Sentence
E	Evidence
S	Summary Statement
T	Transitions

Two Sisters

Although they grew up together, Maggie and Dee, the two sisters in Alice Walker's short story "Everyday Use," are very different. Maggie, who was burned in a fire, is shy and has low self-esteem. When she walks, she shuffles her feet and looks down at the ground. Her sister Dee, however, is confident and outgoing. She looks people in the eye when she talks to them and is very opinionated. Maggie and Dee also have different attitudes toward life. Maggie never complains or asks for anything more than she has. She has remained at home with her mother in rural Georgia. In contrast, Dee has always wanted nicer things. She has gone away to school and hardly ever visits her mother and Maggie. The biggest difference between Maggie and Dee is their attitude toward tradition. Although Maggie values her family's rural American traditions, Dee values her African heritage. Maggie cherishes her family's handmade quilts and furniture, hoping to use them with her own family. In contrast, Dee sees the handmade objects as things to be displayed and shown off, not used every day. The many differences between Maggie and Dee add conflict and tension to the story.

E — Point 1: Different personalities

E — Point 2: Different attitudes toward life

E — Point 3: Different attitudes toward tradition

—Margaret Caracappa (student)

grammar in context

Comparison and Contrast

When you write a comparison-and-contrast paragraph, you should express the points you are comparing in **parallel** terms to highlight their similarities or differences.

NOT PARALLEL Although Maggie values her family's traditions, the African heritage of her family is the thing that Dee values.

PARALLEL Although Maggie values her family's traditions, Dee values her African heritage.

For more information on revising to make ideas parallel, see Chapter 22.

Analyzing a Comparison-and-Contrast Paragraph

Read this comparison-and-contrast paragraph; then, follow the instructions in Practice 8-1.

Virtual and Traditional Classrooms

Taking a course online is very different from taking a course in a traditional classroom. One difference is that students in an online course have more flexibility than students in a traditional course. They can do their schoolwork at any time, scheduling it around other commitments, such as jobs and childcare. Students in a traditional course, however, must go to class at a specific time and place. Another difference is that students in an online course can feel isolated from the teacher and other students because they never actually come into physical contact with them. Students in a traditional classroom, however, are able to connect with the teacher and their classmates because they interact with them in person. A final difference is that in an online course, students use email or a discussion board to discuss course material. A student who is a slow typist or whose Internet connection is unreliable is clearly at a disadvantage. In a traditional course, most of the discussion takes place in the classroom, so technology is not an issue. Because online and traditional courses are so different, students must think carefully about which type of course best fits their needs.

—William Hernandez (student)

PRACTICE

1. Underline the topic sentence of the paragraph above.

2. Does this paragraph deal mainly with similarities or differences?

_____ How do you know? _____

_____

3. Is this paragraph a subject-by-subject or point-by-point comparison?

_____ How do you know? _____

_____

4. List some of the contrasts the writer describes. The first contrast has been listed for you.

When it comes to their schedules, students in an online course have more

flexibility than students in a traditional course do.

_____

_____

_____

_____

_____

5. Circle the transitional words and phrases the writer uses to move from one comparison to the next.

6. Underline the paragraph's summary statement.

PRACTICE

8-2 Following are three topic sentences. For each topic sentence, list three or four similarities or differences between the two subjects. For example, if you were writing a paragraph comparing health care provided by a local clinic with health care provided by a private doctor, you could discuss the cost, the length of waiting time, the quality of care, and the frequency of follow-up visits.

1. My mother (or father) and I are very different (or alike).

2. My friends and I have different views on _____.

3. Two of my college instructors have very different teaching styles.

8b Case Study: A Student Writes a Comparison-and-Contrast Paragraph

Here is how one student, Jermond Love, wrote a comparison-and-contrast paragraph. When Jermond was given this assignment for his composition class, he began by brainstorming to find a topic. When he reviewed his brainstorming notes, he decided that the following topics looked most promising.

Football and soccer

American and Caribbean cooking

The differences between my brother and me

Life in Saint Croix versus life in New York City

After considering each of these topics, Jermond decided to write about the differences between life in Saint Croix, the Caribbean island where he was raised, and life in New York City. He listed various points that he thought he could compare and contrast. Then, he crossed out the ones he didn't want to write about.

Size

~~Economy~~

~~Businesses~~

Lifestyle

~~Politics~~

~~Education~~

~~Music~~

~~Agriculture~~

~~Sports~~

~~Living conditions~~

~~Industry~~

~~Traditions~~

After thinking about the relative sizes of Saint Croix and New York City as well as their respective lifestyles, Jermond brainstormed again to identify some specific differences that he could discuss in his paragraph.

Population: 60,000 versus over 8 million

Laid-back versus hurried lifestyle

Christiansted and Frederiksted versus five boroughs

Friendly versus not friendly

---

list differences

Look over the brainstorming you did in response to the Focus on Writing prompt on page 120, and then cross out the word pairs that you do not want to discuss in your paragraph. On the lines below, list the word pairs you do plan to discuss.

_____

_____

_____

_____

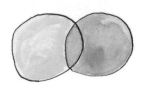

yellow + blue
© Maria Scrivan

After reviewing his list of differences, Jermond drafted the following topic sentence. This sentence told readers that he was going to focus on differences, and it also identified the main point he was going to make in his comparison-and-contrast paragraph.

TOPIC SENTENCE   Life in Saint Croix is very different from life in New York City.

---

write a topic sentence

Review your list of words with new meanings, and then draft a topic sentence for your comparison-and-contrast paragraph.

_____

_____

good for the planet
© Maria Scrivan

At this point, Jermond created the following informal outline, presenting his ideas in the order in which he was going to discuss them in his paragraph.

Size
    Saint Croix
        Small size
        Small population
        Christiansted and Frederiksted
    New York City
        Large size
        Large population
        Five boroughs

Lifestyle
    Saint Croix
        Laid-back
        Friendly
    New York City
        In a hurry
        Not always friendly

Jermond thought that a point-by-point organization would be easier for his readers to follow than a subject-by-subject organization. With this organization, readers would be able to keep track of his comparison as he discussed each of his points, one at a time.

a person you know
© Maria Scrivan

make an outline

Decide whether you will write a subject-by-subject or point-by-point comparison. Then, use the appropriate format (see the paragraph maps on pages 123 and 124) to help you create an outline for your comparison-and-contrast paragraph. Before you begin, decide on the order in which you will present your points—for example, from least to most important. (For a subject-by-subject comparison, begin by deciding which subject you will discuss first.)

Using his informal outline as a guide, Jermond drafted his paragraph. Here is his draft.

Life in Saint Croix is very different from life in New York City. Saint Croix is much smaller than New York City. Saint Croix has a total population of about 60,000 people. The two main towns are Christiansted and Frederiksted. New York City is very large. Its residents are crowded into five boroughs. The lifestyle in Saint Croix is different from the lifestyle of New York City. In Saint Croix, almost everyone operates on "island time." Everyone is friendly. People don't see any point in getting anyone upset. In New York City, most people are always in a hurry. They don't take the time to slow down and enjoy life. As a result, people can seem unfriendly. They don't take the time to get to know anyone. I hope when I graduate I can stay in New York City but visit my home in Saint Croix whenever I can.

draft your paragraph

Using your informal outline as a guide, draft your comparison-and-contrast paragraph.

living matter
© Maria Scrivan

Jermond put his paragraph aside for a day and then reread it. Although he was generally satisfied with what he had written, he thought that his draft could be improved. To help students revise their paragraphs, his instructor divided students into peer-review groups and asked them to read and discuss each other's paragraphs. After working with a class-mate on his draft and **TEST**ing his paragraph, Jermond made the following decisions.

- He decided that his **topic sentence** was clear and specific.
- He saw that he needed more **evidence**—examples and details—to help his readers understand the differences between his two subjects.
- He decided to change his **summary statement** because it didn't clearly reinforce the idea in his topic sentence.
- Finally, he decided that he needed to add **transitional words and phrases** that would show when he was moving from one subject to another.

As Jermond revised his paragraph, he added background about Saint Croix. (The classmate who read his draft had pointed out that many people in the class would not know anything about it.) The final edited and proofread draft includes all the elements Jermond looked for when he **TEST**ed his paragraph.

Saint Croix versus New York City

TEST

T	Topic Sentence
E	Evidence
S	Summary Statement
T	Transitions

E

Life in Saint Croix is very different from life in New York City. One difference between Saint Croix and New York is that Saint Croix is much smaller than New York. Saint Croix, the largest of the United States Virgin Islands, has a population of about 60,000. The two main towns on the island are Christiansted, with a population of about 3,000, and Frederiksted, with a population of only about 830. Unlike Saint Croix, New York City is large. It has a population of over 8 million crowded into the five boroughs of Manhattan, Brooklyn, the Bronx, Queens, and Staten Island. My neighborhood in Brooklyn is more than twice the size of Christiansted and Frederiksted combined. Another difference between Saint Croix and New York City is their lifestyles. Life in Saint Croix is slower than life in New York. In Saint Croix, almost everyone operates on "island time." Things get done, but people don't rush to do them. When workers say "later," they can mean "this afternoon," "tomorrow," or even "next week." No one seems to mind, as long as the job gets done. People don't see any point in getting anyone upset. In New York City however, most people are always in a hurry. They don't take the time to slow down and enjoy life. Everything is fast—fast food, fast cars, fast Internet access. As a result, people can seem unfriendly. Although Saint Croix and New York City are so different, life is interesting in both places.

made naturally in a factory
© Maria Scrivan

TEST · **Revise** · **Edit** · **Proofread**

Look back at the draft of your comparison-and-contrast paragraph. Using the **TEST** checklist below, evaluate your paragraph to make sure it includes a topic sentence, evidence, a summary statement, and transitions. Then, revise your draft accordingly. Finally, edit and proofread your paragraph.

TESTing a comparison-and-contrast paragraph

T opic Sentence Unifies Your Paragraph

☐ Do you have a clearly worded **topic sentence** that states your paragraph's main idea?

☐ Does your topic sentence indicate whether you are focusing on similarities or on differences?

E vidence Supports Your Paragraph's Topic Sentence

☐ Does all your **evidence**—examples and details—support your paragraph's main idea?

☐ Do your examples and details show how your two subjects are alike or different?

☐ Do you need to discuss additional similarities or differences?

S ummary Statement Reinforces Your Paragraph's Unity

☐ Does your paragraph end with a **summary statement** that reinforces your main idea?

T ransitions Add Coherence to Your Paragraph

☐ Do your **transitions** indicate whether you are focusing on similarities or on differences?

☐ Do transitional words and phrases lead readers from one subject or point to the next?

☐ Do you need to add transitions to make your paragraph clearer and to help readers follow your ideas?

9 Descriptive Paragraphs

Richard Levine/Alamy

focus on writing

Look at this picture of bottles of Vitamin Water. The labels of Vitamin Water feature various words (such as *essential* and *endurance*) that attempt to convey a certain image marketers would like to associate with the brand. Imagine you are writing a magazine ad for your favorite beverage, footwear, or cosmetic. Brainstorm to develop a list of characteristics that would enable you to describe the product as persuasively as possible. (If you prefer, you may choose a topic from the list on the following page instead.) You will return to your topic and review your brainstorming later in the chapter when you write your descriptive paragraph.

additional topics for description

Your workplace

An unusual person

Your dream house

A place you would like to visit

A useful gadget or tool

 9a Understanding Description

In a personal email, you may describe a friend or classmate. In a biology lab manual, you may describe the structure of a cell. In a report for a nursing class, you may describe a patient you treated.

When you write a **description**, you use words to paint a picture for your readers. With description, you use language that creates a vivid impression of what you have seen, heard, smelled, tasted, or touched. The more details you include, the better your description will be. (For information on writing descriptive essays, see 16a.)

The following description is flat because it includes very few descriptive details.

FLAT   Today, I saw a beautiful sunrise.

In contrast, the passage below is full of descriptive details that convey the writer's impression of the scene. This revised description relies on sight (*glowed red; turned slowly to pink, to aqua, and finally to blue*), touch (*the soft sandy beach; felt the cold water*), and sound (*heard the waves hit the shore*) to create a vivid picture.

VIVID   Early this morning as I walked along the soft sandy beach,
         I saw the sun rise slowly out of the ocean. At first, the ocean
         glowed red. Then, it turned slowly to pink, to aqua, and
         finally to blue. As I stood watching the sun, I heard the
         waves hit the shore, and I felt the cold water swirl around
         my toes. For a moment, even the small grey and white birds
         that hurried along the shore seemed to stop and watch the
         dazzling sight.

135

When you **TEST** a **descriptive paragraph**, make sure it follows these guidelines:

T A descriptive paragraph should begin with a **topic sentence** that conveys the main idea or general impression you want to communicate in your paragraph—for example, "The woods behind my house may seem ordinary, but to me, they are beautiful" or "The old wooden roller coaster at Lakemont Park is a work of art."

E A descriptive paragraph should present **evidence**—descriptive details—that supports the topic sentence. Details should be presented in a clear **spatial order** that reflects the order in which you observed the person, place, or thing you are describing. For example, you can move from near to far or from top to bottom.

S A descriptive paragraph should end with a **summary statement** that reinforces the paragraph's main idea.

T A descriptive paragraph should include **transitions** that connect details to one another and to the topic sentence.

Some Transitional Words and Phrases for Description

As you arrange your ideas in a descriptive paragraph, be sure to use appropriate transitional words and phrases to lead readers from one detail to another.

above	inside
at the edge	nearby
at the entrance	next to
behind	on
below	on one side . . . on the other side
between	outside
beyond	over
down	spreading out
farther	the first . . . the second
in	the least important . . . the most important
in back of	the next
in front of	under

Paragraph Map: Description

> Topic Sentence
>
> *Detail #1*
>
> *Detail #2*
>
> *Detail #3*
>
> Summary Statement

Model Paragraph: Description

The student writer of the following paragraph uses descriptive details to support the idea that the Lincoln Memorial is a monument to American democracy.

The Lincoln Memorial

The Lincoln Memorial was built to celebrate American democracy. In front of the monument is a long marble staircase that leads from a reflecting pool to the memorial's entrance. Thirty-six columns—which symbolize the thirty-six states reunited after the Civil War—surround the building. Inside the building are three rooms. The first room contains the nineteen-foot statue of Lincoln. Seated in a chair, Lincoln looks exhausted after the long Civil War. One of Lincoln's hands is a fist, showing his strength, and the other is open, showing his kindness. On either side of the first room are the two other rooms. Carved on the wall of the one room is the Gettysburg Address. On the wall of the other room is the Second Inaugural Address. Above the Gettysburg Address is a mural showing an angel freeing the slaves. Above the Second Inaugural Address is another mural, which depicts the people of the North and the South coming back together. As its design shows, the Lincoln Memorial was built to celebrate both the sixteenth president and the nation's struggle for democracy.

—Nicole Lentz (student)

TEST

T	Topic Sentence
E	Evidence
S	Summary Statement
T	Transitions

E Descriptive details arranged in spatial order

grammar in context

Description

When you write a descriptive paragraph, you sometimes use **modifiers**—words and phrases that describe other words in the sentence. A modifier should be placed as close as possible to the word it is supposed to modify. If you place a modifying word or phrase too far from the word it modifies, you create a **misplaced modifier** that will confuse readers.

CONFUSING (MISPLACED MODIFIER)	Seated in a chair, <u>the long Civil War</u> has clearly exhausted Lincoln. (Was the Civil War seated in a chair?)
CLEAR	Seated in a chair, <u>Lincoln</u> looks exhausted after the long Civil War.

For information on how to identify and correct misplaced modifiers, see Chapter 28.

Analyzing a Descriptive Paragraph

Read this descriptive paragraph; then, follow the instructions in Practice 9-1.

Shopping at Ikea

A trip to Ikea is a unique shopping experience. At the entrance to the store, a friendly greeter helps direct customers. Beyond the greeter is a large, white staircase—this is where the adventure begins. Next to the staircase is a bustling restaurant where visitors can take a break from shopping and sample Ikea's famous Swedish meatballs. Once you get past the restaurant, you go on a winding path through the various furniture displays of the store. Ikea visitors can explore elaborate displays for each area of the home: living room, kitchen, bathroom, and office. Typically, one decorating style will be featured to the left, and a different style will be featured to the right. On the floor below are displays of home accessories. Items such as glassware, eating utensils, pots and pans, picture frames, toys, and light fixtures are displayed on tables or in wire bins. In between this merchandise are smaller displays meant to give shoppers an idea of how they can use the accessories in their own home. Finally, the path ends at the warehouse. There are no elaborate displays on this level; once you enter the industrial warehouse it is down to business. Here visitors use a number system to find the boxes that contain the disassembled furniture they would like to take home. Outside the warehouse is the parking lot. Here you are sure to see cars with boxes balanced precariously on their roofs or even hanging out of windows. Ikea isn't the kind of store you stop in quickly on your way home from work; it is a full day of adventure.

PRACTICE

9-1

1. Underline the topic sentence of the paragraph above.

2. In a few words, summarize the main idea of the paragraph.

_____

3. What are some of the details the writer uses to describe the setting in Ikea? The first detail has been listed for you.

friendly greeter _____

_____

_____

_____

_____

_____

4. Circle the transitional words and phrases that the writer uses to lead readers from one detail to another.

5. Underline the paragraph's summary statement.

PRACTICE

9-2   Each of the five topic sentences below states a possible main idea for a descriptive paragraph. For each, list three details that could help convey the main idea. For example, to support the idea that sitting in front of a fireplace is relaxing, you could describe the crackling of the fire, the pine scent of the smoke, and the changing colors of the flames.

1. The most valuable possession I own is _____.

2. The most interesting place I ever visited is _____.

3. One look at my instructor told me that this was going to be a challenging semester.

4. One of my favorite stores to shop at is _____.

5. My neighborhood is full of distinctive sounds and smells.

 # 9b   Case Study: A Student Writes a Descriptive Paragraph

Here is how one student, Jared Lopez, wrote a descriptive paragraph. When Jared was asked to write a descriptive paragraph about someone he admired, he decided to write about his uncle Manuel, who had been a father figure to him.

Because he was very familiar with his paragraph's subject, Jared did not have to brainstorm or freewrite to find material to write about. Instead, he immediately started to list the features of his uncle that he considered the most memorable.

> Looks friendly
> Hands
> Dark eyes
> Distinguished looking
> Tall

list details

List the details that best describe the product that you brainstormed about for the Focus on Writing prompt on p. 134.

Richard Levine/Alamy

After reviewing the list of features he planned to discuss, Jared arranged the features in an informal outline in the order in which he planned to discuss them.

Tall

Looks friendly

Dark eyes

Distinguished looking

Hands

make an outline

Create an informal outline for your paragraph by arranging the details you listed in the order in which you plan to discuss them. You might arrange them in the order in which you observe them—for example, from near to far or from top to bottom—or, as Jared did, in order of importance.

Richard Levine/Alamy

Jared decided to begin his paragraph with a general description of his uncle Manuel and then move on to concentrate on his uncle's most distinctive feature: his hands. Here is the first draft of Jared's paragraph.

My uncle's name is Manuel, but his friends call him Manny. He is over six feet tall. Uncle Manny's eyes are dark brown, almost black. They make him look very serious. When he laughs, however, he looks friendly. His nose is long and straight, and it makes Uncle Manny look very distinguished. Most interesting to me are Uncle Manny's hands. Even though he hasn't worked as a stonemason since he opened his own construction company ten years ago, his hands are still rough and scarred. They are large and strong, but they can be gentle too.

Richard Levine/Alamy

draft your paragraph

Using your informal outline as a guide, draft your descriptive paragraph.

During a conference with his instructor, Jared **TEST**ed his paragraph.

- He decided that he needed to add a **topic sentence** that stated the main idea of his description.
- He decided that he needed to add more descriptive details to give readers more **evidence** of his uncle's strength and gentleness.
- He decided that he needed to add a stronger **summary statement** to unify his paragraph.
- He decided to include more **transitions** to move readers from one part of his description to the next.

After **TEST**ing his paragraph, Jared revised and edited his draft. Then, he proofread carefully for typos. The final draft includes all the elements Jared looked for when he **TEST**ed it.

My Uncle Manny

TEST

T	Topic Sentence
E	Evidence
S	Summary Statement
T	Transitions

My uncle Manuel is a strong but gentle person who took care of my mother and me when my father died. Manuel, or "Manny" as his friends and family call him, is over six feet tall. This is unusual for a Mexican of his generation. The first thing most people notice about my uncle Manny is his eyes. They are large and dark brown, almost black. They make him look very serious. When he laughs, however, the sides of his eyes crinkle up, and he looks warm and friendly. Another thing that stands out is his nose, which is long and straight. My mother says it makes Uncle Manny look strong and distinguished. The most striking thing about Uncle Manny is his hands. Even though he hasn't worked as a stonemason since he opened his own construction company ten years ago, his hands are still rough and scarred from carrying stones. No matter how much he tries, he can't get rid of the dirt under his fingernails. Uncle Manny's hands are big and rough, but they are also gentle and comforting. To me, they show what he really is: a strong and gentle man.

TEST · Revise · Edit · Proofread

Look back at the draft of your descriptive paragraph. Using the **TEST** checklist below, evaluate your paragraph to make sure it includes a topic sentence, evidence, a summary statement, and transitions. Then, revise your draft accordingly. Finally, edit and proofread your paragraph.

Richard Levine/Alamy

TESTing a descriptive paragraph

T opic Sentence Unifies Your Paragraph

☐ Do you have a clearly worded **topic sentence** that states your paragraph's main idea—the general impression you want to convey?

☐ Does your topic sentence identify the person, place, or thing you will describe in your paragraph?

E vidence Supports Your Paragraph's Topic Sentence

☐ Does all your **evidence**—descriptive details—support your paragraph's main idea?

☐ Do you have enough descriptive details, or do you need to include more?

S ummary Statement Reinforces Your Paragraph's Unity

☐ Does your paragraph end with a **summary statement** that reinforces your main idea?

T ransitions Add Coherence to Your Paragraph

☐ Do your **transitions** lead readers from one detail to the next?

☐ Do you need to add transitions to make your paragraph clearer and to help readers follow your ideas?

10 Classification Paragraphs

Hero Images/Getty Images

focus on writing

The picture above shows people at a concert. Brainstorm to identify the types of music that you and your friends listen to. (If you prefer, you may choose a topic from the list on the following page instead.) You will return to this topic and review your brainstorming later in the chapter when you write your classification paragraph.

additional topics for classification

Types of friends

Part-time jobs

Types of drivers

Types of teachers

Kinds of YouTube videos

 10a Understanding Classification

When you **classify**, you sort items (people, things, ideas) into categories or groups. You classify when you organize bills into those you have to pay now and those you can pay later, or when you sort the clothes in a dresser drawer into piles of socks, T-shirts, and underwear.

In a **classification paragraph**, you tell readers how items can be sorted into categories or groups. Each category must be **distinct**. In other words, none of the items in one category should also fit into another category. For example, you would not classify novels into mysteries, romances, and e-books, because both mystery novels and romance novels could also be e-books. (For information on writing classification essays, see 16b.)

When you **TEST** a classification paragraph, make sure it follows these guidelines:

T A classification paragraph should begin with a **topic sentence** that introduces the subject of the paragraph. It may also identify the categories you will discuss (for example, "Before you go camping, you should sort the items you are thinking of packing into three categories: absolutely necessary, potentially helpful, and not really necessary").

E A classification paragraph should discuss one category at a time and should include enough **evidence**—examples and details—to explain each category and show how it is distinct from the other categories. The categories should be arranged in **logical order**—for example, from least to most important or from smallest to largest.

S A classification paragraph should end with a **summary statement** that reinforces the paragraph's main idea.

T A classification paragraph should include **transitions** to introduce the categories you discuss and connect them to one another and to the topic sentence.

145

Some Transitional Words and Phrases for Classification

Transitions tell readers when you are moving from one category to another (for example, *the first type, the second type*). They can also indicate which categories you think are more important than others (for example, *the most important, the least important*).

one kind . . . another kind

one way . . . another way

the first (second, third) category

the first group . . . the last group

the first type . . . the second type

the most (or least) important group

the next part

Paragraph Map: Classification

> **Topic Sentence**
>
> *Category #1*
>
> *Category #2*
>
> *Category #3*
>
> **Summary Statement**

Model Paragraph: Classification

The writer of the following paragraph classifies bosses into three distinct groups.

TEST

T Topic Sentence
E Evidence
S Summary Statement
T Transitions

First type of boss **E**

Types of Bosses

I've had three kinds of bosses in my life: the uninterested boss, the supervisor, and the micromanager. The first type is an uninterested boss. This boss doesn't care what workers do as long as they do the job. When I was a counselor at summer camp, my boss fell into this category. As long as no campers (or worse yet, parents) complained, he left you alone. He never cared if you followed the activity plan for the day or gave the kids an extra snack to keep them quiet. The second type of boss is the supervisor. This kind of boss will check you once in a while and give you helpful advice. You'll have a certain amount of freedom but not too much. When I was a salesperson at the Gap, my boss fell into this category. She helped me through the first few weeks of the job and encouraged me to do my best. At the end of the summer, I had learned a lot about retail business and had good feelings about the job. The last, and worst, type of boss is the micromanager. This kind of boss gets involved in everything. My boss at Taco Bell was this kind of person. No one could do anything right. There was always a better way to do anything you tried to do. If you rolled a burrito one way, he would tell you to do it another way. If you did it the other way, he would tell you to do it the first way. This boss never seemed to understand that people need praise every once in a while. Even though the supervisor expects a lot and makes you work, it is clear to me that this boss is better than the other types.

E Second type of boss

E Last type of boss

—Melissa Burrell (student)

grammar in context

Classification

When you write a classification paragraph, you may list the categories you are going to discuss. If you use a **colon** to introduce your list, make sure that a complete sentence comes before the colon.

INCORRECT Basically, bosses can be divided into: the uninterested boss, the supervisor, and the micromanager.

CORRECT Basically, I've had three kinds of bosses in my life: the uninterested boss, the supervisor, and the micromanager.

For more information on how to use a colon to introduce a list, see 36d.

Analyzing a Classification Paragraph

Read this classification paragraph; then, follow the instructions in Practice 10-1.

Unusual Smartphone Applications

Generally, there are three kinds of unusual smartphone applications: those that are harmlessly entertaining, those that are surprisingly useful, and those that are deadly serious. The first kind is harmlessly entertaining. The purpose of the odd apps in this category is to be amusing, silly, or fun. People enjoy using them to do unimportant things, such as "pop" bubble wrap, choose a pirate name, or look up the height of their favorite celebrity. Goofy apps include Crazy Mouth, which displays animated mouths that you can hold up in front of your face. The second kind of unusual app is also odd but surprisingly useful, helping people accomplish various tasks. For example, FileThis helps users electronically file any type of paper document, and Practice+ helps musicians during practice sessions by offering tools like a metronome, a tuner, and a pitch player. Also in this category is RockMyRun, an app that matches workout songs to a runner's pace. The third kind of unusual app is the serious kind, which can actually help save lives. Often, this kind of app is available only to select groups, not to the general public. For example, trained minesweepers use the PETAL app for the iPhone to help them determine the size and shape of landmines. Another example is TransHeat, the U.S. Army's specialized app for planning travel routes with a minimal risk of being ambushed. Although not equally important, each of these three kinds of apps has its own distinct uses.

—Emily Bentz (student)

PRACTICE
10-1

1. Underline the topic sentence of the paragraph.

2. What is the subject of the paragraph? _____

3. What three categories does the writer describe?

_____

_____

_____

4. Circle the transitional phrases the writer uses to introduce the three categories.

5. Underline the paragraph's summary statement.

PRACTICE

10-2 List items in each of the following groups; then, sort the items into three or four categories.

1. All the items on your desk

2. Buildings on your college campus

3. Websites you visit

4. The various parts of a piece of equipment you use for a course or on the job

 ## 10b Case Study: A Student Writes a Classification Paragraph

Here is how one student, Corey Levin, wrote a classification paragraph. For a college composition course, Corey participated in a service-learning project at a local Ronald McDonald House, a charity that houses families of seriously ill children receiving treatment at nearby hospitals. He met several professional athletes there and was surprised to learn that many of them regularly donate time and money to charity.

When Corey was asked by his composition instructor to write a paragraph about what he had learned from his experience, he decided to write a paragraph that classified the ways in which professional athletes give back to their communities. Based on his experience, he was able to come up with the following three categories.

    Starting charitable foundations
    Guidance
    Responding to emergencies

list categories

Look back at the brainstorming you did in response to the Focus on Writing prompt on page 144, and cross out any categories that you do not plan to discuss. List the remaining categories—the ones that you will discuss in your classification paragraph—on the lines below.

Hero Images/Getty Images

_____

_____

_____

Corey then made an informal outline, listing examples to develop each of the three categories.

Foundations
>Michael Jordan
>Troy Aikman

Guidance
>Shaquille O'Neal
>The Philadelphia 76ers

Responding to emergencies
>Ike Reese
>Vince Carter

Hero Images/Getty Images

make an outline

Create an informal outline by arranging the categories of music you and your friends listen to in the order in which you will discuss them and listing examples to develop each of your categories.

After completing his informal outline, Corey drafted the following topic sentence for his paragraph.

Many high-profile athletes find various ways to give back to their communities.

Hero Images/Getty Images

write a topic sentence

Review your list of categories, and then draft a topic sentence for your classification paragraph.

_____

_____

Then, using his informal outline as a guide, Corey wrote the following draft of his paragraph.

Many high-profile athletes find various ways to give back to their communities. Many athletes as well as teams do a lot to help people. I met some of them when I volunteered at the Ronald McDonald House. For example, Michael Jordan and the Chicago Bulls built a Boys and Girls Club on Chicago's West Side. Shaquille O'Neal's Shaq's Paq provides guidance for inner-city children. Ike Reese, formerly with the Atlanta Falcons, collects clothing and food for families that need help. Vince Carter of the Memphis Grizzlies founded the Embassy of Hope Foundation. It distributes food to needy families at Thanksgiving and hosts a Christmas party for disadvantaged families.

draft your paragraph

Using your informal outline as a guide, draft your classification paragraph.

Hero Images/Getty Images

Following his instructor's suggestion, Corey emailed his draft to a classmate for feedback. In her email reply to Corey, she **TEST**ed his paragraph and made the following suggestions.

- Keep the **topic sentence** the way it is. "Various ways" shows you're writing a classification paragraph.
- Add more specific **evidence**. Give more examples of each category of "giving back" to support the topic sentence. You also need to explain the athletes' contributions in more detail.
- Add a **summary statement** to sum up the paragraph's main idea.
- Add **transitions** to introduce the three specific categories you're discussing.

Corey kept these comments in mind as he revised his paragraph. The final edited and proofread draft includes all the elements Corey looked for when he **TEST**ed his paragraph.

TEST

T Topic Sentence
E Evidence
S Summary Statement
T Transitions

Giving Back

Many high-profile athletes find various ways to give back to their communities. One way to give back is to start a charitable foundation to help young fans. For example, Michael Jordan and the Chicago Bulls built a Boys & Girls Club on Chicago's West Side. In addition, the LeBron James Family Fund spends millions of dollars each year to provide adults with college resources and to help elementary school students learn how to code. Another way athletes give back to their communities is by mentoring, or giving guidance to young people. Many athletes work to encourage young people to stay in school. Shaquille O'Neal's Shaq's Paq, for example, provides guidance for inner-city children. Tennis star Serena Williams is also involved in many charitable causes. She is a UNICEF Goodwill Ambassador, who has helped build schools in Africa and, with UNICEF, has promoted education for children in Asia One more way athletes can contribute to their communities is to respond to emergencies. Football player Ike Reese, formerly with the Atlanta Falcons, collects clothing and food for families that need help. Basketball player Vince Carter of the Memphis Grizzlies founded the Embassy of Hope Foundation. It distributes food to needy families at Thanksgiving and hosts a Christmas party for disadvantaged families. These are just some of the ways that high-profile athletes give back to their communities.

E

Hero Images/Getty Images

TEST · Revise · Edit · Proofread

Look back at the draft of your classification paragraph. Using the **TEST** checklist below, evaluate your paragraph to make sure it includes a topic sentence, evidence, a summary statement, and transitions. Then, revise your draft accordingly. Finally, edit and proofread your paragraph.

TESTing a classification paragraph

T opic Sentence Unifies Your Paragraph

☐ Do you have a clearly worded **topic sentence** that states your paragraph's main idea?

☐ Does your topic sentence identify the categories you will discuss?

E vidence Supports Your Paragraph's Topic Sentence

☐ Does all your **evidence**—examples and details—support your paragraph's main idea?

☐ Do your examples and details explain each category and indicate how each is distinct from the others?

☐ Do you need to include more examples or details?

S ummary Statement Reinforces Your Paragraph's Unity

☐ Does your paragraph end with a **summary statement** that reinforces your main idea?

T ransitions Add Coherence to Your Paragraph

☐ Do your **transitions** clearly indicate which categories are more important than others?

☐ Do you need to add transitions to make your paragraph clearer and to help readers follow your ideas?

11 Definition Paragraphs

Keith Brofsky/UpperCutImage/GettyImages

focus on writing

Look at the word *organic*, printed on an overhead sign at a supermarket, and consider how you would define it. Then, brainstorm to identify some words you have encountered in your college courses for which you could write one-paragraph definitions. (If you prefer, you may choose a topic from the list on the following page instead.) You will return to your topic and review your brainstorming later in the chapter when you write your definition paragraph.

additional topics for definition

A negative quality, such as *jealousy* or *laziness*

A type of person, such as an *optimist* or a *pessimist*

A controversial term, such as *right to life, affirmative action,* or *social justice*

A goal in life, such as *happiness* or *success*

 ## 11a Understanding Definition

During a conversation, you might say that a friend is stubborn, that a stream is polluted, or that a neighborhood is dangerous. In order to make yourself clear, you have to define what you mean by *stubborn, polluted,* or *dangerous.* Like conversations, academic assignments also may involve definition. In a history paper, for example, you might have to define *imperialism*; on a biology exam, you might be asked to define *mitosis.*

A **definition** tells what a word means. When you want your readers to know exactly how you are using a specific term, you define it.

When most people think of definitions, they think of the **formal definitions** they see in a dictionary. Formal definitions have a three-part structure.

- The term to be defined
- The general class to which the term belongs
- The things that make the term different from all other items in the general class to which the term belongs

TERM	CLASS	DIFFERENTIATION
Ice hockey	is a game	played on ice by two teams on skates who use curved sticks to try to hit a puck into the opponent's goal.
Spaghetti	is a pasta	made in the shape of long, thin strands.

A single-sentence formal definition is often not enough to define a specialized term (*point of view* or *premeditation,* for example), an abstract concept (*happiness* or *success*), or a complicated subject (*stem-cell research*). In these cases, you may need to expand the basic formal definition by writing a definition paragraph. In fact, a **definition paragraph** is an expanded formal definition. (For information on writing definition essays, see 16c.)

When you **TEST** a definition paragraph, make sure it follows these guidelines:

T A definition paragraph should begin with a formal definition in the <u>topic sentence</u>.

E A definition paragraph does not follow any one pattern of development; in fact, it may define a term by using any of the patterns discussed in this text. For example, a definition paragraph may explain a concept by *comparing* it to something else or by giving *examples*. For this reason, your discussion of each category should include **evidence**—examples and details—that is appropriate for the pattern of development that you use.

S A definition paragraph should end with a <u>summary statement</u> that reinforces the paragraph's main idea.

T A definition paragraph should include **transitions** that are appropriate for the pattern or patterns of organization you use.

Here is one possible structure for a definition paragraph. Notice that this paragraph uses a combination of **narration** and **exemplification**.

Some Transitional Words and Phrases for Definition

Transitions are important for definition paragraphs. They can signal moves from one narrative event to another. Transitions can also introduce examples.

also	often
for example	one characteristic . . . another characteristic
for men (for women)	one way . . . another way
however	sometimes
in addition	specifically
in particular	the first kind . . . the second kind
in the 1990s (or another time)	until recently
like	

Paragraph Map: Definition

Topic Sentence

> **Point #1**
>
> > Narrative
>
> **Point #2**
>
> > Example
> >
> > Example
>
> **Point #3**
>
> > Example
> >
> > Example
>
> **Summary Statement**

Model Paragraph: Definition

The writer of the following paragraph uses comparison and process to define the *dabbawala* system of food delivery.

The Dabbawala System

T	Topic Sentence
E	Evidence
S	Summary Statement
T	Transitions

<u>Fast food is a common choice for lunch in the United States.</u> Often, this meal is high in calories and full of fat. Many workers in Mumbai, India, <u>however</u>, receive a daily home-cooked lunch by means of the *dabbawala* system. This distribution system consists of people (called *dabbawalas*) who collect freshly made food from the homes of office workers and deliver it to their workplaces. **E** Comparison

<u>First</u>, the worker's wife or mother prepares the meal early in the morning and packs it in a container called a *tiffin*. <u>Next</u>, a dabbawala comes to the door to pick up the tiffin and takes it to the sorting location. <u>Third</u>, the tiffins are coded and loaded on to a train and delivered to offices by local dabbawalas on bicycles or motor scooters. <u>Later</u>, the empty tiffins are collected and returned to the homes. **E** Process

<u>As a result</u> of this system, over 200,000 workers a day in Mumbai have access to healthy, home-cooked meals. **E** Effects

Effects **E** In addition, an important and honorable job exists for the people who pick up and deliver the tiffins. The dabbawala system is so efficient that it has been written up in the *Harvard Business Review* and studied by FedEx.

—Harshil Patel (student)

grammar in context

Definition

A definition paragraph often includes a formal definition of the term or concept you are going to discuss. When you write your formal definition, be careful not to use the phrases *is where* or *is when.*

The *dabbawala system* ~~is when people (called *dabbawalas*)~~ consists of people (called *dabbawalas*) who collect

freshly made food from the homes of office workers and deliver it

to their workplaces.

Analyzing a Definition Paragraph

Read this definition paragraph; then, follow the instructions in Practice 11-1.

Loans That Change Lives

Microloans are small loans given to people who live in extreme poverty. The idea for such loans originated in 1974, when a Bangladeshi economist loaned $27 to a group of local women. The women used the loan to purchase bamboo to make furniture. After they sold the furniture, they repaid the loan and kept a small profit for themselves. As a result of this experience, the economist created a bank for microloans. Similar microcredit banks now exist throughout the world. For example, microcredit banks can be found in Bosnia, Peru, Ethiopia, and Russia. Microloans are different from ordinary loans because they are not awarded on the basis of credit history or financial means; instead, they are based on trust. A microcredit bank trusts a borrower to make money even if he or she has no or little income at the time of the loan. Some people see microloans as a wonderful opportunity for poor businesspeople;

others criticize microloans because they can encourage governments to reduce their support for the poor. Even so, microloans have helped countless people all over the world to lift themselves out of poverty.

PRACTICE

11-1

1. Underline the topic sentence of the preceding paragraph.

2. What is the subject of this definition? _____

3. What is the writer's one-sentence definition of the subject?

_____

4. List some of the specific information the writer uses to define his subject. The first piece of information has been listed for you.

Microloans originated In Bangladesh in 1974.

_____

_____

_____

5. Circle the transitional words and phrases the writer uses.

6. What patterns of development does the writer use in his definition? List them here.

_____

_____

_____

7. Underline the paragraph's summary statement.

PRACTICE

11-2

Following are four possible topic sentences for definition paragraphs. Each topic sentence includes an underlined word. In the space provided, list two possible patterns of development that you could use to develop a definition of the underlined word. For example, you could define the word *discrimination* by giving examples (exemplification) and by telling a story (narration).

1. During the interview, the job candidate made a <u>sexist</u> comment.

    Possible strategy: _____

    Possible strategy: _____

2. <u>Loyalty</u> is one of the chief characteristics of golden retrievers.

    Possible strategy: _____

    Possible strategy: _____

3. More than forty years after President Johnson's Great Society initiative, we have yet to eliminate <u>poverty</u> in the United States.

    Possible strategy: _____

    Possible strategy: _____

4. The problem with movies today is that they are just too <u>violent</u>.

    Possible strategy: _____

    Possible strategy: _____

11b   Case Study: A Student Writes a Definition Paragraph

Here is how one student, Lorraine Scipio, wrote a definition paragraph. On a history exam, Lorraine was asked to write a one-paragraph definition of the term *imperialism*. Lorraine had studied for the exam, so she knew what imperialism was. Because she wanted to make sure that she did not leave anything out of her definition (and because she had a time limit), she quickly listed some supporting examples and details on the inside front cover of her exam book. Then, she crossed out two items that did not seem relevant.

    A policy of control

    Military

    ~~Lenin~~

    Establish empires

    Cultural superiority

    Raw materials and cheap labor

    Africa, etc.

    ~~Cultural imperialism~~

    Nineteenth-century term

list examples and details

Review the brainstorming you did in response to the Focus on Writing prompt on page 154, and choose a word to define. Then, list the examples and details that can best help you develop a definition of that word.

Keith Brofsky/UpperCutImage/
GettyImages

_____

_____

_____

_____

Now, cross out the items on your list that do not seem relevant to your definition.

After reviewing her list of examples and details, Lorraine drafted the topic sentence that appears below.

The goal of imperialism is to establish an empire.

write a topic sentence

Review your list of examples and details, and then draft a topic sentence for your definition paragraph. Include a formal definition of the term you are defining.

Keith Brofsky/UpperCutImage/
GettyImages

_____

_____

Next, Lorraine made an informal outline, quickly arranging her supporting examples and details in the order in which she planned to write about them.

Establish empires
Nineteenth-century term
Cultural superiority
Africa, etc.
Raw materials and cheap labor
A policy of control
Military

make an outline

Create an informal outline for your paragraph by arranging your examples and details in the order in which you plan to discuss them.

Referring to the material on her list, Lorraine wrote the following draft of her definition paragraph. Notice that she uses several different patterns to develop her definition.

The goal of imperialism is to establish an empire. The imperialist country thinks that it is superior to the country it takes over. It justifies its actions by saying that it is helping the other country. But it isn't. Countries such as Germany, Belgium, Spain, and England have been imperialist in the past. The point of imperialism is to take as much out of the occupied countries as possible. Often, imperialist countries sent troops to occupy other countries and to keep order. As a result, imperialism kept the people in occupied countries in poverty and often broke down local governments and local traditions.

draft your paragraph

Using your informal outline as a guide, draft your definition paragraph. Remember, you can use any of the patterns of development discussed in Unit 2 of this text to help you define your term. Begin by identifying the term. Then, you can describe it, give examples, tell how it works, explain its purpose, consider its history or future, or compare it with other similar terms.

After she finished her draft, Lorraine quickly **TEST**ed her paragraph to make sure she had answered the exam question. As a result, she decided that she needed to make the following changes.

- Because the exam question asked for a definition, she rewrote her **topic sentence** as a formal definition.
- She strengthened her **evidence**, explaining her supporting examples and details more fully. She also deleted some vague statements that did not support her topic sentence.

- She added **transitional words and phrases** to make the connections between her ideas clearer.
- She added a **summary statement** to reinforce her explanation of the negative effects of imperialism.

Lorraine made her changes directly on the draft she had written, crossing out unnecessary information and adding missing information. She also edited her paragraph for grammar, punctuation, and mechanical errors. Then, because she had some extra time, she neatly rewrote her paragraph.

Lorraine's revised, edited, and proofread paragraph appears below. (Because this is an exam answer, she does not include a title.) Notice that the final draft includes all the elements Lorraine looked for when she **TEST**ed her paragraph.

Imperialism is the policy by which one country takes over the land or the government of another country. In the nineteenth century, the object of imperialism was to establish an empire. The imperialist country thought that it was superior to the country it took over. It justified its actions by saying that it was helping the other country. For instance, countries such as Germany, Belgium, Spain, and England followed their imperialist ambitions in Africa when they claimed large areas of land. The point of imperialism was to take as much out of the occupied countries as possible. For example, in South America and Mexico, Spain removed tons of gold from the areas it occupied. It made the natives slaves and forced them to work in mines. In order to protect their interests, imperialist countries sent troops to occupy the country and to keep order. As a result, imperialism kept the people in occupied countries in poverty and often broke down local governments and local traditions. Although European imperialism occasionally had benefits, at its worst it brought slavery, disease, and death.

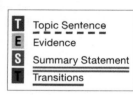

T	Topic Sentence
E	Evidence
S	Summary Statement
T	Transitions

FYI

Writing Paragraph Answers on Exams

When you write paragraph answers on exams, you do not have much time to work, so you need to be well prepared. Know your subject well, and memorize important definitions. You may have time to write an outline, a rough draft, and a final draft, but you will have to work quickly. Even so, your final draft should include all the elements of a good paragraph: a topic sentence, supporting details, transitions, and a summary statement.

Keith Brofsky/UpperCutImage/
GettyImages

TEST · Revise · Edit · Proofread

Look back at the draft of your definition paragraph. Using the **TEST** checklist below, evaluate your paragraph to make sure it includes a topic sentence, evidence, a summary statement, and transitions, and revise your draft accordingly. Finally, edit and proofread your paragraph.

TESTing a definition paragraph

T opic Sentence Unifies Your Paragraph

☐ Do you have a clearly worded **topic sentence** that states your paragraph's main idea?

☐ Does your topic sentence identify the term you are defining?

E vidence Supports Your Paragraph's Topic Sentence

☐ Does all your **evidence**—examples and details—support your paragraph's main idea?

☐ Do you need to add more examples or details to help you define your term?

S ummary Statement Reinforces Your Paragraph's Unity

☐ Does your paragraph end with a **summary statement** that reinforces your main idea?

T ransitions Add Coherence to Your Paragraph

☐ Are your **transitions** appropriate for the pattern (or patterns) of development you use?

☐ Do you need to add transitions to make your paragraph clearer and to help readers follow your ideas?

12 Argument Paragraphs

Marie Kanger-Born/AlamyStockPhoto

focus on writing

Some students, like those pictured above, participate in marches to demonstrate their position on a social or political issue. Brainstorm to develop a list of political issues that interest you. Review your brainstorming, choose one issue, and then write a journal entry exploring your thoughts on this issue. (If you prefer, you may choose a topic from the list on the following page instead.) You will return to your journal entry later in the chapter when you write your argument paragraph.

additional topics for argument

Internet privacy

Campus security

Banning cell phones in class

School speech codes

College debt

 12a   Understanding Argument

When most people hear the word *argument*, they think of heated exchanges on television interview programs. These discussions, however, are more like shouting matches than arguments. True **argument** involves taking a well-thought-out position on a **debatable topic**—a topic about which reasonable people may disagree (for example, "Should convicted felons be allowed to vote?").

In an **argument paragraph**, you take a position on an issue, and your purpose is to persuade readers that your position has merit. You attempt to convince people of the strength of your ideas by presenting **evidence**—in this case, facts and examples. In the process, you address opposing ideas and, if they are strong, you acknowledge their strengths. If your evidence is solid and your logic is sound, you will present a convincing argument. (For information on writing argument essays, see 16d.)

FYI

Evidence

You can use two kinds of evidence in your argument paragraphs: *facts* and *examples*.

1. A **fact** is a piece of information (such as "Alaska officially became a state in 1959") that can be verified. If you make a statement, you should be prepared to support it with facts—using statistics, observations, or statements that are generally accepted as true.

2. An **example** is a specific illustration of a general statement. To be convincing, an example should clearly relate to the point you are making.

When you **TEST** an argument paragraph, make sure it follows these guidelines:

T An argument paragraph should begin with a **topic sentence** that clearly states your position. Using words like *should, should not,* or *ought to* in your topic sentence will make your position clear to your readers.

> The federal government <u>should</u> lower taxes on gasoline.

> The city <u>ought to</u> spend 20 percent of its budget on helping businesses convert to sustainable energy sources.

E An argument paragraph should present points that support the topic sentence in **logical order**. For example, if your purpose is to argue in favor of placing warning labels on unhealthy snack foods, you should give reasons—arranging them from least to most important—why this policy should be instituted. Each of these points should then be supported with **evidence**—facts and examples.

An argument paragraph should also address and **refute** (argue against) opposing arguments. By showing that an opponent's arguments are weak, inaccurate, or misguided, you strengthen your own position. If an opposing argument is particularly strong, you may want to **concede** (accept) its strengths and then point out its shortcomings.

S An argument paragraph should end with a **summary statement** that reinforces the paragraph's main idea—the position you take on the issue.

T An argument paragraph should include **transitions** to connect the points you are making to one another and to the topic sentence.

Some Transitional Words and Phrases for Argument

Transitions are important in argument paragraphs. For example, in the paragraph above, the transitional phrases *the first reason* and *another reason* tell readers they are moving from one point to another. In addition, the transitional phrases *one objection* and *another objection* indicate that the writer is addressing two opposing arguments.

accordingly	certainly	first . . . second . . .
admittedly	consequently	for this reason
after all	despite	however
although	even so	in addition
because	even though	in conclusion
but	finally	in fact

(Continued)

in summary	of course	the first reason
meanwhile	one . . . another	therefore
moreover	on the one hand . . .	thus
nevertheless	on the other hand	to be sure
nonetheless	since	truly

Paragraph Map: Argument

> **Topic Sentence**
>
> **Point #1**
>
> **Point #2**
>
> **Point #3**
>
> **Opposing Argument #1**
> **(plus refutation)**
>
> **Opposing Argument #2**
> **(plus refutation)**
>
> **Summary Statement**

Model Paragraph: Argument

The following paragraph argues in favor of an emergency notification system for college students.

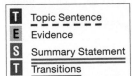

T Topic Sentence
E Evidence
S Summary Statement
T Transitions

Why Our School Should Set Up an Emergency Notification System

Point 1 and support **E**

Our school should set up an emergency notification system that would deliver a text message to students' cell phones in a campus crisis. The first reason why we should set up an emergency notification system is that it is needed. Currently, it takes an hour or two to inform the whole campus of something—for example, that school is closing because of bad weather or that a school event has been canceled. <u>Another reason</u> why we should set up an emergency notification system is that it will make our campus safer by warning students if a crime takes place on campus. For example, when a shooting took place on the campus of Virginia Tech, the school was unable to warn students to evacuate the campus. The result was that more than thirty people were killed. An emergency notification system might have saved the lives of many of these people.

> **E** Point 2 and support

<u>One objection</u> to an instant-messaging emergency notification system is that email notification works just as well. However, although many students check their email just once or twice a day, most students carry cell phones and read text messages whenever they get them.

> **E** Opposing argument 1 (plus refutation)

<u>Another objection</u> is that some students (probably a small number) do not have smartphones. The same system that delivers text messages to students, however, could also deliver messages to digital message boards around campus. <u>Because communicating with students in a crisis situation can save lives, our school should set up an emergency notification system.</u>

> **E** Opposing argument 2 (plus refutation)

—Ashley Phillips (student)

grammar in context

Argument

When you write an argument paragraph, you should use both **compound sentences** and **complex sentences**. By doing this, you not only show the relationship between ideas but also eliminate choppy sentences.

COMPOUND SENTENCE	An emergency notification system will help all of us ~~,and it~~ communicate better. ~~It~~ will ensure our school's safety.
COMPLEX SENTENCE	*Because communicating* ~~Communicating~~ with students in a crisis situation *, our* can save lives. ~~Our~~ school should set up an emergency notification system.

For more information on how to create compound sentences, see Chapter 19.
For more information on how to create complex sentences, see Chapter 20.

Analyzing an Argument Paragraph

Read this argument paragraph; then, follow the instructions in Practice 12-1.

Why We Need Full-Body Scanners

Because of their advantages, airport full-body scanners are a necessary tool in the fight against terrorism. One reason why airport scanners are necessary is that the federal government needs a quick and effective way of screening passengers. Because of their ease of operation, whole-body scanners accomplish this goal. Well over a million people fly throughout the United States each day. A single airport scanner is capable of screening thousands of people a day and is much faster than other methods of screening. Another reason why airport scanners are necessary is that they provide an additional layer of security. For example, scanners are able to detect both metallic and nonmetallic items that are taped to the body. In other words, scanners will detect both weapons and bomb materials that metal detectors might miss. People who oppose scanners say that they are unsafe. However, the literature that the government distributes at airports makes it clear that the latest generation of airport scanners expose passengers to less radiation than they experience when they fly at high altitudes. Opponents also charge that scanners violate the Constitution's guarantee of privacy because they show a three-dimensional image of a person's naked body. To deal with this objection, the Transportation Security Administration has made sure that the TSA officer who operates a scanner never sees the images of the person being scanned. He or she sees only a screen that indicates whether the person has successfully cleared the screening. In addition, the images themselves are deleted immediately after a person has left the screening area. Given the attempts that terrorists have made to attack the United States, airport scanners are a useful and effective way of keeping people safe when they fly.

—Carl Manni (student)

PRACTICE

12-1

1. Underline the topic sentence of the preceding paragraph.

2. What issue is the subject of the paragraph?

_____

3. What is the writer's position?

_____

4. What specific points does the writer use to support his topic sentence?

_____

_____

5. List some evidence (facts and examples) that the writer uses to support his points. The first piece of evidence has been listed for you.

A single full-body scanner is capable of screening thousands of people a day.

_____

_____

_____

6. What other evidence could the writer have used?

_____

_____

_____

7. What opposing arguments does he mention?

_____

8. How does he refute these arguments?

_____

_____

_____

9. Circle the transitional words and phrases the writer uses to move readers through his argument.

10. Underline the paragraph's summary statement.

PRACTICE

12-2   Following are four topic sentences for argument paragraphs. List two or three points that could support each topic sentence. For example, if you were arguing in support of laws requiring motorcycle riders to wear safety helmets, you could say helmets cut down on medical costs and save lives.

1. High school graduates should perform a year of public service before going to college.

2. All student athletes should be paid a salary by their college or university.

3. College students caught cheating should be expelled.

4. The U.S. government should forgive all federal student loans.

PRACTICE

12-3   Choose one of the topic sentences from Practice 12-2. Then, list two types of evidence that could support each point you listed. For example, if you said that wearing safety helmets saves lives, you could list "accident statistics" and "statements by emergency room physicians."

_____

_____

PRACTICE

12-4   List opposing arguments for the topic sentence you selected for Practice 12-3. Then, list the weaknesses of each of these arguments.

Opposing argument #1: _____

Weaknesses: _____

Opposing argument #2: _____

Weaknesses: _____

12b Case Study: A Student Writes an Argument Paragraph

Here is how one student, Phillip Zhu, wrote an argument paragraph. Phillip, a computer science major, was asked to write an argument paragraph on an issue that interested him. Because he was taking a course in computer ethics, he decided to write about an issue that had been discussed in class: the way many employers now search social-networking sites, such as Facebook, to find information about job applicants.

Phillip had already formed an opinion about the issue, so he was ready to write the following topic sentence that expressed his position.

> Employers should not use social-networking sites to find information about job applicants.

write your topic sentence

Look back at the journal entry you wrote in response to the Focus on Writing prompt on the first page of this chapter. Determine your position on the issue you chose to write about, and then draft a topic sentence that clearly states the position you will take in your argument paragraph.

Marie Kanger-Born/AlamyStockPhoto

_____

_____

Phillip then listed the following points that he could use to support his topic sentence.

Social-networking sites should be private

People exaggerate on social-networking sites

Some posts meant to be funny

No one warns applicant

Need email address to register

Expect limited audience

Employers can misinterpret what they find

Employers going where they don't belong

Not an accurate picture

Not fair

Not meant to be seen by job recruiters

Marie Kanger-Born/
AlamyStockPhoto

list your supporting points

Review your topic sentence, and list as many points as you can in support of your position on the issue. Then, look back at your journal entry to find evidence to support your points.

_____

_____

_____

_____

After identifying his three most important supporting points, Phillip arranged them into an informal outline.

Social-networking sites should be private
> Need email address to register
> Expect limited audience
> Employers going where they don't belong

People exaggerate on social-networking sites
> Some posts meant to be funny
> Not meant to be seen by job recruiters
> No one warns applicant

Employers can misinterpret what they find
> Not an accurate picture
> Not fair

Marie Kanger-Born/
AlamyStockPhoto

make an outline

Create an informal outline for your paragraph by arranging the points that support your position in the order that you think will be most convincing to your readers—for example, from the least important point to the most important point. Under each point, list the evidence (facts and examples) that you will use as support.

Once Phillip finished his informal outline, he tried to think of possible arguments against his position because he knew he would have to consider and refute these opposing arguments in his paragraph. He came up with two possible arguments against his position.

1. Employers should be able to find out as much as they can.

2. Applicants have only themselves to blame.

list opposing arguments

Review your informal outline, and then list one or more possible arguments against your position on the lines below.

_____

_____

_____

Marie Kanger-Born/
AlamyStockPhoto

Now, try to think of ways in which these opposing arguments are weak or inaccurate.

Phillip then wrote the following draft of his paragraph.

Employers should not use social-networking sites to find information about job applicants. For one thing, social-networking sites should be private. By visiting these sites, employers are going where they do not belong. People also exaggerate on social-networking sites. They say things that are not true, and they put things on the sites they would not want job recruiters to see. No one ever tells applicants that recruiters search these sites, so they feel safe posting all kinds of material. Employers can misinterpret what they read. Employers and recruiters need to get as much information as they can. They should not use unfair ways to get this information. Applicants have only themselves to blame for their problems. They need to be more careful about what they put up online. Although this is true, most applicants don't know that employers will search social-networking sites.

draft your paragraph

Guided by your informal outline and your list of opposing arguments, draft your argument paragraph. Begin your paragraph with a topic sentence that clearly states the position you are taking on the issue.

Marie Kanger-Born/AlamyStockPhoto

After finishing his draft, Phillip scheduled a conference with his instructor. Together, they went over his paragraph and **TEST**ed it. They agreed that Phillip needed to make the following changes.

- They decided he needed to make his **topic sentence** more specific and more forceful.

- They decided he should add more **evidence** (facts and examples) to his discussion. For example, what social-networking sites is he talking about? Which are restricted? How do employers gain access to these sites?

- They decided he needed to delete the irrelevant discussion blaming job applicants for their problems.

- They decided he should add **transitional words and phrases** to clearly identify the points he is making in support of his argument and also to identify the two opposing arguments he discusses.

- They decided he needed to add a strong **summary statement** to reinforce his position.

As Phillip revised his paragraph, he was guided by these decisions. The final draft below includes all the elements Phillip looked for when he **TEST**ed his paragraph.

Unfair Searching

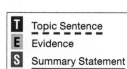

<u>Employers should not use social-networking sites, such as Instagram and Facebook, to find information about job applicants.</u> <u>First,</u> social-networking sites should be private. People who use these sites do not expect employers to access them. However, some employers routinely search social-networking sites to find information about job applicants. Doing this is not right, and it is not fair. By visiting these sites, employers are going where they do not belong. <u>Another reason</u> employers should not use information from social-networking sites is that people frequently exaggerate on them or say things that are not true. They may also put statements and pictures on the sites that they would not want job recruiters to see. Because some applicants don't realize that recruiters search these sites, they feel safe posting embarrassing pictures or making exaggerated claims about drinking or sex. <u>Finally,</u> employers can misinterpret the material they see. As a result, they may reject a good applicant because they take seriously what is meant to be a joke. <u>Of course,</u> employers need to get as much information about a candidate as they can. They should not, however, use unfair tactics to get this information.

T Topic Sentence
E Evidence
S Summary Statement
T Transitions

E

E In addition, prospective employers should realize that the profile they see on a social-networking site may not accurately represent the job applicant. For these reasons, employers should not use social-networking sites to do background checks.

TEST · Revise · Edit · Proofread

Look back at the draft of your argument paragraph. Using the **TEST** checklist that follows, evaluate your paragraph to make sure it includes a topic sentence, evidence, a summary statement, and transitions, and revise your draft accordingly. Finally, edit and proofread your paragraph.

Marie Kanger-Born/
AlamyStockPhoto

TESTing an argument paragraph

T opic Sentence Unifies Your Paragraph

☐ Do you have a clearly worded **topic sentence** that states your paragraph's main idea?

☐ Does your topic sentence state your position on a debatable issue?

E vidence Supports Your Paragraph's Topic Sentence

☐ Does all your **evidence** support your paragraph's main idea?

☐ Have you included enough facts and examples to support your points, or do you need to add more?

☐ Do you summarize and refute opposing arguments?

S ummary Statement Reinforces Your Paragraph's Unity

☐ Does your paragraph end with a strong **summary statement** that reinforces your main idea?

T ransitions Add Coherence to Your Paragraph

☐ Do you use **transitions** to let readers know when you are moving from one point to another?

☐ Do you use transitional words and phrases to indicate when you are addressing opposing arguments?

☐ Do you need to add transitions to make your paragraph clearer and to help readers follow your ideas?

unit
3 Focus on Essays

Focus on Essays

13 Writing an Essay

Allen Creative/Steve Allen/Alamy

focus on writing

People who work in fast-food restaurants, like the one pictured here, have very challenging jobs. Think about the most difficult job you've ever had. This is the topic you will be writing about as you go through this chapter. (If you have never had a job, you may write about a specific task that you disliked or about a difficult job that a friend or relative has had.)

Much of the writing you do in school will be more than just one paragraph. Often, you will be asked to write an **essay**—a group of paragraphs on a single subject. When you write an essay, you follow the same process you follow when you write a paragraph: You begin by planning and then move on to organizing your ideas, drafting, **TEST**ing, revising, editing, and proofreading.

In this chapter, you will see how the strategies you learned for writing paragraphs can help you write essays.

 ## 13a Understanding Essay Structure

Understanding the structure of a paragraph can help you understand the structure of an essay. In a paragraph, the main idea is stated in a **topic sentence**, and the rest of the paragraph supports this main idea with **evidence** (details and examples). **Transitional words and phrases** help readers follow the discussion. The paragraph ends with a **summary statement** that reinforces the main idea.

Paragraph

> The **topic sentence** states the main idea of the paragraph.
>
> **Evidence** supports the main idea.
>
> **Transitional words and phrases** show the connections between ideas.
>
> A **summary statement** reinforces the main idea of the paragraph.

The structure of an essay is similar to the structure of a paragraph:

- The essay's first paragraph—the *introduction*—begins with opening remarks that create interest and closes with a **thesis statement**. This thesis statement, like a paragraph's topic sentence, presents the main idea. (For more on introductions, see 14a.)

- The *body* of the essay contains several paragraphs that support the thesis statement. Each body paragraph begins with a topic sentence that states the main idea of the paragraph. The other sentences in the paragraph support the topic sentence with **evidence** (details and examples).

- **Transitional words and phrases** lead readers from sentence to sentence and from paragraph to paragraph.

- The last paragraph—the *conclusion*—ends the essay. The conclusion includes a **summary statement** that reinforces the thesis. It ends with concluding remarks. (For more on conclusions, see 14b.)

The first letters of these four key elements—**T**hesis statement, **E**vidence, **S**ummary statement, and **T**ransitions—spell **TEST**. Just as you did with paragraphs, you can **TEST** your essays to see whether they include all the elements of an effective essay.

Many of the essays you will write in college will have a **thesis-and-support** structure.

Essay

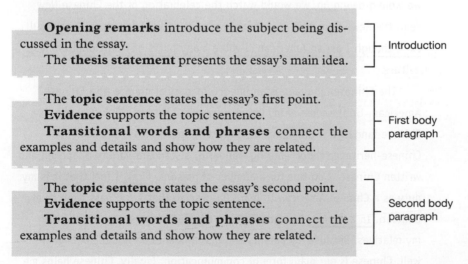

Opening remarks introduce the subject being discussed in the essay.
The **thesis statement** presents the essay's main idea. — Introduction

The **topic sentence** states the essay's first point.
Evidence supports the topic sentence.
Transitional words and phrases connect the examples and details and show how they are related. — First body paragraph

The **topic sentence** states the essay's second point.
Evidence supports the topic sentence.
Transitional words and phrases connect the examples and details and show how they are related. — Second body paragraph

The **topic sentence** states the essay's third point.
Evidence supports the topic sentence.
Transitional words and phrases connect the examples and details and show how they are related.

⎤
⎥ Third body
⎥ paragraph
⎦

The **summary statement** reinforces the thesis, summarizing the essay's main idea.
Concluding remarks present the writer's final thoughts on the subject.

⎤
⎥ Conclusion
⎦

The following essay by Jennifer Chu illustrates the structure of an essay. (Note that transitional words and phrases are underlined in blue.)

Becoming Chinese American

Introduction

Although I was born in Hong Kong, I have spent most of my life in the United States. However, my parents have always made sure that I did not forget my roots. They always tell stories of what it was like to live in Hong Kong. To make sure my brothers and sisters and I know what is happening in China, my parents subscribe to Chinese-language cable channels. When we were growing up, we would watch the celebration of the Chinese New Year, the news from Asia, and Chinese movies and music videos. As a result,

Thesis statement

even though I am an American, I value many parts of traditional Chinese culture.

Topic sentence (states essay's first point)

The Chinese language is an important part of my life as a Chinese American. Unlike some of my Chinese friends, I do not think that the Chinese language is unimportant. In fact, I spend most Saturdays in a

First body paragraph

Chinese-heritage school learning Mandarin, a standard variety of spoken and written Chinese. I do this for a number of reasons. First, I feel that it is my duty as a Chinese American to learn Chinese so that I can pass it on to my children. In addition, knowing Chinese enables me to communicate with

Evidence (supports topic sentence)

my relatives. Because my parents and grandparents do not speak English well, Chinese is our main form of communication. Finally, Chinese helps me identify with my culture. When I speak Chinese, I feel connected to a culture that is over five thousand years old. Without the Chinese language, I would not be who I am.

Chinese food is another important part of my life as a Chinese American. One reason for this is that everything we Chinese people eat has a history and a meaning. At a birthday meal, for example, we serve long noodles and buns in the shape of peaches. This is because we believe that long noodles represent long life and that peaches are served in heaven. Another reason is that to Chinese people, food is a way of reinforcing ties between family and friends. For instance, during a traditional Chinese wedding ceremony, the bride and the groom eat nine of everything. This is because the number nine stands for the Chinese words "together forever." By taking part in this ritual, the bride and groom start their marriage by making Chinese customs a part of their life together.

Religion is the most important part of my life as a Chinese American. At various times during the year, Chinese religious festivals bring together the people I care about the most. During Chinese New Year, my whole family goes to the Buddhist temple, where we say prayers and welcome others with traditional New Year's greetings. After leaving the temple, we all go to Chinatown and eat dim sum until the lion dance starts. As the colorful lion dances its way down the street, people beat drums and throw firecrackers to drive off any evil spirits that may be around. Later that night, parents give children gifts of money in red envelopes that symbolize joy and happiness in the coming year.

My family has taught me how important it is to hold on to my Chinese culture. When I was six, my parents sent me to a Chinese American grade school. My teachers thrilled me with stories of Fa Mulan, the Shang Dynasty, and the Moon God. I will never forget how happy I was when I realized how special it is to be Chinese. This is how I want my own children to feel. I want them to be proud of who they are and to pass their language, history, and culture on to the next generation.

Topic sentence (states essay's second point)

Second body paragraph

Evidence (supports topic sentence)

Topic sentence (states essay's third point)

Third body paragraph

Evidence (supports topic sentence)

Summary statement (reinforces essay's thesis)

Conclusion

PRACTICE

13-1 Following is an essay organized according to the diagram of essay structure on pages 183–184. Read the essay, and then answer the questions that follow.

Enhanced Water

Flavored or "enhanced" water has grown in popularity since it was introduced in the late 1990s. Most enhanced waters are owned by soft drink companies like Coca-Cola and Pepsi. These companies have spent millions of dollars trying to convince consumers that enhanced water is better than ordinary water. In spite of their efforts, however, this is just not true.

There is no question that our bodies need fluid to stay hydrated. In fact, most experts say that people should drink about 64 ounces (eight cups) of water per day. Only athletes and people who are involved in strenuous activities, such as hiking, need to drink significantly more water. These individuals may benefit from the salt and carbohydrates found in sports drinks like Gatorade, but they are the exception. People who exercise at a normal rate, for about an hour a day, need only a few additional cups of plain water to restore lost fluids.

Despite marketing claims, it is not clear that enhanced water is more healthful than regular water. The labels on most enhanced water drinks, such as VitaminWater and SoBe Lifewater, make health claims that have not been scientifically proven. For instance, the label on VitaminWater's drink "Focus" implies that its vitamins and minerals will improve a person's focus and eyesight. Scientists generally agree, however, that this sugary beverage does not improve attention spans or eye health. Another example of a misleading claim appears on the label of SoBe's Blood Orange Mango drink, which lists B12 vitamins that are supposed to boost energy. However, the amount of vitamins found in this drink is too small to provide any health benefits and neither blood oranges nor mangoes are included in the ingredients list. Moreover, many enhanced water drinks actually contain ingredients that the body does not need—for example, caffeine, artificial flavors and colors, and sugar or artificial sweeteners.

In addition to making questionable marketing claims, manufacturers of enhanced waters present nutritional information in a confusing way. For example, just a quick glance at the label for a SoBe Lifewater drink would lead someone to believe that a serving has 40 calories, 16 grams of carbohydrates, and 10 grams of sugar. These amounts may sound reasonable, but a closer look at the label reveals that each 20-ounce bottle actually contains two and a half servings. In other words, a person who drinks the whole bottle is actually consuming 100 calories, 40 grams of carbohydrates, and 25 grams of sugar—more carbohydrates and sugar than in a glazed doughnut.

Even the "zerocalorie" options are concerning. They may seem healthy, but the nutrition labels reveal alarming amounts of sugar, artificial flavor, and dye.

In most cases, regular tap water is all people need to stay healthy and hydrated. The drink manufacturers ignore this fact, saying that enhanced water is lower in calories and sugar than non-diet soft drinks. They also say that, although the herbs and vitamins in their drinks may not have proven health benefits, at least they are not harmful. Finally, the drink manufacturers claim that their products get people to drink more fluids. Although all these claims are partially true, consumers do not need the ingredients in enhanced water or its extra cost.

1. Underline the essay's thesis statement.

2. Underline the topic sentence of each body paragraph.

3. What point does the first body paragraph make? What evidence supports this point?

_____

_____

_____

_____

_____

4. What point does the second paragraph make? What evidence supports this point?

_____

_____

_____

_____

5. What point does the third body paragraph make? What evidence supports this point?

_____

_____

_____

6. What transitions does the essay include? How do they connect the essay's ideas?

_____

_____

_____

_____

7. Where in the conclusion does the writer restate the essay's thesis? Underline this statement.

13b Moving from Assignment to Topic

Many essays you write in college begin as **assignments** given to you by your instructors. Before you focus on any assignment, however, you should take time to think about your **purpose** (what you want to accomplish by writing your essay) and your **audience** (the people who will read your essay). Once you have considered these issues, you are ready to think about the specifics of your assignment.

The following assignments are typical of those given in a composition class.

- Discuss some things you would change about your school.
- What can college students do to improve the environment?
- Discuss an important decision you made during the past three years.

Because these assignments are so general, you need to narrow them before you can start to write. What specific things would you change about your school? Exactly what could college students do to improve the environment? Answering these questions will help you narrow these assignments into **topics** that you can write about.

ASSIGNMENT	TOPIC
Discuss some things you would change about your school.	Three things I would change to improve the quality of life on campus
What can college students do to improve the environment?	The campus recycling project

Jared White, a student in a first-year composition course, was given the following assignment.

ASSIGNMENT

Discuss an important decision you made during the past few years.

Jared narrowed this assignment to the following topic:

TOPIC

Deciding to go back to school

Throughout the rest of this chapter, you will be following Jared's writing process.

PRACTICE

13-2 Decide whether the following topics are narrow enough for an essay of four or five paragraphs. If a topic is suitable, write *OK* in the blank. If it is not, write in the blank a revised version of the same topic that is narrow enough for a brief essay.

Examples

Successful strategies for quitting smoking ___OK_____

Horror movies ___1950s Japanese monster movies_____

1. Instructional design models in elementary education _____

2. Dangers to the environment of Arctic oil drilling _____

3. The minimum wage _____

_____

4. Online retail businesses _____

_____

5. Marketing new smart-phone apps _____

decide on a topic

Look back at the Focus on Writing prompt on the first page of this chapter. To narrow this assignment to a topic you can write about, you need to decide which difficult job to focus on. Begin by listing several jobs you could discuss.

Allen Creative/Steve Allen/Alamy

FYI

Visit the Study Guides and Strategies website (studygs.net/writing/prewriting.htm) to learn how to use one of the graphic organizers or to find other information about the writing process.

13c   Finding Ideas to Write About

Before you start writing about a topic, you need to find ideas to write about. Sometimes ideas may come to you easily. More often, you will have to use specific strategies, such as *freewriting* or *brainstorming*, to help you come up with ideas.

Freewriting

When you **freewrite**, you write for a fixed period of time without stopping. When you do **focused freewriting**, you write with a specific topic in mind. Then, you read what you have written and choose ideas you think you can use.

The following focused freewriting was written by Jared White on the topic "Deciding to go back to school."

Deciding to go back to school. When I graduated high school, I swore I'd never go back to school. Hated it. Couldn't wait to get out. What was I thinking? How was I supposed to support myself? My dad's friend needed help. He taught me how to paint houses. I made good money, but it was boring. I couldn't picture myself doing it forever. Even though I knew I was going to have to go back to school, I kept putting off the decision. Maybe I was lazy. Maybe I was scared— probably both. I had this fear of being turned down. How could someone who had bad grades all through high school go to college? Also, I'd been out of school for six years. And even if I did get in (a miracle!), how would I pay for it? How would I live? Well, here I am—the first one in my family to go to college.

PRACTICE

13-3   Reread Jared White's freewriting. If you were advising Jared, which ideas would you tell him to explore further? Why?

freewrite

Choose two of the difficult jobs you listed, and freewrite about each of them. Then, choose one of the jobs to write about. Circle the ideas about this job that you would like to explore further in an essay.

Brainstorming

When you **brainstorm** (either individually or with others in a group), you write down (or type) all the ideas you can think of about a particular topic. After you have recorded as much material as you can, you look over your notes and decide which ideas are useful and which ones are not.

Here are Jared's brainstorming notes about his decision to go back to school.

Deciding to Go Back to School

Money a problem

Other students a lot younger

Paying tuition—how?

No one in family went to college

Friends not in college

Couldn't see myself in college

Considered going to trade school

Computer programmer?

Grades bad in high school

Time for me to grow up

Wondered if I would get in

Found out about community college

Admission requirements not bad

Afraid—too old, failing out, looking silly

Took time to get used to routine

Found other students like me

Liked studying

PRACTICE

13-4 Reread Jared's brainstorming notes. Which ideas would you advise him to explore further? Why?

Allen Creative/Steve Allen/Alamy

brainstorm

Review your freewriting. Then, brainstorm about the job for which you have found the most interesting ideas. What ideas about this job did you get from brainstorming that you did not get from freewriting?

Keeping a Journal

When you keep a **journal**, you keep an informal record of your thoughts and ideas. As you learned in Chapter 2, your journal can be a computer file or a notebook. In your journal, you record your thoughts about your assignments, identify ideas that you want to explore further, and keep notes about things you read or see. After rereading your journal entries, you can decide to explore an idea further in another journal entry or to use material from a specific entry in an essay.

Following is an entry in Jared's journal that he eventually used in his essay about returning to school.

When I was working as a house painter, I had a conversation that helped convince me to go to college. One day, I started talking to the guy whose house I was painting. I told him that I was painting houses until I figured out what I was going to do with the rest of my life. He asked me if I had considered going to college. I told him that I hadn't done well in high school, so I didn't think college was for me. He told me that I could probably get into the local community college. That night I looked at the community college's website to see if going to college might be a good idea.

write journal entries

Write at least two journal entries for the topic you have been exploring for this chapter: the hardest job you ever had. Which of your entries do you want to explore further? Which could you use in your essay?

Allen Creative/Steve Allen/Alamy

Clustering

Clustering, sometimes called *mapping*, is another strategy you can use to find ideas to write about. When you cluster, you begin by writing your topic in the center of a sheet of paper. Then, you branch out, writing relevant ideas on the page in groups, or clusters, around the topic. As you add new ideas, you circle them and draw lines to connect the ideas to one another and to the topic at the center. (These lines will look like a spiderweb or the spokes of a wheel.) As you move from the center out to the corners of the page, your ideas will be more and more specific.

Jared's cluster diagram on the topic of deciding to go back to school appears below.

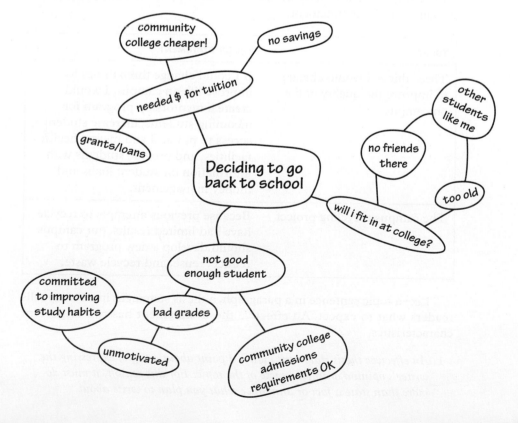

draw a cluster diagram

Draw a cluster diagram for your essay on your most difficult job. Was this method of finding ideas useful? Why or why not?

Allen Creative/Steve Allen/Alamy

 ## 13d   Stating Your Thesis

After you have gathered information about your topic, you need to decide on a thesis for your essay. You do this by reviewing the ideas from your brainstorming, freewriting, and journal entries and then asking, "What is the main point I want to make about my topic?" The answer to this question is the **thesis** of your essay. You express this point in a **thesis statement**: a single sentence that clearly expresses the main idea that you will discuss in the rest of your essay.

Keep in mind that each essay has just *one* thesis statement. The details and examples in the body of the essay all support (add to, discuss, or explain) this thesis statement.

TOPIC	THESIS STATEMENT
Three things I would change to improve the quality of life on campus	If I could change three things to improve life on campus, I would create a mentorship program for incoming students, increase student access to physical and mental health facilities, and provide students with information on student loans and money management.
The campus recycling project	Because previous attempts to recycle have had limited results, our campus should develop a new program to reduce, reuse, and recycle waste.

Like a topic sentence in a paragraph, a thesis statement in an essay tells readers what to expect. An effective thesis statement has two important characteristics.

1. *An effective thesis statement makes a point about a topic, expressing the writer's opinion or unique view of the topic. For this reason, it must do more than state a fact or announce what you plan to write about.*

STATEMENT OF FACT	Many older students are returning to school.
ANNOUNCEMENT	In this essay, I will discuss older students going back to school.

A statement of fact is not an effective thesis statement because it gives you nothing to develop in your essay. After all, how much can you say about the *fact* that many older students are returning to school? Likewise, an announcement of what you plan to discuss gives readers no indication of the position you will take on your topic. Remember, an effective thesis statement makes a point.

  2. *An effective thesis statement is clearly worded and specific.*

VAGUE THESIS STATEMENT	Returning to school is difficult for older students.

The vague thesis statement above gives readers no sense of the ideas the essay will discuss. It does not say, for example, *why* returning to school is difficult for older students. Remember, an effective thesis statement is specific.

FYI

Evaluating Your Thesis Statement

Once you have a thesis statement, you need to evaluate it to determine if it is effective. Asking the following questions will help you decide:

- Is your thesis statement a complete sentence?
- Does your thesis statement clearly express the main idea you will discuss in your essay?
- Is your thesis statement specific and focused? Does it make a point that you can cover within your time and page limits?
- Does your thesis statement make a point about your topic—not just state a fact or announce what you plan to write about?
- Does your thesis statement avoid vague language?
- Does your thesis statement avoid statements like "I think" or "In my opinion"?

After freewriting, brainstorming, and reviewing his journal entries, Jared decided on a topic and wrote the following effective thesis statement for his essay.

EFFECTIVE THESIS   Although I realized it would be difficult in some
     STATEMENT   ways, I decided that if I really wanted to attend
                  college full-time, I could.

Jared knew that his thesis statement had to be a complete sentence that
made a point about his topic and that it should be both clearly worded and
specific. When he reviewed his thesis statement, he felt sure that it satisfied
these criteria and expressed an idea he could develop in his essay.

PRACTICE

13-5   In the space provided, indicate whether each of the following
            items is a statement of fact (*F*), an announcement (*A*), a vague
statement (*VS*), or an effective thesis (*ET*).

Examples

My drive to school takes more than an hour. ____F____

I hate my commute between home and school. ____VS____

1. Students who must commute a long distance to school are at a dis-

   advantage compared to students who live close by. _____

2. In this paper, I will discuss cheating. _____

3. Schools should establish specific policies to discourage students from

   cheating. _____

4. Despite the efforts of the bottled water industry to suggest otherwise,

   plastic water bottles are causing harm. _____

5. Television commercials are designed to sell products. _____

6. Effective television commercials use verbal and visual cues. _____

7. Teenage mothers face many challenges. _____

8. Young people are starting to abuse alcohol and drugs at earlier ages

   than in the past. _____

9. Opioid abuse is a major problem in our society. _____

10. Families can do several things to help children avoid alcohol and

    drugs. _____

PRACTICE

13-6 Rewrite the following vague thesis statements to make them effective.

Example

Making a budget isn't that difficult.

Rewrite: <u>Making a budget is easier than it seems if you follow a few basic</u>

<u>steps.</u>

1. Electric cars have some advantages.

2. Understanding how government works is important.

3. People are interested in alternative energy.

4. Choosing a major is tough.

5. Math is part of everyone's life.

PRACTICE

13-7 Read the following groups of statements. Then, write a thesis statement that could express the main point of each group.

1. Thesis statement _____

_____

- *Gap year* is a term that refers to a year that students take off before they go to college.
- Many college students spend most of their time studying and socializing with their peers.
- Studies show that high school students who take a year off before they go to college get better grades.
- Many students take community-service jobs in order to broaden their interests and to increase their social awareness.

2. Thesis statement _____

_____

- Some people post too much personal information on social-networking sites such as Facebook.
- Child predators frequently use social-networking sites to find their victims.

- Some experts believe that people can become addicted to social-networking sites.
- Employers have fired employees because of information they have seen on their employees' social-networking sites.

3. Thesis statement _____

_____

- Scholarships and grants do not always cover the full cost of tuition.
- Some students enlist in the armed forces and become eligible for tuition-assistance programs.
- Students can apply for federal loans that have lower-interest rates than more traditional loans.
- Some schools offer work-study programs to lower the cost of tuition.

Allen Creative/Steve Allen/Alamy

state your thesis

Review your freewriting, brainstorming, and journal entries. Then, write a thesis statement for your essay.

 ## 13e Choosing Supporting Points

Once you have decided on a thesis statement, look over your freewriting, brainstorming, and journal entries again. Identify **evidence** (details and examples) that best supports your thesis.

Jared made the following list of possible supporting points about his decision to go back to school. When he reviewed his list, he crossed out several points that he thought would not support his thesis.

Deciding to Go Back to School: Pros and Cons

Money a problem

Other students a lot younger

Paying tuition—how?

No one in family went to college

Friends not in college

Couldn't see myself in college

~~Considered going to trade school~~

~~Computer programmer?~~

Grades bad in high school

Wondered if I would get in

Found out about community college

Admission requirements not bad

Afraid—too old, failing out, looking dumb

~~Took time to get used to routine~~

Found other students like me

Liked studying

PRACTICE

13-8 Review Jared's list of supporting points above. Do you see any points he crossed out that you think he should have kept? Do you see any other points he should have crossed out?

13f Making an Outline

After you have selected the points you think will best support your thesis, make an **informal outline**. Begin by arranging your supporting points into groups. Then, arrange them in the order in which you will discuss them (for example, from general to specific or from least to most important).

Arrange the supporting points for each group in the same way. This informal outline can guide you as you write.

When Jared looked over his list of supporting points, he saw that they fell into three groups of excuses for not going back to school: *not being able to pay tuition, not being a good student in high school,* and *not being able to picture himself in college.* He arranged his points under these three headings to create the following informal outline.

Excuse 1: Not being able to pay tuition

 Needed to work to live

 Didn't have much saved

 Found out about community college (low tuition)

 Found out about grants, loans

Excuse 2: Not being a good student in high school

 Got bad grades in high school: wasn't motivated and didn't work

 Looked into admission requirements at community college—doable!

 Made a commitment to improve study habits

Excuse 3: Not being able to picture myself in college

 No college graduates in family

 No friends in college

 Afraid of being too old, looking dumb

 Found other students like me

 Found out I liked studying

PRACTICE

13-9 Look over Jared's informal outline above. Do you think his arrangement is effective? Can you suggest any other ways he might have arranged his points?

FYI

Preparing a Formal Outline

An informal outline like the one that appears above is usually all you need to plan a short essay. However, some writers—especially when they are planning a longer, more detailed essay—prefer to use formal outlines.

Formal outlines use a combination of numbered and lettered headings to show the relationships among ideas. For example, the most important (and most general) ideas are assigned a Roman numeral; the next most important ideas are assigned capital letters. Each level develops the idea above it, and each new level is indented.

Here is a formal outline of the points that Jared planned to discuss in his essay.

Thesis statement: Although I realized it would be difficult in some ways, I decided that if I really wanted to attend college full-time, I could.

  I. Difficulty: Money
     A. Needed to work to live
     B. Didn't have much money saved
     C. Found out about community college (low tuition)
     D. Found out about grants/loans
 II. Difficulty: Academic record
     A. Got bad grades in high school
        1. Didn't care
        2. Didn't work
     B. Found out about reasonable admissions requirements at community college
     C. Committed to improving study habits
III. Difficulty: Imagining myself as a student
     A. Had no college graduates in family
     B. Had no friends in school
     C. Felt anxious
        1. Too old
        2. Out of practice at school
     D. Found other students like me
     E. Discovered I like studying

make an informal outline

Review the freewriting, brainstorming, and journal entries you wrote. Then, list the points you plan to use to support your thesis statement. Cross out any points that do not support your thesis statement. Finally, group the remaining points into an informal outline that will guide you as you write.

Allen Creative/Steve Allen/Alamy

13g Drafting Your Essay

After you have decided on a thesis for your essay and have arranged your supporting points in the order in which you will discuss them, you are ready to draft your essay.

At this stage of the writing process, you should not worry about spelling or grammar or about composing a perfect introduction or conclusion. Your main goal is to get your ideas down so you can react to them. Remember that the draft you are writing will be revised, so leave extra space between lines as you type. Follow your outline, but don't hesitate to depart from it if you think of new points.

As you draft your essay, be sure that it has a **thesis-and-support structure**—that it states a thesis and supports it with evidence. Include a **working title,** a temporary title that you will revise later so that it accurately reflects the content of your completed essay. This working title will help you focus your ideas.

Following is the first draft of Jared's essay.

Going Back to School

I was out of school for six years after I graduated from high school. The decision to return to school was one I had a lot of difficulty making. I had been around enough to know that without more education, I'd never get anywhere in life, but I always found reasons for not taking the plunge. However, after a lot of thinking, I realized that my reasons for not going to college were just excuses. Although I realized it would be difficult in some ways, I decided that if I really wanted to attend college full-time, I could.

My first excuse for not going to college was that I couldn't afford to go to school full-time. I had worked since I finished high school, but I hadn't put much money away. I kept wondering how I would pay for books and tuition. I needed to support myself and pay for rent, food, and car expenses. I was working as a house painter, and a house I was painting belonged to a college instructor. Painting wasn't hard work, but it was boring. I'd start in the morning and work without a break until lunch. We began talking. When I told him about my situation, he told me I should look at our local community college. He also told me about some loans and grants I'd probably be able to apply for. I went online and looked at the college's website. I found out that tuition was one hundred dollars a credit, less than I thought it would be. If I got just one of the grants he mentioned, I might be able to make it.

Now that I had taken care of my first excuse, I had to deal with my second—that I hadn't been a good student in high school. When I was a teenager, I didn't care much about school. School bored me to death.

Probably as a result, I got bad grades. Now that I was considering going back to school, though, I wondered what price I would have to pay for my laziness and immaturity. The answer to this question was not as bad as I thought it would be. According to the community college's website, all I needed to be admitted was a high school diploma and county residence. I would have to take some placement tests, but I would be judged on my ability, not my high school grades. I knew I could do better if I made a real effort to study harder and smarter. The website was easy to navigate, and I had no problem finding information.

I had a hard time picturing myself in college. No one in my family had ever gone to college. My friends were just like me; they all went to work right after high school. I had no role model or mentor who could give me advice. I thought I was just too old for college. After all, I was probably at least six years older than most of the students. How would I be able to keep up with the younger students in the class? I hadn't opened a textbook for years, and I'd never really learned how to study. Most of my fears disappeared during my first few weeks of classes. I saw a lot of students who were as old as I was, and some were even older. Studying didn't seem to be a problem either. I actually enjoyed learning. History, which had put me to sleep in high school, suddenly became interesting. So did math and English. It soon became clear to me that I was going to like being in college.

Going to college as a full-time student has changed my life, both personally and financially. I am no longer the same person I was in high school. I allowed laziness and insecurity to hold me back. Now, I have options that I didn't have before. When I graduate from community college, I plan to transfer to the state university and get a four-year degree.

PRACTICE

13-10 Reread Jared's first draft. What changes would you suggest? What might he have added? What might he have deleted? Which of his supporting details and examples do you find most effective?

draft your essay

Draft an essay about your most difficult job. When you finish your draft, give your essay a working title.

Allen Creative/Steve Allen/Alamy

13h TESTing Your Essay

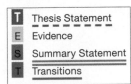

Just as you **TEST** your paragraphs as you begin revising, you should also **TEST** your essays. **TEST**ing will tell you whether your essay includes the basic elements it needs to be effective.

TESTing for a Thesis

The first thing you do when you **TEST** your essay is to make sure it has a clear **thesis statement (T)** that identifies the essay's main idea. By stating the main idea, your thesis statement helps to unify your essay.

When Jared **TEST**ed the draft of his essay, he decided that his thesis statement clearly stated his main idea. (His marginal note appears below.)

Jared's Introduction

I was out of school for six years after I graduated from high school. The decision to return to school was one I had a lot of difficulty making. I had been around enough to know that without more education, I'd never get anywhere in life, but I always found reasons for not taking the plunge. However, after a lot of thinking, I realized that my reasons for not going to college were just excuses. <u>Although I realized it would be difficult in some ways, I decided that if I really wanted to attend college full-time, I could.</u>

Thesis clearly states what I want to say about going to college.

TESTing for Evidence

The next thing you do when you **TEST** your essay is to check your **evidence (E)** to make sure that the body of your essay includes enough examples and details to support your thesis. Remember that without evidence, your essay is simply a series of unsupported general statements. A well-developed essay includes enough evidence to explain, illustrate, and clarify the points you are making.

When Jared **TEST**ed his draft for evidence, he decided that he should add more examples and details in his body paragraphs and delete some irrelevant ones. (His marginal notes appear below.)

Jared's Body Paragraphs

My first excuse for not going to college was that I couldn't afford to go to school full-time. I had worked since I finished high school, but I hadn't put much money away. I kept wondering how I would pay for books and tuition. I needed to support myself and pay for rent, food, and car expenses. I was working as a house painter, and a house I was painting belonged to a college instructor. Painting wasn't hard work, but it was boring. I'd start in the morning and work without a break until lunch. We began talking. When I told him about my situation, he told me I should look at our local community college. He also told me about some loans and grants I'd probably be able to apply for. I went online and looked at the college's website. I found out that tuition was one hundred dollars a credit, less than I thought it would be. If I got just one of the grants he mentioned, I might be able to make it.

E

Are details about painting necessary?

Add more about how I thought I could cover the tuition.

Now that I had taken care of my first excuse, I had to deal with my second—that I hadn't been a good student in high school. When I was a teenager, I didn't care much about school. School bored me to death. Probably as a result, I got bad grades. Now that I was considering going back to school, though, I wondered what price I would have to pay for my laziness and immaturity. The answer to this question was not as bad as I thought it would be. According to the community college's website, all I needed to be admitted was a high school diploma and county residence. I would have to take some placement tests, but I would be judged on my ability, not my high school grades. I knew I could do better if I made a real effort to study harder and smarter. The website was easy to navigate, and I had no problem finding information.

E

Give examples of boredom.

Are details about website relevant?

I had a hard time picturing myself in college. My friends were just like me; they all went to work right after high school. I had no role model or mentor who could give me advice. I thought I was just too old for college. After all, I was probably at least six years older than most of the students. How would I be able to keep up with the younger students in the class? I hadn't opened a textbook for years, and I'd never really learned how to study. Most of my fears disappeared during my first few weeks of classes.

E

Evidence seems OK here

I saw a lot of students who were as old as I was, and some were even older. Studying didn't seem to be a problem, either. I actually enjoyed learning. History, which had put me to sleep in high school, suddenly became interesting. So did math and English. It soon became clear to me that I was going to like being in college.

TESTing for a Summary Statement

The third thing you do when you **TEST** your essay is to look at your conclusion and make sure that it includes a **summary statement (S)**. Most often, your conclusion will begin with this statement, which reinforces your essay's thesis. By reinforcing your thesis, this summary statement helps to **unify** your essay.

When Jared **TEST**ed his draft for a summary statement, he thought that his summary statement adequately reinforced the main idea of his essay. (His marginal note appears below.)

Jared's Conclusion

Conclusion is too short, but summary statement is OK.

<u>Going to college as a full-time student has changed my life, both personally and financially.</u> I am no longer the same person I was in high school. I allowed laziness and insecurity to hold me back. Now, I have options that I didn't have before. When I graduate from community college, I plan to transfer to the state university and get a four-year degree.

TESTing for Transitions

The last thing you do when you **TEST** your essay is to make sure that it includes **transitions (T)**—words and phrases that connect your ideas. Make sure you have included all the transitions you need to tell readers how one sentence (or paragraph) is connected to another. Including transitions makes your essay **coherent**, with its sentences arranged in a clear, logical sequence that helps readers understand your ideas.

By linking sentences and paragraphs, transitions emphasize the relationship between ideas and help readers understand your essay's logic. By reminding readers of what has come before, transitions prepare readers for new information and help them understand how it fits into the discussion. In this sense, transitions are the glue that holds the ideas in your essay together.

Transitions are categorized according to their function. For example, they may indicate **time order** (*first, second, now, next, finally,* and so on), **spatial order** (*above, behind, near, next to, over,* and so on), or **logical order** (*also, although, therefore, in fact,* and so on). (For a full list of transitions, see 3d.)

When Jared **TEST**ed his draft for transitions, he realized that although he had included some transitional words and phrases, he needed to add more of them to connect his ideas. (His marginal notes appear below and on the following pages.)

Jared's Thesis + Body Paragraphs

Although I realized it would be difficult in some ways, I decided that if I really wanted to attend college full-time, I could.

My first excuse for not going to college was that I couldn't afford to go to school full-time. I had worked since I finished high school, but I hadn't put much money away. I kept wondering how I would pay for books and tuition. I needed to support myself and pay for rent, food, and car expenses. I was working as a house painter, and a house I was painting belonged to a college instructor. Painting wasn't hard work, but it was boring. I'd start in the morning and work without a break until lunch. We began talking. When I told him about my situation, he told me I should look at our local community college. He also told me about some loans and grants I'd probably be able to apply for. I went online and looked at the college's website. I found out that tuition was one hundred dollars a credit, less than I thought it would be. If I got just one of the grants he mentioned, I might be able to make it.

Need to show relationship between ideas in this paragraph.

Now that I had taken care of my first excuse, I had to deal with my second—that I hadn't been a good student in high school. When I was a teenager, I didn't care much about school. School bored me to death. Probably as a result, I got bad grades. Now that I was considering going back to school, though, I wondered what price I would have to pay for my laziness and immaturity. The answer to this question was not as bad as I thought it would be. According to the community college's website, all I needed to be admitted was a high school diploma and county residence. I would have to take some placement tests, but I would be judged on my ability, not my high school grades. I knew I could do better if I made a real effort to study harder and smarter. The website was easy to navigate, and I had no problem finding information.

I had a hard time picturing myself in college. No one in my family had ever gone to college. My friends were just like me; they all went to work right after high school. I had no role model or mentor who could give me advice. I thought I was just too old for college. After all, I was probably

Add better transition between these two paragraphs.

Add transition here.

at least six years older than most of the students. How would I be able to keep up with the younger students in the class? I hadn't opened a textbook in years, and I'd never really learned how to study. Most of my fears disappeared during my first few weeks of classes. I saw a lot of students who were as old as I was, and some were even older. Studying didn't seem to be a problem, either. I actually enjoyed learning. History, which had put me to sleep in high school, suddenly became interesting. So did math and English. It <u>soon</u> became clear to me that I was going to like being in college.

Allen Creative/Steve Allen/Alamy

TEST your essay

TEST your draft to make sure it includes all the elements of an effective essay. If any elements are missing, plan to add them when you revise.

 ## 13i Revising Your Essay

When you **revise** your essay, you do not simply correct errors; instead, you resee, rethink, reevaluate, and rewrite your work. Some of the changes you make—such as adding, deleting, or rearranging sentences or paragraphs—will be major. Others—such as adding or deleting words—will be small. Once you have **TEST**ed your essay, you will have a good sense of how your essay can be strengthened. In addition to this self-assessment, you can get feedback for revising from your instructor, peers, or a writing center tutor. The chart below shows you the advantages of each of these revision strategies.

STRATEGIES FOR REVISING	
STRATEGY	**ADVANTAGES**
FACE-TO-FACE CONFERENCE WITH INSTRUCTOR  Hill Street Studios/Blend Images/Alamy	■ Provides one-to-one feedback that you can't get in the classroom ■ Builds a student-teacher relationship ■ Enables you to collaborate with their instructors ■ Allows you to ask questions that they might not ask in a classroom setting

STRATEGY	ADVANTAGES
WRITING CENTER 	■ Offers you a less formal, less stressful environment than an instructor conference ■ Enables you to get help from trained tutors (both students and professionals) ■ Provides a perspective other than the instructor's ■ Offers specialized help to students whose first language is not English
PEER REVIEW 	■ Enables students working on the same assignment to share insights with one another ■ Gives you the experience of writing for a real audience ■ Gives you several different readers' reactions to your work ■ Enables you to benefit from the ideas of your classmates
ELECTRONIC COMMUNICATION WITH INSTRUCTOR 	■ Enables you to submit email questions before a draft is due ■ Gives you quick answers to your questions ■ Enables instructors to give feedback by annotating drafts electronically ■ Enables you to react to your instructor's responses when you have time ■ Eliminates time spent traveling to your instructor's office
REVISION CHECKLIST self-assessment checklist **Revising Your Essay** □ Does your essay have an introduction, a body, and a conclusion? □ Does your introduction include a clearly worded thesis statement that states your essay's main idea? □ Does each body paragraph have a topic sentence? □ Does each topic sentence introduce a point that supports the thesis? □ Does each body paragraph include enough examples and details to support the topic sentence? □ Are the body paragraphs unified, well developed, and coherent? □ Does your conclusion include a concluding statement that restates your thesis or sums up your main idea?	■ Gives you a tool that enables to revise in an orderly way ■ Enables you to learn to revise independently ■ Enables you to focus on specific aspects of your writing

When Jared finished **TEST**ing his essay, he decided to arrange a conference with his instructor to discuss possible revisions. He consulted the FYI box below, "Getting the Most Out of a Conference," in order to prepare for their meeting. During the conference, Jared's instructor pointed out several places where she thought he should add more detail. For example, she thought his introduction started too abruptly and should be expanded. She also thought that Jared should give readers a sense of what he was like as a student in high school.

FYI

Getting the Most Out of a Conference

If you need help at any point in the writing process, you can get it from your instructor or from a tutor in your school's writing center. Following these guidelines will help you get the most out of your conference.

- Make an appointment in advance, either by phone or by email.
- Arrive on time; instructors and tutors often schedule several appointments in a row, and if you are late, you may miss your appointment entirely.
- Bring a copy of your assignment.
- Bring all drafts and prewriting notes for the assignment you are working on.
- Bring a list of specific questions you would like the instructor or tutor to answer.
- Pay attention, ask your questions, and be sure you understand the answers.
- Write the instructor's or tutor's suggestions directly on your latest draft.
- Schedule a follow-up appointment if necessary.

Remember, your instructor or tutor will answer questions and make recommendations, but he or she will *not* revise or edit your work for you. That is your job.

After the conference, Jared revised his essay, using his instructor's feedback, the notes he had created when **TEST**ing his essay, and the self-assessment checklist below.

self-assessment checklist

Revising Your Essay

✔ Does your essay have an introduction, a body, and a conclusion?

✔ Does your introduction include a clearly worded thesis statement that states your essay's main idea?

✔ Does each body paragraph have a topic sentence?

✔ Does each topic sentence introduce a point that supports the thesis?

✔ Does each body paragraph include enough examples and details to support the topic sentence?

✔ Are the body paragraphs unified, well developed, and coherent?

✔ Does your conclusion include a concluding statement that restates your thesis or sums up your main idea?

Here is Jared's revised first draft with his handwritten revisions.

~~Going Back to School~~ Starting Over

I was out of school for six years after I graduated from high school.
The decision to return to school was one I had a lot of difficulty making.
I had been around enough to know that without more education, I'd never
get anywhere in life, but I always found reasons for not taking the plunge.
However, after a lot of thinking, I realized that my reasons for not going to
college were just excuses. Although I realized it would be difficult in some
ways, I decided that if I really wanted to attend college full-time, I could.

My first excuse for not going to college was that I couldn't afford to go
to school full-time. I had worked since I finished high school, but I hadn't
put much money away. I kept wondering how I would pay for books and
tuition. I ̭also needed to support myself and pay for rent, food, and car expenses. The solution to my problem came unexpectedly.
I was working as a house painter, and a house I was painting belonged
to a college instructor. ~~Painting wasn't hard work, but it was boring. I'd~~

The other day, my sociology instructor mentioned that half the students enrolled in college programs across the country are twenty-five or older. His remark caught my attention because I am one of those students.

start in the morning and work without a break until lunch. _{During my lunch break, we} We began

talking. When I told him about my situation, he told me I should look at

our local community college. He also told me about some loans and grants

I'd probably be able to apply for. _{Later,} I went online and looked at the college's

website. I found out that tuition was one hundred dollars a credit, less than

I thought it would be. If I got just one of the grants he mentioned, I might

The money I'd saved, be able to make it.
along with what I could
make painting houses
on the weekends, could
get me through.

    Now that I had taken care of my first excuse, I had to deal with my

second—that I hadn't been a good student in high school. When I was

In class, I would stare a teenager, I didn't care much about school. _{In fact, school} School bored me to death.
out the window or
watch the second
hand on the clock move Probably as a result, I got bad grades. Now that I was considering going
slowly around.
I never bothered with back to school, though, I wondered what price I would have to pay for my
homework. School just
didn't interest me. laziness and immaturity. The answer to this question was not as bad as I

thought it would be. According to the community college's website, all I

needed to be admitted was a high school diploma and county residence.

I would have to take some placement tests, but I would be judged on my

ability, not my high school grades. I knew I could do better if I made a real

effort to study harder and smarter. The website was easy to navigate, and I

had no problem finding information.
    My biggest problem still bothered me:
    I had a hard time picturing myself in college. No one in my family had

ever gone to college. My friends were just like me; they all went to work

right after high school. I had no role model or mentor who could give me

advice. _{Besides,} I thought I was just too old for college. After all, I was probably

at least six years older than most of the students. How would I be able to

keep up with the younger students in the class? I hadn't opened a textbook

for years, and I'd never really learned how to study. _{However, most} Most of my fears

disappeared during my first few weeks of classes. I saw a lot of students who

were as old as I was, and some were even older. Studying didn't seem to be

a problem either. I actually enjoyed learning. *For example, history,* ~~History,~~ which had put me to
sleep in high school, suddenly became interesting. So did math and English.

It soon became clear to me that I was going to like being in college.

Going to college as a full-time student has changed my life, both

personally and financially. I am no longer the same person I was in high

school. *In the past,* I allowed laziness and insecurity to hold me back. Now, I have

options that I didn't have before. When I graduate from community college,

I plan to transfer to the state university and get a four-year degree.

> *The other day, one of my instructors asked me if I had ever considered becoming a teacher. The truth is, I never had, but now I might. I'd like to be able to give kids like me the tough, realistic advice I wish someone had given me.*

PRACTICE

 13-11   Working in a group of three or four students, answer the following questions:

- What kind of material did Jared add to his draft?
- What did he delete?
- Why do you think he made these changes?
- Do you agree with the changes he made?

Be prepared to discuss your reactions to these changes with the class.

---

revise your essay

Using one or two of the additional revision strategies from the Strategies for Revising chart on pages 208–209, continue revising your essay.

Allen Creative/Steve Allen/Alamy

◼ 13j   Editing Your Essay

When you **edit** your essay, you check grammar and sentence structure. Then, you look at punctuation, mechanics, and spelling. As you edit, think carefully about the questions in the following Self-Assessment Checklist. (If you have not already chosen a final title for your essay, this is a good time to do so.)

self-assessment checklist

Editing Your Essay

EDITING FOR COMMON SENTENCE PROBLEMS

✔ Have you avoided run-ons? (See Chapter 24.)

✔ Have you avoided sentence fragments? (See Chapter 25.)

✔ Do your subjects and verbs agree? (See Chapter 26.)

✔ Have you avoided illogical shifts? (See Chapter 27.)

✔ Have you avoided misplaced and dangling modifiers? (See Chapter 28.)

EDITING FOR GRAMMAR

✔ Are your verb forms and verb tenses correct? (See Chapters 29 and 30.)

✔ Have you used nouns and pronouns correctly? (See Chapter 31.)

✔ Have you used adjectives and adverbs correctly? (See Chapter 32.)

EDITING FOR PUNCTUATION, MECHANICS, AND SPELLING

✔ Have you used commas correctly? (See Chapter 34.)

✔ Have you used apostrophes correctly? Have you avoided contractions, which are usually too informal for college writing? (See Chapter 35.)

✔ Have you used capital letters where they are required? (See 36a.)

✔ Have you used quotation marks correctly where they are needed? (See 36b.)

● **13k Proofreading Your Essay**

When you **proofread** your essay, you check for typos, proper formatting, and anything you might have missed while you were editing. Remember that your spell checker and grammar checker are helpful, but they can also introduce errors into your essay. As you proofread, be sure to check the spelling of any words whose spelling you are unsure of. It is also a good idea to print your essay and proofread on the hard copy because it is easy to miss typos and other small errors on a computer screen. After you have checked for typos and other lingering errors, check your essay's format.

The **format** of an essay is the way it looks on a page—for example, the size of the margins, the placement of page numbers, and the amount of space between lines. Most instructors expect you to follow a certain format when you type an essay. The model essay format illustrated below is commonly used in composition classes. Before you hand in an essay, you should make sure that it follows this model (or the format your instructor requires).

Essay Format: Sample

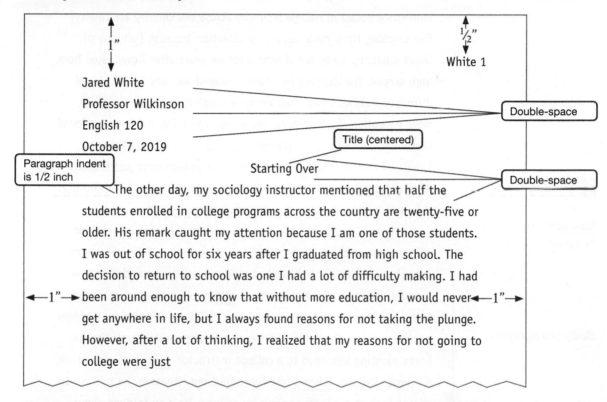

Note: The bottom margin of each page should also be one inch.

When Jared edited and proofread his essay, he deleted all the contractions, which he thought made his serious essay sound too informal. The final version of his essay appears below. (Marginal annotations have been added to highlight key features of his essay.) Note that the final draft includes all the elements Jared looked for when he **TEST**ed his essay.

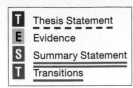

T	Thesis Statement
E	Evidence
S	Summary Statement
T	Transitions

White 1

Jared White

Professor Wilkinson

English 120

October 7, 2019

Starting Over

Introduction

    The other day, my sociology instructor mentioned that half the students enrolled in college programs across the country are twenty-five or older. His remark caught my attention because I am one of those students. I was out of school for six years after I graduated from high school. The decision to return to school was one I had a lot of difficulty making. I had been around enough to know that without more education, I would never get anywhere in life, but I always found reasons for not taking the plunge. However, after a lot of thinking, I realized that my reasons for not going to college were just excuses.

T **Thesis Statement**

Although I realized it would be difficult in some ways, I decided that if I really wanted to attend college full-time, I could.

Topic sentence
(first point)

    My first excuse for not going to college was that I could not afford to go to school full-time. I had worked since I finished high school, but I had not put much money away. I kept wondering how I would pay for books and tuition. I also needed to support myself and pay for rent, food, and car expenses. The solution to my problem came unexpectedly. I was working as a house painter, and a house I was painting belonged to a college instructor. During a lunch break, we began talking. When I told him about my situation, he told me I should look at our local community college. He also told me about some loans and grants I would probably be able to apply for. Later, I went online and looked at the college's website. I found out that tuition was one hundred dollars a credit, less than I thought it would be. If I got just one of the grants he mentioned, I might be able to make it. The money I had saved, along with what I could make painting houses on the weekends, could get me through.

Body paragraphs

E

T **Transitions**

White 2

Now that I had taken care of my first excuse, I had to deal with my second—that I had not been a good student in high school. When I was a teenager, I did not care much about school. In fact, school bored me. In class, I would stare out the window or watch the second hand on the clock move slowly around. I never bothered with homework. School just did not interest me. Probably as a result, I got bad grades. Now that I was considering going back to school, though, I wondered what price I would have to pay for my laziness and immaturity. The answer to this question was not as bad as I thought it would be. According to the community college's website, all I needed to be admitted was a high school diploma and county residence. I would have to take some placement tests, but I would be judged on my ability, not my high school grades. I knew I could do better if I made a real effort to study harder and smarter.

My biggest problem still bothered me: I had a hard time picturing myself in college. No one in my family had ever gone to college. My friends were just like me; they all went to work right after high school. I had no role model or mentor who could give me advice. Besides, I thought I was just too old for college. After all, I was probably at least six years older than most of the students. How would I be able to keep up with the younger students in the class? I had not opened a textbook in years, and I had never really learned how to study. However, most of my fears disappeared during my first few weeks of classes. I saw a lot of students who were as old as I was, and some were even older. Studying did not seem to be a problem, either. I actually enjoyed learning. For example, history, which had put me to sleep in high school, suddenly became interesting. So did math and English. It soon became clear to me that I was going to like being in college.

Topic sentence
(second point)

T Transitions

Body paragraphs

E

Topic sentence
(third point)

Body paragraphs

E

White 3

S Summary

<u>Going to college as a full-time student has changed my life, both personally and financially.</u> I am no longer the same person I was in high school. In the past, I allowed laziness and insecurity to hold me back. Now, I have options that I did not have before. When I graduate from community college, I plan to transfer to the state university and get a four-year degree. The other day, one of my instructors asked me if I had ever considered becoming a teacher. The truth is, I never had, but now I might. I would like to be able to give students like me the tough, realistic advice I wish someone had given me.

Conclusion

PRACTICE

13-12 Reread the final draft of Jared White's essay. Working in a group of three or four students, answer these questions.

- Do you think this draft is an improvement over his first draft (shown in 13g)?
- What other changes could Jared have made?

Be prepared to discuss your group's answers with the class.

Allen Creative/Steve Allen/Alamy

edit and proofread your essay

Edit your draft, using the Self-Assessment Checklist on page 214 to guide you. Then, proofread your essay for typos and other small errors. Finally, make sure your essay's format follows your instructor's guidelines.

EDITING PRACTICE

1. The following student essay is missing its thesis statement and topic sentences and has no summary statement. First, write an appropriate thesis statement on the lines provided. (Make sure your thesis statement clearly communicates the essay's main idea.) Then, fill in the topic sentences for the second, third, and fourth paragraphs. Finally, add a summary statement in the conclusion.

Preparing for a Job Interview

A lot of books and many websites give advice on how to do well on a job interview. Some recommend practicing your handshake, and others suggest making eye contact. This advice is useful, but not many books tell how to get mentally prepared for an interview. [Thesis statement:] _____

_____

_____

_____

[Topic sentence for the second paragraph:] _____

_____

_____

_____

Feeling good about how you look is important, so you should probably wear a dress, or skirt, or pantsuit (or, for males, a jacket and tie or possibly a suit) to an interview. Even if you will not be dressing this formally on the job, try to make a good first impression. For this reason, you should never come to an interview dressed in jeans or shorts. Still, you should be careful not to overdress. For example, wearing a suit or a dressy dress to an interview at a fast-food restaurant might make you feel good, but it could also make you look as if you do not really want to work there.

[Topic sentence for the third paragraph:] _____

_____

_____

Going on an interview is a little like getting ready to compete in a sporting event. You have to go in with the right attitude. If you think you are not going to be successful, chances are that you will not be. So, before you go on any interview, spend some time building your confidence. Tell yourself that you can do the job and that you will do well in the interview. By the time you get to the interview, you will have convinced yourself that you are the right person for the job.

[Topic sentence for the fourth paragraph:] _____

_____

_____

Most people go to an interview knowing little or nothing about the job. They expect the interviewer to tell them what they will have to do. Most interviewers, however, are impressed by someone who has taken the time to do his or her homework. For this reason, you should always do some research before you go on an interview—even for a part-time job. Most of the time, your research can be nothing more than a quick look at the company's website, but this kind of research really pays off. Being able to talk about the job can give you a real advantage over other candidates. Sometimes the interviewer will be so impressed that he or she will offer you a job on the spot.

[Summary statement:] _____

_____

_____

Of course, following these suggestions will not guarantee that you get a job. You still have to do well at the interview itself. Even so, getting mentally prepared for the interview will give you an advantage over people who do almost nothing before they walk in the door.

2. Now, using the topic sentence below, write another body paragraph that you could add to the essay above. (This new paragraph will go right before the essay's conclusion.)

Another way to prepare yourself mentally is to anticipate and answer some typical questions interviewers ask.

_____

_____

_____

_____

COLLABORATIVE ACTIVITY

Working in a group, come up with thesis statements suitable for essays on three of the following topics.

Dealing with a cyberbully	Gun safety
Taxing junk food	Drawbacks of online dating
Voting	Patriotism
Sustainable energy	The effects of divorce
Selecting a major	Making a speech

Then, exchange your group's three thesis statements with those of another group. Choose the best one of the other group's thesis statements. A member of each group can then read the thesis statement to the class and explain why the group chose the thesis statement it did.

review checklist

Writing an Essay

✔ Be sure you understand essay structure. (See 13a.)

✔ Focus on your assignment, purpose, and audience to help you find a topic. (See 13b.)

✔ Find ideas to write about. (See 13c.)

✔ Identify your main idea, and develop an effective thesis statement. (See 13d.)

✔ List the points that best support your thesis, and arrange them in the order in which you plan to discuss them, creating an informal outline of your essay. (See 13e and 13f.)

✔ Write your first draft, making sure your essay has a thesis-and-support structure. (See 13g.)

✔ **TEST** your essay. (See 13h.)

✔ Revise your essay. (See 13i.)

✔ Edit and proofread your essay. (See 13j and 13k.)

✔ Make sure your essay's format is correct. (See 13k.)

14 Introductions and Conclusions

Robert Alexander/Archive Photos/Getty Images

focus on writing

This picture shows a daycare center worker pushing a wagon carrying preschoolers. Like the fast-food workers pictured in Chapter 13, these workers have demanding jobs. Think about what this picture suggests about the work they do, and then print out a copy of the essay you wrote for Chapter 13. At the end of this chapter, you will work on revising the introduction and conclusion of your essay.

In this chapter, you will learn to
- write an introduction (14a)
- choose a title (14a)
- write a conclusion (14b)

When you draft an essay, you usually spend the most time on the **body** because it is the section in which you develop your ideas. A well-constructed essay, however, is more than a series of body paragraphs. It also includes an **introduction** and a **conclusion**, both of which contribute to the essay's overall effectiveness.

14a Writing Introductions

An **introduction** is the first thing people see when they read your essay. If your introduction is interesting, it will make readers want to read further. If it is not, readers may get bored and stop reading.

There are many ways to structure an introduction, but a useful pattern to master is one that moves from general to specific ideas. With this pattern, you begin with some general **opening remarks** that will draw readers into your essay. The **thesis statement**, a specific sentence that presents the main idea of your essay, comes at the end of the introduction. The following diagram illustrates the shape of this type of introduction.

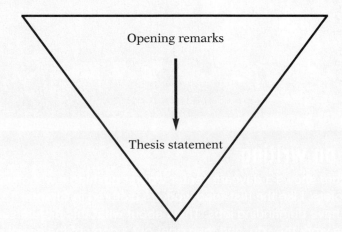

Opening remarks

Thesis statement

Here are some options you can experiment with when you write your introductions. (In each of the sample introductory paragraphs that follow, the thesis statement is underlined and labeled.)

Beginning with a Narrative

You can begin an essay with a narrative drawn from your own experience or from a current news event.

> On the first day my sister and I attended school in America, our parents walked us directly to the entrance of our new classroom. Even though she barely spoke any English, Mom tried earnestly to teach us how to ask for permission to use the bathroom: "Can I go to the bathroom?" Like parrots, she had us repeat this question over and over. At the time, neither of us realized that the proper way of asking for permission is "May I go to the bathroom?" This grammar slip did not matter, though, because we forgot the question as soon as our parents left. Reluctantly, we entered the classroom, more timid than two mice trying not to awaken a sleeping cat. We didn't   Thesis statement
> know yet that going to school where English was the only language spoken would prove to be very difficult.

—Hilda Alvarado (student)

Beginning with a Question (or a Series of Questions)

Asking one or more questions at the beginning of your essay is an effective strategy. Because readers expect you to answer the questions, they will want to read further.

> Could a text message save someone's life? If you are a Crisis Text Line volunteer, the answer is yes. Because many people are more comfortable texting than talking on the phone, Crisis Text Line is an important new service for people of all ages—especially for teenagers. Volunteers take a thirty-four-hour online training program to learn how to provide emotional support and to match people with the resources they need. The training program includes video lessons, role playing, and online observation. Once they complete the program, volunteers are able to offer guidance to the people who contact them each day. Anyone who is looking to help people   Thesis statement
> should consider becoming a Crisis Text Line counselor, crisis-center partner, or supervisor.

—Aleena Abbas (student)

Beginning with a Definition

A definition at the beginning of your essay can give readers important information. As the following introduction shows, a definition can help explain a complicated idea or a confusing concept. When using a definition, however, avoid such cliched phrases as "According to the Merriam-Webster dictionary" or "The dictionary defines the word X as." Instead, put the definition into your own words, and use it to begin discussion that provides a fresh observation or detail.

Thesis statement

> Stereotypes are generalized beliefs about people based on their belonging to a specific group. Stereotypes can be relatively harmless, or they can be quite negative, as in the case of gender or racial stereotypes. Recent research has shown that stereotypes are difficult to change. This is because people tend to select information that confirms their preconceived ideas. Even though most adults claim that they do not have biases, most actually do. The result is that we unconsciously characterize people and act on these misguided beliefs. By understanding the causes of stereotyping, we can take steps to move beyond these generalizations and judge individuals on their personal merits.
>
> —Duc Le (Student)

Beginning with a Quotation

An appropriate saying or some interesting dialogue can draw readers into your essay.

Thesis statement

> According to the environmentalist Paul Watson, "We'll lose more species of plants and animals between 2000 and 2065 than we've lost in the last 65 million years." We humans are causing this problem by over-harvesting, degrading, and destroying habitats. Our activities also threaten entire ecosystems, as when clear-cutting forests or over-planting causes desertification or deforestation. In addition, toxic runoff from farm lands gets into streams and eventually flows into oceans, where it degrades and destroys marine ecosystems. As a result, biodiversity is declining, and a decrease in biodiversity can harm humans. We can slow down and possibly stop this destruction if we act now to increase government support for actions that conserve our natural resources and protect our ecosystems.
>
> —Andres Eckler (student)

Beginning with a Surprising Statement

You can begin your essay with a surprising or unexpected statement. Because your statement takes readers by surprise, it catches their attention.

> In the near future, it is likely that robots will replace us. This may sound like science fiction, but as technology continues to advance, automated machines will take over many of the jobs that humans currently perform. In fact, this has already occurred. For example, car manufacturing is almost completely done by robots. In addition, construction robots lay a brick wall in less time than a team of workers can, and drones are gradually taking the place of traditional home delivery systems. In addition, Google is developing self-driving cars that could soon replace cabdrivers and truckers. As a result, people engaging in any kind of routine or repetitive work are at risk of being replaced by machines. If this trend continues—and it surely will— the country's workforce could lose millions of jobs. For this reason, people should anticipate this trend and begin training for the jobs that are least likely to be automated.

Thesis statement

—Sean Murphy (student)

FYI

What to Avoid in Introductions

When writing an introduction, avoid the following:

- Beginning your essay by announcing what you plan to write about.

  PHRASES TO AVOID

  This essay is about . . .
  In my essay, I will discuss . . .

- Apologizing for your ideas.

  PHRASES TO AVOID

  Although I don't know much about this subject . . .
  I might not be an expert, but . . .

PRACTICE

14-1   Look through the essays in Chapters 15 and 16, and find one introduction you think is particularly effective. Be prepared to explain the strengths of the introduction you chose.

FYI

Choosing a Title

Every essay should have a **title** that suggests the subject of the essay and makes people want to read it. Here are a few tips for properly formatting your title.

- Capitalize all words except for articles (*a, an, the*), prepositions (*at, to, of, around,* and so on), and coordinating conjunctions (*and, but,* and so on), unless they are the first or last word of the title.
- Do not underline or italicize your title or enclose it in quotation marks. Do not type your title in all capital letters.
- Center the title at the top of the first page. Double-space between the title and the first line of your essay.

As you consider a title for your paper, think about the following options.

- *A title can highlight a key word or term that appears in the essay.*
  "Migrant vs. Refugee: What's the Difference?"
- *A title can be a straightforward announcement.*
  "Vaccinations Are for the Good of the Nation"
- *A title can establish a personal connection with readers.*
  "I Owe It All to Community College"
- *A title can be a familiar saying or a quotation from your essay itself.*
  "I Want a Wife"

PRACTICE

14-2 Using the different options for creating titles discussed in the FYI box above, write two titles for each of the essays described below.

1. A student writes an essay about three people who disappeared mysteriously: Amelia Earhart, aviator; Ambrose Bierce, writer; and Jimmy Hoffa, union leader. In the body paragraphs, the student describes the circumstances surrounding their disappearances.

   _____

   _____

2. A student writes an essay describing the harmful effects of steroids on student athletes. In the body paragraphs, he shows the effects on the heart, brain, and other organs.

   _____

   _____

3. A student writes an essay explaining why she joined the Navy Reserve. In the body paragraphs, she discusses her need to earn money for college tuition, her wish to learn a trade, and her desire to see the world.

   _____

   _____

 # 14b Writing Conclusions

A conclusion should reinforce the main point of your essay and bring your essay to a satisfying close. Because your conclusion is the last thing readers see, they often judge your entire essay by its effectiveness. For this reason, conclusions should be planned, drafted, and revised carefully.

Like an introduction, a **conclusion** should be a full paragraph. There are many ways to structure a conclusion, but a useful pattern to master is one that begins with a **summary statement** that reinforces the essay's thesis and ends with some general **concluding remarks**. The following diagram illustrates the general shape of a conclusion.

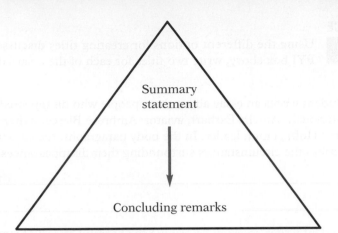

Here are some options you can experiment with when you write your conclusions. (In each of the sample concluding paragraphs that follow, the summary statement is underlined and labeled.)

Concluding with a Narrative

A narrative conclusion can bring an event discussed in the essay to a logical, satisfying close.

Summary statement

> I went to Philadelphia with my boys to share the thing my father and I had shared—a love for history. Unfortunately, they were more interested in horse-and-buggy rides, overpriced knickknacks, the tall buildings, and parades. As we walked into Independence Hall, though, I noticed that the boys became quiet. They felt it. They felt the thick historical air around us. I watched them look around as the guide painted a vivid picture of the times and spoke of the marches down Broad Street and the clashing of ideas as our forefathers debated and even fought for freedom. I felt my husband behind me and took my eyes off of my boys to turn to the left; I could almost see my father. I almost whispered out loud to him, "We were here."
>
> —Shannon Lewis (student)

Concluding with a Recommendation

Once you think you have convinced readers that a problem exists, you can make recommendations in your conclusion about how the problem should be solved.

Solutions for the binge-drinking problem on college campuses are not easy, but both schools and students need to acknowledge the problem and to try to solve it. Schools that have an alcohol-free policy should aggressively enforce it, and schools that do not have such a policy should implement one. In addition, students should take responsibility for their actions and resolve to drink responsibly. No one should get hurt or die from drinking too much, but if something does not change soon, many more students will.

Summary statement

—April Moen (student)

Concluding with a Quotation

A well-chosen quotation—even a brief one—can be an effective concluding strategy. In the following paragraph, the quotation reinforces the main idea of the essay.

The Pure Food and Drug Act is the most important regulatory statute in the history of the United States. In his message to Congress, Theodore Roosevelt announced that the Pure Food and Drug Act would "secure the health and welfare of the consuming public." After weeks of debate, the bill was passed on February 12, 1906. Nearly one hundred years after its passage, this act continues to protect the American public from mislabeled or misrepresented food and drug products. It makes sure that manufacturers list active ingredients and follow standards that are established by law. Since its enactment, millions of consumers have benefitted from improved food quality and the knowledge that products they bought are safe.

Summary statement

—Rose Erlich (student)

Concluding with a Prediction

This type of conclusion not only sums up the thesis but also looks to the future.

Whether people like it or not, texting is not going to go away anytime soon. This generation and future generations are going to use "text speak" and become even more comfortable with communicating via text messages. Texting has already had a large impact on today's world. In fact, texting has helped put the written word back into our lives, making people more comfortable with the skill of writing, & it's a fast, EZ way 2 communic8.

Summary statement

—Courtney Anttila (student)

FYI

What to Avoid in Conclusions

When writing a conclusion, avoid the following:

■ Introducing new ideas. Your conclusion should sum up the ideas you discuss in your essay, not open up new lines of thought.

■ Apologizing for your opinions, ideas, or conclusions. Apologies will undercut your readers' confidence in you.

PHRASES TO AVOID

At least that is my opinion . . .
I could be wrong, but . . .

■ Using unnecessary phrases to announce your essay is coming to a close.

PHRASES TO AVOID

In summary, . . .
In conclusion, . . .

PRACTICE

14-3   Look at the essays in Chapters 15 and 16, and locate one conclusion you think is particularly effective. Be prepared to explain the strengths of the conclusion you chose.

Robert Alexander/Archive
Photos/Getty Images

TEST · revise · edit · proofread

Look back at the essay you wrote for Chapter 13. **TEST** what you have written one more time. Then, revise and edit your introduction and conclusion accordingly. Make sure your introduction creates interest, prepares readers for the essay to follow, and includes a clear thesis statement. Also, make sure your conclusion contains a summary statement and includes general concluding remarks. Finally, make sure your essay has an appropriate and effective title.

EDITING PRACTICE

The following student essay has an undeveloped introduction and conclusion. Decide what introductory and concluding strategies would be best for the essay. Then, rewrite both the introduction and the conclusion. Finally, suggest an interesting title for the essay.

_____

This essay is about three of the most dangerous jobs. They are piloting small planes, logging, and fishing.

Flying a small plane can be dangerous. For example, pilots who fly tiny planes that spray pesticides on farmers' fields do not have to comply with the safety rules for large airplanes. They also have to fly very low in order to spray the right fields. This leaves little room for error. Also, pilots of air-taxis and small commuter planes die in much greater numbers than airline pilots do. In some places, like parts of Alaska, there are long distances and few roads, so many small planes are needed. Their pilots are four times more likely to die than other pilots because of bad weather and poor visibility. In general, flying a small plane can be very risky.

Another dangerous job is logging. Loggers always are at risk of having parts of trees or heavy machinery fall on them. Tree trunks often have odd shapes, so they are hard to control while they are being transported. As a result, they often break loose from equipment that is supposed to move them. In addition, weather conditions, like snow or rain, can cause dangers. Icy or wet conditions increase the risk to loggers, who can fall from trees or slip when they are sawing a tree. Because loggers often work in remote places, it is very hard to get prompt medical aid. For this reason, a wound that could easily be treated in a hospital may be fatal to a logger.

Perhaps the most dangerous occupation is working in the fishing industry. Like loggers, professional fishermen work in unsafe conditions. They use heavy machinery to pull up nets and to move large amounts of fish. The combination of icy or slippery boat decks and large nets and cages makes the job unsafe. The weather is often very bad, so fishermen are at risk of falling overboard during a storm and drowning. In fact, drowning is the most common cause of death in this industry. Also, like logging, fishing is done far from medical help, so even minor injuries can be very serious.

In conclusion, piloting, logging, and fishing are three of the most dangerous occupations.

COLLABORATIVE ACTIVITY

Find a magazine or newspaper article that interests you. Cut off the introduction and conclusion, and bring the body of the article to class. Ask your group to decide on the best strategies for introducing and concluding the article. Then, collaborate on writing new opening and closing paragraphs and an interesting title.

review checklist

Introductions and Conclusions

✔ The introduction of your essay should include opening remarks and a thesis statement. (See 14a.) You can begin an essay with any of the following options.

A narrative   A quotation
A question   A surprising statement
A definition

✔ Your title should suggest the subject of your essay and make people want to read further. (See 14a.)

✔ The conclusion of your essay should include a summary statement and some general concluding remarks. (See 14b.) You can conclude an essay with any of the following options.

A narrative   A quotation
A recommendation   A prediction

15 Patterns of Essay Development

Exemplification, Narration, Process, Cause and Effect, and Comparison and Contrast

Pete Saloutos/GettyImages

In this chapter, you will learn to organize your essays according to the following patterns of development:

- exemplification (15a)
- narration (15b)
- process (15c)
- cause and effect (15d)
- comparison and contrast (15e)

As you learned in Chapters 4 through 12, writers have a variety of options for developing ideas within a paragraph. These options include *exemplification, narration, description, process, cause and effect, comparison and contrast, classification, definition,* and *argument.* When you write an essay, you can use these same patterns of development to help you organize your material.

In your college courses, different assignments and writing situations call for different patterns of essay development.

- If an essay exam question asked you to compare two systems of government, you would use *comparison and contrast.*

- If an English composition assignment asked you to tell about a childhood experience, you would use *narration.*

- If a research paper on environmental pollution in a particular community called for examples of dangerous waste-disposal practices, you would use *exemplification.*

As you will see in this chapter and in the chapter that follows, the skills you learned for writing paragraphs can also be applied to writing essays.

15a Exemplification Essays

Exemplification illustrates a general statement with one or more specific examples. An **exemplification essay** uses specific examples to support a thesis.

When you **TEST** an **exemplification** essay, make sure it includes all these elements:

T **Thesis Statement**—The introduction of an exemplification essay should include a clear **thesis statement** that identifies the essay's main idea—the idea the examples will support.

E **Evidence**—The body paragraphs should present **evidence**, fully developed examples that support the thesis. Each body paragraph should be introduced by a topic sentence that identifies the example or group of related examples that the paragraph will discuss.

S **Summary Statement**—The conclusion of an exemplification essay should include a **summary statement** that reinforces the essay's thesis.

T **Transitions**—An exemplification essay should use appropriate **transitional words and phrases** to connect examples within paragraphs and between one paragraph and another.

Moving from Assignment to Thesis

The wording of your assignment may suggest that you write an exemplification essay. For example, you may be asked to *illustrate* or to *give examples*. Once you decide that your assignment calls for exemplification, you need to develop a thesis that reflects this purpose.

ASSIGNMENT	THESIS STATEMENT
Education Should children be taught only in their native languages or in English as well? Support your answer with examples of specific students' experiences.	The success of students in a bilingual third-grade class suggests the value of teaching elementary school students in English as well as in their native languages.
Literature Does William Shakespeare's *Othello* have to end tragically? Illustrate your position with references to specific characters.	Each of the three major characters in *Othello* contributes to the play's tragic ending.
Composition Discuss the worst job you ever had, including specific examples to support your thesis.	My summer job at a fast-food restaurant was my worst job because of the endless stream of rude customers, the many boring tasks I had to perform, and my manager's insensitivity.

Organizing an Exemplification Essay

In an exemplification essay, each body paragraph can develop a single example or discuss several related examples. Each example you select should clearly support your thesis. The topic sentence should introduce the example (or group of related examples) that the paragraph will discuss.

Essay Map: *One Example per Paragraph*

Essay Map: *Several Related Examples per Paragraph*

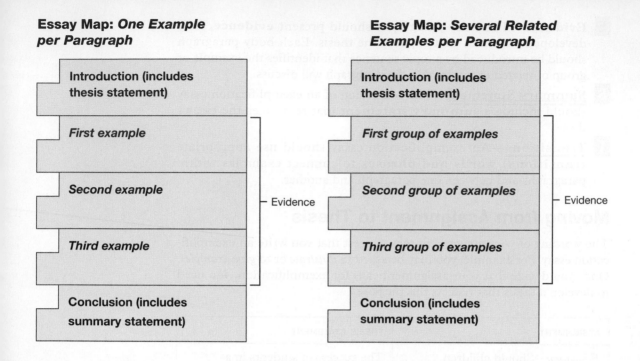

Transitions in Exemplification Essays

For a list of transitions frequently used in exemplification, see Chapter 4, page 81.

Transitional words and phrases should introduce your examples and indicate how one example is related to another.

Case Study: A Student Writes an Exemplification Essay

Kyle Sims, a student in a first-year writing course, was asked to write an essay about a popular hobby or interest. Kyle imagined that most of his classmates would write about topics like video games or sports, and while he knew a lot about sports, his knowledge came from being a spectator, not a participant. He decided to use this knowledge by writing about extreme sports.

Once he had settled on a topic, Kyle did some **freewriting**. When he read over his freewriting, he saw that he had come up with three kinds of information: ideas about the dangers of extreme sports, about the challenges they present, and about the equipment they require. He then wrote a **thesis statement** that identified the three points he wanted to make. After **brainstorming** about each of these points, he decided that he had enough material to begin drafting his essay.

As he wrote his **first draft**, Kyle devoted one paragraph to each point, using examples to develop his body paragraphs. When he finished his draft, he **TEST**ed it. He was satisfied with his thesis, which told readers what points he was going to make about extreme sports and also conveyed the idea that they were not like ordinary sports. His summary statement seemed logical and appropriate. However, realizing that his readers might not know much about extreme sports, Kyle added more examples to illustrate a range of different kinds of extreme sports. He also added more transitions to lead readers from one example to the next.

When Kyle **revised** his draft, he rewrote his topic sentences so they clearly identified the three points he wanted to make about extreme sports. After he finished his revision, he **edited** and **proofread** carefully and checked to make sure his essay met his instructor's **format** requirements.

The following final draft includes all the elements Kyle looked for when he **TEST**ed his essay.

Model Exemplification Essay

Read Kyle's finished essay, and complete the tasks in Practice 15-1.

TEST	
T	Thesis Statement
E	Evidence
S	Summary Statement
T	Transitions

Going to Extremes

Introduction

1   For years, sports like football, baseball, and basketball have been popular in cities, suburbs, and small rural towns. For some young people, however, these sports no longer seem exciting, especially when compared to "extreme sports," such as snowboarding and BMX racing. Extreme sports are different from more familiar sports because they are dangerous, they are physically challenging, and they require specialized equipment.

2   First, extreme sports are dangerous. For example, snowboarders take chances with snowy hills and unpredictable bumps. They zoom down mountains at high speeds, which is typical of extreme sports. In addition, snowboarders and skateboarders risk painful falls as they do their tricks. Also, many extreme sports, like rock climbing, bungee jumping, and skydiving, are performed at very high altitudes. Moreover, the bungee jumper has to jump from a very high place, and there is always a danger of getting tangled with the bungee cord. People who participate in extreme sports accept—and even enjoy—these dangers.

Topic sentence (introduces first point)

E Examples

Body paragraphs

3   In addition, extreme sports are very difficult. For instance, surfers have to learn to balance surfboards while dealing with wind and waves. Bungee jumpers may have to learn how to do difficult stunts while jumping off a high bridge or a dam. Another example of the physical challenge of extreme sports can be found in BMX racing. BMX racers have to learn to steer a lightweight bike on a dirt track that has jumps and banked corners. These extreme sports require skills that most people do not naturally have. These special skills have to be learned, and participants in extreme sports enjoy this challenge.

E Examples

Topic sentence (introduces second point)

Topic sentence
(introduces third point)

Body paragraphs

Examples

E

4   Finally, almost all extreme sports require specialized equipment. For example, surfers need surfboards that are light but strong. They can choose epoxy boards, which are stronger, or fiberglass boards, which are lighter. They can choose shortboards, which are shorter than seven feet and are easier to maneuver, or they can use longboards, which are harder and slower to turn in the water but are easier to learn on. Also, surfers have to get special wax for their boards to keep from slipping as they are paddling out into the water. For surfing in cold water, they need wetsuits that trap their own body heat. Other extreme sports require different kinds of specialized equipment, but those who participate in them are willing to buy whatever they need.

Conclusion

5   Clearly, extreme sports are very different from other sports. Maybe it is because they are so different that they have become so popular in recent years. Already, snowboarding, BMX racing, and other extreme sports are featured in the Olympics. The Summer and Winter X Games are televised on ESPN and ABC, and sports like BMX racing, snowboarding, surfing, and snowmobiling get national attention on these programs. With all this publicity, extreme sports are likely to become even more popular—despite their challenges.

PRACTICE

15-1

1. Restate Kyle's thesis in your own words.

2. What three points about extreme sports does Kyle make in the topic sentences of his body paragraphs?

3. What examples of extreme sports does Kyle give in paragraph 1? What examples of dangers does he give in paragraph 2? In paragraph 4, Kyle discusses surfing, giving examples of the equipment surfers need. List this equipment.

4. Is Kyle's introduction effective? How else might he have opened his essay?

5. Paraphrase Kyle's summary statement.

6. What is this essay's greatest strength? What is its greatest weakness?

grammar in context

Exemplification

When you write an exemplification essay, you may introduce your examples with transitional words and phrases like *First* or *In addition*. If you do, be sure to use a comma after the introductory transitional word or phrase.

<u>First,</u> extreme sports are dangerous.

<u>In addition,</u> extreme sports are very difficult.

<u>Finally,</u> almost all extreme sports require specialized equipment.

For information on using commas with introductory and transitional words and phrases, see 34b.

Step-by-Step Guide: Writing an Exemplification Essay

Now, you are ready to write an exemplification essay on one of the topics listed below (or a topic of your choice).

TOPICS

Reasons to start (or not to start) college right after high school
The three best products ever invented
What kinds of people or images should appear on U.S. postage stamps? Why?
Advantages (or disadvantages) of being a young parent
Athletes who really are role models
Four items students need to survive in college
What messages do rap or hip-hop artists send to listeners?
Study strategies that work
Careers you are considering
Several recent national or world news events that gave you hope

As you write your essay, follow these steps:

- Make sure your topic calls for exemplification, and then find ideas to write about; next, identify your main idea, and write a thesis statement.

- Choose examples to support your thesis; then, arrange your supporting examples in a logical order, making an outline if necessary.

- Draft your essay.

- **TEST** your essay, referring to the **TEST**ing an Exemplification Essay checklist on page 242.

Plan

Organize

Draft

TEST

Revise, edit,
and proofread

- Revise and edit your essay, referring to the two Self-Assessment Checklists in Chapter 13.
- Proofread your essay, and make sure it follows your instructor's format guidelines.

TESTing an exemplification essay

T hesis Statement Unifies Your Essay

☐ Does your introduction include a **thesis statement** that clearly states your essay's main idea?

E vidence Supports Your Essay's Thesis Statement

☐ Do you have enough **evidence**—fully developed examples—to support your thesis?

☐ Do all your examples support your thesis or should some be deleted?

S ummary Statement Reinforces Your Essay's Main Idea

☐ Does your conclusion include a **summary statement** that reinforces your essay's thesis?

T ransitions

☐ Do you include **transitions** that move readers from one example to the next?

Exemplification in Action

In "No, I Do Not Want to Pet Your Dog," Farhad Manjoo uses **exemplification** to structure his essay.

No, I Do Not Want to Pet Your Dog

Farhad Manjoo

Farhad Manjoo was born in South Africa in 1978 and moved with his family to the United States when he was a young boy. He graduated from Cornell University, where he served as the editor of the student newspaper. He has worked as a staff writer for *Slate* and has been a regular contributor to National Public Radio. He currently writes the "State of the Art" column for the *New York Times* and is the author of *True Enough: Learning to Live in a Post-Fact Society* (2008). In "No, I Do Not

Want to Pet Your Dog," which first appeared in *Slate*, Manjoo responds to an everyday irritation by describing an America in which dogs have "achieved dominion" over spaces from which they were once barred. As you read, note how he uses examples to poke fun at the way dog owners talk about and treat their beloved pets.

1   The other day I walked into my gym and saw a dog. A half-dozen people were crowding around him, cooing and petting. He was a big dog, a lean and muscular Doberman with, I later learned, the sort of hair-trigger bark you'd prize if you wanted to protect a big stash of gold bullion.

2   "This is Y.," the dog's owner said. No explanation was offered for the pooch's presence, as if it were the most natural thing in the world to have a dog in a place usually reserved for human beings. *Huh*, I thought.

3   The dog came up to me, because in my experience that's what dogs do when you don't want them to come up to you. They get up real close, touching you, licking you, theatrically begging you to respond. The dog pushed his long face toward my hand, the canine equivalent of a high five. And so—in the same way it's rude to leave a high-fiver hanging, especially if the high-fiver has big teeth and a strong jaw—I was expected to pet him. I ran my hand across his head half-heartedly. I guess I was fairly sure he wouldn't snap and bite me, but stranger things have happened—for instance, dogs snapping and biting people all the time.

4   Anyway, happily, I survived.

5   But wait a second. Come on! Why was this dog here? And why was no one perturbed that this dog was here? When this beast was barking at passersby through the window as we were all working out, why did no one go, *Hey, just throwing this out there, should we maybe not have this distracting, possibly dangerous animal by the free weights?*

6   No one was asking because no one could ask. Sometime in the last decade, dogs achieved dominion over urban America. They are everywhere now, allowed in places that used to belong exclusively to humans, and sometimes only to human adults: the office, restaurants, museums, buses, trains, malls, supermarkets, barber shops, banks, post offices. Even at the park and other places where dogs belong, they've been given free rein. Dogs are frequently allowed to wander off leash, to run toward you and around you, to run across the baseball field or basketball court, to get up in your grill. Even worse than the dogs are the owners, who seem never to consider whether there may be people in the gym/office/restaurant/museum who do not care to be in close proximity to their dogs. After all, what kind of monster would have a problem with a poor innocent widdle doggie? It's a dog's world. We just live in it. And it's awful. Bad dogs!

7   Not everyone agrees with me on this issue. Some people—or maybe even most people, since dogs, like zombies, have an insidious way of turning opponents into allies—love that dogs abound. If you adore dogs but aren't able to keep one, the world is now your dog park, with pooches everywhere to pet and nuzzle and otherwise brighten your day.

WORD POWER
dominion the power to rule

WORD POWER
proximity nearness

WORD POWER
insidious harmful but enticing

8   I am not a dog person. (Could you tell?) It's not that I actively despise mutts; I just don't have much time for them, in the same way I don't have time for crossword puzzles or Maroon 5. Now imagine if, everywhere you went, whatever you did, Maroon 5 was always playing and everyone pretended it was totally normal—that this permanent new situation was not in any way offensive, distracting, dirty, and potentially dangerous.

9   OK, bad example.

10   But here's my problem: There's now a cultural assumption that everyone must love dogs. Dog owners are rarely forced to reckon with the idea that there are people who aren't enthralled by their furry friends, and that taking their dogs everywhere might not be completely pleasant for these folks.

11   Example: If you're in the office and someone has brought her dog in for the day—because, *fun!*—the dog is sure to come around you, get between your legs, rub against your thigh, take a nap on your feet, or do some other annoying thing.

12   If the dog's owner notices these antics, I can promise you she won't apologize for the imposition. Nor will she ask you if you mind her dog doing what he's doing. Nor will she pull on its leash, because there won't be a leash, this being an office, where dogs are as welcome as Wi-Fi and free coffee.

13   Instead, if the owner says anything, it will be on the order of, "Don't worry, he loves people!" Oh, OK then! I guess I'll just take your word for it, and forget for the moment that 1,000 Americans a day go to emergency rooms because of dog bites. More Americans seek medical attention for dog bites than for choking or falls. You're more likely to have to go to a doctor for a bite than to call the fire department for a home fire. Like it or not, American dog owner, your pet is a hazard.

14   But let's leave aside the possibility that I'm scared (maybe legitimately!) of your dog, since you've assured me your dog loves people, and there's no chance you could be wrong. What if I'm allergic? Or what if I just plain hate your dog? What if I think he's dirty, since after all he did just put his nose in another dog's butt? And what if I just want to go through my workday without being slobbered on by an animal?

15   I know this sounds curmudgeonly. You want to shake me and tell me to snap out of it, to get over myself and just love dogs already. But that's because you like dogs and don't see anything but good in them. For you, a dog is like ice cream. What churl doesn't like ice cream? Well, I'm that churl—I'm canine intolerant.

16   To give you a sense of how I feel when I'm accosted by your dog, let's replace that animal with my 2½-year-old son. Now, I love my son, but on any objective scale of socially acceptable behavior, he is the worst. He's loud. He's inconsiderate of people's personal space—if he's left free he won't watch where he's walking and will run into you, either on purpose or accidentally. He's jumpy and fidgety in confined spaces; in an airplane it is physically impossible to restrain him from kicking the seat in front of him.

WORD POWER

curmudgeonly bad tempered

WORD POWER

accosted approached in an aggressive way

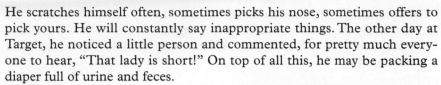

He scratches himself often, sometimes picks his nose, sometimes offers to pick yours. He will constantly say inappropriate things. The other day at Target, he noticed a little person and commented, for pretty much everyone to hear, "That lady is short!" On top of all this, he may be packing a diaper full of urine and feces.

17 Weirdly, irrationally, despite all this, I feel the same way about my son as you do about your dog: I love him unconditionally and just don't understand why even strangers wouldn't want him around all the time. Indeed, I think almost everything he does, even the inappropriate things, is the cutest behavior ever exhibited in human history.

18 And yet, still, I rein him in. I realize that, although he's impossibly cute, it's possible he might aggravate some people. For this reason, whenever I go into public spaces with my toddler, I treat him as if I were handling nuclear waste or a dangerous animal. I keep him confined. I shush him. If he does anything out of turn—screams, touches people—I make a show of telling him to quit it and I apologize profusely. And, finally, there are some places that are completely off-limits to my son: nice restaurants, contemplative adult spaces like grown-up museums and coffee shops, the gym, and the office. Especially the office.

19 Yes, there are parents who don't act this way, awful parents who let their terrible kids run free. The rest of us hate those people because they give all parents a bad name. But I'll submit there are many more such dog owners than there are overindulgent parents. Most parents I know are mortified by the thought that their children might be causing anguish for others. This is evident in the world around you: It's why your coworkers rarely bring their toddlers to work. It's why two-year-olds don't approach you in the park and lick your leg or ask you whether you need to visit the potty. It's why, when a child is being unruly in a supermarket or restaurant, you'll usually see his parents strive to get him to knock it off.

20 But dog owners? They seem to suffer few qualms about their animals' behavior. That's why there are so many dogs running around at the park, jumping up on the bench beside you while you're trying to read a book, the owner never asking if it's OK with you. That's why, when you're at a café, the dog at the neighboring table feels free to curl up under your seat. That's why there's a dog at your office right at this moment and you're having to pretend that he's just the cutest.

21 Well, no more, my fellow doggie skeptics. Let's take back the peace we're owed. The next time your young, happy coworker brings in his dog for the day, tell him the office is not a canine playpen. It's time to take that dog home.

Focus on the Pattern

1. What examples does Manjoo give to support his statement that dogs "are everywhere now" (6)? What evidence does he give to support his belief that this is a problem?

2. In paragraph 10, Manjoo says, "There's now a cultural assumption that everyone must love dogs." Does he give examples to support this statement? If so, where? Can you think of any supporting examples he might add?

Writing Practice

1. Do you agree with Manjoo? Write an exemplification essay that illustrates the problems dogs cause in your own life—for example, in your workplace or on the streets of your community.

2. Do you disagree with Manjoo? Write an exemplification essay that illustrates the benefits of a policy of welcoming dogs in your community, in your workplace, or on your campus.

 # 15b Narrative Essays

Narration tells a story, usually presenting a series of events in chrono-logical (time) order, moving from beginning to end. A **narrative essay** can tell a personal story, or it can recount a recent or historical event or a fictional story.

When you **TEST** a **narrative** essay, make sure it includes all these elements:

T **Thesis Statement**—The introduction of a narrative essay should include a **thesis statement** that communicates the main idea—the point the story is making.

E **Evidence**—The body paragraphs should tell the story, one event at a time, with each event providing **evidence**—examples and details—to support the thesis. Events are usually presented in chronological (time) order.

S **Summary Statement**—The conclusion of a narrative essay should include a **summary statement** that reinforces the essay's main idea.

T **Transitions**—Throughout a narrative essay, **transitional words and phrases** should connect events in time, showing how one event leads to the next.

Moving from Assignment to Thesis

The wording of your assignment may suggest that you write a narrative essay. For example, you may be asked to *tell*, *trace*, *summarize events*, or *recount*. Once you decide that your assignment calls for narration, you need to develop a thesis statement that reflects this purpose.

ASSIGNMENT	THESIS STATEMENT
Psychology Write a case study tracing the treatment of an alcohol-dependent adolescent patient.	With targeted treatment, it is possible for an adolescent to overcome alcohol dependence.
American history Summarize the events that occurred during President Franklin Delano Roosevelt's first one hundred days in office.	Although many thought they were extreme, the measures enacted by Roosevelt during his first one hundred days in office were necessary to fight the economic depression.
Political science Trace the development of the Mississippi Freedom Democratic Party.	As the Mississippi Freedom Democratic Party developed in the 1960s, it found a voice that spoke for equality and justice.

Organizing a Narrative Essay

When you write a narrative essay, you can discuss one event or several in each paragraph of your essay.

Essay Map: *One Event per Paragraph*

Essay Map: *Several Events per Paragraph*

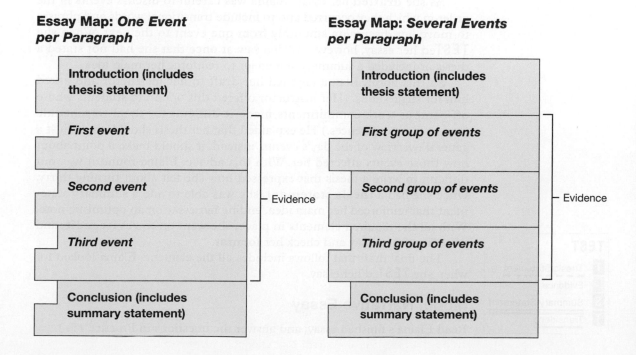

Essay Map: One Event per Paragraph

- Introduction (includes thesis statement)
- First event
- Second event
- Third event
- Conclusion (includes summary statement)

Evidence

Essay Map: Several Events per Paragraph

- Introduction (includes thesis statement)
- First group of events
- Second group of events
- Third group of events
- Conclusion (includes summary statement)

Evidence

For a list of transitions frequently used in narration, see Chapter 6, page 100.

Transitions in Narrative Essays

Sometimes, to add interest to your narrative, you may decide not to use exact chronological order. For example, you might begin with the end of your story and then move back to the beginning to trace the events that led to this outcome. However you arrange the events, carefully worded topic sentences and clear transitional words and phrases will help readers follow your narrative.

Case Study: A Student Writes a Narrative Essay

WORD POWER
milestone an important event; a turning point

Elaina Corrato, a returning student who was older than most of her classmates, wasn't sure how to proceed when her writing instructor gave the class an assignment to write about a milestone in their lives. The first topic that came to mind was her recent thirtieth birthday, but she was reluctant to reveal her age to her classmates. However, when she learned that no one except her instructor would read her essay, she decided to write about this topic.

Elaina began by rereading entries she had made in her **writing journal** in the days before and after her birthday as well as on the day itself. Even before she began to write, she saw that her essay would be a narrative that traced her experiences on that day.

As she **drafted** her essay, Elaina was careful to discuss events in the order in which they occurred and to include transitional words and phrases to move her discussion smoothly from one event to the next. When she **TEST**ed her essay, however, Elaina saw at once that she had not stated a thesis or included a summary statement to reinforce her main idea.

At this point, Elaina emailed her draft to her instructor and asked him for suggestions. (Her instructor offered this option to students whose off-campus work commitments made it difficult for them to schedule face-to-face conferences.) He explained that her thesis should not be just a general overview of the day's events; instead, it should make a point about how those events affected her. With this advice, Elaina found it was not difficult to write a thesis that expressed how she felt about turning thirty. Once she had a **thesis statement**, she was able to add a summary statement that reinforced her main idea, ending her essay on an optimistic note. With all the required elements in place, she went on to **revise**, **edit**, and **proofread** her essay and check her **format**.

The final draft that follows includes all the elements Elaina looked for when she **TEST**ed her essay.

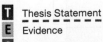

TEST
T Thesis Statement
E Evidence
S Summary Statement
T Transitions

Model Narrative Essay

Read Elaina's finished essay, and answer the questions in Practice 15-2.

Reflections

1   Turning thirty did not bother me at all. My list of "Things to Do before I Die" was far from complete, but I knew I had plenty of time to do them. In fact, turning thirty seemed like no big deal to me. If anything, it was a milestone I was happy to be approaching. <u>Unfortunately, other people had</u> <u>different ideas about this milestone, and eventually their ideas made me</u> <u>rethink my own.</u>

2   <u>As the big day approached, my family kept teasing me about it.</u> My sister kept asking me if I felt any different. She couldn't believe I wasn't upset, but I didn't pay any attention to her. I was looking forward to a new chapter in my life. I liked my job, I was making good progress toward my college degree, and I was healthy and happy. Why should turning thirty be a problem? So, I made no special plans for my birthday, and I decided to treat it as just another day.

Topic sentence (introduces first group of events)

E

Events and details

3   <u>My birthday fell on a Saturday, and I enjoyed the chance to sleep in.</u> After I got up and had breakfast, I did my laundry and then set out for the supermarket. I rarely put on makeup or fixed my hair on Saturdays. After all, I didn't have to go to work or to school. I was only running errands in the neighborhood. <u>Later on,</u> though, as I waited in line at the deli counter, I caught sight of my reflection in the mirrored meat case. <u>At first,</u> I thought it wasn't really me. The woman staring back at me looked so old! She had bags under her eyes, and she even had a few gray hairs. I was so upset by my reflection that on my way home I stopped and bought a mud mask— guaranteed to make me look younger.

Topic sentence (introduces second group of events)

E

Events and details

Body paragraphs

4   <u>As I walked up the street toward my house, I saw something attached</u> <u>to the front railing.</u> When I got closer, I realized that it was a bunch of black balloons. There was also a big sign that said "Over the Hill" in big black letters. I'd been trying to think about my birthday in positive terms, but my family seemed to have other ideas. Obviously, it was time for the mud mask.

Topic sentence (introduces third group of events)

E

Events and details

5   <u>After quickly unloading my groceries, I ran upstairs to apply the</u> <u>mask.</u> The box promised a "rejuvenating look," and that was exactly what I wanted. I spread the sticky brown mixture on my face, and it hardened instantly. <u>As</u> I sat on my bed, waiting for the mask to work its magic, I heard the doorbell ring. <u>Then,</u> I heard familiar voices and my husband calling me to come down, saying that I had company. I couldn't answer him. I couldn't talk (or even smile) without cracking the mask. <u>At this point,</u> I retreated to the bathroom to make myself presentable for my friends and family. This task was not easy.

Topic sentence (introduces fourth group of events)

E

Events and details

Topic sentence
(introduces fifth
group of events)

Body paragraphs

Events and details

Conclusion

E

6   When I managed to scrub off the mud mask, my face was covered with little red pimples. Apparently, my sensitive skin couldn't take the harsh chemicals. At first, I didn't think the promise of "rejuvenated" skin was what I got. I had to admit, though, that my skin did look a lot younger. In fact, when I finally went downstairs to celebrate my birthday, I looked as young as a teenager—a teenager with acne.

7   Despite other people's grim warnings, I discovered that although turning thirty was a milestone, it wasn't a game-changer. I learned a lot that day, and I learned even more in the days that followed. What I finally realized was that I couldn't ignore turning thirty, but having a thirtieth birthday didn't have to mean that my life was over.

PRACTICE

15-2

1. Restate Elaina's thesis statement in your own words.

2. What specific events and details support Elaina's thesis? List as many as you can.

3. Do you think paragraph 2 is necessary? How would the essay be different without it?

4. Paraphrase Elaina's summary statement. Do you think it effectively reinforces her essay's main idea?

5. What is this essay's greatest strength? What is its greatest weakness?

grammar in context

Narration

When you write a narrative essay, you tell a story. When you get caught up in your story, you might sometimes find yourself stringing a list of incidents together without proper punctuation, creating a **run-on**.

INCORRECT   As the big day approached, my family kept teasing me about it, my sister kept asking me if I felt any different.

CORRECT   As the big day approached, my family kept teasing me about it. My sister kept asking me if I felt any different.

For information on how to identify and correct run-ons, see Chapter 24.

Step-by-Step Guide: Writing a Narrative Essay

Now, you are ready to write a narrative essay on one of the topics listed below (or a topic of your choice).

TOPICS

The story of your education
Your idea of a perfect day
The plot summary of a terrible book or movie
A time when you had to make a split-second decision
Your first confrontation with authority
An important historical event
A day on which everything went wrong
A story from your family's history
Your employment history, from first to most recent job
A biography of your pet

As you write your essay, follow these steps:

Plan

Organize

Draft

TEST

Revise, edit, and proofread

- Make sure your topic calls for narration, and then find ideas to write about; next, identify your main idea, and write a thesis statement.

- Choose events and details to support your thesis, and arrange events in chronological order, making an outline if necessary.

- Draft your essay.

- **TEST** your essay, referring to the **TEST**ing a Narrative Essay checklist below.

- Revise and edit your essay, referring to the two Self-Assessment Checklists in Chapter 13.

- Proofread your essay, and make sure it follows your instructor's format guidelines.

TEST ing a narrative essay

T hesis Statement Unifies Your Essay

☐ Does your introduction include a **thesis statement** that clearly states your essay's main idea?

E vidence Supports Your Essay's Thesis Statement

☐ Does all your **evidence**—events and details—support your thesis, or should some be deleted?

☐ Do you include enough specific details to make your narrative interesting?

☐ Are the events you discuss arranged in clear chronological (time) order?

Summary Statement Reinforces Your Essay's Main Idea

☐ Does your conclusion include a **summary statement** that reinforces your essay's thesis?

Transitions

☐ Do you include enough **transitions** to make the sequence of events clear to your reader?

Narration in Action

In "Watching Spider-Man in Santo Domingo," Junot Díaz uses **narration** to structure his essay.

Watching Spider-Man in Santo Domingo

Junot Díaz

Junot Díaz was born in the Dominican Republic and raised in the United States, where he graduated from Rutgers College. His books include *The Brief Wondrous Life of Oscar Wao* (2007), which won the Pulitzer Prize and the National Book Critics Circle Award; *This Is How You Lose Her* (2013), a National Book Award finalist; and the picture book *Islandborn* (2018). Díaz is currently a professor of writing at the Massachusetts Institute of Technology and the fiction editor at *Boston Review*. His many awards include a MacArthur Fellowship, a PEN/Malamud Award, and a Dayton Literary Peace Prize. He has been active in a number of organizations that offer support to immigrants. In this essay, published in 2017 in the *New Yorker*, Díaz explores his first exposure to television and to America.

1   I came late to television. I was five when my neighbor in Santo Domingo bought the first set on our street, the first I'd ever laid eyes on. I can still see it in my mind's eye: a small color TV with long insectoid antennae; an alien device to a kid who had spent most of his childhood with no running water, who considered watching goats climb onto cars and houses serious entertainment.

2   Maybe I would have been O.K. if I'd seen anything else: the news, a variety show, a political debate. But my earliest exposure to television was a Spider-Man cartoon—one of the flipped-out Ralph Bakshi episodes from the late sixties. In other words, the first thing I saw on TV was America.

3   A little context: I had a father in New York City whom I did not remember, and who (it was promised) would one day deliver my family to the States. And here was my first television and my first cartoon and my first superhero—a hero who, like my father, was in America—and somehow it all came together for me in a lightning bolt of longing and imagination. My father's absence made perfect sense. He couldn't come back right away because he was busy fighting crime in N.Y.C. . . . as *Spider-Man*.

4   The diasporic imagination really is its own superpower.

5   I became convinced that I was the son of Spider-Man. Like, seriously. You couldn't tell me otherwise. I went apeshit for climbing trees; sometimes I ran head first into our zinc fence, like the Rhino. (I had no problem playing both hero and villain.) My mother was too busy working to make much of it, but my abuela, who watched my brother and me, was, like, "Algo se le montó."

6   It all ended exactly as you might expect: one overcast day, I plummeted out of our avocado tree with an unheroic shriek and landed belly down on the barbed wire separating our house from our neighbor's.

7   My mother stitched me up herself and promised to knock me out of the next tree she found me in. She didn't have to worry; the hole I'd sliced into my abdomen put an end to my Spider-Man reënactments. I stopped climbing, stayed resolutely terrestrial.

8   But TV—that was something else altogether.

9   No sooner was I allowed out of bed than I was hobbling back to my neighbor's set. That eerie little box had a power that not even evisceration could discourage. Near-gutting or not, I believed I had seen my father on that TV, and if I paid close enough attention it would show him to me again. TV was my scryer's ball, my very own palantír, and, Denethor-like, I consulted it feverishly, searching for signs of my long-lost dad and the new world to come.

10   For the record: my father did eventually return and take us to the States. Not to New York City, as expected, but to central New Jersey. Goes without saying that none of it looked like the Spider-Man cartoon, not even the landfill.

11   Those first years, we had a pretty rough time of it. It's hard to describe the initial shock, the terrible bewilderment, the agonies. No way to talk about it then; barely any way to talk about it now. I had no idea how I was supposed to act or dress or walk or be. I didn't understand what anyone was saying, or why the other black folks in our neighborhood didn't speak Spanish.

12   My father was the worst shock of all. He had no problem laying hands on us kids for the slightest infraction. Beatings like he was making up for lost time. Like he was mad he had a family. Before our first month was out,

> **WORD POWER**
>
> **diasporic** relating to emigration from one's homeland

> **WORD POWER**
>
> **terrestrial** earthly (not of other planets); on land

> **WORD POWER**
>
> **evisceration** removal of the organs

> **WORD POWER**
>
> **infraction** the breaking of rules

he had introduced my brother and me to his side chick as though it were the most normal thing in the world. It turns out the old man did have a secret life in America, but it had nothing to do with fighting crime. No, he was not the hero I had dreamed of, and no amount of wishing could make it so.

13 Are you surprised, then, that I was drawn back to the television? Haunting it as much as it haunted me. Flipping through the channels restlessly. From VHF to UHF, and back. Late into the night, when everyone else was asleep and almost no channels were on. Because I was lost, because I wanted help with my English, because my father was a nightmare. And because I was convinced, foolish little fantasist that I was, that somehow my family and I had ended up in the wrong America and that the country and the father I'd first glimpsed on TV in Santo Domingo, the country and the father I'd been promised, were still out there somewhere.

14 I just had to find them.

15 Never did.

Focus on the Pattern

1. List the key events in Diaz's narrative. What main idea do you think he is trying to get across?

2. What transitional words and phrases does Diaz use to move readers from one event to another? Do you think his essay needs more transitions? If so, where should they be added?

Writing Practice

1. Write a narrative recounting your childhood or adolescent experiences with social media, video games, or another popular electronic pastime that served the same role that television served for Diaz. If it is appropriate, you can open your essay (as Diaz does) with "I came late to _____."

2. Write a narrative about a fictional character who means to you what Spider-Man meant to Diaz. In your essay, trace the development of your relationship with this character.

 ## 15c Process Essays

A **process** is a series of chronological steps that produces a particular result. **Process essays** explain the steps in a procedure, telling how something is (or was) done. A process essay can be organized as either a *process explanation* or a set of *instructions*.

When you **TEST** a **process** essay, make sure it includes all these elements:

T Thesis Statement—A process essay should include a **thesis statement** that expresses the essay's main idea, identifying the process you will discuss and telling why it is important or why you are explaining it.

E Evidence—The body paragraphs should provide **evidence**—examples and details—that explains all the steps in the process and supports the essay's thesis. Each paragraph's topic sentence should identify the step (or group of related steps) that the paragraph will explain. Steps should be presented in strict chronological (time) order.

S Summary Statement—The conclusion of a process essay should include a **summary statement** that reinforces the essay's thesis.

T Transitions—A process essay should include **transitional words and phrases** that link the steps in the process and show how they are related.

Moving from Assignment to Thesis

The wording of your assignment may suggest that you should write a process essay. For example, you may be asked to *explain a process*, *give instructions*, *give directions*, or *give a step-by-step* explanation. Once you decide that your assignment calls for process, you need to develop a thesis statement that reflects this purpose.

ASSIGNMENT	THESIS STATEMENT
American government Explain the process by which a bill becomes a law.	The process by which a bill becomes a law is long and complex, involving numerous revisions and a great deal of compromise.
Pharmacy practice Summarize the procedure for conducting a clinical trial of a new drug.	To ensure that drugs are safe and effective, scientists follow strict procedural guidelines for testing and evaluating the drugs.
Technical writing Write a set of instructions for applying for a student internship in a government agency.	If you want to apply for a government internship, you need to follow several important steps.

If your purpose is simply to help readers understand a process, not actually perform it, you will write a process explanation. **Process explanations**, like the first two examples in the chart above, often use present-tense verbs ("Once a bill *is* introduced in Congress" or "A scientist first *submits* a funding application") to explain how a procedure is generally carried out. However, when a process explanation describes a specific procedure that was completed in the past, it uses past-tense verbs ("The next thing I *did*").

If your purpose is to enable readers to actually perform the steps in a process, you will write instructions. **Instructions**, like the technical writing example above, always use present-tense verbs in the form of commands to tell readers what to do ("First, *meet* with your adviser").

Organizing a Process Essay

Whether your essay is a process explanation or a set of instructions, you can either devote a full paragraph to each step of the process or group a series of minor steps together in a single paragraph.

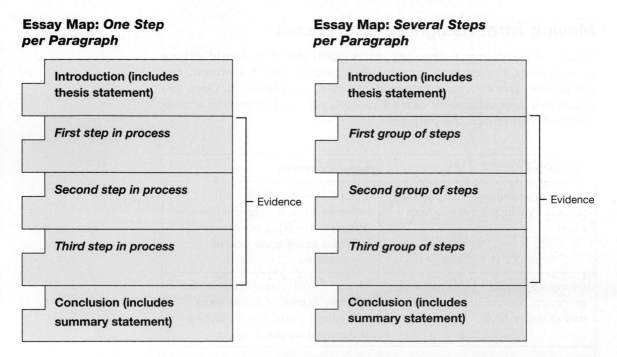

Essay Map: *One Step per Paragraph*

- Introduction (includes thesis statement)
- *First step in process*
- *Second step in process* — Evidence
- *Third step in process*
- Conclusion (includes summary statement)

Essay Map: *Several Steps per Paragraph*

- Introduction (includes thesis statement)
- *First group of steps*
- *Second group of steps* — Evidence
- *Third group of steps*
- Conclusion (includes summary statement)

As you write your process essay, discuss each step in the order in which it is performed, making sure your topic sentences clearly identify each step or group of steps. (If you are writing instructions, you may also include reminders or warnings that readers might need to know when performing the process.)

Transitions in Process Essays

Transitions are extremely important in process essays because they enable readers to follow the sequence of steps in the process and, in the case of instructions, to perform the process themselves.

For a list of transitions frequently used in a process essay, see Chapter 6, page 100.

Case Study: A Student Writes a Process Essay

Jen Rossi, a student in a first-year writing course, was given the following assignment:

> Write a set of instructions for a process that you are very familiar with but that your classmates probably do not know much about. Be sure your readers will be able not just to understand the process but also to perform the steps themselves.

When she considered what she might want to write about, Jen rejected familiar process topics like following a recipe or performing a household repair. Instead, she decided to explain how to sell items at flea markets.

Jen knew a lot about this topic, but she still needed to **brainstorm** to get all the steps down on paper. Next, she **listed the steps,** arranging them in chronological order and checking to make sure that no step was missing. When she **drafted** her essay, she made sure she introduced each step with a transitional word or phrase.

Jen's biggest challenge was developing a **thesis statement**. Before she wrote her draft, she came up with a tentative thesis—"Selling at a flea market is a process that requires a number of steps"—but she knew this sentence was only a placeholder. This thesis statement told readers what she planned to write about, but it didn't tell them why she was explaining this process or how she felt about it.

When she **TEST**ed her draft, Jen saw that while she had a tentative thesis and plenty of support, she had not included a summary statement. She quickly jotted down a placeholder sentence—"These are the steps in selling at a flea market"—that she would revise when she revised her thesis statement.

With the help of classmates in her **peer-review** group, Jen revised her thesis statement and summary statement so they both communicated her essay's main idea: that following a process can establish a routine to make flea market selling easier. She also added a few more examples (for instance, examples of heavy and small items in paragraph 5 and examples of small and large items in paragraph 7) in response to suggestions from her classmates. Once she made these revisions, she went on to **edit** and **proofread** her essay and to check her **format**.

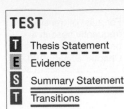

TEST

T Thesis Statement
E Evidence
S Summary Statement
T Transitions

Introduction

Topic sentence
(identifies first step)

Examples and details

Topic sentence
(identifies second step)

Examples and details

Topic sentence
(identifies third step)

Body paragraphs

Examples and details

Topic sentence
(identifies fourth step)

Examples and details

Topic sentence
(identifies fifth step)

Examples and details

Topic sentence
(identifies sixth step)

Examples and details

The final draft that follows includes all the elements Jen looked for when she **TEST**ed her essay.

Model Process Essay

Read Jen's finished essay, and answer the questions in Practice 15-3.

For Fun and Profit

1   Selling items at a flea market can be both fun and profitable. In fact, it can lead to a hobby that will be a continuing source of extra income. Your first flea market can take a lot of work, but establishing a routine will make each experience easier and more rewarding than the last one.

2   The first step in the process is to call to reserve a spot at the flea market. If possible, try to get a spot near the entrance, where there is a lot of foot traffic. Once you have your spot, recruit a helper—for example, one of your roommates—and get to work.

3   The next step is sorting through all the items you've managed to accumulate. Your helper will come in handy here, encouraging you to sell ugly or useless things that you may want to hold on to. Make three piles—keep, sell, and trash—and, one by one, place each item in a pile. (Before you decide to sell or discard an item, check with roommates and family members to make sure you aren't accidentally throwing out one of their prized possessions.)

4   Next, price the items for sale. This can actually be the hardest step in the process. It's always difficult to accept the fact that you might have to set a low price for something that has sentimental value for you (a giant-sized stuffed animal, for example). It can be just as hard to set a high price on the ugly lamp or old record album that might turn out to be someone's treasure. In all likelihood, you will return from your first flea market with a lot of unsold items. You will also probably realize, too late, that you sold some items too cheaply. (Don't worry; you won't make these mistakes again.)

5   The next step is packing up items to be sold. You may want to borrow a friend's truck or van for the heavy, bulky items (boxes of books or dishes, for example). The small items (knickknacks, silk flowers, stray teaspoons) can be transported by car.

6   The final steps in your preparation take place on the day before the event. Borrow a couple of card tables. Then, go to the bank and get lots of dollar bills and quarters, and collect piles of newspaper and grocery bags. Now, your planning is complete, and you are ready for the big day.

7   On the day of the flea market, get up early, and (with your trusty helper's assistance) load your vehicle. When you arrive at the site where the event is to be held, have your helper unload the car. Meanwhile, set things

up, placing small items (such as plates or DVDs) on the card tables and large items (such as your parents' old lawnmower) on the ground near the tables.

8   Now, the actual selling begins. Before you can even set up your tables, people will start picking through your items, offering you cash for picture frames, pots and pans, and old video games. Don't panic! Try to develop a system: one of you can persuade buyers that that old meat grinder or vase is just what they've been looking for; the other person can negotiate the price with prospective buyers. Then, while one of you wraps small items in the newspapers or bags you brought, the other person can take the money and make change.

9   Finally, at the end of the day, the process will come to an end. Now, count your money. (Don't forget to give a share to your helper.) Then, load all the unsold items into your vehicle, and bring them back home. The process ends when you store the unsold items in the back of your closet, ready to pack them all up again and follow the same routine for the next flea market.

Topic sentence (identifies seventh step)

E

Body paragraph

Examples and details

Conclusion

PRACTICE

15-3

1. Restate Jen's thesis statement in your own words.

2. What features identify Jen's essay as a set of instructions rather than a process explanation?

3. Review the transitional words and phrases that link the steps in the process. Are any other transitions needed? If so, where?

4. List the major steps in the process of selling at a flea market. Does Jen present these steps in strict chronological order?

5. Paraphrase Jen's summary statement. Do you think she needs to revise this sentence so it more clearly reinforces her thesis statement?

6. What is the essay's greatest strength? What is its greatest weakness?

grammar in context

Process

When you write a process essay, you may have problems keeping tense, person, and voice consistent throughout. If you shift from one tense, person, or voice to another without good reason, you will confuse your readers.

CONFUSING   <u>Make</u> three piles—keep, sell, and trash—and, one by one, every item <u>should be placed</u> in a pile. (shift from active to passive voice and from present to past tense)

CLEAR   <u>Make</u> three piles—keep, sell, and trash—and, one
by one, <u>place</u> every item in a pile. (consistent voice
and tense)

*For information on how to avoid illogical shifts in tense, person, and voice, see
Chapter 27.*

Step-by-Step Guide: Writing a Process Essay

Now, you are ready to write a process essay on one of the topics listed
below (or a topic of your choice).

TOPICS

An unusual recipe
How to find an apartment
Applying for a job
A religious ritual or cultural ceremony
A complicated task you do at work
A do-it-yourself project that didn't get done
Your own writing process
A self-improvement program (past, present, or future)

As you write your essay, follow these steps:

Plan

Organize

Draft

T E S T

Revise, edit,
and proofread

- Make sure your topic calls for process, and then decide whether you
  want to explain a process or write instructions; next, find ideas to write
  about, identify your main idea, and write a thesis statement.
- Identify the most important steps in the process.
- List the steps in chronological order, making an outline if necessary.
- Draft your essay.
- **TEST** your essay, referring to the **TEST**ing a Process Essay checklist below.
- Revise and edit your essay, referring to the two Self-Assessment
  Checklists in Chapter 13.
- Proofread your essay, and make sure it follows your instructor's format
  guidelines.

TESTing a process essay

Thesis Statement Unifies Your Essay

☐ Does your introduction include a **thesis statement** that
expresses your essay's main idea, identifying the process you
will explain and indicating why you are writing about it?

Evidence Supports Your Essay's Thesis Statement

☐ Does all your **evidence**—examples and details—support your thesis, or should some be deleted?

☐ Do you identify and explain every step that readers will need to understand (or perform) the process? Should any steps in the process be deleted?

☐ Are the steps in the process given in strict chronological order?

☐ If you are writing instructions, have you included all necessary warnings or reminders?

Summary Statement Reinforces Your Essay's Main Idea

☐ Does your conclusion include a **summary statement** that reinforces your essay's thesis?

Transitions

☐ Do you include **transitions** that introduce your steps and clearly show how the steps in the process are related?

Process in Action

In "Slice of Life," Russell Baker uses **process** to structure his essay.

Slice of Life
Russell Baker

Pulitzer Prize–winning columnist and author Russell Baker was known for his keen political insight and sharp social commentary. He was also known for being funny. The source of much of Baker's humor is his deadpan approach, in which he pretends to be completely serious. In "Slice of Life," first published in the *New York Times* in 1974, Baker uses this approach to turn what seems to be a straightforward set of instructions into a humorous discussion of a holiday ritual. As you read, think about your family's Thanksgivings.

1   How to carve a turkey:

2   Assemble the following tools—carving knife, stone for sharpening carving knife, hot water, soap, wash cloth, two bath towels, barbells, meat cleaver. If the house lacks a meat cleaver, an ax may be substituted. If it is, add bandages, sutures, and iodine to above list.

3　Begin by moving the turkey from the roasting pan to a suitable carving area. This is done by inserting the carving knife into the posterior stuffed area of the turkey and the knife-sharpening stone into the stuffed area under the neck.

4　Thus skewered, the turkey may be lifted out of the hot grease with relative safety. Should the turkey drop to the floor, however, remove the knife and stone, roll the turkey gingerly into the two bath towels, wrap them several times around it and lift the encased fowl to the carving place.

5　You are now ready to begin carving. Sharpen the knife on the stone and insert it where the thigh joins the torso. If you do this correctly, which is improbable, the knife will almost immediately encounter a barrier of bone and gristle. This may very well be the joint. It could, however, be your thumb. If not, execute a vigorous sawing motion until satisfied that the knife has been defeated. Withdraw the knife and ask someone nearby, in as testy a manner as possible, why the knives at your house are not kept in better carving condition.

6　Exercise the biceps and forearms by lifting barbells until they are strong enough for you to tackle the leg joint with bare hands. Wrapping one hand firmly around the thigh, seize the turkey's torso in the other hand and scream. Run cold water over hands to relieve pain of burns.

7　Now, take a bath towel in each hand and repeat the above maneuver. The entire leg should snap away from the chassis with a distinct crack, and the rest of the turkey, obedient to Newton's law[1] about equal and opposite reactions, should roll in the opposite direction, which means that if you are carving at the table the turkey will probably come to rest in someone's lap.

8　Get the turkey out of the lap with as little fuss as possible, and concentrate on the leg. Use the meat cleaver to sever the sinewy leather which binds the thigh to the drumstick.

9　If using the alternate, ax method, this operation should be performed on a cement walk outside the house in order to preserve the table.

10　Repeat the above operation on the turkey's uncarved side. You now have two thighs and two drumsticks. Using the wash cloth, soap and hot water, bathe thoroughly and, if possible, go to a movie. Otherwise, look each person in the eye and say, "I don't suppose anyone wants white meat."

11　If compelled to carve the breast anyhow, sharpen the knife on the stone again with sufficient awkwardness to tip over the gravy bowl on the person who started the stampede for white meat.

12　While everyone is rushing about to mop the gravy off her slacks, hack at the turkey breast until it starts crumbling off the carcass in ugly chunks.

13　The alternative method for carving white meat is to visit around the neighborhood until you find someone who has a good carving knife and borrow it, if you find one, which is unlikely.

---

1. Sir Isaac Newton, seventeenth-century physicist and mathematician known for formulating the laws of gravity and light and for inventing calculus.

WORD POWER

gingerly very cautiously or carefully

WORD POWER

execute to do or perform

14 This method enables you to watch the football game on neighbors' television sets and also creates the possibility that somebody back at your table will grow tired of waiting and do the carving herself.

15 In this case, upon returning home, cast a pained stare upon the mound of chopped white meat that has been hacked out by the family carving knife and refuse to do any more carving that day. No one who cares about the artistry of carving can be expected to work upon the mutilations of amateurs, and it would be a betrayal of the carver's art to do so.

Focus on the Pattern

1. How can you tell that this essay is a set of instructions and not an explanation of a process?

2. Do you think the phrase "How to carve a turkey" is an adequate introduction for this essay? What other kind of introduction might Baker have written?

3. Identify the various cautions and warnings that Baker provides for readers. Are they all necessary? Explain.

Writing Practice

1. Write a new introductory paragraph for this essay. Then, turn Baker's instructions into a straightforward process explanation, deleting any material you consider irrelevant to your purpose. Be sure to include all necessary articles (*a*, *an*, *the*) and transitions.

2. List the steps in a recipe for preparing one of your favorite dishes. Then, expand your recipe into an essay, adding transitions and cautions and reminders. Finally, add opening and closing paragraphs that describe the finished product and tell readers why the dish is worth preparing.

15d Cause-and-Effect Essays

A **cause** makes something happen; an **effect** is a result of a particular cause or event. **Cause-and-effect essays** identify causes or predict effects; sometimes, they do both.

When you **TEST** a **cause-and-effect** essay, make sure it includes all these elements:

T **Thesis Statement**—The introduction of a cause-and-effect essay should include a **thesis statement** that communicates the essay's main idea and indicates whether it will focus on causes or on effects.

E **Evidence**—The body paragraphs should include **evidence**—examples and details—to illustrate and explain the causes or effects you examine. The topic sentence of each paragraph should identify the causes or effects the paragraph will discuss.

S **Summary Statement**—The conclusion of a cause-and-effect essay should include a **summary statement** that reinforces the essay's thesis.

T **Transitions**—A cause-and-effect essay should include **transitional words and phrases** that make clear which causes lead to which effects.

Moving from Assignment to Thesis

The wording of your assignment may suggest that you write a cause-and-effect essay. For example, the assignment may ask you to *explain why*, *predict the outcome*, *list contributing factors*, *discuss the consequences*, or tell what *caused* something else or how something is *affected* by something else. Once you decide that your assignment calls for cause and effect, you need to develop a thesis statement that reflects this purpose.

ASSIGNMENT	THESIS STATEMENT
Women's studies What factors contributed to the rise of the women's movement in the 1970s?	The women's movement of the 1970s had its origins in the peace and civil rights movements of the 1960s.
Public health Discuss the possible long-term effects of smoking.	In addition to its well-known negative effects on smokers themselves, smoking also causes significant problems for those exposed to secondhand smoke.
Media and society How has the Internet affected the lives of those who have grown up with it?	The Internet has created a generation of people who learn differently from those in previous generations.

A cause-and-effect essay can focus on causes or on effects. When you write about causes, be sure to examine *all* relevant causes. You should emphasize the cause you consider the most important, but do not forget to consider other causes that may be significant. Similarly, when you write about effects, consider *all* significant effects of a particular cause, not just the first few that you think of.

If your focus is on finding causes, as it is in the first assignment in the chart on page 264, your introductory paragraph should identify the effect (the women's movement). If your focus is on predicting effects, as it is in the second and third assignments in the chart, you should begin by identifying the cause (smoking, the Internet).

Organizing a Cause-and-Effect Essay

In the body of your essay, you will probably devote a full paragraph to each cause (or effect). You can also group several related causes (or effects) together in each paragraph.

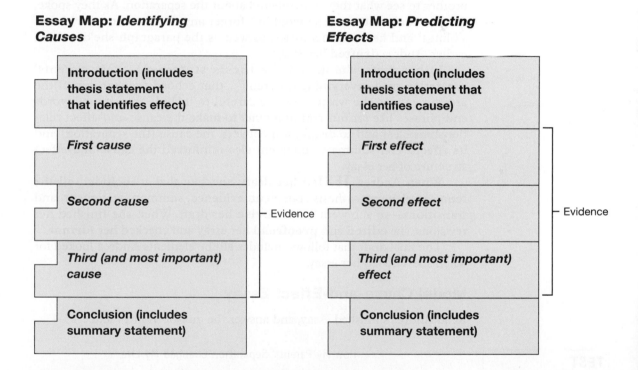

Essay Map: *Identifying Causes*

- Introduction (includes thesis statement that identifies effect)
- First cause
- Second cause
- Third (and most important) cause } Evidence
- Conclusion (includes summary statement)

Essay Map: *Predicting Effects*

- Introduction (includes thesis statement that identifies cause)
- First effect
- Second effect
- Third (and most important) effect } Evidence
- Conclusion (includes summary statement)

Transitions in Cause-and-Effect Essays

Transitions are important in cause-and-effect essays because they establish causal connections, telling readers that A caused B and not the other way around. They also make it clear that events have a *causal* relationship (A *caused* B) and not just a *sequential* relationship (A *came before* B). Remember, when one event follows another, the second is not necessarily the result of the first. For example, an earthquake may occur the day before you fail an exam, but that doesn't mean the earthquake caused you to fail.

For a list of transitions frequently used in cause and effect, see page 111.

Case Study: A Student Writes a Cause-and-Effect Essay

In an orientation course for first-year education majors, Andrea DeMarco was asked to write a personal essay about an event that changed her life. The wording of the assignment indicated to Andrea that her essay would have a cause-and-effect structure. As it happened, she had just written a cause-and-effect paragraph, in response to a composition assignment, about how her parents' separation had led her to grow up quickly. Now, she thought she could develop some of the ideas she had explored in that paragraph into an essay.

Before she wrote her first draft, Andrea talked to her older sister and brother to see what they remembered about the separation. As they spoke, Andrea **took notes** so she wouldn't forget any details. Armed with her siblings' and her own memories, as well as the paragraph she'd written earlier, Andrea **drafted** her essay.

In her draft, she included a **thesis statement**—"My parents' separation made everything different"—that echoed the wording of the assignment. As she wrote, she was careful to include transitional words and phrases like *because* and *as a result* to make the cause-and-effect relationships clear and to distinguish between the cause (the separation) and its effects. Her summary statement also reinforced the cause-and-effect structure of her essay.

When Andrea **TEST**ed her draft, she saw that it included all the required elements—thesis statement, evidence, summary statement, and transitions—so she went on to **revise** her draft. When she finished her revisions, she **edited** and **proofread** her essay and checked her **format**.

The final draft that follows includes all the elements Andrea looked for when she **TEST**ed her essay.

Model Cause-and-Effect Essay

Read Andrea's finished essay, and answer the questions in Practice 15-4.

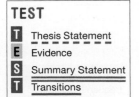

TEST

T Thesis Statement
E Evidence
S Summary Statement
T Transitions

Introduction

How My Parents' Separation Changed My Life

1   Until I was eight, I lived the perfect all-American life with my perfect all-American family. I lived in a suburb of Albany, New York, with my parents, my sister and brother, and our dog, Daisy. We had a Ping-Pong table in the basement, a barbecue in the backyard, and two cars in the garage. My dad and mom were high school teachers, and every summer we took a family vacation. Then, it all changed. My parents' separation made everything different.

2   One day, just before Halloween, when my sister was twelve and my
brother was fourteen (Daisy was seven), our parents called us into the
kitchen for a family conference. We didn't think anything was wrong at first;
they were always calling these annoying meetings. We figured it was time for
us to plan a vacation, talk about household chores, or be nagged to clean
our rooms. As soon as we sat down, though, we knew this was different. We
could tell Mom had been crying, and Dad's voice cracked when he told us the
news. They were separating—they called it a "trial separation"—and Dad
was moving out of our house.

3   After that day, everything seemed to change. Every Halloween we
always had a big jack-o'-lantern on our front porch. Dad used to spend hours
at the kitchen table cutting out the eyes, nose, and mouth and hollowing
out the insides. That Halloween, because he didn't live with us, things were
different. Mom bought a pumpkin, and I guess she was planning to carve it up.
But she never did, and we never mentioned it. It sat on the kitchen counter for
a couple of weeks, getting soft and wrinkled, and then it just disappeared.

4   Other holidays were also different because Mom and Dad were not living
together. Our first Thanksgiving without Dad was pathetic. Christmas was
different, too. We spent Christmas Eve with Dad and our relatives on his side
and Christmas Day with Mom and her family. Of course, we got twice as many
presents as usual. I realize now that both our parents were trying to make
up for the pain of the separation. The worst part came when I opened my big
present from Mom: Barbie's Dream House. This was something I had always
wanted. Even at eight, I knew how hard it must have been for Mom to afford
it. The trouble was, I had gotten the same thing from Dad the night before.

5   The separation affected each of us in different ways. The worst effect
of my parents' separation was not the big events but the disruption in our
everyday lives. Dinner used to be a family time, a chance to talk about
our day and make plans. But after Dad left, Mom seemed to stop eating.
Sometimes she would just have coffee while we ate, and sometimes she
wouldn't eat at all. She would microwave some frozen thing for us or heat up
soup or cook some hot dogs. We didn't care—after all, now she let us watch
TV while we ate—but we did notice.

6   Other parts of our routine changed, too. Because Dad didn't live with
us anymore, we had to spend every Saturday and every Wednesday night at
his apartment, no matter what else we had planned. Usually, he would take
us to dinner at McDonald's on Wednesdays, and then we would go back to
his place and do our homework or watch TV. That wasn't too bad. Saturdays
were a lot worse. We really wanted to be home, hanging out with our friends

Marginal annotations:

Topic sentence (identifies first effect)

Examples and details

Topic sentence (identifies second effect)

Examples and details

Topic sentence (identifies third effect)

Body paragraphs

Examples and details

Topic sentence (identifies fourth effect)

Examples and details

Topic sentence (identifies fifth effect)

Examples and details

Body paragraph

in our own rooms in our own house. Instead, we had to do some planned activity with Dad, like go to a movie or a hockey game.

7   <u><u>As a result</u></u> of what happened in my own family, it is hard for me to believe any relationship is forever. By the end of the school year, my parents had somehow worked things out, and Dad was back home again. That June, at a family conference around the kitchen table, we made our summer vacation plans. We decided on Williamsburg, Virginia, the all-American vacation destination. So, things were back to normal, but I wasn't, and I'm still not. Now, ten years later, my mother and father are all right, but I still worry they'll split up again. And I worry about my own future husband and how I will ever be sure he's the one I'll stay married to.

Conclusion

PRACTICE

1. Restate Andrea's thesis statement in your own words. Does this statement focus on a cause or an effect?

2. List the specific effects of her parents' separation that Andrea identifies.

3. Review the transitional words and phrases Andrea uses to make cause-and-effect connections clear to her readers. Do you think she needs more of these transitions? If so, where?

4. Is Andrea's relatively long concluding paragraph effective? Why or why not? Do you think it should be shortened or divided into two paragraphs? Explain your reasoning.

5. Is Andrea's straightforward title effective, or should she have used a more creative or eye-catching title? Can you suggest an alternative?

6. What is this essay's greatest strength? What is its greatest weakness?

grammar in context

Cause and Effect

When you write a cause-and-effect essay, you may have trouble remembering the difference between *affect* and *effect*.

>   *effect*
> The worst ~~affect~~ of my parents' separation was not the big events
>   ^
> but the disruption in our everyday lives. (*effect* is a noun)
>   *affected*
> The separation ~~effected~~ each of us in different ways.
>   ^
> (*affect* is a verb)

For information on affect *and* effect, *see Chapter 23.*

Step-by-Step Guide: Writing a Cause-and-Effect Essay

Now, you are ready to write a cause-and-effect essay on one of the topics listed below (or a topic of your choice).

TOPICS

A teacher's positive (or negative) effect on you

Why you voted a certain way in a recent election (or why you did not vote)

How your life would be different if you dropped out of school (or quit your job)

How a particular invention has made your life better

Why texting is so popular

A movie or book that changed the way you look at life

How a particular season (or day of the week) affects your mood

How having a child would change (or has changed) your life

How a particular event made you grow up

As you write your essay, follow these steps:

- Make sure your topic calls for cause and effect, and then decide whether your essay will focus on causes, effects, or both; next, find ideas to write about, identify your main idea, and write a thesis statement.

- Choose causes or effects to support your thesis, and arrange causes and effects in an effective order, making an outline if necessary.

- Draft your essay.

- **TEST** your essay, referring to the **TEST**ing a Cause-and-Effect Essay Checklist below.

- Revise and edit your essay, referring to the two Self-Assessment Checklists in Chapter 13.

- Proofread your essay, and make sure it follows your instructor's format guidelines.

Plan

Organize

Draft

TEST

Revise, edit, and proofread

TESTing a cause-and-effect essay

Thesis Statement Unifies Your Essay

☐ Does your introduction include a **thesis statement** that indicates your main idea and makes clear whether your essay will focus on causes or on effects?

E vidence Supports Your Essay's Thesis Statement

☐ Does all your **evidence**—examples and details—support your thesis, or should some be deleted?

☐ Do you identify and explain all causes or effects relevant to your topic, or do you need to add any?

☐ Do you arrange causes and effects to indicate which are more important than others?

☐ Does each body paragraph identify and explain one particular cause or effect (or several closely related causes or effects)?

S ummary Statement Reinforces Your Essay's Main Idea

☐ Does your conclusion include a **summary statement** that reinforces your essay's thesis?

T ransitions

☐ Do you include **transitions** that introduce each of your causes or effects and make your essay's cause-and-effect connections clear?

Cause and Effect in Action

In "Facing the Concussion Risks of Youth Football," Kathleen E. Bachynski and Daniel S. Goldberg use **cause and effect** to structure their essay.

Facing the Concussion Risks of Youth Football

Kathleen E. Bachynski and Daniel S. Goldberg

Kathleen E. Bachynski holds a PhD in sociomedical sciences from Columbia University and an MPH in epidemiology from the University of Michigan. A postdoctoral fellow in medical humanities at NYU Langone, she specializes in the history and ethics of public health, with a focus on injury prevention. Daniel S. Goldberg, JD, PhD, is an associate professor at the Center for Bioethics and Humanities at the University of Colorado. He is trained as an attorney, a historian, and a public health ethicist, and he researches a variety of issues related to health inequalities. This article originally appeared in the Public's Health section of Philly.com in 2014.

1   After years of denying the link between football and brain disease, this month the National Football League's own experts calculated that nearly one third of its players will go on to develop long-term cognitive problems after retirement. The league's new stance might help shift public perceptions of football's extraordinary risks to professional players' brains. From a public health perspective, examining the sport's impact on millions of youth players is of even greater importance.

2   Children as young as seven and eight continue to play tackle football across the United States in far greater numbers than NFL stars. Accumulating evidence suggests that the repeated collisions inherent in the youth sport may cause significant harm. The players might be smaller, but the hits are still dangerous. Researchers have found that nine to twelve year olds can experience head impacts of a similar magnitude to those that occur in high school and college football. Furthermore, because children's brains are still developing and because they have weaker necks than adults, they may be more vulnerable to brain trauma.

3   Why do parents allow their children to participate in a sport that poses significant risks to developing brains? One reason is that organizers of youth football leagues portray the youth game as much safer than the professional game. The Pop Warner website, for example, states that there is "an absence of catastrophic head and neck injuries and disruptive joint injuries found at higher levels" in their league. Such assertions seem to discount the potential severity of concussions, which are common in youth football and can have major short-term and long-term consequences. Parents may not fully appreciate the risks associated with football head injuries. A recent study of over three hundred football parents found that most did not realize that a concussion is considered a mild traumatic brain injury, or that a direct blow to the head is not necessary for a concussion to occur.

4   Yet even if parents acknowledge that concussions are a significant injury, most people believe that strategies such as improved helmets, return-to-play guidelines, and "safer" tackling techniques can help significantly reduce the risks of concussion. Indeed, the NFL has helped promote this prevailing view, most notably with its "Heads Up Football" partnership with youth leagues, intended to teach proper tackling techniques to children.

5   There is no evidence that the "Heads Up Football" program reduces the risk of concussion or of long-term brain damage: As former Denver Broncos tight end Nate Jackson has observed, no matter what tackling technique children use, "you can't remove the head from play in the football field."

6   Unfortunately, improved helmet design is not a silver bullet either. Although helmets are very effective in preventing catastrophic head injuries such as skull fractures, they are not designed to prevent concussions. Even the best designed helmet cannot prevent the forces that occur when the head rotates on the neck. Kevin Walter of the American Academy of Pediatrics' Council on Sports Medicine and Fitness recently stated that currently, "no protective equipment can prevent concussion."

WORD POWER
cognitive related to the mental process of acquiring knowledge; thinking

WORD POWER
inherent a permanent element

7   Although education, training, and improved equipment are all worth encouraging, they do not change the fundamental risks of the sport. Football is a contact game in which repeated full-body collisions place players' brains at risk of chronic trauma. We must acknowledge that the risk of head injuries is inherent to tackle football, even at the youth level, and will remain significant even with new equipment designs or the best tackling techniques.

8   We need to ask different questions. At what point are the risks of head injuries so high or severe that even fully informed parents should not be permitted to let their children play? And at what age can players consent to the risk of brain trauma and the elevated risks of neurological diseases later in life?

9   These are complex ethical issues that involve not only examining the latest concussion research, but also our values and beliefs about how much risk is appropriate for children. Of course, children should be encouraged to play and lead active lives, and experiencing some amount of risk in childhood is inevitable. But how much risk is too much?

10   Addressing this question will require a robust public discussion involving parents, coaches, school administrators, fans, trainers, physicians, sporting goods manufacturers, and the players themselves. While children certainly benefit from participation in team sports, it remains a question whether other sports can offer those same benefits while posing less risk of brain injury than tackle football. Do the risks of America's most popular sport outweigh its benefits for young children?

WORD POWER

inevitable unavoidable

WORD POWER

robust healthy; significant

Focus on the Pattern

1. This essay focuses on the risks of youth football. Are risks the same as causes? Why or why not? What do you think the effects of these risks are for the players, for parents, and for society in general?

2. Write a one-sentence thesis statement for this essay. Include at least one word or phrase (such as *because*, *for this reason*, or *as a result*) that indicates it is a cause-and-effect essay.

Writing Practice

1. Do you think parents are to blame for the negative consequences that may occur if they allow their children to participate in youth football programs? If not, who (or what) do you think is at fault? Write a cause-and-effect essay in response to these questions.

2. Write a cause-and-effect essay in which you discuss the *positive* effects of youth football on players and on their communities. You may briefly acknowledge the possible negative results identified in Bachynski and Goldberg's essay, but be sure to focus on the benefits. If you like, you may use your own experiences to support your thesis.

15e Comparison-and-Contrast Essays

Comparison identifies similarities, and **contrast** identifies differences. **Comparison-and-contrast essays** explain how two things are alike or how they are different; sometimes, they discuss both similarities and differences.

When you **TEST** a **comparison-and-contrast** essay, make sure it includes all these elements:

T Thesis Statement—The introduction of a comparison-and-contrast essay should include a **thesis statement** that communicates the essay's main idea, telling readers what two items you are going to compare or contrast and whether you are going to emphasize similarities or differences.

E Evidence—The body paragraphs should include **evidence**— examples and details—that supports the thesis statement. The topic sentence of each paragraph should identify the similarity or difference the paragraph will examine, and the examples and details should explain that similarity or difference.

S Summary Statement—The conclusion of a comparison-and-contrast essay should include a **summary statement** that reinforces the essay's thesis.

T Transitions—A comparison-and-contrast essay should include **transitional words and phrases** to help readers move from point to point and from subject to subject.

Moving from Assignment to Thesis

The wording of your assignment may suggest that you write a comparison-and-contrast essay. For example, you may be asked to *compare*, *contrast*, *discuss similarities*, or *identify differences*. Once you decide that your assignment calls for comparison and contrast, you need to develop a thesis statement that reflects this purpose.

ASSIGNMENT	THESIS STATEMENT
Philosophy Identify some basic similarities in the beliefs of Henry David Thoreau and Martin Luther King Jr.	Although King was more politically active, both he and Thoreau strongly supported the idea of civil disobedience.
Nutrition How do the diets of native Japanese and Japanese Americans differ?	As they become more and more assimilated, Japanese Americans consume more fats than native Japanese do.

| *Literature*   Contrast the two sisters in Alice Walker's short story "Everyday Use." | Unlike Maggie, Dee—her more successful, better-educated sister—has rejected her family's heritage. |

Organizing a Comparison-and-Contrast Essay

When you organize a comparison-and-contrast essay, you can choose either a *point-by-point* or a *subject-by-subject* arrangement. A **point-by-point** comparison alternates between the two subjects you are comparing or contrasting, moving back and forth from one subject to the other. A **subject-by-subject** comparison treats its two subjects separately, first fully discussing one subject and then moving on to consider the other subject. In both kinds of comparison-and-contrast essays, the same points are discussed in the same order for both subjects.

Essay Map: *Point-by-Point Comparison*   **Essay Map:** *Subject-by-Subject Comparison*

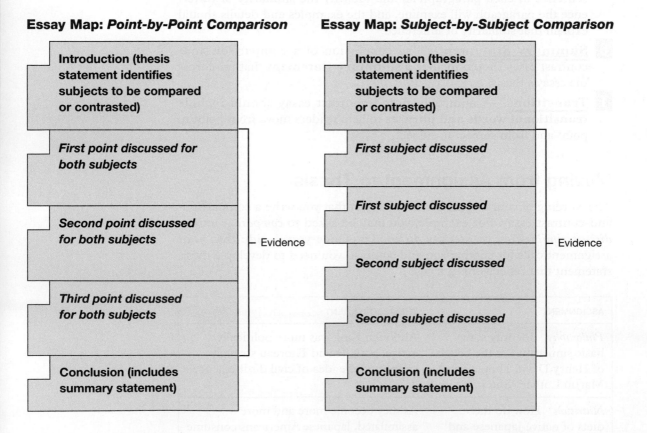

Introduction (thesis statement identifies subjects to be compared or contrasted)

First point discussed for both subjects

Second point discussed for both subjects

Third point discussed for both subjects

Conclusion (includes summary statement)

— Evidence

Introduction (thesis statement identifies subjects to be compared or contrasted)

First subject discussed

First subject discussed

Second subject discussed

Second subject discussed

Conclusion (includes summary statement)

— Evidence

Transitions in Comparison-and-Contrast Essays

For a list of transitions frequently used in comparison and contrast, see page 122.

The transitional words and phrases you use in a comparison-and-contrast essay tell readers whether you are focusing on similarities or on differences. Transitions also help move readers through your essay from one subject to the other and from one point of comparison or contrast to the next.

Case Study: A Student Writes a Comparison-and-Contrast Essay

Nisha Jani, a student in a first-year writing course, was given the following assignment:

> Some people claim that males and females are so different that at times they seem to belong to two different species. Do you agree, or do you think males and females are more alike than different? Write an essay that supports your position.

When Nisha read this assignment, the key words *different* and *alike* suggested to her that the assignment called for a comparison-and-contrast essay. After **brainstorming**, she decided to write about the differences between middle-school boys and girls. She didn't want to write a serious essay, and she thought she could use humor if she wrote about the habits of two typical seventh-graders. When she drafted a **thesis statement** for her essay, Nisha made sure that it focused on differences: "The typical boy and girl lead very different lives."

Once she had a thesis statement, she **listed** some of the most obvious differences between male and female seventh-graders. When she reviewed the ideas on her list, she decided to follow her two subjects (Johnny and Jane) through a typical school day, and this decision led her to structure her essay as a point-by-point comparison that would contrast boys' and girls' behavior at different points of their day.

When Nisha thought she had enough material to write about, she **wrote a draft** of her essay. **TEST**ing her draft showed her that she had included all the required elements, so she felt ready to schedule a **conference** with her instructor. After the conference, she **revised her thesis statement** to make it a bit more specific, added more examples and details, sharpened her summary statement so that it reinforced her essay's main idea, and added more transitions to make the contrast between her two subjects clearer. After she finished these revisions, she **edited** and **proofread** her essay and checked her **format**.

The final draft that follows includes all the elements Nisha looked for when she **TEST**ed her essay.

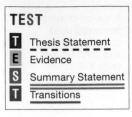

TEST

T	Thesis Statement
E	Evidence
S	Summary Statement
T	Transitions

Introduction

Topic sentence
(identifies first difference)

Examples and details

Body paragraphs

Topic sentence
(identifies second difference)

Examples and details

Model Comparison-and-Contrast Essay

Read Nisha's finished essay, and answer the questions in Practice 15-5.

Another Ordinary Day

1   "Boys are from Jupiter and get stupider / Girls are from Mars and become movie stars / Boys take a bath and smell like trash / Girls take a shower and smell like a flower." As simple playground songs like this one suggest, the two sexes are very different. As adults, men and women have similar goals, values, and occupations, but as children and teenagers, boys and girls often seem to belong to two different species. In fact, from the first moment of the day to the last, the typical boy and girl live very different lives.

2   The sun rises, and the smartphone alarm signals the beginning of another day for Johnny and Jane, two seventh-grade classmates. Johnny, an average thirteen-year-old boy, wakes up late and has to hurry. He throws on jeans or joggers, a hoodie, and a snapback hat. Then, he has a hearty high-cholesterol breakfast and runs out of the house to school, usually forgetting some vital book or homework assignment. Jane, unlike Johnny, wakes up early and takes her time. She takes a long shower and then blow-dries her hair. For Jane, getting dressed can be a very difficult process, one that often includes taking everything out of her closet and calling friends for advice. After she makes her decision, she helps herself to some food (probably low- or no-fat) and goes off to school, making sure she has with her everything she needs.

3   School is a totally different experience for Johnny and Jane. Johnny will probably sit in the back of the classroom with a couple of other guys, throwing paper airplanes and spitballs. These will be directed at the males they do not like and the females they think are kind of cute. (However, if their male friends ever ask the boys about these girls, they will say girls are just losers and deny that they like any of them.) On the opposite side of the classroom, however, Jane is focused on a very different kind of activity. At first, it looks as if she is carefully copying the algebra notes that the teacher is putting on the board, but instead, she is writing a note to her BFF about topics that are much more important to her than the square root of 121. She proceeds to fold the note into a box or other creative shape, which can often put origami to shame. As soon as the teacher turns her back, the note is passed and the process begins all over again.

4   Lunch, a vital part of the school day, is also very different for Johnny and Jane. On the one hand, for Johnny and his friends, it is a time to compare baseball cards, exchange sports facts, and of course tell jokes about every bodily function imaginable. In front of them on the table, their trays are filled with pizza, soda, fries, chips, and items from the vending machines, and this food is their main focus. For Jane, on the other hand, lunch is not about eating; it is a chance to exchange the latest gossip about who is going out with whom. The girls look around to see what people are wearing, what they should do with their hair, and so on. Jane's meal is quite a bit smaller than Johnny's: it consists of a small low-fat yogurt and half a bagel (if she feels like splurging, she will spread some cream cheese on the bagel).

5   After school, Johnny and Jane head in different directions. Johnny rushes home to meet up with his friends. Sometimes they play video games; at other times, they might play pick-up basketball or touch football. Johnny and his friends play with every boy who shows up, whether they know him or not. They may get into physical fights and arguments, but they always assume they will meet up again the next day. In contrast to the boys, Jane and her friends are very selective. Their circle is a small one, and they do everything together. Occasionally, they might go shopping (they will not necessarily buy anything, but they will consider the outing productive anyway because they will have spent time together). Most days, though, they spend their time, alone or together, on their phones, texting, Snapchatting, or posting on their favorite social media sites.

6   At the age of twelve or thirteen, boys and girls do not seem to have very much in common. Given this situation, it is amazing that boys and girls grow up to become men and women who interact as neighbors, friends, and coworkers. What is even more amazing is that so many grow up to share lives and raise families together, treating each other with love and respect.

Topic sentence (identifies third difference)

E   Examples and details

Body paragraphs

Topic sentence (identifies fourth difference)

E   Examples and details

Conclusion

PRACTICE

15-5

1. Restate Nisha's thesis statement in your own words.

2. Does Nisha's opening paragraph identify the subjects she will discuss? Does it tell whether she will focus on similarities or on differences?

3. Nisha's essay is a point-by-point comparison. What four points does she discuss for each of her two subjects (Johnny and Jane)?

4. Review the topic sentences in Nisha's body paragraphs. What part of the day does each topic sentence identify?

5. Review the transitional words and phrases Nisha uses to move readers from one subject (Johnny) to the other (Jane). Do you think these transitions are effective, or should they be revised to make the contrast clearer?

6. What is this essay's greatest strength? What is its greatest weakness?

grammar in context

Comparison and Contrast

When you write a comparison-and-contrast essay, be sure to present the points you are comparing or contrasting in **parallel** terms to highlight their similarities or differences.

⌐ PARALLEL ¬
Johnny, an average thirteen-year-old boy, wakes up late and has

to hurry.

⌐ PARALLEL ¬
Jane, unlike Johnny, wakes up early and takes her time.

For information on revising to make ideas parallel, see Chapter 22.

Step-by-Step Guide: Writing a Comparison-and-Contrast Essay

Now, you are ready to write a comparison-and-contrast essay on one of the topics listed below (or a topic of your choice).

TOPICS

Two coworkers
Two movie heroes or heroines
How you expect your life to be different from the lives of your parents
Men's and women's ideas about their body images
Two ways of studying for an exam
Risk-takers and people who play it safe
Country and city living (or, compare suburban living with either)
Two popular magazines or websites
Leaders and followers
Designer products and counterfeit products
Optimists and pessimists

As you write your essay, follow these steps:

- Make sure your topic calls for comparison and contrast, and then find ideas to write about; next, decide whether you want to discuss similarities, differences, or both, identify your main idea, and write a thesis statement.

- Identify specific points of comparison or contrast to support your thesis, and decide whether to structure your essay as a point-by-point or subject-by-subject comparison; then, arrange your points in a logical order, making an outline if necessary.

- Draft your essay.

- **TEST** your essay, referring to the **TEST**ing a Comparison-and-Contrast Essay checklist below.

- Revise and edit your essay, referring to the two Self-Assessment Checklists in Chapter 13.

- Proofread your essay, and make sure it follows your instructor's format guidelines.

Plan

↓

Organize

↓

Draft

↓

TEST

↓

Revise, edit, and proofread

TESTing a comparison-and-contrast essay

T hesis Statement Unifies Your Essay

☐ Does your introduction include a **thesis statement** that expresses your main idea, identifying the two subjects you will compare and indicating whether your essay will examine similarities or differences?

E vidence Supports Your Essay's Thesis Statement

☐ Do you discuss all significant points of comparison or contrast that apply to your two subjects, explaining each similarity or difference with specific examples and details?

☐ Does all your **evidence**—examples and details—support your thesis, or should some be deleted?

☐ Have you treated similar points for both of your subjects?

☐ Is your essay organized as either a point-by-point comparison or a subject-by-subject comparison?

S ummary Statement Reinforces Your Essay's Main Idea

☐ Does your conclusion include a **summary statement** that reinforces your essay's thesis, reminding readers what your two subjects are and how they are alike or different?

> **T ransitions**
>
> ☐ Do you include **transitions** that introduce each of your points of comparison or contrast and move readers from one subject or point to another?

Comparison and Contrast in Action

In "Migrant vs. Refugee: What's the Difference?" Michael Martinez uses **comparison and contrast** to structure his essay.

Migrant vs. Refugee: What's the Difference?
Michael Martinez

Michael Martinez has worked as a journalist in both print and online media. He was a reporter and war correspondent for the *Chicago Tribune* and is currently a newsdesk writer, editor, and media producer for CNN, where "Migrant vs. Refugee: What's the Difference?" first appeared in 2015. In this piece, Martinez attempts to distinguish the terms *migrant* and *refugee*, two words frequently used interchangeably by the media, resulting in confusion. As you read, ask yourself why the difference between these two similar words matters.

1   The difference between a migrant and a refugee marks a crucial distinction for European countries receiving new arrivals.

2   Refugees, as defined under the 1951 Refugee Convention, are entitled to basic rights under international law, including the right not to be immediately deported and sent back into harm's way.

3   "The practice of granting asylum to people fleeing persecution in foreign lands is one of the earliest hallmarks of civilization," according to the U.N. High Commissioner for Refugees. "References to it have been found in texts written 3,500 years ago, during the blossoming of the great early empires in the Middle East such as the Hittites, Babylonians, Assyrians and ancient Egyptians."

4   A refugee is someone who has been forced to flee his or her home country because of armed conflict or persecution. Syrians are a prime example.

5   The U.N.'s definition of refugee is someone who, "owing to a well-founded fear of being persecuted for reasons of race, religion, nationality, membership of a particular social group or political opinion, is outside the country of his nationality, and is unable to, or owing to such fear, is unwilling to avail himself of the protection of that country."

6 Migrants, however, are processed under the receiving country's immigration laws. So, ultimately, these terms have major implications for those seeking asylum and the countries being asked to grant it.

7 A migrant is someone who chooses to resettle to another country in search of a better life.

8 For example, those fleeing poverty in Nigeria, looking for work in Europe, would not have refugee status and would be considered migrants.

9 Not all migrants then are refugees, but refugees can fall under the migrant umbrella. One of the major differences between the two designations is that while migrants may seek to escape harsh conditions of their own, refugees could face imprisonment, deprivation of basic rights, physical injury or worse.

10 "Refugees have to move if they are to save their lives or preserve their freedom. They have no protection from their own state—indeed it is often their own government that is threatening to persecute them. If other countries do not let them in and do not help them once they are in, then they may be condemning them to death—or to an intolerable life in the shadows, without sustenance and without rights," the U.N. says.

11 So which term should you use?

12 The United Nations notes that both groups are present in Europe and at its shores. It's safe to call all of them migrants because each is migrating, but many of them—especially those fleeing Afghanistan, Eritrea, Syria and Iraq—are also refugees.

Focus on the Pattern

1. Make an informal outline of this essay.

2. Is this essay a point-by-point or a subject-by-subject comparison? How can you tell? Is this structure the best choice for this topic? Why or why not?

3. Why is the distinction between Martinez's two subjects (*migrant* and *refugee*) important?

Writing Practice

1. Write an essay comparing the terms *undocumented immigrants* and *illegal aliens*.

2. Write a comparison-and-contrast essay focusing on two people you know who are immigrants to the United States. How are their personal stories alike and different?

review checklist

Patterns of Essay Development: Exemplification, Narration, Process, Cause and Effect, and Comparison and Contrast

✔ **Exemplification** essays use specific examples to support a thesis. (See 15a.)

✔ **Narrative** essays tell a story by presenting a series of events in chronological order. (See 15b.)

✔ **Process** essays explain the steps in a procedure, explaining how something is (or was) done or how to do something. (See 15c.)

✔ **Cause-and-effect** essays identify causes or predict effects. (See 15d.)

✔ **Comparison-and-contrast** essays explain how two things are alike or how they are different. (See 15e.)

16 Patterns of Essay Development

Description, Classification, Definition, and Argument

sakkmesterke/AlamyStockPhoto

focus on writing

This image is an example of fractal art, a repeating pattern created digitally with a computer algorithm. Throughout this chapter, you will explore a variety of patterns of development for organizing your essays.

16a Descriptive Essays

Description tells what something looks, sounds, smells, tastes, or feels like. A **descriptive essay** uses details to give readers a clear, vivid picture of a person, place, or object.

When you describe a person, place, object, or scene, you can use **objective description**, reporting only what your senses of sight, sound, smell, taste, and touch tell you ("The columns were two feet tall and made of white marble"). You can also use **subjective description**, conveying your attitude or your feelings about what you observe ("The columns were tall and powerful looking, and their marble surface seemed as smooth as ice"). Many essays combine these two kinds of description.

FYI

Figures of Speech

Descriptive writing, particularly subjective description, is frequently enriched by **figures of speech**—language that creates special or unusual effects.

- A **simile** uses *like* or *as* to compare two unlike things.

  Her smile was like sunshine.

- A **metaphor** compares two unlike things without using *like* or *as*.

  Her smile was a light that lit up the room.

- **Personification** suggests a comparison between a nonliving thing and a person by giving the nonliving thing human traits.

  The sun smiled down on the crowd.

When you **TEST** a **descriptive** essay, make sure it includes all these elements:

T Thesis Statement—A descriptive essay should include a **thesis statement** that expresses the essay's main idea.

E Evidence—The body paragraphs should include **evidence**, descriptive details that support the thesis. Details should be arranged in spatial order—for example, from far to near or from top to bottom.

S Summary Statement—The conclusion of a descriptive essay should include a **summary statement** that reinforces the essay's thesis.

T Transitions—A descriptive essay should include **transitional words and phrases** that connect details and show how they are related.

Moving from Assignment to Thesis

The wording of your assignment may suggest that you write a descriptive essay. For example, it may ask you to *describe* or to *tell what* something *looks like*. Once you decide that your assignment calls for description, you need to develop a thesis statement that reflects this purpose.

ASSIGNMENT	THESIS STATEMENT
Composition Describe a room that was important to you when you were a child.	Pink-and-white striped wallpaper, tall shelves of cuddly stuffed animals, and the smell of Oreos dominated the bedroom I shared with my sister.
Scientific writing Describe a piece of scientific equipment.	The mass spectrometer is a complex instrument, but every part is ideally suited to its function.
Art history Choose one modern painting and describe its visual elements.	The disturbing images crowded together in Pablo Picasso's *Guernica* suggest the brutality of war.

Organizing a Descriptive Essay

When you plan a descriptive essay, you focus on selecting details that help your readers see what you see, feel what you feel, and experience what you experience. Your goal is to create a single **dominant impression**, a central theme or idea to which all the details relate—for example, the liveliness of a street scene or the quiet of a summer night. This dominant impression unifies the description and gives readers an overall sense of what the person, place, object, or scene looks like (and perhaps what it sounds, smells, tastes, or feels like).

You can arrange details in a descriptive essay in many different ways. For example, you can move from least to most important details, from top to bottom (or from bottom to top or side to side), or from far to near (or near to far). Each of your essay's body paragraphs may focus on one key characteristic of the subject you are describing or on several related descriptive details.

Essay Map: *Least to Most Important*   **Essay Map: *Top to Bottom/Far to Near***

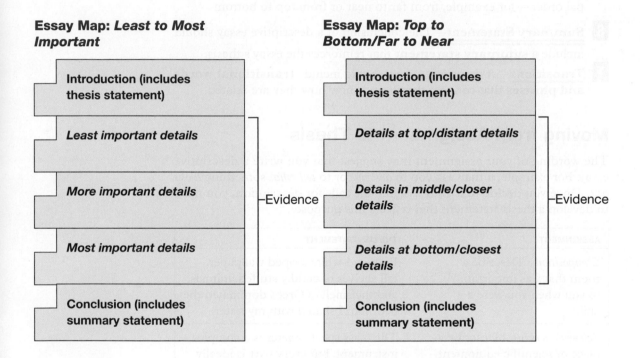

For a list of transitions frequently used in description, see page 136.

Transitions in Descriptive Essays

As you write, use transitional words and expressions to connect details and show how they work together to create a full picture for readers. (Many of these useful transitions indicate location or distance.)

Case Study: A Student Writes a Descriptive Essay

All the students in James Greggs's first-year composition course were also enrolled in sociology, psychology, or education courses with service-learning requirements that reinforced course content. For this reason,

James's composition instructor asked that the students' descriptive essays focus on a person, setting, or item related to their service-learning experiences.

Although James was enjoying his service-learning project—building a deck for elderly residents of a trailer home—he had trouble deciding which aspect of this project to write about. At first, he thought he might describe his team supervisor or one of the other students he worked with, but when he **brainstormed** to find details to include in his essay, he found he had a hard time being objective about his coworkers. However, when he reread entries in the **journal** that he was required to keep for the service-learning component of his sociology class, he found many objective details about the project itself. This discovery led him to the decision to focus on describing the trailer, and the deck he helped to build, rather than the people he worked with.

Consulting photos he had taken of the building site and diagrams he had prepared of the trailer, James wrote a **first draft**, arranging his material from far (the field in which the trailer sat) to near (the trailer itself and the deck he helped to build).

When James **TEST**ed his draft, he saw that his essay had no thesis statement—no sentence that tied all the details together to indicate the main idea he wanted his description to convey. At this point, he emailed his instructor for help, but she reminded him that he had missed her deadline for scheduling appointments and recommended that he make an appointment with a tutor in the writing center.

James's **writing center** tutor suggested that his essay would be more interesting and convincing if his thesis tied the objective details of the project to his conclusions about its value. What did his class contribute? What did they learn? Was the project worth the trouble? She also reviewed his draft with him, suggesting places where he could expand or clarify his description. Because his assignment called for a descriptive essay, not a process essay, she recommended that he delete material that summarized the steps his group took as they built the deck. Finally, she reminded him that he would need to add a summary statement to reinforce his thesis.

When James **revised** his draft, he incorporated his tutor's suggestions and added both a thesis statement and a summary statement. He also added transitional words and phrases to move readers through his description, added more detail, and deleted irrelevant material. Then, he **edited** and **proofread** his essay and checked his **format**.

The following final draft includes all the elements James looked for when he **TEST**ed his essay.

Model Descriptive Essay

Read James's finished essay, and answer the questions in Practice 16-1.

Building and Learning

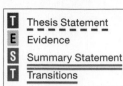

T Thesis Statement
E Evidence
S Summary Statement
T Transitions

Introduction

Topic sentence
(introduces first
group of details)

Descriptive details

Body paragraphs

Topic sentence
(introduces second
group of details)

Descriptive details

Topic sentence
(introduces third
group of details)

Descriptive details

1   Throughout the United States, houses reflect not only the lives of the people who live in them but also the diversity of the American population. Some are large and elaborate, others are modest but well maintained, and still others are in need of repair. Unfortunately, most college students know little about homes other than those in their own neighborhood. I too was fairly sheltered until I participated in a service-learning project for my sociology class. For this project, I, along with some classmates, added a deck to a trailer that was the home of three elderly sisters living on Social Security and disability. It was hard work, but my experience convinced me that all college students should be required to do some kind of service-learning project.

2   The trailer we worked on was located at the end of a small dirt road about thirty minutes from campus. Patches of green and brown grass dotted the land around the trailer, and in the far right-hand corner of the property stood three tall poplar trees. Although the bushes in front of the trailer were trimmed, the woods behind the trailer were beginning to overrun the property. (We were told that members of a local church came once a month to trim the hedges and cut back the trees.) Dominating the right front corner of the lawn, a circular concrete basin looked like a large birdbath. The basin housed a white well pipe with a rusted blue cap. About thirty feet to the left of the concrete basin stood a telephone pole and a bright red metal mailbox.

3   Like the property on which it stood, the trailer was well maintained. It was approximately thirty-five feet long and seven feet high; it rested on cinderblocks, which raised it about three feet off the ground. Under the trailer was an overturned white plastic chair. The trailer itself was covered with sheets of white vinyl siding that ran horizontally, except for the bottom panels on the right side, which ran vertically. The vinyl panels closest to the roof were slightly discolored by dirt and green moss.

4   At the left end of the trailer was a small window—about two feet wide and one foot high. Next to the window was a dark red aluminum door that was outlined in green trim. It had one window at eye level divided by metal strips into four small sections. The number "24" in white plastic letters was glued to the door below this window. To the right of the door was a lightbulb in a black ceramic socket. Next to the light was a large window that was actually two vertical rows of three windows—each the same size as the small window on the left. Further to the right were two smaller windows. Each of these small windows tilted upward and was framed with silver metal strips. On either side of each of these windows was a pair of green metal shutters.

5   The deck we built replaced three wooden steps that had led up to the trailer. A white metal handrail stood on the right side of these steps. It had been newly painted and was connected to the body of the trailer by a heart-shaped piece of metal. In front of the steps, two worn gray wooden boards led to the road.

6   Building the deck was hard work, but the finished deck provided a much better entranceway than the steps did and also gave the trailer a new look. The deck was not very large—ten feet by eight feet—but it extended from the doorway to the area underneath the windows immediately to the right of the door. We built the deck out of pressure-treated lumber so that it wouldn't rot or need painting. We also built three steps that led from the deck to the lawn, and we surrounded the deck with a wooden railing that ran down the right side of the steps. After we finished, we bought two white plastic chairs at a local thrift store and put them on the deck.

7   Now that I look back at the project, I believe that activities like this should be part of every student's college education. Both the residents of the trailer and our class benefited from the service-learning project. The residents of the trailer were happy with the deck because it gave them a place to sit when the weather was nice. They also liked their trailer's new look. Those of us who worked on the project learned that a few days' work could make a real difference in other people's lives.

Topic sentence (introduces fourth group of details)
Descriptive details

Body paragraphs
Topic sentence (introduces fifth group of details)

Descriptive details

Conclusion

PRACTICE

1. Paraphrase James's thesis statement.

2. What determines the order in which James arranges the elements of his description?

3. What details does James provide to describe the property, the trailer, and the deck?

4. What kinds of signals do James's transitions give readers? Do you think he includes enough transitions? Where could he add more?

5. This essay is primarily an objective description. Does it include any subjective details? If so, where?

6. What is this essay's greatest strength? What is its greatest weakness?

grammar in context

Description

When you write a descriptive essay, you may use **modifiers**—words and phrases that describe other words in the sentence—to create a picture of your subject. If you place a modifying word or phrase too far from the word it is supposed to describe, you create a potentially confusing **misplaced modifier**.

> **CONFUSING**   Next to the window <u>outlined in green trim</u> was a dark red aluminum door. (Was the window outlined in green trim?)
>
> **CLEAR**   Next to the window was a dark red aluminum door <u>outlined in green trim</u>.

For information on how to identify and correct misplaced modifiers, see Chapter 28.

Step-by-Step Guide: Writing a Descriptive Essay

Now, you are ready to write a descriptive essay on one of the topics listed below (or a topic of your choice).

TOPICS

An abandoned building
A person or a fictional character
   who makes you laugh (or
   frightens you)
Your room (or your closet
   or desk)
A family photograph

A historical site or monument
An advertisement
An object you cherish
Someone whom everyone notices
Someone whom no one notices
The home page of a website you
   visit often

Plan

Organize

Draft

As you write your essay, follow these steps:

- Make sure your topic calls for description, and then find ideas to write about; next, decide what dominant impression you want to convey, and write a thesis statement that identifies your main idea.

- Choose details that help to convey your dominant impression; then, arrange your details in an effective order, making an outline if necessary.

- Draft your essay.

■ **TEST** your essay, referring to the **TEST**ing a Descriptive Essay checklist below.

■ Revise and edit your essay, referring to the two Self-Assessment Checklists in Chapter 13.

■ Proofread your essay, and make sure it follows your instructor's format guidelines.

TEST

Revise, edit, and proofread

TESTing a descriptive essay

T hesis Statement Unifies Your Essay

☐ Does your introduction include a **thesis statement** that communicates your essay's main idea?

☐ Does your introduction identify the subject of your description?

E vidence Supports Your Essay's Thesis Statement

☐ Does all your **evidence**—your descriptive details—support the dominant impression communicated by your thesis, or should some details be deleted?

☐ Do you describe your subject in enough detail, or do you need to add details to create a more vivid picture?

☐ Are your supporting details arranged in an effective order within your essay and within paragraphs?

S ummary Statement Reinforces Your Essay's Main Idea

☐ Does your conclusion include a **summary statement** that reinforces your essay's thesis?

T ransitions

☐ Do you include **transitions** that introduce your details and move readers smoothly from one aspect of your subject to another?

Description in Action

In "Soweto," Trevor Noah uses **description** to structure his essay.

Soweto

Trevor Noah

Trevor Noah is a comedian, political commentator, and writer. Since 2015, he has hosted *The Daily Show*, a satirical news program. His best-selling autobiography *Born a Crime* (2016) recalls his upbringing in post-apartheid South Africa, the child of a then-illegal relationship between a black mother and a white father. In the excerpt below, Noah depicts his family's life in Soweto, a black township of Johannesburg, under institutionalized racial segregation.

1   There is something magical about Soweto. Yes, it was a prison designed by our oppressors, but it also gave us a sense of self-determination and control. Soweto was ours. It had an aspirational quality that you don't find elsewhere. In America the dream is to make it out of the ghetto. In Soweto, because there was no leaving the ghetto, the dream was to transform the ghetto.

2   For the millions of people who lived in Soweto there were no stores, no bars, no restaurants. There were no paved roads, minimal electricity, inadequate sewerage. But when you put one million people together in one place, they find a way to make a life for themselves. A black-market economy rose up, with every type of business being run out of someone's house: auto mechanics, day care, guys selling refurbished tires.

3   The most common were the *spaza* shops and the shebeens. The *spaza* shops were informal grocery stores. People would build a kiosk in their garage, buy wholesale bread and eggs, and then resell them piecemeal. Everyone in the township bought things in minute quantities because nobody had any money. You couldn't afford to buy a dozen eggs at a time, but you could buy two eggs because that's all you needed that morning. You could buy a quarter loaf of bread, a cup of sugar. The shebeens were unlawful bars in the back of someone's house. They'd put chairs in their backyard and hang out an awning and run a speakeasy. The shebeens were where men would go to drink after work and during prayer meetings and most any other time of day as well.

4   People built homes the way they bought eggs: a little at a time. Every family in the township was allocated a piece of land by the government. You'd first build a shanty on your plot, a makeshift structure of plywood and corrugated iron. Over time, you'd save up money and build a brick wall. One wall. Then you'd save up and build another wall. Then, years later, a third wall and eventually a fourth. Now you had a room, one room for everyone in your family to sleep, eat, do everything. Then you'd save up for a roof. Then windows. Then you'd plaster the thing. Then your daughter would start a family. There was nowhere for them to go, so they'd move in with you. You'd add another corrugated-iron structure onto your brick room and slowly, over years, turn that into a proper room for them as well.

Now your house had two rooms. Then three. Maybe four. Slowly, over generations, you'd keep trying to get to the point where you had a home.

5 My grandmother lived in Orlando East. She had a two-room house. Not a two-bedroom house. A two-room house. There was a bedroom, and then there was basically a living room/kitchen, everything-else room. Some might say we lived like poor people. I prefer "open plan."

6 My mom and I would stay there during school holidays. My aunt and cousins would be there whenever she was on the outs with Dinky. We all slept on the floor in one room, my mom and me, my aunt and my cousins, my uncle and my grandmother and my great-grandmother. The adults each had their own foam mattresses, and there was one big one that we'd roll out into the middle, and the kids slept on that.

Dinky is the name of Noah's uncle, the husband of his aunt mentioned here.

7 We had two shanties in the backyard that my grandmother would rent out to migrants and seasonal workers. We had a small peach tree in a tiny patch on one side of the house and on the other side my grandmother had a driveway. I never understood why my grandmother had a driveway. She didn't have a car. She didn't know how to drive. Yet she had a driveway. All of our neighbors had driveways, some with fancy, cast-iron gates. None of them had cars, either. There was no future in which most of these families would ever have cars. There was maybe one car for every thousand people, yet almost everyone had a driveway. It was almost like building the driveway was a way of willing the car to happen. The story of Soweto is the story of the driveways. It's a hopeful place.

Focus on the Pattern

1. What specific features of Soweto does Noah identify in his description?

2. What dominant impression of Soweto do Noah's details help to convey? Are his memories of Soweto largely positive or negative? Point to details that support your conclusion.

3. Is this a subjective or an objective description? How can you tell?

Writing Practice

1. Write a descriptive essay (subjective or objective) about the neighborhood or community in which you grew up (or the one you live in now).

2. Write a subjective description of your childhood bedroom.

16b Classification Essays

Classification is the act of sorting items into appropriate categories. **Classification essays** divide a whole (your subject) into parts and sort various items into categories.

When you TEST a **classification** essay, make sure it includes all these elements:

T **Thesis Statement**—The introduction of a classification essay should include a **thesis statement** that communicates the essay's main idea and indicates what the essay will classify.

E **Evidence**—The body paragraphs should provide **evidence**—examples and details—to support the thesis statement. The topic sentence of each paragraph should identify the category it will discuss, and the examples and details should explain the category and differentiate it from other categories.

S **Summary Statement**—The conclusion of a classification essay should include a **summary statement** that reinforces the essay's thesis.

T **Transitions**—A classification essay should include **transitional words and phrases** to show how categories are related to one another and to the thesis.

Moving from Assignment to Thesis

The wording of your assignment may suggest that you write a classification essay. For example, you may be asked to consider *kinds, types, categories, components, segments,* or *parts of a whole.* Once you decide that your assignment calls for classification, you need to develop a thesis statement that reflects this purpose.

ASSIGNMENT	THESIS STATEMENT
Business What kinds of courses are most useful for students planning to run their own businesses?	Perhaps surprisingly, courses in communication can be just as useful as courses in accounting, management, and entrepreneurship for future business owners.
Psychology Discuss the kinds of eating disorders that are most common in adolescents.	Although anorexia and bulimia have been widely discussed and studied, binge eating among adolescents, a lesser-known disorder, can be equally serious.
Education Classify elementary school children according to their academic needs.	The elementary school population includes special-needs students, students with reading and math skills at or near grade level, and academically gifted students.

Organizing a Classification Essay

As a rule, each paragraph of a classification essay examines a separate category—a different part of the whole. For example, a paragraph could focus on one kind of course in the college curriculum, one adolescent eating disorder, or one type of child. Within each paragraph, you discuss the individual items that you have put into a particular category—for example, accounting courses, binge eating, or gifted students. If you consider some categories less important than others, you may decide to discuss those minor categories together in a single paragraph, devoting full paragraphs only to the most significant categories.

Essay Map: *One Category in Each Paragraph*

Essay Map: *Major Categories in Separate Paragraphs; Minor Categories Grouped Together*

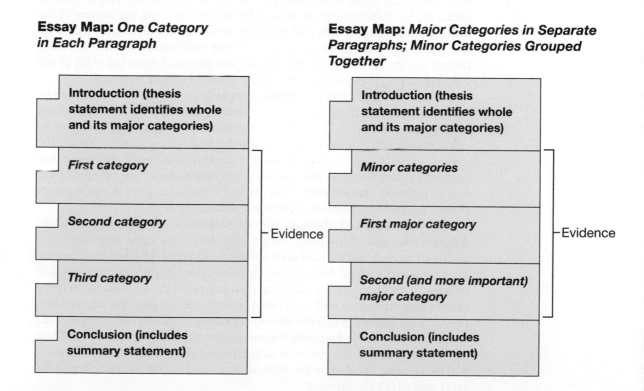

Transitions in Classification Essays

In a classification essay, topic sentences identify the category or categories discussed in each paragraph. Transitional words and phrases signal movement from one category to the next and may also tell readers which categories you consider more (or less) important.

For a list of transitions frequently used in classification, see page 146.

Case Study: A Student Writes a Classification Essay

Rob O'Neal, a student in a first-year writing course, was given the following assignment.

> Write a classification essay focusing on a type of consumer product—for example, smartphones, jeans, mountain bikes, or hair gels. Discuss three or four categories of the product you select, examining the same features for each category.

At first, Rob was overwhelmed by the possibilities; after all, he was a consumer, and there were many products to choose from. Then, stuck in traffic on his way home from school, he started noticing the names of the different cars around him and thinking about all the different models he had learned to identify when he was younger and fascinated by everything related to cars. At this point, he realized that he could write his essay about cars, classifying them on the basis of the kinds of names they had.

When Rob got home, he **brainstormed**, listing all the car names he could think of. Then, he made a **cluster diagram** to help him sort all the names into categories. When he looked over his diagram, he saw that he could organize the car names he had listed into three categories—those that suggest exciting destinations, those that suggest toughness, and those that suggest exploration and discovery. Identifying these three categories led him to a **thesis statement** for his essay: "The names auto manufacturers choose for their cars appeal to Americans' deepest desires."

When he **drafted** his essay, Rob developed each branch of his cluster diagram into one of his body paragraphs and wrote topic sentences that clearly identified and defined each category. When he **TEST**ed his essay, he saw that it included all the required elements, but he still wasn't completely satisfied with his draft. To help him plan his revision, he made a **writing center appointment** and went over his draft with a tutor. She advised him to add more examples of each kind of car name as well as more transitional words and phrases to help readers move smoothly through his essay. When he finished making the revisions suggested by his writing center tutor (as well as some he decided on himself), he went on to **edit** and **proofread** his essay and check his **format**.

The final draft that follows includes all the elements Rob looked for when he **TEST**ed his essay.

Model Classification Essay

Read Rob's finished essay, and answer the questions in Practice 16-2.

Selling a Dream

TEST

T Thesis Statement
E Evidence
S Summary Statement
T Transitions

1   The earliest automobiles were often named after the men who manufactured them—Ford, Studebaker, Nash, Olds, Chrysler, Dodge, Chevrolet, and so on. Over the years, however, American car makers began competing to see what kinds of names would sell the most cars. Many car names seem to have been chosen simply for how they sound: Alero, Corvette, Neon, Probe, Caprice. Many others, however, are designed to sell specific dreams to consumers. Americans always seem to want to be, do, and become something different. They want to be tough and brave, to explore new places, to take risks. The names auto manufacturers choose for their cars appeal to Americans' deepest desires.

Introduction

2   Some American cars are named for places people dream of traveling to. Park Avenue, Malibu, Riviera, Seville, Tahoe, Yukon, Aspen, and Durango are some names that suggest escape—to New York City, California, Europe, the West. Other place names—Sebring, Daytona, and Bonneville, for example—are associated with the danger and excitement of car racing. And then there is the El Dorado, a car named for a fictional paradise: a city of gold.

Topic sentence (identifies first category)

Examples and details

3   Other car names convey rough and tough, even dangerous, images. Animal names fall into this category, with models like Ram, Bronco, and Mustang suggesting powerful, untamed beasts. The "rough and tough" category also includes car names that suggest the wildness of the Old West: Wrangler and Rodeo, for example. Because the American auto industry was originally centered near Detroit, Michigan, where many cities have Indian names, cars named for the cities where they are manufactured inherited these names. Thus, cars called Cadillac, Pontiac, and Cherokee recall the history of Indian nations, and these too might suggest the excitement of the untamed West.

Topic sentence (identifies second category)

Examples and details

Body paragraphs

4   The most interesting car names in terms of the dream they sell, however, were selected to suggest exploration and discovery. Years ago, some car names honored real explorers, like DeSoto and LaSalle. Now, model names only sell an abstract idea. Still, American car names like Blazer, Explorer, Navigator, Journey, Mountaineer, Expedition, Caravan, and Voyager (as well as the names of foreign cars driven by many Americans, such as Nissan's Pathfinder and Quest and Honda's Passport, Pilot, and Odyssey) have the power to make drivers feel they are blazing new trails and discovering new worlds—when in fact they may simply be carpooling their children to a soccer game or commuting to work.

Topic sentence (identifies third category)

Examples and details

Conclusion

5   <u>Most people take cars for granted, but manufacturers still try to make</u> <u>consumers believe they are buying more than just transportation.</u> Today, however, the car is just an ordinary piece of machinery, a necessity for many people. Sadly, the automobile is no longer seen as the amazing invention it once was.

PRACTICE

16-2

1. Restate Rob's thesis statement in your own words.

2. What three categories of car names does Rob discuss in his essay?

3. Is Rob's treatment of the three categories similar? Does he present the same kind of information for each kind of car name?

4. How do Rob's topic sentences move readers from one category to the next? How do they link the three categories?

5. Does Rob consider enough categories? Does he include enough examples in each category? Can you suggest additional categories or examples that he could have discussed?

6. What is this essay's greatest strength? What is its greatest weakness?

grammar in context

Classification

When you write a classification essay, you may want to list the categories you are going to discuss or the examples in each category. If you do, use a **colon** to introduce your list, and make sure that a complete sentence comes before the colon.

> Many car names seem to be chosen simply for how they sound: Alero, Corvette, Neon, Probe, Caprice.

For information on how to use a colon to introduce a list, see 36d.

Step-by-Step Guide: Writing a Classification Essay

Now, you are ready to write a classification essay on one of the topics below (or a topic of your own).

TOPICS

Types of teachers (or bosses)	Traits of oldest children, middle children, and youngest children
Ways to lose (or gain) weight	
Items hanging on your walls	Kinds of desserts
	Kinds of workers you encounter in a typical day
Kinds of stores in your neighborhood	College students' clothing choices
Kinds of learning styles	Kinds of tattoos

As you write your essay, follow these steps:

- Make sure your topic calls for classification, and then find ideas to write about; next, identify your main idea, and write a thesis statement.

- Decide what categories you will discuss, sort examples and details into categories, and arrange your categories in an effective order, making an outline if necessary.

- Draft your essay.

- **TEST** your essay, referring to the **TEST**ing a Classification Essay Checklist that follows.

- Revise and edit your essay, referring to the two Self-Assessment Checklists in Chapter 13.

- Proofread your essay, and make sure it follows your instructor's format guidelines.

Plan

Organize

Draft

TEST

Revise, edit, and proofread

TESTing a classification essay

Thesis Statement Unifies Your Essay

☐ Does your introduction include a **thesis statement** that clearly identifies the subject of your classification and the categories you will discuss?

Evidence Supports Your Essay's Thesis Statement

☐ Does all your **evidence**—examples and details—support your thesis, or should some be deleted? Do you include enough examples and details?

☐ Do you treat each major category similarly and with equal thoroughness?

> **S** ummary Statement Reinforces Your Essay's Main Idea
>
> ☐ Does your conclusion include a **summary statement** that reinforces your essay's thesis?
>
> **T** ransitions
>
> ☐ Do you include **transitions** that introduce your categories and lead readers from one category to the next?

Classification in Action

In "Mother Tongue," Amy Tan uses **classification** to structure her essay.

Mother Tongue
Amy Tan

Amy Tan was born in 1952 in Oakland, California, the daughter of recent Chinese immigrants. In 1984, when she began to write fiction, she started to explore the contradictions she faced as an American daughter of immigrant parents. Three years later, she published *The Joy Luck Club* (1987), a best-selling novel about four immigrant Chinese women and their American-born daughters. Her later works include the novels *Saving Fish from Drowning* (2005) and *The Valley of Amazement* (2013) and the memoir *Where the Past Begins* (2017). In the following 1990 essay, Tan considers her mother's heavily Chinese-influenced English, as well as the different "Englishes" she herself uses, especially in communicating with her mother.

1   I am not a scholar of English or literature. I cannot give you much more than personal opinions on the English language and its variations in this country or others.

2   I am a writer. And by that definition, I am someone who has always loved language. I am fascinated by language in daily life. I spend a great deal of my time thinking about the power of language—the way it can evoke an emotion, a visual image, a complex idea, or a simple truth. Language is the tool of my trade. And I use them all—all the Englishes I grew up with.

3   Recently, I was made keenly aware of the different Englishes I do use. I was giving a talk to a large group of people, the same talk I had already given to half a dozen other groups. The nature of the talk was about my writing, my life, and my book, *The Joy Luck Club*. The talk was going along

well enough, until I remembered one major difference that made the whole talk sound wrong. My mother was in the room. And it was perhaps the first time she had heard me give a lengthy speech, using the kind of English I have never used with her. I was saying things like, "The intersection of memory upon imagination" and "There is an aspect of my fiction that relates to thus-and-thus"—a speech filled with carefully wrought grammatical phrases, burdened, it suddenly seemed to me, with nominalized forms, past perfect tenses, conditional phrases, all the forms of standard English that I had learned in school and through books, the forms of English I did not use at home with my mother.

4   Just last week, I was walking down the street with my mother, and I again found myself conscious of the English I was using, and the English I do use with her. We were talking about the price of new and used furniture and I heard myself saying this: "Not waste money that way." My husband was with us as well, and he didn't notice any switch in my English. And then I realized why. It's because over the twenty years we've been together I've often used that same kind of English with him, and sometimes he even uses it with me. It has become our language of intimacy, a different sort of English that relates to family talk, the language I grew up with.

5   So you'll have some idea of what this family talk I heard sounds like, I'll quote what my mother said during a recent conversation which I videotaped and then transcribed. During this conversation my mother was talking about a political gangster in Shanghai who had the same last name as her family's, Du, and how the gangster in his early years wanted to be adopted by her family, which was rich by comparison. Later, the gangster became more powerful, far richer than my mother's family, and one day showed up at my mother's wedding to pay his respects. Here's what she said in part:

6   "Du Yusong having business like fruit stand. Like off the street kind. He is Du like Du Zong—but not Tsung-ming Island people. The local people call putong, the river east side, he belong to that side local people. The man want to ask Du Zong father take him in like become own family. Du Zong father wasn't looking down on him, but didn't take seriously, until that man big like become a mafia. Now important person very hard to inviting him. Chinese way, come only to show respect, don't stay for dinner. Respect for making big celebration, he shows up. Mean gives lots of respect. Chinese custom. Chinese social life that way. If too important won't have to stay too long. He come to my wedding. I didn't see. I heard it. I gone to boy's side, they have YMCA dinner. Chinese age I was nineteen."

7   You should know that my mother's expressive command of English belies how much she actually understands. She reads the *Forbes* report, listens to *Wall Street Week*, converses daily with her stockbroker, reads all of Shirley MacLaine's books with ease—all kinds of things I can't begin to understand. Yet some of my friends tell me they understand 50 percent of what my mother says. Some say they understand 80 to 90 percent. Some say they understand none of it, as if she were speaking pure Chinese. But to me, my mother's English is perfectly clear, perfectly natural. It's my

WORD POWER

wrought crafted

nominalize to convert a word into a noun

WORD POWER

command the ability to use something

belies disguises

mother's tongue. Her language, as I hear it, is vivid, direct, full of observation and imagery. This was the language that helped shape the way I saw things, expressed things, made sense of the world.

8   Lately, I've been giving more thought to the kind of English my mother speaks. Like others, I have described it to people as "broken" or "fractured" English. But I wince when I say that. It has always bothered me that I can think of no way to describe it other than "broken," as if it were damaged and needed to be fixed, as if it lacked a certain wholeness and soundness. I've heard other terms used, "limited English," for example. But they seem just as bad, as if everything is limited, including people's perceptions of the limited English speaker.

9   I know this for a fact, because when I was growing up, my mother's "limited" English limited *my* perception of her. I was ashamed of her English. I believed that her English reflected the quality of what she had to say. That is, because she expressed them imperfectly her thoughts were imperfect. And I had plenty of empirical evidence to support me: the fact that people in department stores, at banks, and at restaurants did not take her seriously, did not give her good service, pretended not to understand her, or even acted as if they did not hear her.

10   My mother has long realized the limitations of her English as well. When I was fifteen, she used to have me call people on the phone to pretend I was she. In this guise, I was forced to ask for information or even complain and yell at people who had been rude to her. One time it was a call to her stockbroker in New York. She had cashed out her small portfolio and it just so happened we were going to go to New York the next week, our very first trip outside California. I had to get on the phone and say in an adolescent voice that was not very convincing, "This is Mrs. Tan."

11   And my mother was standing in the back whispering loudly, "Why he don't send me check, already two weeks late. So mad he lie to me, losing me money."

12   And then I said in perfect English, "Yes, I'm getting rather concerned. You had agreed to send the check two weeks ago, but it hasn't arrived."

13   Then she began to talk more loudly. "What he want, I come to New York tell him front of his boss, you cheating me?" And I was trying to calm her down, make her be quiet, while telling the stockbroker, "I can't tolerate any more excuses. If I don't receive the check immediately I am going to have to speak to your manager when I'm in New York next week." And sure enough, the following week there we were in front of this astonished stock-broker, and I was sitting there red-faced and quiet, and my mother, the real Mrs. Tan, was shouting at his boss in her impeccable broken English.

14   We used a similar routine just five days ago, for a situation that was far less humorous. My mother had gone to the hospital for an appointment, to find out about a benign brain tumor a CAT scan had revealed a month ago. She said she had spoken very good English, her best English,

WORD POWER

empirical evidence
knowledge gained by experience

guise the way someone or something appears

WORD POWER

benign not dangerous

no mistakes. Still, she said, the hospital did not apologize when they said they had lost the CAT scan and she had come for nothing. She said they did not seem to have any sympathy when she told them she was anxious to know the exact diagnosis, since her husband and son had both died of brain tumors. She said they would not give her any more information until the next time and she would have to make another appointment for that. So she said she would not leave until the doctor called her daughter. She wouldn't budge. And when the doctor finally called her daughter, me, who spoke in perfect English—lo and behold—we had assurances the CAT scan would be found, promises that a conference call on Monday would be held, and apologies for any suffering my mother had gone through for a most regrettable mistake.

15   I think my mother's English almost had an effect on limiting my possibilities in life as well. Sociologists and linguists probably will tell you that a person's developing language skills are more influenced by peers. But I do think that the language spoken in the family, especially in immigrant families which are more insular, plays a large role in shaping the language of the child. And I believe that it affected my results on achievement tests, IQ tests, and the SAT. While my English skills were never judged as poor, compared to math, English could not be considered my strong suit. In grade school I did moderately well, getting perhaps B's, sometimes B-pluses, in English and scoring perhaps in the sixtieth or seventieth percentile on achievement tests. But those scores were not good enough to override the opinion that my true abilities lay in math and science, because in those areas I achieved A's and scored in the ninetieth percentile or higher.

> **WORD POWER**
>
> **insular** uninterested in things outside of one's experiences

16   This was understandable. Math is precise; there is only one correct answer. Whereas, for me at least, the answers on English tests were always a judgment call, a matter of opinion and personal experience. Those tests were constructed around items like fill-in-the-blank sentence completion, such as "Even though Tom was _____, Mary thought he was _____." And the correct answer always seemed to be the most bland combinations of thoughts, for example, "Even though Tom was shy, Mary thought he was charming," with the grammatical structure "even though" limiting the correct answer to some sort of semantic opposites, so you wouldn't get answers like, "Even though Tom was foolish, Mary thought he was ridiculous." Well, according to my mother, there were very few limitations as to what Tom could have been and what Mary might have thought of him. So I never did well on tests like that.

> **WORD POWER**
>
> **semantic** relating to language

17   The same was true with word analogies, pairs of words in which you were supposed to find some sort of logical, semantic relationship—for example, "*Sunset* is to *nightfall* as _____ is to _____." And here you would be presented with a list of four possible pairs, one of which showed the same kind of relationship: *red* is to *stoplight, bus* is to *arrival, chills* is to *fever, yawn* is to *boring.* Well, I could never think that way. I knew what the tests were asking, but I could not block out of my mind the images already created by the first pair, "*sunset* is to *nightfall*"—and I would see a burst of colors

against a darkening sky, the moon rising, the lowering of a curtain of stars. And all the other pairs of words—red, bus, stoplight, boring—just threw up a mass of confusing images, making it impossible for me to sort out something as logical as saying: "A sunset precedes nightfall" is the same as "a chill precedes a fever." The only way I would have gotten that answer right would have been to imagine an associative situation, for example, my being disobedient and staying out past sunset, catching a chill at night, which turns into feverish pneumonia as punishment, which indeed did happen to me.

18   I have been thinking about all this lately, about my mother's English, about achievement tests. Because lately I've been asked, as a writer, why there are not more Asian Americans represented in American literature. Why are there few Asian Americans enrolled in creative writing programs? Why do so many Chinese students go into engineering? Well, these are broad sociological questions I can't begin to answer. But I have noticed in surveys—in fact, just last week—that Asian students, as a whole, always do significantly better on math achievement tests than in English. And this makes me think that there are other Asian-American students whose English spoken in the home might also be described as "broken" or "limited." And perhaps they also have teachers who are steering them away from writing and into math and science, which is what happened to me.

19   Fortunately, I happen to be rebellious in nature and enjoy the challenge of disproving assumptions made about me. I became an English major my first year in college, after being enrolled as pre-med. I started writing nonfiction as a freelancer the week after I was told by my former boss that writing was my worst skill and I should hone my talents toward account management.

20   But it wasn't until 1985 that I finally began to write fiction. And at first I wrote using what I thought to be wittily crafted sentences, sentences that would finally prove I had mastery over the English language. Here's an example from the first draft of a story that later made its way into *The Joy Luck Club*, but without this line: "That was my mental quandary in its nascent state." A terrible line, which I can barely pronounce.

21   Fortunately, for reasons I won't get into today, I later decided I should envision a reader for the stories I would write. And the reader I decided upon was my mother because these were stories about mothers. So with this reader in mind—and in fact she did read my early drafts—I began to write stories using all the Englishes I grew up with: the English I spoke to my mother, which for lack of a better term might be described as "simple"; the English she used with me, which for lack of a better term might be described as "broken"; my translation of her Chinese, which could certainly be described as "watered down"; and what I imagined to be her translation of her Chinese if she could speak in perfect English, her internal language,

WORD POWER

hone improve

and for that I sought to preserve the essence, but neither an English nor a Chinese structure. I wanted to capture what language ability tests can never reveal: her intent, her passion, her imagery, the rhythms of her speech and the nature of her thoughts.

22   Apart from what any critic had to say about my writing, I knew I had succeeded where it counted when my mother finished reading my book and gave me her verdict: "So easy to read."

Focus on the Pattern

1. What is Tan classifying in this essay? What categories does she discuss?

2. Why is classification a good choice for the subject of Tan's essay? What other patterns of essay development might she have used to structure her essay?

Writing Practice

1. What different languages do you use when you speak (or write) as a student, employee, friend, or son or daughter? Write a classification essay discussing these different levels of speech or writing.

2. Think about the mothers you know best (in addition to your own). Then, write a classification essay that assigns each of these women to one of these three categories on the basis of how closely they supervise their children: helicopter parents, free-range parents, and those who fall somewhere in the middle. In your essay's thesis, state which kind of mother is superior to the others.

16c   Definition Essays

Definition explains the meaning of a term or concept. A **definition essay** presents an *extended definition*, using various patterns of development to move beyond a simple dictionary definition.

When you **TEST** a **definition** essay, make sure it includes all these elements:

T   Thesis Statement—The introduction of a definition essay should include a **thesis statement** that communicates the essay's main idea and identifies the term you are going to define.

E   Evidence—The body paragraphs should include **evidence**— examples and details—that supports the thesis statement and defines your term. Body paragraphs may use different patterns of development.

S   **Summary Statement**—The conclusion of a definition essay should include a **summary statement** that reinforces the essay's thesis.

T   **Transitions**—A definition essay should include **transitional words and phrases** to move readers from one section of the definition to the next.

Moving from Assignment to Thesis

The wording of your assignment may suggest that you write a definition essay. For example, you may be asked to *define* or *explain* or to answer the question *What is x?* or *What does x mean?* Once you decide that your assignment calls for definition, you need to develop a thesis statement that reflects this purpose.

ASSIGNMENT	THESIS STATEMENT
Art Explain the meaning of the term *performance art*.	Unlike more conventional forms of art, *performance art* extends beyond the canvas.
Biology Define Darwin's concept of *natural selection*.	The term *natural selection*, popularly known as "survival of the fittest," is the idea that organisms whose traits are best suited to their environments will survive to pass those traits to offspring.
Psychology What is *attention deficit disorder*?	*Attention deficit disorder* (ADD), once narrowly defined as a childhood problem, is now known to affect adults as well as children.

Organizing a Definition Essay

As the thesis statements above suggest, definition essays can be developed in various ways. For example, you can define something by telling how it occurred (narration), by describing its appearance (description), by giving a series of examples (exemplification), by telling how it operates (process), by telling how it is similar to or different from something else (comparison and contrast), or by discussing its parts (classification).

Some definition essays use a single pattern of development; others combine several patterns of development, perhaps using a different one in each paragraph.

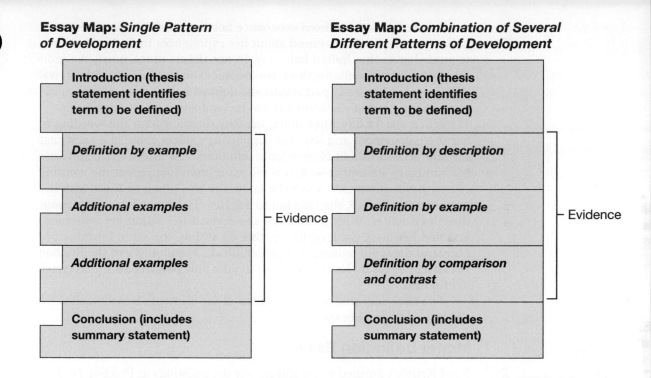

Essay Map: *Single Pattern of Development*

- Introduction (thesis statement identifies term to be defined)
- *Definition by example*
- *Additional examples* ⎤
- *Additional examples* ⎦ Evidence
- Conclusion (includes summary statement)

Essay Map: *Combination of Several Different Patterns of Development*

- Introduction (thesis statement identifies term to be defined)
- *Definition by description* ⎤
- *Definition by example* ⎥ Evidence
- *Definition by comparison and contrast* ⎦
- Conclusion (includes summary statement)

Transitions in Definition Essays

The kinds of transitions used in a definition essay depend on the specific pattern or patterns of development in the essay.

For a list of transitions frequently used in definition, see page 156.

Case Study: A Student Writes a Definition Essay

Kristin Whitehead, a student in a first-year writing course, was given the following assignment:

> From the attached list, choose a slang term, an abbreviation or short-hand used in text messages, or a technical term used in one of your classes. Write an essay in which you define this term, developing your definition with any patterns that seem appropriate.

Because her instructor gave the class a list of topics to choose from, Kristin was able to decide on a topic quickly. She chose to define *street smart*, a term with which she was very familiar. She was particularly interested in defining this term because she thought of herself as a street-smart person and was impatient with some of her fellow first-year students, who she felt lacked this important trait.

Kristin had learned from experience how important it was to be street smart, and she **brainstormed** about her experiences to find information to guide her as she drafted her essay. In her **thesis statement**, she indicated why she was defining this term (because she saw it as a "vital survival skill"), and in her body paragraphs she defined her term by giving examples of behavior that she considered to be (and *not* to be) street smart.

When she TESTed her draft, she was satisfied with the wording of her thesis statement and with her supporting evidence, but she knew that she still needed to add clearer topic sentences; she also needed to revise her summary statement so that it did more than just repeat the wording of her thesis statement. Since she knew she was going to meet with her **peer-review** group, she decided to ask her classmates for advice about these two issues. With their help, she revised her summary statement and tied her body paragraphs together by adding the same introductory phrase to the topic sentences of paragraphs 2, 3, and 4. When she finished **revising** her essay, Kristin went on to **edit** and **proofread** it and check her **format**.

The final draft that follows includes all the elements Kristin looked for when she TESTed her essay.

Model Definition Essay

Read Kristin's finished essay, and answer the questions in Practice 16-3.

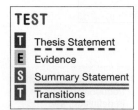

Introduction

Thesis statement

Topic sentence
(identifies first point)

Body paragraphs

Examples and details

Street Smart

1   I grew up in a big city, so I was practically born street smart. I learned the hard way how to act and what to do, and so did my friends. To us, being *street smart* meant having common sense. We wanted to be cool, but we needed to be safe, too. Now I go to college in a big city, and I realize that not everyone here grew up the way I did. Many students are from suburbs or rural areas, and they are either terrified of the city or totally ignorant of city life. The few suburban or rural students who are willing to venture downtown are not street smart—but they should be. Being street smart is a vital survival skill, one that everyone should learn.

2   For me, being street smart means knowing how to protect my possessions. Friends of mine who are not used to city life insist on wearing all their jewelry when they go downtown. I think this is asking for trouble, and I know better. I always tuck my chain under my shirt and leave my gold earrings home. Another thing that surprises me is how some of my friends wave their money around. They always seem to be standing on the street, trying to count their change or stuff dollars into their wallets. Street-smart people make sure to put their money safely away in their pockets or purses before they leave a store. A street-smart person will also carry a backpack,

a purse strapped across the chest, or no purse at all. A person who is not street smart carries a purse loosely over one shoulder or dangles it by its handle. Again, these people are asking for trouble.

3   Being street smart also means protecting myself. It means being aware of my surroundings at all times and looking alert. A lot of times, I have been downtown with people who kept stopping on the street to talk about where they should go next or walking up and down the same street over and over again. A street-smart person would never do this. It is important that I look as if I know where I am going at all times, even if I don't. Whenever possible, I decide on a destination in advance, and I make sure I know how to get there. Even if I am not completely sure where I am headed, I make sure my body language conveys my confidence in my ability to reach my destination.

Topic sentence (identifies second point)

Examples and details

Body paragraphs

4   Finally, being street smart means protecting my life. A street-smart person does not walk alone, especially after dark, in an unfamiliar neighborhood. A street-smart person does not ask random strangers for directions; when lost, he or she asks a shopkeeper for help. A street-smart person takes main streets instead of side streets. When faced with danger or the threat of danger, a street-smart person knows when to run, when to scream, and when to give up money or possessions to avoid violence.

Topic sentence (identifies third point)

Examples and details

5   Being street smart is vitally important—sometimes even a matter of life and death. Some people think it is a gift, but I think it is something almost anyone can learn. Probably the best way to learn how to be street smart is to hang out with people who know where they are going.

Conclusion

PRACTICE

16-3

1. Restate Kristin's thesis statement in your own words.

2. In your own words, define the term *street smart*. Why does this term require more than a one-sentence definition?

3. Where does Kristin use examples to develop her definition? Where does she use comparison and contrast? What other patterns of development could she have used?

4. What phrase does Kristin repeat in her topic sentences to tie her essay's three body paragraphs together?

5. Kristin's conclusion is quite a bit shorter than her other paragraphs. Do you think she should expand this paragraph? If so, what should she add?

6. What is this essay's greatest strength? What is its greatest weakness?

grammar in context

Definition

When you write a definition essay, you may begin with a one-sentence definition that you expand in the rest of your essay. When you write your definition sentence, do not use the phrase *is when* or *is where*.

For me, being street smart ~~is when I know~~ how to protect my
^{means knowing}

possessions.

Being street smart is also ~~where I protect~~ myself.
^{means protecting}

For information on how to structure a definition sentence, see the Grammar in Context box in 11a.

Step-by-Step Guide: Writing a Definition Essay

Now, you are ready to write a definition essay on one of the topics listed below (or a topic of your choice).

Plan

Organize

Draft

TEST

Revise, edit,
and proofread

TOPICS

Upward mobility	Responsibility	Courage
Peer pressure	Procrastination	Happiness
Success	Security	Home
Loyalty	Ambition	Family

As you write your essay, follow these steps:

- Make sure your topic calls for definition, and then find ideas to write about; next, identify your main idea, and write a thesis statement.
- Decide what patterns of development to use to support your thesis, and arrange supporting examples and details in an effective order, making an outline if necessary.
- Draft your essay.
- **TEST** your essay, referring to the **TEST**ing a Definition Essay checklist below.
- Revise and edit your essay, referring to the two Self-Assessment Checklists in Chapter 13.
- Proofread your essay, and make sure it follows your instructor's format guidelines.

Definition in Action

In "I Want a Wife," Judy Brady uses **definition** to structure her essay.

I Want a Wife

Judy Brady

Writer and activist Judy Brady helped found the Toxic Links Coalition, an organization dedicated to exposing the dangers of environmental toxins and their impact on public health, and Greenaction for Health and Environmental Justice. She was also active in the women's movement, and her classic essay "I Want a Wife" was published in the first issue of *Ms.* magazine (1971).

1   I belong to that classification of people known as wives. I am A Wife. And, not altogether incidentally, I am a mother.

2   Not too long ago a male friend of mine appeared on the scene fresh from a recent divorce. He had one child, who is, of course, with his ex-wife. He is looking for another wife. As I thought about him while I was ironing one evening, it suddenly occurred to me that I, too, would like to have a wife. Why do I want a wife?

3   I would like to go back to school so that I can become economically independent, support myself, and, if need be, support those dependent upon me. I want a wife who will work and send me to school. And while I am going to school I want a wife to take care of my children. I want a wife to keep track of the children's doctor and dentist appointments. And to keep track of mine, too. I want a wife to make sure my children eat properly and are kept clean. I want a wife who will wash the children's clothes and keep them mended. I want a wife who is a good nurturant attendant to my children, who arranges for their schooling, makes sure that they have an adequate social life with their peers, takes them to the park, the zoo, etc. I want a wife who takes care of the children when they are sick, a wife who arranges to be around when the children need special care, because, of course, I cannot miss classes at school. My wife must arrange to lose time at work and not lose the job. It may mean a small cut in my wife's income from time to time, but I guess I can tolerate that. Needless to say, my wife will arrange and pay for the care of the children while my wife is working.

WORD POWER

nurturant providing physical and emotional care

4   I want a wife who will take care of *my* physical needs. I want a wife who will keep my house clean. A wife who will pick up after my children, a wife who will pick up after me. I want a wife who will keep my clothes clean, ironed, mended, replaced when need be, and who will see to it that my personal things are kept in their proper place so that I can find what I need the minute I need it. I want a wife who cooks the meals, a wife who is a *good* cook. I want a wife who will plan the menus, do the necessary grocery shopping, prepare the meals, serve them pleasantly, and then do the cleaning up while I do my studying. I want a wife who will care for me when I am sick and sympathize with my pain and loss of time from school. I want a wife to go along when our family takes a vacation so that someone can continue to care for me and my children when I need a rest and change of scene.

5   I want a wife who will not bother me with rambling complaints about a wife's duties. But I want a wife who will listen to me when I feel the need to explain a rather difficult point I have come across in my course of studies. And I want a wife who will type my papers for me when I have written them.

6   I want a wife who will take care of the details of my social life. When my wife and I are invited out by my friends, I want a wife who will take care of the babysitting arrangements. When I meet people at school that I like and want to entertain, I want a wife who will have the house clean, will prepare a special meal, serve it to me and my friends, and not interrupt when I talk about things that interest me and my friends. I want a wife who will have arranged that the children are fed and ready for bed before my guests arrive so that the children do not bother us. I want a wife who takes care of the needs of my guests so that they feel comfortable, who makes sure that they have an ashtray, that they are passed the hors d'oeuvres, that they are

offered a second helping of the food, that their wine glasses are replenished when necessary, that their coffee is served to them as they like it. And I want a wife who knows that sometimes I need a night out by myself.

7   I want a wife who is sensitive to my sexual needs, a wife who makes love passionately and eagerly when I feel like it, a wife who makes sure that I am satisfied. And, of course, I want a wife who will not demand sexual attention when I am not in the mood for it. I want a wife who assumes the complete responsibility for birth control, because I do not want more children. I want a wife who will remain sexually faithful to me so that I do not have to clutter up my intellectual life with jealousies. And I want a wife who understands that *my* sexual needs may entail more than strict adherence to monogamy. I must, after all, be able to relate to people as fully as possible.

8   If, by chance, I find another person more suitable as a wife than the wife I already have, I want the liberty to replace my present wife with another one. Naturally, I will expect a fresh new life; my wife will take the children and be solely responsible for them so that I am left free.

9   When I am through with school and have a job, I want my wife to quit working and remain at home so that my wife can more fully and completely take care of a wife's duties.

10   My God, who *wouldn't* want a wife?

WORD POWER

replenished made full or complete again

WORD POWER

adherence steady or faithful attachment

monogamy having one spouse or sexual partner at a time

Focus on the Pattern

1. Does Brady include a formal definition of *wife* anywhere in her essay? If so, where? If not, do you think she should?

2. Brady develops her definition with examples. What are some of her most important examples?

3. Besides exemplification, what other patterns of development does Brady use to develop her definition?

Writing Practice

1. Assume you are Brady's husband and feel unjustly attacked by her essay. Write her a letter in which you define *husband*, using as many examples as you can to show how overworked and underappreciated you are.

2. Write an essay in which you define your ideal teacher, parent, spouse, or boss.

16d Argument Essays

An **argument** takes a stand on a debatable issue—that is, an issue that has two sides (and can therefore be debated). An **argument essay** uses different kinds of *evidence*—facts, examples, and sometimes expert opinion—to persuade readers to accept a position.

When you **TEST** an **argument** essay, make sure it includes all these elements:

T   <u>Thesis Statement</u>—The introduction of an argument essay should introduce the issue you will discuss and include a **thesis statement** that expresses the essay's main idea: the position you will take on the issue.

E   Evidence—The body paragraphs should include **evidence**—facts, examples, and expert opinion—to support the thesis statement convincingly. The topic sentence of each body paragraph should identify one point of support for your thesis.

S   <u>Summary Statement</u>—The conclusion of an argument essay should include a strong **summary statement** that reinforces the essay's thesis.

T   **Transitions**—An argument essay should include logical **transitional words and phrases** that show how your points are related and move readers through your argument.

Moving from Assignment to Thesis

The wording of your assignment may suggest that you write an argument essay. For example, you may be asked to *debate, argue, consider, give your opinion, take a position,* or *take a stand.* Once you decide that your assignment calls for argument, you need to develop a thesis statement that takes a position on the topic you will write about in your essay.

ASSIGNMENT	THESIS STATEMENT
Composition Explain your position on a current social issue.	People should be able to invest some of their Social Security contributions in the stock market.
American history Do you believe that General Lee was responsible for the South's defeat at the Battle of Gettysburg? Why or why not?	Because Lee refused to listen to the advice given to him by General Longstreet, he is largely responsible for the South's defeat at the Battle of Gettysburg.
Ethics Should physician-assisted suicide be legalized?	Although many people think physician-assisted suicide should remain illegal, it should be legal in certain situations.

Organizing an Argument Essay

An argument essay can be organized *inductively* or *deductively*. An **inductive argument** moves from the specific to the general—that is, from a group of specific observations to a general conclusion based on these observations. An essay on the first topic in the chart above, for example, could be an inductive argument. It could begin by presenting facts, examples, and expert opinion about the benefits of investing in the stock market and end with the conclusion that people should be able to invest part of their Social Security contributions in the stock market.

A **deductive argument** moves from the general to the specific. A deductive argument begins with a **major premise** (a general statement that the writer believes his or her audience will accept) and then moves to a **minor premise** (a specific instance of the belief stated in the major premise). It ends with a **conclusion** that follows from the two premises. For example, an essay on the last topic in the chart above could be a deductive argument. It could begin with the major premise that all terminally ill patients who are in great pain should be given access to physician-assisted suicide. It could then go on to state and explain the minor premise that a particular patient is both terminally ill and in great pain, offering facts, examples, and the opinions of experts to support this premise. The essay could conclude that this patient should, therefore, be allowed the option of physician-assisted suicide. The deductive argument presented in the essay would have three parts.

MAJOR PREMISE   All terminally ill patients who are in great pain should be allowed to choose physician-assisted suicide.

MINOR PREMISE   John Lacca is a terminally ill patient who is in great pain.

CONCLUSION   Therefore, John Lacca should be allowed to choose physician-assisted suicide.

Before you present your argument, think about whether your readers are likely to be hostile toward, neutral toward, or in agreement with your position. Once you understand your audience, you can decide which points to make to support your argument. As you write, focus on being fair: try to achieve a balanced, moderate tone, and avoid name-calling or personal attacks.

Begin each paragraph of your argument essay with a topic sentence that clearly introduces a point in support of your thesis. Throughout your essay, include specific examples that will make your arguments persuasive. Keep in mind that arguments that rely on generalizations alone are not as convincing as those that include vivid details and specific examples.

In addition to supporting your position, your essay should also briefly summarize arguments *against* your position and **refute** them (that is, argue against them) by identifying factual errors or errors in logic. If an opposing argument is particularly strong, concede its strength—but try to point out some weaknesses as well. If you deal with opposing arguments in this way, your audience will see you as a fair and reasonable person.

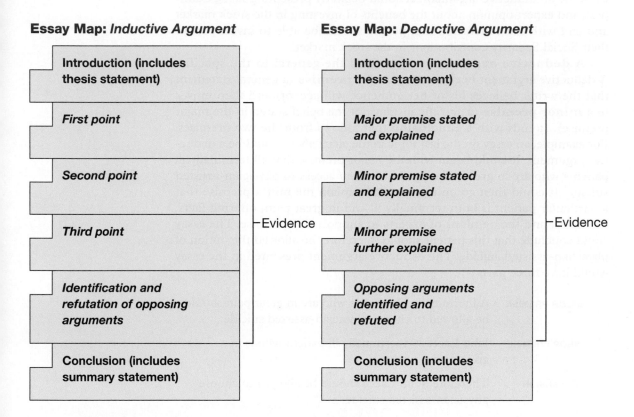

Essay Map: *Inductive Argument*

- Introduction (includes thesis statement)
- First point
- Second point
- Third point
- Identification and refutation of opposing arguments
- Conclusion (includes summary statement)

⎤Evidence

Essay Map: *Deductive Argument*

- Introduction (includes thesis statement)
- Major premise stated and explained
- Minor premise stated and explained
- Minor premise further explained
- Opposing arguments identified and refuted
- Conclusion (includes summary statement)

⎤Evidence

For a list of transitions frequently used in argument, see page 167.

Transitions in Argument Essays

Transitions are extremely important in argument essays because they not only signal the movement from one part of the argument to another but also relate specific points to one another and to the thesis statement.

Case Study: A Student Writes an Argument Essay

Alex Norman, a student in a first-year writing course, was assigned to write an argument essay on a controversial issue of his choice. His instructor suggested that students find a topic by reading campus and local news papers, going online to read national news stories and political blogs, and perhaps watching public affairs programs on television. Alex followed this advice and also talked about his assignment with friends and family members.

The issue that most interested him was one about which he had already written an argument paragraph for an earlier assignment: the question of whether the federal government should do more to subsidize the cost of college for low-income students. Now, he thought he could do some additional work to develop some of that paragraph's ideas into an argument essay.

Alex began by **brainstorming**, recording all his ideas on this complex issue, including those he had discussed in his earlier paragraph. He also included ideas he developed as he spoke to his sister, a recent college graduate, and to his boss at the bank where he worked part-time. When he read over his brainstorming notes, he saw that he had good arguments both for and against increasing government funding for low-income students. Although Alex sympathized with students who needed help paying for school, he questioned whether taxpayers should have to foot the bill. At this point, he wasn't sure what position to take in his essay, so he scheduled an appointment for a **conference** with his instructor.

Alex's instructor pointed out that he could make a good case either for or against greater government subsidies; like many controversial issues, this one had no easy answers. She encouraged him to support the position that seemed right to him and to use the information on the opposing side to present (and refute) opposing arguments. She also recommended that Alex email his first draft to her so she could review it.

After he thought about his instructor's comments, Alex decided to argue in favor of increasing government grants to help low-income students pay for college. Before he began to draft his essay, he wrote a **thesis statement** that presented his position on the issue; then, he arranged supporting points from his brainstorming notes into an **outline** that he could follow as he wrote. As he **drafted** his essay, Alex made sure to support his thesis with evidence and to explain his position as clearly and thoroughly as possible. He paid special attention to choosing transitional words and phrases that would indicate how his points were logically connected to one another.

When Alex finished his draft, he **TEST**ed it, taking a quick inventory to make sure he had included all four necessary components of an essay. Then, he emailed the draft to his instructor. Following her suggestions, he **revised** his draft, this time focusing on his topic sentences, his presentation (and refutation) of opposing arguments, and his introductory and concluding paragraphs. When he was satisfied with his revisions, he **edited** and **proofread** his paper and checked his **format**.

The final draft that follows includes all the elements Alex looked for when he **TEST**ed his essay.

TEST
T Thesis Statement
E Evidence
S Summary Statement
T Transitions

Introduction

Topic sentence
(introduces first point)

Body paragraphs

Facts, examples,
expert opinion

Topic sentence
(introduces second point)

Facts, examples,
or expert opinion

Topic sentence
(introduces third point)

Model Argument Essay

Read Alex's finished essay, and answer the questions in Practice 16-4.

Increase Grant Money for Low-Income College Students

1   The price of college tuition has more than doubled over the last two decades. Today, low-income students are finding it especially difficult (and sometimes impossible) to pay for school. Should the government help these students more than it does now? If so, what form should that help take? Rather than reducing aid or asking students to borrow more, the government should give larger grants to subsidize tuition for low-income students.

2   If the United States is a country that is committed to equal opportunity, then college should be affordable for all. To compete in today's high-tech job market, people need a college degree. However, students' access to college is too often determined by their parents' income. This unfairly excludes many people. Therefore, the government should make it a priority to support students who are being priced out of a college education. Specifically, the government should give larger grants to low-income students. Although some critics see these grants as unnecessary "handouts," such awards are the best way for the government to invest in the future and maintain our nation's core values. After all, the country's economy benefits when more of its citizens earn college degrees. Even more important, by giving low-income students the same opportunities to succeed as their more affluent peers, the United States keeps its promise to treat all its citizens fairly.

3   Some people argue that the best way to help students who are struggling to pay for college is to offer them more loans at a lower interest rate. However, this solution is inadequate, unfair, and short-sighted. First of all, lowering the interest rate on student loans only reduces the average monthly payments by a few dollars. Second, student loans already unfairly burden low-income students. Why should they have to take on more debt simply because their parents make less money? The government should reduce the amount these students have to borrow, not increase it. Finally, forcing graduates to start their careers with a heavy financial burden hurts the country's economy. Although loans might cost the government less in the short term, in the long term student debt makes it more difficult for Americans to be successful and competitive.

4   The federal government does have Pell Grant funding to help students who demonstrate need, but this program needs to be expanded. As Sara Goldrick-Rab reports, although Pell Grants once allowed students to focus

their time and energy on school instead of work, the proportion of tuition the grants now cover is so low that this balance is no longer possible. In fact, according to the Office of Federal Student Aid, for 2018-19, Pell Grants are limited to $6,095, not nearly enough to cover tuition at most four-year colleges and universities. At most, Pell Grants cover only a third of average college costs. Meanwhile, the education gap between rich and poor is growing. As education policy expert Andrew J. Rotherham observes, while 75 percent of wealthy students earn a four-year degree by age 24, less than 10 percent of low-income students do. To help close this gap, the government should offer more funding to those most in need of financial assistance.

> Facts, examples, or expert opinion
>
> *Body paragraphs*

5   Some would argue, however, that the government should do just the opposite. One of the most common criticisms of government subsidies is that they are to blame for the rising costs of college. Critics point out that by supplying money to colleges, government grants only make it easier for them to charge more. This may be true, but, as Andrew Rotherham points out, the government could do more to regulate college tuition. For example, the government could offer incentives to schools that keep their costs down or award more generous grants to students who attend affordable schools. Ultimately, withdrawing aid and abandoning students to the free market is irresponsible as well as counterproductive. Instead, the government should take steps to prevent colleges from taking advantage of its generosity.

> Topic sentence (introduces fourth point)
>
> Facts, examples, or expert opinion

6   With the cost of college continuing to rise, now is the time for the government to help the hardest-hit students by offering them more help to pay for their education. Rather than cutting spending on student aid, the government should increase grants to low-income students. However, it must do so in ways that discourage irresponsible increases in tuition. By acting wisely and prudently, the government can improve access to higher education for all and support the country's economic future.

> *Conclusion*

Works Cited

Goldrick-Rab, Sara. "The Real College Barrier for Working-Poor Families." *Inside Higher Ed,* 10 Dec. 2013, www.insidehighered.com/ views/2013/12/10/federal-aid-needy-students-inadequate-essay.

Rotherham, Andrew J. "How to Fix Pell Grants." *Time*, 24 May 2012, ideas. time.com/2012/05/24/how-to-fix-pell-grants/.

U.S. Department of Education. "Federal Student Aid at a Glance." Federal Student Aid, 9 Sept. 2017, https://studentaid.ed.gopdfv/sa/sites/ default/files/aid-glance-2018-19.

PRACTICE

16-4   1. In your own words, summarize the position Alex takes in his essay.

2. List the facts and examples Alex uses to support his thesis. Where does he include expert opinion?

3. Can you think of any other supporting evidence that Alex should have included but didn't?

4. Review the transitional words and phrases Alex uses. How do they move readers from one point to another? Should he add any transitions?

5. What opposing arguments does Alex address? How does he refute them? Can you think of other arguments he should have considered?

6. What is this essay's greatest strength? What is its greatest weakness?

grammar in context

Argument

When you write an argument essay, you need to show the relationships between your ideas by combining sentences to create **compound sentences** and **complex sentences**.

The federal government does have a program in place to help

students who demonstrate need, Pell Grant funding needs to be
                                 ,but

expanded. (compound sentence)

Although some critics
Some critics see these grants as unnecessary "handouts," Such
                                                       , such

awards are the best way for the government to invest in the future

and to maintain our nation's core values. (complex sentence)

For information on how to create compound sentences, see Chapter 19.
For information on how to create complex sentences, see Chapter 20.

Step-by-Step Guide: Writing an Argument Essay

Now, you are ready to write an argument essay on one of the topics listed below (or a topic of your choice).

TOPICS

Teenagers who commit serious crimes should (or should not) be tried as adults.

All citizens without criminal records should (or should not) be permitted to carry concealed weapons.

Human beings should (or should not) be used as subjects in medical research experiments.

College financial aid should (or should not) be based solely on merit.

Government funds should (or should not) be used to support the arts.

The minimum wage should (or should not) be raised.

College athletes should (or should not) be paid to play.

Convicted felons should (or should not) lose the right to vote.

As you write your essay, follow these steps:

- Make sure your topic calls for argument, and then find ideas to write about; next, decide on the position you will support, and write a thesis statement that clearly expresses that position.

- List the key points in support of your thesis, and arrange these points identify in an effective order; then, identify evidence (facts, examples, and expert opinion) in support of each point, list arguments against your position, and make an outline that includes key supporting and opposing points.

- Draft your essay.

- **TEST** your essay, referring to the **TEST**ing an Argument Essay checklist below.

- Revise and edit your essay, referring to the two Self-Assessment Checklists in Chapter 13.

- Proofread your essay, and make sure it follows your instructor's format guidelines.

Plan

↓

Organize

↓

Draft

↓

TEST

↓

Revise, edit, and proofread

TESTing an argument essay

T hesis Statement Unifies Your Essay

☐ Does your introduction include a **thesis statement** that clearly expresses your position on the issue you will discuss? Is this issue debatable—that is, does it really have two sides?

E vidence Supports Your Essay's Thesis Statement

☐ Does all your **evidence**—facts, examples, and expert opinion—support your thesis, or should some evidence be deleted?

☐ Do you have enough evidence to support your points?

☐ Have you considered whether readers are likely to be hostile toward, neutral toward, or in agreement with your position—and have you chosen your points accordingly?

☐ Have you presented your evidence in a clear inductive or deductive order?

S ummary Statement Reinforces Your Essay's Main Idea

☐ Does your conclusion include a **summary statement** that reinforces your essay's thesis?

T ransitions

☐ Do you include **transitions** that introduce your points?

☐ Do you include enough transitional words and phrases to help readers follow the logic of your argument?

Argument in Action

In "Vaccinations Are for the Good of the Nation," Ben Carson uses **argument** to structure his essay.

Vaccinations Are for the Good of the Nation
Ben Carson

Ben Carson served as the director of pediatric neurosurgery at Johns Hopkins Hospital from 1984 until 2013, when he retired. He won the Presidential Medal of Freedom in 2008 for his contributions to the medical field, including separating conjoined twins. Originally from

Detroit, Michigan, Carson is the author of many essays and books on his medical career, including 2014's *One Nation: What We Can All Do to Save America's Future*. In 2016, he made an unsuccessful bid to become the Republican Party's nominee for president of the United States. In this 2015 op-ed for the *National Review*, Carson draws on his medical experience to caution against the dangers of the anti-vaccination movement. As you read, think about whether you trust Carson's opinion more than other writers' positions, given his medical background.

1   There has been much debate recently over vaccination mandates, particularly in response to the measles outbreak currently taking place throughout the country.

2   At this juncture, there have been 102 confirmed measles cases in the U.S. during 2015, with 59 of them linked to a December 2014 visit to the Disneyland theme park in Southern California. (It is important to note that eleven of the cases associated with Disneyland were detected last year and, consequently, fall within the 2014 measles count.) This large outbreak has spread to at least a half-dozen other states, and the Centers for Disease Control and Prevention is currently requesting that all health-care professionals "consider measles when evaluating patients with febrile rash and ask about a patient's vaccine status, recent travel history and contact with individuals who have febrile rash illness."

3   One must understand that there is no specific antiviral therapy for measles and that 90 percent of those who are not vaccinated will contract measles if they are indeed exposed to the virus. This explains why Arizona health officials are monitoring more than 1,000 people after potential exposure to measles. These are pretty staggering numbers that should concern not only parents and children, but also the general populace.

4   I have been asked many times throughout the past week for my thoughts concerning the issue of vaccines. The important thing is to make sure the public understands that there is no substantial risk from vaccines and that the benefits are very significant. Although I strongly believe in individual rights and the rights of parents to raise their children as they see fit, I also recognize that public health and public safety are extremely important in our society. Certain communicable diseases have been largely eradicated by immunization policies in this country. We should not allow those diseases to return by foregoing safe immunization programs for philosophical, religious, or other reasons when we have the means to eradicate them.

5   Obviously, there are exceptional situations to virtually everything, and we must have a mechanism whereby those can be heard. Nevertheless, there is public policy and health policy that we must pay attention to regarding this matter. We already have policies in place at schools that require immunization records—this is a positive thing. Studies have shown over the course of time that the risk-benefit ratio for vaccination is grossly in favor of being vaccinated as opposed to not.

WORD POWER

mandates rules

juncture point in time

WORD POWER

febrile related to a fever

WORD POWER

communicable infectious

eradicated ended; destroyed

means ways

6   There is no question that immunizations have been effective in eliminating diseases such as smallpox, which was devastating and lethal. When
you have diseases that have been demonstrably curtailed or eradicated by
immunization, why would you even think about not doing it? Certain people have discussed the possibility of potential health risks from vaccinations. I am not aware of scientific evidence of a direct correlation. I think
there probably are people who may make a correlation where one does not
exist, and that fear subsequently ignites, catches fire, and spreads. But it is
important to educate the public about what evidence actually exists.

7   I am very much in favor of parental rights on certain types of things.
I am in favor of you and me having the freedom to drive a car. But do we
have a right to drive without wearing our seatbelts? Do we have a right to
text while we are driving? Studies have demonstrated that those are dangerous things to do, so it becomes a public-safety issue. You have to be
able to distinguish our rights versus the rights of the society in which we
live, because we are all in this thing together. We have to be cognizant of
the other people around us, and we must always bear in mind the safety
of the population. That is key, and that is one of the responsibilities of
government.

8   I am a small-government person, and I greatly oppose government
intrusion into everything. Still, it is essential that we distinguish between
those things that are important and those things that are just intruding
upon our basic privacy. Whether to participate in childhood immunizations
would be an individual choice if individuals were the only ones affected,
but our children are part of our larger community. None of us lives in iso-
lation. Your decision does not affect only you—it also affects your fellow
Americans.

WORD POWER

correlation
relationship

WORD POWER

cognizant aware

Focus on the Pattern

1. Restate Carson's thesis in your own words. Where does he state this
   thesis? What evidence does he use to support his position?

2. Where does Carson introduce opposing arguments? Does he refute
   them effectively?

3. Is this argument organized inductively or deductively? Explain.

Writing Practice

1. Write an argument essay in which you support the position that certain individuals or groups should have the right not to vaccinate their
   children.

2. Write an argument essay with the title "——————— Is/Are for the
   Good of the Nation." In your essay, explain why you support a particular law or regulation (for example, requiring bicycle riders to wear
   helmets or limiting the size of soda containers) despite some people's
   objections.

review checklist

Patterns of Essay Development: Description, Classification, Definition, and Argument

✔ **Descriptive** essays use details to give readers a clear, vivid picture of a person, place, or object. (See 16a.)

✔ **Classification** essays divide a whole into parts and sort various items into categories. (See 16b.)

✔ **Definition** essays use various patterns to develop an extended definition. (See 16c.)

✔ **Argument** essays take a stand on a debatable issue, using evidence to persuade readers to accept a position. (See 16d.)

17 Writing with Sources

In this chapter, you will learn to

- find and evaluate information (17a)
- paraphrase, summarize, and quote sources (17b)
- synthesize two or more sources (17b)
- use sources ethically (17c)
- follow MLA documentation style (17d)
- follow APA documentation style (17e)

17a Finding and Evaluating Information

When you do research, you—like most students—probably go straight to the Internet. If you do this, however, you are shortchanging yourself. Your college library gives you access to valuable resources that are available nowhere else. In addition, unlike the material on the Internet, where anything and everything is posted, the material in the library has been screened by librarians (as well as instructors) and, in many cases, conforms to academic standards of reliability. For this reason, you should always begin your research by visiting the library's website.

Finding Information in the Library

Once you connect to the library's website, you should consult the library's **online catalog**—a database of all the library's holdings. Many libraries subscribe to a **discovery service**—an online research tool that allows you to use a single search box to access all of the library's print and electronic holdings—including print books, e-books, full-text journal articles, government documents, streaming video, and DVDs. The result is a Google-like search experience that ranks results by relevancy.

You search the online catalog (or discovery service) just as you would search the Internet: by carrying out a *keyword search* or a *subject search*.

1. You do a **keyword search** the same way you would search using Google—by entering your keywords in a search box to retrieve a list of books, periodicals, and other materials that are relevant to your topic. The more specific your keywords are, the more focused your search will be. Thus, the keywords *Facebook privacy* will yield more specific (and useful) results than the words *social networking* would.

2. You do a **subject search** by entering a subject heading related to your topic. Unlike keywords, subject headings are predetermined and come from a list of subject headings published by the Library of Congress. Many online catalogs provide lists of subject headings you can use. A subject search is best when you want information about a general topic—for example, *rap music*, *discography*, or *Mark Twain*.

As you carry out your search, make sure you look at the material in the library's electronic databases (such as InfoTrac and ProQuest). These databases enable you to access articles from newspapers, magazines, and journals that you cannot freely access on the Internet. In addition, database sources usually contain the full text of articles as well as complete bibliographic information, sometimes in the form of a works-cited entry.

If your library subscribes to a discovery service, you can search all the library's electronic databases at once from a search box. If not, you will have to search each database individually. (Most online catalogs list the databases to which your college library subscribes.)

Evaluating Library Sources

Even though the sources in the library are generally more reliable than those on the Internet, they still need to be evaluated. In other words, you have to determine their usefulness and reliability before you use them in your essay.

- Consider the source's **purpose and audience**. Does the source aim to inform, entertain, persuade, or sell something? Is the information intended for scholars or for a general audience? Is the language simple or technical?

- Determine the **date** the source was published. How current is the information in the source? For your topic, how important is it that source information be current?

- Consider the **author**. Is he or she an expert in the subject the source explores? Does the author strive for objectivity, or does he or she seem to be advancing a particular point of view?

- Consider the **publisher**. Is the publisher a university press or a commercial press? Is the publisher known to have an editorial bias? How might this bias affect the information in the source?

- Determine the **credibility** (believability) of a source. For example, an article in a respected periodical, such as the *New York Times* or *Wall Street Journal*, is more credible than one in a tabloid, such as the *National Enquirer* or the *Sun*.

> **WORD POWER**
> **tabloid** a newspaper that emphasizes stories with sensational content

Your instructor or college librarian can help you select sources that are both appropriate and reliable.

Finding Information on the Internet

The Internet can give you access to a great deal of information that can help you support your ideas and develop your essay. Unlike the resources available in your college library, however, no one is responsible for checking the accuracy of information or the credentials of people who post on the Internet. For this reason, it is your responsibility (and obligation) to determine the trustworthiness of an Internet source and decide whether it is appropriate for your paper.

Once you are online, you need to connect to a **search engine**, which helps you find information by sorting through the millions of documents that are available on the Internet. Among the most popular search engines are Google, Yahoo!, and Bing.

There are two ways to use a search engine to access information.

1. *You can do a keyword search.* All search engines let you do a keyword search. You type a term (or terms) into a box, and the search engine looks for documents that contain the term, listing all the hits that it finds.

2. *You can paste a URL.* Every web page has a unique electronic address called a **URL** (uniform resource locater). You can copy a URL and paste it into your browser's search box. Click Search, and you will be connected to the website or web page you want.

Evaluating Internet Sources

You evaluate Internet sources the same way you evaluate library sources. With the Internet, however, you have problems you do not have with the sources in your college library. Because anyone can post information on a website, it can be difficult—if not impossible—to judge the credentials of an author or sometimes even to identify an author. Dates can also be missing, so it may be difficult to tell when information was posted and when it was updated. Finally, it can be challenging to determine whether or not the website is trying to sell something or advance a political or social agenda. If it is, it may contain information that is misleading, biased, or incorrect.

You can evaluate websites (and the information posted on them) by asking the following basic questions.

- *Who is the author of the site?* Avoid information written by unnamed authors or by authors with questionable credentials.

- *Who is the sponsoring organization?* Be especially careful of using information from websites that are sponsored by companies trying to sell something or organizations that have a particular agenda.

- *Can you verify information posted on the site?* Make sure that you are able to check the source of the information. For example, you should see if an article on a site includes documentation. Also, cross-check information you find there. Does the same information appear in other sources that are reliable?

- *Does the site contain errors?* In addition to factual errors, look out for mistakes in grammar or spelling. Errors such as these should raise a red flag about the accuracy of the information on the site you are visiting.

- *Do the links on the site work?* Make sure that the links on the site are "live." The presence of "dead" links is a good indication that a site is not being properly maintained.

- *Is the information up-to-date?* Make sure that the site's information is current. Avoid sites that contain information that seems old or outdated. A reliable site will usually include the date information was posted and the date it was revised.

When in doubt, the surest strategy for determining whether a website is reliable is to check with a reference librarian or with your instructor. Unless you can be certain that a site is reliable, do not use it as a source.

FYI

Using Wikipedia as a Source

Most college students regularly consult Wikipedia, the open-source online encyclopedia. The rationale behind Wikipedia is that if a large number of people review information, errors will eventually be discovered and corrected. Because there are no full-time professional editors, however, Wikipedia articles can (and do) contain inaccurate as well as biased information. In addition, anyone—not just experts—can write and edit entries. Understandably, some instructors distrust—or at least question—the accuracy of Wikipedia entries. For this reason, they do not consider them suitable for academic research. Even though Wikipedia may not be a credible research source, you can use it to familiarize yourself with a topic or to find acceptable sources by checking the bibliographic entries at the end of an article. (Keep in mind that many instructors do not consider articles from any encyclopedia—print or electronic—acceptable for college research.)

17b   Using Sources in Your Writing

Once you have gathered your source material, you need to transfer relevant information into computer files or onto index cards. **Taking notes**, however, involves more than simply copying down or cutting and pasting information.

As you record information, you should put it into a form that you can use when you write your essay. This strategy allows you to keep track of your source material and eliminates the possibility of accidentally committing plagiarism. For this reason, when you take notes, you should *paraphrase*, *summarize*, or *quote* the information from your sources.

FYI

Avoiding Plagiarism

When you transfer information from websites into your notes, you may carelessly cut and paste text without recording where the material came from. If you then copy this material into your essay without citing the source, you are committing **plagiarism**—stealing someone else's ideas. Also keep in mind that you must document *all* material that you get from the Internet, just as you document material that you get from print sources. For information on documentation, see 17d. For information on plagiarism, see 17c.

Paraphrasing

When you **paraphrase**, you use your own words to convey a source's key ideas. You paraphrase when you want to include detailed information from the source but not the author's exact words. Paraphrasing is useful when you want to make a difficult discussion easier to understand while still presenting a comprehensive overview of the original.

Writing a Paraphrase

1. Read the passage until you understand it.

2. Note the main idea of the passage, and list key supporting points.

3. Draft your paraphrase, beginning with the source's main idea and then presenting the source's most important supporting points.

4. When you revise, make sure you have used your own words and phrasing, not the words or sentence structure of the original. Use quotation marks to identify any unique or memorable phrases you have borrowed from the source.

5. Document your source.

Here is a passage from the article "Hot Fakes," by Joanie Cox, followed by a student's paraphrase.

ORIGINAL

Always pay close attention to the stitching. On a Kate Spade bag, the logo is stitched perfectly straight; it's not a sticker. Most designers stitch a simple label to the inside of their purses. On Chanel bags, however, the interior label is usually stamped and tends to match the color of the exterior. Study the material the bag is made from. A real Chanel Ligne Cambon multipocket bag, for example, is constructed from buttery lambskin leather, not vinyl.

PARAPHRASE

It is often possible to tell a fake designer handbag from a genuine one by looking at the details. For example, items such as logos should not be crooked. You should also look for the distinctive features of a particular brand of handbag. Counterfeiters will not take the time to match colors, and they may use vinyl instead of expensive leather (Cox).

Note that this paraphrase does not simply change a word here and there. Instead, the student has taken the time to make sure she fully understands the main idea and supporting points of the passage and has restated the source's ideas in her own words.

Summarizing

Unlike a paraphrase, which presents the key points of a source in detail, a **summary** is a general restatement, in your own words, of just the main idea of a passage. For this reason, a summary is always much shorter than the original.

> **Writing a Summary**
>
> 1. Read the passage until you understand it.
> 2. Jot down the main idea of the passage.
> 3. As you write, make sure you use your own words, not those of your source.
> 4. When you revise, make sure your summary contains only the ideas of the source.
> 5. Document your source.

Here is a student's summary of the original passage on the previous page.

SUMMARY

Buyers who want to identify fake handbags should check details such as the way the label is sewn and the material the item is made from (Cox).

Quoting

When you **quote**, you use an author's exact words as they appear in the source, including all punctuation and capitalization. Enclose all words from your source in quotation marks—*followed by appropriate documentation*. Because quotations can distract readers, use them only when you think that the author's exact words will add to your discussion.

When to Quote

1. Quote when the words of a source are so memorable that to put them into your own words would lessen their impact.

2. Quote when the words of a source are so precise that a paraphrase or summary would change the meaning of the original.

3. Quote when the words of a source add authority to your discussion. The exact words of a recognized expert can help you make your point convincingly.

Here is how a student writer incorporated a quotation from the original passage on page 332 into her notes.

QUOTATION

Someone who wants to buy an authentic designer handbag should look carefully at the material the purse is made from. For example, there is a big difference between vinyl and Chanel's "buttery lambskin leather" (Cox).

Working Sources into Your Writing

To show readers why you are using a source and to help you blend source material smoothly into your essay, introduce paraphrases, summaries, and quotations with **identifying tags** (sometimes called *signal phrases*)—phrases that name the source or its author. You can position an identifying tag at various places in a sentence.

> <u>As one celebrity fashion columnist points out,</u> "A real Chanel Ligne Cambon multipocket bag, for example, is constructed from buttery lambskin leather, not vinyl" (Cox).

> "A real Chanel Ligne Cambon multipocket bag, for example," <u>says one celebrity fashion columnist,</u> "is constructed from buttery lambskin leather, not vinyl" (Cox).

> "A real Chanel Ligne Cambon multipocket bag, for example, is constructed from buttery lambskin leather, not vinyl," <u>observes one celebrity fashion columnist</u> (Cox).

FYI

Identifying Sources

Instead of repeating the word *says*, you can use one of the following words or phrases to identify the source of a quotation, paraphrase, or summary.

admits	concludes	points out
believes	explains	remarks
claims	notes	states
comments	observes	suggests

Synthesizing

When you **synthesize,** you combine ideas from two or more sources with your own ideas. The goal of a synthesis is to use sources to develop your own point about a topic. In a synthesis, then, your own ideas, not those of your sources, should dominate the discussion. In a sense, every time you weave together paraphrase, summary, and quotation to support a point, you are writing a synthesis.

Using Sources in Your Writing **17b** 335

Writing a Synthesis

1. Decide on the point you want to develop.

2. Select at least two or three sources to support your point.

3. Read each source carefully, taking note of how they are alike, how they are different, and how they relate to your point.

4. Begin your synthesis by clearly stating the point you are going to develop.

5. Use specific examples (paraphrases, summaries, and quotations) from your sources to support your point.

6. When you revise, make sure that you have used appropriate transitions to indicate the movement from one source to another. Also be sure that you have clearly identified each source that you discuss.

7. Document all words and ideas that you borrow from your sources.

Here is a paragraph from a student's research paper in which she incorporates material from three different sources. (You can read the full paper on pages 345–347.) Notice how she uses source material (underlined) to develop her point that buying counterfeit items is really stealing.

What most people choose to ignore is that buying counterfeit items is stealing. In 2016, U.S. Customs and Border Protection and U.S. Immigration and Customs Enforcement seized a record number of counterfeit goods. Leading the list of seized items were designer watches and jewelry as well as handbags and wallets ("CBP"). The FBI estimates that in the United States alone, companies lose about $250 billion as a result of counterfeits (Wallace). In addition, buyers of counterfeit items avoid state and local taxes that legitimate companies pay. Thus, New York City alone loses about a billion dollars a year as a result of counterfeit merchandise ("Counterfeit Goods"). When this happens, everyone loses. After all, a billion dollars would pay for a lot of police officers and teachers, would fill a lot of potholes, and would pave a lot of streets. Even though buyers of counterfeit designer goods do not think of themselves as thieves, that is exactly what they are.

17c Using Sources Ethically

When you write a research essay, you must use your sources ethically. In other words, you must document (give source information for) all words, ideas, or statistics from an outside source. You must also document all visuals—tables, graphs, photographs, and so on—that you do not create yourself. (It is not necessary, however, to document **common knowledge**—factual information widely available in various reference works.)

When you present information from another source as if it is your own (whether you do it intentionally or unintentionally), you commit **plagiarism**—and plagiarism is theft. Although most plagiarism is accidental, the penalties can still be severe. You can avoid plagiarism by understanding what you must document and what you do not have to document. (See 17d and 17e for more on documentation.)

FYI

What to Document

You should document the following.

- All quotations from a source
- All summaries and paraphrases of source material
- All ideas—opinions, judgments, and insights—of others
- All tables, graphs, charts, and statistics from a source

You do not need to document the following.

- Your own ideas
- Common knowledge
- Familiar quotations

Read the following paragraph from "Agencies Can Improve Efforts to Address Risks Posed by Changing Counterfeit Markets," a report by the U.S. Senate Committee on Finance, and the four guidelines that follow it. This material will help you understand the most common causes of plagiarism and show you how to avoid it.

ORIGINAL

Counterfeit goods may pose risks to the health and safety of consumers. CBP [U.S. Customs and Border Protection] and ICE [U.S. Immigration and Customs Enforcement] have seized and investigated counterfeit goods, such as health and personal care products and consumer electronics, that carried a number of health and safety risks. For example, CBP has seized counterfeit versions of personal care products such as contact lenses, perfume, hair removal devices, hair curlers and straighteners, skin cleansing devices, and condoms, which pose risks to the consumer that include damage to skin or eyes caused by dangerous chemicals and bacteria, burning or electrocution due to nonstandardized wiring, or ineffectual family planning protection. ICE has also investigated IP crimes involving counterfeit airbags, phone accessories, pharmaceuticals, and other items that present risks to the health and safety of consumers. Counterfeit electronics and batteries can also pose significant risks, including the risk of injury or death, according to CBP. For instance, in December 2015, CBP seized 1,378 hoverboards with counterfeit batteries that carried a risk of causing fires.

Rule 1: Document Ideas from Your Sources

PLAGIARISM

Counterfeit goods—especially personal care products and pharmaceuticals—may pose a great risk to consumers.

Even though the student writer does not quote her source directly, she must identify the article as the source of this material because it expresses the article's ideas, not her own.

CORRECT

Counterfeit goods—especially personal care products and pharmaceuticals—can be dangerous (Senate Committee on Finance 8).

Rule 2: Place Borrowed Words in Quotation Marks

PLAGIARISM

Counterfeit goods, such as personal care products and pharmaceuticals, may pose risks to the health and safety of consumers (Senate Committee on Finance 8).

Although the student writer cites the source, the passage incorrectly uses the source's exact words without quoting them. In order to avoid plagiarizing her source, she must quote the borrowed words.

CORRECT (BORROWED WORDS IN QUOTATION MARKS)

Counterfeit goods, such as personal care products and pharmaceuticals, "may pose risks to the health and safety of consumers" (Senate Committee on Finance 8).

Rule 3: Use Your Own Phrasing

PLAGIARISM

Is buying counterfeit goods without risk? Not at all. The counterfeit goods, such as personal care products and pharmaceuticals, can create problems for consumers. In addition, the CBP and ICE have seized counterfeit contact lenses as well as hair straighteners and skin cleansing devices. Other consumer products, such as batteries and airbags, can actually be dangerous (Senate Committee on Finance 8).

Even though the student writer acknowledges her source and even though she does not use the source's exact words, her passage closely follows the order, emphasis, sentence structure, and phrasing of the original.

In the following passage, the student writer uses her own wording, quoting one distinctive phrase from the source.

CORRECT

According to a report from the Senate Committee on Finance, counterfeit goods are not an insignificant problem. In fact, they "may pose risks to the health and safety of consumers." The poor quality of most counterfeit goods ensures that they will cause harm. For example, counterfeit contact lenses can damage a person's eyes and counterfeit airbags can cause injury or even death when they don't deploy properly (Senate Committee on Finance 8).

Note: The quotation does not require separate documentation because the identifying tag, "According to a report from the Senate Committee on Finance," makes it clear that all the borrowed material in the passage is from the same source.

Rule 4: Distinguish Your Ideas from the Source's Ideas

PLAGIARISM

> The CPB and ICE have investigated may cases of counterfeit merchandise being smuggled into the United States. These goods include personal care products, electronic items, and pharmaceuticals. The poor quality of these goods makes it likely that they will "pose significant risks to the health and safety of consumers" (Senate Committee on Finance 8).

In the passage above, it appears that only the quotation in the last sentence is borrowed from the Senate Committee repost. In fact, however, the ideas in the first two sentences also come from Meyer's article.

In the following passage, the student writer uses an identifying tag to acknowledge the borrowed material in the second sentence.

CORRECT

> According to a report from the Senate Committee on Finance, the CPB and ICE have investigated many cases of counterfeit merchandise being smuggled into the United States. These goods include personal care products, electronic items, and pharmaceuticals. The poor quality of these items makes it likely that they will "pose significant risks to the health and safety of consumers" (Senate Committee on Finance 8).

17d MLA Documentation Style

Whenever you use information from a source, you have to **document** it—that is, you need to indicate to readers where you found it. By doing this, you identify your source and you enable readers to locate the information you use. Because conventions differ from discipline to discipline, there is no single documentation style that you can use in all of your courses. For this reason, you should ask your instructors which format they require. Two of the most widely used documentation styles are those recommended by the **Modern Language Association** (MLA), preferred in the humanities, and the **American Psychological Association** (APA), preferred in the social sciences. This section covers MLA style; APA style is covered in 17e.

MLA In-Text Citations

MLA documentation requires you to make a brief citation in the body of your essay immediately following material you are using from another source. Readers can use these **in-text citations** to find detailed information on specific sources in your **works-cited list** at the end of the paper.

The in-text citation names the author of your source and provides a page number (if there is one). A typical in-text citation consists of the author's last name and the page number in parentheses (Brown 2). Notice that there is no comma and no *p* or *p.* before the page number.

Whenever possible, introduce information from a source with a phrase that includes the author's name. (If you do this, include only the page number in parentheses.) Place documentation so that it does not interrupt the flow of your ideas, preferably at the end of a sentence.

> As Jonathan Brown observes in "Demand for Fake Designer Goods Is Soaring," as many as 70 percent of buyers of luxury goods are willing to wear designer brands alongside of fakes (2).

Here are some specific guidelines for four special situations.

1. CITING A WORK BY TWO AUTHORS

> Instead of buying nonbranded items of similar quality, many customers are willing to pay extra for the counterfeit designer label (Grossman and Shapiro 79).

2. CITING A WORK WITHOUT PAGE NUMBERS

> A seller of counterfeited goods in California "now faces 10 years in prison and $20,000 in fines" (Cox).

3. CITING A WORK WITHOUT A LISTED AUTHOR OR PAGE NUMBERS

> More counterfeit goods come from China than from any other country ("Counterfeit Goods").

Note: Material from the Internet frequently lacks some publication information—for example, page or paragraph numbers. For this reason, the parenthetical references that cite it may contain just the author's name (as in example 2) or just a shortened title (as in example 3) if the article appears without an author.

4. CITING A STATEMENT BY ONE AUTHOR THAT IS QUOTED IN A WORK BY ANOTHER AUTHOR

> Speaking of consumers' buying habits, designer Miuccia Prada says, "There is a kind of an obsession with bags" (qtd. in Thomas A23).

FYI

Formatting Quotations in an MLA Paper

1. **Short quotations** Quotations of no more than four typed lines are run into the text of your essay. End punctuation comes after the parenthetical reference, which follows the quotation marks.

   According to Dana Thomas, customers often "pick up knockoffs for one-tenth the legitimate bag's retail cost, then pass them off as real" (A23).

2. **Long quotations** Quotations of more than four lines are set off from the text of your essay. Begin a long quotation on a new line, indented one-half inch from the left-hand margin, and do not enclose it in quotation marks. Do not indent the first line of a single paragraph. If a quoted passage has more than one paragraph, indent the first line of each paragraph (including the first) an extra one-quarter inch. Introduce a long quotation with a complete sentence followed by a colon, and place the parenthetical reference one space *after* the end punctuation.

   The editorial "Terror's Purse Strings" describes a surprise visit to a factory that makes counterfeit purses:

   > On a warm winter afternoon in Guangzhao, I accompanied Chinese police officers on a raid in a decrepit tenement. We found two dozen children, ages 8 to 13, gluing and sewing together fake luxury-brand handbags. The police confiscated everything, arrested the owner and sent the children out. Some punched their timecards, hoping to still get paid. (Thomas A23)

The Works-Cited List

The works-cited list includes all the works you **cite** (refer to) in your essay. Use the guidelines in the "Preparing the Works-Cited List" FYI box on page 344 to help you prepare your list.

The following sample works-cited entries cover the situations you will encounter most often.

Periodicals

JOURNALS

A **journal** is a periodical aimed at readers who know a lot about a particular subject—literature or history, for example.

When citing an article from a journal, include the journal's volume number and issue number, as well as the season and year of publication.

Following the date of publication, include page numbers, if there are any. Include the name of the online database (such as Academic Search Premier) if you used one to find the source. For all web sources, add the URL or **DOI** (digital object identifier) for the source.

Article in a Print Journal

Gioia, Dana. "Robert Frost and the Modern Narrative." *Virginia Quarterly Review,* vol. 89, no. 2, Spring 2013, pp. 185–93.

Article in a Journal Accessed through a Library Database

Coles, Kimberly Anne. "The Matter of Belief in John Donne's Holy Sonnets." *Renaissance Quarterly,* vol. 68, no. 3, Fall 2015, pp. 899–931. *JSTOR,* doi:10.1086/683855.

MAGAZINES

A **magazine** is a periodical aimed at general readers, rather than people who already know a lot about a subject. Frequently, an article in a magazine is not printed on consecutive pages. For example, it may begin on page 40, skip to page 47, and continue on page 49. If this is the case, your citation should include only the first page, followed by a plus sign.

Article in a Print Magazine

Poniewozik, James. "Why I Watch Reality TV with My Kids." *Time* 17 June 2013, pp. 54–55.

Isaacs, Matt. "Sheldon Adelson Goes All In." *Mother Jones* March/April 2016, pp. 18+.

Article in a Magazine Accessed through a Library Database

Sharp, Kathleen. "The Rescue Mission." *Smithsonian,* Nov. 2015, pp. 40–49. *OmniFile Full Text Select,* web.b.ebscohost.com.ezproxy.bpl.org/.

NEWSPAPERS

List page numbers, section numbers, and any special edition information (such as "late ed.") as provided by the source. If the article falls into a special category, such as an editorial, a letter to the editor, or a review, add this label to your entry, after the title.

Article in a Print Newspaper

Shah, Neil. "More Young Adults Live with Parents." *The Wall Street Journal* 28 Aug. 2013, p. A2.

Article from a Newspaper Accessed through a Library Database

"The Road toward Peace." *The New York Times,* 15 Feb. 1945, p. 18. Editorial. *ProQuest Historical Newspapers: The New York Times,* search.proquest.com /hnpnewyorktimes.

Books

Books by One Author

List the author with last name first. Italicize the title. Include a shortened form of the publisher's name—for example, *Bedford* for *Bedford/St. Martin's*. Use the abbreviation *UP* for *University Press*, as in *Princeton UP* and *U of Chicago P*. Include the date of publication.

> Mantel, Hilary. *Bring up the Bodies*. Holt, 2012.

Books by Two or More Authors

For books with more than one author, list second and subsequent authors with first name first, in the order in which they are listed on the book's title page.

> Mooney, Chris, and Sheril Kirshenbaum. *Unscientific America: How Scientific Illiteracy Threatens Our Future*. Basic, 2009.

For books with more than three authors, you may list only the first author, followed by the abbreviation *et al.* ("and others").

> Heti, Sheila, *et al. Women in Clothes*. Blue Rider Press, 2014.

Two or More Books by the Same Author

List two or more books by the same author in alphabetical order according to title. In each entry after the first, use three unspaced hyphens (followed by a period) instead of the author's name.

> Eggers, Dave. *The Circle*. Random, 2013.
> ---. *A Hologram for the King*. McSweeney's, 2012.

Edited Book

> Austen, Jane. *Persuasion: An Annotated Edition*. Edited by Robert Morrison. Belknap-Harvard UP, 2011.

Anthology

> Adler, Frances P., Debra Busman, and Diana Garcia, editors. *Fire and Ink: An Anthology of Social Action Writing*. U of Arizona P, 2009.

Essay in an Anthology or Chapter of a Book

> Weise, Matthew J. "How the Zombie Changed Videogames." *Zombies Are Us: Essays on the Humanity of the Walking Dead*. Edited by Christopher M. Moreman and Cory James Rushton, McFarland, 2011, pp. 151–68.

Internet Sources

Full source information is not always available for Internet sources. When citing Internet sources, include whatever information you can find—ideally, the name of the author (or authors), the title of the article or other document (in quotation marks), the title of the site (italicized), the sponsor or publisher, and the date of publication or last update.

Be sure to include a Digital Object Indicator (DOI) or a web address (URL) when citing an electronic source.

Document within a Website

Enzinna, Wes. "Syria's Unknown Revolution." *Pulitzer Center on Crisis Reporting*, 24 Nov. 2015, pulitzercenter.org/projects /middle-east-syria-enzinna-war-rojava.

Entire Website

Railton, Stephen. *Mark Twain in His Times*. Stephen Railton/U of Virginia Library, 2012, twain.lib.virginia.edu/.

Article in an Online Reference Book or Encyclopedia

Hall, Mark. "Facebook (American Company)." *The Enyclopaedia Britannica*, 2 Jul. 2014, www.britannica.com/topic/Facebook.

Article in an Online Newspaper

Crowell, Maddy. "How Computers Are Getting Better at Detecting Liars." *The Christian Science Monitor*, 12 Dec. 2015, www .csmonitor.com/Science/Science-Notebook/2015/1212 /How-computers-are-getting-better-at-detecting-liars.

FYI

Preparing the Works-Cited List

- Begin the works-cited list on a new page after the last page of your essay.
- Number the works-cited page as the next page of your essay.
- Center the heading "Works Cited" one inch from the top of the page; do not italicize the heading or place it in quotation marks.
- Double-space the list.
- List entries alphabetically according to the author's last name.
- Alphabetize unsigned articles according to the first major word of the title.
- Begin typing each entry at the left-hand margin.
- Indent second and subsequent lines of each entry one-half inch.
- Separate major divisions of each entry—author, title, and publication information—by a period and one space.

Sample MLA Essay

On the pages that follow is an essay on the topic of counterfeit designer goods. The essay uses MLA documentation style and format and includes a works-cited page.

Compton 1

May Compton
Professor DiSalvo
English 100
29 Apr. 2019

Center your title: do not italicize or underline

The True Price of Counterfeit Goods

At purse parties in city apartments and suburban homes, customers can buy "designer" handbags at impossibly low prices. On street corners, sidewalk vendors sell name brand-perfumes and sunglasses for much less than their list prices. On the Internet, buyers can buy fine watches for a fraction of the prices charged by manufacturers. Is this too good to be true? Of course it is. All of these "bargains" are knockoffs—counterfeit copies of the real thing. What the people who buy these items do not know (or prefer not to think about) is that the money they are spending supports organized crime—and, sometimes, terrorism. For this reason, people should not buy counterfeit designer merchandise, no matter how tempted they are to do so.

People who buy counterfeit designer merchandise defend their actions by saying that designer products are very expensive. This is certainly true. According to Dana Thomas, the manufacturers of genuine designer merchandise charge ten times more than what it costs to make it (A23). A visitor from Britain, who bought an imitation Gucci purse in New York City for fifty dollars, said, "The real thing is so overpriced. To buy a genuine Gucci purse, I would have to pay over a thousand dollars" (qtd. in "Counterfeit Goods"). Even people who can easily afford to pay the full amount buy fakes. For example, movie stars like Jennifer Lopez openly wear counterfeit goods, and many customers think that if it is all right for celebrities like Lopez to buy fakes, it must also be all right for them, too (Malone). However, as the well-known designer Giorgio Armani points out, counterfeiters create a number of problems for legitimate companies because they use the brand name but do not maintain quality control.

Marginal notes:

Include your last name and the page number in the upper right-hand corner of every page.

Include your name, instructor's name, course title, and date on first page.

Introduction

Thesis statement

Paragraph combines paraphrase, quotation, and May's own ideas.

Compton 2

What most people choose to ignore is that buying counterfeit items is stealing. In 2016, U.S. Customs and Border Protection and U.S. Immigration and Customs Enforcement seized a record number of counterfeit goods. Leading the list of seized items were designer watches and jewelry as well as handbags and wallets ("CBP"). The FBI estimates that in the United States alone, companies lose about $250 billion as a result of counterfeits (Wallace). In addition, buyers of counterfeit items avoid the state and local sales taxes that legitimate companies pay. Thus, New York City alone loses about a billion dollars every year as a result of the sale of counterfeit merchandise ("Counterfeit Goods"). When this happens, everyone loses. After all, a billion dollars would pay for a lot of police officers and teachers, would fill a lot of potholes, and would pave a lot of streets. Buyers of counterfeit designer goods do not think of themselves as thieves, but that is exactly what they are.

Buyers of counterfeit merchandise also do not realize that the sale of knockoffs is a criminal activity. Most of the profits go to the criminal organization that either makes or imports the counterfeit goods—not to the person who sells the items. In fact, the biggest manufacturer and distributor of counterfeit items is organized crime ("Trafficking"). Michael Kessler, who heads a company that investigates corporate crime, makes this connection clear when he describes the complicated organization that is needed to make counterfeit perfume:

> They need a place that makes bottles, a factory with pumps to fill the bottles, a printer to make the labels, and a box manufacturer to fake the packaging. Then, they need a sophisticated distribution network, as well as all the cash to set everything up. (qtd. in Malone)

Kessler concludes that only an organized crime syndicate—not an individual—has the money to support this illegal activity. For this reason, anyone who buys counterfeits may also be supporting activities such as prostitution, drug distribution, smuggling of illegal immigrants, gang warfare, extortion, and murder (Nellis). In addition, the people who make counterfeits often work in sweatshops where labor and environmental laws are ignored. As Dana Thomas points out, a worker in China who makes counterfeits earns only a fraction of the salary of a worker who makes the real thing (A23).

Paragraph synthesizes May's own ideas with material from three articles.

Long quotation is set off one-half inch from the left-hand margin. No quotation marks are used.

Finally, and perhaps most shocking, is the fact that some of the money earned from the sale of counterfeit designer goods also supports international terrorism. For example, Kim Wallace reports in her *Times Daily* article that during Al-Qaeda training, terrorists are advised to sell fakes to get money for their operations. According to Interpol, an international police organization, the bombing of the World Trade Center in 1993 was paid for in part by the sale of counterfeit T-shirts. Also, evidence suggests that associates of the 2001 World Trade Center terrorists may have been involved with the production of imitation designer goods (Malone). Finally, the 2004 bombing of commuter trains in Madrid was financed in part by the sale of counterfeits. In fact, an intelligence source states, "It would be more shocking if Al-Qaeda *wasn't* involved in counterfeiting. The sums involved are staggering—it would be inconceivable if money were not being raised for their terrorist activities" (qtd. in Malone).

> Paragraph contains May's own ideas as well as a paraphrase and a quotation.

Consumers should realize that when they buy counterfeits, they are actually breaking the law. By doing so, they are making it possible for organized crime syndicates and terrorists to earn money for their illegal activities. Although buyers of counterfeit merchandise justify their actions by saying that the low prices are impossible to resist, they might reconsider if they knew the uses to which their money was going. The truth of the matter is that counterfeit designer products, such as handbags, sunglasses, jewelry, and T-shirts, are luxuries, not necessities. By resisting the temptation to buy knockoffs, consumers could help to eliminate the companies that hurt legitimate manufacturers, exploit workers, and even finance international terrorism.

> Conclusion contains May's original ideas, so no documentation is necessary.

Compton 4

Works Cited

Armani, Giorgio. "10 Questions for Giorgio Armani." *Time*, 12 Feb. 2009, content
.time.com/time/magazine/article/0,9171,1879189,00.html.

"CBP, ICE Seize Record Number of Shipments with Intellectual Property Rights
Violations in FY2016." U.S. Customs and Border Protection, Department of
Homeland Security, 24 Nov. 2017, www.cbp.gov/newsroom/national-media
-release/cbp-ice-seize-record-number-shipments-intellectual-property-rights.

"Counterfeit Goods Are Linked to Terror Groups." *The International Herald Tribune*,
12 Feb. 2007, www.nytimes.com/2007/02/12/business/worldbusiness
/12iht-fake.4569452.html?_r=0.

Malone, Andrew. "Revealed: The True Cost of Buying Cheap Fake Goods." *Daily Mail*,
29 July 2007, www.dailymail.co.uk/news/article-471679/Revealed-The-true
-cost-buying-cheap-fakegoods.html.

Nellis, Cynthia. "Faking It: Counterfeit Fashion." *About.com*, www.about.com/cs
/tipsadvice/a/fakingit.htm.

Thomas, Dana. "Terror's Purse Strings." *The New York Times*, 30 Aug. 2007, p. A23.
Editorial. *Proquest*, search.proquest.com/hnpnewyorktimes.

"Trafficking in Illicit Goods and Counterfeiting." *Interpol*, www.interpol.int/Crime
-areas/Trafficking-in-illicit-goods-and-counterfeiting/Trafficking
-in-illicit-goods-and-counterfeiting.

Wallace, Kim. "A Counter-Productive Trade." *TimesDaily.com*, 28 July 2007,
timesdaily.com/opinion/editorials/counter-productive-trade.

Works-cited list starts a new page.

This Internet source has no listed author, so it is alphabetized in the list by the title.

First lines of entries are set flush left; subsequent lines are indented one-half inch.

17e APA Documentation Style

APA documentation requires you to make a brief citation in the body of your essay when using material from another source. Readers can use these **in-text citations** to find detailed information on specific sources in your **references list** at the end of the paper.

APA In-Text Citations

In-text citations refer readers to sources in the list of references at the end of the paper. In general, these citations are placed in parentheses at the end of the sentence where the source is first used and include the author's last name and the year of publication: (Diamond, 2012). If you are quoting directly from a source, the reference should also include page numbers: (Diamond, 2012, p. 137). If, however, you refer to the author's name in your text, include only the year of publication in parentheses: Diamond asserted . . . (2012). When quoting directly, include the page number as well: Diamond asserted . . . (2012, p. 137).

Once you have cited a source, you can refer to the author again within that same paragraph, without the publication date, so long as it is clear you are referring to the same source: Diamond also found. . . .

Here are some specific guidelines for five special situations.

1. CITING A WORK BY MULTIPLE AUTHORS

When a work has two authors, cite both names and the year (Reid & Boyer, 2013). Use the word *and* between the authors' names when you mention the authors in your text, but use an ampersand (&) in the parenthetical reference. For three to five authors, cite all authors in the first reference, along with the year (Jung, Pick, Schluter-Muller, Schmeck, & Goth, 2013). For subsequent references, cite only the first author followed by *et al.* and the year (Jung et al., 2013).

When a work has six or more authors, use only the first author's name, followed by *et al.* and the year (Malm et al., 2012).

2. CITING A WORK THAT HAS NO PAGE NUMBERS

Omit page numbers if you are quoting from a source that does not include them, as is the case with many online sources. (Try to find a PDF version of an online source if it is an option; it will usually include page numbers.) If a source shows paragraph numbers, you can use these instead of page numbers, preceded by the abbreviation *para*. If a source has neither page nor paragraph numbers but has headings, you can cite a shortened version of the heading in quotation marks followed by the number of the paragraph.

3. CITING A WORK THAT HAS NO NAMED AUTHOR

If no author is identified, use a shortened version of the title of the work ("Mind," 2013).

4. CITING A SOURCE THAT IS QUOTED IN ANOTHER SOURCE

If you quote a source found in another source, indicate the original author and the source in which you found it.

As Hatzes asserted, "If one analysis produces a planet and another doesn't, that's not robust" (as cited in Cowen, 2013, p. 25).

5. CITING PERSONAL COMMUNICATIONS

Include parenthetical references to personal communications and interviews that you conducted by providing the person's name, the phrase *personal communication*, and the date (J. Smith, personal communication, February 12, 2014). Do **not** include these sources in your reference list.

FYI

Formatting Quotations in an APA Paper

1. **Short quotations**   If a direct quotation is fewer than forty words long, set it within quotation marks without separating it from the rest of the text. The parenthetical reference follows, and if the quotation is at the end of the sentence, the period follows the final parenthesis.

   Scientists use mice in these experiments on smell because "the rodent olfactory system provides a good functional model for at least some aspects of the human system" (Yantis, 2014, p. 438).

2. **Long quotations**   When quoting a passage that is forty or more words long, set it off from the rest of your paper. Indent the entire block of quoted text one-half inch from the left margin, begin it on a new line, and do not enclose it in quotation marks. If a quoted passage has more than one paragraph, indent the first line of subsequent paragraphs an extra half-inch. The quoted passage should be double-spaced, like the rest of the paper. Place your parenthetical reference after the final punctuation of the quotation.

   Perceptual organization is critical to vision, as Yantis has noted:

   > Perceptual organization is the visual system's way of dealing with scenes containing multiple overlapping objects—it makes object recognition within complex scenes possible. Without perceptual organization, the visual system would be overwhelmed by the jumbled pattern of brightness and color in the retinal image of most real scenes. (2014, p. 123)

The References List

The reference list includes all the works you cite in your essay. Use the guidelines in the "Preparing the References List" FYI box on page 353 to help you prepare your list.

The following sample reference-list entries cover the situations you will encounter most often.

Note: For all sources with authors, give the authors' last name first, followed by a comma and initials. The authors' names are followed by the publication year in parentheses.

Periodicals

Capitalize only the first word of the title and subtitle and any names; do not use quotation marks or italics. Give the title of the publication (journal, magazine, or newspaper) in italics, with all major words capitalized. For journals and magazines, add the volume number, italicized and preceded by a comma, and, if the issue paginates the publication, follow the volume number with the issue number in parentheses. After a comma, give the page numbers of the article. Use the abbreviation *p.* or *pp.* only for newspaper articles.

Because websites change and disappear without warning, many publishers, particularly journal publishers, have started adding a digital object identifier (DOI) to their articles. A DOI is a unique number that can be retrieved no matter where the article ends up on the web. If an article, electronic or print, has a DOI, include it at the end of your reference-list entry, with no final period.

Article in a Print Journal

Heyns, C., & Srinivasan, S. (2013). Protecting the right to life of journalists: The need for a higher level of engagement. *Human Rights Quarterly, 35*, 304–332. doi: 10.1353/hrq.2013.0030

Article in a Journal Accessed through an Online Database

The name and URL of the database are not required for citations. If the article has a DOI, use the DOI. If no DOI is available, provide the home page URL of the journal or other periodical.

Almeroth, K., & Zhang, H. (2013). Alternatives for monitoring and limiting network access to students in network-connected classrooms. *Journal of Interactive Learning Research, 24*, 237–265. Retrieved from http://www.aace.org/pubs/jilr/

Article in a Print Magazine

Kenny, P. J. (2013, September). The food addiction. *Scientific American, 309*(3), 44–49.

Article in a Print Newspaper

> Smith, P. A. (2013, August 27). A quest for even safer drinking water. *The New York Times*, p. D3.

Books

Give book titles in italics, and capitalize only the first word of the title and subtitle and any names. For place of publication, give the city followed by a comma and the two-letter abbreviation for the state. Following a colon, give a shortened form of the publisher's name.

Books by One Author

> McCrum, R. (2010). *Globish: How the English language became the world's language.* New York, NY: Norton.

Books by Two to Seven Authors

For works with up to seven authors, give all authors' names, with an ampersand before the last author.

> Acemoglu, D., & Robinson, J. (2012). *Why nations fail: The origins of power, prosperity, and poverty.* New York, NY: Crown.

Books by Eight or More Authors

Include the names of the first six authors and then add three ellipsis points and the name of the last author.

> Wolfe, J. M., Kluender, K. R., Levi, D. M., Bartoshuk, L. M., Herz, R. S., Klatzky, R. L., . . . Merfeld, D. M. (2012). *Sensation & perception* (3rd ed.). Sunderland, MA: Sinauer.

Edited Book

> Sarat, A., Douglas, L., & Umphrey, M. M. (Eds.). (2011). *Law as punishment /Law as regulation.* Stanford, CA: Stanford University Press.

Essay or Chapter in an Edited Book

> Gleiser, M. (2012). We are unique. In J. Brockman (Ed.), *This will make you smarter* (pp. 3–5). New York, NY: Harper.

Internet Sources

Include the Information that your readers will need in order to be able to retrieve your sources. As discussed above, when a DOI is not available, provide a URL.

Document within a Website

In your retrieval statement, give the website and its URL.

Roushdy, R., Sieverding, M., & Radwan, H. (2012). *The impact of water supply and sanitation on child health: Evidence from Egypt* (Poverty, Gender, and Youth Working Paper No. 24). Retrieved from Population Council website: http://www.popcouncil.org/

Blog Post or Video Blog Post

In brackets after the title, describe the source type—for example, as *Web log post* or *Video file*.

Siegel, E. (2013, August 30). How would you figure out whether global warming is real? Part 3 [Web log post]. Retrieved from http://scienceblogs.com/startswithabang/2013/08/30/how-would-you-figure-out-whether-global-warming-is-real-part-3/

FYI

Preparing the References List

- Start your list of references on a separate page at the end of your paper.
- Center the title References at the top of the page.
- Begin each reference flush with the left margin, and indent subsequent lines one-half inch.
- Double-space the list.
- List your references alphabetically by the author's last name (or by the first major word of the title if no author is identified).
- If the list includes references for two sources by the same author, list them in order by the year of publication, starting with the earliest.
- Italicize the titles of books and periodicals. Do not italicize article titles or enclose them in quotation marks.
- For the titles of books and articles, capitalize only the first word of the title and subtitle as well as any proper nouns. Capitalize words in a periodical title as in the original.

Sample APA Paper

On the pages that follow are excerpts from the student essay on the topic of counterfeit designer goods, showing the differences in formatting from MLA. It has been annotated to show you the proper formatting and elements of a research paper.

Title page

The True Price of Counterfeit Goods

May Compton

Drexel University

Running head: THE TRUE PRICE OF COUNTERFEIT GOODS   1

> Title of paper appears top left on each page in capital letters. On the title page, it follows the words "Running head:" If the title is more than 50 characters, use a shortened version. Page number is placed top right.

> Full title of paper, author's name and school are centered halfway down the page. Do not bold, underline, or italicize.

Author Note

> Author note with course title and instructor's name can be placed at the bottom of the page. Check with your instructor for his or her preferences.

This paper was prepared for English 100, taught by Professor Mandell

Abstract page

THE TRUE PRICE OF COUNTERFEIT GOODS   2

Abstract

> The abstract, a brief summary of the paper, appears on the second page.

Many people buy "designer" goods, such as watches, jewelry, handbags, and wallets, at bargain prices online or from street vendors. Few are aware that they are committing theft and aiding criminals. Mass production of fake goods requires significant capital and is often financed by organized crime. Goods are produced by low-paid workers in sweatshops, no state or local taxes are paid, and the profits are often used to subsidize illegal activities, such as prostitution, drug distribution, gang warfare, the smuggling of illegal immigrants, and even terrorism. This paper explores the consequences of buying counterfeit goods and the arguments for avoiding participation in illegal activities by refusing to buy discounted "designer" items.

First page of paper

THE TRUE PRICE OF COUNTERFEIT GOODS   3

The True Price of Counterfeit Goods

> The running head and the title, centered, appear on page 3, followed by the text of the paper.

Paragraph showing APA parenthetical references

People who buy counterfeit designer merchandise defend their actions by saying that designer products are expensive. This is certainly true. According to Thomas (2007), the manufacturers of genuine designer merchandise charge more than ten times what it costs to make it (p. A23). A visitor from Britain, who bought an imitation Gucci purse in New York City for fifty dollars, said, "The real thing is so overpriced. To buy a genuine Gucci purse, I would have to pay over a thousand dollars" (as cited in "Counterfeit goods," 2007). Even people who can easily afford to pay the full amount buy fakes. For example, movie stars like Jennifer Lopez openly wear counterfeit goods, and many customers think that if it is all right for celebrities like Lopez to buy fakes, it is all right for them too (Malone, 2007). However, as the well-known designer Giorgio Armani (2009) points out, counterfeiters create a number of problems for legitimate companies because they use the brand name but do not maintain quality control.

> Note that in APA style, the authors' names and/or dates of publication appear in parenthetical references, separated by commas. Titles are used if there is no author.

References page

Start the references list on a new page, center the title, and double-space throughout. List sources alphabetically by last names of authors or editors or first word of title if no one named.

References   7

Armani, G. (2009, February 12). 10 questions for Giorgio Armani. *Time*. Retrieved
    from time.com/

CBP, ICE seize record number of shipments with intellectual property rights
    violations in FY2016. (2017, November 24). Retrieved from U.S. Customs and
    Border Protection, Department of Homeland Security: https://www.cbp.gov/

Counterfeit goods are linked to terror groups. (2007, February 12). *International
    Herald Tribune*. Retrieved from https://www.nytimes.com/

Malone, A. (2007, July 29). Revealed: The true cost of buying cheap fake goods.
    Daily Mail. Retrieved from www.dailymail.co.uk/

Nellis, C. (2009). Faking it: Counterfeit fashion. *About.com*. Retrieved from www.
    about.com/

Thomas, D. (2007, August 30). Terror's purse strings [Editorial]. *The New York
    Times*, p. A23. Retrieved from https://www.nytimes.com/

Wallace, K. (2007, July 28). A counter-productive trade. *Times Daily*. Retrieved from
    www.timesdaily.com/

First lines of entries are set flush left; subsequent lines are indented one-half inch. Note that titles are set lowercase, except for the first word of the title or subtitle, dates are included after author names, and "Retrieved from" is placed before URLs. Review the Sample Reference List Entries section for more details.

EDITING PRACTICE

Read the paragraph below from *The New York Times* article "The New Math on Campus" by Alex Williams. Then, read the three student paragraphs that use this article as a source. In each of these paragraphs, student writers have accidentally committed plagiarism. On the line below each student paragraph, explain the problem. Then, edit the paragraph so that it correctly documents the source and avoids plagiarism.

North Carolina, with a student body that is nearly 60 percent female, is just one of many large universities that at times feel eerily like women's colleges. Women have represented about 57 percent of enrollments at American colleges since at least 2000, according to a recent report by the American Council on Education. Researchers there cite several reasons: Women tend to have higher grades; men tend to drop out in disproportionate numbers; and female enrollment skews higher among older students, low-income students, and black and Hispanic students.

1. About 60% female, the University of North Carolina is an example of large universities with many more women than men. According to a report from the American Council on Education, one reason is that "female enrollment skews higher among older students, low-income students, and black and Hispanic students" (Williams). If this is true, what will this mean for the black and Hispanic communities?

   _____

   _____

2. In recent years, colleges and universities have taken on a very different atmosphere. The reason is clear to anyone who takes a casual look around at just about any college campus. Women now outnumber men, so much so that some colleges at times feel eerily like women's colleges (Williams). This situation seems likely to continue in the years to come.

   _____

   _____

3. Why do women outnumber men in today's colleges? Researchers at the American Council on Education mention a few reasons: Women often have higher grades, men tend to drop out in larger numbers, and female enrollment is especially high for some groups such as older students, low-income students, and black and Hispanic students (Williams). These reasons may all be true at our school, which certainly has more women than men.

_____

_____

COLLABORATIVE ACTIVITY

Create an MLA or APA works-cited list using three different types of sources (such as a book, an article in an online newspaper, and a document within a website). Make sure that you arrange the entries in alphabetical order and that you use the correct format for each type of source.

review checklist

✔ Whenever you use information from a source in your writing, you have to document it, indicating for readers where you found it so they can also locate it. Documentation styles vary by discipline, but two of the most common are MLA (see 17d) and APA (see 17e). Before writing, check what style your instructor requires.

✔ Both MLA and APA use parenthetical references within the body of the text that lead readers to alphabetized listings of complete source information at the end of the paper (see MLA In-Text Citations, p. 340, and APA Parenthetical References, p. 349, for details).

✔ In MLA, the list of works you cited in your paper is called a Works-Cited List (see The Works-Cited List on p. 341 for details).

✔ In APA, the list of works you cited in your paper is titled References (see The References List on p. 351 for details).

Unit

4 Revising and Editing Your Writing

Parts of Speech

The English language has eight basic parts of speech: nouns, pronouns, verbs, adjectives, adverbs, prepositions, conjunctions, and interjections.

Nouns

A **noun** names a person, an animal, a place, an object, or an idea.

<u>Christine</u> brought her <u>dog</u> <u>Bailey</u> to obedience <u>school</u> in <u>Lawndale</u>.
   noun   *noun* *noun*   *noun*   *noun*

Pronouns

A **pronoun** refers to and takes the place of a noun or another pronoun.

Bailey did very well in <u>her</u> lessons and seemed to enjoy <u>them</u>.
noun   *pronoun noun*   *pronoun*

Verbs

A **verb** tells what someone or something does, did, or will do.

Sometimes Bailey <u>rolls</u> over, but earlier today she <u>refused</u>.
                  verb   *verb*

Maybe she <u>will change</u> someday.
                verb

Adjectives

An **adjective** identifies or describes a noun or a pronoun.

<u>This</u> <u>dog</u> is a <u>small</u> <u>beagle</u> with a <u>brown</u> and <u>white</u> <u>coat</u> and <u>long</u> <u>ears</u>.
adj *noun*   *adj*   *noun*   *adj*   *adj*   *noun*   *adj*   *noun*

Adverbs

An **adverb** identifies or describes a verb, an adjective, or another adverb.

Bailey is old, so she moves <u>very</u> <u>slowly</u> and <u>seldom</u> barks.
                       verb *adverb adverb*   *adverb*   *verb*

Prepositions

A **preposition** is a word—such as *to*, *on*, or *with*—that introduces a noun or pronoun and connects it to other words in a sentence.

Bailey likes sitting quietly <u>in</u> her box <u>at</u> the foot <u>of</u> the stairs.

Conjunctions

A **conjunction** is a word that connects parts of a sentence.

People say you can't teach an old dog new tricks, <u>but</u> Bailey might be an exception.

Interjections

An **interjection** is a word—such as *Oh!* or *Hey!*—that is used to express emotion.

<u>Wow!</u> Bailey finally rolled over!

The eight basic parts of speech can be combined to form **sentences**, which always include at least one **subject** and one **verb**. The subject tells who or what is being talked about, and the verb tells what the subject does, did, or will do.

<u>Bailey</u> <u>graduated</u> from obedience school at the head of her class.
S   *V*

18 Writing Simple Sentences

A **sentence** is a group of words that expresses a complete thought. Every sentence includes both a subject and a verb. A **simple sentence** consists of a single **independent clause**: one <u>subject</u> and one <u>verb</u>.

<u>Service animals</u> <u>help</u> people with disabilities.

18a Identifying Subjects

Every sentence includes a subject. The **subject** of a sentence tells who or what is being talked about in the sentence. Without a subject, a sentence is not complete. In each of the following three sentences, the subject is underlined.

<u>Derek Walcott</u> won the Nobel Prize in Literature.

<u>He</u> was born in St. Lucia.

<u>St. Lucia</u> is an island in the Caribbean.

The subject of a sentence can be a noun or a pronoun. A **noun** names a person, place, or thing—*Derek Walcott*, *St. Lucia*. A **pronoun** takes the place of a noun—*I, you, he, she, it, we, they*, and so on.

The subject of a sentence can be *singular* or *plural*. A **singular subject** is one person, place, or thing (*Derek Walcott, St. Lucia, he*).

A **plural subject** is more than one person, place, or thing (*poets, people, they*).

<u>Readers</u> admire Walcott's poems.

A plural subject that joins two subjects with *and* is called a **compound subject**.

<u>St. Lucia and Trinidad</u> are Caribbean islands.

361

PRACTICE

18-1 In the following paragraph, underline the subject of each sentence.

Example: <u>Zombies</u> have been a part of folklore for centuries.

(1) In today's popular culture, zombies seem to be everywhere. (2) However, this trend is not a recent phenomenon. (3) For example, African slaves in seventeenth- and eighteenth-century Haiti sometimes longed for escape in death but feared becoming zombies. (4) Zombies can also be found throughout modern literature. (5) Frankenstein's monster—although not a zombie himself—inspired later interpretations of the undead. (6) In addition, zombies are popular in film. (8) *Night of the Living Dead* (1968) is a classic film featuring zombies. (9) *World War Z* (2013) continues the tradition. (10) Television has also been overrun by zombie tales, such as *The Walking Dead*. (11) In fact, zombies are popular in everything from comic books and video games to Halloween costumes. (12) The website of the Centers for Disease Control even features a Zombie Apocalypse Survival Guide.

PRACTICE

18-2 Underline the subject in each sentence. Then, write *S* above singular subjects and *P* above plural subjects. Remember, compound subjects are plural.

                                              P

Example: <u>Renewable energy sources</u> are being developed to replace fossil fuels.

1. For years, fossil fuels have been the main source of energy around the world.

2. Fossil fuels, which include coal, oil, and natural gas, are nonrenewable.

3. They are not replenished once they have been used.

4. In contrast, the sun and wind are renewable energy sources.

5. The sun's energy is collected through solar panels and converted into electricity.

6. Solar power can be used to produce electricity without being connected to a grid.

7. Turbines capture the wind's energy and convert it into electricity.

8. To produce energy, turbines require strong and consistent winds.

9. Other renewable energy sources include hydropower, biomass, and geothermal energy.

10. Despite some obstacles, renewable energy will play an important role in the future.

18b Identifying Prepositional Phrases

A **prepositional phrase** consists of a **preposition** (a word such as *on*, *to*, *in*, or *with*) and its **object** (the noun or pronoun it introduces).

PREPOSITION	+	OBJECT	=	PREPOSITIONAL PHRASE
on		the stage		on the stage
to		Nia's house		to Nia's house
in		my new car		in my new car
with		them		with them

Because the object of a preposition is a noun or a pronoun, it may seem to be the subject of a sentence. However, the object of a preposition can never be the subject of a sentence. To identify a sentence's true subject, cross out each prepositional phrase. (Remember, every prepositional phrase is introduced by a preposition.)

> SUBJECT PREP PHRASE
> The cost of the repairs was astronomical.

> PREP PHRASE   PREP PHRASE   SUBJECT
> At the end of the novel, after an exciting chase, the lovers flee
> PREP PHRASE
> to Mexico.

Frequently Used Prepositions

about	at	during	off	under
above	before	except	on	underneath
according to	behind	for	onto	until
across	below	from	out	up
after	beneath	in	outside	upon
against	beside	inside	over	with
along	between	into	through	within
among	beyond	like	throughout	without
around	by	near	to	
as	despite	of	toward	

PRACTICE

18-3   Each of the following sentences includes at least one prepositional phrase. To identify each sentence's subject, begin by crossing out each prepositional phrase. Then, underline the subject of the sentence.

Example: <u>Bicycling</u> ~~on busy city streets~~ can be dangerous.

(1) In many American cities, cyclists are concerned about sharing the road with cars. (2) For this reason, people are becoming more interested in "green" lanes. (3) These bike lanes are different from traditional bike lanes in one important way. (4) Green lanes are separated from the road by curbs, planters, or parked cars. (5) For years, people in Europe have been creating and using these protected bike lanes. (6) Until recently, however, few green lanes were created in the United States. (7) Now, with the help of the Bikes Belong Foundation and the Federal Highway Administration, several U.S. cities are installing green lanes. (8) For their supporters, these bike lanes are a positive step toward healthier, safer cities. (9) However, some critics worry about reduced space for traffic lanes and parking. (10) Still, despite the criticism, green lanes are increasing the number of bike riders and reducing the number of bike accidents.

18c Identifying Verbs

In addition to its subject, every sentence also includes a verb. This **verb** (also called a **predicate**) tells what the subject does or connects the subject to words that describe or rename it. Without a verb, a sentence is not complete.

Action Verbs

An **action verb** tells what the subject does, did, or will do.

> Serena Williams <u>plays</u> tennis.
>
> Amelia Earhart <u>flew</u> across the Atlantic.
>
> Renee <u>will drive</u> to Tampa on Friday.

Action verbs can also show mental and emotional actions.

> Travis always <u>worries</u> about his job.

Sometimes the subject of a sentence performs more than one action. In this case, the sentence includes two or more action verbs that form a **compound predicate**.

> He <u>hit</u> the ball, <u>threw</u> down his bat, and <u>ran</u> toward first base.

PRACTICE

 18-4 In the following sentences, underline each action verb twice. Some sentences contain more than one action verb.

Example: Invasive species <u>cause</u> billions of dollars in damage every year.

1. Invasive plant species include weeds as well as flowering plants, shrubs, trees, and vines.

2. Invasive plants thrive outside their native range.

3. These plants tolerate many soil types and weather conditions.

4. They grow rapidly and spread easily, usually by wind, water, or animals.

5. They outcompete native species for food, sunlight, soil, and space.

6. Typically, human actions introduce an invasive plant species to a habitat.

7. People often choose these plants because of their favorable qualities.

8. For instance, Americans first imported Japanese honeysuckle and kudzu for erosion control.

9. Unfortunately, these two invasive vines smother, strangle, and kill other vegetation.

10. Invasive plants harm the environment, the economy, and even human health.

Linking Verbs

A **linking verb** does not show action. Instead, it connects the subject to a word or words that describe or rename it. The linking verb tells what the subject is (or what it was, will be, or seems to be).

A googolplex <u>is</u> an extremely large number.

Many linking verbs, like *is*, are forms of the verb *be*. Other linking verbs refer to the senses (*look*, *feel*, and so on).

The photocopy <u>looks</u> blurry.

Some people <u>feel</u> anxious about the future.

> ### Frequently Used Linking Verbs
>
> | | | |
> |---|---|---|
> | act | feel | seem |
> | appear | get | smell |
> | be (am, is, are, | grow | sound |
> | was, were) | look | taste |
> | become | remain | turn |

PRACTICE

18-5 In each of the following sentences, underline every verb twice. Remember that a verb can be an action verb or a linking verb.

Example: Airplane pilots and investment bankers <u>use</u> checklists.

(1) In *The Checklist Manifesto,* surgeon Atul Gawande argues for using checklists in operating rooms. (2) Gawande reminds readers of the complexity of modern medicine. (3) Currently, there are 6,000 drugs and 4,000 medical and surgical procedures. (4) Each year, the number of drugs and procedures increases. (5) As a result, even knowledgeable and highly trained surgeons make mistakes. (6) For some types of patients, the error rate is very high. (7) For example, doctors deliver inappropriate care to 40 percent of patients with coronary artery disease. (8) Luckily, checklists make a big difference for these and other patients. (9) In fact, checklists reduce complications by more than one-third. (10) It is hard to imagine an argument against such a simple and effective tool.

Helping Verbs

Many verbs consist of more than one word. For example, the verb in the following sentence consists of two words.

Minh <u>must make</u> a decision about his future.

In this sentence, *make* is the **main verb**, and *must* is a **helping verb**.

Frequently Used Helping Verbs

does	was	must	should
did	were	can	would
do		could	will
is	have	may	
are	has	might	
am	had		

A sentence's **complete verb** is made up of a main verb plus any helping verbs that accompany it. In the following sentences, the complete verb is underlined twice, and the helping verbs are checkmarked.

Minh should have gone earlier. ✓ ✓

Did Minh ask the right questions? ✓

Minh will work hard.

Minh can really succeed. ✓

FYI

Helping Verbs with Participles

Participles, such as *going* and *gone*, cannot stand alone as main verbs in a sentence. They need a helping verb to make them complete.

INCORRECT	Minh going to the library.
CORRECT	Minh is going to the library.
INCORRECT	Minh gone to the library.
CORRECT	Minh has gone to the library.

PRACTICE

18-6   The verbs in the sentences that follow consist of a main verb and one or more helping verbs. In each sentence, underline the complete verb twice, and put a check mark above each helping verb.

Example: In 1954, the Salk polio vaccine was given to more than a ✓
million schoolchildren.

(1) By the 1950s, polio had become a serious problem throughout the United States. (2) For years, it had puzzled doctors and researchers. (3) Thousands had become ill each year in the United States alone. (4) Children should have been playing happily. (5) Instead, they would get very sick. (6) Polio was sometimes called infantile paralysis. (7) In fact, it did cause paralysis in children and in adults as well. (8) Some patients could breathe only with the help of machines called iron lungs. (9) Others would remain in wheelchairs for life. (10) By 1960, Jonas Salk's vaccine had reduced the incidence of polio in the United States by more than 90 percent.

EDITING PRACTICE

Read the following student essay. Underline the subject of each sentence once, and underline the complete verb of each sentence twice. If you have trouble locating the subject, try crossing out the prepositional phrases. The first sentence has been done for you.

A New Way to Learn

Salman Khan founded the nonprofit online Khan Academy in 2006. Khan Academy promises "a free world-class education for anyone anywhere." With the help of short videos, people can learn a subject like physics or economics at their own pace. According to some, Khan Academy is in the process of revolutionizing education.

Salman Khan was born in New Orleans in 1976. His parents had moved to Louisiana from Bangladesh. During his childhood, Khan attended public schools in New Orleans. After high school, he earned three degrees from MIT and one degree from Harvard. His degrees are in math, engineering, computer science, and business. He had never considered a career in education. However, in 2008, Khan's cousin asked him for help with algebra. He made some short YouTube videos for her. To his surprise, the lessons became extremely popular. He had a talent for teaching. With a small donation from an investor that same year, Salman Khan started Khan Academy.

Khan Academy has succeeded well beyond Khan's expectations. Now, the organization receives millions of dollars in donations. The Khan Academy website has thousands of videos. Every video is available for free to anyone. Khan teaches many of the lessons himself. He researches his subjects. Then, without a script, he records each video in one take. These videos are not traditional lectures. The audience never sees his face. Throughout each lesson, his writing appears on the screen. Related images appear as well. For viewers, each lesson feels like a one-on-one tutoring session.

The site also offers exercises for students and tools for teachers. Students can practice subjects by themselves. They can progress at their own speed. Some schools are even using Khan Academy lessons in their classrooms. With the help of Khan's videos, teachers can create a "flipped" classroom. Students learn basic concepts at night on their computers. Then, at school, students work on problems with the teacher's help. This means more time for questions. For some students, this method has been extremely effective.

Without any training in education, Salman Khan has changed people's ideas about learning. Around the world, people are using his website. They are learning new ideas. Khan is happy about this. In his view, education should be accessible for all.

COLLABORATIVE ACTIVITY

Fold a sheet of paper in half vertically. Working in a group of three or four students, spend two minutes listing as many nouns as you can in the column to the left of the fold. When your time is up, exchange papers with another group of students, and write an appropriate action verb beside each noun. (Each noun will now be the subject of a short sentence.)

Then, choose five of your sentences, and collaborate with the other students in your group to create more fully developed sentences. First, expand each subject by adding words or prepositional phrases that give more information about the subject. (For example, you could expand *boat* to *the small, leaky boat with the red sail*.) Then, expand each sentence further, adding ideas after the verb. (For example, the sentence *The boat bounced* could become *The small, leaky boat with the red sail bounced helplessly on the water*.)

review checklist

Writing Simple Sentences

✔ A sentence expresses a complete thought. The subject tells who or what is being talked about in the sentence. (See 18a.)

✔ A prepositional phrase consists of a preposition and its object (the noun or pronoun it introduces). (See 18b.)

✔ The object of a preposition cannot be the subject of a sentence. (See 18b.)

✔ An action verb tells what the subject does, did, or will do. (See 18c.)

✔ A linking verb connects the subject to a word or words that describe or rename it. (See 18c.)

✔ Many verbs are made up of more than one word. The complete verb in a sentence includes the main verb plus any helping verbs. (See 18c.)

19 Writing Compound Sentences

The most basic kind of sentence, a **simple sentence**, consists of a single **independent clause**: one <u>subject</u> and one <u>verb</u>.

Many European <u>immigrants</u> <u>arrived</u> at Ellis Island.

A **compound sentence** is made up of two or more simple sentences (independent clauses).

◆ 19a Using Coordinating Conjunctions

One way to form a compound sentence is by joining two independent clauses with a **coordinating conjunction** preceded by a comma.

Many European immigrants arrived at Ellis Island, <u>but</u> many Asian immigrants arrived at Angel Island.

COORDINATING CONJUNCTIONS			
and	for	or	yet
but	nor	so	

FYI

Use the letters that spell *FANBOYS* to help you remember the coordinating conjunctions.

F	for
A	and
N	nor
B	but
O	or
Y	yet
S	so

Coordinating conjunctions join two ideas of equal importance. They describe the relationship between two ideas, showing how and why the ideas are related. Different coordinating conjunctions have different meanings.

- To indicate addition, use *and*.

  He acts like a child, <u>and</u> people think he is cute.

- To indicate contrast or contradiction, use *but* or *yet*.

  He acts like a child, <u>but</u> he is an adult.

  He acts like a child, <u>yet</u> he wants to be taken seriously.

- To indicate a cause-and-effect relationship, use *so* or *for*.

  He acts like a child, <u>so</u> we treat him like one.

  He acts like a child, <u>for</u> he needs attention.

- To present alternatives, use *or*.

  Either he acts like a child, <u>or</u> he is ignored.

- To eliminate alternatives, use *nor*.

  He does not act like a child, <u>nor</u> does he look like one.

FYI

Commas with Coordinating Conjunctions

When you use a coordinating conjunction to join two independent clauses into a single compound sentence, always put a comma before the coordinating conjunction.

We can stand in line all night, or we can go home now.

PRACTICE

19-1 Fill in the coordinating conjunction—*and, but, for, nor, or, so,* or *yet*—that most logically links the two parts of each compound sentence. Remember to insert a comma before each coordinating conjunction.

Example: Fairy tales have been told by many people around the world, ___ *but* ___ the stories by two German brothers may be the
_∧
most famous.

(1) Jakob and Wilhelm Grimm lived in the nineteenth century _____ they wrote many well-known fairy tales. (2) Most people think fondly of fairy tales _____ the Brothers Grimm wrote many unpleasant and violent stories. (3) In their best-known works, children are abused _____ endings are not always happy. (4) Either innocent children are brutally punished for no reason _____ they are neglected. (5) For example, in "Hansel and Gretel," the stepmother mistreats the children _____ their father abandons them in the woods. (6) In this story, the events are horrifying _____ the ending is still happy. (7) The children outwit the evil adults _____ they escape unharmed. (8) Apparently, they are not injured physically _____ are they harmed emotionally. (9) Nevertheless, their story can hardly be called pleasant _____ it remains a story of child abuse and neglect.

PRACTICE

19-2 Add coordinating conjunctions to combine some of the simple sentences in the following paragraph. Remember to put a comma before each coordinating conjunction you add.

, but today,

Example: Years ago, few Americans lived to be one hundred, ~~Today,~~
_∧
there are over 70,000 centenarians.

(1) Diet, exercise, and family history may explain centenarians' long lives. (2) This is not the whole story. (3) A recent study showed surprising similarities among centenarians. (4) They did not all avoid tobacco and alcohol. (5) They did not have low-fat diets. (6) In fact, they ate relatively large amounts of fat, cholesterol, and sugar. (7) Diet could not explain their long lives. (8) They did, however, share four key traits. (9) First, all

the centenarians were optimistic about life. (10) All were positive thinkers. (11) They also had deep religious faith. (12) In addition, they had all continued to lead physically active lives. (13) They remained mobile even as elderly people. (14) Finally, all were able to adapt to loss. (15) They had all lost friends, spouses, or children. (16) They were able to get on with their lives.

PRACTICE

19-3 Write another simple sentence to follow each of the sentences below. Then, connect the sentences with a coordinating conjunction and the correct punctuation.

Example: Many patients need organ transplants,␣ , but there is a serious

shortage of organ donors. _____

1. Secondhand smoke is dangerous. _____

   _____

2. Kangaroos carry their young in pouches. _____

   _____

3. Motorcycle helmets are not required in every state. _____

   _____

4. Many juice drinks actually contain very little real fruit juice. _____

   _____

5. People tend to resist change. _____

   _____

19b Using Semicolons

Another way to create a compound sentence is by joining two simple sentences (independent clauses) with a **semicolon**. A semicolon connects clauses whose ideas are closely related.

The AIDS Memorial Quilt contains thousands of panels; each panel represents a life lost to AIDS.

Also use a semicolon to show a strong contrast between two ideas.

> With new drugs, people can live with HIV for years; many people, however, cannot get these drugs.

FYI

Avoiding Fragments

A semicolon can only join two complete sentences (independent clauses). A semicolon cannot join a sentence and a fragment.

FRAGMENT

INCORRECT   Because millions worldwide are still dying of AIDS; more research is needed.

SENTENCE

CORRECT   Millions worldwide are still dying of AIDS; more research is needed.

PRACTICE

19-4   Each of the following items consists of one simple sentence. Create a compound sentence for each item by changing the period to a semicolon and then adding another simple sentence.

Example: My brother is addicted to fast food; *he eats it every day.*

1. Fast-food restaurants are an American institution._____

   _____

2. Families often eat at these restaurants. _____

   _____

3. Many teenagers work there. _____

   _____

4. Many fast-food restaurants promote "healthy" options. _____

   _____

5. Some offer recyclable packaging. _____

   _____

6. Some even have playgrounds. _____

   _____

19c Using Transitional Words and Phrases

Another way to create a compound sentence is by combining two simple sentences (independent clauses) with a **transitional word or phrase**. When you use a transitional word or phrase to join two sentences, always place a semicolon *before* the transitional word or phrase and a comma *after* it.

Many college students apply for grants; in addition, they often have to take out loans.

He had a miserable time at the party; besides, he lost his wallet.

Frequently Used Transitional Words

also	instead	still
besides	later	subsequently
consequently	meanwhile	then
eventually	moreover	therefore
finally	nevertheless	thus
furthermore	now	otherwise
however		

Frequently Used Transitional Phrases

after all	in comparison
as a result	in contrast
at the same time	in fact
for example	in other words
for instance	of course
in addition	on the contrary

Adding a transitional word or phrase makes the connection between ideas in a sentence clearer and more precise than it would be if the ideas were linked with just a semicolon. Different transitional words and phrases convey different meanings.

- Some signal addition (*also, besides, furthermore, in addition, moreover,* and so on).

   I have a lot on my mind; <u>also</u>, I have a lot of things to do.

- Some make causal connections (*therefore, as a result, consequently, thus,* and so on).

   I have a lot on my mind; <u>therefore</u>, it is hard to concentrate.

- Some indicate contradiction or contrast (*nevertheless, however, in contrast, still,* and so on).

   I have a lot on my mind; <u>still</u>, I must try to relax.

- Some present alternatives (*instead, on the contrary, otherwise,* and so on).

   I have a lot on my mind; <u>otherwise</u>, I could relax.

   I will try not to think; <u>instead</u>, I will relax.

- Some indicate time sequence (*eventually, finally, at the same time, later, meanwhile, now, subsequently, then,* and so on).

   I have a lot on my mind; <u>meanwhile</u>, I still have work to do.

PRACTICE

19-5 Add semicolons and commas where required to set off transitional words and phrases that join two independent clauses.

Example: Ketchup is a popular condiment; therefore, it is available in almost every restaurant.

(1) Andrew F. Smith, a food historian, wrote a book about the tomato later he wrote a book about ketchup. (2) This book, *Pure Ketchup*, was a big project in fact Smith worked on it for five years. (3) The word *ketchup* may have come from a Chinese word however Smith is not certain of the word's origins. (4) Ketchup has existed since ancient times in other words it is a very old product. (5) Ketchup has changed a lot over the years for example special dyes were developed in the nineteenth century to make it red. (6) Smith discusses many other changes for instance preservative-free

ketchup was invented in 1907. (7) Ketchup is now used by people in many cultures still salsa is more popular than ketchup in the United States. (8) Today, designer ketchups are being developed meanwhile Heinz once introduced green and purple ketchup in squeeze bottles. (9) Some of today's ketchups are chunky in addition some ketchups are spicy. (10) Ketchup continues to evolve meanwhile Smith has written books about hamburgers, sugar, and fast food.

PRACTICE

19-6   Consulting the lists of transitional words and phrases on page 377, choose a word or phrase that logically connects each pair of simple sentences in the following paragraph into one compound sentence. Be sure to punctuate appropriately.

> **Example:** Red-light cameras are used worldwide; however, some ~~Some~~ people believe these cameras should be illegal.

(1) Red-light cameras are a form of traffic enforcement. The cameras have proven to be controversial. (2) Cars trigger the camera. The camera photographs the car. (3) A law-enforcement official reviews the photos. The officer issues tickets to drivers who ran the red light. (4) The cameras enforce traffic rules. They should reduce the number of crashes. (5) Some say the cameras are not a safety feature . They primarily increase revenue. (6) Opponents are concerned about danger. Drivers may stop to avoid running a red light. (7) Some people are concerned about the pictures. They think the cameras violate their privacy. (8) The risks and rewards of red-light cameras are not necessarily clear. Several states have banned their use. (9) The red-light camera controversy will likely continue for years to come. It is every driver's responsibility to drive safely. (10) Drivers should obey traffic rules. Everyone should want safe roads.

PRACTICE

19-7   Add the suggested transitional word or phrase to each of the following simple sentences. Then, add a new independent clause after it. Be sure to punctuate correctly.

   Example: Commuting students do not really experience campus life. (however)

   Commuting students do not really experience campus life; however,

   there are some benefits to being a commuter.

1. Campus residents may have a better college experience. (still)

   _____

   _____

2. Living at home gives students access to home-cooked meals. (in contrast)

   _____

   _____

3. Commuters have a wide choice of jobs in the community. (on the other hand)

   _____

   _____

4. Commuters get to see their families every day. (however)

   _____

   _____

5. There are also some disadvantages to being a commuter. (for example)

   _____

   _____

   _____

6. Unlike campus residents, many commuters have family responsibilities. (in fact)

   _____

   _____

7. Commuters might need a car to get to school. (consequently)

_____

_____

8. Commuting to college has pros and cons. (therefore)

_____

_____

PRACTICE

19-8   Using the specified transitional words or phrases, create two compound sentences for each of the topics listed below. Be sure to punctuate appropriately.

Example

Topic: gluten-free menu items
Transitional phrases: for example; as a result

Many chain restaurants now offer gluten-free menu items; for example,

Chili's, Outback Steakhouse, and Ruby Tuesday all offer gluten-free options.

Many chain restaurants offer gluten-free menu items; as a result, people

sensitive to gluten have more dining options.

1. *Topic:* male nurses
    Transitional phrases: in addition; after all

_____

_____

2. *Topic:* gay couples as adoptive parents
    Transitional words: however; now

_____

_____

3. *Topic:* dangerous high-school sports
    Transitional words: instead; consequently

_____

_____

CHAPTER REVIEW

EDITING PRACTICE

Read the following student essay. Then, create compound sentences by linking pairs of simple sentences where appropriate, joining them with a coordinating conjunction, a semicolon, or a transitional word or phrase. Remember to put commas before coordinating conjunctions and to use semicolons and commas correctly with transitional words and phrases. The first two sentences have been combined for you.

My Grandfather's Life

, but they

My great-grandparents were born in Ukraine/ ~~They~~ raised my grandfather
                                              ^
in western Pennsylvania. The ninth of their ten children, he had a life I cannot

begin to imagine. To me, he was my big, strong, powerful grandfather. He was

also a child of poverty.

My great-grandfather worked for the American Car Foundry. The family

lived in a company house. They shopped at the company store. In 1934, my

great-grandfather was laid off. He went to work digging sewer lines for the

government. At that time, the family was on welfare. Every week, they were

entitled to get food rations. My grandfather would go to pick up the food.

The family desperately needed the prunes, beans, flour, margarine, and other

things.

For years, my grandfather wore his brothers' hand-me-down clothes. He

wore thrift-shop shoes with cardboard over the holes in the soles.

He was often hungry. He would sometimes sit by the side of the railroad

tracks, waiting for the engineer to throw him an orange. My grandfather

would do any job to earn a quarter. Once, he weeded a mile-long row of

tomato plants. For this work, he was paid twenty-five cents and a pack of

NECCO wafers.

My grandfather saved his pennies. Eventually, he was able to buy a used bicycle for two dollars. He dropped out of school at fourteen and got a job. The family badly needed his income. He woke up every day at 4 a.m. He rode his bike to his job at a meatpacking plant. He worked for fifty cents a day.

In 1943, at the age of seventeen, my grandfather joined the U.S. Navy. He discovered a new world. For the first time in his life, he had enough to eat. He was always first in line at the mess hall. He went back for seconds and thirds before anyone else. After the war ended in 1945, he was discharged from the Navy. He went to work in a meat market in New York City. The only trade he knew was the meat business. Three years later, when he had saved enough to open his own store, Pete's Quality Meats, he knew his life of poverty was finally over.

COLLABORATIVE ACTIVITY

Working in a small group, pair each of the simple sentences in the left-hand column below with a sentence in the right-hand column to create ten compound sentences. Use as many different coordinating conjunctions as you can to connect the independent clauses. Be sure each coordinating conjunction you choose conveys a logical relationship between ideas, and remember to put a comma before each one. You may use some of the listed sentences more than once. *Note:* Many different combinations—some serious and factually accurate, some humorous—are possible.

Some dogs wear little sweaters.	Many are named Hamlet.
Pit bulls are raised to fight.	They live in groups.
Bonobos are pygmy chimpanzees.	One even sings Christmas carols.
Many people fear Dobermans.	They can wear bandanas.
Leopards have spots.	They can play Frisbee.
Dalmatians can live in fire-houses.	Many live in equatorial Zaire.
Horses can wear blankets.	Some people think they are gentle.
	They don't get cold in winter.

All mules are sterile.   They are half horse and half
Great Danes are huge dogs.   donkey.
Parrots can often speak.   They can be unpredictable.

review checklist

Writing Compound Sentences

✔ A compound sentence is made up of two simple sentences (independent clauses).

✔ A coordinating conjunction—*and, but, for, nor, or, so,* or *yet*—can join two independent clauses into one compound sentence. A comma always comes before the coordinating conjunction. (See 19a.)

✔ A semicolon can join two independent clauses into one compound sentence. (See 19b.)

✔ A transitional word or phrase can also join two independent clauses into one compound sentence. When it joins two independent clauses, a transitional word or phrase is always preceded by a semicolon and followed by a comma. (See 19c.)

20 Writing Complex Sentences

 ## 20a Identifying Complex Sentences

As you learned in Chapters 19, an **independent clause** can stand alone as a sentence.

> INDEPENDENT CLAUSE The <u>exhibit</u> was controversial.

However, a **dependent clause** cannot stand alone as a sentence.

> DEPENDENT CLAUSE Because the exhibit was controversial

What happened because the exhibit was controversial? To answer this question, you need to add an independent clause that completes the idea begun in the dependent clause. The result is a **complex sentence**—a sentence that consists of one independent clause and one or more dependent clauses.

> COMPLEX SENTENCE
> ┌──────────DEPENDENT CLAUSE──────────┐
> Because the exhibit was controversial,
> ┌──── INDEPENDENT CLAUSE ────┐
> many people came to see it.

PRACTICE

20-1 In the blank after each of the following items, indicate whether the group of words is an independent clause (*IC*) or a dependent clause (*DC*).

Example: When novelist Toni Morrison was born in Ohio in 1931.

_____*DC*_____

1. As a young reader, Toni Morrison liked the classic Russian novelists.

   _____

2. After she graduated from Howard University with a bachelor's degree in English. _____

3. Morrison based her novel *The Bluest Eye* on a childhood friend's prayers to God for blue eyes. _____

4. While she raised two sons as a single mother and worked as an editor at Random House. _____

5. As her reputation as a novelist grew with the publication of *Song of Solomon* and *Tar Baby.* _____

6. Her picture appeared on the cover of *Newsweek* in 1981. _____

7. Before her novel *Beloved* won the 1988 Pulitzer Prize for Fiction. _____

8. *Beloved* was made into a film starring Oprah Winfrey. _____

9. In 1993, Morrison became the first African American woman to win the Nobel Prize in Literature. _____

10. Who published the novel *God Help the Child* in 2015 to favorable reviews. _____

 ## 20b Using Subordinating Conjunctions

One way to form a complex sentence is to use a **subordinating conjunction**—a word such as *although* or *because*—to join two simple sentences (independent clauses). When the subordinating conjunction is added to the beginning of one simple sentence, the sentence becomes dependent for its meaning on the other simple sentence.

> **WORD POWER**
>
> **subordinate** (adj)
> lower in rank or
> position; secondary in
> importance

TWO SIMPLE SENTENCES	Muhammad Ali was stripped of his heavyweight title for refusing to serve in the army. Many people admired his antiwar position.

————————————DEPENDENT CLAUSE————————————

COMPLEX SENTENCE	Although Muhammad Ali was stripped of his heavyweight title for refusing to serve in the army, many people admired his antiwar position.

Frequently Used Subordinating Conjunctions

after	even though	since	whenever
although	if	so that	where
as	if only	than	whereas
as if	in order that	that	wherever
as though	now that	though	whether
because	once	unless	while
before	provided that	until	
even if	rather than	when	

As the chart below shows, different subordinating conjunctions express different relationships between dependent and independent clauses.

Relationship between Clauses	Subordinating Conjunction	Example
Time	after, before, since, until, when, whenever, while	When the whale surfaced, Ahab threw his harpoon.
Reason or cause	as, because	Scientists scaled back the project because the government cut funds.
Result or effect	in order that, so that	So that students' math scores will improve, many schools have begun special programs.
Condition	even if, if, unless	The rain forest may disappear unless steps are taken immediately.
Contrast	although, even though, though	Although Thomas Edison had almost no formal education, he was a successful inventor.
Location	where, wherever	Pittsburgh was built where the Allegheny and Monongahela Rivers meet.

FYI

Punctuating with Subordinating Conjunctions

In a complex sentence, use a comma after the dependent clause.

```
   ┌─── DEPENDENT CLAUSE ───────────┐ ┌─ INDEPENDENT CLAUSE ──┐
   Although she wore the scarlet letter, Hester carried herself
   ┌─────────┐
   proudly.
```

Do not use a comma after the independent clause.

```
   ┌─── INDEPENDENT CLAUSE ────────┐ ┌─── DEPENDENT CLAUSE ─────────────┐
   Hester carried herself proudly although she wore the scarlet letter.
```

PRACTICE

20-2   In the blank in each of the sentences below, write an appropriate subordinating conjunction. Be sure to choose a conjunction that expresses the logical relationship between the two clauses it links.

Example: Movie cowboys are usually portrayed as white *even though* many were African American.

(1) Few people today know about black cowboys _____ they were once common. (2) _____ the transcontinental railroad was built, cowboys were in high demand. (3) The ranchers hired cowboys to drive their cattle to the Midwest, _____ the cows were loaded on trains headed to eastern cities. (4) Many former slaves became cowboys _____ they wanted a new start. (5) Many African Americans also became cowboys _____ they had experience working with horses and cattle on Southern plantations or farms. (6) However, black cowboys faced difficulties _____ they arrived in the West. (7) African American cowboys often had to work much harder than whites _____ earn the same pay and respect. (8) _____ almost one-fourth of cowboys were black, few writers wrote about them. (9) The myth of the white-only cowboy was spread in novels, films, and television shows _____ black cowboys never existed. (10) Black cowboys did appear in some films of the 1970s _____ by this time Westerns were

no longer popular. (11) The situation started to change in the 1970s

_____ several museums honored black, Indian, and Mexican

cowboys. (12) _____ African American cowboys have finally

received some recognition, their history can now be more fully understood.

 20c Using Relative Pronouns

Another way to form a complex sentence is to use **relative pronouns**
(*who*, *that*, *which*, and so on) to join two simple sentences (independent
clauses).

TWO SIMPLE SENTENCES	Harry Potter is an adolescent wizard. He attends Hogwarts School of Witchcraft and Wizardry.

	DEPENDENT CLAUSE
COMPLEX SENTENCE	Harry Potter, who attends Hogwarts School of Witchcraft and Wizardry, is an adolescent wizard.

Note: The relative pronoun always refers to a word or words in the independent clause. (In the complex sentence above, *who* refers to *Harry Potter*.)

Relative Pronouns

that	which	whoever	whomever
what	who	whom	whose

A relative pronoun indicates the relationships between the ideas in the
independent and dependent clauses it links.

TWO SIMPLE SENTENCES	Nadine Gordimer lived in South Africa. She won the Nobel Prize in Literature in 1991.
COMPLEX SENTENCE	Nadine Gordimer, who won the Nobel Prize in Literature in 1991, lived in South Africa.
TWO SIMPLE SENTENCES	Last week I had a job interview. It went very well.
COMPLEX SENTENCE	Last week I had a job interview that went very well.

TWO SIMPLE SENTENCES	Transistors have replaced vacuum tubes in radios and televisions. They were invented in 1948.
COMPLEX SENTENCE	Transistors, which were invented in 1948, have replaced vacuum tubes in radios and televisions.

PRACTICE

20-3   In each of the following complex sentences, underline the dependent clause once, and underline the relative pronoun twice. Then, draw an arrow from the relative pronoun to the word or words to which it refers.

Example: Research shows that vampire legends, which you may have thought were fiction, have some truth to them.

1. Vampires, which were thought of as terrifying but imaginary, have been shown to have a basis in reality, have been proven to be "real."

2. Recently released research challenges the myth that vampires are only found in fiction.

3. Vampire rumors, which began when a person died, started because close family members often died at the same time.

4. Fear quickly turned into panic that inspired the vampire folklore.

5. People assumed that the deceased, who they imagined to be returning from the dead, wanted to consume the blood of their family members.

6. Actually, the so-called vampires did not suck anyone's blood, which is important to note, or return from the dead.

7. The real issue, which many people did not understand at the time, was germs.

8. Poor hygiene, which came from a lack of basic health knowledge, led to diseases that spread quickly.

9. Doctors, who were limited by the knowledge of the era, exhumed the bodies and removed the heart of the deceased was the only way to prevent the rise of vampires.

10. Researchers, who are still discovering "real" vampire stories, now know that the vampire myth began with misinformation.

PRACTICE

20-4 Combine each of the following pairs of simple sentences into one complex sentence. Use the relative pronoun that follows each pair.

Example: Elias Howe invented an early type of zipper. He was too busy with his other invention—the sewing machine—to work on it. (who)

Elias Howe, who invented an early type of zipper, was too busy with his other invention— the sewing machine—to work on it.

1. Early zippers were just hooks and eyes. These hooks and eyes were fastened to a cloth tape. (that)

_____

_____

2. Gideon Sundback invented the first useful zipper. He worked endless hours to help him stop grieving for his wife. (who)

_____

_____

3. Their "high" price kept early zippers from becoming popular. It was about eighteen cents. (which)

_____

_____

4. The word *zipper* began as a brand name. It was coined by a company executive. (which)

_____

_____

5. At first, zipper manufacturers could not convince people to use zippers in clothing. They sold many zippers for boots. (who)

_____

_____

CHAPTER REVIEW

EDITING PRACTICE

Read the following student essay. Then, revise it by combining pairs of simple sentences with subordinating conjunctions or relative pronouns that indicate the relationship between them. Be sure to punctuate correctly. The first two sentences have been combined for you.

Community Art

~~A~~ city has a crime problem, ~~The~~ police and the courts try to solve it.
When a ... *, the*

Some cities have come up with creative ways to help young people stay out of trouble. One example is the Philadelphia Mural Arts Program. It offers free art education for high school students.

In the 1960s, Philadelphia had a serious problem. The problem was graffiti. Graffiti artists had painted on buildings all over the city. A solution to the problem was the Philadelphia Anti-Graffiti Network. This offered graffiti artists an alternative. The artists would give up graffiti. They would not be prosecuted. The artists enjoyed painting. They could paint murals on public buildings instead. They could create beautiful landscapes, portraits of local heroes, and abstract designs. The graffiti artists had once been lawbreakers. They could now help beautify the city.

The Mural Arts Program began in 1984 as a part of the Philadelphia Anti-Graffiti Network. By 1996, the Philadelphia Anti-Graffiti Network was focusing on eliminating graffiti, and its Mural Arts Program was working to improve the community. It no longer worked with graffiti offenders. It ran after-school and summer programs for students. The Mural Arts Program got national recognition in 1997. That is when President Bill Clinton helped paint a mural. So far, the Mural Arts Program has completed more than 3,600 murals. This is more than any other public art program in the country.

Over 20,000 students have taken part in the Mural Arts Program. The students come from all parts of the city. In one part of the program, students work alongside professional artists. The students get to paint parts of the artists' murals themselves. The artwork is on public buildings. The artwork can be seen by everyone.

The Mural Arts Program continues to build a brighter future for students and their communities. It is now over a quarter of a century old. Students help bring people together to create a mural. They feel a stronger connection to their community and more confidence in themselves. They leave the program. They are equipped to make a positive difference in their communities and in their own lives.

COLLABORATIVE ACTIVITY

Working in a group of four students, make a list of three or four of your favorite television shows. Then, divide into pairs, and with your partner, write two simple sentences describing each show. Next, use subordinating conjunctions or relative pronouns to combine each pair of sentences into one complex sentence. With your group, discuss how the ideas in each complex sentence are related, and make sure you have used the subordinating conjunction or relative pronoun that best conveys this relationship.

Example: *The Walking Dead* is a dystopian series set in a world overrun by zombies. It appeals to many of today's viewers.

The Walking Dead, which appeals to many of today's viewers, is a dystopian series set in a world overrun by zombies.

review checklist

Writing Complex Sentences

✔ A complex sentence consists of one independent clause (simple sentence) combined with one or more dependent clauses. (See 20a.)

✔ Subordinating conjunctions—dependent words such as *although*, *after*, *when*, *while*, and *because*—can join two independent clauses into one complex sentence. (See 20b.)

✔ Relative pronouns—dependent words such as *who*, *which*, and *that*—can also join two independent clauses into one complex sentence. The relative pronoun shows the relationship between the ideas in the two independent clauses that it links. (See 20c.)

21 Writing Varied Sentences

Sentence variety is important because a paragraph of varied sentences flows more smoothly, is easier to read and understand, and is more interesting than one in which all the sentences are structured in the same way.

 ## 21a Varying Sentence Types

Most English sentences are **statements**. Others are **questions** or **exclamations**. One way to vary your sentences is to use an occasional question or exclamation where it is appropriate.

In the following paragraph, a question and an exclamation add variety.

> Jacqueline Cochran, the first woman pilot to break the sound barrier, was one of the most important figures in aviation history. In 1996, the United States Postal Service issued a stamp honoring Cochran; the words "Pioneer Pilot" appear under her name. <u>What did she do to earn this title and this tribute?</u> Cochran broke more flight records than anyone else in her lifetime and won many awards, including the United States Distinguished Service Medal in 1945 and the United States Air Force Distinguished Flying Cross in 1969. During World War II, she helped form the WASPs, the Women's Air Force Service Pilots program, so that women could fly military planes to their bases (even though they were not allowed to go into combat). Remarkably, she accomplished all this with only three weeks of flying instruction. She only got her pilot's license in the first place because she wanted to start her own cosmetics business and flying would enable her to travel quickly around the country. Although she never planned to be a pilot, once she discovered flying she quickly became the best. <u>Not surprisingly, when the Postal Service honored Jacqueline Cochran, it was with an airmail stamp!</u>

Question

Exclamation

PRACTICE

21-1 Revise the following paragraph by changing one of the statements into a question and one of the statements into an exclamation.

395

Example: Lewis Carroll first applied the term *portmanteau words* to certain English words. (statement)

Did Lewis Carroll first apply the term *portmanteau words* to certain

English words? (question)

(1) Many words in the English language are actually two words combined into one. (2) For example, combining the words *breakfast* and *lunch* creates the word *brunch*. (3) A person who works too much might be called a *workaholic*, a word we get from combining the words *work* and *alcoholic*. (4) Words like these have a name. (5) Such word combinations are called *portmanteau words*. (6) In nineteenth-century English, *portmanteau* was the name for a suitcase opening into two equal halves. (7) The two halves comprise the whole suitcase, just as the two words form a portmanteau. (8) Popular English is always developing new portmanteau words. (9) For example, a combination fork and spoon is called a *spork*, and a *turducken* is a chicken inside a duck, which is inside a turkey. (10) In fact, even the coined names of Hollywood couples, such as *Brangelina* (*Brad* plus *Angelina*), might be considered portmanteau words.

21b Varying Sentence Openings

When all the sentences in a paragraph begin the same way, your writing is likely to seem dull and repetitive. In the following paragraph, for example, every sentence begins with the subject.

> Scientists have been observing a disturbing phenomenon. The population of frogs, toads, and salamanders has been declining. This decline was first noticed in the mid-1980s. Some reports blamed chemical pollution. Some biologists began to suspect that a fungal disease was killing these amphibians. The most reasonable explanation seems to be that the amphibians' eggs are threatened by solar radiation. This radiation penetrates the thinned ozone layer, which used to shield them from the sun's rays.

WORD POWER

amphibians cold-blooded vertebrates, such as frogs, that live both in the water and on land

Beginning with Adverbs

Instead of opening every sentence in a paragraph with the subject, you can try beginning some sentences with one or more **adverbs**.

> Scientists have been observing a disturbing phenomenon. <u>Gradually but steadily,</u> the population of frogs, toads, and salamanders has been declining. This decline was first noticed in the mid-1980s. Some reports blamed chemical pollution. Some biologists began to suspect that a fungal disease was killing these amphibians. <u>However,</u> the most reasonable explanation seems to be that the amphibians' eggs are threatened by solar radiation. This radiation penetrates the thinned ozone layer, which used to shield them from the sun's rays.

PRACTICE

21-2   Underline the adverb in each of the following sentences, and then rewrite the sentence so that the adverb appears at the beginning. Be sure to punctuate correctly.

Example: An internship is <u>usually</u> a one-time work or service experience related to a student's career plans.

Usually, an internship is a one-time work or service experience related to

a student's career plans.

1. Internships are sometimes paid or counted for academic credit.

_____

2. A prospective student intern should first talk to an academic adviser.

_____

3. The student should next write a résumé listing job experience, education, and interests.

_____

_____

4. The student can then send the résumé to organizations that are looking for interns.

_____

_____

5. Going to job fairs and networking are often good ways to find internships.

_____

PRACTICE

21-3

In each of the following sentences, fill in the blank with an appropriate adverb. Be sure to punctuate correctly.

Example: ___Slowly,___ the sun crept over the horizon.

1. _____ the speeding car appeared from out of nowhere.

2. _____ it crashed into the guardrail.

3. _____ the car jackknifed across the highway.

4. _____ drivers behind the car slammed on their brakes.

5. _____ someone called 911.

6. _____ a wailing siren could be heard.

7. _____ the ambulance arrived.

8. _____ emergency medical technicians went to work.

9. _____ a police officer was on hand to direct traffic.

10. _____ no one was badly hurt in the accident.

Beginning with Prepositional Phrases

Another way to create sentence variety is to begin some sentences with prepositional phrases. A **prepositional phrase** (such as *along the river* or *near the diner*) is made up of a preposition and its object.

> In recent years, scientists have observed a disturbing phenomenon. Gradually but steadily, the population of frogs, toads, and salamanders has been declining. This was first noticed in the mid-1980s. At first, some reports blamed chemical pollution. After a while, some biologists began to suspect that a fungal disease was killing them. However, the most reasonable explanation seems to be that the amphibians' eggs are threatened by solar radiation. This radiation penetrates the thinned ozone layer, which used to shield them from the sun's rays.

PRACTICE

21-4

Underline the prepositional phrase in each of the following sentences, and then rewrite the sentence so that the prepositional phrase appears at the beginning. Be sure to punctuate correctly.

Example: Very few American women did factory work <u>before the 1940s.</u>

Before the 1940s, very few American women did factory work.

1. Many male factory workers became soldiers during World War II.

   _____

2. The U.S. government encouraged women to take factory jobs in the war's early years.

   _____

   _____

3. Over six million women took factory jobs between 1942 and 1945.

   _____

4. A new female image emerged with this greater responsibility and independence.

   _____

   _____

5. Many women wore pants for the first time.

   _____

6. Most women lost their factory jobs after the war and returned to "women's work."

   _____

   _____

PRACTICE

21-5 In each of the following sentences, fill in the blank with an appropriate prepositional phrase. Be sure to punctuate correctly.

Example: <u>At the start of the New York Marathon,</u> Justin felt as if he could run forever.

1. _____ he warmed up by stretching and bending.

2. _____ all the runners were crowded together.

3. _____ they crossed a bridge over the Hudson River.

4. _____ the route became more and more challenging.

5. _____ Justin grabbed some water from a helpful onlooker.

6. _____ he staggered across the finish line.

PRACTICE

21-6 Every sentence in the following paragraph begins with the subject, but several contain prepositional phrases or adverbs that could be moved to the beginning. To vary the sentence openings, move prepositional phrases to the beginnings of four sentences, and move adverbs to the beginnings of two other sentences. Be sure to place a comma after these introductory phrases.

Example: ~~Everyone~~ had heard of Venus and Serena Williams ~~by the early 2000s~~.

By the early 2000s, everyone

(1) Venus and Serena Williams are famous for their tennis skills in the sports world. (2) Venus is older, but the sisters are just one year apart. (3) The Williams sisters were playing tennis professionally by the time they were teenagers. (4) They have played both as opponents and as doubles partners. (5) The sisters won several gold medals at the 2012 Olympics. (6) They still support each other as sisters, bravely facing intense competition. (7) Venus and Serena have also written books and produced popular fashion lines, successfully developing business careers. (8) The Williams sisters had to overcome the challenges of their childhood in a tough neighborhood in Compton, California, to achieve their dreams.

21c Combining Sentences

You can also create sentence variety by experimenting with different ways of combining sentences.

Using *-ing* Modifiers

A **modifier** identifies or describes other words in a sentence. You can use an *-ing* modifier to combine two sentences.

TWO SENTENCES	Duke Ellington composed more than a thousand songs. He worked hard to establish his reputation.
COMBINED WITH *-ING* MODIFIER	<u>Composing</u> <u>more than a thousand songs</u>, Duke Ellington worked hard to establish his reputation.

When the two sentences above are combined, the -*ing* modifier (*composing more than a thousand songs*) describes the new sentence's subject (*Duke Ellington*).

PRACTICE

21-7 Use an -*ing* modifier to combine each of the following pairs of sentences into a single sentence. Eliminate any unnecessary words, and place a comma after each -*ing* modifier.

Example: Many American colleges are setting an example for the rest of the country. They are going green.

Setting an example for the rest of the country, many American colleges

are going green.

1. Special lamps in the dorms of one Ohio college change from green to red. They warn of rising energy use.

   _____

   _____

2. A Vermont college captures methane from dairy cows. It now needs less energy from other sources.

   _____

   _____

3. Student gardeners at a North Carolina college tend a campus vegetable plot. They supply the cafeteria with organic produce.

   _____

   _____

4. A building on a California campus proves that recycled materials can be beautiful. It is built from redwood wine casks.

   _____

   _____

5. Some colleges are preparing students to take the green revolution beyond campus. They offer courses in sustainability.

   _____

   _____

Using *-ed* Modifiers

You can also use an *-ed* modifier to combine two sentences.

TWO SENTENCES	Nogales is located on the border between Arizona and Mexico. It is a bilingual city.
COMBINED WITH *-ED* MODIFIER	<u>Located</u> on the border between Arizona and Mexico, Nogales is a bilingual city.

When the two sentences above are combined, the *-ed* modifier (*located on the border between Arizona and Mexico*) describes the new sentence's subject (*Nogales*).

PRACTICE

21-8   Use an *-ed* modifier to combine each of the following pairs of sentences into a single sentence. Eliminate any unnecessary words, and use a comma to set off each *-ed* modifier. When you are finished, underline the *-ed* modifier in each sentence.

Example: Potato chips and cornflakes were invented purely by accident. They are two of America's most popular foods.

<u>Invented purely by accident</u>, potato chips and cornflakes are two of

America's most popular foods.

1. George Crum was employed as a chef in a fancy restaurant. He was famous for his french fries.

   _____

   _____

2. A customer was dissatisfied with the fries. He complained and asked for thinner fries.

   _____

3. The customer was served thinner fries. He was still not satisfied and complained again.

   _____

4. Crum was now very annoyed. He decided to make the fries too thin and crisp to eat with a fork.

   _____

   _____

5. The customer was thrilled with the extra-thin and crisp potatoes. He ate them all.

_____

6. Potato chips were invented to get even with a customer. They are the most popular snack food in America today.

_____

_____

7. Dr. John Kellogg was concerned about the diet of patients at his hospital. He and his brother set out to make healthy foods.

_____

_____

8. The brothers were called away on an urgent matter. They left a pot of boiled wheat on the stove.

_____

_____

9. The wheat had hardened by the time they returned. It broke into flakes when they rolled it.

_____

_____

10. The brothers were delighted with the results. They came up with a new flake made of corn.

_____

Using a Series of Words

Another way to vary your sentences is to combine a group of sentences into one sentence that includes a **series** of words (nouns, verbs, or adjectives). Combining sentences in this way eliminates a boring string of similar sentences and repetitive phrases and also makes your writing more concise.

GROUP OF SENTENCES College presidents want to improve athletes' academic performance. Coaches too want to improve athletes' academic performance. The players themselves also want to improve their academic performance.

COMBINED (SERIES OF NOUNS)	College <u>presidents</u>, <u>coaches</u>, and the <u>players</u> themselves want to improve athletes' academic performance.
GROUP OF SENTENCES	Arundhati Roy published her first novel, *The God of Small Things*, in 1997. She won the Man Booker Prize for Fiction that year. She published her second novel, *The Ministry of Utmost Happiness*, in 2017.
COMBINED (SERIES OF VERBS)	Arundhati Roy published her first novel, The God of Small Things, in 1997; won the Man Booker Prize for Fiction that year; and published her second novel in 2017.
GROUP OF SENTENCES	As the tornado approached, the sky grew dark. The sky grew quiet. The sky grew threatening.
COMBINED (SERIES OF ADJECTIVES)	As the tornado approached, the sky grew <u>dark</u>, <u>quiet</u>, and <u>threatening</u>.

PRACTICE

 Combine each of the following groups of sentences into one sentence that includes a series of nouns, verbs, or adjectives.

Example: Many years ago, Pacific Islanders from Samoa settled in Hawaii. Pacific Islanders from Fiji also settled in Hawaii. Pacific Islanders from Tahiti settled in Hawaii, too.

Many years ago, Pacific Islanders from Samoa, Fiji, and Tahiti settled in

Hawaii.

1. In the eighteenth century, the British explorer Captain Cook came to Hawaii. Other explorers also came to Hawaii. European travelers came to Hawaii, too.

_____

_____

2. Explorers and traders brought commerce to Hawaii. They brought new ideas. They brought new cultures.

_____

_____

3. Missionaries introduced the Christian religion. They introduced a Hawaiian-language bible. Also, they introduced a Hawaiian alphabet.

_____

_____

4. In the mid-nineteenth century, pineapple plantations were established in Hawaii. Sugar plantations were established there as well. Other industries were also established.

_____

_____

5. By 1900, Japanese people were working on the plantations. Chinese people were also working on the plantations. In addition, native Hawaiians were working there.

_____

_____

6. People of many different races and religions now live in Hawaii. People of many different races and religions now go to school in Hawaii. People of many different races and religions now work in Hawaii.

_____

_____

7. Schoolchildren still study the Hawaiian language. They learn about the Hawaiian kings and queens. They read about ancient traditions.

_____

_____

8. Now, Hawaii is well known for its tourism. It is well known too for its weather. It is especially well known for its natural beauty.

_____

_____

9. Tourists can swim. They can surf. They can play golf. They can ride in outrigger canoes.

_____

_____

10. Today, the state of Hawaii remains lively. It remains culturally diverse. It remains very beautiful.

_____

_____

Using Appositives

WORD POWER

adjacent next to

An **appositive** is a word or word group that identifies, renames, or describes an adjacent noun or pronoun. Creating an appositive is often a good way to combine two sentences about the same subject.

TWO SENTENCES   C. J. Walker was the first American woman to become a self-made millionaire. She marketed a line of hair-care products for black women.

COMBINED WITH APPOSITIVE   C. J. Walker, the first American woman to become a self-made millionaire, marketed a line of hair-care products for black women.

In the example above, the appositive appears in the middle of a sentence. However, an appositive can also come at the beginning or at the end of a sentence.

The first American woman to become a self-made millionaire, C. J. Walker marketed a line of hair-care products for black women. (appositive at the beginning)

Several books have been written about C. J. Walker, the first American woman to become a self-made millionaire. (appositive at the end)

PRACTICE

21-10   Combine each of the following pairs of sentences into one sentence by creating an appositive. Note that the appositive may appear at the beginning, in the middle, or at the end of the sentence. Be sure to use commas appropriately.

Example: *Hamilton* ~~is~~, a Broadway musical; ~~It~~ is based on a biography of Alexander Hamilton ^by Ron Chernow.

(1) *Hamilton* is an award-winning show about Alexander Hamilton. He was the first U.S. treasury secretary. (2) He was an immigrant from the West Indies. He was killed in a famous duel with Vice President Aaron Burr. (3) The musical numbers in *Hamilton* were influenced by hip-hop. They have won rave reviews. (4) The play's words and lyrics were written by Lin-Manual Miranda. Lin-Manual Miranda is the actor who originated the role of Alexander Hamilton on Broadway. (5) Other characters in the play include George Washington, Thomas Jefferson, and James Madison. They are all played by African American or Hispanic actors. (6) This innovative musical has already changed the way theatergoers see American history. Some of these theatergoers are inner-city students. (7) A Rockefeller Foundation grant enabled 20,000 New York City students to see *Hamilton* for just ten dollars. It subsidized the cost of tickets. (8) Hamilton was the winner of eleven Tony awards. The show is now performed around the world.

21d Mixing Long and Short Sentences

A paragraph of short, choppy sentences—or a paragraph of long, rambling sentences—can be monotonous. By mixing long and short sentences, perhaps combining some simple sentences to create **compound** and **complex** sentences, you can create a more interesting paragraph.

In the following paragraph, the sentences are all short, and the result is boring and hard to follow.

> The world's first drive-in movie theater opened on June 6, 1933. This drive-in was in Camden, New Jersey. Automobiles became more popular. Drive-ins did, too. By the 1950s, there were more than four thousand drive-ins in the United States. Over the years, the high cost of land led to a decline in the number of drive-ins. So did the rising

popularity of television. Soon, the drive-in movie theater had almost disappeared. It was replaced by the multiplex. In 1967, there were forty-six drive-ins in New Jersey. Today, only one is still open. That one is the Delsea Drive-in in Vineland, New Jersey.

The revised paragraph that follows is more interesting and easier to read. (Note that the final short sentence is retained for emphasis.)

> The world's first drive-in movie theater opened on June 6, 1933, in Camden, New Jersey. As automobiles became more popular, drive-ins did, too, and by the 1950s, there were more than four thousand drive-ins in the United States. Over the years, the high cost of land and the rising popularity of television led to a decline in the number of drive-ins. Soon, the drive-in movie theater had almost disappeared, replaced by the multiplex. In 1967, there were forty-six drive-ins in New Jersey, but today, only one is still open. That one is the Delsea Drive-in in Vineland, New Jersey.

PRACTICE

21-11 The following paragraph contains a series of short, choppy sentences that can be combined. Revise the paragraph so that it mixes long and short sentences. Be sure to use commas and other punctuation appropriately.

Example: Kente cloth has special significance for many African
Americans, ~~Some~~ ⟨, but some⟩ other people do not understand this significance.

(1) Kente cloth is made in western Africa. (2) It is produced primarily by the Ashanti people. (3) It has been worn for hundreds of years by African royalty. (4) They consider it a sign of power and status. (5) Many African Americans wear kente cloth. (6) They see it as a link to their heritage. (7) Each pattern on the cloth has a name. (8) Each color has a special significance. (9) For example, red and yellow suggest a long and healthy life. (10) Green and white suggest a good harvest. (11) African women may wear kente cloth as a dress or head wrap. (12) African American women, like men, usually wear strips of cloth around their shoulders. (13) Men and women of African descent wear kente cloth as a sign of racial pride. (14) It often decorates college students' gowns at graduation.

EDITING PRACTICE

The following student essay lacks sentence variety. All of its sentences begin with the subject, and the essay includes a number of short, choppy sentences. Using the strategies discussed in this chapter as well as strategies for creating compound and complex sentences, revise the essay to achieve greater sentence variety. The first sentence has been edited for you.

Toys by Accident

Many popular toys and games are the result of accidents, ~~People~~ when people try to invent one thing but discover something else instead. Sometimes they are not trying to invent anything at all. They are completely surprised to find a new product.

Play-Doh is one example of an accidental discovery. Play-Doh is a popular preschool toy. Play-Doh first appeared in Cincinnati. A company made a compound to clean wallpaper. They sold it as a cleaning product. The company then realized that this compound could be a toy. Children could mold it like clay. They could use it again and again. The new toy was an immediate hit. Play-Doh was first sold in 1956. Since then, more than two billion cans have been sold.

The Slinky was discovered by Richard James. He was an engineer. At the time, he was trying to invent a spring to keep ships' instruments steady at sea. He tested hundreds of springs of varying sizes, metals, and tensions. None of them worked. One spring fell off the desk and "walked" down a pile of books. It then went end over end onto the floor. He thought his children might enjoy playing with it. James took the spring home. They loved it. Every child in the neighborhood wanted one. The first Slinky was demonstrated at Gimbel's Department Store in Philadelphia in 1945. All four hundred Slinkys were sold within ninety minutes. The Slinky is simple and inexpensive. The Slinky is still popular with children today.

The Frisbee was also discovered by accident. According to one story, a group of Yale University students were eating pies from a local bakery. The bakery was called Frisbies. They finished eating the pies. They started throwing the empty pie tins around. A carpenter in California made a plastic version. He called it the Pluto Platter. The Wham-O company bought the patent on the product. Wham-O renamed it the Frisbee after the bakery. This is how the Frisbee came to be.

Some new toys are not developed by toy companies. Play-Doh, the Frisbee, and the Slinky are examples of very popular toys that were discovered by accident. Play-Doh started as a cleaning product. The Slinky was discovered by an engineer who was trying to invent something else. The Frisbee was invented by students having fun. The toys were discovered unexpectedly. All three toys have become classics.

COLLABORATIVE ACTIVITY

Read the following list of sentences. Working in a small group, change one sentence to a question and one to an exclamation. Then, add adverbs or prepositional phrases at the beginning of several of the sentences in the list.

Many well-known African American writers left the United States in the years following World War II.
Many went to Paris.
Richard Wright was a novelist.
He wrote *Native Son* and *Black Boy*.
He wrote *Uncle Tom's Children*.
He left the United States for Paris in 1947.
James Baldwin wrote *Another Country*, *The Fire Next Time*, and *Giovanni's Room*.
He also wrote essays.
He came to Paris in 1948.
Chester Himes was a detective story writer.
He arrived in Paris in 1953.
William Gardner Smith was a novelist and journalist.
He also left the United States for Paris.
These expatriates found Paris more hospitable than America.
They also found it less racist.

Finally, use the strategies discussed and illustrated in 21c and 21d to help you combine the sentences listed above and on the previous page into a paragraph. (You may keep the sentences in the order in which they appear.)

review checklist

Writing Varied Sentences

✔ Vary sentence types. (See 21a.)

✔ Vary sentence openings. (See 21b.)

✔ Combine sentences. (See 21c.)

✔ Mix long and short sentences. (See 21d.)

22 Using Parallelism

 22a Recognizing Parallel Structure

Parallelism is the use of matching words, phrases, clauses, and sentence structure to highlight similar ideas in a sentence. When you use parallelism, you are telling readers that certain ideas are related and have the same level of importance. By repeating similar grammatical patterns to express similar ideas, you create sentences that are clearer, more concise, and easier to read.

In the following examples, the parallel sentences highlight similar ideas; the other sentences do not.

PARALLEL	NOT PARALLEL
Please leave <u>your name</u>, <u>your number</u>, and <u>your message</u>.	Please leave <u>your name</u>, <u>your number</u>, and <u>you should also leave a message</u>.
I plan to <u>graduate</u> from high school and <u>become</u> a nurse.	I plan to <u>graduate</u> from high school, and then <u>becoming</u> a nurse would be a good idea.
The grass was <u>soft</u>, <u>green</u>, and <u>sweet smelling</u>.	The grass was <u>soft</u>, <u>green</u>, and <u>the smell was sweet</u>.
<u>Making</u> the team was one thing; <u>staying on it</u> was another.	<u>Making the team</u> was one thing, but it was very difficult <u>to stay on it</u>.
We can <u>register</u> for classes in person, or <u>we can register</u> by email.	We can <u>register</u> for classes in person, or <u>registering</u> by email is another option.

PRACTICE

22-1   In the following sentences, decide whether the underlined words and phrases are parallel. If so, write *P* in the blank. If not, rewrite the sentences so that the underlined ideas are presented in parallel terms.

Examples: The missing dog had <u>brown fur</u>, <u>a red collar</u>, and <u>a long tail</u>.   _____P_____

Signs of drug abuse in teenagers include <u>falling grades</u>, <u>mood swings</u>, and ~~they lose~~ weight‸^{loss.}

1. The food in the cafeteria is <u>varied</u>, <u>tasty</u>, and <u>it is healthy</u>. _____

2. Do you want the job done <u>quickly</u>, or do you want it done <u>well</u>?

   _____

3. Last summer I <u>worked at the library</u>, <u>babysat for my neighbor's</u> daughter, and <u>there was a soup kitchen where I volunteered</u>.

   _____

4. Pandas eat <u>bamboo leaves</u>, and <u>eucalyptus leaves are eaten by</u> koalas. _____

5. Skydiving is <u>frightening</u> but <u>fun</u>. _____

6. A number of interesting people work at the co-op with me, including <u>an elderly German man</u>, <u>there is a middle-aged Chinese woman</u>, and <u>a teenaged Mexican boy</u>. _____

7. <u>The bell rang</u>, and <u>the students stood up</u>. _____

8. To conserve energy while I was away, I <u>unplugged the television</u>, <u>closed the curtains</u>, and <u>the thermostat was set at 65 degrees</u>. _____

9. He <u>wore</u> jeans, a T-shirt, and <u>had on</u> running shoes. _____

10. For several weeks after the storm, the supermarkets had <u>no eggs</u>, <u>they were out of milk</u>, and <u>they did not have any bread</u>. _____

⬢ 22b Using Parallel Structure

Parallel structure is especially important in *paired items*, *items in a series*, and *items in a list or in an outline*.

Paired Items

Use parallel structure when you connect ideas with a **coordinating conjunction**—*and*, *but*, *for*, *nor*, *or*, *so*, and *yet*.

George believes in <u>doing a good job</u> and <u>minding his own business</u>.

You can <u>pay me now</u> or <u>pay me later</u>.

You should also use parallel structure for paired items joined by *both . . . and, not only . . . but also, either . . . or, neither . . . nor,* and *rather . . . than.*

Jan is <u>both</u> <u>skilled in writing</u> <u>and</u> <u>fluent in French</u>.

The group's new recording <u>not only</u> <u>has a dance beat</u> <u>but also</u> <u>has thought-provoking lyrics</u>.

Louis XVI was a weak monarch who would <u>rather</u> <u>repair locks</u> <u>than</u> <u>govern</u>.

Items in a Series

Use parallel structure for items in a series—words, phrases, or clauses. (Be sure to use commas to separate three or more items in a series. Never put a comma after the final item.)

The immediate causes of World War I were <u>imperialism</u>, <u>militarism</u>, and <u>nationalism</u>. (three words)

<u>Increased demand</u>, <u>high factory output</u>, and <u>a strong dollar</u> will help the economy. (three phrases)

She is a champion because she <u>stays in excellent physical condition</u>, <u>puts in long hours of practice</u>, and <u>has an intense desire to win</u>. (three clauses)

Items in a List or in an Outline

Use parallel structure for items in a numbered or bulleted list.

There are three reasons to open an Individual Retirement Account (IRA):

1. To save money
2. To reduce taxes
3. To be able to retire

Use parallel structure for the elements in an outline.

A. Types of rocks
   1. Igneous
   2. Sedimentary
   3. Metamorphic

PRACTICE

22-2 Fill in the blanks in the following sentences with parallel words, phrases, or clauses of your own that make sense in context.

Example: At the lake, we can ___go for a swim,___, ___paddle a canoe,___, and ___play volleyball.___.

1. When I get too little sleep, I am _____, _____, and _____.

2. I am good at _____ but not at _____.

3. My ideal mate is _____ and _____.

4. I personally define success not only as _____ but also as _____.

5. I use my computer for both _____ and _____.

6. I like _____ and _____.

7. You need three qualities to succeed in college: _____, _____, and _____.

8. I enjoy not only _____ but also _____.

9. I would rather _____ than _____.

10. Football _____, but baseball _____.

PRACTICE

22-3 Rewrite the following sentences so that matching ideas are presented in parallel terms. Add punctuation as needed.

Example: *Game of Thrones* has been filmed in Northern Ireland and Iceland, and also some filming was done in Morocco.

Game of Thrones has been filmed in Northern Ireland, Iceland, and Morocco.

1. *Game of Thrones* is a television series on HBO that features more than 20 main characters, and 250 additional characters are also featured.

_____

_____

2. True *Game of Thrones* fans know that the story originated in a series of novels titled *A Song of Ice and Fire*, and George R. R. Martin wrote these novels, as true fans also know.

_____

_____

_____

3. The complex plot lines follow the Stark family, and the Lannisters are also followed, as well as the Targaryens.

_____

4. In the media, *Game of Thrones* has been both praised for the performance of its actors, and many have criticized it because of its extreme violence.

_____

_____

5. *Game of Thrones* has received many honors, including Emmys and Golden Globes, and another award, a Peabody, was also won.

_____

_____

EDITING PRACTICE

Read the following student essay, which contains examples of faulty parallelism. Identify the sentences you think need to be corrected, and make the changes required to achieve parallelism. Be sure to supply all words necessary for clarity, grammar, and sense. Add punctuation as needed. The first error has been edited for you.

Self-Made Men and Women Helping Others

Many self-made people go from poverty to ~~achieving~~ success. Quite a few of them not only achieve success but also they help others. Three of these people are Oprah Winfrey, Alfredo Quiñones-Hinojosa, and Geoffrey Canada. Their lives are very different, but all possess great strength, being determined, and concern for others.

Oprah is one of the most influential people in the world, and she has more money than almost anyone in the world. She came from a very poor family. First, she lived with her grandmother on a Mississippi farm, and then her mother in Milwaukee. During this time, she was abused by several relatives. When she was thirteen, she was sent to Nashville to live with her father. He used strict discipline, and she was taught by him to value education. Through her own determination and because she was ambitious, Winfrey got a job at a local broadcasting company. This started her career. However, Oprah was not satisfied with being successful. Through Oprah's Angel Network and the Oprah Winfrey Leadership Academy, she helps others and making the world a better place.

Today, Alfredo Quiñones-Hinojosa is a top brain surgeon and conducting research on new ways to treat brain cancer. At age nineteen, however, he was an illegal immigrant from Mexico, worked in the fields, and without any English. When he told his cousin he wanted to learn English and get a better job, his cousin told him he was crazy. Then, while he was a welder on a railroad crew, he fell into an empty petroleum tank and was almost dying from the fumes. However, he overcame these hardships. He enrolled in a community college, and with determination and by working hard, he began to change his life. He won a scholarship to Berkeley, went on to medical school at Harvard, and eventually winding up as director of the brain tumor program at Johns Hopkins University. In 1997, he became a citizen of the United States. At each step of the way, he has made a special effort to reach out to students from low-income backgrounds and to inspire others.

Geoffrey Canada grew up in a New York City neighborhood that was poor, dangerous, and where violence was not uncommon. His mother was a single parent who struggled to support him and his three brothers. Canada learned to survive on the streets, but he also studied a lot in school. Thanks to this hard work, he won a scholarship to Bowdoin College in Maine and went on to a master's degree from Harvard and a career in education. Deciding to leave his neighborhood in New York wasn't hard, but to decide to come back wasn't hard either. He wanted to help children in poor families to succeed in school and so they could have better lives. With this in mind, he started the Harlem Children's Zone (HCZ). HCZ includes workshops for parents, a preschool and three charter schools, and running health programs for children and families. President Obama has said he would like to see more programs like HCZ.

Oprah Winfrey, Alfredo Quiñones-Hinojosa, and Geoffrey Canada have very different careers—in entertainment, in medicine, and educating children. However, all three overcame great adversity, all three have achieved enormous success, and they have helped others. They have helped their communities, their country, and have contributed to the world.

COLLABORATIVE ACTIVITY

Working in a group, list three or four qualities that you associate with each word in the following pairs.

Brothers/sisters
Teachers/students
Parents/children
City/country
Fast food/organic food
Movies/TV shows
Work/play

Then, write a compound sentence comparing the two words in each pair. Use a coordinating conjunction to join the clauses, and make sure each sentence uses clear parallel structure, mentions both words, and includes the qualities you listed for the word pairs.

review checklist

Using Parallelism

✔ Use matching words, phrases, clauses, and sentence structure to highlight similar items or ideas. (See 22a.)

✔ Use parallel structure with paired items. (See 22b.)

✔ Use parallel structure for items in a series. (See 22b.)

✔ Use parallel structure for items in a list or in an outline. (See 22b.)

23 Using Words Effectively

 ## 23a Using Specific Words

Specific words refer to particular people, places, things, ideas, or qualities. **General words** refer to entire classes or groups. Sentences that contain specific words are more precise and vivid than those that contain only general words.

SENTENCES WITH GENERAL WORDS	SENTENCES WITH SPECIFIC WORDS
While walking in the woods, I saw an <u>animal</u>.	While walking in the woods, I saw a <u>baby skunk</u>.
<u>Someone</u> decided to run for Congress.	<u>Rebecca</u> decided to run for Congress.
Plessy v. Ferguson was a <u>bad</u> Supreme Court decision.	*Plessy v. Ferguson* <u>institutionalized</u> the "separate but equal" doctrine of racial apartheid.
Acid rain is a <u>problem</u>.	Acid rain <u>erodes buildings</u>, <u>damages crops</u>, and <u>creates pollution</u>.
Almost from the beginning, Europeans <u>deceived</u> Native Americans.	Almost from the beginning, Europeans <u>lied</u>, <u>broke treaties</u>, and <u>stole land</u> from Native Americans.

FYI

Using Specific Words

One way to strengthen your writing is to avoid general words like *good*, *nice*, or *great*. Take the time to think of more specific words. For example, when you say the ocean looked *pretty*, do you really mean that it *sparkled*, *glistened*, *rippled*, *foamed*, *surged*, or *billowed*?

PRACTICE

23-1 In the following passage, underline the specific words that help you imagine the scene the writer describes. The first sentence has been done for you.

Last summer, I spent three weeks backpacking through <u>the remote rural province of Yunnan in China</u>. One day, I came across four farm women playing a game of mahjong on a patch of muddy ground. Squatting on rough wooden stools around a faded green folding table, the women picked up and discarded the smooth ivory mahjong tiles as if they were playing cards. In the grassy field around them, their chestnut-colored horses grazed with heavy red and black market bags tied to their backs. A veil of shimmering white fog hung over a nearby hill, and one woman sat under a black umbrella to shelter herself from the sun. A fifth woman watched, with her wrinkled hands on her hips and a frown on her face. The only sound was the sharp click of the tiles and the soft musical talk of the women as they played.

PRACTICE

23-2 The following one-paragraph job-application letter uses many general words. Rewrite the paragraph, substituting specific words and adding details where necessary. Start by making the first sentence, which identifies the job, more specific: for example, "I would like to apply for the <u>dental technician</u> position you advertised on <u>March 15 in the *Post*</u>." Then, add information about your background and <u>qualifications</u>. Expand the original paragraph into a three-paragraph letter.

I would like to apply for the position you advertised in today's paper. I graduated from high school and am currently attending college. I have taken several courses that have prepared me for the duties the position requires. I also have several personal qualities that I think you would find useful in a person holding this position. In addition, I have had certain experiences that qualify me for such a job. I would appreciate the opportunity to meet with you to discuss your needs as an employer. Thank you.

23b Using Concise Language

Concise language says what it has to say in as few words as possible. Too often, writers use words and phrases that add nothing to a sentence's meaning. A good way to test a sentence for these words is to see if crossing them out changes the sentence's meaning. If the sentence's meaning does not change, you can assume that the words you crossed out are unnecessary.

          The
~~It is clear that the~~ United States was not ready to fight World War II.

   To   ^
~~In order to~~ follow the plot, you must make an outline.
    ^

Sometimes you can replace several unnecessary words with a single word.

~~Due to the fact that~~ I was tired, I missed my first class.
(Because)

Einstein ~~believed but could not confirm~~ the existence of black holes.
(assumed)

FYI

Using Concise Language

The following wordy phrases add nothing to a sentence. You can usually delete or condense them with no loss of meaning.

WORDY	CONCISE
It is clear that	(delete)
It is a fact that	(delete)
The reason is because	Because
The reason is that	Because
It is my opinion that	I think/I believe
Due to the fact that	Because
Despite the fact that	Although
At the present time	Today/Now
At that time	Then
In most cases	Usually
In order to	To
In the final analysis	Finally
Subsequent to	After

Unnecessary repetition—saying the same thing twice for no reason—can also make your writing wordy. When you revise, delete repeated words and phrases that add nothing to your sentences.

My instructor told me the book was ~~old-fashioned and~~ outdated. (An old-fashioned book *is* outdated.)

The ~~terrible~~ tragedy of the fire could have been avoided. (A tragedy is *always* terrible.)

PRACTICE

23-3 To make the following sentences more concise, eliminate any unnecessary repetition, and delete or condense wordy expressions.

Example: When the movie *Hidden Figures* came out ~~a few years ago~~ in
2016, people ~~in audiences everywhere~~ were introduced to three ~~heroic~~
                                                          heroes
~~individuals~~ in NASA's space program.

(1) Based on a book written by Margot Lee Shetterly, *Hidden Figures*
version is about the story of NASA mathematicians Katherine Johnson,
Dorothy Vaughan, and Mary Jackson. (2) At the time that these women
worked for NASA, segregation laws were still very much in effect.
(3) Because of the fact that they were African Americans, they came face
to face with discrimination in their jobs as "human computers." (4) On
top of that, as women, they faced sexist attitudes typical of that time in
history. (5) Despite having to confront many difficulties and challenges,
the women were able to overcome the obstacles and achieve several mile-
stones during their careers at NASA. (6) Dorothy Vaughan became the first
African American supervisor at the space center. (7) Mary Jackson rose
from her position as a computer and took advanced engineering classes on
her way to becoming NASA's first ever African American female engineer.
(8) Katherine Johnson played a key role in many NASA missions. As just an
example, she calculated the trajectory for, the first flight to the moon. For her
many, many contributions to the space program, Katherine Johnson,
received the Presidential Medal of Freedom in 2015.

23c Avoiding Slang

Slang is nonstandard language that calls attention to itself. It is usually
associated with a particular social group—Twitter users or video gamers,
for example. Some slang eventually spreads beyond its original context and
becomes widely used. Often, it is used for emphasis or to produce a surprising or original effect. In any case, because it is very informal, slang is
not acceptable in your college writing.

                                                      easy.
My psychology exam was really ~~sweet.~~

                    relax ^
On the weekends, I like to ~~chill~~ and watch movies on my laptop.
                        ^

If you have any question about whether a term is slang or not, look it up in a dictionary. If the term is identified as *slang* or *informal*, find a more suitable term.

FYI

Avoiding Abbreviations and Shorthand

While abbreviations and shorthand such as *BC*, *BTW*, *IMO*, and *2day* are acceptable in informal electronic communication, they are not acceptable in your college writing, in emails to your instructors, or in online class discussions.

In my opinion,
~~IMO~~ your essay needs a strong thesis statement.
^   *you*   *today.*
I would like to meet with ~~u~~ for a conference ~~2day.~~
                          ^   ^

PRACTICE

23-4　Edit the following sentences, replacing the slang expressions with clearer, more precise words and phrases.

                    yelled at me
Example: My father ~~lost it~~ when I told him I crashed the car.
                       ^

1. Whenever I get bummed, I go outside and jog.

2. Tonight I'll have to leave by 11 because I'm wiped out.

3. I'm not into movies or television.

4. Whenever we argue, my boyfriend knows how to push my buttons.

5. I really lucked out when I got this job.

 ## 23d Avoiding Clichés

Clichés are expressions—such as "easier said than done" and "last but not least"—that have been used so often that they have lost their meaning. These worn-out expressions get in the way of clear communication.

When you identify a cliché in your writing, replace it with a direct statement—or, if possible, with a fresher expression.

CLICHÉ   When school was over, she felt free ~~as a bird~~.

                                       seriously ill

CLICHÉ   These days, you have to be ~~sick as a dog~~ before you are

admitted to a hospital.

FYI

Avoiding Clichés

Here are examples of some clichés you should avoid in your writing.

a perfect storm	play God
back in the day	pushing the envelope
better late than never	reality check
bottom line	skill set
connect the dots	think outside the box
cutting edge	touched base
give 110 percent	tried and true
groupthink	water under the bridge
it goes without saying	what goes around comes
it is what it is	around
keep your eye on the	
ball	

PRACTICE

23-5   Cross out any clichés in the following sentences. Then, either substitute a fresher expression or restate the idea more directly.

                                    free of financial worries

Example: Lottery winners often think they will be ~~on easy street~~ for

the rest of their lives.

(1) Many people think that a million-dollar lottery jackpot allows the winner to stop working like a dog and start living high on the hog. (2) All things considered, however, the reality for lottery winners is quite different. (3) For one thing, lottery winners who hit the jackpot do not always receive their winnings all at once; instead, yearly payments—for example, $50,000—can be paid out over twenty years. (4) Of that

$50,000 a year, close to $20,000 goes to taxes and anything else the lucky stiff already owes the government, such as student loans. (5) Next come relatives and friends with their hands out, leaving winners between a rock and a hard place. (6) They can either cough up gifts and loans or wave bye-bye to many of their loved ones. (7) Adding insult to injury, many lottery winners lose their jobs because employers think that, now that they are "millionaires," they no longer need to draw a salary. (8) Many lottery winners wind up way over their heads in debt within a few years. (9) In their hour of need, many might like to sell their future payments to companies that offer lump-sum payments of forty to forty-five cents on the dollar. (10) This is easier said than done, however, because most state lotteries do not allow winners to sell their winnings.

 ## 23e Using Similes and Metaphors

A **simile** is a comparison of two unlike things that uses *like* or *as*.

His arm hung at his side <u>like</u> a broken branch.
He was <u>as</u> content <u>as</u> a cat napping on a windowsill.

A **metaphor** is a comparison of two unlike things that does not use *like* or *as*.

Invaders from another world, the dandelions conquered my garden.
He was a beast of burden, hauling cement from the mixer to the building site.

The impact of similes and metaphors comes from the surprise of seeing two seemingly unlike things being compared. Used in moderation, similes and metaphors can make your writing more lively and more interesting.

PRACTICE

23-6   Use your imagination to complete each of the following items by creating three original similes.

Example: A boring class is like _____ toast without jam. _____

_____ a four-hour movie. _____

_____ a bedtime story. _____

1. A good friend is like _____

_____

_____

2. A thunderstorm is like _____

_____

_____

3. A workout at the gym is like _____

_____

_____

23f Avoiding Sexist Language

Sexist language refers to men and women in insulting terms. Sexist language is not just words such as *stud* or *babe*, which people may find objectionable. It can also be words or phrases that unnecessarily call attention to gender or that suggest a job or profession is held only by a man (or only by a woman) when it actually is not.

You can avoid sexist language by using a little common sense. There is always an acceptable nonsexist alternative for a sexist term.

SEXIST	NONSEXIST
man, mankind	humanity, humankind, the human race
businessman	executive, businessperson
fireman, policeman, mailman	firefighter, police officer, letter carrier
male nurse, woman engineer	nurse, engineer
congressman	member of Congress, representative
stewardess, steward	flight attendant
man and wife	man and woman, husband and wife
manmade	synthetic
chairman	chair, chairperson
anchorwoman, anchorman	anchor
actor, actress	actor
waiter, waitress	server

FYI

Avoiding Sexist Language

Do not use *he* when your subject could be either male or female.

> **SEXIST** Everyone should complete <u>his</u> assignment by next week.

You can correct this problem in three ways.

- *Use* he or she *or* his or her.

  > Everyone should complete <u>his or her</u> assignment by next week.

- *Use plural forms.*

  > Students should complete <u>their</u> assignments by next week.

- *Eliminate the pronoun.*

  > Everyone should complete <u>the</u> assignment by next week.

PRACTICE

23-7 Edit the following sentences to eliminate sexist language.

or her (or omit "his")

Example: A doctor should be honest with his patients.

1. Many people today would like to see more policemen patrolling the streets.

2. The attorneys representing the plaintiff are Geraldo Diaz and Mrs. Barbara Wilkerson.

3. Every soldier picked up his weapons.

4. Ivy R. Taylor is the female mayor of San Antonio, Texas.

5. Travel to other planets will be a significant step for man.

23g Commonly Confused Words

Accept/Except   *Accept* means "to receive something." *Except* means "with the exception of" or "to leave out or exclude."

> "I <u>accept</u> your challenge," said Alexander Hamilton to Aaron Burr.
>
> Everyone <u>except</u> Darryl visited the museum.

Affect/Effect   *Affect* is a verb meaning "to influence." *Effect* is a noun meaning "result."

> Carmen's job could <u>affect</u> her grades.
>
> Overexposure to sun can have a long-term <u>effect</u> on skin.

All ready/Already   *All ready* means "completely prepared." *Already* means "previously, before."

> Serge was <u>all ready</u> to take the history test.
>
> Gina had <u>already</u> been to Italy.

Brake/Break   *Brake* is a noun that means "a device to slow or stop a vehicle." *Break* is a verb meaning "to smash" or "to detach" and sometimes a noun meaning either "a gap" or "an interruption" or "a stroke of luck."

> Peter got into an accident because his foot slipped off the <u>brake</u>.
>
> Babe Ruth thought no one would ever <u>break</u> his home run record.
>
> The baseball game was postponed until there was a <u>break</u> in the bad weather.

Buy/By   *Buy* means "to purchase." *By* is a preposition meaning "close to," "next to," or "by means of."

> The Stamp Act forced colonists to <u>buy</u> stamps for many public documents.
>
> He drove <u>by</u> but did not stop.
>
> He stayed <u>by</u> her side all the way to the hospital.
>
> Malcolm X wanted "freedom <u>by</u> any means necessary."

Conscience/Conscious   *Conscience* is a noun that refers to the part of the mind that urges a person to choose right over wrong. *Conscious* is an adjective that means "aware" or "deliberate."

After he cheated at cards, his <u>conscience</u> started to bother him.

As she walked through the woods, she became <u>conscious</u> of the hum of insects.

Elliott made a <u>conscious</u> decision to stop smoking.

Everyday/Every day *Everyday* is a single word that means "ordinary" or "common." *Every day* is two words that mean "occurring daily."

Friends was a successful comedy show because it appealed to <u>everyday</u> people.

<u>Every day</u>, the six friends met at the Central Perk café.

Fine/Find *Fine* means "superior quality" or "a sum of money paid as a penalty." *Find* means "to locate."

He sang a <u>fine</u> solo at church last Sunday.

Demi had to pay a <u>fine</u> for speeding.

Some people still use a willow rod to <u>find</u> water.

Hear/Here *Hear* means "to perceive sound by ear." *Here* means "at or in this place."

I moved to the front so I could <u>hear</u> the speaker.

My great-grandfather came <u>here</u> in 1883.

Its/It's *Its* is the possessive form of *it*. *It's* is the contraction of *it is* or *it has*.

The airline canceled <u>its</u> flights because of the snow.

<u>It's</u> twelve o'clock, and we are late.

Ever since <u>it's</u> been in the accident, the car has rattled.

Know/No/Knew/New *Know* means "to have an understanding of" or "to have fixed in the mind." *No* means "not any," "not at all," or "not one." *Knew* is the past tense form of the verb *know*. *New* means "recent or never used."

I <u>know</u> there will be a lunar eclipse tonight.

You have <u>no</u> right to say that.

He <u>knew</u> how to install a <u>new</u> light switch.

Lie/Lay *Lie* means "to rest or recline." The past tense of *lie* is *lay*. *Lay* means "to put or place something down." The past tense of *lay* is *laid*.

Every Sunday, I <u>lie</u> in bed until noon.

They <u>lay</u> on the grass until it began to rain, and then they went home.

Tammy told Carl to <u>lay</u> his cards on the table.

Brooke and Cassia finally <u>laid</u> down their hockey sticks.

Loose/Lose   *Loose* means "not fixed or rigid" or "not attached securely." *Lose* means "to mislay" or "to misplace" or "to not win."

In the 1940s, many women wore <u>loose</u>-fitting pants.

I always <u>lose</u> my car keys.

I never gamble because I hate to <u>lose</u>.

Passed/Past   *Passed* is the past tense of the verb *pass*. It means "moved by" or "succeeded in." *Past* is a noun or an adjective meaning "earlier than the present time."

The car that <u>passed</u> me was doing more than eighty miles an hour.

David finally <u>passed</u> his driving test.

The novel was set in the <u>past</u>.

The statement said that the bill was <u>past</u> due.

Peace/Piece   *Peace* means "the absence of war" or "calm." *Piece* means "a part of something."

The British prime minister tried to achieve <u>peace</u> with honor.

My <u>peace</u> of mind was destroyed when the flying saucer landed.

"Have a <u>piece</u> of cake," said Marie.

Principal/Principle   *Principal* means "first" or "highest" or "the head of a school." *Principle* means "a law or basic assumption."

She had the <u>principal</u> role in the movie.

I'll never forget the day the <u>principal</u> called me into his office.

It was against his <u>principles</u> to lie.

Quiet/Quit/Quite   *Quiet* means "free of noise" or "still." *Quit* means "to leave a job" or "to give up." *Quite* means "actually" or "very."

Jane looked forward to the <u>quiet</u> evenings at the lake.

Sammy <u>quit</u> his job and followed the girls into the parking lot.

"You haven't <u>quite</u> got the hang of it yet," she said.

After practicing all summer, Tamika got <u>quite</u> good at tennis.

Raise/Rise *Raise* means "to elevate" or "to increase in size, quantity, or worth." The past tense of *raise* is *raised*. *Rise* means "to stand up" or "to move from a lower position to a higher position." The past tense of *rise* is *rose*.

Carlos <u>raises</u> his hand whenever the teacher asks for volunteers.

They finally <u>raised</u> the money for the down payment.

The crowd <u>rises</u> every time their team scores a touchdown.

Kim <u>rose</u> before dawn so she could see the eclipse.

Sit/Set *Sit* means "to assume a sitting position." The past tense of *sit* is *sat*. *Set* means "to put down or place" or "to adjust something to a desired position." The past tense of *set* is *set*.

I usually <u>sit</u> in the front row at the movies.

They <u>sat</u> at the clinic waiting for their names to be called.

Elizabeth <u>set</u> the mail on the kitchen table and left for work.

Every semester I <u>set</u> goals for myself.

Suppose/Supposed *Suppose* means "to consider" or "to assume." *Supposed* is both the past tense and the past participle of *suppose*. *Supposed* also means "expected" or "required." (Note that when *supposed* has this meaning, it is always followed by *to*.)

<u>Suppose</u> researchers were to find a cure for cancer.

We <u>supposed</u> the movie would be over by ten o'clock.

You were <u>supposed</u> to finish a draft of the report by today.

Their/There/They're *Their* is the possessive form of the pronoun *they*. *There* means "at or in that place." *There* is also used in the phrases *there is* and *there are*. *They're* is the contraction of *they are*.

They wanted poor people to improve <u>their</u> living conditions.

I put the book over <u>there</u>.

<u>There</u> are three reasons I will not eat meat.

<u>They're</u> the best volunteer firefighters I've ever seen.

Then/Than *Then* means "at that time" or "next in time." *Than* is used in comparisons.

He was young and naive <u>then</u>.

I went to the job interview and <u>then</u> stopped off for coffee.

My dog is smarter <u>than</u> your dog.

Threw/Through   *Threw* is the past tense of *throw*. *Through* means "in one side and out the opposite side" or "finished."

> Satchel Paige threw a baseball more than ninety-five miles an hour.
>
> It takes almost thirty minutes to go through the tunnel.
>
> "I'm through," said Clark Kent, storming out of Perry White's office.

To/Too/Two   *To* means "in the direction of." *Too* means "also" or "more than enough." *Two* denotes the numeral 2.

> During spring break, I am going to Disney World.
>
> My roommates are coming too.
>
> The microwave popcorn is too hot to eat.
>
> "If we get rid of the Tin Man and the Cowardly Lion, the two of us can go to Oz," said the Scarecrow to Dorothy.

Use/Used   *Use* means "to put into service" or "to consume." *Used* is both the past tense and the past participle of *use*. *Used* also means "accustomed." (Note that when *used* has this meaning, it is followed by *to*.)

> I use a soft cloth to clean my glasses.
>
> "Hey! Who used all the hot water?" he yelled from the shower.
>
> Marisol had used all the firewood during the storm.
>
> After two years in Alaska, they got used to the short winter days.

Weather/Whether   *Weather* refers to temperature, humidity, precipitation, and so on. *Whether* is used to introduce alternative possibilities.

> The *Farmer's Almanac* says that the weather this winter will be severe.
>
> Whether or not this prediction will be correct is anyone's guess.

Where/Were/We're   *Where* means "at or in what place." *Were* is the past tense of *are*. *We're* is the contraction of *we are*.

> Where are you going, and where have you been?
>
> Charlie Chaplin and Mary Pickford were popular stars of silent movies.
>
> We're doing our back-to-school shopping early this year.

Whose/Who's *Whose* is the possessive form of *who*. *Who's* is the contraction of either *who is* or *who has*.

My roommate asked, "Whose book is this?"

"Who's there?" squealed the second little pig as he leaned against the door.

Who's been blocking the driveway?

Your/You're *Your* is the possessive form of *you*. *You're* is the contraction of *you are*.

"You should have worn your running shoes," said the hare as he passed the tortoise.

"You're too kind," said the tortoise sarcastically.

EDITING PRACTICE

Read the following student essay carefully, and then revise it. Make sure that your revision is concise, uses specific words, and includes no slang, sexist language, clichés, or confused words. Add an occasional simile or metaphor if you like. The first sentence has been edited for you.

Unexpected Discoveries

            hear   , like dented fenders and broken glass.

When we ~~here~~ the word "accident," we think of bad things. But accidents can be good, too. Modern science has made advances as a result of accidents. It is a fact that a scientist sometimes works like a dog for years in his laboratory, only to make a weird discovery because of a mistake.

The most famous example of a good, beneficial accident is the discovery of penicillin. A scientist, Alexander Fleming, had seen many soldiers die of infections after they were wounded in World War I. All things considered, many more soldiers died due to the fact that infections occurred than from wounds. Fleming wanted to find a drug that could put an end to these terrible, fatal infections. One day in 1928, Fleming went on vacation, leaving a pile of dishes in the lab sink. As luck would have it, he had been growing bacteria in those dishes. When he came back, he noticed that one of the dishes looked moldy. What was strange was that near the mold, the bacteria were dead as a doornail. It was crystal clear to Fleming that the mold had killed the bacteria. He had discovered penicillin, the first antibiotic.

Everyone has heard the name "Goodyear." It was Charles Goodyear who made a discovery that changed and revolutionized the rubber industry. In the early nineteenth century, rubber products became thin and runny in hot weather and cracked in cold weather. One day in 1839, Goodyear accidentally dropped some rubber mixed with sulfur on a hot stove. It changed color and turned black. After being cooled, it could be stretched, and it would return to its original size and shape. This kind of rubber is now used in tires and in many other products.

Another thing was also discovered because of a lab accident involving rubber. In 1953, Patsy Sherman, a female chemist for the 3M company, was trying to find a new type of rubber. She created a batch of man-made liquid rubber. Some of the liquid accidentally spilled onto a lab assistant's new white canvas sneaker. Her assistant used everything but the kitchen sink to clean the shoe, but nothing worked. Over time, the rest of the shoe became dirty, but the part where the spill had hit was still clean as a whistle. Sherman new that she had found something that could actually keep fabrics clean by doing a number on dirt. The 3M Corporation named it's brand new product Scotchgard.

A scientist can be clumsy and careless, but sometimes his mistakes lead to great and important discoveries. Penicillin, better tires, and Scotchgard are examples of products that were the result of scientific accidents.

COLLABORATIVE ACTIVITY

Photocopy two or three paragraphs of description from a romance novel, a western novel, or a mystery novel, and bring your paragraphs to class. Working in a group, choose one paragraph that seems to need clearer, more specific language. As a group, revise the paragraph you chose, making it as specific as possible and eliminating any clichés or sexist language. Then, exchange your revised paragraph with the paragraph revised by another group, and check the other group's work. Make any additional changes you think the paragraph needs.

review checklist

Using Words Effectively

✔ Use specific words that convey your ideas clearly and precisely. (See 23a.)

✔ Use concise language that says what it has to say in the fewest possible words. (See 23b.)

✔ Avoid slang. (See 23c.)

✔ Avoid clichés. (See 23d.)

✔ When appropriate, use similes and metaphors to make your writing more lively and more interesting. (See 23e.)

✔ Avoid sexist language. (See 23f.)

✔ Avoid commonly confused words. (See 23g.)

24 Run-Ons

 ## 24a Recognizing Run-Ons

A **sentence** consists of at least one independent clause—one subject and one verb.

> College costs are rising.

A **run-on** is an error that occurs when two sentences are joined incorrectly. There are two kinds of run-ons: *fused sentences* and *comma splices.*

- A **fused sentence** occurs when two sentences are joined without any punctuation.

  FUSED SENTENCE   [College costs are rising] [many students are concerned.]

- A **comma splice** occurs when two sentences are joined with just a comma.

  COMMA SPLICE   [College costs are rising], [many students are concerned.]

PRACTICE

24-1   Some of the sentences in the following paragraph are correct, but others are run-ons. In the answer space after each sentence, write *C* if the sentence is correct, *FS* if it is a fused sentence, and *CS* if it is a comma splice.

Example: Using a screen reader is one way for visually impaired people to access the web, two popular programs are JAWS for Windows and Window-Eyes. __*CS*__

(1) The Internet should be accessible to everyone, this is not always the case. _____ (2) Many visually impaired computer users have trouble finding information on the web. _____ (3) Often, this is the result of poor web design it is the designer's job to make the site accessible.

_____ (4) Most visually impaired people use special software called screen readers, this technology translates text into speech or Braille.

_____ (5) However, screen readers do not always work well the information is sometimes hard to access. _____ (6) Websites need to be understandable to all Internet users. _____ (7) The rights of visually impaired Internet users may be protected by the Americans with Disabilities Act (ADA)._____ (8) We will have to wait for more cases to come to trial then we will know more. _____ (9) Meanwhile, we have to rely on software companies to make the necessary changes, this will take some time. _____ (10) However, there are incentives for these companies, the more than 1.5 million visually impaired computer users are all potential customers. _____

24b Correcting Run-Ons

FYI

> ### Correcting Run-Ons
> You can correct run-ons in five ways:
> 1. *Use a period to create two separate sentences.*
>   College costs are rising. Many students are concerned.
> 2. *Use a coordinating conjunction* (and, but, for, nor, or, so, *or* yet) *to connect ideas.*
>   College costs are rising, and many students are concerned.
> 3. *Use a semicolon to connect ideas.*
>   College costs are rising; many students are concerned.
> 4. *Use a semicolon followed by a transitional word or phrase to connect ideas.*
>   College costs are rising; as a result, many students are concerned.
> 5. *Use a dependent word* (although, because, when, *and* so on) *to connect ideas.*
>   Because college costs are rising, many students are concerned.

The pages that follow explain and illustrate the five different ways to correct run-ons.

1. *Use a period to create two separate sentences.* Be sure each sentence begins with a capital letter and ends with a period.

INCORRECT **(FUSED SENTENCE)**	Elizabeth Gilbert wrote the poem "Florida"_Maya Angelou wrote a poem called "My Arkansas."
INCORRECT **(COMMA SPLICE)**	Elizabeth Gilbert wrote the poem "Florida," Maya Angelou wrote a poem called "My Arkansas."
CORRECT	Elizabeth Gilbert wrote the poem "Florida." Maya Angelou wrote a poem called "My Arkansas."

PRACTICE

24-2　Correct each of the following run-ons by using a period to create two separate sentences. Be sure both of your new sentences begin with a capital letter and end with a period.

Example: Stephen Colbert used to have a show called *The Colbert Report,* now, he hosts *The Late Show.*
(edited to: *The Colbert Report.* Now, he hosts *The Late Show.*)

1. Margaret Thatcher was the first woman chosen as prime minister of the United Kingdom Teresa May was the second.

2. New York–style pizza usually has a thin crust Chicago-style "deep-dish pizza" has a thick crust.

3. Last week, Soraya won a texting contest the prize for texting the fastest was five hundred dollars.

4. In some parts of Canada's Northwest Territory, the only way to transport supplies is over frozen lakes, being an ice road trucker is one of the most dangerous jobs in the world.

5. In 1961, the first Six Flags opened in Arlington, Texas, the six flags represent the six former ruling governments of Texas.

2. *Use a coordinating conjunction to connect ideas.* If you want to indicate a particular relationship between ideas—for example, cause and effect or contrast—you can connect two independent clauses with a coordinating conjunction that makes this relationship clear. Always place a comma before the coordinating conjunction.

Coordinating Conjunctions

and	for	or	yet
but	nor	so	

INCORRECT (FUSED SENTENCE)	Some schools require students to wear uniforms other schools do not.
INCORRECT (COMMA SPLICE)	Some schools require students to wear uniforms, other schools do not.
CORRECT	Some schools require students to wear uniforms, but other schools do not. (clauses connected with the coordinating conjunction *but*, preceded by a comma)

PRACTICE

24-3 Correct each of the following run-ons by using a coordinating conjunction (*and, but, for, nor, or, so,* or *yet*) to connect ideas. Be sure to put a comma before each coordinating conjunction.

Example: Many college students use Snapchat and Instagram to share photos ‸ they also use these apps to keep up with their friends.
, and

1. A car with soft tires gets poor gas mileage, keeping tires inflated is a good way to save money on gas.

2. Once it was difficult for football fans to see the first-down line on television, the computer-generated yellow line makes it much easier.

3. Indonesia has more volcanoes than any other country the United States has the biggest volcano in the world, Hawaii's Mauna Loa.

4. Chefs can become famous for cooking at popular restaurants they can gain fame by hosting television shows.

5. Overcrowded schools often purchase portable classrooms or trailers this is only a temporary solution.

3. ***Use a semicolon to connect ideas.***   If you want to indicate a particularly close connection—or a strong contrast—between two ideas, use a semicolon.

> **INCORRECT (FUSED SENTENCE)**   Most professional basketball players have gone to college most professional baseball players have not.
>
> **INCORRECT (COMMA SPLICE)**   Most professional basketball players have gone to college, most professional baseball players have not.
>
> **CORRECT**   Most professional basketball players have gone to college; most professional baseball players have not. (clauses connected with a semicolon)

PRACTICE

24-4   Correct each of the following run-ons by using a semicolon to connect ideas. Do not use a capital letter after the semicolon unless the word that follows it is a proper noun.

Example: From 1930 until 2006, Pluto was known as a planet;it is now known as a "dwarf planet."

1. Of all the states, Alaska has the highest percentage of Native American residents 16 percent of Alaskans are of Native American descent.

2. Satellites and global positioning systems (GPS) can help farmers to better understand the needs of their crops, these tools are part of a trend called "precision agriculture."

3. Enforcing traffic laws can be difficult some cities use cameras to photograph cars at intersections.

4. Old landfills can sometimes be made into parks, Cesar Chavez Park in Berkeley, California, is one example.

5. Freestyle motocross riders compete by doing jumps and stunts some famous FMX riders are Carey Hart, Nate Adams, and Travis Pastrana.

4. *Use a semicolon followed by a transitional word or phrase to connect ideas.* To show how two closely linked ideas are related, add a transitional word or phrase after the semicolon. The transition will indicate the specific relationship between the two clauses.

INCORRECT (**FUSED SENTENCE**)	Finding a part-time job can be challenging some-times it is even hard to find an unpaid internship.
INCORRECT (**COMMA SPLICE**)	Finding a part-time job can be challenging, some-times it is even hard to find an unpaid internship.
CORRECT	Finding a part-time job can be challenging; in fact, sometimes it is even hard to find an unpaid intern-ship. (clauses connected with a semicolon followed by the transitional phrase *in fact*)

Some Frequently Used Transitional Words and Phrases

after all	for this reason	now
also	however	still
as a result	in addition	then
eventually	in fact	therefore
finally	instead	thus
for example	moreover	unfortunately
for instance	nevertheless	

For more complete lists of transitional words and phrases, see 19c.

PRACTICE
24-5 Correct each of the following run-ons by using a semicolon, followed by the transitional word or phrase in parentheses, to connect ideas. Be sure to put a comma after the transitional word or phrase.

Example: When babies are first born, they can only see black and
; still,
white most infant toys are made in primary colors. (still)
      ^

1. Restaurant goers can expect to see different condiments in different

   regions of the country, few tables in the Southwest are without a

   bottle of hot sauce. (for example)

2. Every year, millions of people participate in TV-Turnoff Week by not watching television they read, spend time with family and friends, and generally enjoy their free time. (instead)

3. Today, few workers can count on company pension plans, forty years ago, most workers could. (however)

4. Many Americans see bottled water as a waste of money tap water is free. (after all)

5. Owners of "puppy mills" are only concerned with making money they are not concerned with the dogs' well-being. (unfortunately)

FYI

Connecting Ideas with Semicolons

Run-ons often occur when you use a transitional word or phrase to join two independent clauses *without also using a semicolon.*

INCORRECT (FUSED SENTENCE)	It is easy to download information from the Internet however it is not always easy to evaluate the information.
INCORRECT (COMMA SPLICE)	It is easy to download information from the Internet, however it is not always easy to evaluate the information.

To avoid this kind of run-on, always put a semicolon before the transitional word or phrase and a comma after it.

CORRECT	It is easy to download information from the Internet; however, it is not always easy to evaluate the information.

5. *Use a dependent word to connect ideas.* When one idea is dependent on another, you can connect the two ideas by adding a dependent word, such as *when, who, although,* or *because.*

INCORRECT (FUSED SENTENCE)	American union membership was high in the mid-twentieth century it has declined in recent years.

INCORRECT (COMMA SPLICE)	American union membership was high in the mid-twentieth century, it has declined in recent years.
CORRECT	Although American union membership was high in the mid-twentieth century, it has declined in recent years. (clauses connected with the dependent word *although*)
CORRECT	American union membership, which was high in the mid-twentieth century, has declined in recent years. (clauses connected with the dependent word *which*)

Some Frequently Used Dependent Words

after	even though	until
although	if	when
as	since	which
because	that	who
before	unless	

For complete lists of dependent words, including subordinating conjunctions and relative pronouns, see 20b and 20c.

PRACTICE

24-6 Correct each run-on in the following paragraph by adding a dependent word. Consult the list above to help you choose a logical dependent word. Be sure to add correct punctuation where necessary.

until
Example: Harlem was a rural area ^improved transportation linked it to lower Manhattan.

(1) Contemporary historians have written about the Harlem Renaissance, its influence is still not widely known. (2) Harlem was populated mostly by European immigrants at the turn of the last century, it saw an influx of African Americans beginning in 1910. (3) This migration from the South continued Harlem became one of the largest African American communities in the United States. (4) Many black artists and writers settled in

Harlem during the 1920s. African American art flourished. (5) This "Harlem Renaissance" was an important movement in American literary history it is not even mentioned in some textbooks. (6) Scholars recognize the great works of the Harlem Renaissance, they point to the writers Langston Hughes and Countee Cullen and the artists Henry Tanner and Sargent Johnson. (7) Zora Neale Hurston moved to Harlem from her native Florida in 1925, she began writing a book of African American folklore. (8) Harlem was an exciting place in the 1920s people from all over the city went there to listen to jazz and to dance. (9) The white playwright Eugene O'Neill went to Harlem to audition actors for his play *The Emperor Jones*, he made an international star of the great Paul Robeson. (10) The Great Depression occurred in the 1930s it led to the end of the Harlem Renaissance.

PRACTICE

24-7 Correct each of the following run-ons in one of these four ways: by creating two separate sentences, by using a coordinating conjunction, by using a semicolon, or by using a semicolon followed by a transitional word or phrase. Remember to put a semicolon before, and a comma after, each transitional word or phrase.

> **Example:** Some fish-and-chip shops in Scotland sell deep-fried
> . Children
> MARS bars ~~children~~ are the biggest consumers of these calorie-rich
> bars.

1. Fourteen percent of Americans have one or more tattoos there are over 20,000 tattoo parlors in the United States.

2. The ancient Greeks built their homes facing south this practice took advantage of light and heat from the winter sun.

3. Flamenco—a Spanish style of dancing, singing, and clapping— was traditionally informal and unplanned it has been compared to improvisational American jazz.

4. In Acadia National Park in Maine, large stones line the edges of steep trails the stones are called "Rockefeller's teeth" in honor of the trails' patron.

5. Allen Ginsberg was charged with obscenity for his book *Howl* the charges were dismissed.

PRACTICE

24-8 Correct each run-on in the following paragraph in the way that best indicates the relationship between ideas. Be sure to use appropriate punctuation.

Example: E. L. Doctorow's *Homer and Langley* tells the story of two
eccentric brothers it shows that truth can be stranger than fiction.
         , and
              ^

(1) The Collyer brothers were wealthy and educated they lived and died alone in a filthy apartment. (2) Langley and Homer Collyer were the sons of a doctor and an opera singer the brothers seemed to be as talented and motivated as their parents. (3) Langley played piano and studied engineering Homer had a law degree. (4) However, in their twenties and thirties, the brothers did not have jobs they lived with their parents in a Manhattan apartment. (5) Their parents died Langley and Homer inherited the apartment. (6) Gradually, they became frightened of outsiders they boarded up the windows and set traps for burglars. (7) They stopped paying their bills their heat, water, and electricity were shut off. (8) They also became compulsive hoarders, they could not throw anything away. (9) They accumulated thousands and thousands of books, numerous bundles of old newspapers, and fourteen pianos, they saved tons of garbage. (10) They got their water from a public park they collected discarded food from grocery stores and butcher shops. (11) Eventually, Langley was caught in one of his own burglar traps, the trap sent three bundles of newspapers and a suitcase tumbling on top of him. (12) Langley died of his injuries Homer died by his side, surrounded by mountains of trash.

CHAPTER REVIEW

EDITING PRACTICE: PARAGRAPH

Read the following student paragraph, and revise it to eliminate run-ons. Correct each run-on in the way that best indicates the relationship between ideas. Be sure to use appropriate punctuation. The first error has been corrected for you.

Cold Cases

Cold cases are criminal investigations that have not been solved, ^so they are not officially closed. New evidence is found, cold cases may be reexamined. DNA tests might provide new clues, a witness may come forward with new testimony. The new evidence might lead to new suspects it might change the nature of the crime. In some cases, an accident might be reclassified a homicide, in other cases a murder might be ruled a suicide. Sometimes a person who was convicted of a crime is found to be innocent. Cold cases usually involve violent crimes, rape and murder are two examples. Investigators sometimes reopen very old cold cases, they usually focus on more recent cases with living suspects. For serious crimes, there is no time limit, a criminal may be convicted many years after the crime was committed. When cold cases are solved, the crime is not undone, nevertheless victims' families finally feel that justice has been served.

EDITING PRACTICE: ESSAY

Read the following student essay, and revise it to eliminate run-ons. Correct each run-on in the way that best indicates the relationship between ideas, and be sure to punctuate correctly. The first error has been corrected for you.

Feng Shui

Feng shui is an ancient Chinese practice it was developed over 3,000 years ago to balance energies and ensure both health and good fortune. A room organized according to feng shui practices is said to bring good fortune to the occupants, a room assembled without feng shui will bring bad fortune.

Two tools are used for feng shui: the Compass and the Bagua. The Compass is also referred to as a Luo-Pan its purpose is to discover hidden details about a site or a building. The Compass is composed of layers of circles surrounding a magnetic needle. The Bagua is a grid in the shape of an octagon, a symbol in each section of the grid represents an ancient oracle. The purpose of the Bagua is to analyze the energy of the room the Bagua also reveals connections between the space and certain areas of the occupants' lives.

One of the main principles of feng shui is yin and yang this means balance. One common example of yin and yang is black and white, another is heavy and light. Balancing the chi, or the energy in the room, is about achieving a balance between yin and yang. The Compass and the Bagua are the tools used to determine balance, everyone's version of balance will be different.

Many people spend several hours a day at their desks either working or studying, for this reason, it makes sense to apply the concepts of feng shui to workspaces. Some people may want to improve several areas of their work lives, focusing on just one or two areas is usually best. For example, the back left corner of the desk represents wealth, a plant could be placed there. The center left of the desk represents family, that may be an ideal place for a family photo.

Feng shui does not guarantee immediate improvements, however, its practitioners report feeling calmer and more relaxed. Perhaps practitioners have already cleaned and organized their living spaces, perhaps the feng shui practice itself makes a difference. No one knows for sure. Feng shui is an ancient art, it will undoubtedly be practiced for many years to come.

COLLABORATIVE ACTIVITY

Find an interesting paragraph in a newspaper or magazine article or on the web. Working in a small group, recopy the paragraph onto a separate sheet of paper, creating run-ons. Exchange exercises with another group. Then, work in your own group to correct each fused sentence and comma splice in an exercise prepared by another group of students. When you have finished, return the exercise to the group that created it. Finally, continuing to work with members of your group, evaluate the other group's work on your exercise, comparing it to the original newspaper, magazine, or online paragraph.

review checklist

Run-Ons

✔ A run-on is an error that occurs when two sentences are joined incorrectly. There are two kinds of run-ons: fused sentences and comma splices. (See 24a.)

✔ A fused sentence occurs when two sentences are incorrectly joined without any punctuation. (See 24a.)

✔ A comma splice occurs when two sentences are joined with just a comma. (See 24a.)

✔ Correct a run-on in one of the following ways:

1. by creating two separate sentences _____ . _____ .

2. by using a coordinating conjunction _____ , [coordinating conjunction] _____ .

3. by using a semicolon _____ ; _____ .

4. by using a semicolon followed by a transitional word or phrase _____ ; [transitional word or phrase], _____ .

5. by using a dependent word [Dependent word] _____ , _____ . _____ [dependent word] (See 24b.)

25 Fragments

25a Recognizing Fragments

A **fragment** is an incomplete sentence. Every sentence must include at least one subject and one verb, and every sentence must express a complete thought. If a group of words does not do *both* these things, it is a fragment and not a sentence—even if it begins with a capital letter and ends with a period.

The following is a complete sentence.

                          S   **V**

SENTENCE   The actors in the play were very talented. (The sentence includes both a subject and a verb and expresses a complete thought.)

Because a sentence must have both a subject and a verb and express a complete thought, the following groups of words are not complete sentences; they are fragments.

FRAGMENT (NO VERB)   The actors in the play. (What point is being made about the actors?)

FRAGMENT (NO SUBJECT)   Were very talented. (Who were very talented?)

FRAGMENT (NO SUBJECT OR VERB)   Very talented. (Who was very talented?)

FRAGMENT EXPRESS (DOES NOT COMPLETE THOUGHT)   Because the actors in the play were very talented. (What happened because they were very talented?)

FYI

Spotting Fragments

Fragments almost always appear next to complete sentences.

   ┌─── COMPLETE SENTENCE ───┐ ┌─────── FRAGMENT ───────┐
Celia took two electives. Physics 320 and Spanish 101.

The fragment above does not have a subject or a verb. The complete sentence that comes before it, however, has both a subject (*Celia*) and a verb (*took*).

Often, you can correct a fragment by attaching it to an adjacent sentence that supplies the missing words. (This sentence will usually appear right before the fragment.)

Celia took two electives, Physics 320 and Spanish 101.

> **WORD POWER**
> **adjacent** next to

PRACTICE

25-1   Some of the following items are fragments, and others are complete sentences. On the line following each item, write *F* if it is a fragment and *S* if it is a complete sentence.

    Example: Star formations in the night sky. _____F_____

1. To save as much as possible for college. _____

2. The judge gave her a two-year sentence. _____

3. A birthday on Christmas Day. _____

4. Because he lost ten pounds on his new diet. _____

5. Working in the garden and fixing the roof. _____

6. Sonya flew to Mexico. _____

7. Starts in August in many parts of the country. _____

8. And slept in his own bed last night. _____

9. Famous for her movie roles. _____

10. Phones that also play music and take photos. _____

PRACTICE

25-2   In the following paragraph, some of the numbered groups of words are missing a subject, a verb, or both. First, underline each fragment. Then, decide how each fragment could be attached to a nearby word group to create a complete new sentence. Finally, rewrite the entire paragraph, using complete sentences, on the lines provided.

    Example: Gatorade was invented at the University of Florida.
    To help the Florida Gators fight dehydration.

    Rewrite: Gatorade was invented at the University of Florida to help the Florida Gators fight dehydration.

    (1) Doctors discovered that football players were losing electrolytes and carbohydrates. (2) Through their sweat. (3) They invented a drink. (4) That replaced these important elements. (5) Gatorade tasted terrible.

(6) But did its job. (7) The Florida Gators survived a very hot season. (8) And won most of their games. (9) Now, Gatorade is used by many college and professional football teams. (10) As well as baseball, basketball, tennis, and soccer teams.

Rewrite:

_____

_____

_____

_____

_____

_____

 ## 25b Missing-Subject Fragments

Every sentence must include both a subject and a verb. If the subject is left out, the sentence is incomplete. In the example on the following page, the first word group is a sentence. It includes both a subject (*He*) and a verb (*packed*). However, the second word group is a fragment. It includes a verb (*took*), but it does not include a subject.

```
┌────── SENTENCE ──────────┐ ┌────────── FRAGMENT ──────────┐
He packed his books and laptop. And also took an umbrella.
```

The best way to correct this kind of fragment is to attach it to the sentence that comes right before it. This sentence will usually contain the missing subject.

> **CORRECT**   He packed his books and laptop <u>and</u> also took an umbrella.

Another way to correct this kind of fragment is to add the missing subject.

> **CORRECT**   He packed his books and laptop. <u>He</u> also took an umbrella.

PRACTICE

25-3 Each of the following items includes a missing-subject fragment. Using one of the two methods explained above, correct each fragment.

Example: Back-to-school sales are popular with students. And with their parents.

Back-to-school sales are popular with students and with their parents. *or*

Back-to-school sales are popular with students. The sales are also

popular with their parents.

1. Some retailers make large donations to charity. And even donate part of their profits.

2. Geography bees resemble spelling bees. But instead test the contestants' knowledge of countries around the world.

3. School uniforms are often preferred by parents. And also favored by many school principals.

4. Pro-football linemen can weigh more than 300 pounds. But are still able to run fast.

5. Using an electric toothbrush strengthens the teeth. And promotes healthy gums.

25c Phrase Fragments

Every sentence must include a subject and a verb. A **phrase** is a group of words that is missing a subject or a verb or both. When you punctuate a phrase as if it is a sentence, you create a fragment.

If you spot a phrase fragment in your writing, you can often correct it by attaching it to the sentence that comes directly before it.

Appositive Fragments

An **appositive** identifies, renames, or describes an adjacent noun or pronoun. An appositive cannot stand alone as a sentence.

To correct an appositive fragment, attach it to the sentence that comes right before it. (This sentence will contain the noun or pronoun that the appositive describes.)

INCORRECT   He decorated the room in his favorite colors.
┌── FRAGMENT ──┐
Brown and black.

CORRECT   He decorated the room in his favorite colors, brown and black.

Sometimes a word or expression like *especially, except, including, such as, for example,* or *for instance* introduces an appositive. Even if an appositive is introduced by one of these expressions, it is still a fragment.

┌ FRAGMENT ─
INCORRECT   A balanced diet should include high-fiber foods. Such as leafy vegetables, fruits, beans, and whole-grain bread.

CORRECT   A balanced diet should include high-fiber foods, such as leafy vegetables, fruits, beans, and whole-grain bread.

Prepositional Phrase Fragments

A **prepositional phrase** consists of a preposition and its object. A prepositional phrase cannot stand alone as a sentence. To correct a prepositional phrase fragment, attach it to the sentence that comes immediately before it.

┌─── FRAGMENT ───┐
INCORRECT   She promised to stand by him. In sickness and in health.

CORRECT   She promised to stand by him in sickness and in health.

Infinitive Fragments

An **infinitive** consists of *to* plus the base form of the verb (*to be, to go, to write*). An infinitive phrase (*to be free, to go home, to write a novel*) cannot stand alone as a sentence. You can usually correct an infinitive fragment by attaching it to the sentence that comes directly before it.

┌── FRAGMENT ──

INCORRECT   Eric considered dropping out of school. To start his

own business.

CORRECT   Eric considered dropping out of school to start his

own business.

You can also add the words needed to complete the sentence.

CORRECT   Eric considered dropping out of school. He wanted

to start his own business.

PRACTICE

25-4   In the following paragraph, some of the numbered groups of words are phrase fragments. First, underline each fragment. Then, decide how each fragment could be attached to an adjacent sentence to create a complete new sentence. Finally, rewrite the entire paragraph, using complete sentences, on the lines provided.

Example: Florence Nightingale worked as a nurse. During the

Crimean War.

Rewrite: Florence Nightingale worked as a nurse during the Crimean War.

(1) Nurses' uniforms have changed a lot. (2) Over the years. (3) Originally, nurses' uniforms looked like nuns' habits because nuns used to provide care. (4) To sick people. (5) In the late 1800s, a student of Florence Nightingale created a brown uniform. (6) With a white apron and cap. (7) This uniform was worn by student nurses at her school. (8) The Florence Nightingale School of Nursing and Midwifery. (9) Eventually, nurses began to wear white uniforms, white stockings, white shoes, and starched white caps. (10) To stress the importance of cleanliness. (11) Many older people remember these uniforms. (12) With affection. (13) Today,

most nurses—both male and female—wear bright, comfortable scrubs.

(14) To help patients (especially children) feel more at ease.

Rewrite:

_____

_____

_____

_____

_____

_____

_____

_____

_____

_____

PRACTICE

25-5 Each of the following items is a phrase fragment, not a sentence. Correct each fragment by adding any words needed to turn the fragment into a complete sentence. (You may add words before or after the fragment.)

Example: During World War I. _A flu epidemic killed millions of people_

during World War I. or During World War I, a flu epidemic killed millions

of people.

1. To be the best player on the team. _____

_____

2. From a developing nation in Africa. _____

_____

3. Such as tulips or roses. _____

_____

4. Behind door number 3. _____

_____

5. Including my parents and grandparents. _____

_____

6. With a new car in the driveway. _____

_____

7. To make a difficult career decision. _____

_____

8. For a long time. _____

_____

9. Turkey, stuffing, mashed potatoes, and cranberry sauce. _____

_____

10. In less than a year. _____

_____

25d *-ing* Fragments

Every sentence must include a subject and a verb. If the verb is incomplete, a word group is a fragment, not a sentence.

An *-ing* verb cannot be a complete verb. It needs a **helping verb** to complete it. An *-ing* verb, such as **looking**, cannot stand alone in a sentence without a helping verb (*is looking, was looking, were looking*, and so on). When you use an *-ing* verb without a helping verb, you create a fragment.

┌─────── FRAGMENT ───────┐

INCORRECT   The twins are full of mischief. Always looking for trouble.

The best way to correct an *-ing* fragment is to attach it to the sentence that comes right before it.

CORRECT   The twins are full of mischief, always looking for trouble.

Another way to correct an *-ing* fragment is to add a subject and a helping verb.

CORRECT   The twins are full of mischief. They are always looking for trouble.

FYI

Being

As you write, be careful not to use the *-ing* verb *being* as if it were a complete verb.

> **INCORRECT** I decided to take a nap. The outcome <u>being</u> that I slept through calculus class.

To correct this kind of fragment, substitute a form of the verb *be* that can serve as the main verb in a sentence—for example, *is*, *was*, *are*, or *were*.

> **CORRECT** I decided to take a nap. The outcome <u>was</u> that I slept through calculus class.

PRACTICE
25-6

Each of the following items includes an *-ing* fragment. In each case, correct the fragment by attaching it to the sentence before it.

Example: Students can use several strategies to pay back their loans early. Saving money in the long run.

Students can use several strategies to pay back their loans early,

saving money in the long run.

1. Most student loans have a grace period. Giving borrowers time to start earning an income before loan payments begin.

_____

_____

2. Use the grace period to create a budget. Building it around how much you owe.

_____

_____

3. If you have several student loans, you can consolidate them during the grace period. Combining them into one payment.

_____

_____

4. Try to pay more than the minimum. Setting up automatic payments with the extra amount included.

_____

_____

5. Apply any tax refund to your student loan. Using this extra money to reduce your debt.

_____

_____

PRACTICE

25-7   Each of the following items is an *-ing* fragment. Turn each fragment into a complete sentence by adding a subject and a helping verb. Write your revised sentence on the line below each fragment.

Example: Running up and down the stairs.

Revised: Jane and her dog are always running up and down the stairs.

1. Trying to decide where to live.

Revised: _____

_____

2. Really feeling optimistic about the future.

Revised: _____

_____

3. Always complaining about the lab manual.

Revised: _____

_____

4. Deciding whether or not to get a new cell phone.

Revised: _____

_____

5. Minding their own business.

Revised: _____

_____

 ## 25e Dependent-Clause Fragments

Every sentence must include a subject and a verb. Every sentence must also express a complete thought.

A **dependent clause** is a group of words that is introduced by a dependent word, such as *although, because, that,* or *after.* A dependent clause includes a subject and a verb, but it does not express a complete thought. Therefore, it cannot stand alone as a sentence. To correct a dependent-clause fragment, you must complete the thought.

The following dependent clause is incorrectly punctuated as if it were a sentence.

FRAGMENT   After Simon won the lottery.

This fragment includes both a subject (*Simon*) and a complete verb (*won*), but it does not express a complete thought. What happened after Simon won the lottery? To turn this fragment into a sentence, you need to complete the thought.

SENTENCE   After Simon won the lottery, he quit his night job.

Some dependent clauses are introduced by dependent words called **subordinating conjunctions**.

FRAGMENT   Although Marisol had always dreamed of visiting California.

This fragment includes a subject (*Marisol*) and a complete verb (*had dreamed*), but it is not a sentence; it is a dependent clause introduced by the subordinating conjunction *although*.

To correct this kind of fragment, attach it to an **independent clause** (a simple sentence) to complete the idea. (You can often find the independent clause you need right before or right after the fragment.)

SENTENCE   Although Marisol had always dreamed of visiting California, she did not have enough money for the trip until last year.

Subordinating Conjunctions

after	even though	since	whenever
although	if	so that	where
as	if only	than	whereas
as if	in order that	that	wherever
as though	now that	though	whether
because	once	unless	while
before	provided that	until	
even if	rather than	when	

For information on how to use subordinating conjunctions, see 20b.

FYI

Correcting Dependent-Clause Fragments

The simplest way to correct a dependent-clause fragment is to cross out the dependent word that makes the idea incomplete.

~~Although~~ Marisol had always dreamed of visiting California.

However, when you delete the dependent word, readers may have trouble seeing the connection between the new sentence and the one before or after it. A better way to revise is to attach the dependent-clause fragment to an adjacent independent clause, as illustrated in the example sentence at the top of this page.

Some dependent clauses are introduced by dependent words called **relative pronouns**.

FRAGMENT   Novelist Richard Wright, <u>who</u> came to Paris in 1947.

FRAGMENT   A quinceañera, <u>which</u> celebrates a Latina's fifteenth birthday.

FRAGMENT   A key World War II battle <u>that</u> was fought on the Pacific island of Guadalcanal.

Each of the above fragments includes a subject (*Richard Wright*, *quinceañera*, *battle*) and a complete verb (*came, celebrates, was fought*). However, they are not sentences because they do not express complete thoughts. In each case, a relative pronoun creates a dependent clause.

To correct each of these fragments, add the words needed to complete the thought.

SENTENCE Novelist Richard Wright, who came to Paris in 1947, <u>spent the rest of his life there.</u>

SENTENCE A quinceañera, which celebrates a Latina's fifteenth birthday, <u>signifies her entrance into womanhood.</u>

SENTENCE A key World War II battle that was fought on the Pacific island of Guadalcanal <u>took place in 1943.</u>

Relative Pronouns

that	who	whomever
what	whoever	whose
which	whom	

For information on how to use relative pronouns, see 20c.

PRACTICE

25-8 Correct each of the following dependent-clause fragments by attaching it to the sentence before or after it. If the dependent clause comes at the beginning of a sentence, place a comma after it.

Example: Before it became a state. West Virginia was part of Virginia.

<u>Before it became a state, West Virginia was part of Virginia.</u>

1. Because many homeless people are mentally ill. It is hard to find housing for them. _____

_____

2. People do not realize how dangerous raccoons can be. Even though they can be found in many parts of the United States. _____

_____

_____

3. I make plans to be better organized. Whenever a new semester begins.

_____

4. Until something changes. We will just have to accept the situation.

_____

5. Because it is a very controversial issue. My parents and I have agreed not

to discuss it. _____

_____

PRACTICE
25-9

Correct each of these dependent-clause fragments by adding the words needed to complete the idea.

Example: Many minor species of animals, which are rapidly disappearing.

Many minor species of animals, which are rapidly disappearing, need to

be protected.

1. The film that frightened me. _____

_____

2. People who drink and drive. _____

_____

3. Some parents who are very strict with their children. _____

_____

4. The Vietnam War, which many Americans did not support. _____

_____

5. Animals that are used in medical research. _____

_____

PRACTICE

25-10 Each of the following is a fragment. Some fragments are missing a subject, some are phrases incorrectly punctuated as sentences, others do not have a complete verb, and still others are dependent clauses punctuated as sentences. Turn each fragment into a complete sentence, writing the revised sentence on the line below the fragment. Whenever possible, try creating two different revisions.

Example: Part of a healthy diet.

Revised: Many people enjoy fruit as part of a healthy diet.

Revised: Fruit can be enjoyed as part of a healthy diet.

1. To participate in campus activities.

Revised: _____

_____

Revised: _____

_____

2. Apps that help users create a budget.

Revised: _____

_____

Revised: _____

_____

3. On the way to the gym.

Revised: _____

_____

Revised: _____

_____

4. Because many employers want to hire bilingual workers.

Revised: _____

_____

Revised: _____

_____

5. Taking notes on a laptop.

Revised: _____

_____

Revised: _____

_____

6. Tried a new recipe.

Revised: _____

_____

Revised: _____

_____

EDITING PRACTICE: PARAGRAPH

Read the following student paragraph, which includes incomplete sentences. Underline each fragment. Then, correct the fragment by attaching it to a nearby sentence that completes the thought. The first fragment has been underlined and corrected for you.

Student Debt

Debt is a serious concern, ~~That~~ that many students face after graduation. Students have different options for funding their education. Such as savings, scholarships, and grants. One of the most popular options is student loans. More than 40 million people carry debt. From financing their college educations. A difficult job market has made it hard for some to repay their loans. In response to the increasing burden. President Obama introduced the Student Aid Bill of Rights. No one has the solution to this problem yet. But progress is being made. Perhaps one day in the future. Higher education will be affordable. For all students.

EDITING PRACTICE: ESSAY

Read the following student essay, which includes incomplete sentences. Underline each fragment. Then, correct the fragment by attaching it to an adjacent sentence that completes the idea. Be sure to punctuate correctly. The first fragment has been underlined and corrected for you.

A New Face

Have you ever thought about the people whose portraits appear on our paper money? Most of us are so used to seeing George Washington on the one-dollar bill that we hardly even notice him. The same goes for the rest of our paper money, ~~Which~~ , which is dominated by presidents and founding fathers. Several denominations will be updated in the near future. So it is time to consider a change. New bills would let us recognize people who have made a mark on history in different ways. Going beyond the usual choices. One

467

person who deserves to be considered is Jeannette Rankin. The first woman elected to Congress.

First, here is some background. About money. The secretary of the treasury selects the people whose faces appear on our currency. By law, only someone who is deceased may appear. On U.S. money. The portraits on paper money today were adopted long ago. In 1929. Bills are being redesigned now to improve security features. And to include a touch feature that will assist blind people.

Former presidents dominate the money we use today. With two exceptions. The $10 bill features Alexander Hamilton, the first treasury secretary. And the $100 bill features Benjamin Franklin, a signer of the Declaration of Independence. The only woman who has appeared (so far) on U.S. paper currency is Martha Washington. Our first First Lady. Her portrait was featured on silver certificates. In the 1880s. Two other women who appeared on American money were Susan B. Anthony and Sacagawea. But their portraits were on coins.

Jeannette Rankin could be one of the first women to appear on modern paper currency. Rankin was a pioneer for women's rights. And a lifelong peace activist. She served two terms in Congress. In 1917–1919 and again in 1940–1942. In her first term, she helped pass the 19th Amendment. Giving women the right to vote. She also argued for a Constitutional amendment banning child labor. And she was the only member of Congress to vote against U.S. participation in both World War I and World War II. After she left politics, she kept working for peace. Leading a march to Capitol Hill at the age of 87 to protest the Vietnam War. She was considering another run for office when she died. at age 92.

In 2020. The United States will celebrate the 100th anniversary of the 19th Amendment. As one of the people who fought hardest for a woman's right to vote. Jeannette Ranking has earned her place in history. The treasury secretary may decide to reveal new currency designs as part of the 100th anniversary celebration. Making it even more appropriate for Jeannette Rankin's face to appear on one of those bills.

The idea of putting a female face on our paper money is not new. And there are many worthy candidates. For example, among the most popular suggestions are Eleanor Roosevelt and Rosa Parks. Jeannette Rankin may not be as well known. But as the first woman in Congress, she paved the way for others. The face of this independent, dedicated American is a fitting choice for the first woman on U.S. paper currency.

COLLABORATIVE ACTIVITY

Working in a group of three or four students, build as many sentences as you can from the fragments listed below. Use your imagination to create as many creative sentences as you can.

Example

FRAGMENT   Knowing he has an incredible memory

SENTENCES   Zack, knowing he has an incredible memory, wonders how he managed to forget everything he learned about chemistry.
Knowing he has an incredible memory, Monty the Magnificent is confident that he can amaze his audience.

FRAGMENTS

1. Wandering in the desert
2. Never worrying about anything
3. Looking for his ideal mate
4. Always using as much ketchup as possible
5. Starting a new job

review checklist

Fragments

✔ A fragment is an incomplete sentence. Every sentence must include a subject and a verb and express a complete thought. (See 25a.)

✔ Every sentence must include a subject. (See 25b.)

✔ Phrases cannot stand alone as sentences. (See 25c.)

✔ Every sentence must include a complete verb. (See 25d.)

✔ Dependent clauses cannot stand alone as sentences. (See 25e.)

26 Subject-Verb Agreement

26a Understanding Subject-Verb Agreement

A sentence's subject (a noun or a pronoun) and its verb must **agree**: singular subjects take singular verbs, and plural subjects take plural verbs.

The <u>museum</u> <u>opens</u> at ten o'clock. (singular noun subject *museum* takes singular verb *opens*)

Both <u>museums</u> <u>open</u> at ten o'clock. (plural noun subject *museums* takes plural verb *open*)

<u>She</u> always <u>watches</u> the eleven o'clock news. (singular pronoun subject *she* takes singular verb *watches*)

<u>They</u> always <u>watch</u> the eleven o'clock news. (plural pronoun subject *they* takes plural verb *watch*)

Subject-Verb Agreement with Regular Verbs

	SINGULAR	PLURAL
First person	I play	Molly and I/we play
Second person	you play	you play
Third person	he/she/it plays	they play
	the man plays	the men play
	Molly plays	Molly and Sam play

PRACTICE

26-1 Underline the correct form of the verb in each of the following sentences. Make sure the verb agrees with its subject.

Example: Sometimes local farmers (<u>grow</u>/grows) unusual vegetables.

(1) Locavores (choose/chooses) to eat locally grown food for a number of reasons. (2) Some locavores (eat/eats) local food simply because they (like/likes) the taste. (3) When food (travel/travels) a long distance, it (lose/loses) some of its flavor and freshness. (4) By eating locally grown food, locavores also (hope/hopes) to decrease the use of fossil fuels. (5) After all, food transportation (require/requires) a lot of energy. (6) In addition, locavores (visit/visits) farmers' markets to support local producers. (7) Local farmers (need/needs) their community's support to survive. (8) In some cases, local food supporters (buy/buys) only food produced within 50 or 100 miles. (9) In colder or drier regions, however, the climate (make/makes) such a strict policy difficult. (10) More often, a locavore diet (contain/contains) a mix of food from local and faraway places.

26b Compound Subjects

The subject of a sentence is not always a single word. It can also be a **compound subject**, made up of two or more subjects joined by *and* or *or*. To avoid subject-verb agreement problems with compound subjects, follow these two rules.

1. When the parts of a compound subject are connected by *and*, the compound subject takes a plural verb.

   $\overset{s}{\underline{\text{France and } \overset{v}{\text{Germany}}}} \underline{\text{share}}$ the euro as an official currency.

2. When the parts of a compound subject are connected by *or*, the verb agrees with the part of the subject that is closer to it.

$$\text{s} \qquad\qquad\qquad\qquad \text{v}$$
<u>The mayor or the council members</u> <u>meet</u> with community groups.

$$\text{s} \qquad\qquad\qquad\qquad \text{v}$$
<u>The council members or the mayor</u> <u>meets</u> with community groups.

PRACTICE

26-2   Underline the correct form of the verb in each of the following sentences. Make sure that the verb agrees with its compound subject.

Example: Every summer, wind and rain (<u>pound</u>/pounds) the small shack on the beach.

1. Trophies and medals (fill/fills) my sister's bedroom.

2. Mashed potatoes and gravy (come/comes) with all our chicken dinners.

3. The instructor or his graduate students (grade/grades) the final exams.

4. A voice coach and a piano instructor (teach/teaches) each of the gifted students.

5. Pollen or cat hair (trigger/triggers) allergies in many people.

 ## 26c *Be, Have,* and *Do*

The verbs *be, have,* and *do* are irregular in the present tense. Memorizing their present tense forms is the only sure way to avoid agreement problems.

Subject-Verb Agreement with *Be*

	SINGULAR	PLURAL
First person	I am	we are
Second person	you are	you are
Third person	he/she/it is	they are
	Tran is	Tran and Ryan are
	the boy is	the boys are

Subject-Verb Agreement with *Have*

	SINGULAR	PLURAL
First person	I have	we have
Second person	you have	you have
Third person	he/she/it has	they have
	Shana has	Shana and Robert have
	the student has	the students have

Subject-Verb Agreement with *Do*

	SINGULAR	PLURAL
First person	I do	we do
Second person	you do	you do
Third person	he/she/it does	they do
	Ken does	Ken and Mia do
	the book does	the books do

PRACTICE

26-3   Fill in the blank with the correct present tense form of the verb *be, have,* or *do.*

Example: Sometimes people ___do___ damage without really meaning to. (do)

(1) Biologists _____ serious worries about the damage that invading species of animals can cause. (have) (2) The English sparrow _____ one example. (be) (3) It _____ a role in the decline in the number of bluebirds. (have) (4) On the Galapagos Islands, cats _____ another example. (be) (5) Introduced by early explorers, they currently _____ much damage to the eggs of the giant tortoises that live on the islands. (do) (6) Scientists today _____ worried now about a new problem. (be) (7) This _____ a situation caused by wildlife agencies that put exotic fish into lakes and streams. (be) (8) They _____ this to please those who enjoy fishing. (do) (9) Although popular with people who fish, this policy _____ major drawbacks. (have) (10) It _____ one drawback in particular: many native species of fish have been pushed close to extinction. (have)

26d Words between Subject and Verb

Remember that a verb must always agree with its subject. Words (for example, a prepositional phrase) that come between the subject and the verb do not affect subject-verb agreement.

CORRECT High <u>levels</u> of mercury <u>occur</u> in some fish.

CORRECT <u>Water</u> in the fuel lines <u>causes</u> an engine to stall.

CORRECT <u>Food</u> between the teeth <u>leads</u> to decay.

An easy way to identify the subject of the sentence is to cross out the words that come between the subject and the verb.

High levels ~~of mercury~~ occur in some fish.

Water ~~in the fuel lines~~ causes an engine to stall.

Food ~~between the teeth~~ leads to decay.

FYI

Words between Subject and Verb

Look out for words such as *in addition to*, *along with*, *together with*, *as well as*, *except*, and *including*. Phrases introduced by these words do not affect subject-verb agreement.

<u>St. Thomas</u>, ~~along with St. Croix and St. John,~~ <u>is</u> part of the United States Virgin Islands.

PRACTICE

26-4 In each of the following sentences, cross out the words that separate the subject and the verb. Then, underline the subject of the sentence once and the verb that agrees with the subject twice.

Example: The <u>messages</u> ~~on the phone~~ (<u>say</u>/says) that Carol is out of town.

1. Each summer, fires from lightning (cause/causes) great damage.

2. Books downloaded onto an eReader usually (cost/costs) less than print books.

3. One out of ten men (gets/get) prostate cancer.

4. The woodstove in the living room (heat/heats) the entire house.

5. Trans fat in a variety of foods (lead/leads) to increased rates of heart disease.

 26e Collective Noun Subjects

Collective nouns are words (such as *family* and *audience*) that name a group of people or things but are singular. Because they are singular, they take singular verbs.

The <u>team</u> <u>practices</u> five days a week in the gym.
$\overset{s}{}$ $\overset{v}{}$

> ### Frequently Used Collective Nouns
>
> | | | | |
> |---|---|---|---|
> | army | club | family | jury |
> | association | committee | gang | mob |
> | band | company | government | team |
> | class | corporation | group | union |

PRACTICE

26-5 Fill in the blank with the correct present tense form of the verb.

Example: Our government _____is_____ democratically elected by the people. (be)

1. The Caribbean Culture Club _____ on the first Thursday of every month. (meet)

2. The company no longer _____ health insurance for part-time employees. (provide)

3. The basketball team _____ competing in the division finals next week. (be)

4. After two days, the jury _____ been unable to reach a verdict. (have)

5. The union _____ guaranteed raises for its members. (want)

26f Indefinite Pronoun Subjects

Indefinite pronouns—*anybody*, *everyone*, and so on—do not refer to a particular person, place, or idea.

Most indefinite pronouns are singular and take singular verbs.

>   s   v
> No one likes getting up early.

>   s   v
> Everyone likes to sleep late.

>   s   v
> Somebody likes beets.

Singular Indefinite Pronouns			
another	either	neither	somebody
anybody	everybody	nobody	someone
anyone	everyone	no one	something
anything	everything	nothing	
each	much	one	

A few indefinite pronouns (*both*, *many*, *several*, *few*, *others*) are plural and take plural verbs.

>   s   v
> Many were left homeless by the flood.

FYI

Indefinite Pronouns as Subjects

If a prepositional phrase comes between the indefinite pronoun and the verb, cross out the prepositional phrase to help you identify the sentence's subject.

>   s   v
> Each of the boys has a bike.

>   s   v
> Many of the boys have bikes.

PRACTICE

26-6 Underline the correct verb in each sentence.

Example: As my friends and I know, anything (<u>helps</u>/help) when it comes to paying for college.

1. One of my friends (has/have) an academic scholarship.

2. Everybody (says/say) that work-study jobs are best.

3. Many of the most interesting work-study jobs (is/are) located on campus.

4. Some of the work-study jobs (tends/tend) to be better than a regular job.

5. Several of the jobs (is/are) full-time.

 ## 26g Verbs before Subjects

A verb always agrees with its subject—even if the verb comes *before* the subject. In questions, for example, word order is reversed, with the verb coming before the subject or with the subject coming between two parts of the verb.

>   V   S
> Where is the bank?
>
> V   S   V
> Are you going to the party?

If you have trouble identifying the subject of a question, answer the question with a statement. (In the statement, the subject will come before the verb.)

>   V   S   S   V
> Where is the bank? The bank is on Walnut Street.

FYI

There Is and *There Are*

When a sentence begins with *there is* or *there are*, the word *there* is not the subject of the sentence. The subject comes after the form of the verb *be*.

>   V   S
> There is one chief justice on the Supreme Court.
>
>   V   S
> There are nine justices on the Supreme Court.

PRACTICE

26-7   Underline the subject of each sentence, and circle the correct form of the verb.

Example: Who (is/are) the baseball <u>player</u> who broke Hank Aaron's home-run record?

1. Where (do/does) snakes go in the winter?

2. Why (do/does) people who cannot afford them buy lottery tickets?

3. (Is/Are) there any states that do not follow Daylight Savings Time?

4. How (do/does) an immigrant become a citizen?

5. There (is/are) three branches of government in the United States.

EDITING PRACTICE: PARAGRAPH

Read the following student paragraph, which includes errors in subject-verb agreement. Decide whether each of the underlined verbs agrees with its subject. If it does not, cross out the verb, and write in the correct form. If it does, write *C* above the verb. The first sentence has been done for you.

Conflict Diamonds

Today, many people <u>know</u> [*C*] about conflict diamonds, and most <u>wants</u> [*want*] this violent trade to end. These illegal diamonds <u>comes</u> from countries where there <u>are</u> civil war. Most often, the origin of these stones <u>is</u> an unstable central or West African nation. Rebel groups in these countries <u>mines</u> the diamonds and <u>sells</u> them to raise money for weapons. In the process, local people, who <u>does</u> not benefit from the sale of the diamonds, often <u>gets</u> hurt or killed. How <u>does</u> a person who wants to buy a diamond avoid buying a conflict diamond? Once a diamond <u>reach</u> a store, neither a customer nor a gem expert <u>have</u> the ability to determine its history just by looking at it. However, a consumer can ask for proof that the diamond <u>is</u> "conflict-free." Each of the diamonds in a store <u>are</u> supposed to have an official certificate to prove that it <u>is</u> legal.

EDITING PRACTICE: ESSAY

Read the following student essay, which includes errors in subject-verb agreement. Decide whether each of the underlined verbs agrees with its subject. If it does not, cross out the verb, and write in the correct form. If it does, write *C* above the verb. The first sentence has been done for you.

Making Your Own Dream Team

Every August, Sean and a group of friends <u>gathers</u> [*gather*] at his place for a very important meeting. There <u>is</u> chili on the stove and there <u>is</u> sodas in the cooler. The centerpiece on Sean's kitchen table <u>is</u> not a bowl of fruit or a vase of flowers. It <u>is</u> a large, golden trophy bearing the words "League Champion." As people arrive, everyone <u>smile</u> at the trophy and some even <u>shake</u> Sean's hand. What <u>are</u> the meeting about? Sean's fantasy football league <u>is</u> kicking off a new season.

Like sports fans everywhere, Sean and his friends <u>has</u> discovered the fun of fantasy sports leagues. (You <u>do</u> not have to be a sports fan to enjoy fantasy sports leagues, but it <u>help</u>.) Fantasy sports leagues have an online element, but friends often <u>joins</u> a league together. Game days <u>is</u> even more interesting when you and your friends <u>has</u> your own dream teams.

There <u>is</u> different stories about how fantasy sports leagues began, but most <u>say</u> golf was the first fantasy sport. Today, there <u>are</u> a fantasy league for every major sport, including football, baseball, basketball, hockey, tennis, and cricket. People can be in more than one fantasy league for more than one sport. For example, Sean <u>is</u> in two different football leagues with his friends as well as a tennis league with his grandparents.

A fantasy league <u>imitate</u> the real thing. In professional sports, owners and managers <u>create</u> a team with the best players they can get. The same happens in fantasy sports leagues. You <u>chooses</u> real players from a professional sport. You <u>researches</u> the players and <u>puts</u> together a team with a player for each position, depending on the sport. Each fantasy player <u>is</u> a real person from a real team, but the fantasy team <u>have</u> a mix of players from different teams. For instance, Sean's fantasy football team <u>have</u> a quarterback from the Atlanta Falcons and a kicker from the Kansas City Chiefs. Your fantasy baseball team might have a pitcher from the Houston Astros and a first baseman from the Detroit Tigers.

The goal <u>is</u> to choose the best performing athletes during a certain season. Participants <u>uses</u> their own knowledge of their favorite sports. In addition, they <u>looks</u> at actual statistics for players, such as speed, agility, and points scored. For a fantasy team draft, participants <u>combine</u> their own knowledge with players' statistics. Each participant <u>choose</u> a line-up and <u>draft</u> (or <u>pick</u>) those players. Everyone <u>take</u> turns selecting players, so it is important to be prepared. You may not get your first choice, or even your third.

Once the season <u>start</u>, fantasy teams <u>compete</u> based on how players <u>perform</u> in actual games. Each real-life player <u>gain</u> or <u>lose</u> points for a fantasy team. A fantasy team might get 20 points for a good performance by one player but zero points for a bad performance by another player. Each team's total <u>determine</u> who wins the league that week. If you are the manager of the fantasy team, you <u>makes</u> strategic decisions based on a player's performance. You <u>trade</u> players, <u>cut</u> players from the team, and <u>sign</u> new players. Most fantasy leagues <u>requires</u> you to choose new players every season. Other leagues <u>lets</u> you keep some or all of your players for the next season.

For most people in fantasy sports leagues, the biggest thrill <u>come</u> at the end of the season. Anyone can have a good week along the way, but only one person <u>get</u> the trophy. Everyone else <u>wait</u> until next year.

COLLABORATIVE ACTIVITY

Working in a group of four students, list ten nouns (five singular and five plural)—people, places, or things—along the left-hand side of a sheet of paper. Beside each noun, write the present tense form of a verb that could logically be used with the noun. Then, expand each noun-and-verb combination you listed into a complete sentence. Next, write a sentence that could logically follow each of these sentences, using a pronoun as the subject of the new sentence. Make sure the pronoun you choose refers to the noun in the previous sentence, as in this example: *Max watches three movies a week. <u>He</u> is addicted to films.* Check to be certain the subjects in your sentences agree with the verbs.

review checklist

Subject-Verb Agreement

✔ Singular subjects (nouns and pronouns) take singular verbs, and plural subjects take plural verbs. (See 26a.)

✔ Special rules govern subject-verb agreement with compound subjects. (See 26b.)

✔ The irregular verbs *be*, *have*, and *do* often present problems with subject-verb agreement in the present tense. (See 26c.)

✔ Words that come between the subject and the verb do not affect subject-verb agreement. (See 26d.)

✔ Collective nouns are singular and take singular verbs. (See 26e.)

✔ Most indefinite pronouns, such as *no one* and *everyone*, are singular and take a singular verb when they serve as the subject of a sentence. A few are plural and take plural verbs. (See 26f.)

✔ A sentence's subject and verb must always agree, even if the verb comes before the subject. (See 26g.)

27 Illogical Shifts

A **shift** occurs whenever a writer changes **tense**, **person**, or **voice**. As you write and revise, be sure that any shifts you make are **logical**—that is, that they occur for a reason.

 ## 27a Shifts in Tense

Tense is the form a verb takes to show when an action takes place or when a situation occurs. Some shifts in tense are necessary—for example, to indicate a change from past time to present time.

> LOGICAL SHIFT   When they first <u>came</u> out, cell phones <u>were</u> large and bulky, but now they <u>are</u> small and compact.

An **illogical shift in tense** occurs when a writer shifts from one tense to another for no apparent reason.

> ILLOGICAL SHIFT IN TENSE   The dog <u>walked</u> to the fireplace. Then, he <u>circles</u> twice and <u>lies</u> down in front of the fire. (shift from past tense to present tense)

> REVISED   The dog <u>walked</u> to the fireplace. Then, he <u>circled</u> twice and <u>lay</u> down in front of the fire. (consistent use of past tense)

> REVISED   The dog <u>walks</u> to the fireplace. Then, he <u>circles</u> twice and <u>lies</u> down in front of the fire. (consistent use of present tense)

PRACTICE

27-1   Edit the sentences in the following paragraph to correct illogical shifts in tense. If a sentence is correct, write *C* in the blank.

Example: The 100th Battalion of the 442nd Infantry is the only remaining United States Army Reserve ground combat unit that fought in World War II.   _____*C*_____

483

(1) During World War II, the 100th Battalion of the 442nd Combat Infantry Regiment was made up of young Japanese Americans who are eager to serve in the U.S. Army. _____ (2) At the start of World War II, 120,000 Japanese Americans were sent to relocation camps because the government feared that they might be disloyal to the United States. _____ (3) However, in 1943, the United States needed more soldiers, so it sends recruiters to the camps to ask for volunteers.

_____ (4) The Japanese American volunteers are organized into the 442nd Combat Infantry Regiment. _____ (5) The soldiers of the 442nd Infantry fought in some of the bloodiest battles of the war, including the invasion of Italy at Anzio and a battle in Bruyeres, France, where they capture over two hundred enemy soldiers. _____ (6) When other U.S. troops are cut off by the enemy, the 442nd Infantry soldiers were sent to rescue them. _____ (7) The Japanese American soldiers suffered the highest casualty rate of any U.S. unit and receive over eighteen thousand individual decorations. _____

 ## 27b Shifts in Person

Person is the form a pronoun takes to show who is speaking, spoken about, or spoken to.

Person

	SINGULAR	PLURAL
First person	I	we
Second person	you	you
Third person	he, she, it	they

An **illogical shift in person** occurs when a writer shifts from one person to another for no apparent reason.

ILLOGICAL SHIFT IN PERSON	The <u>hikers</u> were told that <u>you</u> had to stay on the trail. (shift from third person to second person)
REVISED	The <u>hikers</u> were told that <u>they</u> had to stay on the trail. (consistent use of third person)
ILLOGICAL SHIFT IN PERSON	<u>Anyone</u> can learn to cook if <u>you</u> practice. (shift from third person to second person)
REVISED	<u>You</u> can learn to cook if <u>you</u> practice. (consistent use of second person)
REVISED	<u>Anyone</u> can learn to cook if <u>he or she</u> practices. (consistent use of third person)

PRACTICE

27-2 The sentences in the following paragraph contain illogical shifts in person. Edit each sentence so that it uses pronouns consistently. Be sure to change any verbs that do not agree with the new subjects.

Example: Before a person finds a job in the fashion industry, ~~you have~~ *he or she has* to have some experience.

(1) Young people who want careers in the fashion industry do not always realize how hard you will have to work. (2) They think that working in the world of fashion will be glamorous and that you will make a lot of money. (3) In reality, no matter how talented you are, a recent college graduate entering the industry is paid only about $22,000 a year. (4) The manufacturers who employ new graduates expect you to work at least three years at this salary before you are promoted. (5) A young designer may get a big raise if you are very talented, but this is unusual. (6) New employees have to pay their dues, and you soon realize that most of your duties are boring. (7) An employee may land a job as an assistant designer but then find that you have to color in designs that have already been drawn.

(8) Other beginners discover that you spend most of your time typing up orders. (9) If a person is serious about working in the fashion industry, you have to be realistic. (10) For most newcomers to the industry, the ability to do what you are told to do is more important than your talent.

27c Shifts in Voice

Voice is the form a verb takes to indicate whether the subject is acting or is acted upon. When the subject is acting, the sentence is in the **active voice**. When the subject is acted upon, the sentence is in the **passive voice**.

> ACTIVE VOICE   Nat Turner <u>organized</u> a slave rebellion in August 1831. (Subject *Nat Turner* is acting.)

> PASSIVE VOICE   A slave <u>rebellion</u> <u>was organized</u> by Nat Turner in 1831. (Subject *rebellion* is acted upon.)

An **illogical shift in voice** occurs when a writer shifts from active to passive voice or from passive to active voice for no apparent reason.

> ILLOGICAL SHIFT IN VOICE   J. D. Salinger <u>wrote</u> *The Catcher in the Rye*, and *Frannyand Zooey* <u>was also written</u> by him. (active to passive)

> REVISED   J. D. Salinger <u>wrote</u> *The Catcher in the Rye*, and he also <u>wrote</u> *Franny and Zooey*. (consistent use of active voice)

> ILLOGICAL SHIFT IN VOICE   Radium <u>was discovered</u> by Marie Curie in 1910, and she <u>won</u> a Nobel Prize in chemistry in 1911. (passive to active)

> REVISED   Marie Curie <u>discovered</u> radium in 1910, and she <u>won</u> a Nobel Prize in chemistry in 1911. (consistent use of active voice)

FYI

Correcting Illogical Shifts in Voice

You should usually use the active voice in your college writing because it is stronger and more direct than the passive voice.

To change a sentence from the passive to the active voice, determine who or what is acting, and make this noun the subject of a new active voice sentence.

PASSIVE VOICE Gunpowder was invented by the Chinese in the ninth century. (*The Chinese* are acting.)

ACTIVE VOICE The Chinese invented gunpowder in the ninth century.

PRACTICE

27-3 The following sentences contain illogical shifts in voice. Revise each sentence by changing the underlined passive voice verb to the active voice.

Example:

Two teachers believed they could help struggling students in New York City schools, so "Chess in the Schools" was founded by them.

Two teachers believed they could help struggling students in New York City schools, so they founded "Chess in the Schools."

1. Chess develops critical-thinking skills, and self-discipline and self-esteem are developed by players, too.

   _____

   _____

2. Because players face complicated chess problems, good problem-solving skills are developed by them.

   _____

   _____

3. Student chess players improve their concentration, and reading and math skills <u>can be improved</u> through this better concentration.

_____

_____

4. Chess teaches students how to lose as well as win, and that ability <u>will be needed</u> by students throughout their lives.

_____

_____

5. "Chess in the Schools" also helps keep students out of trouble because of the conflict-resolution skills <u>developed</u> by them.

_____

_____

EDITING PRACTICE: PARAGRAPH

Read the following student paragraph, which includes illogical shifts in tense, person, and voice. Edit the passage to eliminate the unnecessary shifts, making sure subjects and verbs agree. The first error has been corrected for you.

The Origin of Baseball Cards

The first baseball cards appeared in the late 1800s. These cardboard pictures ~~are~~ *were* inserted in packs of cigarettes. Some people collected the cards, and the cigarette companies use the cards to encourage people to buy their products. By the early twentieth century, it was found by candy makers that one could use baseball cards to sell candy to children, so they developed new marketing plans. For example, each Cracker Jack box contains a baseball card. In 1933, gum manufacturers packaged bubble gum with baseball cards to make "bubble gum cards." Children could trade these cards. Sometimes children would put cards in the spokes of their bike wheels. The cards made noise when the wheels turns. Eventually, the bubble gum is dropped by the card manufacturers, and people just bought the cards. Still, collecting baseball cards was seen as a hobby for children until the 1970s, when dealers began to sell their rarest cards at high prices. Today, baseball-card collectors were mainly adults who are interested in investment, not baseball. For example, in 2007, a rare Honus Wagner baseball card sells for a record $2.8 million.

EDITING PRACTICE: ESSAY

Read the following essay, which includes illogical shifts in tense, person, and voice. Edit the passage to eliminate the illogical shifts, making sure subjects and verbs agree. The first sentence has been edited for you.

A Different Kind of Vacation

During our upcoming winter break, my sister and I ~~were~~ ^are^ going to Belize to help build a school. Like many people, we want to travel and see new places, but we did not want to be tourists who only see what is in a guidebook. We also want to help people who are less fortunate than we were. Volunteering gives us the opportunity to combine travel with community service and to get to know a different culture at the same time.

These days, many people are using his or her vacation time to do volunteer work. Lots of charitable organizations offer short-term projects during school or holiday breaks. For most projects, no experience was necessary. All people need is his or her interest in other people and a desire to help.

For example, last year my aunt goes to Tanzania to work in a health clinic. She loved her experience volunteering in a poor rural community where you help local doctors. She also loved the host family who shared their modest house with her. Before she left Tanzania, she and some of the other volunteers climb Mount Kilimanjaro. She said it was the best vacation she had ever had.

Although many volunteer vacations focus on improving schools or health care, a wide range of projects was available. Everyone can find work that suits their interests. For instance, people can volunteer to help preserve the environment, or you can work to protect women's rights. Countries all over the world welcome volunteers because help is needed by a lot of people.

My sister and I decided to help with the school in Belize because we believe a clean and safe place to learn is deserved by everyone. We are also eager to do some construction, get to know the local people, and enjoy the warm weather. If we have enough time, we hoped to visit some Mayan ruins as well. All in all, we are looking forward to a rewarding and unforgettable experience.

COLLABORATIVE ACTIVITY

Working in a group of three or four students, make up a test with five sentences containing illogical shifts in tense, person, and voice. Exchange tests with another group in the class. After you have taken their test, compare your answers with theirs.

review checklist

Illogical Shifts

✔ An illogical shift in tense occurs when a writer shifts from one tense to another for no apparent reason. (See 27a.)

✔ An illogical shift in person occurs when a writer shifts from one person to another for no apparent reason. (See 27b.)

✔ An illogical shift in voice occurs when a writer shifts from active to passive voice or from passive to active voice for no apparent reason. (See 27c.)

28 Misplaced and Dangling Modifiers

A **modifier** is a word or word group that identifies or describes another word in a sentence. Many word groups that act as modifiers are introduced by *-ing* (present participle) or *-ed* (past participle) modifiers.

Working in his garage, Steve Jobs invented the personal computer.

Rejected by Hamlet, Ophelia goes mad and drowns herself.

Used correctly, *-ing* and *-ed* modifiers provide useful information. Used incorrectly, however, these types of modifiers can be very confusing.

The two most common problems with modification are *misplaced modifiers* and *dangling modifiers*.

28a Correcting Misplaced Modifiers

A **misplaced modifier** appears to modify the wrong word because it is placed incorrectly in the sentence. To avoid confusion, move the modifier so it is as close as possible to the word it is supposed to modify (usually directly before or after it).

INCORRECT Dressed in a raincoat and boots, I thought my son was prepared for the storm. (Who was dressed in a raincoat and boots?)

CORRECT I thought my son, dressed in a raincoat and boots, was prepared for the storm.

INCORRECT Holden Caulfield went to New York wearing his hunting hat backwards. (Was New York wearing the hunting hat?)

CORRECT Wearing his hunting hat backwards, Holden Caulfield went to New York.

PRACTICE

28-1 Underline the modifier in each of the following sentences. Then, draw an arrow to the word it modifies.

Example: <u>Helping people worldwide</u>, Doctors Without Borders is a group of volunteer medical professionals.

1. Suffering from famine and other disasters, some people are unable to help themselves.

2. Feeding and healing them, Doctors Without Borders improves their lives.

3. Responding to a recent earthquake, doctors arrived within three days to help with the relief effort.

4. Setting up refugee camps in Thailand, the group quickly helped its first survivors.

5. Some doctors, chartering a ship called *The Island of Light*, once provided medical aid to people escaping Vietnam by boat.

PRACTICE

28-2 Rewrite the following sentences, which contain misplaced modifiers, so that each modifier clearly refers to the word it logically modifies.

Example: Mark ate a pizza standing in front of the refrigerator.
Standing in front of the refrigerator, Mark ate a pizza.
_____

1. Running across my bathroom ceiling, I saw two large, hairy bugs.

_____

_____

2. Lori looked at the man sitting in the chair with red hair.

_____

_____

3. The deer was hit by a car running across the street.

_____

_____

4. Dressed in a beautiful wedding gown, the groom watched the bride walk down the aisle.

_____

_____

5. The exterminator sprayed the insect wearing a mask.

_____

_____

 ## 28b Correcting Dangling Modifiers

A **dangling modifier** "dangles" because the word it modifies does not appear in the sentence. Often, a dangling modifier comes at the beginning of a sentence and appears to modify the noun or pronoun that follows it.

Using my computer, the report was finished in two days.

In the sentence above, the modifier *Using my computer* seems to be modifying *the report*. But this makes no sense. (How can the report use a computer?) The word the modifier should logically refer to is missing.

Using my computer, I finished the report in two days.

To correct a dangling modifier, supply a word to which the modifier can logically refer.

INCORRECT Moving the microscope's mirror, the light can be directed onto the slide. (Can the light move the mirror?)

CORRECT Moving the microscope's mirror, you can direct the light onto the slide.

INCORRECT Ruling as emperor for many years, Charlemagne's kingdom prospered. (Was Charlemagne's kingdom ruling?)

CORRECT Ruling as emperor for many years, Charlemagne brought prosperity to his kingdom.

| INCORRECT | Paid in advance, the furniture was delivered. (Was the furniture paid in advance?) |
| CORRECT | Paid in advance, the movers delivered the furniture. |

PRACTICE

28-3 Each of the following sentences contains a dangling modifier. To correct each sentence, add a word to which the modifier can logically refer.

Example: Waiting inside, my bus passed by.

Waiting inside, I missed my bus.

1. Pushing on the brakes, my car would not stop for the red light.

_____

_____

2. Working overtime, his salary almost doubled.

_____

_____

3. Angered by the noise, the concert was called off.

_____

_____

4. Using the correct formula, the problem was easily solved.

_____

_____

5. Tired and hungry, the assignment was finished by midnight.

_____

_____

PRACTICE

28-4   Complete the following sentences, making sure to include a word to which each modifier can logically refer.

Example: Dancing with the man of her dreams, *she decided it was time to wake up.*

1. Blocked by the clouds, _____
_____.

2. Applying for financial aid, _____
_____.

3. Settled into his recliner chair, _____
_____.

4. Fearing that they might catch a cold, _____
_____.

5. Hearing strange noises through the wall, _____
_____.

EDITING PRACTICE: PARAGRAPH

Read the following student paragraph, which includes modification errors. Rewrite sentences where necessary to correct misplaced and dangling modifiers. In some cases, you may have to supply a word to which the modifier can logically refer. The first incorrect sentence has been corrected for you.

Beyond Mickey Mouse

For more than twenty years, Pixar computer animation studios have produced movies. Sketched by hand before Pixar, ~~artists provided thousands of pictures~~ *thousands of pictures were provided by artists* for traditional animated films. In 2006, Disney bought Pixar for $7.4 billion. Now, the company that pioneered traditional animation eighty years ago owns Pixar. Led by Steve Jobs, animation was revolutionized by Pixar. Working with computers, special software was used by animators to create movement. Invented by Pixar, animators were able to achieve startling lifelike effects. The first commercially successful Pixar film was *Toy Story*. Completed in 1995, the use of computer animation made *Toy Story* a success. Fourteen more films were created by Pixar since the debut of *Toy Story*. The most recent film, *Inside Out,* is about a young girl named Riley. With the help of her personified emotions, Riley navigates life in a new town. This typical Pixar emotional development plot resonates with audiences. Bringing in more than $9 billion in worldwide box office sales, audiences make Pixar movies very successful.

EDITING PRACTICE: ESSAY

Read the following student essay, which includes modification errors. Rewrite sentences to correct dangling and misplaced modifiers. In some cases, you will have to supply a word to which the modifier can logically refer. The first sentence has been corrected for you.

Eating as a Sport

often

After eating a big meal, ~~the food often makes~~ you feel stuffed. Imagine
how someone participating in competitive eating feels. To win, you have
to eat more food faster than anyone else. Training for days, many different
kinds of food are eaten in these contests. For example, contestants eat
chicken wings, pizza, ribs, hot dogs, and even matzo balls. Training for
events, competitive eating is considered a sport by participants. By winning,
a good living can be made by a competitive eater. Considered dangerous
by some, competitive eaters and their fans nevertheless continue to
grow.

The way it works is that each competitor eats the same weight or
portion of food. Giving the signal, the competitors begin eating. Breaking
the food in pieces or just eating the food whole, any technique can be
used. The competitors, soaked in water, can make the food softer. They can
even eat hot dogs separately from their buns. Good competitors are usually
not overweight. In fact, some are quite thin. Keeping the stomach from
expanding, competitors are hurt by extra fat. By drinking large amounts of
water, their stomachs stretch and increase their chances of winning. This is
one technique many competitors use when they train.

The International Federation of Competitive Eating watches over
the contests to make sure they are fair and safe. Providing the dates and
locations, contests are listed on its website. Often, contests are held at
state fairs. Also listing participants, prizes, and rankings of winners, new
participants are invited. Before entering the contests, their eating specialty
and personal profile must be indicated by new participants. Competitors
must also be at least eighteen years old.

Many competitive eaters participate in lots of contests. For example,
weighing only 100 pounds, 8.1 pounds of sausage was eaten in only

10 minutes by Sonya Thomas. At another contest, she ate 46 crab cakes in 10 minutes. Held in the United States, some participants come from other countries. For instance, Takeru Kobayashi, who comes from Japan, once ate 18 pounds of cow brains in 15 minutes. Winners usually get cash prizes. The largest prize, $20,000, was awarded in a hot dog–eating contest at Coney Island, which was televised by ESPN. By eating 66 hot dogs and their buns in 12 minutes, the contest was won by Joey Chestnut, a professional speed eater. Almost 50,000 people attended the contest in person, and millions watched on television.

There is some concern about competitive eating. By stretching the stomach, a person's health may be affected. There is also concern about obesity and overeating. Worried about choking, events should have doctors present some people argue. Still, many people like to watch these contests, and they seem to be getting more popular each year.

COLLABORATIVE ACTIVITY

Working in a group of five or six students, make a list of five modifiers that end in *-ing* and five modifiers that end in *-ed*. Exchange your list with another group, and complete each other's sentences.

Examples

Typing as fast as he could, John could not wait to finish his screenplay.

Frightened by a snake, the horse ran away.

review checklist

> **Misplaced and Dangling Modifiers**
>
> ✔ Correct a misplaced modifier by placing the modifier as close as possible to the word it modifies. (See 28a.)
>
> ✔ Correct a dangling modifier by supplying a word to which the modifier can logically refer. (See 28b.)

29 Verbs: Past Tense

Tense is the form a verb takes to show when an action or situation takes place. The **past tense** indicates that an action occurred in the past.

 ## 29a Regular Verbs

Regular verbs form the past tense by adding either *-ed* or *-d* to the **base form** of the verb (the present tense form of the verb that is used with *I*).

We regist<u>ed</u> for classes yesterday.

Walt Disney produce<u>d</u> short cartoons in 1928.

Regular verbs that end in *-y* form the past tense by changing the *y* to *i* and adding *-ed*.

| tr<u>y</u> | tried |
| app<u>ly</u> | appl<u>ied</u> |

PRACTICE

29-1 Change the regular verbs below to the past tense.

visited
Example: Every year, my mother ~~visits~~ her family in Bombay.

(1) My mother always returns from India with henna designs on her hands and feet. (2) In India, henna artists create these patterns. (3) Henna originates in a plant found in the Middle East, India, Indonesia, and northern Africa. (4) Many women in these areas use henna to color their hands, nails, and parts of their feet. (5) Men dye their beards as well as the manes and hooves of their horses. (6) They also color animal skins with henna. (7) In India, my mother always celebrates the end of the Ramadan religious fast by going to a "henna party." (8) A professional henna artist attends the

party to apply new henna decorations to the women. (9) After a few weeks, the henna designs wash off. (10) In the United States, my mother's henna designs attract the attention of many people.

 ## 29b Irregular Verbs

Unlike regular verbs, whose past tense forms end in -*ed* or -*d*, **irregular verbs** have irregular forms in the past tense. In fact, their past tense forms may look very different from their present tense forms.

The following chart lists the base form and past tense form of many of the most commonly used irregular verbs. (The past tense of other irregular verbs can be found in a dictionary.)

Irregular Verbs in the Past Tense

BASE FORM	PAST	BASE FORM	PAST
awake	awoke	feel	felt
be	was, were	fight	fought
beat	beat	find	found
become	became	fly	flew
begin	began	forgive	forgave
bet	bet	freeze	froze
bite	bit	get	got
blow	blew	give	gave
break	broke	go (goes)	went
bring	brought	grow	grew
build	built	have	had
buy	bought	hear	heard
catch	caught	hide	hid
choose	chose	hold	held
come	came	hurt	hurt
cost	cost	keep	kept
cut	cut	know	knew
dive	dove (dived)	lay (to place)	laid
do	did	lead	led
draw	drew	learn	learnt (learned)
drink	drank	leave	left
drive	drove	let	let
eat	ate	lie (to recline)	lay
fall	fell	light	lit
feed	fed	lose	lost

(Continued)

BASE FORM	PAST	BASE FORM	PAST
make	made	speak	spoke
meet	met	spend	spent
pay	paid	spring	sprang
quit	quit	stand	stood
read	read	steal	stole
ride	rode	stick	stuck
ring	rang	sting	stung
rise	rose	swear	swore
run	ran	swim	swam
say	said	take	took
see	saw	teach	taught
sell	sold	tear	tore
send	sent	tell	told
set	set	think	thought
shake	shook	throw	threw
shine	shone	understand	understood
	(shined)	wake	woke
sing	sang	wear	wore
sit	sat	win	won
sleep	slept	write	wrote

PRACTICE

29-2   Fill in the correct past tense form of each irregular verb in parentheses, using the Irregular Verbs chart to help you. If you cannot find a particular verb on the chart, look it up in a dictionary.

Example: Security on Campus _____*was*_____ (be) founded in 1987.

(1) After their daughter, Jeanne, _____ (be) murdered at Lehigh University, Connie and Howard Clery _____ (begin) a movement to improve safety on college campuses. (2) Jeanne _____ (think) she was safe. (3) However, her attacker _____ (get) into her dorm room through three different doors that had all been left unlocked. (4) Shockingly, Jeanne's attacker actually _____ (go) to Lehigh. (5) Shattered by the loss of their daughter, her parents _____ (do) not withdraw into their pain. (6) Instead, they _____ (feel) that the best memorial to their daughter would be the prevention of similar crimes, so they founded Security on

Campus, Inc. (7) SOC _____ (make) legal information available to victims of crimes on college campuses. (8) Because of the efforts of SOC, Congress _____ (write) a law that forced colleges to disclose their crime statistics.

 ## 29c Problem Verbs: *Be*

The irregular verb *be* causes problems because it has two different past tense forms—*was* for singular subjects and *were* for second-person singular subjects as well as for plural subjects. (All other English verbs have just one past tense form.)

> Carlo <u>was</u> interested in becoming a city planner. (singular)

> They <u>were</u> happy to help out at the school. (plural)

Past Tense Forms of the Verb *Be*

	SINGULAR	PLURAL
First person	I <u>was</u> tired.	We <u>were</u> tired.
Second person	You <u>were</u> tired.	You <u>were</u> tired.
Third person	He <u>was</u> tired.	
	She <u>was</u> tired.	They <u>were</u> tired.
	It <u>was</u> tired.	
	The man <u>was</u> tired.	Frank and Billy <u>were</u> tired.

PRACTICE

29-3 Edit the following passage for errors in the use of the verb *be*. Cross out any underlined verbs that are incorrect, and write the correct forms above them. If a verb form is correct, label it *C*.

Example: Before 1990, there <u>~~was~~</u> *were* no female Hispanic astronauts in the NASA program.

(1) Although there had never been a Hispanic woman astronaut, it <u>was</u> impossible for NASA to ignore Ellen Ochoa's long career in physics and engineering. (2) When Ochoa <u>was</u> young, her main interests <u>was</u> music,

math, and physics. (3) After getting a degree in physics at San Diego State University, she <u>were</u> considering a career in music or business. (4) However, she <u>was</u> convinced by her mother to continue her education. (5) In 1983, Ochoa <u>was</u> studying for a doctorate in electrical engineering at Stanford University when the first female astronaut, Sally Ride, flew on the space shuttle. (6) Ochoa <u>were</u> inspired by Sally Ride to become an astronaut. (7) In 1993, Ochoa <u>was</u> the first Hispanic woman to fly into space. (8) After retiring as an astronaut, she <u>were</u> appointed Deputy Director of the Johnson Space Center, and in 2013 became its director.

 ## 29d   Problem Verbs: *Can/Could* and *Will/Would*

The helping verbs *can/could* and *will/would* present problems because their past tense forms are sometimes confused with their present tense forms.

Can/Could

Can, a present tense verb, means "is able to" or "are able to."

> First-year students <u>can</u> apply for financial aid.

Could, the past tense of *can*, means "was able to" or "were able to."

> Escape artist Harry Houdini claimed that he <u>could</u> escape from any prison.

Will/Would

Will, a present tense verb, talks about the future from a point in the present.

> A solar eclipse <u>will</u> occur in ten months.

Would, the past tense of *will*, talks about the future from a point in the past.

> I told him yesterday that I <u>would</u> think about it.

Would is also used to express a possibility or wish.

If we stuck to our budget, we <u>would</u> be better off.

Laurie <u>would</u> like a new stuffed animal.

FYI

Will and *Would*

Note that *will* is used with *can* and that *would* is used with *could*.

I <u>will</u> feed the cats if I <u>can</u> find their food.

I <u>would</u> feed the cats if I <u>could</u> find their food.

PRACTICE

29-4 Circle the appropriate helping verb from the choices in parentheses.

Example: Anyone who doesn't want to throw things away (can, could) rent a self-storage unit.

(1) Today's self-storage units (can, could) make life easier for people with limited space and many belongings. (2) In the past, warehouse storage (will, would) provide a place to store excess items. (3) However, people (will, would) have to hire moving vans and (can, could) hardly ever have access to their stored items. (4) They (will, would) have to sign an expensive long-term contract. (5) Now, however, they (can, could) take advantage of another option, self-storage. (6) With Self-storage, they (can, could) store possessions in a space as small as a closet or as large as a house. (7) People (can, could) easily move their belongings in and out of the storage unit. (8) When they need more space, they (will, would) be able to get it. (9) In face, the managers of self-storage facilities (can, could) suggest how much space owners (will, would) need. (10) The only person who (can, could) get into the self-storage unit is the person who has rented it. (11) If people need a hand truck to move their belongings, they (can, could) usually borrow one. (12) All in all, using self-storage (can, could) solve a lot of problems for people.

CHAPTER REVIEW

EDITING PRACTICE

Read the following student essay, which includes errors in past tense verb forms. Decide whether each of the underlined past tense verbs is correct. If the verb is correct, write *C* above it. If it is not, cross out the verb, and write in the correct past tense form. The first sentence has been corrected for you. (If necessary, consult the list of irregular verbs on pages 501–502.)

Healing

The window seat ~~were~~ ^{was} our favorite place to sit. I piled pillows on the ledge and spended several minutes rearranging them. Then, my friend and I lied on our backs and propped our feet on the wall. We sat with our arms around our legs and thinked about the mysteries of life.

We stared at the people on the street below and wonder who they was and where they was going. We imagined that they can be millionaires, foreign spies, or drug smugglers. We believed that everyone except us leaded wonderful and exciting lives.

I heard a voice call my name. Reluctantly, I standed up, tearing myself away from my imaginary world. My dearest and oldest friend—my teddy bear—and I came back to the real world. I grabbed Teddy and brung him close to my chest. Together, we go into the cold dining room, where twelve other girls sit around a table eating breakfast. None of them looked happy.

In the unit for eating disorders, meals was always tense. Nobody wants to eat, but the nurses watched us until we eated every crumb. I set Teddy on the chair beside me and stared gloomily at the food on our plate. I closed my eyes and taked the first bite. I feeled the calories adding inches of ugly fat. Each swallow were like a nail being ripped from my finger. At last, it was over. I had survived breakfast.

Days passed slowly. Each passing minute <u>was</u> a victory. After a while,
I learned how to eat properly. I learned about other people's problems. I also
learned that people loved me. Eventually, even Teddy stopped feeling sorry for
me. I <u>begun</u> to smile—and laugh. Sometimes I even considered myself happy. My
doctors challenged me—and, surprisingly, I <u>rised</u> to the occasion.

COLLABORATIVE ACTIVITY

Form a group with three other students. What national or world events do
you remember most clearly? Take ten minutes to list news events that you
think have defined the last five years. On your own, write a few paragraphs
in which you discuss the significance of the three or four events that the
members of your group agree were the most important.

review checklist

Verbs: Past Tense

✔ The past tense is the form a verb takes to show that an action
occurred in the past.

✔ Regular verbs form the past tense by adding either -*ed* or -*d* to the
base form of the verb. (See 29a.)

✔ Irregular verbs have irregular forms in the past tense. (See 29b.)

✔ *Be* has two different past tense forms—*was* for singular subjects
and *were* for second-person singular subjects as well as for plural
subjects. (See 29c.)

✔ *Could* is the past tense of *can*. *Would* is the past tense of *will*.
(See 29d.)

30 Verbs: Past Participles

 ## 30a Regular Past Participles

Every verb has a past participle form. The **past participle** form of a regular verb is identical to its past tense form. Both are formed by adding either -*ed* or -*d* to the **base form** of the verb (the present tense form of the verb that is used with the pronoun *I*).

PAST TENSE	PAST PARTICIPLE
He earned a fortune.	He has earned a fortune.

PAST TENSE	PAST PARTICIPLE
He created a work of art.	He has created a work of art.

PRACTICE

30-1 Fill in the correct past participle form of each regular verb in parentheses.

Example: For years, volunteer vacationers have _____visited_____ (visit) remote areas to build footpaths, cabins, and shelters.

(1) Rece cationers have _____ (discover) some new opportunities to get away from it all and to do good at the same time. (2) Groups such as Habitat for Humanity, for example, have _____ (offer) volunteers a chance to build homes in low-income areas. (3) Habitat's Global Village trips have _____ (raise) awareness about the lack of affordable housing in many countries. (4) Participants in Sierra Club programs have _____ (donate) thousands of work hours all over the United States. (5) Sometimes these volunteers have _____ (join) forest service workers to help restore wilderness areas. (6) They have _____ (clean) up trash at campsites.

(7) They have also _____ (remove) nonnative plants.

(8) Some volunteer vacationers have _____ (travel) to countries such as Costa Rica, Russia, and Thailand to help with local projects.

(9) Other vacationers have _____ (serve) as English teachers.

(10) Volunteering vacations have _____ (help) to strengthen cross-cultural understanding.

 # 30b Irregular Past Participles

Irregular verbs nearly always have irregular past participles. Irregular verbs do not form the past participle by adding -ed or -d to the base form of the verb.

The following chart lists the base form, the past tense form, and the past participle of the most commonly used irregular verbs.

Irregular Past Participles

BASE FORM	PAST TENSE	PAST PARTICIPLE
awake	awoke	awoken
be (am, are)	was (were)	been
beat	beat	beaten
become	became	become
begin	began	begun
bet	bet	bet
bite	bit	bitten
blow	blew	blown
break	broke	broken
bring	brought	brought
build	built	built
buy	bought	bought
catch	caught	caught
choose	chose	chosen
come	came	come
cost	cost	cost
cut	cut	cut

(Continued)

(continued from previous page)

BASE FORM	PAST TENSE	PAST PARTICIPLE
dive	dove, dived	dived
do	did	done
draw	drew	drawn
drink	drank	drunk
drive	drove	driven
eat	ate	eaten
fall	fell	fallen
feed	fed	fed
feel	felt	felt
fight	fought	fought
find	found	found
fly	flew	flown
forgive	forgave	forgiven
freeze	froze	frozen
get	got	got, gotten
give	gave	given
go	went	gone
grow	grew	grown
have	had	had
hear	heard	heard
hide	hid	hidden
hold	held	held
hurt	hurt	hurt
keep	kept	kept
know	knew	known
lay (to place)	laid	laid
lead	led	led
leave	left	left
let	let	let
lie (to recline)	lay	lain
light	lit	lit
lose	lost	lost
make	made	made
meet	met	met
pay	paid	paid
quit	quit	quit

BASE FORM	PAST TENSE	PAST PARTICIPLE
read	read	read
ride	rode	ridden
ring	rang	rung
rise	rose	risen
run	ran	run
say	said	said
see	saw	seen
sell	sold	sold
send	sent	sent
set	set	set
shake	shook	shaken
shine	shone, shined	shone, shined
sing	sang	sung
sit	sat	sat
sleep	slept	slept
speak	spoke	spoken
spend	spent	spent
spring	sprang	sprung
stand	stood	stood
steal	stole	stolen
stick	stuck	stuck
sting	stung	stung
swear	swore	sworn
swim	swam	swum
take	took	taken
teach	taught	taught
tear	tore	torn
tell	told	told
think	thought	thought
throw	threw	thrown
understand	understood	understood
wake	woke, waked	woken, waked
wear	wore	worn
win	won	won
write	wrote	written

PRACTICE

30-2 Edit the following paragraph for errors in irregular past participles. Cross out any underlined past participles that are incorrect, and write in the correct form above them. If the verb form is correct, label it *C*.

                                                       kept
Example: Banned book lists have ~~keeped~~ many people from reading
                                                       ^
great novels.

(1) Banning books has <u>became</u> a controversial topic. (2) Many people have <u>spoke</u> out about banning books, particularly in relation to freedom of speech. (3) It's very likely that some of your most beloved books have <u>be</u> put on banned book lists. (4) For example, *Alice in Wonderland* had <u>made</u> the list in Hunan, China, in 1931. (5) In Australia, the *Twilight* books have <u>rised</u> to the top of the banned list in several schools. (6) Many books have <u>made</u> the banned list in the United States as well. (7) In 2006, a Kansas school district had <u>taked</u> *Charlotte's Web* off of bookshelves. (8) Recently, the annual Banned Books Week celebration has <u>grew</u> in popularity. (9) Banned Books Week has <u>builded</u> awareness about censorship issues. (10) Organizers hope that if more people have <u>readed</u> banned books, then more people will protest the censorship of those books.

 30c   The Present Perfect Tense

The past participle can be combined with the present tense forms of *have* to form the **present perfect tense**.

> **The Present Perfect Tense**
> (*have* or *has* + past participle)
>
> **SINGULAR**   **PLURAL**
> I <u>have gained.</u>   We <u>have gained.</u>
> You <u>have gained.</u>   You <u>have gained.</u>
> He <u>has gained.</u>   They <u>have gained.</u>
> She <u>has gained.</u>
> It <u>has gained.</u>

■ Use the present perfect tense to indicate an action that began in the past and continues into the present.

> **PRESENT PERFECT** The <u>nurse</u> <u>has worked</u> at the clinic for two years. (The working began in the past and continues into the present.)

■ Use the present perfect tense to indicate that an action has just occurred.

> **PRESENT PERFECT** <u>I</u> <u>have</u> just <u>eaten</u>. (The eating has just occurred.)

PRACTICE

30-3 Fill in the appropriate tense (past tense or present perfect) of the verb in parentheses.

Example: Now, cell phones fit easily into a pocket, but the first mobile-phone users __*carried*__ (carry) devices that were more than a foot long.

(1) In recent years, the size of many everyday items _____ (change) considerably. (2) Cell phones and computers _____ _____ (undergo) the biggest changes. (3) There was a time, not long ago, when a single computer _____ (fill) an entire room and a cell phone weighed as much as two pounds. (4) Since then, we _____ _____ (invent) smaller and smaller devices. (5) Now, we _____ (become) accustomed to tiny devices that act as both phone and computer yet weigh only a few ounces. (6) However, while these items have shrunk, other things _____ (get) bigger. (7) For example, flat-screen TVs now come in sizes up to 100 inches. (8) Moreover, as Americans _____ _____ (grow) heavier, hospital equipment has had to get sturdier. (9) Ten years ago, manufacturers _____ (build) operating tables that supported a maximum of 700 pounds. (10) Now, medical supply companies _____ _____ (develop) a standard table that supports up to 1,200 pounds.

(11) To accommodate the growing number of overweight people, movie theater seats and caskets _____ (increase) in size as well. (12) While movie-goers in the 1980s _____ (sit) in 20-inch seats, today's viewers sit in 26-inch seats. (13) Similarly, standard-size caskets have expanded in width from 24 to 28 inches, and some companies _____ (start) making plus-size caskets as large as 52 inches across. (14) Clearly, consumers prefer some items to be smaller even as they themselves _____ (get) bigger.

 ## 30d The Past Perfect Tense

The past participle can also be used to form the **past perfect tense**, which consists of the past tense of *have* plus the past participle.

The Past Perfect Tense

(*had* + past participle)

SINGULAR	PLURAL
<u>I</u> <u>had returned.</u>	<u>We</u> <u>had returned.</u>
<u>You</u> <u>had returned.</u>	<u>You</u> <u>had returned.</u>
<u>He</u> <u>had returned.</u>	<u>They</u> <u>had returned.</u>
<u>She</u> <u>had returned.</u>	
<u>It</u> <u>had returned.</u>	

Use the past perfect tense to show that an action occurred before another past action.

PAST PERFECT TENSE   PAST TENSE

<u>Chief Sitting Bull</u> <u>had fought</u> many battles before <u>he</u> <u>defeated</u> General Custer. (The fighting was done before Sitting Bull defeated Custer.)

PRACTICE

30-4 Underline the appropriate verb tense (present perfect or past perfect) from the choices in parentheses.

Example: Although he (has missed/<u>had missed</u>) his second free throw, the crowd cheered for him anyway.

1. Meera returned to Bangladesh with the money she (has raised/had raised).

2. Her contributors believe that she (has shown/had shown) the ability to spend money wisely.

3. The planner told the commission that she (has found/had found) a solution to the city's traffic problem.

4. It seems clear that traffic cameras (have proven/had proven) successful in towns with similar congestion problems.

5. Emily says she (has saved/had saved) a lot of money by driving a motor scooter instead of a car.

6. She sold the car she (has bought/had bought) three years before.

7. Because they are huge fans, Esteban and Tina (have camped/had camped) out in front of the theater to buy tickets.

8. The people who (have waited/had waited) all night were the first to get tickets.

9. Sam and Ryan volunteer at Habitat for Humanity, where they (have learned/had learned) many useful skills.

10. After they (have completed/had completed) five hundred hours of work, they were eligible to get their own house.

30e   Past Participles as Adjectives

In addition to functioning as verbs, past participles can function as adjectives modifying nouns that follow them.

I cleaned up the broken glass.

The exhausted runner finally crossed the finish line.

Past participles are also used as adjectives after **linking verbs**, such as *seemed* or *looked*.

Jason seemed surprised.

He looked shocked.

PRACTICE

30-5   Edit the following passage for errors in past participle forms used as adjectives. Cross out any underlined participles that are incorrect, and write the correct form above them. If the participle form is correct, label it *C*.

>   inspired
> **Example:** I am ~~inspire~~ by the lost boys of Sudan.
>   ^

(1) Many people are interesting in the story of the lost boys of Sudan. (2) The young boys were force to leave their homes when civil war broke out. (3) The frightening boys traveled to Ethiopia on foot. (4) Many boys died because they were dehydrate. (5) The story of the lost boys of Sudan fascinate people around the world, inspiring them to help. (6) In 2000, approximately three thousand surprised boys learned that they would be relocated to the United States. (7) Since many of them felt overwhelm by life in the United States, volunteers were recruited to help them adjust. (8) Concern groups formed fundraising efforts to help support the lost boys. (9) Although many of the boys (now men) are still locate in the United States, others have returned to Sudan to help rebuild their country.

EDITING PRACTICE

Read the following student essay, which includes errors in the use of past participles and perfect tenses. Decide whether each of the underlined verbs or participles is correct. If it is correct, write *C* above it. If it is not, write in the correct verb form. The first error has been corrected for you.

The Flash Mob Phenomenon

The first flash mob ~~had take~~ *took* place in 2003 when two hundred people assembled in a New York City Macy's store. Since then, these strange spontaneous gatherings had popped up in cities around the world and have involve all kinds of unusual behaviors. Occasionally, a group has organized a flash mob for criminal purposes, but in most cases, flash mobs had been harmless acts of group expression.

Organizer Bill Wasik had actually intend the first flash mob to be a social commentary. Wasik has wanted to make fun of "hipster" New Yorkers who showed up at events simply because other people did. However, almost no one had saw the first flash mob that way. In fact, people mostly have thought it was cool. As a result, admirers started organizing their own flash mobs.

So far, few of the subsequent flash mobs had have a political or social purpose. Typically, people had participate simply because these gatherings are fun. For example, over the years, people have gathered in cities around the world to dance to Michael Jackson's "Thriller." People had also enjoyed getting together in public spaces for massive pillow fights. In addition, several groups have coordinated group "freeze frames," in which participants all "freeze" at the same moment. Organized quietly by text messages or social media, most flash mobs have not publicize their plans in traditional media. Consequently, passers-by have enjoyed the feeling that the group had gathered spontaneously.

Although the majority of flash mob organizers <u>have create</u> these brief performances to entertain, people <u>have</u> occasionally <u>use</u> flash mobs to commit crimes. Over the last few years, several groups <u>have robbed</u> stores by entering in large numbers, stealing merchandise, and then separating quickly. Worse, several groups <u>have came</u> together to commit violent acts or destroy property. Most of today's flash mobs, however, are peaceful.

Over the last decade, flash mobs <u>have became</u> more popular than anyone could have imagined. Although they have not had the impact that creator Bill Wasik <u>had hoped</u> for, they <u>given</u> a lot of people a lot of enjoyment. Flash mobs allow people to be creative, to work together, and to have fun. Although a few flash mobs <u>have done</u> harm, most <u>have offer</u> people a way to be a part of something memorable.

COLLABORATIVE ACTIVITY

Assume that you are a restaurant employee who has been nominated for the Employee-of-the-Year Award. To win this award (along with a thousand-dollar prize), you have to explain in writing what you have done during the past year to deserve this honor. Write a letter to your supervisor and the awards committee. When you have finished, trade papers with another student and edit his or her letter. Read all the letters to the class, and have the class decide which is the most convincing.

review checklist

Verbs: Past Participles

✔ The past participle of regular verbs is formed by adding *-ed* or *-d* to the base form. (See 30a.)

✔ Irregular verbs usually have irregular past participles. (See 30b.)

✔ The past participle is combined with the present tense forms of *have* to form the present perfect tense. (See 30c.)

✔ The past participle is used to form the past perfect tense, which consists of the past tense of *have* plus the past participle. (See 30d.)

✔ The past participle can function as an adjective. (See 30e.)

31 Nouns and Pronouns

 ## 31a Identifying Nouns

A **noun** is a word that names a person (*singer, Beyoncé*), an animal (*dolphin, Flipper*), a place (*downtown, Houston*), an object (*game, Scrabble*), or an idea (*happiness, Darwinism*).

A **singular noun** names one thing. A **plural noun** names more than one thing.

FYI

When to Capitalize Nouns

Most nouns, called **common nouns**, begin with lowercase letters.

character   holiday

Proper nouns name particular people, animals, places, objects, or events. A proper noun always begins with a capital letter.

Homer Simpson   Labor Day

 ## 31b Forming Plural Nouns

Most nouns that end in consonants add *-s* to form plurals. Other nouns add *-es* to form plurals. For example, most nouns that end in *-o* add *-es* to form plurals. Other nouns, whose singular forms end in *-s, -ss, -sh, -ch, -x,* or *-z*, also add *-es* to form plurals. (Some nouns that end in *-s* or *-z* double the *s* or *z* before adding *-es*.)

SINGULAR	PLURAL
street	streets
tomato	tomatoes
gas	gases
class	classes
bush	bushes
church	churches
fox	foxes
quiz	quizzes

519

Irregular Noun Plurals

Some nouns form plurals in unusual ways.

- Nouns whose plural forms are the same as their singular forms

SINGULAR	PLURAL
a deer	a few deer
this species	these species
a television series	two television series

- Nouns ending in -*f* or -*fe*

SINGULAR	PLURAL
each half	both halves
my life	our lives
a lone thief	a gang of thieves
one loaf	two loaves
the third shelf	several shelves

Exceptions: *roof* (plural *roofs*), *proof* (plural *proofs*), *belief* (plural *beliefs*)

- Nouns ending in -*y*

SINGULAR	PLURAL
another baby	more babies
every worry	many worries

Note that when a vowel (*a, e, i, o, u*) comes before the *y*, the noun has a regular plural form: *monkey* (plural *monkeys*), *day* (plural *days*).

- Hyphenated compound nouns

SINGULAR	PLURAL
Lucia's sister-in-law	Lucia's two favorite sisters-in-law
a mother-to-be	twin mothers-to-be
the first runner-up	all the runners-up

Note that the plural ending is attached to the compound's first word: *sister, mother, runner*.

- Miscellaneous irregular plurals

SINGULAR	PLURAL
that child	all children
a good man	a few good men
the woman	lots of women
my left foot	both feet
a wisdom tooth	my two front teeth
this bacterium	some bacteria

PRACTICE

31-1

                     circuses

Example: Like other ~~circusses~~ around the world, America's

first circus featured a variety of animals.

    (1) A tradition for many <u>familys</u> ended on May 21, 2017, when Ringling Brothers and Barnum & Bailey Circus gave its final performance. (2) The <u>origines</u> of "The Greatest Show on Earth" go back to 1806, when Hachaliah Bailey first established his traveling show. (3) Selling <u>tickets</u> for Bailey was a young P. T. Barnum, who became one of the <u>founderrs</u> of Barnum & Bailey's Circus. (4) The Ringling <u>brothers</u> started their own circus and then bought Barnum & Bailey and combined the two <u>companys</u>. (5) Under the big top, the ringmaster announced the show by calling out, "<u>Ladys</u> and <u>Gentleman</u>! <u>Children</u> of all ages!" (6) The millions of fans answering the call over the <u>years</u> were amazed by the <u>skillz</u> of both <u>humans</u> and <u>animals</u>. (7) <u>Audience</u> cheered as <u>performeres</u> were shot out of <u>cannons</u>, walked across <u>tightropes</u>, and flew from one trapeze to another. (8) The circus was as famous for <u>clownes</u>, <u>acrobats</u>, and <u>jugglers</u> as it was for <u>tigers</u>, <u>horsess</u>, <u>lions</u>, and of course, <u>elephantes</u>. (9) In 2016, the <u>elephants</u> performed for the last time and then were moved to a preserve where they would spend the rest of their <u>lifes</u>. (10) Ringling Brothers and Barnum & Bailey closed within a year, citing high operating <u>costes</u> and declining ticket <u>sale</u>, after the <u>elephants</u> left the show.

 # 31c **Identifying Pronouns**

A **pronoun** is a word that refers to and takes the place of a noun or another pronoun. In the following sentence, the pronouns *she* and *her* take the place of the noun *Michelle*.

    Michelle was really excited because <u>she</u> had finally found a job that made <u>her</u> happy. (*She* refers to *Michelle*; *her* refers to *she*.)

Pronouns, like nouns, can be singular or plural.

- Singular pronouns (*I*, *he*, *she*, *it*, *him*, *her*, and so on) always take the place of singular nouns or pronouns.

  Geoff left his jacket at work, so <u>he</u> went back to get <u>it</u> before <u>it</u> could be stolen. (*He* refers to *Geoff*; *it* refers to *jacket*.)

- Plural pronouns (*we*, *they*, *our*, *their*, and so on) always take the place of plural nouns or pronouns.

  Jessie and Dan got up early, but <u>they</u> still missed <u>their</u> train. (*They* refers to *Jessie and Dan*; *their* refers to *they*.)

- The pronoun *you* can be either singular or plural.

  When the volunteers met the mayor, they said, "We really admire <u>you</u>." The mayor replied, "I admire <u>you</u>, too." (In the first sentence, *you* refers to *the mayor*; in the second sentence, *you* refers to *the volunteers*.)

FYI

Demonstrative Pronouns

Demonstrative pronouns—*this*, *that*, *these*, and *those*—point to one or more items.

- *This* and *that* point to one item: This is a <u>work</u> of fiction, and <u>that</u> is a nonfiction <u>book</u>.

- *These* and *those* point to more than one item: These are <u>fruits</u>, but <u>those</u> are <u>vegetables</u>.

PRACTICE

31-2   In the following sentences, fill in each blank with an appropriate pronoun.

Example: Installing operating system updates can help ___**you**___

protect ___**your**___ personal information.

(1) _____ can help keep _____ personal information safe online by following some "always" and "never" rules. (2) When _____ are shopping or banking online, always check to make sure that the site is encrypted.

(3) If _____ is secure, the web address will begin with "https." (4) Always be sure to shop only at well-known retailers; _____ are more likely to offer protection in case of fraud. (5) Never send _____ bank account number or other sensitive information over a public Wi-Fi network. (6) Always protect _____ passwords by keeping _____ private and secure. (7) Even if _____ have created the perfect password, never use _____ for more than one account. (8) Always copy important data onto a backup drive and then store _____ in a safe place so you can get to _____ even if your device is compromised. (9) Always make sure that apps are safe before you install _____, and never click on suspicious email links or websites. (10) Finally, always disconnect from the Internet and turn off _____ computer when you are finished using _____.

31d   Understanding Pronoun-Antecedent Agreement

The word that a pronoun refers to is called the pronoun's **antecedent**. In the following sentence, the noun *leaf* is the antecedent of the pronoun *it*.

The <u>leaf</u> turned yellow, but <u>it</u> did not fall.

A pronoun must always agree with its antecedent. If an antecedent is singular, as it is in the sentence above, the pronoun must be singular. If the antecedent is plural, as it is in the sentence below, the pronoun must also be plural.

The <u>leaves</u> turned yellow, but <u>they</u> did not fall.

If an antecedent is feminine, the pronoun that refers to it must also be feminine.

<u>Melissa</u> passed <u>her</u> driver's exam with flying colors.

If an antecedent is masculine, the pronoun that refers to it must also be masculine.

Matt wondered what courses he should take.

If an antecedent is **neuter** (neither masculine nor feminine), the pronoun that refers to it must also be neuter.

The car broke down, but they refused to fix it again.

PRACTICE

31-3   In the following sentences, circle the antecedent of each underlined pronoun. Then, draw an arrow from the pronoun to the antecedent it refers to.

Example: Navajo Indians were recruited by the U.S. military because they spoke a language that very few could understand.

(1) During World War II, approximately 400 Navajos participated in a top-secret military program in which they served as "code talkers." (2) The U.S. Marine Corps recruited Navajos to assist them with guarding military secrets. (3) Philip Johnston, a World War I veteran, developed the idea of the "code talkers" because ___he___ grew up on a Navajo reservation. (4) The Navajos used only oral communication, and their language's syntax and vocabulary were not recorded in writing. (5) In addition, the language is so specific and complex that often Navajo tribes could not even understand their neighboring tribes. (6) These features of the language made ___it___ ideal for a secret military project. (7) One major obstacle was that the Navajos did not have language for military words, so they had to improvise. (8) All in all, the Navajos proved they were important contributors to the war effort. (9) Because the code-talker program was top secret, ___it___ was not made public until 2000. (10) Today, the Navajos are honored for their important contributions to the war effort.

PRACTICE

31-4 Fill in each blank in the following passage with an appropriate pronoun.

Example: Americans celebrate July 4 because _____it_____ is Independence Day.

(1) For some Germans, November 9 is a day to celebrate positive change; for others, _____ recalls the human potential for violence and destruction. (2) November 9, designated "World Freedom Day," is important because _____ is the day the Berlin Wall fell. (3) On that day in 1989, residents of East and West Germany were allowed to cross the barrier that had separated _____ since 1961. (4) However, Germans have mixed feelings about this date because November 9 also reminds _____ of a dark moment in their history. (5) On the night of November 9, 1938, Nazis took sledgehammers and axes to as many Jewish businesses, synagogues, and homes as _____ could find. (6) In German, this violent event is called *Kristallnacht*; in English, _____ is known as the "Night of Broken Glass." (7) Because November 9 has been so important in German history, journalists sometimes refer to _____ as Germany's "day of fate." (8) Coincidentally, Albert Einstein, a German Jew, received the Nobel Prize on November 9, 1921; the theories _____ described have changed the way scientists think. (9) In short, November 9 in Germany is a day of opposites; like so many dates in human history, _____ marks both triumph and tragedy.

31e Identifying Problem Areas with Agreement

Certain kinds of antecedents can be challenging for writers because they cannot easily be identified as singular or plural.

Compound Antecedents

A **compound antecedent** consists of two or more words connected by *and* or *or.*

- Compound antecedents connected by *and* are plural, and they are used with plural pronouns.

  During World War II, <u>Belgium and France</u> tried to protect <u>their</u> borders.

- Compound antecedents connected by *or* may take a singular or a plural pronoun. The pronoun always agrees with the word that is closer to it.

  Is it possible that European nations or <u>Russia</u> may send <u>its</u> [not *their*] troops?

  Is it possible that Russia or European <u>nations</u> may send <u>their</u> [not *its*] troops?

PRACTICE
31-5

In each of the following sentences, underline the compound antecedent, and circle the connecting word (*and* or *or*). Then, underline the appropriate pronoun in parentheses.

Example: <u>Romeo (and) Juliet</u> fell in love against the wishes of (his or her/<u>their</u>) families.

1. Both Savannah, Georgia, and Charleston, South Carolina, are popular tourist' destinations because of (its/their) Southern charm.

2. In *Game of Thrones,* Jon Snow and Daenerys Targaryen are portrayed as strong leaders who want the best for (his or her/their) people.

3. When you travel to a new place, either TripAdvisor or Yelp can be helpful for (its/their) online reviews of restaurants and hotels.

4. In 1903, Marie and Pierre Curie were awarded the Nobel Prize for Physics for (his or her/their) work on radioactivity.

5. One challenge for either vegetarians or vegans can be including enough protein in (his or her/their) diets.

6. For more than a hundred years, Sherlock Holmes and John Watson have entertained (his/their) fans as they investigate mysterious cases.

7. On Cyber Monday, shoppers may go to Amazon or another online retailer offering (its/their) products at bargain prices.

8. This summer, Katie and her sister Liz are planning to drive to Denver to visit (her/their) cousin.

9. Weather forecasters predicted that either the Virgin Islands or Puerto Rico could be devastated if Hurricane Maria continued (its/their) course.

Indefinite Pronoun Antecedents

Most pronouns refer to a specific person or thing. However, **indefinite pronouns** do not refer to any particular person or thing.

Most indefinite pronouns are singular.

Singular Indefinite Pronouns

another	everybody	no one
anybody	everyone	nothing
anyone	everything	one
anything	much	somebody
each	neither	someone
either	nobody	something

When an indefinite pronoun antecedent is singular, use a singular pronoun to refer to it.

Everything was in its place. (*Everything* is singular, so it is used with the singular pronoun *its*.)

FYI

Indefinite Pronouns with *Of*

The singular indefinite pronouns *each, either, neither,* and *one* are often used in phrases with *of—each of, either of, neither of,* or *one of—*followed by a plural noun. Even in such phrases, these indefinite pronoun antecedents are always singular and take singular pronouns.

Each of the routes has its [not *their*] own special challenges.

A few indefinite pronouns are plural.

Plural Indefinite Pronouns

both	others
few	several
many	

When an indefinite pronoun antecedent is plural, use a plural pronoun to refer to it.

They all wanted to graduate early, but few received their diplomas in January. (*Few* is plural, so it is used with the plural pronoun *their.*)

FYI

Using *His* or *Her* with Indefinite Pronouns

Even though the indefinite pronouns *anybody, anyone, everybody, everyone, somebody, someone,* and so on are singular, many people use plural pronouns to refer to them.

Everyone must hand in their completed work by 2 p.m.

Although this usage is widely accepted in spoken English, indefinite pronouns like *everyone* are singular, so written English requires a singular pronoun here instead of the plural *their.* However, using the singular pronoun *his* to refer to *everyone* excludes women, suggesting that *everyone* refers only to a male. Because the indefinite pronoun can refer to either a male or a female, using *his* or *her* is more accurate.

Everyone must hand in his or her completed work by 2 p.m.

When used over and over again, *he or she, him or her,* and *his or her* can create wordy or awkward sentences. Also, some people chose not to identify with a specific gender, and this language does not include them. Whenever possible, use plural forms.

<u>All students</u> must hand in <u>their</u> completed work by 2 p.m.

PRACTICE

31-6 Edit the following sentences for errors in pronoun-antecedent agreement. When you edit, you have two options: either substitute *its* or *his or her* for *their* to refer to the singular antecedent, or replace the singular antecedent with a plural word.

Examples: Everyone can help prevent the spread of germs by washing
his or her
~~their~~ hands.
        ^
All
~~Each~~ of the passengers presented their tickets at the gate.
     ^

1. Each of the programs has their advantages and disadvantages.

2. Anyone who tries out for the play is responsible for learning their lines.

3. Everyone had to show their registration card to attend the free seminar.

4. Several people agreed to meet at the rally but few kept his or her promise

   because of the rain.

5. Everybody waits until fall to get their flu shots.

6. Every school in the district changed their starting times to 8:30.

7. Neither of the buildings had their own parking lot.

8. Anyone who needs to take a make-up test must write their name on the

   list.

9. One of the companies moved their headquarters across town.

10. Each employee had a chance to ask questions about their benefits.

Collective Noun Antecedents

Collective nouns are words (such as *band* and *team*) that name a group of people or things but are singular. Because they are singular, collective noun antecedents are used with singular pronouns.

The band played on, but it never played our song.

> ### Frequently Used Collective Nouns
>
> | | | | |
> |---|---|---|---|
> | army | club | gang | mob |
> | association | committee | government | posse |
> | band | company | group | team |
> | class | family | jury | union |

PRACTICE

31-7 Circle the collective noun antecedent in each of the following sentences. Then, circle the correct pronoun in parentheses.

Example: The jury returned with (its / their) verdict.

1. The company offers comprehensive benefits to (its / their) employees.

2. All five study groups must hand in (its / their) projects by Tuesday.

3. Any government should be concerned about the welfare of (its / their) citizens.

4. The Asian Students Union is sponsoring an event to celebrate (its / their) twentieth anniversary.

5. Every family has (its / their) share of problems.

6. To join the electricians' union, applicants had to pass (its / their) test.

7. Even the best teams have (its / their) bad days.

8. The orchestra just signed a contract for (its / their) first recording.

9. The math class did very well with (its / their) new instructor.

10. The club voted to amend (its / their) charter.

PRACTICE

31-8 Edit the following passage for correct pronoun-antecedent agreement. First, circle the antecedent of each underlined pronoun. Then, cross out any pronoun that does not agree with its antecedent, and write the correct form above it. If the pronoun is correct, write *C* above it.

Example: Many Americans believe that the ⟨country⟩ is ready for its̲ *C*
first female president.

(1) The history of woman suffrage in the United States shows that women were determined to achieve her̲ equal rights. (2) Before 1920, most American women were not allowed to vote for the candidates they̲ preferred. (3) Men ran the government, and a woman could not express their̲ views at the ballot box. (4) However, in the mid-1800s, women began to demand her̲ right to vote—or "woman suffrage." (5) Supporters of woman suffrage believed everyone, regardless of their̲ gender, should be able to vote. (6) At the first woman suffrage convention, Elizabeth Cady Stanton and Lucretia Mott gave speeches explaining his or her̲ views. (7) Susan B. Anthony started the National Woman Suffrage Association, which opposed the Fifteenth Amendment to the Constitution because it̲ gave the vote to black men but not to women. (8) The first state to permit women to vote was Wyoming, and soon other states became more receptive to her̲ cause. (9) Many women participated in marches where he or she̲ carried banners and posters for their̲ cause. (10) During World War I, the U.S. government found that the co-operation of women was essential to their̲ military success. (11) Finally, in 1919, the House of Representatives and the states gave its̲ approval to the Nineteenth Amendment, which gave American women the right to vote.

31f Vague and Unnecessary Pronouns

Vague and unnecessary pronouns clutter up your writing and make it hard to understand. Eliminating them will make your writing clearer and easier for readers to follow.

Vague Pronouns

A pronoun should always refer to a specific antecedent. When a pronoun—such as *they* or *it*—has no antecedent, readers may be confused.

> **VAGUE PRONOUN** On the news, <u>they</u> said baseball players would strike. (Who said baseball players would strike?)

> **VAGUE PRONOUN** <u>It</u> says in today's paper that our schools are overcrowded. (Who says schools are overcrowded?)

If a pronoun does not refer to a specific word in the sentence, replace the pronoun with a noun.

> **REVISED** On the news, the <u>sportscaster</u> said baseball players would strike.

> **REVISED** An <u>editorial</u> in today's paper says that our schools are overcrowded.

Unnecessary Pronouns

When a pronoun comes directly after its antecedent, it is unnecessary.

> **UNNECESSARY PRONOUN** The librarian, <u>he</u> told me I should check the database.

In the sentence above, the pronoun *he* serves no purpose. Readers do not need to be directed back to the pronoun's antecedent (the noun *librarian*) because it appears right before the pronoun. The pronoun should therefore be deleted.

> **REVISED** The librarian told me I should check the database.

PRACTICE

31-9 The following sentences contain vague or unnecessary pronouns. Revise each sentence on the line below it.

Example: On their website, they advertised a special offer.

On its website, the Gap advertised a special offer.

1. In Jamaica, they love their spectacular green mountains.

   _____

2. My hamster, he loves his exercise wheel.

   _____

3. On *Jeopardy!* they have to give the answers in the form of questions.

   _____

4. On televisions all over the world, they watched the moon landing.

   _____

5. In Sociology 320, they do not use a textbook.

   _____

 # 31g Understanding Pronoun Case

A **personal pronoun** refers to a particular person or thing. Personal pronouns change form according to their function in a sentence. Personal pronouns can be *subjective*, *objective*, or *possessive*.

Personal Pronouns

SUBJECTIVE	OBJECTIVE	POSSESSIVE
I	me	my, mine
he	him	his
she	her	her, hers
it	it	its
we	us	our, ours
you	you	your, yours
they	them	their, theirs
who	whom	whose
whoever	whomever	

Subjective Case

When a pronoun is a subject, it is in the **subjective case**.

> Finally, <u>she</u> realized that dreams could come true.

Objective Case

When a pronoun is an object, it is in the **objective case**.

> If Joanna hurries, she can stop <u>him</u>. (The pronoun *him* is the object of the verb *can stop*.)
>
> Professor Miller sent <u>us</u> information about his research. (The pronoun *us* is the object of the verb *sent*.)
>
> Marc threw the ball to <u>them</u>. (The pronoun *them* is the object of the preposition *to*.)

Possessive Case

When a pronoun shows ownership, it is in the **possessive case**.

> Hieu took <u>his</u> lunch to the meeting. (The pronoun *his* indicates that the lunch belongs to Hieu.)
>
> Debbie and Kim decided to take <u>their</u> lunches, too. (The pronoun *their* indicates that the lunches belong to Debbie and Kim.)

PRACTICE

31-10   In the following passage, fill in the blank after each pronoun to indicate whether the pronoun is subjective (*S*), objective (*O*), or possessive (*P*).

Example: Between 1932 and 1934, famous criminals Bonnie and Clyde committed their _____P_____ robberies and murders in broad daylight.

(1) Bonnie Parker and Clyde Barrow are remembered today because they _____ were the first celebrity criminals. (2) With their _____ gang, Bonnie and Clyde robbed a dozen banks as well as many

stores and gas stations (3) In small towns, they _____ terrorized the police. (4) Capturing them _____ seemed impossible. (5) To many Americans, however, their _____ crimes seemed exciting. (6) Because Bonnie was a woman, she _____ was especially fascinating to them _____. (7) During their _____ crimes, Bonnie and Clyde would often carry a camera, take photographs of themselves, and then send them _____ to the newspapers, which were happy to publish them _____. (8) By the time they _____ were killed in an ambush by Texas and Louisiana law officers, Bonnie and Clyde were famous all over the United States.

◼ 31h Identifying Problem Areas with Pronoun Case

When you are trying to determine which pronoun case to use in a sentence, three kinds of pronouns can present challenges: pronouns in compounds, pronouns in comparisons, and the pronouns *who* and *whom* (or *whoever* and *whomever*).

Pronouns in Compounds

Sometimes a pronoun is linked to a noun or to another pronoun with *and* or *or* to form a **compound**.

> The teacher and I met for an hour.

> He or she can pick up Jenny at school.

To determine whether to use the subjective or objective case for a pronoun in the second part of a compound, follow the same rules that apply for a pronoun that is not part of a compound.

■ If the compound is a subject, use the subjective case.

> Toby and I [not *me*] like jazz.

> He and I [not *me*] went to the movies.

■ If the compound is an object, use the objective case.

The school sent <u>my father and me</u> [not *I*] the financial-aid forms.

This argument is between <u>Kate and me</u> [not *I*].

FYI

Choosing Pronouns in Compounds

To determine which pronoun case to use in a compound that joins a noun and a pronoun, rewrite the sentence with just the pronoun.

Toby and [*I* or *me*?] like jazz.

<u>I</u> like jazz. (not *Me like jazz*)

Toby and <u>I</u> like jazz.

PRACTICE

31-11   In the following passage, the underlined pronouns are parts of compounds. Check them for correct subjective or objective case. If the pronoun is incorrect, cross it out, and write the correct form above it. If the pronoun is correct, write *C* above it.

Example: My classmates and $\overset{C}{\underline{I}}$ were surprised by the results of a study on listening.

(1) According to a recent study, the average listener remembers only 50 percent of what <u>him</u> or <u>her</u> hears. (2) Two days later, <u>he</u> or <u>she</u> can correctly recall only 25 percent of the total message. (3) My friend Alyssa and <u>me</u> decided to ask our school to sponsor a presentation about listening in the classroom. (4) One point the speaker made was especially helpful to Alyssa and <u>I</u>. (5) We now know that <u>us</u> and the other students in our class each have four times more mental "room" than we need for listening. (6) The presenter taught the other workshop participants and <u>we</u> how to use this extra space. (7) Now, whenever one of our professors pauses to write on the board or take a sip of water, Alyssa and <u>I</u> remember to silently

summarize the last point <u>he</u> or <u>she</u> made. (8) Throughout the lecture, we pay attention to the big ideas and overall structure that the professor wants the other students and <u>us</u> to take away. (9) Also, to keep ourselves actively thinking about the topic, we try to predict where the professor will lead our classmates and <u>us</u> next. (10) Above all, we do not waste our mental energy on distractions that other students and <u>us</u> ourselves create, such as dropped books or our own worries. (11) Comedian Lily Tomlin's advice to "listen with an intensity most people save for talking" now makes a lot of sense to Alyssa and <u>me</u>.

Pronouns in Comparisons

Sometimes a pronoun appears after the word *than* or *as* in the second part of a **comparison**.

> John is luckier <u>than I</u>.
> The inheritance changed Raymond as much <u>as her</u>.

- If the pronoun is a subject, use the subjective case.

> John is luckier <u>than I</u> [am].

- If the pronoun is an object, use the objective case.

> The inheritance changed Raymond as much <u>as</u> [it changed] <u>her</u>.

FYI

Choosing Pronouns in Comparisons

Sometimes the pronoun you use can change your sentence's meaning. For example, if you say, "I like Cheerios more than *he*," you mean that you like Cheerios more than the other person likes them.

> I like Cheerios more than <u>he</u> [does].

If, however, you say, "I like Cheerios more than *him*," you mean that you like Cheerios more than you like the other person.

> I like Cheerios more than [I like] <u>him</u>.

PRACTICE

31-12 Each of the following sentences includes a comparison with a pronoun following the word *than* or *as*. Write in each blank the correct form (subjective or objective) of the pronoun in parentheses. In brackets, add the word or words needed to complete the comparison.

Example: Many people are better poker players than _____I [am]_____ (I/me).

1. The survey showed that most people like the candidate's family as much as _____ (he/him).

2. No one enjoys shopping more than _____ (she/her).

3. My brother and Aunt Cecile were very close, so her death affected him more than _____ (I/me).

4. No two people could have a closer relationship than _____ (they/ them).

5. My neighbor drives better than _____ (I/me).

6. He may be as old as _____ (I/me), but he does not have as much work experience.

7. That jacket fits you better than _____ (I/me).

8. The other company had a lower bid than _____ (we/us), but we were awarded the contract.

Who and *Whom*, *Whoever* and *Whomever*

To determine whether to use *who* or *whom* (or *whoever* or *whomever*), you need to know how the pronoun functions within the clause in which it appears.

■ When the pronoun is the subject of the clause, use *who* or *whoever*.

I wonder <u>who</u> wrote that song. (*Who* is the subject of the clause *who wrote that song.*)

I will vote for <u>whoever</u> supports the youth center. (*Whoever* is the subject of the clause *whoever supports the youth center.*)

■ When the pronoun is the object, use *whom* or *whomever*.

Whom do the police suspect? (*Whom* is the direct object of the verb *suspect*.)

I wonder whom the song is about. (*Whom* is the object of the preposition *about* in the clause *whom the song is about*.)

Vote for whomever you prefer. (*Whomever* is the object of the verb *prefer* in the clause *whomever you prefer*.)

FYI

Who and *Whom*

To determine whether to use *who* or *whom*, try substituting another pronoun for *who* or *whom* in the clause. If you can substitute *he* or *she*, use *who*; if you can substitute *him* or *her*, use *whom*.

[Who/Whom] wrote a love song? He wrote a love song.

[Who/Whom] was the song about? The song was about her.

The same test will work for *whoever* and *whomever*.

PRACTICE

31-13 Circle the correct form—*who* or *whom* (or *whoever* or *whomever*)—in parentheses in each sentence.

Example: With (who/ⓦhom) did Rob collaborate?

1. The defense team learned (who / whom) was going to testify for the prosecution.

2. (Who/ Whom) does she think she can find to be a witness?

3. The contestant (who/whom) eats the most hot dogs will be the winner.

4. They will argue their case to (whoever /whomever) will listen.

5. It will take time to decide (who /whom) is the record holder.

6. Take these forms to the clerk (who/whom) is sitting at the front desk.

7. We will have to penalize (whoever /whomever) misses the first practice.

8. (Who/ Whom) did Kobe take to the prom?

9. We saw the man (who/whom) fired the shots.

10. To (who/whom) am I speaking?

31i   Identifying Reflexive and Intensive Pronouns

Two special kinds of pronouns, *reflexive pronouns* and *intensive pronouns*, end in *-self* (singular) or *-selves* (plural). Although the functions of the two kinds of pronouns are different, their forms are identical.

Reflexive and Intensive Pronouns

Singular Forms

ANTECEDENT	REFLEXIVE OR INTENSIVE PRONOUN
I	myself
you	yourself
he	himself
she	herself
it	itself

Plural Forms

ANTECEDENT	REFLEXIVE OR INTENSIVE PRONOUN
we	ourselves
you	yourselves
they	themselves

Reflexive Pronouns

Reflexive pronouns indicate that people or things did something to themselves or for themselves.

Rosanna lost herself in the novel.

You need to watch yourself when you mix those solutions.

Mehul and Paul made themselves cold drinks.

Intensive Pronouns

Intensive pronouns always appear directly after their antecedents, and they are used for emphasis.

I myself have had some experience in sales and marketing.

The victim himself collected the reward.

They themselves were uncertain of the significance of their findings.

PRACTICE

31-14 Fill in the correct reflexive or intensive pronoun in each of the following sentences.

Example: The opening act was exciting, but the main attraction _____itself_____ was boring.

1. Morticia told her visitors to make _____ at home.

2. Migrating birds can direct _____ through clouds, storms, and moonless nights.

3. The Queen _____ gave a short speech at the ceremony.

4. We all finished the project without injuring _____.

5. Even though the government promised to help flood victims, the residents _____ did most of the rebuilding.

6. Sometimes he finds _____ daydreaming in class.

7. The guide warned us to watch _____ on the slippery path.

8. The senators were not happy about committing _____ to a shorter recess.

9. She gave _____ a manicure.

10. Although everyone else in my family can sing or play a musical instrument, I _____ am tone-deaf.

CHAPTER REVIEW

EDITING PRACTICE

Read the following student essay, which includes noun and pronoun errors. Check for errors in plural noun forms, pronoun case, and pronoun-antecedent agreement. Then, make any editing changes you think are necessary. The first paragraph has been edited for you.

Swimming to Safety

Swimming is a favorite summertime activity for many children and adults, but it is not enjoyable for everyone. For those who cannot swim, being in or near the water can be a terrifying experience. The Swimming Saves Lives Foundation is one organization that is trying to make a difference for ~~a person~~ _people_ who never learned how to swim.

It is important for children to start swimming lessons at a young age. Children should learn how to keep himself or herself safe near the water. The Swimming Saves Lives Foundation believes that water-safety lessons are important for all children, but particularly for minorities. Reports suggest that approximately 70 percent of African American children and 60 percent of Latino children are not strong swimmeres. For all children, drowning is a common cause of death. Whom wants to take that risk? Even if a child does not want to swim recreationally, him or her should understand basic water safety.

Some adult seem to think that it is too late to learn how to swim. The Swimming Saves Lives Foundation offers their services to anyone who wants to learn to swim. Local program are available in many states. Anyone who wants to participate can sign themselves up online.

For many adults, learning to swim leads him to a new favorite sport. For these people, the Swimming Saves Lives Foundation offers a Masters Swimming program. In this program, adults can continue to refine his or her swimming skills.

Approximately 37 percent of adults cannot swim the length of the pool, and it is time for that number to drop. Thanks to the Swimming Saves Lives Foundation, whomever wants to swim has a greater opportunity to learn. Even if adults do not choose to swim recreationally, he or she can still learn practical water safety and teach it to their children.

COLLABORATIVE ACTIVITY

Working in a group, fill in the following chart, writing one noun on each line. If the noun is a proper noun, be sure to capitalize it.

CARS	TREES	FOODS	FAMOUS COUPLES	CITIES
____	____	____	____	____
____	____	____	____	____
____	____	____	____	____
____	____	____	____	____
____	____	____	____	____
____	____	____	____	____

Now, using as many of the nouns listed above as you can, write a one-paragraph news article that describes an imaginary event. Exchange your work with another group, and check the other group's article to be sure the correct pronoun refers to each noun. Return the articles to their original groups for editing.

review checklist

Nouns and Pronouns

✔ A noun is a word that names something. A singular noun names one thing; a plural noun names more than one thing. (See 31a.)

✔ Most nouns add -*s* or -*es* to form plurals. Some nouns have irregular plural forms. (See 31b.)

✔ A pronoun is a word that refers to and takes the place of a noun or another pronoun. (See 31c.)

✔ The word a pronoun refers to is called the pronoun's antecedent. A pronoun and its antecedent must always agree. (See 31d.)

✔ Compound antecedents connected by *and* are plural and are used with plural pronouns. Compound antecedents connected by *or* may take singular or plural pronouns. (See 31e.)

✔ Most indefinite pronoun antecedents are singular and are used with singular pronouns; some are plural and are used with plural pronouns. (See 31e.)

✔ Collective noun antecedents are singular and are used with singular pronouns. (See 31e.)

✔ A pronoun should always refer to a specific antecedent. (See 31f.)

✔ Personal pronouns can be in the subjective, objective, or possessive case. (See 31g.)

✔ Pronouns present special problems when they are used in compounds and comparisons. The pronouns *who* and *whom* and *whoever* and *whomever* can also cause problems. (See 31h.)

✔ Reflexive and intensive pronouns must agree with their antecedents. (See 31i.)

32 Adjectives and Adverbs

32a Identifying Adjectives and Adverbs

Adjectives and adverbs are words that modify (identify or describe) other words. They help make sentences more specific and more interesting.

An **adjective** answers the question *What kind? Which one?* or *How many?* Adjectives modify nouns or pronouns.

The Turkish city of Istanbul spans two continents. (*Turkish* modifies the noun *city*, and *two* modifies the noun *continents*.)

It is fascinating because of its location and history. (*Fascinating* modifies the pronoun *it*.)

FYI

Demonstrative Adjectives

Demonstrative adjectives—*this*, *that*, *these*, and *those*—do not describe other words. They simply identify particular nouns.

This and *that* identify singular nouns and pronouns.

This website is much more current than that one.

These and *those* identify plural nouns.

These words and phrases are French, but those expressions are Creole.

An **adverb** answers the question *How? Why? When? Where?* or *To what extent?* Adverbs modify verbs, adjectives, or other adverbs.

Traffic moved steadily. (*Steadily* modifies the verb *moved*.)

Still, we were quite impatient. (*Quite* modifies the adjective *impatient*.)

Very slowly, we moved into the center lane. (*Very* modifies the adverb *slowly*.)

FYI

Distinguishing Adjectives from Adverbs

Many adverbs are formed when -*ly* is added to an adjective form.

ADJECTIVE	ADVERB
slow	slowly
nice	nicely
quick	quickly
real	really

ADJECTIVE   Let me give you one quick reminder.
(*Quick* modifies the noun *reminder*.)

ADVERB   He quickly changed the subject.
(*Quickly* modifies the verb *changed*.)

PRACTICE

32-1   In the following sentences, circle the correct form (adjective or adverb) from the choices in parentheses.

Example: Beatles enthusiasts all over the world have formed tribute bands devoted to the (famous/famously) group's music.

(1) To show appreciation for their favorite musicians, tribute bands go to (great/greatly) lengths. (2) Fans who have a (real/really) strong affection for a particular band may decide to play its music and copy its style. (3) Sometimes they form their own groups and have successful careers (simple/simply) performing that band's music. (4) These groups are (usual/usually) called *tribute bands*. (5) Most tribute bands are (passionate/passionately) dedicated to reproducing the original group's work. (6) They not only play the group's songs but (careful/carefully) imitate the group's look. (7) They study the band members' facial expressions and body movements and create (exact/exactly) copies of the band's costumes and instruments. (8) Some more (inventive/inventively)

tribute bands take the original band's songs and interpret them (different/ differently). (9) For example, by performing Beatles songs in the style of Metallica, the tribute band Beatallica has created a (unique/uniquely) sound. (10) Some people believe such tributes are the (ultimate/ultimately) compliment to the original band; others feel (sure/surely) that tribute groups are just copycats who (serious/seriously) lack imagination.

FYI

Good and Well

Be careful not to confuse *good* and *well*. Unlike regular adjectives, whose adverb forms add *-ly*, the adjective *good* is irregular. Its adverb form is *well*.

ADJECTIVE	Fred Astaire was a good dancer. (*Good* modifies the noun *dancer*.)
ADVERB	He danced especially well with Ginger Rogers. (*Well* modifies the verb *danced*.)

Always use *well* when you are describing a person's health.

He really didn't feel well [not *good*] after eating the entire pizza.

PRACTICE

32-2

Circle the correct form (*good* or *well*) in the sentences below.

Example: It can be hard for some people to find a (good/ well) job that they really like.

(1) Some people may not do (good/well) sitting in an office. (2) Instead, they may prefer to find jobs that take advantage of their (good/well) physical condition. (3) Such people might consider becoming smoke jumpers—firefighters who are (good/well) at parachuting from small planes into remote areas to battle forest fires. (4) Smoke jumpers must be able to work (good/well) even without much sleep. (5) They must also

handle danger (good/well). (6) They look forward to the (good/well) feeling of saving a forest or someone's home. (7) As they battle fires, surrounded by smoke and fumes, smoke jumpers may not feel very (good/well). (8) Sometimes things go wrong; for example, when their parachutes fail to work (good/well), jumpers may be injured or even killed. (9) Smoke jumpers do not get paid particularly (good/well). (10) However, they are proud of their strength and endurance and feel (good/well) about their work.

32b Understanding Comparatives and Superlatives

The **comparative** form of an adjective or adverb compares two people or things. Adjectives and adverbs form the comparative with *-er* or *more*. The **superlative** form of an adjective or adverb compares more than two things. Adjectives and adverbs form the superlative with *-est* or *most*.

ADJECTIVES	This film is <u>dull</u> and <u>predictable</u>.
COMPARATIVE	The film I saw last week was even <u>duller</u> and <u>more predictable</u> than this one.
SUPERLATIVE	The film I saw last night was the <u>dullest</u> and <u>most predictable</u> one I've ever seen.
ADVERBS	For a beginner, Jane did needlepoint <u>skillfully</u>.
COMPARATIVE	After she had watched the demonstration, Jane did needlepoint <u>more skillfully</u> than Rosie.
SUPERLATIVE	Of the twelve beginners, Jane did needlepoint the <u>most skillfully</u>.

Forming Comparatives and Superlatives

Adjectives

■ One-syllable adjectives generally form the comparative with *-er* and the superlative with *-est*.

great	greater	greatest

- Adjectives with two or more syllables form the comparative with *more* and the superlative with *most*.

wonderful	more wonderful	most wonderful

Exception: Two-syllable adjectives ending in *-y* add *-er* or *-est* after changing the *y* to an *i*.

funny	funnier	funniest

Adverbs

- All adverbs ending in *-ly* form the comparative with *more* and the superlative with *most*.

efficiently	more efficiently	most efficiently.

- Some other adverbs form the comparative with *-er* and the superlative with *-est*.

soon	sooner	soonest

Solving Special Problems with Comparatives and Superlatives

The following rules will help you avoid errors with comparatives and superlatives.

- Never use both *-er* and *more* to form the comparative or both *-est* and *most* to form the superlative.

Nothing could have been <u>more awful</u>. (not *more awfuller*)

Space Mountain is the <u>most frightening</u> (not *most frighteningest*) ride at Disney World.

- Never use the superlative when you are comparing only two things.

This is the <u>more serious</u> (not *most serious*) of the two problems.

- Never use the comparative when you are comparing more than two things.

This is the <u>worst</u> (not *worse*) day of my life.

PRACTICE

32-3 Fill in the correct comparative form of the word supplied in parentheses.

Example: Children tend to be _____noisier_____ (noisy) than adults.

1. Traffic always moves _____ (slow) during rush hour than late at night.

2. The weather report says temperatures will be _____ (cold) tomorrow.

3. Some elderly people are _____ (healthy) than younger people.

4. It has been proven that pigs are _____ (intelligent) than dogs.

5. When someone asks you to repeat yourself, you usually answer _____ (loud).

6. The _____ (tall) of the two buildings was damaged by the earthquake.

7. They want to teach their son to be _____ (respectful) of women than many young men are.

8. Las Vegas is _____ (famous) for its casinos than for its natural resources.

9. The WaterDrop is _____ (wild) than any other ride in the amusement park.

10. You must walk _____ (quick) if you expect to catch the bus.

PRACTICE

32-4 In the following passage, fill in the correct superlative form of the word supplied in parentheses.

Example: *Match.com* and *eHarmony* are two of the _____most popular_____ (popular) online dating sites.

(1) Niche dating sites are becoming some of the _____ (popular) places to find a date online. (2) Although more general-interest

sites, such as *Match.com* and *eHarmony*, are still widely used, the

_____ (specialized) sites are creating new ways for people

to connect. (3) For example, *FarmersOnly.com* is a dating site for people

who are the _____ (enthusiastic) about the farming lifestyle.

(4) If you love *Star Trek*, then *Trek Passions* is the dating site that is the

_____ (likely) to help you find a like-minded Trekkie. (5) Fans

of Apple products will find *Cupidtino* the _____ (simple) way

to find other fans. (6) Even salad fanatics can find love using *SaladMatch*,

an app that connects people with their _____ (compatible)

mate based on their favorite salad toppings. (7) Many users of dating sites

have proclaimed niche sites to be the _____ (effective) way to

find love online. (8) Identifying common ground is the _____

(easy) way to start a conversation, and these communities emphasize users'

common interests. (9) With new sites appearing all the time, even the

_____ (unusual) interests are represented. (10) With so many

options, choosing one site might be the _____ (intimidating)

part of the process.

FYI

Good/Well and *Bad/Badly*

Most adjectives and adverbs form the comparative with *-er* or *more* and
the superlative with *-est* or *most*. The adjectives *good* and *bad* and their
adverb forms *well* and *badly* are exceptions.

ADJECTIVE	COMPARATIVE FORM	SUPERLATIVE FORM
good	better	best
bad	worse	worst

ADVERB	COMPARATIVE FORM	SUPERLATIVE FORM
well	better	best
badly	worse	worst

PRACTICE

32-5 Fill in the correct comparative or superlative form of *good*, *well*, *bad*, or *badly*.

Example: My sister is a _____better_____ (good) runner than I am.

1. Neela was certain she was the _____ (good) chef in the competition.

2. Because he studied more, Helio earned _____ (good) grades than his sister.

3. An optimist, Mara always thinks she will do _____ (well) next time.

4. Many people drive the _____ (badly) when they are in a hurry.

5. Of all the mortgage companies Ramon researched, Plains Bank had the _____ (good) interest rate.

6. I feel bad when I get rejected, but I feel _____ (bad) when I do not try.

7. For nontraditional students, access to education is _____ (good) than it used to be.

8. Jamie sings badly, but Simon sings _____ (badly).

9. I learn the _____ (well) when I am not distracted.

10. After looking at every painting in the gallery, they decided that the landscapes were definitely the _____ (bad) paintings there.

EDITING PRACTICE

Read the following student essay, which includes errors in the use of adjectives and adverbs. Make any changes necessary to correct adjectives incorrectly used for adverbs and adverbs incorrectly used for adjectives. Also, correct any errors in the use of comparatives and superlatives and in the use of demonstrative adjectives. Finally, try to add some adjectives and adverbs that you feel would make the writer's ideas clearer or more specific. The first sentence has been edited for you.

Starting Over

A wedding can be the ~~joyfullest~~ ^{most joyful} occasion in two people's lives, the beginning of a couple's most happiest years. For some unlucky women, however, a wedding can be the worse thing that ever happens; it is the beginning not of their happiness but of their battered lives. As I went through the joyful day of my wedding, I wanted bad to find happiness for the rest of my life, but what I hoped and wished for did not come true.

I was married in the savannah belt of the Sudan in the eastern part of Africa, where I grew up. I was barely twenty-two years old. The first two years of my marriage progressed peaceful, but problems started as soon as our first child was born.

Many American women say, "If my husband hit me just once, that would be it. I'd leave." But those attitude does not work in cultures where tradition has overshadowed women's rights and divorce is not accepted. All women can do is accept their sadly fate. Battered women give many reasons for staying in their marriages, but fear is the commonest. Fear immobilizes these women, ruling their decisions, their actions, and their very lives. This is how it was for me.

Of course, I was real afraid whenever my husband hit me. I would run to my mother's house and cry, but she would always talk me into going back and being more patiently with my husband. Our tradition discourages divorce, and wife-beating is taken for granted. The situation is really quite ironic: the religion I practice sets harsh punishments for abusive husbands, but tradition has so overpowered religion that the laws do not really work very good.

One night, I asked myself whether life had treated me fair. True, I had a high school diploma and two of the beautifullest children in the world, but all this was not enough. I realized that to stand up to the husband who treated me so bad, I would have to achieve more a better education than he had. That night, I decided to get a college education in the United States. My husband opposed my decision, but with the support of my father and mother, I was able to begin to change my life. My years as a student and single parent in the United States have been real difficult for me, but I know I made the right choice.

COLLABORATIVE ACTIVITY

Working in a small group, write a plot summary for an imaginary film. Begin with one of the following three sentences.

- Dirk and Clive were sworn enemies, but that night on Boulder Ridge they vowed to work together just this once, for the good of their country.
- Genevieve entered the room in a cloud of perfume, and when she spoke, her voice was like velvet.
- The desert sun beat down on her head, but Susanna was determined to protect what was hers, no matter what the cost.

Now, exchange summaries with another group, and add as many adjectives and adverbs as you can to the other group's summary. Finally, reread your own group's plot summary, and edit it carefully, paying special attention to the way adjectives and adverbs are used.

review checklist

Adjectives and Adverbs

✔ Adjectives modify nouns or pronouns. (See 32a.)

✔ Adverbs modify verbs, adjectives, or other adverbs. (See 32a.)

✔ To compare two people or things, use the comparative form of an adjective or adverb. To compare more than two people or things, use the superlative form of an adjective or adverb. (See 32b.)

✔ The adjectives *good* and *bad* and their adverb forms *well* and *badly* have irregular comparative and superlative forms. (See 32b.)

33 Grammar and Usage for Multilingual Writers

Learning English as a second language involves more than just learning grammar. In fact, if you have been studying English as a second language, you may know more about English grammar than many native speakers do. However, you will still need to learn the conventions and rules that most native speakers already know.

 ## 33a   Subjects in Sentences

English requires that every sentence state its subject. Every independent clause and every dependent clause must also have a subject.

> **INCORRECT**   Elvis Presley was only forty-two years old when died. (When who died?)
>
> **CORRECT**   Elvis Presley was only forty-two years old when <u>he</u> died.

When the real subject follows the verb and the normal subject position before the verb is empty, it must be filled by a "dummy" subject, such as *it* or *there*.

> **INCORRECT**   ___ Is hot in this room.
>
> **CORRECT**   <u>It</u> is hot in this room.
>
> **INCORRECT**   ___ Are many rivers in my country.
>
> **CORRECT**   <u>There</u> are many rivers in my country.

Standard English also does not permit a two-part subject in which the second part of the subject is a pronoun referring to the same person or thing as the first part.

INCORRECT   The <u>Caspian Sea</u> it is the largest lake in the world.

CORRECT   The <u>Caspian Sea</u> is the largest lake in the world.

PRACTICE

33-1   Each of the following sentences is missing the subject of a dependent or an independent clause. On the lines provided, rewrite each sentence, adding an appropriate subject. Then, underline the subject you have added.

Example: Because college students often have very little money, are always looking for inexpensive meals.

<u>Because college students often have very little money, they</u> are always

looking for inexpensive meals.

1. Ramen noodles are a popular choice for students because are cheap, tasty, and easy to prepare.

_____

_____

2. In minutes, a student can enjoy hot noodles flavored with chicken, shrimp, or beef, and sell vegetarian versions, too.

_____

_____

3. Although high in carbohydrates (a good source of energy), also contain saturated and trans fats and few vitamins or minerals.

_____

_____

4. Cookbooks provide special recipes for preparing ramen noodles; include "Ramen Shrimp Soup" and "Ramen Beef and Broccoli."

_____

_____

5. Ramen noodles are not just popular with American college students; are also popular in many other countries around the world.

_____

_____

6. The noodles have even found their way to the International Space Station, where enjoy them in space.

_____

_____

7. The noodles originated in China many years ago, where were deep fried so that they could be stored for a long time without spoiling.

_____

_____

8. For today's college students, however, spoilage is not a problem because are usually eaten long before their expiration date.

_____

_____

PRACTICE

33-2 The following sentences contain unnecessary two-part subjects. Cross out the unnecessary pronoun. Then, rewrite each sentence correctly on the lines provided.

Example: Travelers to China ~~they~~ often visit the Great Wall.

Travelers to China often visit the Great Wall.

1. The first parts of the Great Wall they were built around 200 BCE.

_____

_____

2. The Great Wall it was built to keep out invading armies.

_____

_____

3. The sides of the Great Wall they are made of stone, brick, and earth.

_____

_____

4. The top of the Great Wall it is paved with bricks, forming a roadway for horses.

_____

_____

5. The Great Wall it is so huge that it can be seen by astronauts in space.

_____

_____

 ## 33b Count and Noncount Nouns

A **count noun** names one particular thing or a group of particular things that can be counted: *a teacher, a panther, a bed, an ocean, a cloud, an ice cube, two teachers, many panthers, three beds, two oceans, several clouds, some ice cubes.* A **noncount noun** names things that cannot be counted: *gold, cream, sand, blood, smoke, water.*

Count nouns usually have a singular form and a plural form: *cube, cubes.* Noncount nouns usually have only a singular form: *water.* Note how the nouns *cube* and *water* differ in the way they are used in sentences.

CORRECT	The glass is full of ice cubes.
CORRECT	The glass is full of water.
INCORRECT	The glass is full of waters.
CORRECT	The glass contains five ice cubes.
CORRECT	The glass contains some water.
INCORRECT	The glass contains five waters.

Often, the same idea can be expressed with either a count noun or a noncount noun.

COUNT	NONCOUNT
people (plural of *person*)	humanity [*not* humanities]
tables, chairs, beds	furniture [*not* furnitures]
letters	mail [*not* mails]
supplies	equipment [*not* equipments]
facts	information [*not* informations]
guns	ammunition [*not* ammunitions]

Some words can be either count or noncount, depending on the meaning intended.

COUNT   He had many interesting <u>experiences</u> at his first job.

NONCOUNT   It is often difficult to get a job if you do not have <u>experience</u>.

FYI

Guidelines for Using Count and Noncount Nouns

- Use a count noun to refer to a living animal, but use a noncount noun to refer to the food that comes from that animal.

    COUNT   There are three live <u>lobsters</u> in the tank.

    NONCOUNT   This restaurant specializes in <u>lobster</u>.

- If you use a noncount noun for a substance or class of things that can come in different varieties, you can often make that noun plural if you want to talk about those varieties.

    NONCOUNT   <u>Cheese</u> is a rich source of calcium.

    COUNT   Many different <u>cheeses</u> come from Italy.

- If you want to shift attention from a concept in general to specific examples of it, you can often use a noncount noun as a count noun.

    NONCOUNT   You have a great deal of <u>talent</u>.

    COUNT   My <u>talents</u> do not include singing.

PRACTICE

33-3   In each of the following sentences, decide if the underlined word is being used as a count or a noncount noun. If it is being used as a noncount noun, circle the *N* following the sentence. If it is being used as a count noun, circle the *C*.

Examples: As a Peace Corps volunteer in Ecuador, Dave Schweiden-
back realized how important bicycles could be.   N Ⓒ

Using his imagination, Dave figured out an effective way to recycle
America's unwanted bicycles. Ⓝ C

1. Pedals for Progress is an American nonprofit organization.   N   C

2. The group collects and repairs old bicycles and sends them to
   countries where they are needed.   N   C

3. Pedals for Progress aims to reduce the amount of bicycle waste that
   ends up in American landfills.   N   C

4. People in the United States throw away millions of bikes and bike
   parts every year.   N   C

5. At the same time, lack of transportation is a serious problem for many
   people in developing countries.   N   C

6. Without an efficient and affordable way to get to work, a person
   cannot hold a job.   N   C

7. A working bicycle provides an easy and environmentally friendly way
   to get around.   N   C

8. Bicycles from Pedals for Progress only cost the user a small amount of
   money.   N   C

9. To help maintain these recycled bikes, the organization also helps to
   establish local repair shops.   N   C

10. By making it easier for people to work, Pedals for Progress hopes to
    reduce poverty.   N   C

33c Determiners with Count and Noncount Nouns

Determiners are adjectives that *identify* rather than describe the nouns they modify. Determiners may also *quantify* nouns (that is, indicate an amount or a number).

Determiners include the following words.

- Articles: *a, an, the*
- Demonstrative pronouns: *this, these, that, those*
- Possessive pronouns: *my, our, your, his, her, its, their*
- Possessive nouns: *Sheila's, my friend's,* and so on
- *Whose, which, what*
- *All, both, each, every, some, any, either, no, neither, many, most, much, a few, a little, few, little, several, enough*
- All numerals: *one, two,* and so on

When a determiner is accompanied by one or more other adjectives, the determiner always comes first. For example, in the phrase *my expensive new digital watch, my* is a determiner; you cannot put *expensive, new, digital,* or any other adjective before *my.*

A singular count noun must always be accompanied by a determiner—for example, *my watch* or *the new digital watch,* not just *watch* or *new digital watch.* However, noncount nouns and plural count nouns sometimes have determiners but sometimes do not. *This honey is sweet* and *Honey is sweet* are both acceptable as are *These berries are juicy* and *Berries are juicy.* (In each case, the meaning is different.) You cannot say, *Berry is juicy,* however; say instead, *This berry is juicy, Every berry is juicy,* or *A berry is juicy.*

FYI

Determiners

Some determiners can be used only with certain types of nouns.

- *This* and *that* can be used only with singular nouns (count or noncount): *this berry, that honey.*
- *These, those, a few, few, many, both,* and *several* can be used only with plural count nouns: *these berries, those apples, a few ideas, few people, many students, both sides, several directions.*
- *Much, little,* and *a little* can be used only with noncount nouns: *much affection, little time, a little honey.*

- *Some, enough, all,* and *most* can be *used* only with noncount or plural count nouns: *some* honey, *some* berries; *enough* trouble, *enough* problems; *all* traffic, *all* roads; *most* money, *most* coins.

- *A, an, every, each, either,* and *neither* can be used only with singular count nouns: *a* berry, *an* elephant, *every* possibility, *each* citizen, *either* option, *neither* candidate.

PRACTICE

33-4 In each of the following sentences, circle the more appropriate choice from each pair of words or phrases in parentheses.

Examples: Volcanoes are among the most destructive of (all/ every) natural forces on earth.

People have always been fascinated and terrified by (this/ these) force of nature.

1. Not (all/every) volcano is considered a danger.

2. In (major some/ some major) volcanic eruptions, huge clouds rise over the mountain.

3. In 2010, ash from a volcano in Iceland caused (many/ much) disruption for airline passengers throughout Europe.

4. (A few violent / Violent a few) eruptions are so dramatic that they blow the mountain apart.

5. (Most / Much) volcanic eruptions cannot be predicted.

6. Since the 1400s, (many/much) people—almost 200,000—have lost their lives in volcanic eruptions.

7. When a volcano erupts, (little /a little) can be done to prevent property damage.

8. By the time people realize an eruption is about to take place, there is rarely (many/enough) time to escape.

9. Volcanoes can be dangerous, but they also produce (a little/some) benefits.

10. For example, (a few/a little) countries use energy from underground steam in volcanic areas to produce electric power.

33d Articles

The **definite article** *the* and the **indefinite articles** *a* and *an* are determiners that tell readers whether the noun that follows is one they can identify (*the book*) or one they cannot yet identify (*a book*).

The Definite Article

When the definite article *the* is used with a noun, the writer is saying to readers, "You can identify which particular thing or things I have in mind. The information you need to make that identification is available to you. Either you have it already, or I am about to give it to you."

Readers can find the necessary information in the following ways.

■ By looking at other information in the sentence

Meet me at <u>the</u> corner of Main Street and Lafayette Road.

In this example, *the* is used with the noun *corner* because other words in the sentence tell readers which particular corner the writer has in mind: the one located at Main and Lafayette.

■ By looking at information in other sentences

Aisha ordered a slice of pie and a cup of coffee. <u>The</u> pie was delicious. She asked for a second slice.

Here, *the* is used before the word *pie* in the second sentence to indicate that it is the same pie identified in the first sentence. Notice, however, that the noun *slice* in the third sentence is preceded by an indefinite article (*a*) because it is not the same slice referred to in the first sentence.

■ By drawing on general knowledge

<u>The</u> earth revolves around <u>the</u> sun.

Here, *the* is used with the nouns *earth* and *sun* because readers are expected to know which particular things the writer is referring to.

FYI

The Definite Article

Always use *the* (rather than *a* or *an*) in the following situations:

■ Before the word *same*: <u>*the same day*</u>

■ Before the superlative form of an adjective: <u>*the youngest son*</u>

■ Before a number indicating order or sequence: <u>*the third time*</u>

Indefinite Articles

When an indefinite article is used with a noun, the writer is saying to readers, "I don't expect you to have enough information right now to identify a particular thing that I have in mind. I do, however, expect you to recognize that I'm referring to only one item."

Consider the following sentences.

We need a table for our computer.
I have a folding table; maybe you can use that.

In the first sentence, the writer is referring to a hypothetical table, not an actual one. Because the table is indefinite to the writer, it is clearly indefinite to the reader, so *a* is used, not *the*. The second sentence refers to an actual table, but because the writer does not expect the reader to be able to identify the table specifically, it is also used with *a* rather than *the*.

> **WORD POWER**
>
> **hypothetical**
> assumed or supposed;
> not supported by
> evidence

FYI

Indefinite Articles

Unlike the definite article (*the*), the indefinite articles *a* and *an* occur only with singular count nouns. *A* is used when the next sound is a consonant, and *an* is used when the next sound is a vowel. In choosing *a* or *an*, pay attention to sound rather than to spelling: *a house, a year, a union,* but *an hour, an uncle.*

No Article

Only noncount and plural count nouns can stand without articles: *butter, chocolate, cookies, strawberries* (but *a cookie* or *the strawberry*).

Nouns without articles can be used to make generalizations.

Infants need affection as well as food.

Here, the absence of articles before the nouns *infants, affection,* and *food* indicates that the statement is not about particular infants, affection, or food but about infants, affection, and food in general. Remember not to use *the* in such sentences; in English, a sentence like *The infants need affection as well as food* can only refer to particular, identifiable infants, not to infants in general.

Articles with Proper Nouns

Proper nouns can be divided into two classes: names that take *the* and names that take no article.

- Names of people usually take no article unless they are used in the plural to refer to members of a family, in which case they take *the*: *Napoleon, Mahatma Gandhi* (but *the Parkers*).

- Names of places that are plural in form usually take *the*: *the Andes, the United States*.

- The names of most places on land (cities, states, provinces, and countries) take no article: *Salt Lake City, Mississippi, Alberta, Japan*. The names of most bodies of water (rivers, seas, and oceans, although not lakes or bays) take *the*: *the Mississippi, the Mediterranean, the Pacific* (but *Lake Erie, San Francisco Bay*).

- Names of streets take no article: *Main Street*. Names of unnumbered highways take *the*: *the Belt Parkway*.

PRACTICE

33-5   In the following passage, decide whether each blank needs a definite article (*the*), an indefinite article (*a* or *an*), or no article. If a definite or an indefinite article is needed, write it in the space provided. If no article is needed, leave the space blank.

Example: Football _____is_____ a popular sport, but its players take some serious health risks.

Football has been (1) _____ popular American pastime for many years. Recently, more and more experts have become concerned about (2) _____ sport. Even though football players wear protective gear, (3) _____ helmets do not always protect them from severe concussions. Experts now believe that concussions are (4) _____ reason some players experience memory loss and depression. Although much of (5) _____ media coverage on this issue has been about professional football, the concern extends to college, high school, and youth football. Today, some parents are encouraging their children to choose other sports because of (6) _____ risks of football. As a result of (7) _____ increasing concern, new technology is being developed to address the problem of concussions on the field. For example, some professional players are given (8) _____ helmet with a device that records the speed of the impact when two players crash together.

This technology may help doctors to better understand (9) _____ risks (10) _____ player takes and how to prevent serious injury. (11) Football is _____ essential part of American culture, so it is important that steps are taken to keep players safe.

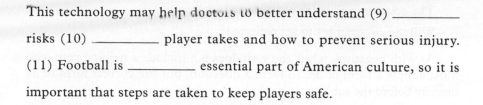

33e Negative Statements and Questions

Negative Statements

To form a negative statement, add the word *not* directly after the first helping verb of the complete verb.

> Global warming has been getting worse.

> Global warming has <u>not</u> been getting worse.

When there is no helping verb, a form of the verb *do* must be inserted before *not*.

> Automobile traffic contributes to pollution.

> Automobile traffic <u>does not</u> contribute to pollution.

However, if the main verb is *am, is, are, was,* or *were*, do not insert a form of *do* before *not*: *Harry was late. Harry was <u>not</u> late.*

Remember that when *do* is used as a helping verb, the form of *do* used must match the tense and number of the original main verb. Note that in the negative statement above, the main verb loses its tense and appears in the base form (*contribute*, not *contributes*).

Questions

To form a question, move the helping verb that follows the subject to the position directly before the subject.

> The governor <u>is</u> trying to compromise.

> <u>Is</u> the governor trying to compromise?

> The governor <u>is</u> working on the budget.

> <u>Is</u> the governor working on the budget?

The same rule applies even when the verb is in the past or future tense.

> The governor <u>was</u> trying to lower state taxes.

> <u>Was</u> the governor trying to lower state taxes?

The governor <u>will</u> try to get reelected.

<u>Will</u> the governor try to get reelected?

As with negatives, when the verb does not include a helping verb, you must supply a form of *do*. To form a question, put the correct form of *do* directly before the subject.

The governor <u>works</u> hard.

<u>Does</u> the governor <u>work</u> hard?

The governor <u>improved</u> life in his state.

<u>Did</u> the governor <u>improve</u> life in his state?

However, if the main verb is *am*, *is*, *are*, *was*, or *were*, do not insert a form of *do* before the verb. Instead, move the main verb before the subject: *Harry was late. Was Harry late?*

Note: The helping verb never comes before the subject if the subject is a question word, such as *who* or *which*.

<u>Who</u> is talking to the governor?

<u>Which</u> bills have been vetoed by the governor?

PRACTICE

33-6   Rewrite each of the following sentences in two ways: first, turn the sentence into a question; then, rewrite the original sentence as a negative statement.

Example: Her newest book is selling as well as her first one.

Question: <u>Is her newest book selling as well as her first one?</u>

Negative statement: <u>Her newest book is not selling as well as her first one.</u>

1. Converting metric measurements to the system used in the United States is difficult.

   Question: _____

   _____

   Negative statement: _____

   _____

2. The early frost damaged some crops.

   Question: _____

   _____

   Negative statement: _____

   _____

3. That family was very influential in the early 1900s.

   Question: _____

   _____

   Negative statement: _____

   _____

4. Most stores in malls are open on Sundays.

   Question: _____

   _____

   Negative statement: _____

   _____

5. Choosing the right gift is a difficult task.

   Question: _____

   _____

   Negative statement: _____

   _____

6. Most great artists are successful during their lifetimes.

   Question: _____

   _____

   Negative statement: _____

   _____

7. The lawyer can verify the witness's story.

   Question: _____

   _____

   Negative statement: _____

   _____

8. American cities are as dangerous as they were thirty years ago.

   Question: _____

   _____

   Negative statement: _____

   _____

9. The British royal family is loved by most of the British people.

   Question: _____

   _____

   Negative statement: _____

   _____

10. Segregation in the American South ended with the Civil War.

    Question: _____

    _____

    Negative statement: _____

    _____

 ## 33f Verb Tense

In English, a verb's form must indicate when an action took place (for instance, in the past or in the present). Always use the appropriate tense of the verb even if the time is obvious or if the sentence includes other indications of time (such as *two years ago* or *at present*).

INCORRECT Albert Einstein <u>emigrate</u> from Germany in 1933.

CORRECT Albert Einstein <u>emigrated</u> from Germany in 1933.

 # 33g Stative Verbs

Stative verbs usually tell that someone or something is in a state that will not change, at least for a while.

Hiro <u>knows</u> American history very well.

Most English verbs show action, and these action verbs can be used in the progressive tenses. The **present progressive** tense consists of the present tense of *be* plus the present participle (*I am going*). The **past progressive** tense consists of the past tense of *be* plus the present participle (*I was going*). Unlike most verbs, however, stative verbs are rarely used in the progressive tenses.

INCORRECT Hiro <u>is knowing</u> American history very well.

CORRECT Hiro <u>knows</u> American history very well.

FYI

Stative Verbs

Verbs that are stative—such as *know, understand, think, believe, want, like, love,* and *hate*—often refer to mental states. Other stative verbs include *be, have, need, own, belong, weigh, cost,* and *mean.* Certain verbs of sense perception, like *see* and *hear,* are also stative even though they can refer to momentary events as well as to unchanging states.

Many verbs have more than one meaning, and some of these verbs are active with one meaning but stative with another. An example is the verb *weigh.*

ACTIVE The butcher <u>weighs</u> the meat.

STATIVE The meat <u>weighs</u> three pounds.

In the first sentence above, the verb *weigh* means "to put on a scale"; it is active, not stative. In the second sentence, however, the same verb means "to have weight," so it is stative, not active. It would be unacceptable to say "The meat is weighing three pounds," but "The butcher is weighing the meat" would be correct.

PRACTICE

33-7 In each of the following sentences, circle the verb or verbs. Then, correct any problems with stative verbs by crossing out the incorrect verb tense and writing the correct verb tense above the line. If the verb is correct, write *C* above it.

                        know   C
Example: Police officers ~~are knowing~~ that fingerprint identification ⓘⓢ one of the best ways to catch criminals.

1. As early as 1750 BC, ancient Babylonians were signing their identities with fingerprints on clay tablets.

2. By 220 BCE, the Chinese were becoming aware that ink fingerprints could identify people.

3. However, it was not until the late 1800s that anyone was believing that criminal identification was possible with fingerprints.

4. Today, we know that each person is having unique patterns on the tips of his or her fingers.

5. When police study a crime scene, they want to see whether the criminals have left any fingerprint evidence.

6. There is always a layer of oil on the skin, and police are liking to use it to get fingerprints.

7. Crime scene experts are often seeing cases where the criminals are touching their hair and pick up enough oil to leave a good fingerprint.

8. The police are needing to judge whether the fingerprint evidence has been damaged by sunlight, rain, or heat.

9. In the courtroom, juries often weigh fingerprint evidence before they are deciding on their verdict.

10. The FBI is collecting millions of fingerprints, which police departments can compare with the fingerprints they find at crime scenes.

33h Gerunds

A **gerund** is a verb form ending in *-ing* that acts as a noun.

> <u>Reading</u> the newspaper is one of my favorite things to do on Sundays.

Just like a noun, a gerund can be used as a subject, a direct object, a subject complement, or the object of a preposition.

- A gerund can be a subject.

  <u>Playing</u> tennis is one of my hobbies.

- A gerund can be a direct object.

  My brother influenced my <u>racing</u>.

- A gerund can be a subject complement.

  The most important thing is <u>winning</u>.

- A gerund can be the object of a preposition.

  The teacher rewarded him for <u>passing</u>.

PRACTICE

33-8 To complete the sentences below, fill in the blanks with the gerund form of the verb provided in parentheses.

Example: _____Typing_____ (type) is a skill that used to be taught in high school.

1. _____ (eat) five or six smaller meals throughout the day is healthier than eating two or three big meals.

2. The household task I dread the most is _____ (clean).

3. Her parents praised her for _____ (remember) their anniversary.

4. I did not like his _____ (sing).

5. The best way to prepare for the concert is by _____ (practice).

33i   Choosing Prepositions

A **preposition** introduces a noun or pronoun and links it to other words in the sentence. The word the preposition introduces is called the **object** of the preposition.

A preposition and its object combine to form a **prepositional phrase**: *on the table, near the table, under the table.*

> I thought I had left the book on the table or somewhere near the table, but I found it under the table.

The prepositions *at, in,* and *on* sometimes cause problems for non-native speakers of English. For example, to identify the location of a place or an event, you can use *at, in,* or *on.*

- The preposition *at* specifies an exact point in space or time.

  > The museum is at 1000 Fifth Avenue. Let's meet there at 10:00 tomorrow morning.

- Expanses of space or time are treated as containers and therefore require *in.*

  > Women used to wear long skirts in the early 1900s.

- *On* must be used in two cases: with names of streets (but not with exact addresses) and with days of the week or month.

  > We will move into our new office on 18th Street either on Monday or on March 12.

FYI

Using Prepositions in Familiar Expressions

Many familiar expressions end in prepositions. The following pairs of expressions have similar meanings.

acquainted with, familiar with	interested in, fascinated by
addicted to, hooked on	interfere with, disrupt
angry with (a person), upset with	meet with, get together with
bored with, tired of	object to, oppose
capable of, able to	pleased with, happy with
consist of, have	protect against, guard against
contain, include	reply to, answer

deal with, address (a problem)

depend on, rely on

differ from (something else),
  be different from

differ with (someone else),
  disagree

emigrate from, move from
  (another country)

grateful for (a favor),
  thankful for

immigrate to, move to
  (another country)

responsible for, accountable for

similar to, almost the
  same as

succeed in, attain success in

take advantage of, use an
  opportunity to

wait for (something to
  happen), expect

wait on (in a restaurant),
  serve

PRACTICE

33-9 In the following passage, fill in each blank with the correct preposition.

Example: Like other struggling artists, writers often make a living

working ____*in*____ restaurants and waiting ____*on*____ customers.

(1) Most writers, even those who succeed _____ the literary

world, need day jobs to help pay _____ food and rent. (2) Many

_____ them work _____ related fields—for example, _____

bookstores, _____ publishing houses, or _____ newspapers.

(3) Some take advantage _____ their talents and devote them-

selves _____ teaching others _____ language and literature.

(4) For example, _____ the 1990s, *Harry Potter* author J. K. Rowling

worked as a teacher _____ Portugal and _____ Britain.

(5) _____ the 1960s and '70s, students _____ Howard University

_____ Washington, D.C., could enroll _____ classes taught

_____ Nobel Prize winner Toni Morrison. (6) Other writers work

_____ fields unrelated _____ writing. (7) For instance, poet

William Carlos Williams was a medical doctor who wrote poetry only
_____ the evenings. (8) Science fiction writer Isaac Asimov worked
_____ Boston University _____ the department _____
biochemistry. (9) Occasionally, an aspiring writer has friends and family who approve _____ his or her goals, and he or she can depend
_____ them _____ financial help. (10) However, many family members, wanting to protect young writers _____ poverty, try to encourage them to focus _____ other goals.

33j   Prepositions in Phrasal Verbs

A **phrasal verb** consists of two words, a verb and a preposition, that are joined to form an idiomatic expression. Many phrasal verbs are **separable**. This means that a direct object can come between the verb and the preposition. However, some phrasal verbs are **inseparable**; that is, the preposition must always come immediately after the verb.

Separable Phrasal Verbs

In many cases, phrasal verbs may be split, with the direct object coming between the two parts of the verb. When the direct object is a noun, the second word of the phrasal verb can come either before or after the object.

In the sentences below, *fill out* is a phrasal verb. Because the object of the verb *fill out* is a noun (*form*), the second word of the verb can come either before or after the verb's object.

> **CORRECT**   Please fill out the form.

> **CORRECT**   Please fill the form out.

When the object is a pronoun, however, these phrasal verbs must be split, and the pronoun must come between the two parts of the verb.

> **INCORRECT**   Please fill out it.

> **CORRECT**   Please fill it out.

Some Common Separable Phrasal Verbs

ask out	give away	put back	throw away
bring up	hang up	put on	try out
call up	leave out	set aside	turn down
carry out	let out	shut off	turn off
drop off	make up	take down	wake up
fill out	put away	think over	

Remember, when the object of the verb is a pronoun, these phrasal verbs must be split, and the pronoun must come between the two parts (for example, *take it down*, *put it on*, *let it out*, and *make it up*).

Inseparable Phrasal Verbs

Some phrasal verbs, however, cannot be separated; that is, the preposition cannot be separated from the verb. This means that a direct object cannot come between the verb and the preposition.

INCORRECT   Please go the manual over carefully.

CORRECT   Please go over the manual carefully.

Notice that in the correct sentence above, the direct object (*manual*) comes right after the preposition (*over*).

Some Common Inseparable Phrasal Verbs

come across	run across	show up
get along	run into	stand by
go over	see to	

PRACTICE

33-10   In each of the following sentences, look closely at the phrasal verb, and decide whether the preposition is placed correctly in the sentence. If it is, write *C* in the blank after the sentence. If the preposition needs to be moved, edit the sentence.

Example: People who live in American suburbs are often surprised to come across wild animals in their neighborhoods. _____*C*_____

1. In one case, a New Jersey woman was startled when a hungry bear woke up her from a nap one afternoon. _____

2. She called the police, hung up the phone, and ran for her life.

   _____

3. Actually, although it is a good idea to stay from bears away, most wild bears are timid. _____

4. When there is a drought, people are more likely to run into bears and other wild animals. _____

5. The amount of blueberries and other wild fruit that bears eat usually drops in dry weather off._____

6. Bears need to put on weight before the winter, so they may have to find food in suburban garbage cans. _____

7. It is a good idea for families to go their plans over to safeguard their property against bears.

8. People should not leave pet food out overnight, or else their dog may find that a hungry bear has eaten its dinner. _____

9. If people have a bird feeder in the yard, they should put away it during the autumn. _____

10. As the human population grows, more and more houses are built in formerly wild areas, so bears and people have to learn to get along with each other. _____

EDITING PRACTICE

Read the following student essay, which includes errors in the use of subjects, nouns, articles, determiners, and stative verbs, as well as errors with phrasal verbs. Check each underlined word or phrase. If it is not used correctly, write in any necessary changes. If the underlined word or phrase is correct, write *C* above it. The title of the essay has been edited for you.

in
How to Succeed ~~on~~ Multinational Business
^

Success in multinational business often <u>depends in</u> the ability to understand other countries' cultures. Understanding how cultures <u>differ to</u> our own, however, is only one key to <u>these</u> success. Also, <u>is</u> crucial that businesses learn to adapt to different cultures. <u>The ethnocentrism</u> is the belief that one's own culture has <u>a</u> best way of doing things. In international business, <u>is</u> necessary to <u>set aside</u> this belief. A company cannot <u>be using</u> the same methods or sell the same products overseas as it does at home. Although making these changes requires a lot of work, companies that choose to adjust to new markets are usually <u>happy with</u> their decision.

<u>It is</u> many aspects of a country that must be understood before successful international business can be <u>carried out</u>. To protect itself <u>from</u> legal errors, a company needs to understand the country's legal system, which may be very different from its home country's legal system. <u>May</u> <u>be</u> necessary to get licenses to export products <u>onto</u> other countries. The role of <u>women</u> is also likely to be different; without knowing this, businesspeople might unintentionally offend people. Also, <u>much</u> personal interactions in other countries may give the wrong impression to someone who is inexperienced. For example, in Latin American countries, people <u>are often standing</u> close together and touch each other when they are talking. Americans may feel uncomfortable in such a situation <u>unless understand</u> it.

To succeed in international business, companies are also needing to understand what people buy and why. To avoid problems, a company that wants to sell its product internationally it should do a few market research. For example, when McDonald's opened restaurants on India, realized that beef burgers would not work in a country where many people believe that cows are sacred. Instead, burgers were made from ground chickens. For India's many vegetarians, McDonald's created several different vegetable patties. McDonald's understood that both the religious and the cultural characteristic of India had to be considered if its new restaurants were going to succeed.

Looking to attract new customers in today's international market, companies they are noticing a growing demand for *halal* goods and services. The word *halal* indicates an object or action that is permissible by Islamic law. Businesses are realizing that world's Muslims depend in companies to provide acceptable *halal* foods, banks, hotels, magazines, and other services. Nestlé, KFC, Subway, LG, and Nokia are just a few of the well-known companies that have been successfully remaking their products to appeal in Muslim consumers. Because these high-quality items also appeal to non-Muslims, many of this companies are discovering that meeting cultural needs and desires are simply good business.

Over time, the marketplace is becoming more global. In those setting, individuals from numerous cultures come together. To take advantage from opportunities and perform effectively, an international company must hire people with the right experiences. To deal with other cultures, multinational companies inside today's global market must have good informations and show other cultures the highest respects.

COLLABORATIVE ACTIVITY

Working in a small group, make a list of ten prepositional phrases that include the prepositions *above, around, at, between, from, in, on, over, under,* and *with*. Use appropriate nouns as objects of these prepositions, and use as many modifying words as you wish. (Try, for example, to write something like *above their hideous wedding portrait*, not just *above the picture*.) Now, work together to compose a list of ten sentences, each including one of your ten prepositional phrases.

review checklist

Grammar and Usage for Multilingual Writers

✔ English sentences must state their subjects. (See 33a.)

✔ English nouns may be count nouns or noncount nouns. A count noun names one particular thing or a group of particular things (*a teacher, oceans*). A noncount noun names something that cannot be counted (*gold, sand*). (See 33b.)

✔ Determiners are adjectives that identify rather than describe the nouns they modify. Determiners may also indicate amount or number. (See 33c.)

✔ The definite article *the* and the indefinite articles *a* and *an* are determiners that indicate whether the noun that follows is one readers can identify (*the book*) or one they cannot yet identify (*a book*). (See 33d.)

✔ To form a negative statement, add the word *not* directly after the first helping verb of the complete verb. To form a question, move the helping verb that follows the subject to the position directly before the subject. (See 33e.)

✔ A verb's form must indicate when an action took place. (See 33f.)

✔ Stative verbs indicate that someone or something is in a state that will not change, at least for a while. Stative verbs are rarely used in the progressive tenses. (See 33g.)

✔ A gerund is a verb form ending in *-ing* that is always used as a noun. (See 33h.)

✔ The prepositions *at, in,* and *on* sometimes cause problems for nonnative speakers of English. (See 33i.)

✔ A phrasal verb consists of two words, a verb and a preposition, that are joined to form an idiomatic expression. (See 33j.)

34 Using Commas

A **comma** is a punctuation mark that separates words or groups of words within sentences. In this way, commas keep ideas distinct from one another.

 ## 34a Commas in a Series

Use commas to separate all elements in a **series** of three or more words, phrases, or clauses.

> <u>Leyla</u>, <u>Zack</u>, and <u>Kathleen</u> campaigned for Representative Lewis.

> <u>Leyla</u>, <u>Zack</u>, or <u>Kathleen</u> will be elected president of Students for Lewis.

> Leyla <u>made phone calls</u>, <u>licked envelopes</u>, and <u>ran errands</u> for the campaign.

> <u>Leyla is president</u>, <u>Zack is vice president</u>, and <u>Kathleen is treasurer</u>.

FYI

Using Commas in a Series

Newspapers and magazines usually omit the comma before the coordinating conjunction in a series. However, in college writing, you should always use a comma before the coordinating conjunction.

> Leyla, Zack, and Kathleen worked on the campaign.

Exception: Do not use *any* commas if all the items in a series are separated by coordinating conjunctions.

> Leyla <u>or</u> Zack <u>or</u> Kathleen will be elected president of Students for Lewis.

PRACTICE

34-1   Edit the following sentences for the use of commas in a series. If the sentence is correct, write *C* in the blank.

Examples

Costa Rica produces bananas, cocoa, and sugarcane. ———*C*———

The pool rules state that there is no running/ or jumping/ or diving. ————

1. The musician plays guitar bass and drums. ————

2. The organization's goals are feeding the hungry, housing the homeless and helping the unemployed find work. ————

3. *The Price Is Right*, *Wheel of Fortune*, and *Jeopardy!* are three of the longest-running game shows in television history. ————

4. In native Hawaiian culture, yellow was worn by the royalty red was worn by priests and a mixture of the two colors was worn by others of high rank. ————

5. The diary Anne Frank kept while her family hid from the Nazis is insightful, touching and sometimes humorous. ————

6. A standard bookcase is sixty inches tall forty-eight inches wide and twelve inches deep. ————

7. Most coffins manufactured in the United States are lined with bronze, or copper, or lead. ————

8. Young handsome and sensitive, Leonardo DiCaprio was the 1990s answer to the 1950s actor James Dean. ————

9. California's capital is Sacramento, its largest city is Los Angeles and its oldest settlement is San Diego. ————

10. Playing soccer, playing video games, and riding his bicycle are some of my ten-year-old son's favorite pastimes. ————

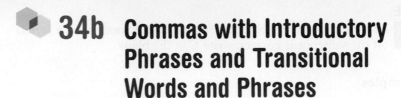

34b Commas with Introductory Phrases and Transitional Words and Phrases

Introductory Phrases

Use a comma to set off an **introductory phrase** from the rest of the sentence.

> <u>In the event of a fire,</u> proceed to the nearest exit.
> <u>Walking home,</u> Nelida decided to change her major.
> <u>To keep fit,</u> people should try to exercise regularly.

PRACTICE

34-2 Edit the sentences in the following passage for the use of commas with introductory phrases. If the sentence is correct, write *C* in the blank.

Examples

For some medical conditions effective treatments are hard to find.

_____

After taking placebos, some depressed patients experience relief from their symptoms. _____

(1) Sometimes known as sugar pills placebos contain no actual medicine. _____ (2) Despite this fact, placebos sometimes have positive effects on patients who take them. _____ (3) For years researchers have used placebos in experiments. _____ (4) To evaluate the effectiveness of a medication scientists test the drug on volunteers. _____ (5) To ensure that the experiment's results are reliable, researchers always have a control group. _____ (6) Instead of taking the drug the control group takes a placebo. _____ (7) Thinking

they are taking an actual medicine patients in the control group may experience the "placebo effect." _____ (8) After receiving treatment with a placebo, they feel better. _____ (9) In some cases patients feel better even when they know they have taken a placebo. _____ (10) Puzzling to researchers, this "honest placebo effect" is the subject of several new scientific studies. _____

Transitional Words and Phrases

Also use commas to set off **transitional words or phrases**, whether they appear at the beginning, in the middle, or at the end of a sentence.

> In fact, Thoreau spent only one night in jail.
>
> He was, of course, bailed out by a friend.
>
> He did spend more than two years at Walden Pond, however.

FYI

Using Commas in Direct Address

Always use commas to set off the name of someone whom you are addressing (speaking to) directly, whether the name appears at the beginning, in the middle, or at the end of a sentence.

> Molly, come here and look at this.
>
> Come here, Molly, and look at this.
>
> Come here and look at this, Molly.

PRACTICE

34-3 Edit the sentences in the following passage for the use of commas with transitional words and phrases. If the sentence is correct, write *C* in the blank.

> **Example:** In general, many people agree that mandatory minimum sentence laws should be reformed.

(1) Recently mandatory minimum sentences have been called into question. _____ (2) Nonviolent drug offenders for example are often incarcerated when addiction treatment would be a better course of action. _____ (3) In fact an increasing percentage of the total prison population is composed of these nonviolent offenders. _____ (4) As a result taxpayers are increasingly burdened by the rising costs associated with keeping people behind bars. _____ (5) Of course, there should be consequences for breaking the law. _____ (6) For this reason supporters of mandatory minimum sentences say that they are necessary to deter people from committing crimes. _____ (7) Lawmakers in both parties have been working on reform however. _____ (8) In 2014 the Obama administration endorsed a proposal to reduce mandatory minimum sentences for nonviolent drug offenders. _____ (9) In December 2019, Congress approved the FIRST STEP Act, a criminal justice reform bill that includes provisions for reducing some sentences.

_____

 ## 34c   Commas with Appositives

Use commas to set off an **appositive**—a word or word group that identifies, renames, or describes a noun or a pronoun.

> I have visited only one country, Canada, outside the United States. (*Canada* is an appositive that identifies the noun *country*.)

> Carlos Santana, leader of the group Santana, played at Woodstock in 1969. (*Leader of the group Santana* is an appositive that identifies *Carlos Santana*.)

> A really gifted artist, he is also a wonderful father. (*A really gifted artist* is an appositive that describes the pronoun *he*.)

FYI

Using Commas with Appositives

Most appositives are set off by commas, whether they fall at the beginning, in the middle, or at the end of a sentence.

A dreamer, he spent his life thinking about what he could not have.

He always wanted to build a house, a big white one, overlooking the ocean.

He finally built his dream house, a log cabin.

PRACTICE

34-4 Underline the appositive in each of the following sentences. Then, check each sentence for the correct use of commas to set off appositives, and add any missing commas. If the sentence is correct, write *C* in the blank.

Example: Wendy Kopp, a college student, developed the Teach For America program to help minority students get a better education.

_____

1. Guglielmo Marconi a young Italian inventor, sent the first wireless message across the Atlantic Ocean in 1901. _____

2. A member of the boy band 'N Sync Justin Timberlake went on to establish a successful career as a solo musician and an actor. _____

3. HTML hypertext markup language, is the set of codes used to create web documents. _____

4. William Filene, founder of Filene's Department Store, invented the "bargain basement." _____

5. Known as NPR National Public Radio presents a wide variety of programs. _____

6. On the southwest coast of Nigeria lies Lagos a major port. _____

7. Prospective home of the 2022 Olympics, Beijing continues to have serious problems with its air quality. _____

8. Lightning a strong electrical charge can be both beautiful and
dangerous. _____

9. A plant that grows on mountains and in deserts, the fern is
surprisingly adaptable. _____

10. Golf a game developed in Scotland, is very popular in the United
States. _____

 ## 34d Commas with Nonrestrictive Clauses

Clauses are often used to add information within a sentence. In some
cases, commas are needed to set off these clauses; in other cases, commas
are not required.

Use commas to set off **nonrestrictive clauses**, those that are not
essential to a sentence's meaning. Do not use commas to set off **restrictive
clauses**.

- A **nonrestrictive clause** does *not* contain essential information.
  Nonrestrictive clauses are set off from the rest of the sentence by
  commas.

  Telephone scams, which cost consumers millions of dollars a
  year, are becoming increasingly common.

  Here, the clause between the commas (underlined) provides extra
  information to help readers understand the sentence, but the sentence
  would still communicate the same idea without this information.

  Telephone scams are becoming increasingly common.

- A **restrictive clause** contains information that is essential to a sentence's meaning. Restrictive clauses are *not* set off from the rest of the
  sentence by commas.

  Many rock stars who recorded hits in the 1950s made little
  money from their songs.

  In the sentence above, the clause *who recorded hits in the 1950s* supplies
  specific information that is essential to the idea the sentence is
  communicating: it tells readers which group of rock stars made little
  money. Without the clause, the sentence does not communicate the
  same idea because it does not tell which rock stars made little money.

Many rock stars made little money from their songs.

Compare the meanings of the following pairs of sentences with non-restrictive and restrictive clauses.

NONRESTRICTIVE Young adults, who text while driving, put themselves and others in danger. (This sentence says that all young adults text while driving and all pose a danger.)

RESTRICTIVE Young adults who text while driving put themselves and others in danger. (This sentence says that only those young adults who text and drive pose a danger.)

NONRESTRICTIVE Student loans, which are based on need, may not be fair to middle-class students. (This sentence says that all student loans are based on need and all may be unfair to middle-class students.)

RESTRICTIVE Student loans that are based on need may not be fair to middle-class students. (This sentence says that only those student loans that are based on need may be unfair to middle-class students.)

FYI

Which, *That*, and *Who*

■ *Which* always introduces a nonrestrictive clause.

The job, which had excellent benefits, did not pay well.
(clause set off by commas)

■ *That* always introduces a restrictive clause.

He accepted the job that had the best benefits. (no commas)

■ *Who* can introduce either a restrictive or a nonrestrictive clause.

RESTRICTIVE Many parents who work feel a lot of stress. (no commas)

NONRESTRICTIVE Both of my parents, who have always wanted the best for their children, have worked two jobs for years. (clause set off by commas)

PRACTICE

34-5 Edit the sentences in the following passage so that commas set off all nonrestrictive clauses. (Remember, commas are *not* used to set off restrictive clauses.) If a sentence is correct, write *C* in the blank.

Example: A museum exhibition that celebrates the Alaska highway tells the story of its construction. ———*C*———

(1) During the 1940s, a group of African American soldiers who defied the forces of nature and human prejudice were shipped to Alaska. ————— (2) They built the Alaska highway which stretches twelve hundred miles across Alaska. ————— (3) The troops who worked on the highway have received little attention in most historical accounts. ————— (4) The highway which cut through some of the roughest terrain in the world was begun in 1942. ————— (5) The Japanese had just landed in the Aleutian Islands which lie west of the tip of the Alaska Peninsula. ————— (6) Military officials, who oversaw the highway project, doubted the ability of the African American troops. ————— (7) As a result, they made them work under conditions, that made construction difficult. ————— (8) The troops who worked on the road proved their commanders wrong by finishing the highway months ahead of schedule. ————— (9) In one case, white engineers, who surveyed a river, said it would take two weeks to bridge. ————— (10) To the engineers' surprise, the soldiers who worked on the project beat the estimate. ————— (11) A military report that was issued in 1945 praised them. ————— (12) It said the goals that the African American soldiers achieved would be remembered through the ages. —————

34e Commas in Dates and Addresses

Dates

Use commas in dates to separate the day of the week from the month and the day of the month from the year.

> The first Cinco de Mayo we celebrated in the United States was Tuesday, May 5, 1998.

When a date that includes commas does not fall at the end of a sentence, place a comma after the year.

> Tuesday, May 5, 1998, was the first Cinco de Mayo we celebrated in the United States.

Addresses

Use commas in addresses to separate the street address from the city and the city from the state or country.

> The office of the famous fictional detective Sherlock Holmes was located at 221b Baker Street, London, England.

When an address that includes commas falls in the middle of a sentence, place a comma after the state or country.

> The office at 221b Baker Street, London, England, belonged to the famous fictional detective Sherlock Holmes.

PRACTICE

34-6 Edit the following sentences for the correct use of commas in dates and addresses. Add any missing commas, and cross out any unnecessary commas. If the sentence is correct, write *C* in the blank.

Examples

Usher's album *Looking 4 Myself* was released on June 8ˏ2012. _____

The entertainer grew up in ChattanoogaˏTennessee. _____

1. On Sunday September 27, 2015, and Monday, September 28 2015, people around the world witnessed the rare astronomical phenomenon known as the super blood moon eclipse. _____

2. For traditional Venezuelan food, locals go to Café Casa Veroes on Avenida Norte in Caracas Venezuela. _____

3. Stefani Joanne Angelina Germanotta, more commonly known as Lady Gaga, was born on March 28 1986 in New York New York. _____

4. Jake Arrieta of the Chicago Cubs pitched a no-hitter on August 30, 2015. _____

5. Donations can be sent to the American Red Cross at P. O. Box 4002018 in Des Moines, Iowa. _____

6. To visit the New York Transit Museum, visitors must travel to 130 Livingston Street in Brooklyn New York. _____

7. The Anne Frank House in Amsterdam the Netherlands became a museum on May 3 1960. _____

8. First released on November 1 1997, *Titanic* remains one of the highest-grossing movies of all time. _____

9. Fans from around the world travel to visit Ernest Hemingway's houses in Key West Florida and San Francisco de Paula, Cuba. _____

10. Oprah addressed the graduating class at Smith College on Sunday May 21, 2017 in Northampton Massachusetts. _____

34f   Unnecessary Commas

In addition to knowing where commas are required, it is also important to know when *not* to use commas.

- Do not use a comma before the first item in a series.

  INCORRECT   The 1933 film *Duck Soup* starred, Groucho, Chico, and Harpo Marx.

  CORRECT   The 1933 film *Duck Soup* starred Groucho, Chico, and Harpo Marx.

■ Do not use a comma after the last item in a series.

INCORRECT	Groucho, Chico, and Harpo Marx, starred in the 1933 film *Duck Soup*.
CORRECT	Groucho, Chico, and Harpo Marx starred in the 1933 film *Duck Soup*.

■ Do not use a comma between a subject and a verb.

INCORRECT	Students and their teachers, should try to respect one another.
CORRECT	Students and their teachers should try to respect one another.

■ Do not use a comma before the coordinating conjunction that separates the two parts of a compound predicate.

INCORRECT	The transit workers voted to strike, and walked off the job.
CORRECT	The transit workers voted to strike and walked off the job.

■ Do not use a comma before the coordinating conjunction that separates the two parts of a compound subject.

INCORRECT	The transit workers, and the sanitation workers voted to strike.
CORRECT	The transit workers and the sanitation workers voted to strike.

■ Do not use a comma to set off a restrictive clause.

INCORRECT	People, who live in glass houses, should not throw stones.
CORRECT	People who live in glass houses should not throw stones.

■ Finally, do not use a comma before a dependent clause that follows an independent clause.

INCORRECT	He was exhausted, because he had driven all night.
CORRECT	He was exhausted because he had driven all night.

PRACTICE

34-7   Some of the following sentences contain unnecessary commas. Edit to eliminate unnecessary commas. If the sentence is correct, write *C* in the blank following it.

Example: Both the Dominican Republic, and the republic of Haiti occupy the West Indian island of Hispaniola. _____

1. The capital of the Dominican Republic, is Santo Domingo. _____

2. The country's tropical climate, generous rainfall, and fertile soil, make the Dominican Republic suitable for many kinds of crops. _____

3. Some of the most important crops are, sugarcane, coffee, cocoa, and rice. _____

4. Mining is also important to the country's economy, because the land is rich in many ores. _____

5. Spanish is the official language of the Dominican Republic, and Roman Catholicism is the state religion. _____

6. In recent years, resort areas have opened, and brought many tourists to the country. _____

7. Tourists who visit the Dominican Republic, remark on its tropical beauty. _____

8. Military attacks, and political unrest have marked much of the Dominican Republic's history. _____

9. Because the republic's economy has not always been strong, many Dominicans have immigrated to the United States. _____

10. However, many Dominican immigrants maintain close ties to their home country, and return often to visit. _____

EDITING PRACTICE

Read the following student essay, which includes errors in comma use. Add commas where necessary between items in a series and with introductory phrases, transitional words and phrases, appositives, and nonrestrictive clauses. Cross out any unnecessary commas. The first sentence has been edited for you.

Earn While You Learn

What is an apprentice? If you watch reality TV, you might think of the people on *The Celebrity Apprentice*. On that show celebrities raised money for charity and, competed for the title of "apprentice." If you are a fan of old Disney movies you might picture Mickey Mouse in his role as the "sorcerer's apprentice," the sorcerer's magical assistant in *Fantasia*. In real life though apprentices do not fit either description. Generally an apprentice is someone who works for a skilled person, while learning a trade on the job.

In Europe and around the world apprenticeships have been used for a long time. They have provided a path to jobs in many fields, from skilled trades, to health care, to banking. Apprenticeship programs are a normal part of life in Switzerland for example where seventy percent of teenagers participate in apprenticeships. Australia, has a strong apprenticeship system, as well.

In the United States however apprenticeships were traditionally for jobs in skilled blue-collar trades, such as construction, and plumbing. Today that is changing. A wide variety of industries, offer apprenticeships for both blue-collar and white-collar jobs. In addition to skilled trades apprenticeships are offered by insurance companies hospital systems and cybersecurity firms. All kinds of companies want to take part, in these "earn-and-learn" programs.

No matter what the industry is the focus of an apprenticeship is on hands-on training. Apprentices usually begin with simple tasks which become more complicated as they gain experience skills and knowledge. In a typical apprenticeship program professional skills are taught through a combination of paid on-the-job training, and classroom instruction. The length of an apprenticeship program depends on the employer the job and other factors. Programs can be as short as one year or as long as six years.

In today's market jobs that start with apprenticeships include plumbers electricians and carpenters as well as dental assistants solar panel installers and information-technology specialists. Apprenticeships are offered by corporations and by departments of the federal government including the Centers for Disease Control and Prevention and, the Bureau of Engraving and Printing. Employers who use apprenticeship programs have been pleased with the results reporting higher productivity and lower turnover.

Congress has shown support for apprenticeships setting aside money to go with apprenticeship grants given to colleges states and companies. Apprenticeship programs also got a boost from the original host, of *The Celebrity Apprentice*. In 2017 President Donald Trump signed an executive order expanding access to apprenticeship programs. In addition the order promotes apprenticeships to business leaders, in a wide range of industries, including manufacturing and health care. It, also, encourages colleges and universities to incorporate apprenticeship programs into their courses of study.

COLLABORATIVE ACTIVITY

Bring a homemaking, sports, or fashion magazine to class. Working in a small group, look at the people pictured in the ads. In what roles are men most often depicted? In what roles are women presented? Identify the three or four most common roles for each sex, and give each kind of character a descriptive name—*athlete* or *mother*, for example.

Working on your own, choose one type of character, and write a paragraph in which you describe his or her typical appearance and habits. Then, circle every comma in your paragraph, and work with your group to explain why each comma is used. If no one in your group can explain why a particular comma is used, cross it out.

review checklist

Using Commas

✔ Use commas to separate all elements in a series of three or more words or word groups. (See 34a.)

✔ Use commas to set off introductory phrases and transitional words and phrases from the rest of a sentence. (See 34b.)

✔ Use commas to set off appositives from the rest of a sentence. (See 34c.)

✔ Use commas to set off nonrestrictive clauses. (See 34d.)

✔ Use commas to separate parts of dates and addresses. (See 34e.)

✔ Avoid unnecessary commas. (See 34f.)

35 Using Apostrophes

An **apostrophe** is a punctuation mark that is used in two situations: to form a contraction and to form the possessive of a noun or an indefinite pronoun.

 ## 35a Apostrophes in Contractions

A **contraction** is a word that uses an apostrophe to combine two words. The apostrophe takes the place of omitted letters.

> I <u>didn't</u> (*did not*) realize how late it was.

> <u>It's</u> (*it is*) not right for cheaters to go unpunished.

Frequently Used Contractions

I + am = I'm	can + not = can't
we + are = we're	do + not = don't
you + are = you're	will + not = won't
it + is = it's	should + not = shouldn't
I + have = I've	let + us = let's
I + will = I'll	that + is = that's
there + is = there's	who + is = who's
is + not = isn't	who + has = who's
are + not = aren't	

PRACTICE

35-1 In the following sentences, add apostrophes to contractions if needed. If the sentence is correct, write *C* in the blank.

               What's
Example: ~~Whats~~ the deadliest creature on earth? _____
      ^

(1) Bacteria and viruses, which we cant see without a microscope,

kill many people every year. _____ (2) When we speak about the deadliest creatures, however, usually were talking about creatures that cause illness or death from their poison, which is called *venom*. _____ (3) After your bitten, stung, or stuck, how long does it take to die? _____ (4) The fastest killer is a creature called the sea wasp, but it isn't a wasp at all. _____ (5) The sea wasp is actually a fifteen-foot-long jellyfish, and although its not aggressive, it can be deadly. _____ (6) People who've gone swimming off the coast of Australia have encountered this creature. _____ (7) While jellyfish found off the Atlantic coast of the United States can sting, they arent as dangerous as the sea wasp, whose venom is deadly enough to kill sixty adults. _____ (8) A person whos been stung by a sea wasp has anywhere from thirty seconds to four minutes to get help or die. _____ (9) Oddly, it's been found that something as thin as pantyhose worn over the skin will prevent these stings. _____ (10) Also, theres an antidote to the poison that can save victims._____

 ## 35b Apostrophes in Possessives

Possessive forms of nouns and pronouns show ownership. Nouns and indefinite pronouns do not have special possessive forms. Instead, they use apostrophes to indicate ownership.

Singular Nouns and Indefinite Pronouns

To form the possessive of **singular nouns** (including names) and **indefinite pronouns**, add an apostrophe plus an *s*.

> Cesar Chavez's goal (*the goal of Cesar Chavez*) was justice for American farmworkers.

> The strike's outcome (*the outcome of the strike*) was uncertain.

> Whether it would succeed was anyone's guess (*the guess of anyone*).

FYI

Singular Nouns Ending in -s

Even if a singular noun already ends in -s, add an apostrophe plus an s to form the possessive.

The <u>class's</u> next assignment was a research paper.

<u>Dr. Ramos's</u> patients are participating in a clinical trial.

Plural Nouns

Most plural nouns end in -s. To form the possessive of **plural nouns ending in -s** (including names), add just an apostrophe (not an apostrophe plus an s).

The two <u>drugs'</u> side effects (*the side effects of the two drugs*) were quite different.

The <u>Johnsons'</u> front door (*the front door of the Johnsons*) is red.

Some irregular noun plurals do not end in -s. If a plural noun does not end in -s, add an apostrophe plus an s to form the possessive.

The <u>men's</u> room is right next to the <u>women's</u> room.

PRACTICE

35-2   Rewrite the following phrases, changing the noun or indefinite pronoun that follows *of* to the possessive form. Be sure to distinguish between singular and plural nouns.

Examples

the mayor of the city *the city's mayor*

the uniforms of the players *the players' uniforms*

1. the video of the singer _____

2. the scores of the students _____

3. the favorite band of everybody _____

4. the office of the boss _____

5. the union of the players _____

6. the specialty of the restaurant _____

7. the bedroom of the children _____

8. the high cost of the tickets _____

9. the dreams of everyone _____

10. the owner of the dogs _____

 ## 35c Incorrect Use of Apostrophes

Be careful not to confuse a plural noun (*boys*) with the singular possessive form of the noun (*boy's*). Never use an apostrophe with a plural noun
unless the noun is possessive.

> Termites can be dangerous <u>pests</u> [not *pest's*].

> The <u>Velezes</u> [not *Velez's*] live on Maple Drive, right next door to the
> <u>Browns</u> [not *Brown's*].

Also remember not to use apostrophes with possessive pronouns that
end in *-s*: *theirs* (not *their's*), *hers* (not *her's*), *its* (not *it's*),
ours (not *our's*), and *yours* (not *your's*).

Be especially careful not to confuse possessive pronouns with sound-
alike contractions. Possessive pronouns never include apostrophes.

POSSESSIVE PRONOUN	CONTRACTION
The dog bit <u>its</u> master.	<u>It's</u> (*it is*) time for breakfast.
The choice is <u>theirs</u>.	<u>There's</u> (*there is*) no place like home.
<u>Whose</u> house is this?	<u>Who's</u> (*who is*) on first base?
Is this <u>your</u> house?	<u>You're</u> (*you are*) late again.

PRACTICE

35-3 Check the underlined words in the following sentences for correct use of apostrophes. If a correction needs to be made, cross
out the word and write the correct version above it. If the noun or pronoun
is correct, write *C* above it.

> **Example:** The <u>governor's</u> [C] views were presented after several other
> ~~speaker's~~ [speakers] first presented ~~their's~~ [theirs].

1. <u>Parent's</u> should realize that when it comes to disciplining children, the responsibility is <u>their's</u>.

2. <u>It's</u> also important that parents offer praise for a <u>child's</u> good behavior.

3. In <u>it's</u> first few <u>week's</u> of life, a dog is already developing a personality.

4. His and <u>her's</u> towels used to be popular with <u>couple's</u>, but <u>it's</u> not so common to see them today.

5. All the <u>Ryan's</u> spent four <u>year's</u> in college and then got good jobs.

6. Kanye told Kim, "<u>You're</u> the one <u>who's</u> love I've been waiting for."

7. If you expect to miss any <u>class's</u>, you will have to make arrangements with someone <u>who's</u> willing to tell you <u>you're</u> assignment.

8. No other <u>school's</u> cheerleading squad tried as many stunts as <u>our's</u> did.

9. Surprise <u>test's</u> are common in my economics <u>teacher's</u> class.

10. <u>*Jazz's*</u> influence on many mainstream <u>musician's</u> is one of the <u>book's</u> main <u>subject's</u>.

EDITING PRACTICE

Read the following student essay, which includes errors in the use of apostrophes. Edit it to eliminate errors by crossing out incorrect words and writing corrections above them. (Note that this essay is an informal response, so contractions are acceptable.) The first sentence has been edited for you.

The Women of Messina

In William ~~Shakespeares'~~ Shakespeare's play *Much Ado about Nothing*, the women of Messina, whether they are seen as love objects or as ~~shrew's,~~ shrews, have very few options. A womans role is to please a man. She can try to resist, but she will probably wind up giving in.

The plays two women, Hero and Beatrice, are very different. Hero is the obedient one. Heroes cousin, Beatrice, tries to challenge the rules of the mans world in which she lives. However, in a place like Messina, even women like Beatrice find it hard to get the respect that should be their's.

Right from the start, we are drawn to Beatrice. Shes funny, she has a clever comment for most situation's, and she always speaks her mind about other peoples behavior. Unlike Hero, she tries to stand up to the men in her life, as we see in her and Benedicks conversations. But even though Beatrice's intelligence is obvious, she often mocks herself. Its clear that she doesn't have much self-esteem. In fact, Beatrice is'nt the strong woman she seems to be.

Ultimately, Beatrice does get her man, and she will be happy—but at what cost? Benedicks' last word's to her are "Peace! I will stop your mouth." Then, he kisses her. The kiss is a symbolic end to their bickering. It is also the mark of Beatrices defeat. She has lost. Benedick has silenced her. Now, she will be Benedick's wife and do what he wants her to do. Granted, she will

WORD POWER

shrew a scolding woman

603

have more say in her marriage than Hero will have in her's, but she is still defeated.

Shakespeares audience might have seen the plays ending as a happy one. For contemporary audience's, however, the ending is disappointing. Even Beatrice, the most rebellious of Messinas women, finds it impossible to achieve anything of importance in this male-dominated society.

COLLABORATIVE ACTIVITY

Bring to class a book, magazine, or newspaper whose style is informal—for example, a romance novel, *People*, your school newspaper, or even a comic book. Working in a group, circle every contraction you can find on one page of each publication, and substitute for each contraction the words it combines. Are your substitutions an improvement? (You may want to read a few paragraphs aloud before you reach a conclusion.)

review checklist

Using Apostrophes

✔ Use apostrophes to form contractions. (See 35a.)

✔ Use an apostrophe plus an *s* to form the possessive of singular nouns and indefinite pronouns, even when a noun ends in -*s*. (See 35b.)

✔ Use an apostrophe alone to form the possessive of plural nouns ending in -*s*, including names. If a plural noun does not end in -*s*, add an apostrophe plus an *s*. (See 35b.)

✔ Do not use apostrophes with plural nouns unless they are possessive. Do not use apostrophes with possessive pronouns. (See 35c.)

36 **Understanding Mechanics**

36a Capitalizing Proper Nouns

A **proper noun** names a particular person, animal, place, object, or idea. Proper nouns are always capitalized. The list that follows explains and illustrates specific rules for capitalizing proper nouns.

- Always capitalize names of **races, ethnic groups, tribes, nationalities, languages, and religions**.

   The census data revealed a diverse community of Caucasians, African Americans, and Asian Americans, with a few Latino and Navajo residents. Native languages included English, Korean, and Spanish. Most people identified themselves as Catholic, Protestant, or Muslim.

- Capitalize names of **specific people and the titles that accompany them**. In general, do not capitalize titles used without a name.

   In 1994, President Nelson Mandela was elected to lead South Africa.

   The newly elected fraternity president addressed the crowd.

- Capitalize names of **specific family members and their titles**. Do not capitalize words that identify family relationships, including those introduced by possessive pronouns.

   The twins, Aunt Edna and Aunt Evelyn, are Dad's sisters.

   My aunts, my father's sisters, are twins.

- Capitalize names of **specific countries, cities, towns, bodies of water, streets, and so on**. Do not capitalize words that do not name specific places.

   The Seine runs through Paris, France.

   The river runs through the city.

- Capitalize names of **specific geographical regions**. Do not capitalize such words when they specify direction.

    William Faulkner's novels are set in the South.

    Turn right at the golf course, and go south for about a mile.

- Capitalize names of **specific groups, clubs, teams, and associations**. Do not capitalize general references to such groups.

    The Teamsters Union represents workers who were at the stadium for the Republican Party convention, the Rolling Stones concert, and the Phillies-Astros game.

    The union represents workers who were at the stadium for the political party's convention, the rock group's concert, and the baseball teams' game.

- Capitalize **brand names**. Do not capitalize general references to kinds of products.

    While Jeff waited for his turn at the Xerox machine, he drank a can of Coke.

    While Jeff waited for his turn at the copier, he drank a can of soda.

- Capitalize **titles of specific academic courses**. Do not capitalize names of general academic subject areas, except for proper nouns—for example, a language or a country.

    Are Introduction to American Government and Biology 200 closed yet?

    Are the introductory American government course and the biology course closed yet?

- Capitalize **days of the week, months of the year, and holidays**. Do not capitalize the names of seasons.

    The Jewish holiday of Passover usually falls in April.

    The Jewish holiday of Passover falls in the spring.

Note: Also capitalize names of specific buildings and monuments; names of specific historical periods, events, and documents; and names of businesses, government agencies, schools, and other institutions.

PRACTICE

36-1 Edit the following passage, capitalizing letters or changing capitals to lowercase where necessary.

Example: The third-largest ⊄ity in the ᵤnited ˢtates is ⊄hicago,
ᵢllinois.

(1) Located in the midwest on lake Michigan, chicago is an important port city, a rail and highway hub, and the site of o'hare international airport, one of the Nation's busiest. (2) The financial center of the city is Lasalle street, and the lakefront is home to Grant park, where there are many Museums and monuments. (3) To the North of the city, soldier field is home to the chicago bears, the city's football team, and wrigley field is home to the chicago cubs, a national league Baseball Team. (4) In the mid-1600s, the site of what is now Chicago was visited by father jacques marquette, a catholic missionary to the ottawa and huron tribes, who were native to the area. (5) By the 1700s, the city was a trading post run by john kinzie. (6) The city grew rapidly in the 1800s, and immigrants included germans, irish, italians, poles, greeks, and chinese, along with african americans who migrated from the south. (7) In 1871, much of the city was destroyed in one of the worst fires in united states history; according to legend, the fire started when mrs. O'Leary's Cow kicked over a burning lantern. (8) Today, Chicago's skyline has many Skyscrapers, built by businesses like the john hancock company, sears, and amoco. (9) I know Chicago well because my Mother grew up there and my aunt jean and uncle amos still live there. (10) I also got information from the Chicago Chamber of Commerce when I wrote a paper for introductory research writing, a course I took at Graystone high school.

36b Punctuating Direct Quotations

A **direct quotation** shows the *exact* words of a speaker or writer. Direct quotations are always placed in quotation marks.

A direct quotation is usually accompanied by an **identifying tag**, a phrase (such as "she said") that names the person being quoted. In the following sentences, the identifying tag is underlined.

<u>Lauren said</u>, "My brother and Tina have gotten engaged."

A <u>famous advertising executive wrote</u>, "Don't sell the steak; sell the sizzle."

When a quotation is a complete sentence, it begins with a capital letter and ends with a period (or a question mark or exclamation point). When a quotation falls at the end of a sentence (as in the two examples above) the period is placed *before* the quotation marks.

If the quotation is a question or an exclamation, the question mark or exclamation point is also placed *before* the closing quotation mark.

The instructor asked, "Has anyone read Toni Morrison's *Sula*<u>?"</u>

Officer Warren shouted, "Hold it right there<u>!"</u>

If the quotation itself is not a question or an exclamation, the question mark or exclamation point is placed *after* the closing quotation mark.

Did Joe really say, "I quit<u>"?</u>

I can't believe he really said, "I quit<u>"!</u>

FYI

Indirect Quotations

A direct quotation shows someone's *exact* words, but an **indirect quotation** simply summarizes what was said or written.

Do not use quotation marks with indirect quotations.

DIRECT QUOTATION	Martin Luther King Jr. said, <u>"I have a dream."</u>
INDIRECT QUOTATION	Martin Luther King Jr. said that he had a dream.

The rules for punctuating direct quotations with identifying tags are summarized below.

Identifying Tag at the Beginning

When the identifying tag comes *before* the quotation, it is followed by a comma.

> Theodore Roosevelt said, "Speak softly and carry a big stick."

Identifying Tag at the End

When the identifying tag comes at the *end* of a quoted sentence, it is followed by a period. A comma (or, sometimes, a question mark or an exclamation point) inside the closing quotation mark separates the quotation from the identifying tag.

> "Life is like a box of chocolates," stated Forrest Gump.
>
> "Is that so?" his friends wondered.
>
> "That's amazing!" he cried.

Identifying Tag in the Middle

When the identifying tag comes in the *middle* of the quoted sentence, it is followed by a comma. The first part of the quotation is also followed by a comma, placed inside the closing quotation mark. Because the part of the quotation that follows the identifying tag is not a new sentence, it does not begin with a capital letter.

> "This is my life," Bette insisted, "and I'll live it as I please."

Identifying Tag between Two Sentences

When the identifying tag comes *between two* quoted sentences, it is preceded by a comma and followed by a period. (The second quoted sentence begins with a capital letter.)

> "Producer Berry Gordy is an important figure in the history of music," Tony explained. "He was the creative force behind Motown records."

PRACTICE

36-2 The following sentences contain direct quotations. First, underline the identifying tag. Then, punctuate the quotation correctly, adding capital letters as necessary.

Example: " Why " Darryl asked " are teachers so strict about deadlines? "

1. We who are about to die salute you said the gladiators to the emperor.

2. The bigger they are said boxer John L. Sullivan the harder they fall.

3. If you believe the celebrity gossip my friend always says then you'll believe anything.

4. When asked for the jury's verdict, the foreperson replied we find the defendant not guilty.

5. I had felt for a long time that if I was ever told to get up so a white person could sit Rosa Parks recalled I would refuse to do so.

 # 36c   Setting Off Titles

Some titles are typed in *italics*. Others are enclosed in quotation marks. The following box shows how to set off different kinds of titles.

Italics or Quotation Marks?

ITALICIZED TITLES

Books: *How the García Girls Lost Their Accents*
Newspapers: *Miami Herald*
Magazines: *People*
Long poems: *John Brown's Body*
Plays: *Death of a Salesman*
Films: *The Hunger Games*
Television or radio series or podcast: *Game of Thrones*
Paintings and sculpture: *American Gothic*
Video games: *Call of Duty Black Ops 4*

TITLES IN QUOTATION MARKS

Book chapters: "Understanding Mechanics"
Short stories: "The Tell-Tale Heart"
Essays and articles: "Mother Tongue"
Short poems: "Richard Cory"
Songs and speeches: "America the Beautiful"; "The Gettysburg Address"
Individual episodes of television or radio series or podcast: "The Montgomery Bus Boycott" (an episode of the PBS series *Eyes on the Prize*)

FYI

Capital Letters in Titles

Capitalize the first letters of all important words in a title. Do not capitalize an **article** (*a, an, the*), a **preposition** (*to, of, around,* and so on), the *to* in an infinitive, or a **coordinating conjunction** (*and, but,* and so on)—unless it is the first or last word of the title or subtitle (<u>O</u>n the Road; "<u>T</u>o an Athlete Dying Young"; No Way <u>O</u>ut; <u>A</u>nd Quiet Flows the Don).

PRACTICE

36-3

Edit the following sentences, capitalizing letters as necessary in titles.

Example: *New york times* best-seller *three cups of tea* is about Greg

Mortenson's work building schools in Pakistan and Afghanistan.

1. In 2009, aziz ansari began appearing in *parks and recreation*; in 2017, he began playing dev shah in the Netflix series *master of none*.

2. In 2009, David Blaine delivered his famous TED Talk "how i held my breath for 17 minutes."

3. After nearly losing her life for supporting education for young girls, Malala Yousafzai published a memoir titled *i am malala: the girl who stood up for education and was shot by the taliban.*

4. Actor Johnny Depp plays the pirate Captain Jack Sparrow in the films *the curse of the black pearl, dead man's chest, at world's end,* and *on stranger tides.*

5. Singer-songwriter Bruno Mars has written songs that were performed by other artists, such as "billionaire," as well as songs he has performed himself, such as "just the way you are."

PRACTICE

36-4 In the following sentences, underline titles to indicate italics or place them in quotation marks. (Remember that titles of books and other long works are italicized, and titles of stories, essays, and other shorter works are enclosed in quotation marks.)

Example: In an article in <u>The New Yorker</u> called "Scoop Dreams," Shonda Rhimes recalls a job she had when she was a teenager.

1. BusinessWeek reports that many young workers do not contribute regularly to a retirement account.

2. At the beginning of most major American sporting events, the crowd stands for The Star-Spangled Banner.

3. People who want to purchase new cars often compare the different models in Consumer Reports magazine.

4. U2's song Pride (in the Name of Love) is about Martin Luther King Jr.

5. Edgar Allan Poe wrote several mysterious short stories, two of which are called The Tell-Tale Heart and The Black Cat.

6. The popular Broadway show Hamilton was based on Ron Chernow's 2004 book Alexander Hamilton.

7. Aasif Mandvi, a comedian who was a correspondent on The Daily Show, also wrote the book No Land's Man.

8. In a college textbook called Sociology: A Brief Introduction, the first chapter is titled The Essence of Sociology.

36d Using Semicolons, Colons, Dashes, and Parentheses

Correct usage of semicolons, colons, dashes, and parentheses will help you to communicate your ideas effectively.

The Semicolon

Use a **semicolon** to join independent clauses in a compound sentence.

Twenty years ago, smartphones did not exist; today, many people cannot imagine life without them.

The Colon

■ Use a **colon** to introduce a quotation.

Our family motto is a simple one: "Accept no substitutes."

■ Use a colon to introduce an explanation, a clarification, or an example.

Only one thing kept him from climbing Mt. Everest: fear of heights.

■ Use a colon to introduce a list.

I left my job for four reasons: boring work, poor working conditions, low pay, and a terrible supervisor.

The Dash

Use **dashes** to set off important information.

She parked her car—a red Firebird—in a tow-away zone.

Parentheses

Use **parentheses** to enclose material that is relatively unimportant.

The weather in Portland (a city in Oregon) was overcast.

PRACTICE

36-5 Add semicolons, colons, dashes, and parentheses to the following sentences where necessary.

Example: Megachurches (those with more than two thousand worshippers at a typical service) have grown in popularity since the 1950s.

1. Megachurches though they are Protestant are not always affiliated with the main Protestant denominations.

2. Services in megachurches are creative preaching is sometimes accompanied by contemporary music and video presentations.

3. Although many of these churches are evangelical actively recruiting new members, people often join because of friends and neighbors.

4. Megachurches tend to keep their members because they encourage a variety of activities for example, hospitality committees and study groups.

5. Worshippers say that their services are upbeat they are full of joy and spirituality.

6. Megachurches in nearly all cases use technology to organize and communicate with their members.

7. The largest of these churches with ten thousand members would be unable to function without telecommunications.

8. Some even offer services in a format familiar to their younger members the podcast.

9. Critics of megachurches and there are some believe they take up too much tax-exempt land.

10. Other critics fear that smaller churches already struggling to keep members will lose worshippers to these huge congregations and eventually will have to close.

EDITING PRACTICE

Read the following student essay, which includes errors in capitalization and punctuation and in the use of direct quotations and titles. Correct any errors you find. The first sentence has been edited for you.

A Threat to Health

Pandemics are like ~~E~~epidemics, only more widespread, perhaps even spreading throughout the World. In a pandemic, a serious Disease spreads very easily. In the past, there have been many pandemics. In the future, in spite of advances in Medicine, there will still be pandemics. In fact, scientists agree that not every pandemic can be prevented, so pandemics will continue to be a threat.

Probably the best-known pandemic is the bubonic plague. It killed about one-third of the Population of europe during the middle ages. Some areas suffered more than others. According to Philip ziegler's book the black Death, at least half the people in florence, Italy, died in one year. Many years later, in 1918, a flu pandemic killed more than fifty million people worldwide, including hundreds of thousands in the United states.

Unfortunately, pandemics have not disappeared. AIDS, for example, is a current pandemic. Philadelphia the 1993 movie starring denzel washington and tom hanks is still one of the most moving depictions of the heartbreak of AIDS. The rate of AIDS infection is over 30 percent in parts of africa, the disease continues to spread on other Continents as well. So far, efforts to find an AIDS vaccine have failed. Dr. anthony s. Fauci discussed this problem, as well as recent AIDS research on NPR's series All things considered in a program called Search for an HIV vaccine expands.

Although some pandemic diseases, such as Smallpox, have been wiped out by Vaccination, new pandemics remain a threat. Many viruses and Bacteria change in response to treatment, so they may become resistant to Vaccination and Antibiotics. Also, with modern transportation, a disease can move quickly from Country to Country. For example, the disease known as severe acute respiratory syndrome (SARS) began in china but was spread to other countries by travelers. Hundreds died as a result of the SARS pandemic between November 2002 and july 2003.

Birds also remain a threat because they can transmit disease. It is obviously impossible to prevent birds from flying from one country to another. Markos kyprianou, health commissioner of the European union, has said that I am concerned that birds in Turkey had been found with the bird flu Virus. He said, There is a direct relationship with viruses found in Russia, Mongolia and china. If this Virus changes so that it can move easily from birds to Humans, bird flu could become the next pandemic.

Public Health Officials are always on the lookout for diseases with three characteristics they are new, they are dangerous, and they are very contagious. Doctors try to prevent these diseases from becoming Pandemics. However, they continue to warn that some Pandemics cannot be prevented.

COLLABORATIVE ACTIVITY

Working in pairs, write a conversation between two characters, real or fictional, who have very different positions on a particular issue. Place all direct quotations within quotation marks, and include identifying tags that clearly indicate which character is speaking. (Begin a new paragraph each time a new person speaks.)

Exchange your conversation with another pair, and check their work to see that directly quoted speech is set within quotation marks and that capital letters and other punctuation are used correctly.

review checklist

Understanding Mechanics

✔ Capitalize proper nouns. (See 36a.)

✔ Always place direct quotations within quotation marks. (See 36b.)

✔ In titles, capitalize all important words. Use italics or quotation marks to set off titles. (See 36c.)

✔ Use semicolons to join independent clauses in a compound sentence. (See 36d.)

✔ Use colons, dashes, and parentheses to set off material from the rest of a sentence. (See 36d.)

Unit
5 Reading Essays

37 Readings for Writers 620

37 Readings for Writers

The following twelve essays by professional writers offer interesting material to read, react to, think critically about, discuss, and write about. In addition, these essays illustrate some of the ways you can organize ideas in your own writing.

The essays in this chapter use many of the patterns of essay development you learned about in Chapters 15 and 16 of this book. Of course, these patterns are not your only options for arranging ideas in essays; in fact, many essays combine several patterns of development. Still, understanding how patterns work will help you to choose the most effective organization strategy when you are writing for a particular purpose and audience.

Each of the essays that follow is preceded by a short **headnote**, an introduction that tells you something about the writer and suggests what to look for as you read, and an "As you read" sentence that suggests what to focus on as you approach the essay. **Word Power** boxes define words that may be unfamiliar to you. Following each essay are four sets of questions and two writing prompts.

- **Focus on Reading** questions offer suggestions for previewing, marking up, and annotating the essay.
- **Focus on Meaning** questions help you to assess your understanding of the basic ideas the essay communicates.
- **Focus on Strategy and Critical Thinking** questions ask you to consider the writer's purpose and intended audience, the essay's opening and closing strategies, and the thesis statement. These questions often ask you to make judgments about the writer's rhetorical choices.
- **Focus on Language and Style** questions ask you to think about the writer's stylistic decisions and word choices as well as the connotations (meanings associated with words) and denotations (dictionary definitions).
- **Focus on Writing** prompts offer suggestions for writing in response to each essay.

As you read each of the essays in this chapter, follow the active reading process outlined in Chapter 1–previewing, marking up, and annotating each essay–to help you understand what you are reading and prepare for writing an essay of your own. You can use **TEST** to help you identify the essay's key elements.

T **Thesis**—Look for the thesis or **main idea**, which is sometimes stated directly, often (but not always) in the opening paragraphs. Try to decide why the writer placed the main idea where it is. If the main idea is **implied** (suggested), try to decide why it is not explicitly stated. Try to write a sentence that states the main idea in your own words.

E **Evidence**—Look for the evidence that supports the writer's main idea. This evidence can be in the form of examples, statistics, or anecdotes based on the writer's observations or experiences, or the opinions of experts. Think about why the writer chose these types of evidence rather than others. Consider whether different evidence or additional support is needed and whether any evidence is irrelevant or unnecessary. Think about what you can **infer** from the evidence presented (see 5e).

S **Summary**—Look for a statement that lists or summarizes the writer's key points or the essay's main idea. Often, this summary appears in the closing paragraphs. If no summary is included, write a sentence that could serve as a summary statement.

T **Transitions**—Look for transitional words and expressions that connect ideas within and between paragraphs. How do these transitions help you to understand the writer's ideas and follow his or her train of thought? Look for **transitional paragraphs**, paragraphs whose purpose is not to supply evidence, but rather to move readers from one section of the essay to the next.

The Case against E-Readers: Why Reading Paper Books Is Better for Your Mind

Naomi S. Baron

Naomi S. Baron has a PhD in linguistics from Stanford University. She has taught at Brown University, Emory University, Southwestern University, and American University, where she has been the executive director of the Center for Teaching, Research, and Learning since 2011. Baron's research includes a focus on language in the computer age. Her recent books include *Always On: Language in an Online and Mobile World* (2008) and *Words Onscreen: The Fate of Reading in a Digital World* (2015). In this 2015 essay from *The Washington Post*, Baron discusses the limitations of reading on screens.

As you read, think about why you prefer either reading on paper or reading electronically.

1   You got an e-reader over the holidays. What should you load it up with?

2   Beach reads? Sure. *Ulysses*?[1] Probably not.

[1]Novel written by Irish writer James Joyce, published in 1922.

3   We know a lot about the pros and cons of reading a hard-copy book vs. reading electronically. The problem is, many of us refuse to listen.

4   Don't get me wrong: Digital reading has some real advantages. Ask people what they like most about reading on digital screens (a question I've put to several hundred university students in the United States, Germany, Japan, and Slovakia), and you hear over and over again about convenience: "easy to carry" and "compact." We also know electronic texts (especially when they are open-access or donated) are vital for democratizing learning opportunities. Just look at projects like the Digital Public Library of America or Worldreader.

5   More points for digital reading: e-books tend to be cheaper than print versions (though outside America, tax structures sometimes complicate the comparison). There's also the environmental argument. Think of the trees!

6   Yet the soundness of this case is arguable. The earth metals we're using up to build e-readers and tablets are not just rare but highly toxic. And think about all that energy needed to run servers and cooling fans. And remember, trees are a renewable resource.

7   Then, there's the appeal of a hard copy. What fascinates me is how many people—from teenagers to millennials to those of a certain age—prefer print when reading both for pleasure and for school or work. Drawing examples from my own research, some of the reasons are aesthetic ("charm of actually turning pages" and "scent of a new book"). Others involve a sense of accomplishment ("able to see how much I read"), ease of annotation ("I can write on the pages"), and navigation ("easy to locate where I was"). In contrast, I hear abundant complaints about eye strain and headaches when using screens.

8   Much of what students liked about reading print involved their minds. They said "it's easier to focus," "my spatial memory works best," and "feel like the content sticks in my head more easily." Some also acknowledged they took more time with printed text and read more carefully—not really a surprise, since digital screens encourage scrolling and hasten us along to grab the next website or tweet.

9   But the real nail in the coffin for one-size-fits-all electronic reading is concentration. Over 92 percent of those I surveyed said they concentrate best when reading a hard copy. The explanation is hardly rocket science. When a digital device has an Internet connection, it's hard to resist the temptation to jump ship: I'll just respond to that text I heard come in, check the headlines, order those boots that are on sale.

10   Readers are human. If you dangle distractions in front of us (or if we know they are just a click or swipe away), it's hard not to take the bait.

11   Which brings us back to the question of what sorts of reading it makes sense to do onscreen and which to reserve for paper. If digital interruptions don't threaten your enjoyment or understanding of a text (but here, you have to be honest), then medium may not matter. Casual reading like Baldacci?[2] If you break to check sports scores, little harm done. Just don't expect to understand much of Joyce this way.

[2]David Baldacci, a best-selling American thriller writer.

WORD POWER

open-access online information that is free of all restrictions

WORD POWER

democratizing making more equal for all

WORD POWER

soundness validity; truth

WORD POWER

aesthetic concerned with beauty

WORD POWER

hasten to be quick to do something

Focus on Reading

1. In the margins of this essay, label the advantages and disadvantages of digital reading and reading hard copy.

2. Construct a brief informal outline of this essay.

3. **TEST** Baron's essay. Does she include all four **TEST** elements? If not, why not?

Focus on Meaning

1. According to Baron, what are the advantages of reading electronically versus reading a hard copy?

2. What kinds of readings does Baron think are better suited to digital reading? Why? What kinds of readings does she think should be read in a hard-copy book? Why?

Focus on Strategy and Critical Thinking

1. What audience does Baron seem to be addressing? Does she expect this audience to have a preference for one kind of reading over the other?

2. Baron's title expresses her preference for "paper books" over e-readers. Do you think she makes a convincing case for hard-copy books? Why or why not?

3. This essay is organized as a comparison and contrast. Is this the best choice? Why or why not? What other pattern of development could Baron have used to structure her essay?

Focus on Language and Style

1. In paragraph 9, Baron uses three clichés: "nail in the coffin," "hardly rocket science," and "jump ship." What does each of these expressions mean? Does Baron's use of these clichés undercut her credibility, or does it add to her essay's effectiveness? Explain.

2. What is a "beach read" (2)? Why do you think Baron uses this expression instead of a more formal term?

Focus on Writing

1. Write an essay in which you compare two texts you have read—one more suitable for digital reading and one more suitable for reading as hard copy. Why is each book better suited to one method of reading than to another?

2. Write an essay that compares the way you would read an online news article or textbook passage versus the way you would read the same text in a paper book.

Real Solutions for Curtailing Gun Violence

John Carlson

John Carlson is a conservative political activist and a talk radio host on KVI-AM in Washington state, where he received a bachelor's degree in political science from the University of Washington. In the 1990s, Carlson coauthored two state anticrime ballot initiatives, "Three Strikes and You're Out" (which influenced similar laws in dozens of other states) and "Hard Time for Armed Crime." After their passage, he successfully campaigned for a state ballot initiative prohibiting affirmative action in public employment, education, and contracting. He currently hosts a morning radio show called *The Commute with Carlson*. In this 2018 article for the *Wall Street Journal*, he adds his voice to the debate about gun violence.

As you read, think about some recent incidents of gun violence that you have read about or witnessed.

1   The most predictable fallout from last week's school shooting in Florida is the impassioned reactions from both sides of the gun divide, which guarantee nothing will change. Gun-control supporters demonize firearms and Second Amendment supporters, blaming the National Rifle Association for mass murder. Conservatives see their critics as caring little about the Constitution and knowing next to nothing about firearms.

2   But people of good faith can find common ground and help reduce gun violence in the U.S.

3   Let's begin with a statistic: The number of guns in America rose nearly 50% between 1993 and 2013. During the same period, gun homicides fell by nearly 50%. The notion that more guns mean more crime is simplistic and false.

4   Yet we still see frightening outbursts of armed violence—whether sudden, as in 17 dead within minutes at Marjory Stoneman Douglas High School, or in slow motion, as in 20 dead during January in Chicago—an improvement from last year.

5   A University of Chicago study found that only 3% of Windy City gun crimes were committed with legally purchased guns. A federal study in 2004 put the percentage of gun crimes committed with legal guns at 11%. By and large the problem isn't guns—it's that people who shouldn't have them are getting them and using them.

6   As for mass shootings, almost all of them have involved mentally ill young men. Some used pistols, some used rifles, some had both—but as with street crime, people who shouldn't have weapons got them.

7   So, what to do? Here are three suggestions.

8   First, to reduce street violence, dramatically increase penalties for stealing a firearm. According to FBI statistics, in the four years from 2012–15, 1.2 million guns were stolen from people, and another 22,000 were stolen from gun stores. Criminals respond to incentives like everybody

else. A mandatory four-year prison term for illegally possessing a firearm, and a six-year term per gun for selling stolen firearms, would, if seriously enforced, escalate the risk of the crime past the point of anticipated benefits. Sentences should be so severe that a burglar would *avoid* taking the victim's guns rather than face the consequences of being caught with them. Similarly harsh sentences should apply to felons carrying firearms. We don't need a war on guns, but we do need a war on illegal guns. This will save more lives than any other single policy change.

9   Second, enforce the law against straw purchases of handguns. A straw purchase happens when someone who is legally allowed to buy a gun walks into a store, completes the required paperwork, takes possession of the firearm—and then gives it or sells it to someone who isn't allowed to own one. Federal law makes it a crime punishable by up to 10 years in prison and a $250,000 fine.

10   But those laws are rarely enforced. In the eyes of the federal government (and straw purchasers) it's a low priority. If that changed, illegal guns from straw purchases would start to dry up. This requires no change in laws, only priorities. The president and attorney general could make it happen immediately.

11   Third, find practical, legal ways of preventing seriously mentally ill people from acquiring firearms. Nikolas Cruz, the confessed killer of 17 in Florida last week, had been investigated by Florida's child-protective agency in late 2016 after cutting himself in an online video. He stated he was going out to buy a gun (which he did). The investigating agency "found him stable enough not to be hospitalized."

12   Two months later, Mr. Cruz, a chronic troublemaker who had been repeatedly suspended from school, was referred for a "threat assessment." Records show he attended half a dozen schools, including one for students with emotional problems. The FBI received a tip from someone who knew Mr. Cruz, cited concerns about his behavior and guns, and expressed concerns he could attack a school. The FBI has confirmed that it did not follow protocol in handling the reports. Nor did it follow up on a tip from a YouTube blogger after Mr. Cruz left a comment declaring: "Im [sic] going to be a professional school shooter." The local sheriff said his office had received more than 20 calls about Mr. Cruz. Police had been called out to his house more than three dozen times.

13   And he was able to buy a gun.

14   Pre-emptively denying someone a constitutional right requires navigating a social, legal and political minefield. It is a tough job that needs to be done. The president should announce a task force to make clear recommendations to Congress on where that line should be drawn. Attempts to deny some Social Security Disability recipients gun rights recently ran afoul not only of Congress and the president, but also the American Civil Liberties Union and a host of disability-rights groups as well. But conservatives and liberals can agree that someone like Nikolas Cruz shouldn't be allowed to legally buy a gun.

15   All Americans want less gun violence. The way to get there is to keep guns away from people who have no business owning them, and punishing them when they do obtain or possess guns illegally.

WORD POWER

protocol regulations, plan of procedure

WORD POWER

pre-emptively as a preventive measure against something expected

WORD POWER

ran afoul of came into conflict with

Focus on Reading

1. Underline Carlson's thesis statement. In the margin beside this statement, rewrite it in your own words.

2. Number the three suggestions Carlson makes in paragraphs 8 through 11. Put a star beside the suggestion you think is the most important.

3. **TEST** Carlson's essay. Does he include all four **TEST** elements? If not, why not?

Focus on Meaning

1. According to Carlson, what positions do "gun-control supporters" and "conservatives" (1) take on gun violence?

2. In your own words, what are the three suggestions Carlson offers to solve the problem of gun violence? Which do you see as the most important? Why?

Focus on Strategy and Critical thinking

1. Do you agree with Carlson that "people of good faith can find common ground" on this issue? Why or why not? Do you agree with his position in paragraph 15? Explain.

2. In paragraph 3, Carlson says, "Let's begin with a statistic." Why does he introduce his argument with this statistic?

3. In paragraph 5, Carlson says, "By and large the problem isn't guns—it's that people who shouldn't have them are getting them and using them." Does he support this claim? If so, where?

Focus on Language and Style

1. Why does Carlson set off the sentences in paragraphs 2, 7, and 13 as single paragraphs? Should he have combined any of these sentences with the paragraphs before or after them? Why or why not?

2. What do you think Carlson means by "street violence" (8)? What connotations does this term have? What other terms could he have used to characterize this kind of gun violence?

Focus on Writing

1. Choose one of Carlson's three solutions to the problem of gun violence, and write an essay explaining why you believe it will or will not work. Be specific, and be sure to address Carlson's position, quoting from his essay where appropriate.

2. Write an essay in which you take the position that video games, movies, and television encourage or do not encourage gun violence. Be sure your essay has a clear thesis statement, and support your thesis by referring to specific video games, movies, or television shows.

Should Driverless Cars Kill Their Own Passengers to Save a Pedestrian?

Olivia Goldhill

Olivia Goldhill grew up in London. She received a bachelor's degree in philosophy from Harvard and a master's degree in journalism from City University in London. She was a features writer for *The Telegraph* and now combines her two areas of interest by writing about philosophy and psychology for *Quartz*. In the following *Quartz* article from 2015, Goldhill examines the ethical implications of a developing technology.

As you read, think about what you already know about driverless cars.

1   Imagine you're in a self-driving car, heading towards a collision with a group of pedestrians. The only other option is to drive off a cliff. What should the car do? Philosophers have been debating a similar moral conundrum for years, but the discussion has a new practical application with the advent of self-driving cars, which are expected to be commonplace on the road in the coming years.

2   Specifically, self-driving cars from Google, Tesla, and others will need to address a much-debated thought experiment called The Trolley Problem. In the original set-up, a trolley is headed towards five people. You can pull a lever to switch to a different track, where just one person will be in the trolley's path. Should you kill the one to save five?

3   Many people believe they should, but this moral instinct is complicated by other scenarios. For example: You're standing on a footbridge above the track and can see a trolley hurtling towards five people. There's a fat man standing next to you, and you know that his weight would be enough to stop the trolley. Is it moral to push him off the bridge to save five people?

> **WORD POWER**
>
> **Conundrum** a challenging or unsolvable problem

Go off the cliff

4   When non-philosophers were asked how driverless cars should handle a situation where the death of either passenger or pedestrian is inevitable, most believed that cars should be programmed to avoid hurting bystanders, according to a paper uploaded to the scientific research site Arxiv this month.

5   The researchers, led by psychologist Jean-François Bonnefon from the Toulouse School of Economics, presented a series of collision scenarios to around 900 participants in total. They found that 75% of people thought the car should always swerve and kill the passenger, even to save just one pedestrian.

6   Among the philosophers debating moral theory, this solution is complicated by various arguments that appeal to our moral intuitions but point to different answers. The Trolley Problem is fiercely debated precisely because it is a clear example of the tension between our moral duty not to cause harm, and our moral duty not to do bad things.

7   The former school of thought argues that the moral action is that which causes the maximum happiness to the maximum number of people, a theory known as utilitarianism. Based on this reasoning, a driverless

car should take whatever action would save the greatest number of people, regardless of whether they are passenger or pedestrian. If five people inside the car would be killed in a collision with the wall, then the driverless car should continue on even if it means hitting an innocent pedestrian. The reasoning may sound simplistic, but the details of Utilitarian theory, as set out by John Stuart Mill, are difficult to dispute.

Who is responsible?

8   However, other philosophers who have weighed in on the Trolley Problem argue that utilitarianism is a crude approach, and that the correct moral action doesn't just evaluate the consequences of the action, but also considers who is morally responsible.

9   Helen Frowe, a professor of practical philosophy at Stockholm University, who has given a series of lectures on the Trolley Problem, says self-driving car manufactures should program vehicles to protect innocent bystanders, as those in the car have more responsibility for any danger.

10   "We have pretty stringent obligations not to kill people," she tells Quartz. "If you decided to get into a self-driving car, then that's imposing the risk."

11   The ethics are particularly complicated when Frowe's argument points to a different moral action than utilitarian theory. For example, a self-driving car could contain four passengers, or perhaps two children in the backseat. How does the moral calculus change? If the car's passengers are all adults, Frowe believes that they should die to avoid hitting one pedestrian, because the adults have chosen to be in the car and so have more moral responsibility.

12   Although Frowe believes that children are not morally responsible, she still argues that it's not morally permissible to kill one person in order to save the lives of two children. "As you increase the number of children, it will be easier to justify killing the one. But in cases where there are just adults in the car, you'd need to be able to save a lot of them—more than ten, maybe a busload—to make it moral to kill one."

It's better to do nothing

13   Pity the poor software designers (and, undoubtedly, lawyers) who are trying to figure this out, because it can get much more complicated. What if a pedestrian acted recklessly, or even stepped out in front of the car with the intention of making it swerve, thereby killing the passenger? (Hollywood screenwriters, start your engines.) Since driverless cars cannot judge pedestrians' intentions, this ethical wrinkle is practically very difficult to take into account.

14   Philosophers are far from a solution despite the scores of papers that debate every tiny ethical detail. For example, is it more immoral to actively swerve the car into a lone pedestrian than to simply do nothing and allow the vehicle to hit someone? Former UCLA philosophy professor Warren Quinn explicitly rejected the utilitarian idea that morality should maximize happiness. Instead, he argued that humans have a duty to respect other persons, and so an action that directly and intentionally causes harm is ethically worse than an indirect action that happens to lead to harm.

15   Of course, cars will very rarely be in a situation where ~~it~~ there are only two courses of action, and the car can compute, with 100% certainty, that either decision will lead to death. But with enough driverless cars on the road, it's far from implausible that software will someday have to make such a choice between causing harm to a pedestrian or passenger. Any safe driverless car should be able to recognize and balance these risks.

16   Self-driving car manufacturers have yet to reveal their stance on the issue. But, given the lack of philosophical unanimity, it seems unlikely they'll find a universally acceptable solution. As for philosophers, time will tell if they enjoy having their theories tested in a very real way.

Focus on Reading

1. Skim this essay, and put a checkmark beside each example of expert opinion Goldhill presents.

2. This essay includes three boldfaced headings. Are they necessary? Helpful? Distracting? Explain.

3. **TEST** Goldhill's essay. Does she include all four **TEST** elements? If not, why not? What, if anything, should be added?

Focus on Meaning

1. In paragraph 2, Goldhill mentions "a much-debated thought experiment called the Trolley Problem." What is the Trolley Problem? How does it apply to driverless cars?

2. What is *utilitarianism*? How is it relevant to the scenarios Goldhill presents?

Focus on Strategy and Critical Thinking

1. Is Goldhill trying to convince readers of something, or is she just presenting information? Explain your conclusion.

2. What kind of examples do you find most convincing in this essay—scenarios, research findings, or expert opinions? Why?

3. What other ethical or practical problems might driverless cars create? Who do you think should be responsible for solving these problems? Why?

Focus on Language and Style

1. This essay's title is presented in the form of a question. Where else does Goldhill pose questions? Why do you think she does this? Does she provide answers?

2. Goldhill uses the terms *driverless cars* and *self-driving cars* interchangeably. Do they mean the same thing? How are the connotations of these two terms different?

Focus on Writing

1. Do you think driverless cars are primarily beneficial or problematic for our society? Write an essay in which you consider the pros and cons

of this technology, and take a position on which you see as more significant. Support your thesis with specific examples of the benefits or problems you foresee.

2. Apply the Trolley Problem to some ethical issues of your choice. (You can find some possible scenarios described online.) Using each scenario as an example in support of your thesis, take a stand on whether you think it is ethical to "kill. . .one to save five" (2).

I Owe It All to Community College

Tom Hanks

Tom Hanks, one of the biggest boxoffice stars and most respected actors in America, has also worked as a screenwriter, director, and producer. Hanks received two Academy Awards for Best Actor, for *Philadelphia* (1993) and *Forrest Gump* (1994); four Golden Globes for acting, including his performances in *Big* (1989) and *Cast Away* (2001); and seven Emmy Awards, one of which honored his directing for *Band of Brothers* (2002). Among numerous other honors, he has been awarded the Kennedy Center Honors Medallion and the Presidential Medal of Freedom. In this 2015 essay originally published in *The New York Times*, Hanks discusses his life-changing experience at community college.

As you read, consider how Hanks's experiences are similar to and different from your own.

1   In 1974, I graduated from Skyline High School in Oakland, Calif., an underachieving student with lousy SAT scores. Allowed to send my results to three colleges, I chose M.I.T. and Villanova, knowing such fine schools would never accept a student like me but hoping they'd toss some car stickers my way for taking a shot. I couldn't afford tuition for college anyway. I sent my final set of stats to Chabot, a community college in nearby Hayward, Calif., which, because it accepted everyone and was free, would be my alma mater.

2   For thousands of commuting students, Chabot was our Columbia, Annapolis, even our Sorbonne,[1] offering courses in physics, stenography, auto mechanics, certified public accounting, foreign languages, journalism—name the art or science, the subject or trade, and it was probably in the catalog. The college had a nursing program that churned out graduates, sports teams that funneled athletes to big-time programs, and parking for a few thousand cars—all free but for the effort and the cost of used textbooks.

3   Classmates included veterans back from Vietnam, women of every marital and maternal status returning to school, middle-aged men wanting

> **WORD POWER**
> **alma mater** a school a person once attended

[1]Columbia is an Ivy League university in New York City; Annapolis is the site of the U.S. Naval Academy in Maryland; and the Sorbonne, in Paris, France, was one of the first universities in the world.

to improve their employment prospects and paychecks. We could get our general education requirements out of the way at Chabot—credits we could transfer to a university—which made those two years an invaluable head start. I was able to go on to the State University in Sacramento (at $95 a semester, just barely affordable) and study no other subject but my major, theater arts. (After a year there I moved on, enrolling in a little thing called the School of Hard Knocks, a.k.a. Life.)

4   By some fluke of the punch-card computer era, I made Chabot's dean's list taking classes I loved (oral interpretation), classes I loathed (health, a requirement), classes I aced (film as art—like Jean Renoir's "Golden Coach" and Luis Buñuel's "Simon of the Desert"), and classes I dropped after the first hour (astronomy, because it was all math). I nearly failed zoology, killing my fruit flies by neglect, but got lucky in an English course, The College Reading Experience. The books of Carlos Castaneda were incomprehensible to me (and still are), but my assigned presentation on the analytic process called structural dynamics was hailed as clear and concise, though I did nothing more than embellish the definition I had looked up in the dictionary.

5   A public speaking class was unforgettable for a couple of reasons. First, the assignments forced us to get over our self-consciousness. Second, another student was a stewardess, as flight attendants called themselves in the '70s. She was studying communications and was gorgeous. She lived not far from me, and when my VW threw a rod and was in the shop for a week, she offered me a lift to class. I rode shotgun that Monday-Wednesday-Friday totally tongue-tied. Communicating with her one on one was the antithesis of public speaking.

6   Classes I took at Chabot have rippled through my professional pond. I produced the HBO mini-series *John Adams* with an outline format I learned from a pipe-smoking historian, James Coovelis, whose lectures were riveting. Mary Lou Fitzgerald's Studies in Shakespeare taught me how the five-act structures of *Richard III*, *The Tempest*, and *Othello* focused their themes.

7   In Herb Kennedy's Drama in Performance, I read plays like *The Hot L Baltimore* and *Desire Under the Elms*, then saw their productions. I got to see the plays he taught, through student rush tickets[2] at the American Conservatory Theater in San Francisco and the Berkeley Repertory Theater. Those plays filled my head with expanded dreams. I got an A.

8   Of course, I goofed off between classes eating French fries and looking at girls; such are the pleasures, too, of schools that cost thousands of bucks a semester. Some hours I idled away in the huge library that anchored Chabot's oval quad. It's where I first read the *New York Times*, frustrated by its lack of comics.

9   If Chabot's library still has its collection of vinyl records, you will find my name repeatedly on the takeout slip of Jason Robards's performance of

WORD POWER
embellish to make more interesting by adding details, mostly untrue

WORD POWER
antithesis opposite

WORD POWER
idled to do nothing

---

[2]Discounted tickets sold on the same day as the performance.

the monologues of Eugene O'Neill.[3] On Side B he was Hickey, from *The Iceman Cometh*, a recording I listened to twenty times at least. When I worked with Mr. Robards on the 1993 film *Philadelphia*, he Confessed to recording those monologues at ten in the morning after lots and lots of coffee.

10   President Obama hopes to make two years of free community college accessible for up to nine million Americans. I'm guessing the new Congress will squawk at the $60 billion price tag, but I hope the idea sticks, because more veterans, from Iraq and Afghanistan this time, as well as another generation of mothers, single parents and workers who have been out of the job market, need lower obstacles between now and the next chapter of their lives. High school graduates without the finances for a higher education can postpone taking on big loans and maybe luck into the class that will redefine their life's work. Many lives will be changed.

11   Chabot College is still in Hayward, though Mr. Coovelis, Ms. Fitzgerald, and Mr. Kennedy are no longer there. I drove past the campus a few years ago with one of my kids and summed up my two years there this way: "That place made me what I am today."

Focus on Reading

1. Skim this essay, circling words you consider to be informal. Try substituting a more formal word for each of these words. Do your substitutions improve the essay?

2. Mark up paragraph 5. What did you underline? Did you use any symbols? Should you add any?

3. **TEST** Hanks's essay. Does he include all four **TEST** elements? If not, why not?

Focus on Meaning

1. Why did Hanks end up enrolling at Chabot Community College?

2. In paragraph 11, Hanks says that Chabot "made me what I am today." In what sense did Chabot do this?

Focus on Strategy and Critical Thinking

1. In paragraph 10, Hanks discusses a proposal made by President Obama. Does this paragraph explain Hanks's purpose for writing this essay, or did he have another motive? Explain.

2. Do you think Hanks should have discussed the background and academic experiences of his fellow students? Why or why not?

3. Do you agree with Hanks that community colleges are a vital part of our higher education system? What benefits do they provide that four-year schools do not?

[3]Eugene O'Neill (1888–1957): famous American playwright.

Focus on Language and Style

1. What exactly is the "School of Hard Knocks" (3)? What is the origin of this expression? In what sense is it an appropriate choice here?

2. In his introduction, Hanks mentions his "lousy SAT scores." What other negative attributes does he describe to characterize his younger self? Why does he do this?

Focus on Writing

1. Watch the 2011 film *Larry Crowne*, which Hanks says was inspired by the time he spent at Chabot Community College. Take notes as you watch. Then, write an essay identifying specific elements that link the film to this essay. In your essay, evaluate the film's effectiveness in conveying Hanks's personal experiences to his audience.

2. Have your own experiences adjusting to college been similar to Hanks's? Write an essay exploring the challenges you have faced, and suggest some steps your school could take to make the adjustment process easier for students like you.

Don't Know the Difference between Emoji and Emoticons? Let Me Explain

Alex Hern

Alex Hern has been a staff writer for the *New Statesman* and is now a technology reporter for *The Guardian*. His writing covers topics including policy, Internet culture, cryptocurrency, and the dark net. In the following 2015 article from *The Guardian*, Hern defines two types of graphic symbols and explains their differences.

As you read, think about the occasions on which you use emoji, and consider when they are appropriate and when they are not.

1   Emoji and emoticons are not the same thing and the continued confusion of the two will not stand.

2   In *The New York Times*, under the headline "At Silk Road Trial, Lawyers Fight to Include Evidence They Call Vital: Emoji," the two were treated as interchangeable.

3   "At issue" in the court's debates "was a piece of information that [the Silk Road founder Ross Ulbricht's] lawyer suggested was critically important, yet was omitted by federal prosecutors: an emoji.

4   "And not just any emoji, or emoticon, as the symbol is sometimes called—it was the gold standard. A version of a smiley face."

WORD POWER

portmanteau a word whose form and meaning are created by a combination of two other words.

WORD POWER

pictograph an image that symbolizes a word or phrase

5   And on the BBC, under the headline "Emoticons in texts can rack up huge bills" is a news story which exclusively discusses emoji.

6   An **emoticon** is a typographic display of a facial representation, used to convey emotion in a text only medium. Like so: ;-).

7   Invented multiple times over human history, its internet-era genesis is widely considered to have occurred in September 1982, when computer scientist Scott Fahlman suggested to the Carnegie Mellon University message board that :-) and :-(could be used to distinguish jokes from serious statements online. Shortly thereafter came the name, a portmanteau of the phrase "emotion icon".

8   In contrast to the grassroots creation of the emoticon, **emoji** were created in the late 1990s by NTT DoCoMo, the Japanese communications firm. The name is a contraction of the words *e* and *moji*, which roughly translates to pictograph.

9   Unlike emoticons, emoji are actual pictures, of everything from a set of painted nails (💅) to a slightly whimsical ghost (👻). And where emoticons were invented to portray emotion in environments where nothing but basic text is available, emoji are actually extensions to the character set used by most operating systems today, Unicode.

10   In essence, emoji are treated by the computer as letters from a non-western language, in much the same way as Japanese and Chinese characters are. But that also means that the software has to explicitly support them—otherwise it is forced to display a placeholder icon, or even just a blank space (which you might see between the brackets in the paragraph above if your browser doesn't support emoji).

11   It also means that each company has to provide its own interpretations of what the emoji descriptions should actually look like—and they don't always agree. Take the implementations of the "dancer" emoji: for Twitter and Apple, it's a female flamenco dancer. But for Google, it was, until recently, a John Travolta lookalike dancing disco style. And now it's a weird blobby thing. So if you're about to tell someone "you look gorgeous, like a 🕺," make sure they aren't reading it on a new Android phone.

12   To complicate matters, some emoji are also emoticons. The standard for the characters breaks them apart into sets by theme. Most are filed under "Miscellaneous Symbols and Pictographs", but the emoji which depict emotive faces are separated out as "emoticons".

13   There's more.

14   Although the name's not much used in the west, it's probably best to distinguish **kaomoji** from emoticons in general. Independently invented around the same time as emoticons, they make the most of the fuller character set necessary to write in Japanese, and can be read head-on. They may be as simple as (*_*), or as complex as (/❛ヮ❛)/*:・゚✧. or ಠ_ಠ.

15   Oh, and then there's **stickers**, the custom pictures used in a number of instant messaging clients such as Facebook Messenger or Line. Some apps refer to them as emoji, but they're fully specific to the app, and can't be cut and pasted anywhere else except when they're treated as an image.

16   With that much variation, is it surprising that people get a little (╯°□°)╯ ︵ ┻━┻ if you confuse :-) with ☺?

Focus on Reading

1. Scan this essay to locate the definitions of the two terms being compared. Then, underline these definitions.

2. Construct a brief outline to identify the main points of contrast between *emoticon* and *emoji*.

3. **TEST** Hern's essay. Does he include all four **TEST** elements? If not, why not? What, if anything, should be added?

Focus on Meaning

1. In one sentence, define *emoticon*; then, define *emoji* in a single sentence.

2. How did emoticons originate? How were emoji created?

3. What are *kaomoji*? How are they different from "emoticons in general" (14)? What are *stickers*? How are they different from emoji?

Focus on Strategy and Critical Thinking

1. What is Hern's thesis? Where does he state it? Is his purpose in this essay to make a point or just to amuse or entertain? Explain your answer.

2. Should Hern have used more examples of *emoticons* or *emoji* to define these two terms? Should he have used more visuals—for example, a chart—to distinguish one from the other?

3. Paragraph 12 begins with the phrase "To complicate matters. . ." Does this paragraph just "complicate matters," or does it provide information that is central to Hern's comparison? Explain.

4. Do you think the distinction between emoticons and emoji is important? Why or why not?

Focus on Language and Style

1. What is a *portmanteau* word? Using the example given in paragraph 7 (*emotion* + *icon* = *emoticon*) as a model, try to think of five additional portmanteau words.

2. Some of the paragraphs in this essay are quite short; several, in fact, are each just one sentence long. Is this a strength or a weakness of the essay? Should any of the single-sentence paragraphs be combined with paragraphs that precede or follow them? If so, which ones?

Focus on Writing

1. Write an essay in which you compare the kinds of situations in which emoji and emoticons are and are not appropriate or helpful.

2. Assemble emoji so they briefly summarize a familiar fairy tale. Then, use words to retell the same story. Now, write an essay comparing the visual language of emoji with the language of words. What advantages and disadvantages of each can you identify?

If You Want Women to Move Up, You Have to Accommodate Mothers

Rebecca Johnson

Rebecca Johnson holds an MA and a PhD in government from Georgetown University as well as a Master of Divinity from Wesley Theological Seminary. Johnson has taught in the fields of public policy and international service at American University and Georgetown University and served as academic director at the University of South Carolina; she has also been a research fellow at the Brookings Institution. Since 2015, she has been Dean of Academics and Deputy Director at the Marine Corps War College. In this essay, originally published in *The Wall Street Journal* in 2018, Johnson discusses the challenges she and other mothers face in professional settings.

As you read, think about what employers might do to make work more rewarding and less stressful for their employees who are parents.

1 I got mixed reactions when I brought my 6-month-old daughter to a recent professional conference. Several people pointedly ignored us. One person asked if I was the speaker's wife; another rushed over to me in the plenary session to say she was "proud" of me for being so "brave" as to take my baby to a conference. Many stared, and I heard a couple of comments about the need for better maternity leave and conference day care.

2 As someone fairly senior in my organization, I have been encouraged, supported and welcomed as a mother. It was surprising to have people react to my daughter as if she were an alien in this similar professional space.

3 Between panels, I did what I have done thousands of times—sent a quick tweet commenting on my day: "At a massive professional conference. Brought the baby. People seen astounded. Here's the thing: If you want women in positions of authority, you have to get comfortable with motherhood. You're welcome."

4 The tweet went viral. In the first day, it received roughly 1,000 "likes" an hour. I was inundated with comments from women and men who shared

> **WORD POWER**
>
> **plenary session** a conference session attended by all members

stories about how their mom brought them to conferences, the lab, class or on rounds at the hospital, helping to spark a passion for their current profession and shape their adult lives. Women also told of being turned away from professional settings because they brought their still-nursing infants with them.

5   In subsequent discussions with women concerning what it would mean for organizations to "get comfortable with motherhood," two themes emerged: Working moms need flexibility in how they get their job done, and they want recognition of their professional commitment and abilities. To the extent organizations can meet these two needs, they are well-positioned to retain female talent and enjoy the advantages of a diverse leadership team.

6   Hands down, the greatest need working mothers articulate is for increased flexibility at work. People, particularly women, lose significant control over their daily lives when they become parents. Day care won't take kids with fevers. Children with chronic health issues or developmental challenges can spend a lot of time at appointments. Snow days, teacher work days, a sick babysitter—any of these can require a quick change in a working mom's day.

7   Working mothers recognize their responsibility to meet their organization's mission. "Flexibility" does not mean absolution from responsibility. It may mean having the ability to work from home, video-conference to a meeting, work fewer but longer days each week, or another arrangement that allows the mom to get the job done without needing to be in the office during business hours every day.

> **WORD POWER**
> **absolution** release from obligations

8   Companies can make organizational shifts to support flexibility—using a project-based, as opposed to hours-based, system of personnel accounting; providing child care on-site to reduce commute time; providing hospital-grade pumps in lactation rooms with locking doors at multiple points across the organization.

9   More ambitiously, companies could allow employees to "job share" for a time—for example, one employee assumes the local responsibilities for a position, while a different employee covers the travel requirements for that job. Companies might also allow working mothers to "ramp down" at reduced pay. Instead of working on five projects simultaneously, a working mom could work on three until her child enters preschool (or over the summer), then return to her normal load.

10   As more millennials enter the workforce, corporations might consider how flexible work plans could benefit employees beyond working mothers. Adopting these alternative work arrangements for working mothers today can allow managers to figure out which options fit the culture and tempo of their organization, in order to roll them out to wider groups of workers over time. This would enable not only working moms but anyone who doesn't perform optimally in an 8-to-5 desk job to thrive professionally.

11   Women I talked to also noted the desire for recognition. Every working mom knows she has to carry her weight. If that were the only requirement,

working mothers would be likelier to stay in the workforce and continue to advance. Unfortunately, they also have to fight well-documented bias that automatically identifies working mothers as less committed and less capable than their peers who are fathers.

12 Leaders who counter that prejudice by providing clear, practical acknowledgment of those women's accomplishments—in staff meetings, company newsletters, team lead selection, annual performance reviews and bonuses—are likely to retain and promote motivated, effective women.

13 Mothers who work in environments that maintain a gender- and parent-neutral culture of recognition are cultivated professionally in reinforcing ways—by managers who publicly acknowledge their talent and performance, and over time by peers who are made aware of these women's accomplishments by leadership. Over time, public recognition erodes the biases working mothers face. This motivates mothers to stay in the workforce for longer periods of time, to continue to push themselves professionally in anticipation of future recognition, and ultimately to be in a position to advance to more-senior levels.

14 Flexibility and recognition are the keys to working mothers' ability to thrive. While these insights are hardly revolutionary, they could bring significant change to organizations that take them seriously. The greatest change will be more highly qualified, high-performing women in positions of authority—and a more welcoming environment for my daughter when she reaches working age.

> **WORD POWER**
>
> **cultivated**
> encouraged

Focus on Reading

1. In a marginal annotation beside the paragraph where Johnson states her thesis, restate it in your own words.

2. Mark up and annotate this essay's conclusion. What key terms did you identify? Sum up the paragraph's main idea in a marginal note.

3. **TEST** Johnson's essay. Does she include all four **TEST** elements? If not, why not?

Focus on Meaning

1. According to Johnson, what is working mothers' greatest need? What else does she say they need? Can you think of anything she doesn't mention?

2. In paragraphs 8 through 10, Johnson offers some suggestions for how employers could accommodate mothers. What does she suggest? Can you think of any reasons why any of these suggestions might not work?

3. How does Johnson suggest employers can show recognition to working mothers? Can you suggest other strategies they might use?

Focus on Strategy and Critical Thinking

1. Johnson opens her essay by describing the "mixed reactions" to her baby daughter's presence at a professional meeting. What do you think your reaction would be? Why?

2. Do you think Johnson intends her recommendations in this essay to apply to fathers as well as mothers? Why or why not? Do you think "working fathers" need the same accommodations?

3. Does Johnson present the employer's position as well as the position of the employees? If so, where? If not, should she have done so?

Focus on Language and Style

1. Read Johnson's definition of *flexibility* in paragraph 7. In your own words, what does she mean—and what doesn't she mean—by this term?

2. Although Johnson's title uses the word *mothers*, elsewhere in her essay she uses the phrase "working moms" (5) as well. What are the advantages and disadvantages of using the word *moms* instead of *mothers*?

Focus on Writing

1. Choose one of the suggestions Johnson makes in paragraphs 8 through 10, and write a proposal to an employer (your own or one you imagine) supporting this accommodation. Be sure to identify any problems that might occur and explain how they might be overcome.

2. Think about a particular workplace where a mother you know was (or is) employed. What workplace challenges did the mother face when her children were very young? When they got older? How, specifically, could these problems have been eliminated? Write an essay in which you make recommendations for how this employer should treat working mothers.

How to Have a Dog's Life

Caroline Knapp

After graduating from Brown University, Caroline Knapp (1959–2012) spent seven years writing and editing for *The Boston Phoenix*. Knapp invented an alter ego named Alice K for her popular column, "Out There"; some of these columns were collected and published as her first book in 1994. Her best-selling memoir, *Drinking: A Love Story* (1996), bluntly discusses her two-decade struggle with alcoholism. *Pack of Two* (1998), Knapp's next book, which examines the relationships between humans and dogs, was also a best seller. Two of her books have been published posthumously: *Appetites: Why Women Want* (2003) and *The Merry Recluse: A Life in Essays* (2004). In "How to Have a Dog's Life," which originally appeared in *The Boston Phoenix* in 1995, Knapp humorously details the many ways in which having a dog changes a person's life.

As you read, think about the pets you've had—or consider why you've never had one.

1   Have you ever considered, or are you currently considering, acquiring a canine companion? If so, understand in advance that your life will change dramatically. When asking you to contemplate life with a dog, most experts ask you to consider a fairly standard set of questions about leisure time and household space: how many hours a day might the dog be left alone; do you have a yard where the dog can play; are you willing to train the dog; and so on. The experts also outline a fairly predictable set of general expectations: you'll need certain equipment for the dog (dish, leash), and you'll need to walk the dog, and here and there you'll have to take it to the vet. These are all important questions and factors, but acquiring a dog is actually a far more complex matter. This is what you are likely to go through.

2   *1. You idealize.* This happens before you get the dog. You have a charming set of images about man's best friend. Dogs are wonderful, obedient, intuitive creatures, correct? You will acquire one for yourself, and occasionally you will walk it and feed it, but for the most part you will go about your business as before while the dog sits quietly by your side and gazes lovingly into your eyes.

3   *2. You have a quick reality-check.* You acquire the dog. In the car on the way home from the animal shelter, the dog sits quietly by your side and gazes lovingly into your eyes. You beam with pride at your fine judgment and wise decision. Ten minutes later, you open the door to your boyfriend's apartment, shout "Look what I got!" and watch as the new pup trots up to the boyfriend and defecates on the rug. In shame, you hustle the pup over to your own home, where she promptly urinates all over the kitchen floor. Reality sinks in: this is all going to be a little more complicated than you thought.

4   *3. You lose your life.* Once upon a time, you were a busy, active, articulate young professional who spent the bulk of her time engaged in serious activities: working, reading, discussing important matters with friends and co-workers. Suddenly, within the course of three days, you become a frenzied, confused person who spends the bulk of her time standing in a stooped position with her arms dangling by her sides ready to swoop the urinating, defacating puppy up off the floor and outside. Your vocabulary has degenerated with amazing speed and now appears to consist of only two or three key words and phrases. "Yes!" "No!" "Drop it!" "No . . . no . . . no! outside! outside!" Stoop-and-swoop, stoop-and-swoop: this is what your life has become.

5   *4. You fall in love.* So, who minds a little stooping and scooping? By day two or three, you are so enchanted with the new pup you can hardly

WORD POWER

articulate
well-spoken

stand it. Everything she does is cute: her paws and ears and sharp little teeth are cute, the way she curls in a circle on the farthest corner of the sofa is cute, even the way she squats to pee is cute. You worry you might literally cuddle her to death and you periodically forget your boyfriend's name ("Who?"). At first, the pup slept in a crate. Then on the floor by your bed. Now she's on, and in, the bed. Your side. You are so smitten that you find yourself doing things like standing in the kitchen boiling her a chicken for dinner. Free-range chicken, from Bread & Circus. (Notably, you have a fight with your boyfriend about this: you haven't cooked him dinner in three years.) You suddenly appreciate why people join bereavement groups when their dogs die: you're already worrying about how you'll handle your dog's demise and she isn't even four months old yet.

6   5. *You freak out.* This phase immediately follows. You wake up at 3 a.m. on the second or third day with your dog and you think, Oh my God, what have I gotten myself into?! This helpless, alien creature is totally dependent upon you and you feel completely inadequate to the task of caring for it. You worry about your inability to anticipate its needs. You worry about your basic character, your capacity for giving and nurturance. You worry about failing the dog in some fundamental way, scarring it for life. You feel completely sandbagged by these feelings—no one told you a tiny pup could generate such a flood of emotion and self-doubt and intensity—and you worry that you're in way over your head.

7   As the pup develops, other anxieties follow. You begin to act like the mother of a toddler. You take the dog to the park and find yourself worrying about her social skills: will she get along with the other dogs? Does she have the right toys? You become way overidentified with the dog: if she refuses to obey a simple command (sit; heel; stop trying to follow the pizza-delivery guy out to his car), you take it as a sign of personal failure. If she rests her head sweetly on your boyfriend's knee instead of yours, you feel betrayed and paranoid: you haven't bonded with her sufficiently; you're not good enough for her; she hates you. You realize you've got way more emotions than you anticipated tied up in this tiny creature and you find yourself actually discussing your relationship with the dog in therapy. You ponder the irony: at $125 per hour, this is vastly more expensive than the dog was.

8   6. *You become obnoxious.* As the dog's social skills improve, yours deteriorate. You realize you are having conversations about such topics as canine stool color and consistency with total strangers at the park, often at great length. You stand on street corners and enthuse loudly, wildly, as your dog pees in public. You begin to bore your friends with lengthy descriptions of the latest incredibly cute thing the pup did, and finally, you exact a promise from your family: if they ever—ever find that you've added the dog's name to your answering machine message, they will take you out and shoot you.

9   7. *Your social world changes.* You develop a new set of acquaintances, many of whom meet each morning at the same park to walk their dogs: the dogs romp and play; the humans stand in a clump and oooh and aaaah like mothers at a sandbox. The dogs in this particular group have names

like Max, Marty, Murray, Rita, Sadie, Frannie, and Lucille. You all stand around discussing the animals, sounding as though you're talking about a group of old Jewish people in the Catskills.

10   8. *You develop canine empathy.* Five or six weeks pass and you begin to settle in. The pup is house-trained (mostly), the two of you have established a set of routines, and you are through the most acute phases of adjustment. You notice at this point that you have begun to think like a dog, probably because you have read nothing but tomes on dog psychology for the last month. You now consider the pup a member of your pack and you are confident about your role as the leader, or alpha wolf. You understand that your pup thinks of you as the head of the pack, and you empathize with her interpretation of the world around her. Thus, when you return from your morning foray to the bakery to purchase breakfast, you blaze into the house with a flourish and announce proudly to the dog that you've been out hunting and killing scones. The dog looks excited by this, so later, when the guy from Bertucci's comes to deliver a large pepperoni pie, you emerge from the front hall with the box and inform the dog that your alpha wolf skills are so sophisticated and acute that a pizza has actually come and died at your front door. The dog wags her tail; your heart swells with pride.

11   Later that night, you're actually engaged in something non-canine related (reading, watching TV), when you look up and notice: sitting across the room, the dog is gazing lovingly into your eyes. You gaze lovingly back. Then you stop for an instant and relish the moment: this is it; this is the combined result of all that love, all that anxiety, all that work. This is joy, the purest sort.

WORD POWER

tomes long scholarly books

Focus on Reading

1. In your own words, list the stages a potential dog owner goes through when acquiring a dog. Write each step in the margin beside each of Knapp's numbered steps.

2. In the margin next to the concluding paragraph, write down a few alternative titles for this final step.

3. **TEST** Knapp's essay. Does she include all four **TEST** elements? If not, why not?

Focus on Meaning

1. Look carefully at each step in this process, and consider what it actually means. Then, rewrite each step so that its meaning is clearer and more specific.

2. According to Knapp, how does a person's life change when he or she acquires a dog?

3. What misconceptions about dog ownership does Knapp think most people have? How are these mistaken assumptions different from the reality of dog ownership?

Focus on Strategy and Critical Thinking

1. Knapp begins her essay by summarizing the advice "experts" usually give to potential pet owners. Why does she introduce her essay in this way?

2. What kind of audience is Knapp writing for? Experienced dog owners? Potential first-time dog owners? Both? Explain.

3. Do you think the essay's last paragraph is necessary? Should it be a separate step in the process? If so, what would you call this step?

4. Knapp includes both positive and negative details about dog ownership. All in all, is this essay's view of owning a dog positive or negative?

Focus on Language and Style

1. The steps in this process are introduced by numbered headings. Are these headings necessary, or are they distracting?

2. Knapp speaks directly to her readers in this essay, addressing them as "you." What are the advantages and disadvantages of this strategy?

3. What does the expression "a dog's life" mean? Does it have positive or negative connotations? What does it mean in the context of this essay's title?

Focus on Writing

1. Write an essay advising potential dog owners of the drawbacks of owning a dog. Use a descriptive heading to identify each drawback, discussing them in the order in which they become apparent to the owner. Your goal here is to discourage your readers from dog ownership.

2. Writing from a dog's point of view, explain the steps you would take to evaluate and select a potential owner.

What Really Keeps Women Out of Tech

Eileen Pollack

Eileen Pollack is a fiction and essay writer whose books include the short story collection *In the Mouth* (2008), the nonfiction book *Woman Walking Ahead: In Search of Catherine Weldon and Sitting Bull* (2003), and the novels *Breaking and Entering* (2012) and *The Bible of Dirty Jokes* (2018). Her book *The Only Woman in the Room: Why Science Is Still a Boys' Club* (2015) explores the discrepancy between the number of women and men in math- and science-based industries, a subject she also discusses in the following 2015 essay from *The New York Times*.

As you read, think about what you know about the roles of men and women in the tech industry.

1   Technology companies know they have a gender and diversity problem in their work force, and they are finally taking steps to try to fix it. But where are those new employees going to come from if women and minority students aren't opting to study computer science or engineering?

2   Figuring out why people who choose not to do something don't in fact do it is like attempting to interview the elves who live inside your refrigerator but come out only when the light is off. People already working for a company might tell you what makes them unhappy. But these complaints won't necessarily pinpoint the factors that keep women and minorities away from studying computer science in the first place.

3   As a woman who earned a bachelor of science degree in physics in the 1970s but left the field because I felt I didn't belong, I have long been interested, and focus here, on women in science and math. I was fascinated, but not surprised, to learn that many young women today avoid studying computer science because they, too, fear they won't fit in.

4   For the past six years, Sapna Cheryan, a psychology professor at the University of Washington, has been studying why girls in high school are significantly less likely than boys to sign up for a class in computer science, take the Advanced Placement exam in that subject, or express interest in computer science as a career, and why female college students are four times less likely than men to major in computer science or engineering, even though they test extremely well in math.

5   Over and over, Dr. Cheryan and her colleagues have found that Female students are more interested in enrolling in a computer class if they are shown a classroom (whether virtual or real) decorated not with "Star Wars" posters, science-fiction books, computer parts and tech magazines, but with a more neutral décor—art and nature posters, coffee makers, plants and general-interest magazines.

6   The researchers also found that cultural stereotypes about computer scientists strongly influenced young women's desire to take classes in the field. At a young age, girls already hold stereotypes of computer scientists as socially isolated young men whose genius is the result of genetics rather than hard work. Given that many girls are indoctrinated to believe that they should be feminine and modest about their abilities, as well as brought up to assume that girls are not innately gifted at science or math, it is not surprising that so few can see themselves as successful computer scientists.

7   In another experiment, Dr. Cheryan and her colleagues arranged for female undergraduates to talk to an actor pretending to be a computer science major. If the actor wore a T-shirt that said "I CODE THEREFORE I AM" and claimed to enjoy video games, the students expressed less interest in studying computer science than if the actor wore a solid shirt and claimed to enjoy hanging out with friends—even if the T-shirt-clad actor was another woman.

8   Such superficial stereotypes might seem laughably outdated. And yet, studies show that the public's image of a scientist hasn't changed since the 1950s. And such stereotypes do have a basis in reality. Who could fail to notice that only one of the eight people awarded Nobel Prizes in science or medicine last week was a woman?

> **WORD POWER**
>
> **indoctrinated** taught to accept certain beliefs without questioning

> **WORD POWER**
>
> **innately** naturally

9 The percentage of women studying computer science actually has fallen since the 1980s. Dr. Cheryan theorizes that this decline might be partly attributable to the rise of pop-culture portrayals of scientists as white or Asian male geeks in movies and TV shows like *Revenge of the Nerds* and *The Big Bang Theory.* The media's intense focus on start-up culture and male geniuses such as Steve Jobs and Bill Gates might also have inspired more young men than women to enter the field.

10 Men sometimes scoff that if young women let such nebulous factors deter them from careers in physics or computer science, the women are exercising their own free choice, and if girls were tough enough, such exaggerated stereotypes and feelings of discomfort wouldn't discourage them.

11 Yet I wonder how many young men would choose to major in computer science if they suspected they might need to carry out their coding while sitting in a pink cubicle decorated with posters of *Sex and the City*, with copies of *Vogue* and *Cosmo* scattered around the lunchroom. In fact, Dr. Cheryan's research shows that young men tend not to major in English for the same reasons women don't pick computer science: They compare their notions of who they are to their stereotypes of English majors and decide they won't fit in.

12 All this meshes with my own experience. Even though I felt more comfortable wearing a T-shirt and jeans than a skirt and high heels, after four years of studying physics at Yale I felt so much pressure to dress and act like a man that I became extremely uncomfortable about my identity as a woman. I loved teaching myself to program the university's new IBM mainframe. What a miracle it seemed that boxes of punched cardboard cards could produce pages and pages of a printed simulation of a collision between a K meson and a proton.

13 But the summer I worked as a programmer at Oak Ridge National Laboratory in Tennessee, I felt out of place among my mostly male colleagues because I hated drinking beer and didn't like being mocked for reading novels. Not to mention that the men who controlled access to the computer made me listen to a barrage of sexist teasing if I wanted to be given that day's code to run my program.

14 Despite my passion for physics, I didn't feel what Dr. Cheryan calls "an ambient sense of belonging" and left science. As this new research demonstrates, young women today still are avoiding technical disciplines because, like me, they are afraid they won't fit in.

15 To make computer science more attractive to women, we might help young women change how they think about themselves and what's expected of them. But we might also diversify the images of scientists they see in the media, along with the décor in the classrooms and offices in which they might want to study or work.

16 As Dr. Cheryan points out, stereotypes are only partly true, and women who actually take classes in computer science don't hold the same prejudices as women who get their ideas from pop culture.

17 This is why Mayor Bill de Blasio's recent announcement that within ten years all of New York City's public schools must offer at least some

WORD POWER
attributable resulting from a specific cause

WORD POWER
nebulous vague

WORD POWER
meshes matches

WORD POWER
ambient related to the immediate surroundings of something

training in computer science is so important. All students will have the opportunity to decide for themselves if they like this work.

18 At the college level, some fairly simple changes have proved stunningly effective. At Harvey Mudd College, strategies such as creating separate introductory classes for students with no programming experience and renaming courses ("Introduction to programming in Java" became "Creative approaches to problem solving in science and engineering using Python") led to an increase in the percentage of computer science majors who are female, from 10 to 40 percent, in four years.

19 Computer scientists and engineers are going to be designing the future that everyone inhabits. We need women and minorities to enjoy an ambient sense of belonging in those professions if the future they create is going to be one in which all of us feel at home.

Focus on Reading

1. Reread paragraph 5. Do your own experiences support this paragraph's claim? Write a marginal note that conveys your reaction to this paragraph.

2. Mark up paragraph 6. In marginal annotations, create a mini-outline of this paragraph.

3. **TEST** Pollack's essay. Does she include all four **TEST** elements? If not, why not?

Focus on Meaning

1. According to Pollack, what factors "keep women out of tech"? What changes does she propose to improve this situation?

2. According to Pollack's summary of Cheryan's research, "young men tend not to major in English for the same reasons women don't pick computer science" (paragraph 11). What are those reasons? Does your own experience support this claim?

Focus on Strategy and Critical Thinking

1. Where does Pollack include information about her own experiences? Do you find these passages irrelevant or distracting, or do you think they help her make her point? Explain.

2. Is Pollack's explanation of the problem—largely based on Cheryan's research—convincing? Oversimplified? What other factors might explain why so few women enter tech fields?

3. In paragraphs 1 and 2 and in her conclusion, Pollack suggests that minorities face the same challenges as women in tech. Do you think she should delete these references and just focus on women? Change her essay's title? Weave a more thorough discussion of minorities in tech into her essay? Explain.

Focus on Language and Style

1. If you were writing a flyer for an open house for prospective computer science majors, what adjectives would you include to attract women? Which words would you avoid? Why?

2. In paragraph 2, Pollack explains a concept by comparing it to "the elves who live inside your refrigerator but come out only when the light is off." Is this a useful description? Is it appropriate for this essay?

Focus on Writing

1. In paragraph 8, Pollack mentions stereotypical views of scientists. What is your image of a scientist? Write an essay explaining how your experiences shaped this view.

2. What fields do you see as female? Why? What factors keep men from entering these fields in greater numbers? What steps can (or should) be taken to make them more appealing to men?

Make Your Own Waste Pie Chart

Roger Spranz

Born in Germany, Roger Spranz has a master's degree in cultural anthropology from the University of Freiburg. As a PhD candidate in environmental behavior at the University of Bremen, Spranz is researching ways to reduce plastic bag use in Indonesia. He is the cofounder of Making Oceans Plastic Free, an initiative facilitating behavioral change toward ocean conservation. In this piece, which appeared on the initiative's blog in 2017, Spranz explains and illustrates the process of one clean-up campaign.

As you read, think about the different kinds of items you might find discarded on a street or in a park in your neighborhood.

Our real waste pie chart has been a great success at the launch of UNEP's[1] #cleanseas campaign at the World Ocean Summit, and with the help of Bye Bye Plastic Bags it has already been shared on Facebook more than 500 times. Find out what kind of waste is most common at your next beach clean up event! We show you here how to do it yourself!

How to Make a Waste Pie Chart

1. **Draw a circle into the sand:**

   You can use your finger, or a stick.

   Tip: You make it more perfect when you use a rope! Your friend holds the rope in the middle, and you - holding the rope on the other hand - walk around him while your finger is drawing the line into the sand.

[1]United Nations Environment Programme

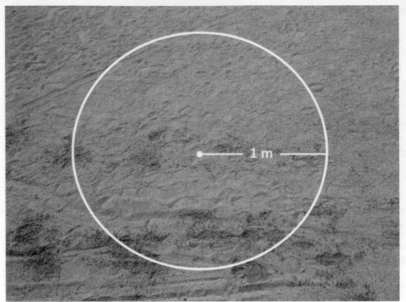

2. **Cut it like a pie-in 10 pieces:**

   Draw straight lines into the sand, to create 10 equal sections. Use this image for orientation for where to draw the lines.

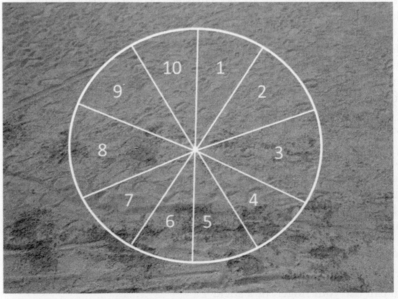

3. **Collect, Sort and Count:**

   (a) **Collect**. For the waste pie chart you only need to collect one bag of waste. Make sure you are the one walking across the beach before the others of your group. You need to pick up every non-organic piece of waste you come across. You can stop when the bag is full.

(b) **Sort**. You may want to sort them differently (check Ocean Conservancy—https://oceanconservancy.org—for standards), but we used following categories: Straws, Plastic Bottles and Cups, Plastic Bags, Food Wrappings, Other Plastic Items, Shoes/Sandals, Glass Pieces/Bottles, Cigarette Ends, Cans.

(c) **Count the items in each category**.

4. **Calculate (it's easy) and fill the chart**:

(a) **Total**. Once you know how many items you have in each category, add them up to get your total number of waste items.

(b) **Divide each category by the total**. To get the percentage and know how to fill the pie you need to do this: You calculate e.g. # of Straws/ total # of waste items. You can use the calculator on your phone: You will get a number like 0.1521, which means 15% of the waste you collected is straws. Do this calculation for each category.

(c) **Put waste into the pie slices**. Once you have the percentage of each category, you can start filling the pie with waste. Each of your 10 pie slices is 10%. So, if you have 15% straws, you will fill one slice and another 1/2 slice with straws. You continue like this with all waste categories.

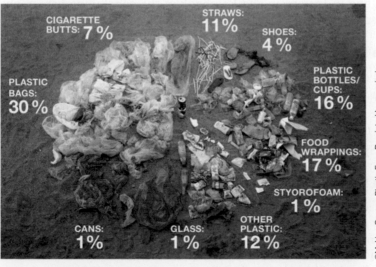

Congratulations, your waste pie chart is done! You may want to edit the photo into an info-graphic and add percentages for each category. #MakeOceansPlasticFree and post it on Instagram or Facebook so we can gather different waste pie charts and learn what others have found.

Focus on Reading

1. Write a one-paragraph summary of this essay, taking care to include all the steps.

2. Now, write a one-sentence summary of the paragraph you wrote for question 1.

3. TEST Spranz's essay. Does he include all four TEST elements? If not, why not?

Focus on Meaning

1. What is a pie chart? What does it usually look like? (You can find many examples online.)

2. In what respects is a pie chart an appropriate model for sorting different kinds of waste?

3. Would this essay's explanations and steps be clear without the images? Why or why not?

Focus on Strategy and Critical Thinking

1. Why does Spranz advise readers to make their own waste pie charts? What does he want them to get out of this experience?

2. What do Spranz's references to Facebook in the introductory paragraph and to Instagram and Facebook in the concluding paragraphs suggest about what he wants his process essay to accomplish?

Focus on Language and Style

1. Is this essay an explanation of a process or a set of instructions? What stylistic features identify it as one or the other?

2. Where does Spranz include the cautions and reminders that are often found in process essays? Does he need more? Why or why not?

3. Does Spranz need to add any transitional words and phrases? If so, where?

Focus on Writing

1. Draw a pie chart for the various items on your desk or in your car, listing items in the sections of the chart. Then, write a process essay explaining how you assembled and distributed the items. Be sure to give each section of the chart a descriptive name, and describe the contents of each section in detail.

2. Write an essay explaining how you would create a pie chart to represent the kinds of items you would want to pass down to your children and grandchildren. Steps in the process might include choosing categories, giving each category a name, and deciding what percentage of the pie to assign to each category.

The Flight from Conversation

Sherry Turkle

Sherry Turkle received a PhD in sociology and personality psychology from Harvard University. She is a licensed clinical psychologist, a professor at MIT, and the founding director of the MIT Initiative on Technology and Self. Turkle writes about people's relationship with technology. Her books include *Life on the Screen: Identity in the Age of the Internet* (1995), *Alone Together: Why We Expect More from Technology and Less from Each Other* (2011), and *Reclaiming Conversation: The Power of Talk in a Digital Age* (2015). In "The Flight from Conversation," Turkle contrasts face-to-face conversation and technological connection and identifies some of the effects of people's shift in communication styles.

As you read, think about how much time you spend on social media each day.

1   We live in a technological universe in which we are always communicating. And yet we have sacrificed conversation for mere connection.

2   At home, families sit together, texting and reading email. At work, executives text during board meetings. We text (and shop and go on Facebook) during classes and when we're on dates. My students tell me about an important new skill: it involves maintaining eye contact with someone while you text someone else; it's hard, but it can be done.

3   Over the past 15 years, I've studied technologies of mobile connection and talked to hundreds of people of all ages and circumstances about their plugged-in lives. I've learned that the little devices most of us carry around are so powerful that they change not only what we do, but also who we are.

4   We've become accustomed to a new way of being "alone together." Technology-enabled, we are able to be with one another, and also elsewhere, connected to wherever we want to be. We want to customize our lives. We want to move in and out of where we are because the thing we value most is control over where we focus our attention. We have gotten used to the idea of being in a tribe of one, loyal to our own party.

5   Our colleagues want to go to that board meeting but pay attention only to what interests them. To some this seems like a good idea, but we can end up hiding from one another, even as we are constantly connected to one another.

6   A businessman laments that he no longer has colleagues at work. He doesn't stop by to talk; he doesn't call. He says that he doesn't want to interrupt them. He says they're "too busy on their e-mail." But then he pauses and corrects himself. "I'm not telling the truth. I'm the one who doesn't want to be interrupted. I think I should. But I'd rather just do things on my BlackBerry."

7   A 16-year-old boy who relies on texting for almost everything says almost wistfully, "Someday, someday, but certainly not now, I'd like to learn how to have a conversation."

8 In today's workplace, young people who have grown up fearing conversation show up on the job wearing earphones. Walking through a college library or the campus of a high-tech startup, one sees the same thing: we are together, but each of us is in our own bubble, furiously connected to keyboards and tiny touch screens. A senior partner at a Boston law firm describes a scene in his office. Young associates lay out their suite of technologies: laptops, iPods and multiple phones. And then they put their earphones on. "Big ones. Like pilots. They turn their desks into cockpits." With the young lawyers in their cockpits, the office is quiet, a quiet that does not ask to be broken.

9 In the silence of connection, people are comforted by being in touch with a lot of people—carefully kept at bay. We can't get enough of one another if we can use technology to keep one another at distances we can control: not too close, not too far, just right. I think of it as a Goldilocks effect.

10 Texting and e-mail and posting let us present the self we want to be. This means we can edit. And if we wish to, we can delete. Or retouch: the voice, the flesh, the face, the body. Not too much, not too little—just right.

11 Human relationships are rich; they're messy and demanding. We have learned the habit of cleaning them up with technology. And the move from conversation to connection is part of this. But it's a process in which we shortchange ourselves. Worse, it seems that over time we stop caring, we forget that there is a difference.

12 We are tempted to think that our little "sips" of online connection add up to a big gulp of real conversation. But they don't. Email, Twitter, Facebook, all of these have their places—in politics, commerce, romance and friendship. But no matter how valuable, they do not substitute for conversation.

13 Connecting in sips may work for gathering discrete bits of information or for saying, "I am thinking about you." Or even for saying, "I love you." But connecting in sips doesn't work as well when it comes to understanding and knowing one another. In conversation we tend to one another. (The word itself is kinetic; it's derived from words that mean to move, together.) We can attend to tone and nuance. In conversation, we are called upon to see things from another's point of view.

14 Face-to-face conversation unfolds slowly. It teaches patience. When we communicate on our digital devices, we learn different habits. As we ramp up the volume and velocity of online connections, we start to expect faster answers. To get these, we ask one another simpler questions; we dumb down our communications, even on the most important matters. It is as though we have all put ourselves on cable news. Shakespeare might have said, "We are consum'd with that which we were nourish'd by."

15 And we use conversation with others to learn to converse with ourselves. So our flight from conversation can mean diminished chances to learn skills of self-reflection. These days, social media continually asks us what's "on our mind," but we have little motivation to say something truly

---

WORD POWER

discrete separate; individual

self-reflective. Self-reflection in conversation requires trust. It's hard to do anything with 3,000 Facebook friends except connect.

16   As we get used to being shortchanged on conversation and to getting by with less, we seem almost willing to dispense with people altogether. Serious people muse about the future of computer programs as psychiatrists. A high school sophomore confides to me that he wishes he could talk to an artificial intelligence program instead of his dad about dating; he says the A.I. would have so much more in its database. Indeed, many people tell me they hope that as Siri, the digital assistant on Apple's iPhone, becomes more advanced, "she" will be more and more like a best friend—one who will listen when others won't.

17   During the years I have spent researching people and their relationships with technology, I have often heard the sentiment "No one is listening to me." I believe this feeling helps explain why it is so appealing to have a Facebook page or a Twitter feed—each provides so many automatic listeners. And it helps explain why—against all reason—so many of us are willing to talk to machines that seem to care about us. Researchers around the world are busy inventing sociable robots, designed to be companions to the elderly, to children, to all of us.

18   One of the most haunting experiences during my research came when I brought one of these robots, designed in the shape of a baby seal, to an elder-care facility, and an older woman began to talk to it about the loss of her child. The robot seemed to be looking into her eyes. It seemed to be following the conversation. The woman was comforted.

19   And so many people found this amazing. Like the sophomore who wants advice about dating from artificial intelligence and those who look forward to computer psychiatry, this enthusiasm speaks to how much we have confused conversation with connection and collectively seem to have embraced a new kind of delusion that accepts the simulation of compassion as sufficient unto the day. And why would we want to talk about love and loss with a machine that has no experience of the arc of human life? Have we so lost confidence that we will be there for one another?

20   We expect more from technology and less from one another and seem increasingly drawn to technologies that provide the illusion of companionship without the demands of relationship. Always-on/always-on-you devices provide three powerful fantasies: that we will always be heard; that we can put our attention wherever we want it to be; and that we never have to be alone. Indeed our new devices have turned being alone into a problem that can be solved.

21   When people are alone, even for a few moments, they fidget and reach for a device. Here connection works like a symptom, not a cure, and our constant, reflexive impulse to connect shapes a new way of being.

22   Think of it as "I share, therefore I am." We use technology to define ourselves by sharing our thoughts and feelings as we're having them. We used to think, "I have a feeling; I want to make a call." Now our impulse is, "I want to have a feeling; I need to send a text."

23   So, in order to feel more, and to feel more like ourselves, we connect. But in our rush to connect, we flee from solitude, our ability to be separate and gather ourselves. Lacking the capacity for solitude, we turn to other people but don't experience them as they are. It is as though we use them, need them as spare parts to support our increasingly fragile selves.

24   We think constant connection will make us feel less lonely. The opposite is true. If we are unable to be alone, we are far more likely to be lonely. If we don't teach our children to be alone, they will know only how to be lonely.

25   I am a partisan for conversation. To make room for it, I see some first, deliberate steps. At home, we can create sacred spaces: the kitchen, the dining room. We can make our cars "device-free zones." We can demonstrate the value of conversation to our children. And we can do the same thing at work. There we are so busy communicating that we often don't have time to talk to one another about what really matters. Employees asked for casual Fridays; perhaps managers should introduce conversational Thursdays. Most of all, we need to remember—in between texts and e-mails and Facebook posts—to listen to one another, even to the boring bits, because it is often in unedited moments, moments in which we hesitate and stutter and go silent, that we reveal ourselves to one another.

26   I spend the summers at a cottage on Cape Cod, and for decades I walked the same dunes that Thoreau once walked. Not too long ago, people walked with their heads up, looking at the water, the sky, the sand and at one another, talking. Now they often walk with their heads down, typing. Even when they are with friends, partners, children, everyone is on their own devices.

27   So I say, look up, look at one another, and let's start the conversation.

> **WORD POWER**
>
> **partisan** strong supporter

Focus on Reading

1. Scan this essay to identify all the words that suggest communication. Then, circle those words.

2. In the margin beside paragraph 10, write a one-sentence summary of the paragraph.

3. **TEST** Turkle's essay. Does she include all four **TEST** elements? If not, why not?

Focus on Meaning

1. What has caused the situation Turkle describes? What results of the "flight from conversation" does she identify? Are all these results negative?

2. Central to this essay is a comparison between two kinds of communication. What are they? How are they alike? How are they different?

3. What does Turkle mean by "connecting in sips" (12–13)? What, according to her, is wrong with this kind of connection? How is it different from face-to-face conversation?

Focus on Strategy and Critical Thinking

1. In her essay's first paragraph, Turkle says that we "have sacrificed conversation for mere connection." What distinction is she making? Is this her essay's thesis? Explain.

2. In paragraph 3, Turkle notes that she has studied "technologies of mobile connection" for fifteen years and has interviewed hundreds of people. Later, in paragraph 17, she mentions that she has spent "years. . . researching people and their relationships with technology." Why does she provide this information?

3. At one point, Turkle suggests that people today "seem almost willing to dispense with people altogether (16). Do you think she is being serious here, or do you think she is exaggerating? Explain your answer.

4. In paragraph 25, Turkle makes some recommendations for solving the problem she has described. Do any of these recommendations make sense (or seem feasible) to you? Explain.

5. This essay was written in 2012. Does it seem dated, or do you think Turkle's conclusions make sense today? Do they perhaps make *more* sense today?

Focus on Language and Style

1. What does Turkle mean by "'alone together'" (4)? How does she illustrate this paradox?

2. What is the "Goldilocks effect" (9)? How does this term help Turkle make her point?

3. In paragraph 15, Turkle mentions the "flight from conversation" that is also the essay's title. Consider the connotations of the word *flight*. Is this the best choice of words? Can you think of another word that might express the concept more effectively?

4. In paragraph 24, Turkle makes a distinction between being *alone* and being *lonely*. What is the difference?

Focus on Writing

1. Do you recognize yourself in the scenarios Turkle presents here? For example, have you come to "expect more from technology and less from [others]" (paragraph 20)? Do you find yourself spending more time on social media than in face-to-face conversation? Write an essay in which you consider how social media has affected your life in the years since your early adolescence. Do you see this increased influence as entirely negative, as Turkle seems to, or can you identify some positive effects?

2. Write an essay in which you trace the way a friend of yours has moved from being a face-to-face friend to being just a social-media friend—or vice versa. What led to the change in status?

My First Police Stop

Hanif Willis-Abdurraqib

Hanif Willis-Abdurraqib was born in 1983 and grew up in Columbus, Ohio. He is a poet, essayist, and cultural critic whose work has appeared in periodicals including *Medium,* the *New Yorker,* and *Pitchfork.* Willis-Abdurraqib has written the poetry collection *The Crown Ain't Worth Much* (2016), which explores the generational history and shifting landscape of his home city, and the essay collection *They Can't Kill Us Until They Kill Us* (2017). In "My First Police Stop," published in *The New York Times* in 2016, Willis-Abdurraqib recounts a personal experience through sensory and emotional detail.

As you read, think about what image comes to mind when you picture a police officer.

1   My father went with me to the used-car lot on a summer day before my senior year in high school. We paid $1,995, from savings left to me after my mother's death, for a 1994 Nissan Maxima.

2   It was an odd shade of brown, with a thin gold stripe painted along the body, and it had a small exhaust leak, which made the engine loud. Still, it was mine.

3   Almost immediately, the car had issues. The alarm went off whenever you unlocked the driver's door because of an electrical problem that, I was told, would cost almost as much to fix as I had paid for the car.

4   This resulted in two solutions: Either I had to unlock the driver's door and quickly start the engine (to stop the blaring horn and flashing lights), or I would have to unlock the passenger-side door (which did not trigger the alarm) and climb toward the driver's seat.

5   It was a typical high school car. It was imperfect, a bit of a wreck and I loved it.

6   During the school year, Capital University, in Bexley, Ohio, recruited me to play soccer. At 17, with an offer from a college a few miles from my father's house, I didn't really consider what it would be like to exist as black in a community that had managed to keep itself white.

7   So in the late summer of 2001, before the start of my freshman year in college, I stepped onto the field for a preseason practice session as the first American-born player of color in the soccer program's history.

8   By that time I had learned to deal with the Nissan's quirks; I decided whether or not to endure the burst of the car's alarm depending on the area I was in. If I found myself in a place where my existence might raise suspicion, I chose the safer but more difficult route of going in through the passenger door.

9   On a September night, eager to escape a house imprisoned by a thick cloud of body heat and drink, I skipped out of a college party and rushed to my car. I slid the key into the driver's door. But before turning it, I

checked the street: the towering and expensive homes, the paved sidewalks, the darkness and silence.

10   I opted for what my father would say was the smarter choice: I went in through the passenger-side door. The engine let out a rumble that cut through the suburban night. As I pulled away from the curb, I saw the flashing lights of a police car.

11   I spend a lot of time trying to pinpoint how fear is learned. Or, rather, how we decide that fear is a necessary animal that grows out of our expectation to survive at all costs, and how I have been afraid and feared at the same time.

12   When I reflect, I think the fact that I had gone 17 years without having developed a direct fear of the police meant that I was lucky.

13   I knew the warnings from my father: Don't go on a run at night, don't reach into your pockets too quickly, be polite in front of them. And I had seen the police make life difficult for other people in my home neighborhood, and yet I never learned to be afraid.

14   Until this early fall night in 2001, with its unseasonable cold, the Midwest wind like daggers.

15   Bexley sits on the east side of Columbus. A small and flourishing mostly white suburb, it is sandwiched by two significantly poorer, mostly black neighborhoods. One of these is where I grew up.

16   When you are asked to step out of a car that you own, your body no longer belongs to you, but instead to the lights drowning it. There are two sides of the night that you can end up on: one where you see the sunrise again and one where you do not. You may not consider this in the moment.

17   That particular night, the police officers—first two, and then three more—were responding to a call of suspicious behavior. I was asked to exit my car before I was asked for ID. When I mentioned that this was my own vehicle, I was silenced and held by two officers while the others huddled around a squad car.

18   When I was finally asked to produce ID, I reached into a pocket, only to remember that it was in the book bag I had left in the trunk. I moved to get it. That's when I was grabbed and forcefully held down in the grass.

19   People who had been watching out of windows now emerged from their homes. I wondered which one of them had called the police. I thought about my pants, a pair of new Old Navy jeans purchased with money I had gotten as a graduation gift, now stained with grass, and I thought about how much they had cost me.

20   I thought about how much the car had cost me. How much it had cost me to get here, to Bexley, just five miles away from a neighborhood that no one from the nearby homes would venture to. But mostly I thought about how I perhaps owned nothing. Not even my hands, now pressed behind my back.

21   I was eventually pulled up from the grass after what felt like hours, but must have been about five minutes. My car ransacked, my book bag's contents scattered across the otherwise empty street.

22 A police officer stared at my face, stared at my ID, and he mumbled: "Interesting name. Sorry for the trouble."

23 After the officers were gone, I sat on the curb and watched my hands shake. No one who lived in the nearby homes offered to help or asked if I was O.K.

24 I didn't hate the police that night. Even today, while being critical of the institution of police and systems of policing, I feel no hatred toward the men and women themselves.

25 I have had many interactions with police officers since then, some better, a few just as bad. But I go into each one expecting to fear and to be feared. And when I see the news of another unarmed person's death, I wonder how their stories began.

26 If they began something like mine.

Focus on Reading

1. If you have not already done so, write a question in the margin beside a paragraph that confuses or puzzles you.

2. To help you identify the individual stages of the narrative, add a descriptive heading to introduce each section. How does the addition of headings change the essay?

3. **TEST** this essay. Does it include all four **TEST** elements? If not, why not?

Focus on Meaning

1. Why does Willis-Abdurraqib think it is important for readers to know that his car was "a bit of a wreck" (5) and that he was driving by "towering and expensive homes" (9)?

2. On the night he describes, why does Willis-Abdurraqib enter his car "through the passenger-side door" (10)? Was this "the smarter choice" (10)? Explain.

3. What does Willis-Abdurraqib mean when he says he has been "afraid and feared at the same time" (11)? (Note that this paradox is echoed in paragraph 25.)

4. Generally speaking, what is Willis-Abdurraqib's current view of the police? What was his view of the police at the time of the incident he describes?

Focus on Strategy and Critical Thinking

1. Why do you think Willis-Abdurraqib was stopped by the police? Why does he think he was stopped? Do you think his characterization of the incident is fair and accurate, or do you think he might be exaggerating? Explain.

2. Reread the last sentence of paragraph 6. What information does the word *managed* tell you about Willis-Abdurraqib? Is this the essay's thesis statement? Explain.

3. Why do you think Willis-Abdurraqib does not give a physical description of the police officers who stop him? Was this a good decision, or should he have provided some description? In the absence of description, how do you picture the officers?

4. In the newspaper in which this essay appeared, it was labeled a "rite of passage" column. What is a *rite of passage*? In what respects does the incident described here qualify as a rite of passage?

Focus on Language and Style

1. What does the word *first* in the essay's title suggest to you? Do you think the title is effective? What other title might work?

2. What adjectives does Willis-Abdurraqib use to describe his car? The neighborhood in which he is driving? Himself?

3. Willis-Abdurraqib is a poet. Can you identify any language in this essay that you would consider "poetic"? Explain.

Focus on Writing

1. Write a narrative report of this incident from the point of view of one of the responding police officers.

2. In a narrative essay called "My First _____," write about a rite of passage you experienced. What happened? How did the incident change you? What did you learn? What did the experience mean to you at the time, and what does it mean to you now?

When a Southern Town Broke a Heart
Jacqueline Woodson

Jacqueline Woodson grew up in South Carolina and Brooklyn in the 1960s and '70s. She is known for her children's literature for a range of ages. Woodson's writing includes picture books such as *Each Kindness* (2012), middle grade titles such as the Newbery Honor-winning *After Tupac and D Foster* (2008), and young adult books such as *Brown Girl Dreaming* (2014), winner of the Coretta Scott King Award and the National Book Award. Her most recent book is the novel *Another Brooklyn* (2016). Woodson is the 2018–2019 National Ambassador for Young People's Literature. In her 2016 *New York Times* article "When a Southern Town Broke a Heart," Woodson describes a childhood memory and a shifting perception of home.

As you read, think about a place where you felt safe when you were a child.

1   Greenville, S.C., in the 1970s is a rolling green dream in my memory now. Always in that memory are the smell of pine and the red dirt wafting up around our summer shoes—new blue Keds with thick white soles, red by the end of our first day "home." Because for me, South Carolina had always been home. Even years after my family joined the Great Migration and my mother moved us from Greenville to Brooklyn, each summer we returned to the Southern town of my mother's childhood.

2   There, the friendly neighbors who knew us before we "were even a thought" and remembered our mama "when she was a little girl in pig-tails" opened their arms to us every summer, welcoming us home. Vegetable gardens filled with collards, berries, pole beans and cucumbers grew beside the small houses. Raised flower beds brightened front yards. And, always, the smell of honeysuckle beckoned my siblings and me to its vine where we sipped sweet nectar from the flowers until, as always, my grandmother called from the kitchen window, "Let that honeysuckle grow like y'all try-ing to grow," and we ran off to whatever next thing the summer brought us. We were safe. We were home.

3   But the summer I was 9 years old, the town I had always loved mor-phed into a beautifully heartbreaking and complicated place. That sum-mer, like other summers and many Brooklyn children, we left the city only days after school ended.

4   My mother was a single mom whose days were spent as a customer service rep at Con Edison in downtown Brooklyn. When school ended with a half-day party of sugary Kool-Aid, cookies and report cards, my sister, brothers and I took the No. 52 Gates Avenue bus to downtown Brooklyn, waiting outside of J. W. Mays until my mother, nearly six feet tall, appeared in the crowd of people moving along Fulton Street.

5   Mays was a discount chain that eventually, like other discount chains—Orbach's, Korvettes, Alexander's—went out of business. But back then, it was an affordable one-stop shopping spot where my mother, in antic-ipation of our trip home and wanting to make sure her four children represented what it meant to leave the oppressive Jim Crow South for the economic and educational opportunity of New York, filled a cart with blue Keds, cotton dresses, T-shirts and underwear. We would return home well-dressed and well-spoken, products of the North's unbroken promise.

6   In other years, we had traveled back to Greenville by bus, but that year, for the first time, we took a train home, our uncle accompanying my sister, brothers and me. For the four of us, an overnight train brought a free-dom we'd never dreamed—our overly permissive uncle letting us run from train car to train car, eat the small bags of candy he'd bought us before we even pulled the waxed paper-wrapped sandwiches and fruit my mother had packed from our new school bags.

WORD POWER

morphed turned into

7   The train left New York in the late afternoon, arriving in Greenville before daybreak. As we disembarked, my sleepy-eyed siblings and I exaggerated deep inhalations of "country air."

8   The fleeting moments of childhood are etched deep in my memory—the salty indentations of baby teeth newly gone, the tug of hairbrushes through knotted hair, the heat and smell of the straightening comb, my mother's broad shoulders and easy smile—and a summer in South Carolina, when the deep green beauty revealed my place and time in history and laid claim to that moment all children know, when the tendrils of adulthood move toward us, showing themselves long before we are ready to see.

9   For so many summers, we'd been warned to stay away from the small patch of poison ivy that grew around the base of the one tree in my grandparents' backyard. But until that year, the consequence had been as theoretical as the segregation surrounding us. We saw the white people when we went downtown or as we drove through their neighborhoods on our way to visit relatives.

10   We knew the ones our family members worked for as maids and handymen and how they sometimes sent home bags of not so gently-used clothing that were thankfully accepted then redonated. A "No thank you" would have been as unacceptable as leaving off a "Ma'am" or "Sir" or heading downtown to march against Jim Crow. The poison ivy crept up the base of the tree on the roadside but grew low to the ground on the house side. "Don't go on the other side of that tree," our grandmother warned us. "And don't touch those leaves."

11   I would love to write that I remember the tree—that it was an old, solid oak or a stunning pine tree. Or one of the beautiful willows that seemed to weep all over South Carolina. I would love to bring the metaphor sorrowfully back somehow to Billie Holiday's "Strange Fruit" or Buffy Sainte-Marie's "Tall Trees in Georgia."

12   But what I remember of that summer is not the actual tree but the sap running from it, the thick shine of it moving along a gnarled and blackened trunk. And at the foot of that trunk, the poison ivy's oily leaves circling the base then climbing up into the tree on the road side. At 5, 6 and 7, I spent long periods of the day bent over the ivy, fascinated by the promise of its danger— a danger I believed I was protected from—and would continue to be.

13   But that summer, the poison ivy found its way to my older brother's legs, then along his hands and arms. As he suffered what we discovered was an allergic reaction to the ivy, the clammy heat rose in South Carolina and a fiery rash settled itself over my brother's neck and throat until, finally, my grandmother took him to the one white doctor who would treat black patients in our segregated town.

14   Dr. M. had a jar in the reception room filled with rock candy that he gave out to both his patients and their sugar-loving siblings. He's a kind man, my grandmother said. Other doctors wouldn't even look at colored people, let alone treat them. It was the early '70s. In our Brooklyn school we were being taught that segregation was a thing of the past, that what King

WORD POWER

tendrils long, thin, curling strands (usually of hair)

and Parks, Tubman and Turner, Phillis Wheatley and Crispus Attucks had struggled for was all behind us. But in Greenville, we lived in Nicholtown, a segregated neighborhood inside of a segregated town. I realized that either Greenville was cheating or Brooklyn was lying.

15   Coming home from Dr. M.'s my grandmother trailed the four of us to the back of the bus where other blacks had settled themselves. I sat, as I always did, in a window seat leaning into my grandmother—for safety? For assuredness? For comfort? For love. I watched downtown Greenville become Nicholtown again. We had left "home" the first time with my mother for the dream of New York. At 9, I felt as though home was turning its back on me now without so much as a wave goodbye.

Focus on Reading

1. Circle the term *Great Migration* in paragraph 1. Look up this term, and briefly explain it in a marginal note.

2. In the margin beside paragraph 11, write a question about the paragraph's content that you would like Woodson to answer.

3. **TEST** Woodson's essay. Does it include all four **TEST** elements? If not, why not?

Focus on Meaning

1. What is the meaning of the essay's title? How did Greenville break Woodson's heart?

2. What does Woodson mean by "the North's unbroken promise" (5)? How, according to Woodson, were she and her family products of this promise?

3. What is the Great Migration (1)? What is Jim Crow (10)? Why are these references important for this essay?

4. In paragraph 14, Woodson says, "I realized that either Greenville was cheating or Brooklyn was lying." What does she mean? Which of these two alternatives does her essay support?

5. In paragraph 1, Woodson says that for her, "South Carolina had always been home"; in her concluding paragraph, she says that she "felt as though home was turning its back on me now. . ." (15). What, specifically, changed her mind?

Focus on Strategy and Critical Thinking

1. What is this essay's main idea—the central point or dominant impression—that Woodson wants to make about her subject?

2. In paragraph 12, Woodson says that when she looked at the poison ivy, she was "fascinated by the promise of its danger." What exactly do

you think "fascinated" her? What kind of danger do you think she was anticipating?

3. In what sense do you see this essay as a description of a time (the early 1970s) as well as a place?

Focus on Language and Style

1. In addition to describing what things look like, Woodson gives a great deal of information on the way things smelled. Give some examples. How do these memories of odors help to paint a picture of Greenville?

2. In paragraphs 10 through 14, Woodson discusses the poison ivy the children were warned against. In what sense is this poison ivy a symbol as well as an actual plant? Beyond its literal significance, what might the poison ivy stand for?

Focus on Writing

1. Find the lyrics to the two songs Woodson mentions in paragraph 11. Then, write a descriptive essay in which you analyze the lyrics of one of these songs.

2. In paragraph 2, Woodson says that when she was a child in Greenville, she and her three siblings "were safe. We were home." In what childhood location did you feel "safe" and "at home"? Why? Write an essay describing that place and the sense of security it gave you.

Acknowledgments

Kathleen E. Bachynski and Daniel S. Goldberg, "Facing the Concussion Risks of Youth Football," Philly.com, September 26, 2014. Copyright © 2014 by Kathleen E. Bachynski and Daniel S. Goldberg. Reprinted by permission of the authors.

Russell Baker, "Slice of Life," *New York Times*, November 24, 1974. Copyright © 1974 The New York Times. All rights reserved. Used under license.

Naomi S. Baron, "The Case Against E-Readers," *Washington Post*, January 12, 2015. Copyright © 2015 by Naomi S. Baron. Reprinted by permission of the author.

Judy Brady, "I Want a Wife." Copyright © 1970 by Judy Brady. Reprinted by permission of the author.

John Carlson, "Real Solutions for Curtailing Gun Violence," *Wall Street Journal*, February 20, 2018. Copyright © 2018 by Dow Jones & Company. Republished with permission of Dow Jones & Company; permission conveyed through Copyright Clearance Center, Inc.

Ben Carson, "Vaccinations Are for the Good of the Nation," *National Review*, February 11, 2015. Copyright © 2015 National Review. Reprinted by permission.

Junot Díaz, "Watching Spiderman in Santa Domingo," *The New Yorker*, November 13, 2017. Reprinted by permission of Aragi, Inc. on behalf of the author.

Olivia Goldhill, "Should Driverless Cars Kill Their Own Passengers to Dave a Pedestrian?" *Quartz*, November 1, 2015. Copyright © 2015 by Quartz. Republished with permission of Quartz; permission conveyed through Copyright Clearance Center, Inc.

Tom Hanks, "I Owe It All to Community College," *New York Times*, January 14, 2015, A25, https://www.nytimes.com/2015/01/14/opinion/tom-hanks-on-his-two-years-at-chabot-college.html. Copyright © 2015 The New York Times. All rights reserved. Used by permission and protected by the Copyright Laws of the United States. The printing, copying, redistribution, or retransmission of this Content without express written permission is prohibited.

Alex Hern, "Don't Know the Difference between Emoji and Emoticons? Let Me Explain," *Guardian*, February 6, 2015. Copyright Guardian News & Media Ltd., 2018. Reprinted by permission.

Rebecca Johnson, "If You Want Women to Move Up, You Have to Accommodate Mothers," *Wall Street Journal*, January 4, 2018. Copyright © 2018 by Dow Jones & Company. Republished with permission of Dow Jones & Company; permission conveyed through Copyright Clearance Center, Inc.

Caroline Knapp, "How to Have a Dog's Life," from *The Merry Recluse: A Life in Essays.* Copyright © 2004 by Caroline Knapp. Reprinted by permission of Counterpoint Press.

Farhad Manjoo, "No, I Do Not Want to Pet Your Dog," Slate.com, May 9, 2013. Copyright © 2013 by the Slate Group. All rights reserved. Used by permission and protected by the Copyright Laws of the United States. The printing, copying, redistribution, or retransmission of this Content without express written permission is prohibited.

Michael Martinez, "Migrant vs. Refugee: What's the Difference?" CNN, September 8, 2015, https://www.cnn.com/2015/09/08/world/what-is-difference-migrants-refugees/index.html. Copyright © 2015 Turner Broadcast Systems. All rights reserved. Used by permission and protected by the Copyright Laws of the United States. The printing, copying, redistribution, or retransmission of this Content without express written permission is prohibited.

Trevor Noah, excerpt(s) from *Born a Crime: Stories From a South African Childhood.* Copyright © 2016 by Trevor Noah. Used by permission of Spiegel & Grau, an imprint of Random House, a division of Penguin Random House LLC. All rights reserved.

Eileen Pollack, "What Really Keeps Women Out of Tech," *New York Times*, October 11, 2015, SR3, https://www.nytimes.com/2015/10/11/opinion/sunday/what-really-keeps-women-out-of-tech.html. Copyright © 2015 The New York Times. All rights reserved. Used by permission and protected by the Copyright Laws of the United States. The printing, copying, redistribution, or retransmission of

Index

Note: Page numbers in **bold** type indicate pages on which terms are defined.

Revision Symbols

This chart lists symbols that many instructors use to point out writing problems in student papers. Next to each problem is the chapter of *Focus on Writing*, Fifth Edition, where you can find help with that problem. If your instructor uses different symbols from those shown here, write them in the space provided.

INSTRUCTOR'S SYMBOL	STANDARD SYMBOL	PROBLEM
	adj	problem with use of adjective 32
	adv	problem with use of adverb 32
	agr	agreement problem (subject-verb) 26 agreement problem (pronoun-antecedent) 31
	apos	apostrophe missing or used incorrectly 35
	awk	awkward sentence structure 27, 28
	cap or triple underline [example]	capital letter needed 36
	case	problem with pronoun case 31
	cliché	cliché 21
	coh	lack of paragraph coherence 2
	combine	combine sentences 19, 25
	cs	comma splice 24
	d or wc	diction (poor word choice) 23
	dev	lack of paragraph development 2
	frag	fragment 25
	fs	fused sentence 24
	ital	italics or underlining needed 36
	lc or diagonal slash [Example]	lowercase; capital letter not needed 36
	para or ¶	indent new paragraph 2
	pass	overuse of passive voice 27
	prep	nonstandard use of preposition 33
	ref	pronoun reference not specific 31
	ro	run-on sentence 24
	shift	illogical shift 27
	sp	incorrect spelling 36
	tense	problem with verb tense 29, 30
	trans	transition needed 3
	unity	paragraph not unified 3
	w	wordy, not concise 21
	//	problem with parallelism 22
	⊙	problem with comma use 34
	⊙	problem with semicolon use 36
	⟨" "⟩	problem with quotation marks 36
	⊃ *[ex ample]*	close up space
	^	insert
	⟍ *[exa mple]*	delete
	∿ *[words example]*	reversed letters or words
	X	obvious error
	✓	good point, well put
	# *[example words]*	add a space

Bedford/St. Martin's puts writers *first*

From day one, our goal has been simple: to provide inspiring resources that are grounded in best practices for teaching reading and writing. For more than 35 years, Bedford/St. Martin's has partnered with the field, listening to teachers, scholars, and students about the support writers need.

Contact your Bedford/St. Martin's sales representative or visit **macmillanlearning.com** to learn more.

Looking for digital formats?

- *Innovative digital learning space*
  Bedford/St. Martin's suite of digital tools makes it easy to get everyone on the same page by putting student writers at the center. For details, visit **macmillanlearning.com/college/us/englishdigital**.

- *Popular e-book formats*
  For details about our e-book partners, visit **macmillanlearning.com/ebooks**.

Focus for Success

Focus on Writing, Fifth Edition, offers clear, thorough coverage of college writing, with a chapter design that puts writing first. The Focus on Writing strand in Chapters 2-17 prompts students to write, learn essential concepts as they follow a student model, and apply those concepts to their own writing in a series of manageable steps. The text also empowers students with a unique tool for assessing and revising their work: the easy-to-grasp, easy-to-remember **TEST** (**T**opic sentence or **T**hesis statement, **E**vidence, **S**ummary statement, and **T**ransitions). A complete three-in-one text, *Focus on Writing,* Fifth Edition, not only covers the process of writing paragraphs and essays but also includes a grammar guide with exercises and an essay collection.

This book does not have a traditional binding; its pages are loose and 2-hole punched to provide flexibility and a low price to students.

Cover image: PJPhoto69 / E+ / Getty Images

macmillanlearning.com

bedford/st.martin's
Macmillan Learning

ISBN 978-1-319-22993-1

90000